# Scaling Networks v6
## Companion Guide

Cisco Networking Academy

**Cisco Press**

800 East 96th Street

Indianapolis, Indiana 46240 USA

# Scaling Networks v6 Companion Guide

Cisco Networking Academy

Copyright © 2018 Cisco Systems, Inc.

Published by:
Cisco Press
800 East 96th Street
Indianapolis, IN 46240 USA

Printed in the United States of America

1   17

Library of Congress Control Number: 2017946462

ISBN-13: 978-1-58713-434-0

ISBN-10: 1-58713-434-9

## Warning and Disclaimer

This book is designed to provide information about the Cisco Networking Academy Scaling Networks course. Every effort has been made to make this book as complete and as accurate as possible, but no warranty or fitness is implied.

The information is provided on an "as is" basis. The authors, Cisco Press, and Cisco Systems, Inc. shall have neither liability nor responsibility to any person or entity with respect to any loss or damages arising from the information contained in this book or from the use of the discs or programs that may accompany it.

The opinions expressed in this book belong to the author and are not necessarily those of Cisco Systems, Inc.

**Editor-in-Chief**
Mark Taub

**Alliances Manager, Cisco Press**
Ron Fligge

**Product Line Manager**
Brett Bartow

**Executive Editor**
Mary Beth Ray

**Managing Editor**
Sandra Schroeder

**Development Editor**
Ellie C. Bru

**Senior Project Editor**
Tonya Simpson

**Copy Editor**
Kitty Wilson

**Technical Editor**
Rick McDonald

**Editorial Assistant**
Vanessa Evans

**Cover Designer**
Ockomon House

**Composition**
codeMantra

**Indexer**
Erika Millen

**Proofreader**
Abigail Manheim

# Trademark Acknowledgments

All terms mentioned in this book that are known to be trademarks or service marks have been appropriately capitalized. Cisco Press or Cisco Systems, Inc., cannot attest to the accuracy of this information. Use of a term in this book should not be regarded as affecting the validity of any trademark or service mark.

# Special Sales

For information about buying this title in bulk quantities, or for special sales opportunities (which may include electronic versions; custom cover designs; and content particular to your business, training goals, marketing focus, or branding interests), please contact our corporate sales department at corpsales@pearsoned.com or (800) 382-3419.

For government sales inquiries, please contact governmentsales@pearsoned.com.

For questions about sales outside the U.S., please contact intlcs@pearson.com.

# Feedback Information

At Cisco Press, our goal is to create in-depth technical books of the highest quality and value. Each book is crafted with care and precision, undergoing rigorous development that involves the unique expertise of members from the professional technical community.

Readers' feedback is a natural continuation of this process. If you have any comments regarding how we could improve the quality of this book, or otherwise alter it to better suit your needs, you can contact us through email at feedback@ciscopress.com. Please make sure to include the book title and ISBN in your message.

We greatly appreciate your assistance.

·ı|ıı·ı|ıı
CISCO.

| Americas Headquarters | Asia Pacific Headquarters | Europe Headquarters |
| --- | --- | --- |
| Cisco Systems, Inc. | Cisco Systems (USA) Pte. Ltd. | Cisco Systems International BV Amsterdam, |
| San Jose, CA | Singapore | The Netherlands |

Cisco has more than 200 offices worldwide. Addresses, phone numbers, and fax numbers are listed on the Cisco Website at **www.cisco.com/go/offices**.

Cisco and the Cisco logo are trademarks or registered trademarks of Cisco and/or its affiliates in the U.S. and other countries. To view a list of Cisco trademarks, go to this URL: www.cisco.com/go/trademarks. Third party trademarks mentioned are the property of their respective owners. The use of the word partner does not imply a partnership relationship between Cisco and any other company. (1110R)

## About the Contributing Authors

**Bob Vachon** is a professor at Cambrian College in Sudbury, Ontario, Canada, where he teaches network infrastructure courses. He has worked and taught in the computer networking and information technology field since 1984. Since 2002, he has collaborated on various CCNA, CCNA Security, CCNP, Cybersecurity, and IoT projects for the Cisco Networking Academy as team lead, lead author, and subject matter expert. He enjoys playing guitar and being outdoors.

**Allan Johnson** entered the academic world in 1999, after 10 years as a business owner/operator, to dedicate his efforts to his passion for teaching. He holds both an MBA and an MEd in training and development. He taught CCNA courses at the high school level for seven years and has taught both CCNA and CCNP courses at Del Mar College in Corpus Christi, Texas. In 2003, Allan began to commit much of his time and energy to the CCNA Instructional Support Team, providing services to Networking Academy instructors worldwide and creating training materials. He now works full time for Cisco Networking Academy as curriculum lead.

# Contents at a Glance

# Contents

# Reader Services

**Register your copy** at www.ciscopress.com/title/9781587134340 for convenient access to downloads, updates, and corrections as they become available. To start the registration process, go to www.ciscopress.com/register and log in or create an account*. Enter the product ISBN 9781587134340 and click Submit. When the process is complete, you will find any available bonus content under Registered Products.

*Be sure to check the box that you would like to hear from us to receive exclusive discounts on future editions of this product.

# Command Syntax Conventions

The conventions used to present command syntax in this book are the same conventions used in the IOS Command Reference. The Command Reference describes these conventions as follows:

- **Boldface** indicates commands and keywords that are entered literally as shown. In actual configuration examples and output (not general command syntax), boldface indicates commands that are manually input by the user (such as a **show** command).

- *Italic* indicates arguments for which you supply actual values.

- Vertical bars (|) separate alternative, mutually exclusive elements.

- Square brackets ([ ]) indicate an optional element.

- Braces ({ }) indicate a required choice.

- Braces within brackets ([{ }]) indicate a required choice within an optional element.

# Introduction

*Scaling Networks v6 Companion Guide* is the official supplemental textbook for the Cisco Network Academy CCNA Routing & Switching Scaling Networks course. Cisco Networking Academy is a comprehensive program that delivers information technology skills to students around the world. The curriculum emphasizes real-world practical application, while providing opportunities for you to gain the skills and hands-on experience needed to design, install, operate, and maintain networks in small to medium-sized businesses, as well as enterprise and service provider environments.

This book provides a ready reference that explains the same networking concepts, technologies, protocols, and devices as the online curriculum. This book emphasizes key topics, terms, and activities and provides some alternate explanations and examples than are available in the course. You can use the online curriculum as directed by your instructor and then use this book's study tools to help solidify your understanding of all the topics.

## Who Should Read This Book

The book, as well as the course, is designed as an introduction to data network technology for those pursuing careers as network professionals as well as those who need only an introduction to network technology for professional growth. Topics are presented concisely, starting with the most fundamental concepts and progressing to a comprehensive understanding of network communication. The content of this text provides the foundation for additional Cisco Networking Academy courses and preparation for the CCNA Routing and Switching certification.

## Book Features

The educational features of this book focus on supporting topic coverage, readability, and practice of the course material to facilitate your full understanding of the course material.

### Topic Coverage

The following features give you a thorough overview of the topics covered in each chapter so that you can make constructive use of your study time:

- **Objectives:** Listed at the beginning of each chapter, the objectives reference the core concepts covered in the chapter. The objectives match the objectives stated in the corresponding chapters of the online curriculum; however, the question format in this book encourages you to think about finding the answers as you read the chapter.

- **Notes:** These are short sidebars that point out interesting facts, timesaving methods, and important safety issues.

- **Chapter summaries:** At the end of each chapter is a summary of the chapter's key concepts. It provides a synopsis of the chapter and serves as a study aid.

- **Practice:** At the end of chapter is a full list of the labs, class activities, and Packet Tracer activities to refer to for study time.

## Readability

The following features have been updated to assist your understanding of the networking vocabulary:

- **Key terms:** Each chapter begins with a list of key terms, along with a page-number reference from within the chapter. The terms are listed in the order in which they are explained in the chapter. This handy reference allows you to find a term, flip to the page where the term appears, and see the term used in context. The Glossary defines all the key terms.

- **Glossary:** This book contains an all-new Glossary with more than 250 terms.

## Practice

Practice makes perfect. This new Companion Guide offers you ample opportunities to put what you learn into practice. You will find the following features valuable and effective in reinforcing the instruction that you receive:

- **"Check Your Understanding" questions and answer key:** Updated review questions are presented at the end of each chapter as a self-assessment tool. These questions match the style of questions that you see in the online course. Appendix A, "Answers to the 'Check Your Understanding' Questions," provides an answer key to all the questions and includes an explanation of each answer.

Packet Tracer
☐ Activity

Video

- **Labs and activities:** Throughout each chapter, you will be directed back to the online course to take advantage of the activities created to reinforce concepts. In addition, at the end of each chapter, there is a practice section that collects a list of all the labs and activities to provide practice with the topics introduced in the chapter. The labs, class activities, and Packet Tracer instructions are available in the companion *Scaling Networks v6 Labs & Study Guide* (ISBN 9781587134333). The Packet Tracer PKA files are found in the online course.

- **Page references to online course:** After headings, you will see, for example, (1.1.2.3). This number refers to the page number in the online course so that you can easily jump to that spot online to view a video, practice an activity, perform a lab, or review a topic.

## Lab Study Guide

The supplementary book *Scaling Networks v6 Labs & Study Guide*, by Allan Johnson (ISBN 9781587134333), includes a Study Guide section and a Lab section for each chapter. The Study Guide section offers exercises that help you learn the concepts, configurations, and troubleshooting skill crucial to your success as a CCNA exam candidate. Some chapters include unique Packet Tracer activities available for download from the book's companion website. The Labs and Activities section contains all the labs, class activities, and Packet Tracer instructions from the course.

Packet Tracer
☐ **Activity**

## About Packet Tracer Software and Activities

Interspersed throughout the chapters you'll find many activities to work with the Cisco Packet Tracer tool. Packet Tracer allows you to create networks, visualize how packets flow in the network, and use basic testing tools to determine whether the network would work. When you see this icon, you can use Packet Tracer with the listed file to perform a task suggested in this book. The activity files are available in the course. Packet Tracer software is available only through the Cisco Networking Academy website. Ask your instructor for access to Packet Tracer.

## How This Book Is Organized

This book corresponds closely to the Cisco Academy Scaling Networks course and is divided into 10 chapters, one appendix, and a Glossary of key terms:

- **Chapter 1, "LAN Design":** This chapter discusses strategies that can be used to systematically design a highly functional network, such as the hierarchical network design model and appropriate device selections. The goals of network design are to limit the number of devices impacted by the failure of a single network device, provide a plan and path for growth, and create a reliable network.

- **Chapter 2, "Scaling VLANs":** This chapter examines the implementation of inter-VLAN routing using a Layer 3 switch. It also describes issues encountered when implementing VTP, DTP and inter-VLAN routing.

- **Chapter 3, "STP":** This chapter focuses on the protocols used to manage Layer 2 redundancy. It also covers some of the potential redundancy problems and their symptoms.

- **Chapter 4, "EtherChannel and HSRP":** This chapter describes EtherChannel and the methods used to create an EtherChannel. It also focuses on the operations and configuration of Hot Standby Router Protocol (HSRP), a first-hop redundancy protocol. Finally, the chapter examines a few potential redundancy problems and their symptoms.

- **Chapter 5, "Dynamic Routing":** This chapter introduces dynamic routing protocols. It explores the benefits of using dynamic routing protocols, how different routing protocols are classified, and the metrics routing protocols use to determine the best path for network traffic. In addition, the characteristics of dynamic routing protocols and the differences between the various routing protocols are examined.

- **Chapter 6, "EIGRP":** This chapter introduces EIGRP and provides basic configuration commands to enable it on a Cisco IOS router. It also explores the operation of the routing protocol and provides more detail on how EIGRP determines the best path.

- **Chapter 7, "EIGRP Tuning and Troubleshooting":** This chapter describes EIGRP tuning features, the configuration mode commands to implement these features for both IPv4 and IPv6, and the components and commands used to troubleshoot OSPFv2 and OSPFv3.

- **Chapter 8, "Single-Area OSPF":** This chapter covers basic single-area OSPF implementations and configurations.

- **Chapter 9, "Multiarea OSPF":** This chapter discusses basic multiarea OSPF implementations and configurations.

- **Chapter 10, "OSPF Tuning and Troubleshooting":** This chapter describes OSPF tuning features, the configuration mode commands to implement these features for both IPv4 and IPv6, and the components and commands used to troubleshoot OSPFv2 and OSPFv3.

- **Appendix A, "Answers to the Review Questions":** This appendix lists the answers to the "Check Your Understanding" review questions that are included at the end of each chapter.

- **Glossary:** The Glossary provides you with definitions for all the key terms identified in each chapter.

# CHAPTER 1

# LAN Design

## Objectives

Upon completion of this chapter, you will be able to answer the following questions:

- What are the appropriate hierarchical network designs for small businesses?

- What are the considerations for designing a scalable network?

- What switch hardware features are appropriate to support network requirements in small to medium-sized business networks?

- What types of routers are available for small to medium-sized business networks?

- What are the basic configuration settings for a Cisco IOS device?

## Key Terms

This chapter uses the following key terms. You can find the definitions in the Glossary.

mission-critical services   Page 3

enterprise network   Page 3

network operations center (NOC)   Page 5

hierarchical design model   Page 6

access layer   Page 7

distribution layer   Page 7

core layer   Page 7

collapsed core design   Page 7

multilayer switch   Page 9

Redundant links   Page 9

link aggregation   Page 9

redundancy   Page 10

Spanning Tree Protocol (STP)   Page 10

failure domain   Page 11

wireless access point (AP)   Page 12

building switch block   Page 13

departmental switch block   Page 13

EtherChannel   Page 13

port channel interface   Page 14

load balancing   Page 14

Open Shortest Path First (OSPF)   Page 15

Enhanced Interior Gateway Routing Protocol (EIGRP)   Page 15

link-state routing protocol   Page 15

single-area OSPF   Page 15

multiarea OSPF   Page 15

distance vector routing protocol   Page 16

form factor   Page 17

# Introduction (1.0.1.1)

There is a tendency to discount a network as just simple plumbing, to think that all you have to consider is the size and the length of the pipes or the speeds and feeds of the links, and to dismiss the rest as unimportant. Just as the plumbing in a large stadium or high rise has to be designed for scale, purpose, redundancy, protection from tampering or denial of operation, and the capacity to handle peak loads, a network requires similar consideration. As users depend on a network to access the majority of the information they need to do their jobs and to transport their voice or video with reliability, the network must be able to provide resilient, intelligent transport.

As a business grows, so does its networking requirements. Businesses rely on the network infrastructure to provide *mission-critical services*. Network outages can result in lost revenue and lost customers. Network designers must design and build an *enterprise network* that is scalable and highly available.

The campus local area network (LAN) is the network that supports devices people use within a location to connect to information. The campus LAN can be a single switch at a small remote site up to a large multi-building infrastructure, supporting classrooms, office space, and similar places where people use their devices. The campus design incorporates both wired and wireless connectivity for a complete network access solution.

This chapter discusses strategies that can be used to systematically design a highly functional network, such as the hierarchical network design model and appropriate device selections. The goals of network design are to limit the number of devices impacted by the failure of a single network device, provide a plan and path for growth, and create a reliable network.

**Class Activity 1.0.1.2: Network by Design**

Refer to *Scaling Networks v6 Labs & Study Guide* and the online course to complete this activity.

Your employer is opening a new branch office. You have been reassigned to the site as the network administrator, and your job will be to design and maintain the new branch network. The network administrators at the other branches used the Cisco three-layer hierarchical model when designing their networks. You decide to use the same approach. To get an idea of what using the hierarchical model can do to enhance the design process, you research the topic.

# Campus Wired LAN Designs (1.1)

Enterprise networks come in all sizes. There are small networks consisting of a few hosts, medium-sized networks consisting of a few hundred hosts, and large networks consisting of thousands of hosts. Besides the number of hosts these networks must support, consideration must be given to the applications and services that must be supported to meet the organizational goals.

Fortunately, proven methods are available to design all types of networks. The Cisco Enterprise Architecture is an example of a proven campus network design.

In this section, you will learn why it is important to design a scalable hierarchical network.

## Cisco Validated Designs (1.1.1)

Networks must be scalable, which means they must be able to accommodate an increase or a decrease in size. The focus of this topic is to discover how the hierarchical design model is used to help accomplish this task.

### The Need to Scale the Network (1.1.1.1)

Businesses increasingly rely on their network infrastructure to provide mission-critical services. As businesses grow and evolve, they hire more employees, open branch offices, and expand into global markets. These changes directly affect the requirements of a network.

The LAN is the networking infrastructure that provides access to network communication services and resources for end users and devices spread over a single floor or building. A campus network is created by interconnecting a group of LANs that are spread over a small geographic area.

Campus network designs include small networks that use a single LAN switch, up to very large networks with thousands of connections. For example, in Figure 1-1, the company is located in a single location with one connection to the Internet.

**Figure 1-1**   A Small, Single-Location Company

In Figure 1-2, the company grows to multiple locations in the same city.

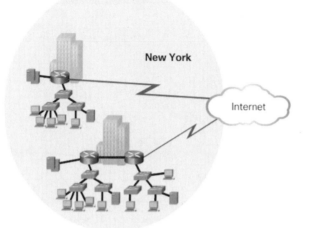

**Figure 1-2**   The Company Grows to Multiple Locations in the Same City

In Figure 1-3, the company continues to grow and expands to more cities. It also hires and connects teleworkers.

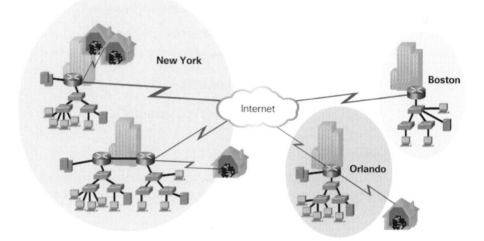

**Figure 1-3**   Enterprise Grows to Multiple Cities and Adds Teleworkers

In Figure 1-4, the company expands to other countries and centralizes management in a *network operations center (NOC)*.

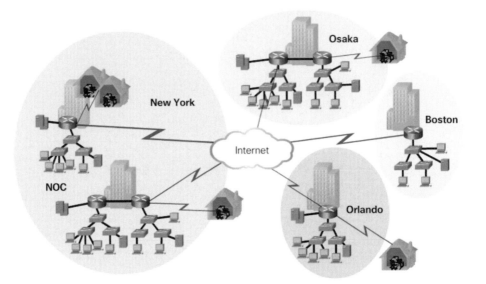

**Figure 1-4**    Enterprise Becomes Global and Centralizes Network Operations

In addition to supporting physical growth, a network must also support the exchange of all types of network traffic, including data files, email, IP telephony, and video applications for multiple business units.

Specifically, all enterprise networks must:

- Support mission-critical services and applications
- Support converged network traffic
- Support diverse business needs
- Provide centralized administrative control

To help campus LANs meet these requirements, a *hierarchical design model* is used.

## Hierarchical Design Model (1.1.1.2)

The campus wired LAN enables communications between devices in a building or group of buildings, as well as interconnection to the WAN and Internet edge at the network core.

Early networks used a flat or meshed network design, in which large numbers of hosts were connected in the same network. Changes affected many hosts in this type of network architecture.

Campus wired LANs now use a hierarchical design model that divides network design into modular groups or layers. Dividing (or *breaking*) the network design into layers enables each layer to implement specific functions. This simplifies the network design and the deployment and management of the network.

A hierarchical LAN design consists of the following three layers, as shown in Figure 1-5:

- Access layer
- Distribution layer
- Core layer

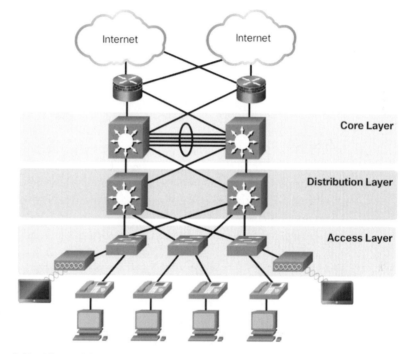

**Figure 1-5**   Hierarchical Design Model

Each layer is designed to meet specific functions.

The *access layer* provides endpoints and users direct access to the network. The *distribution layer* aggregates access layers and provides connectivity to services. Finally, the *core layer* provides connectivity between distribution layers for large LAN environments. User traffic is initiated at the access layer and passes through the other layers if the functionality of those layers is required.

Medium-sized to large enterprise networks commonly implement the three-layer hierarchical design model. However, some smaller enterprise networks may implement a two-tier hierarchical design, referred to as a *collapsed core design*. In a two-tier hierarchical design, the core and distribution layers are collapsed into one layer, reducing cost and complexity, as shown in Figure 1-6.

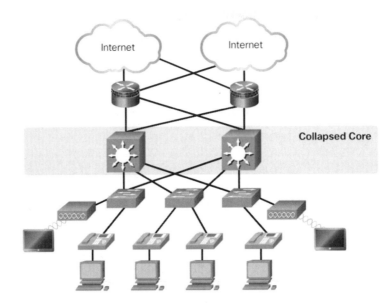

**Figure 1-6**  Collapsed Core

In flat or meshed network architectures, changes tend to affect a large number of systems. Hierarchical design helps constrain operational changes to a subset of the network, which makes it easy to manage and improves resiliency. Modular structuring of the network into small, easy-to-understand elements also facilitates resiliency via improved fault isolation.

# Expanding the Network (1.1.2)

Networks must be scalable, which means they must be able to accommodate an increase or a decrease in size. The focus of this topic is to discover how the hierarchical design model is used to help accomplish this task.

## Design for Scalability (1.1.2.1)

To support a large, medium, or small network, the network designer must develop a strategy to enable the network to be available and to scale effectively and easily. Included in a basic network design strategy are the following recommendations:

- Use expandable, modular equipment or clustered devices that can be easily upgraded to increase capabilities. Device modules can be added to the existing equipment to support new features and devices without requiring major equipment upgrades. Some devices can be integrated in a cluster to act as one device to simplify management and configuration.

- Design a hierarchical network to include modules that can be added, upgraded, and modified as necessary, without affecting the design of the other functional areas of the network. For example, you might create a separate access layer that can be expanded without affecting the distribution and core layers of the campus network.

- Create an IPv4 or IPv6 address strategy that is hierarchical. Careful address planning eliminates the need to re-address the network to support additional users and services.

- Use a router or *multilayer switch* to limit broadcasts and filter other undesirable traffic from the network. Use Layer 3 devices to filter and reduce traffic to the network core.

As shown in Figure 1-7, more advanced network design requirements include:

**A.** *Redundant links*—Implementing redundant links in the network between critical devices and between access layer and core layer devices.

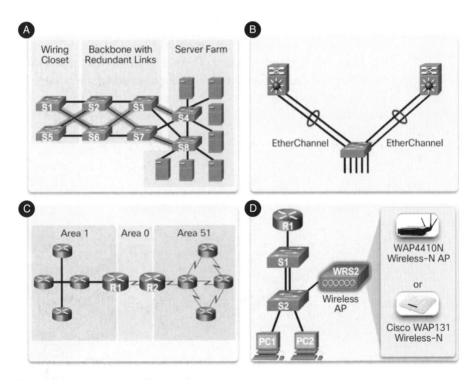

**Figure 1-7**   Design for Scalability

**B.** *Link aggregation*—Implementing multiple links between equipment, with either link aggregation (EtherChannel) or equal-cost load balancing, to increase bandwidth. Combining multiple Ethernet links into a single, load-balanced EtherChannel configuration increases the available bandwidth. EtherChannel implementations can be used when budget restrictions prohibit purchasing high-speed interfaces and fiber runs.

**C.** **Scalable routing protocols**—Using a scalable routing protocol such as multiarea OSPF and implementing features within that routing protocol to isolate routing updates and minimize the size of the routing table.

**D.** **Wireless mobility**—Implementing wireless connectivity to allow for mobility and expansion.

## Planning for Redundancy (1.1.2.2)

For many organizations, the availability of the network is essential to supporting business needs. *Redundancy* is an important part of network design for preventing disruption of network services by minimizing the possibility of a single point of failure. One method of implementing redundancy is to install duplicate equipment and provide failover services for critical devices.

Another method of implementing redundancy is using redundant paths, as shown in Figure 1-8. Redundant paths offer alternate physical paths for data to traverse the network. Redundant paths in a switched network support high availability. However, due to the operation of switches, redundant paths in a switched Ethernet network may cause logical Layer 2 loops. For this reason, *Spanning Tree Protocol (STP)* is required.

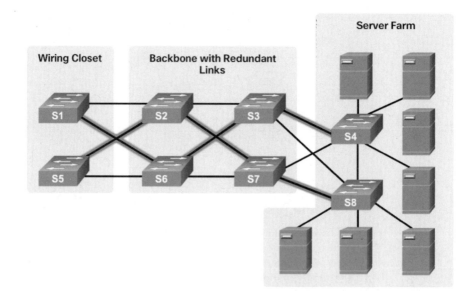

**Figure 1-8**   LAN Redundancy

STP eliminates Layer 2 loops when redundant links are used between switches. It does this by providing a mechanism for disabling redundant paths in a switched network until the path is necessary, such as when failures occur. STP is an open standard protocol used in a switched environment to create a loop-free logical topology.

Chapter 3, "STP," provides more details about LAN redundancy and the operation of STP.

## Failure Domains (1.1.2.3)

A well-designed network not only controls traffic but also limits the size of failure domains. A *failure domain* is the area of a network that is impacted when a critical device or network service experiences problems.

The function of the device that initially fails determines the impact of a failure domain. For example, a malfunctioning switch on a network segment normally affects only the hosts on that segment. However, if the router that connects this segment to others fails, the impact is much greater.

The use of redundant links and reliable enterprise-class equipment minimizes the chance of disruption in a network. Smaller failure domains reduce the impact of a failure on company productivity. They also simplify the troubleshooting process, thereby shortening the downtime for all users.

Figure 1-9 shows an example of the failure domain for a router.

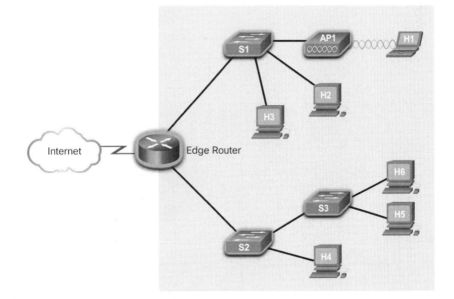

**Figure 1-9**   Failure Domain—Router

Figure 1-10 shows an example of the failure domain for a switch.

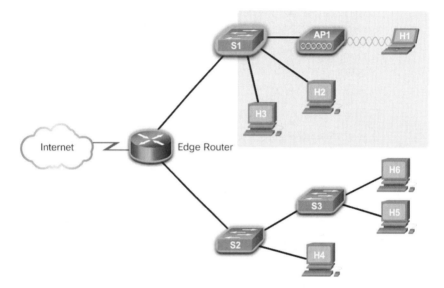

**Figure 1-10**   Failure Domain—Switch

Figure 1-11 shows an example of the failure domain for a *wireless access point (AP)*.

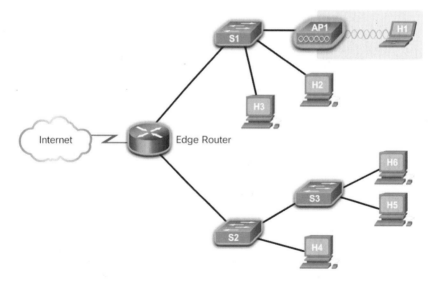

**Figure 1-11**   Failure Domain—Wireless Access Point

Because a failure at the core layer of a network can have a potentially large impact, the network designer often concentrates on efforts to prevent failures. These efforts can greatly increase the cost of implementing the network.

In the hierarchical design model, it is easiest and usually least expensive to control the size of a failure domain in the distribution layer. Limiting the size of failure domains in the distribution layer confines network errors to a smaller area and thereby affects fewer users. When using Layer 3 devices at the distribution layer, every router functions as a gateway for a limited number of access layer users.

Routers or multilayer switches are usually deployed in pairs, with access layer switches evenly divided between them. This configuration is referred to as a *building switch block* or a *departmental switch block*. Each switch block acts independently of the others. As a result, the failure of a single device does not cause the network to go down. Even the failure of an entire switch block does not affect a significant number of end users.

## Increasing Bandwidth (1.1.2.4)

In hierarchical network design, some links between access and distribution switches may need to process a greater amount of traffic than other links. As traffic from multiple links converges onto a single, outgoing link, it is possible for that link to become a bottleneck.

Link aggregation allows an administrator to increase the amount of bandwidth between devices by creating one logical link by grouping several physical links together. *EtherChannel* is a form of link aggregation used in switched networks, as shown in Figure 1-12.

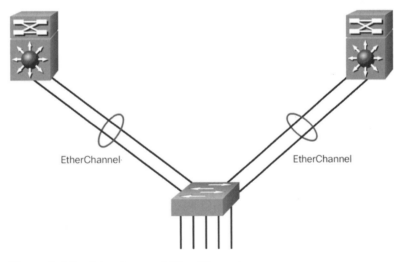

**Figure 1-12**  Advantages of EtherChannel

EtherChannel uses the existing switch ports. Therefore, additional costs to upgrade the link to a faster and more expensive connection are not necessary. The EtherChannel is seen as one logical link, using an EtherChannel interface.

On a Cisco Catalyst switch, an EtherChannel is configured as a *port channel interface*. Most configuration tasks are done on the port channel interface instead of on each individual port to ensure configuration consistency throughout the links.

Finally, the EtherChannel configuration takes advantage of *load balancing* between links that are part of the same EtherChannel, and depending on the hardware platform, one or more load balancing methods can be implemented.

EtherChannel operation and configuration are covered in more detail Chapter 4, "EtherChannel and HSRP."

## Expanding the Access Layer (1.1.2.5)

A network must be designed to be able to expand network access to individuals and devices as needed. An increasingly important aspect of extending access layer connectivity is wireless connectivity. Providing wireless connectivity offers many advantages, such as increased flexibility, reduced costs, and the ability to grow and adapt to changing network and business requirements.

To communicate wirelessly, end devices require a wireless network interface card (NIC) that incorporates a radio transmitter/receiver and the required software driver to make it operational. In addition, a wireless router or a wireless access point (AP) is required for users to connect, as shown in Figure 1-13.

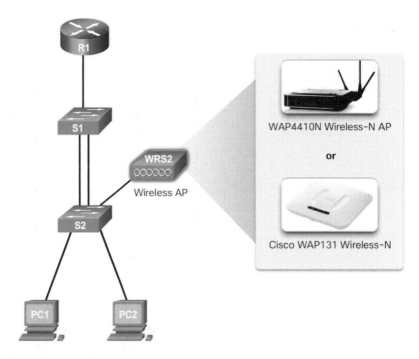

**Figure 1-13**   Wireless LANs

Implementing a wireless network involves many considerations, such as the types of wireless devices to use, wireless coverage requirements, interference considerations, and security considerations.

### Fine-tuning Routing Protocols (1.1.2.6)

Advanced routing protocols, such as *Open Shortest Path First (OSPF)* and *Enhanced Interior Gateway Routing Protocol (EIGRP)*, are used in large networks.

A *link-state routing protocol* such as OSPF, as shown in Figure 1-14, works well for larger hierarchical networks where fast convergence is important.

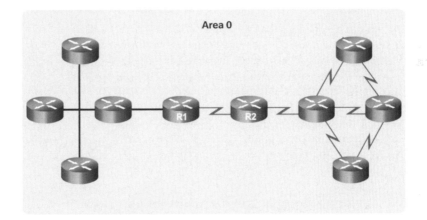

**Figure 1-14**   Single-Area OSPF

OSPF routers establish and maintain neighbor adjacency or adjacencies with other connected OSPF routers. When routers initiate an adjacency with neighbors, an exchange of link-state updates begins. Routers reach a FULL state of adjacency when they have synchronized views on their link-state database. With OSPF, link-state updates are sent when network changes occur. *Single-area OSPF* configuration and concepts are covered in Chapter 8, "Single-Area OSPF."

In addition, OSPF supports a two-layer hierarchical design, referred to as *multiarea OSPF*, as shown in Figure 1-15.

All multiarea OSPF networks must have an Area 0, also called the backbone area. Non-backbone areas must be directly connected to area 0. Chapter 9, "Multiarea OSPF," introduces the benefits, operation, and configuration of multiarea OSPF. Chapter 10, "OSPF Tuning and Troubleshooting," covers more advanced features of OSPF.

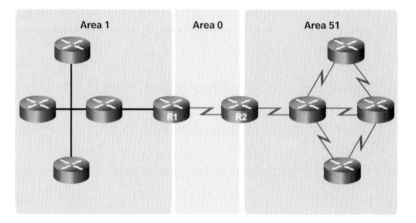

**Figure 1-15**   Multiarea OSPF

Another popular routing protocol for larger networks is EIGRP. Cisco developed EIGRP as a proprietary *distance vector routing protocol* with enhanced capabilities. Although configuring EIGRP is relatively simple, the underlying features and options of EIGRP are extensive and robust. For example, EIGRP uses protocol-dependent modules (PDM), which enable support for IPv4 and IPv6 routing tables, as shown in Figure 1-16.

| Neighbor Table – IPv6 | | |
| --- | --- | --- |
| Neighbor Table – IPv4 | | 2 Neighbor Tables |
| Net-Hop Router | Interface | |

| Topology Table – IPv6 | | |
| --- | --- | --- |
| Topology Table – IPv4 | | 2 Topology Tables |
| Destination1 | Successor | |
| Destination2 | Feasible Successor | |

| Routing Table – IPv6 | | |
| --- | --- | --- |
| Routing Table – IPv4 | | 2 Routing Tables |
| Destination1 | Successor | |

**Figure 1-16**   EIGRP Protocol-Dependent Modules (PDM)

EIGRP contains many features that are not found in any other routing protocols. It is an excellent choice for large multiprotocol networks that use primarily Cisco devices.

Chapter 6, "EIGRP," introduces the operation and configuration of the EIGRP routing protocol, and Chapter 7, "EIGRP Tuning and Troubleshooting," covers some of the more advanced configuration options of EIGRP.

**Interactive Graphic**

**Activity 1.1.2.7: Identify Scalability Terminology**

Refer to the online course to complete this activity.

# Selecting Network Devices (1.2)

Switches and routers are core network infrastructure devices. Therefore, selecting them appears to be a fairly simple task. However, many different models of switches and routers are available. Different models provide various numbers of ports, different forwarding rates, and unique feature support.

In this section, you will learn how to select network devices based on feature compatibility and network requirements.

## Switch Hardware (1.2.1)

Various types of switch platforms are available. Each platform differs in terms of physical configuration and *form factor*, the number of ports, and the features supported, including *Power over Ethernet (PoE)* and routing protocols.

The focus of this topic is on how to select the appropriate switch hardware features to support network requirements in small to medium-sized business networks.

### Switch Platforms (1.2.1.1)

When designing a network, it is important to select the proper hardware to meet current network requirements, as well as allow for network growth. Within an enterprise network, both switches and routers play a critical role in network communication.

There are five categories of switches for enterprise networks, as shown in Figure 1-17:

- *Campus LAN switch*—To scale network performance in an enterprise LAN, there are core, distribution, access, and compact switches. These switch platforms vary from fanless switches with eight fixed ports to 13-blade switches supporting hundreds of ports. Campus LAN switch platforms include the Cisco 2960, 3560, 3650, 3850, 4500, 6500, and 6800 Series.

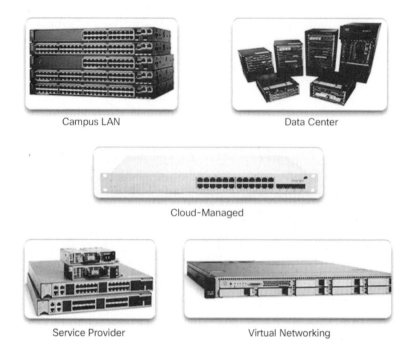

**Figure 1-17** Switch Platforms

- *Cloud-managed switch*—The Cisco Meraki cloud-managed access switches enable virtual stacking of switches. They monitor and configure thousands of switch ports over the web, without the intervention of onsite IT staff.

- *Data center switch*—A data center should be built based on switches that promote infrastructure scalability, operational continuity, and transport flexibility. The data center switch platforms include the Cisco Nexus Series switches and the Cisco Catalyst 6500 Series switches.

- *Service provider switch*—Service provider switches fall under two categories: aggregation switches and Ethernet access switches. Aggregation switches are carrier-grade Ethernet switches that aggregate traffic at the edge of a network. Service provider Ethernet access switches feature application intelligence, unified services, virtualization, integrated security, and simplified management.

- *Virtual networking switch*—Networks are becoming increasingly virtualized. Cisco Nexus virtual networking switch platforms provide secure multitenant services by adding virtualization intelligence technology to the data center network.

When selecting switches, network administrators must determine the switch form factors. These include *fixed configuration* (Figure 1-18), *modular configuration* (Figure 1-19), or *stackable configuration* (Figure 1-20).

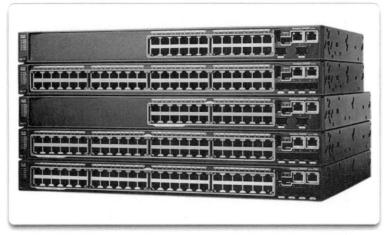

Features and options are limited to those that originally come with the switch.

**Figure 1-18**   Fixed Configuration Switches

The chassis accepts line cards that contain the ports.

**Figure 1-19**   Modular Configuration Switches

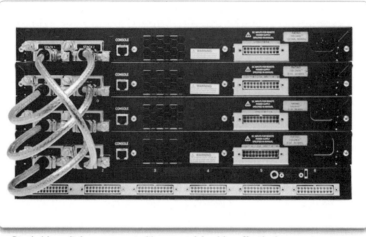

Stackable switches, connected by a special cable, effectively operate as one large switch.

**Figure 1-20**  Stackable Configuration Switches

The amount of space that a device occupies in a network rack is also an important consideration. *Rack unit* is a term used to describe the thickness of a rack-mountable network device. Defined in EIA-310, a unit (U) describes a device with a standard height of 4.45 centimeters (1 3/4 inches) and width of 48.26 centimeters (19 inches). For example, the fixed configuration switches shown in Figure 1-18 are all one rack unit (1U).

Besides the device form factor, other device selection considerations must be made. Table 1-1 describes some of these considerations.

**Table 1-1**  Considerations When Selecting Network Devices

| Consideration | Description |
|---|---|
| Cost | The cost of a switch depends on the number and speed of the interfaces, supported features, and expansion capability. |
| Port density | The port density describes how many ports are available on the switch. Network switches must support the appropriate number of devices on the network. |
| Port speed | The speed of the network connection is of primary concern to end users. |
| Forwarding rate | This rate defines the processing capabilities of a switch by rating how much data the switch can process per second. For instance, distribution layer switches should provide higher forwarding rates than access layer switches. |

| Consideration | Description |
|---|---|
| Size of frame buffers | Switches with large frame buffers are better able to store frames when there are congested ports to servers or other areas of the network. |
| PoE support | Power over Ethernet (PoE) is used to power access points, IP phones, security cameras, and even compact switches. Demand for PoE is increasing. |
| Redundant power | Some stackable and modular chassis-based switches support redundant power supplies. |
| Reliability | Switches should provide continuous access to the network. Therefore, select switches with reliable redundant features including redundant power supplies, fans, and *supervisor engines*. |
| Scalability | The number of users on a network typically grows over time. Therefore, select switches that provide the opportunity for growth. |

Some of these considerations are now described in more detail.

## Port Density (1.2.1.2)

The *port density* of a switch refers to the number of ports available on a single switch. Figure 1-21 shows the port densities of three different switches.

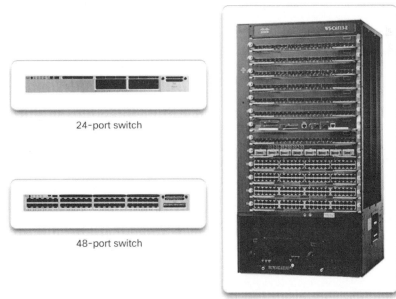

24-port switch

48-port switch

Modular switch with up to 1000+ ports

**Figure 1-21**   Port Densities

Fixed configuration switches support a variety of port density configurations. The Cisco Catalyst 3850 24-port and 48-port switches are shown on the left in the figure. The 48-port switch has an option for 4 additional ports for *small form-factor plug-gable (SFP)* devices. SFPs are small compact, hot-pluggable transceivers used on some switches to provide flexibility when choosing network media. SPF transceivers are available for copper and fiber Ethernet, Fibre Channel networks, and more.

Modular switches can support very high port densities through the addition of multiple switch port line cards. The modular Catalyst 6500 switch shown on the right in the figure can support in excess of 1000 switch ports.

Large networks that support many thousands of network devices require high-density modular switches to make the best use of space and power. Without high-density modular switches, a network would need many fixed configuration switches to accommodate the number of devices that need network access—and this approach can consume many power outlets and a lot of closet space.

A network designer must also consider the issue of uplink bottlenecks: A series of fixed configuration switches may consume many additional ports for bandwidth aggregation between switches, for the purpose of achieving target performance. With a single modular switch, bandwidth aggregation is less problematic because the backplane of the chassis can provide the necessary bandwidth to accommodate the devices connected to the switch port line cards.

## Forwarding Rates (1.2.1.3)

*Forwarding rates* define the processing capabilities of a switch by rating how much data the switch can process per second. Switch product lines are classified by forwarding rates, as shown in Figure 1-22.

Forwarding rates are an important consideration when selecting a switch. If its forwarding rate is too low, a switch cannot accommodate full wire-speed communication across all of its switch ports. *Wire speed* is a term used to describe the data rate that each Ethernet port on the switch is capable of attaining. Data rates can be 100 Mb/s, 1 Gb/s, 10 Gb/s, or 100 Gb/s.

For example, a typical 48-port gigabit switch operating at full wire speed generates 48 Gb/s of traffic. If the switch supports a forwarding rate of only 32 Gb/s, it cannot run at full wire speed across all ports simultaneously.

Access layer switches are usually physically limited by their uplinks to the distribution layer. However, they typically do not need to operate at full wire speed. Therefore, less expensive, lower-performing switches can be used at the access layer. The more expensive, higher-performing switches can be used at the distribution and core layers, where the forwarding rate has a greater impact on network performance.

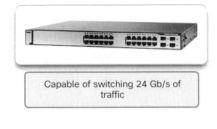

24-port Gigabit Ethernet Switch

Capable of switching 24 Gb/s of traffic

48-port Gigabit Ethernet Switch

Capable of switching 48 Gb/s of traffic

**Figure 1-22**   Forwarding Rate

## Power over Ethernet (1.2.1.4)

PoE allows a switch to deliver power to a device over the existing Ethernet cabling. This feature can be used by IP phones and some wireless access points. Figure 1-23 shows PoE ports on various devices.

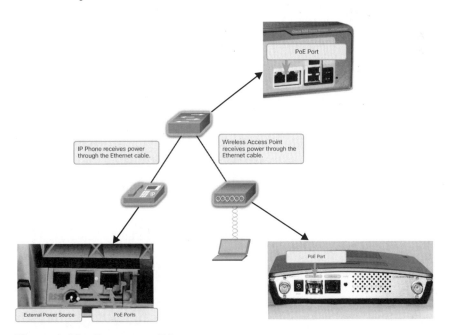

**Figure 1-23**   Power over Ethernet

PoE increases flexibility when installing wireless access points and IP phones because these devices can be installed anywhere that there is an Ethernet cable. Therefore, a network administrator should ensure that the PoE features are required because switches that support PoE are expensive.

The Cisco Catalyst 2960-C and 3560-C Series compact switches support PoE pass-through. PoE pass-through allows a network administrator to power PoE devices connected to the switch, as well as the switch itself, by drawing power from certain upstream switches. Figure 1-24 shows the PoE ports on a Cisco Catalyst 2960-C.

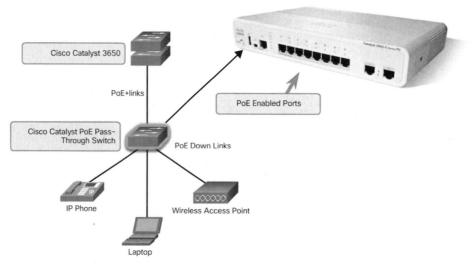

**Figure 1-24**   PoE Pass-through

## Multilayer Switching (1.2.1.5)

Multilayer switches are typically deployed in the core and distribution layers of an organization's switched network. Multilayer switches are characterized by their capability to build a routing table, support a few routing protocols, and forward IP packets at a rate close to that of Layer 2 forwarding. Multilayer switches often support specialized hardware, such as *application-specific integrated circuits (ASIC)*. ASICs along with dedicated software data structures can streamline the forwarding of IP packets independently of the CPU.

There is a trend in networking toward a pure Layer 3 switched environment. When switches were first used in networks, none of them supported routing; now, almost all switches support routing. It is likely that soon all switches will incorporate a route processor because the cost is decreasing relative to other constraints.

As shown in Figure 1-25, the Catalyst 2960 switches illustrate the migration to a pure Layer 3 environment. With IOS versions prior to 15.x, these switches supported only one active switched virtual interface (SVI). With IOS 15.x, these switches now support multiple active SVIs. This means that a Catalyst 2960 switch can be remotely accessed via multiple IP addresses on distinct networks.

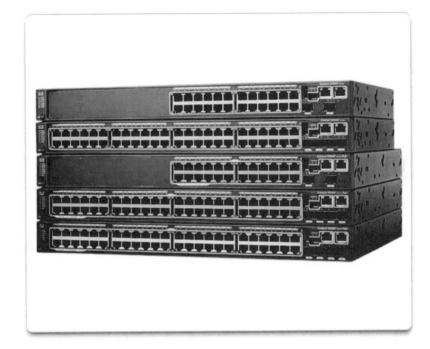

**Figure 1-25**   Cisco Catalyst 2960 Series Switches

**Activity 1.2.1.6: Selecting Switch Hardware**

Refer to the online course to complete this activity.

**Packet Tracer 1.2.1.7: Comparing 2960 and 3560 Switches**

In this activity, you will use various commands to examine three different switching topologies and compare the similarities and differences between the 2960 and 3560 switches. You will also compare the routing table of a 1941 router with a 3560 switch.

## Router Hardware (1.2.2)

Various types of router platforms are available. Like switches, routers differ in physical configuration and form factor, the number and types of interfaces supported, and the features supported.

The focus of this topic is on how to describe the types of routers available to support network requirements in small to medium-sized business networks.

### Router Requirements (1.2.2.1)

In the distribution layer of an enterprise network, routing is required. Without the routing process, packets cannot leave the local network.

Routers play a critical role in networking by determining the best path for sending packets. They connect multiple IP networks by connecting homes and businesses to the Internet. They are also used to interconnect multiple sites within an enterprise network, providing redundant paths to destinations. A router can also act as a translator between different media types and protocols. For example, a router can accept packets from an Ethernet network and re-encapsulate them for transport over a serial network.

Routers use the network portion of the destination IP address to route packets to the proper destination. They select an alternate path if a link or path goes down. All hosts on a local network specify the IP address of the local router interface in their IP configuration. This router interface is the default gateway. The ability to route efficiently and recover from network link failures is critical to delivering packets to their destination.

Routers also serve other beneficial functions, as shown in Figure 1-26:

- Provide broadcast containment
- Provide enhanced security
- Connect remote locations
- Group users logically by application or department

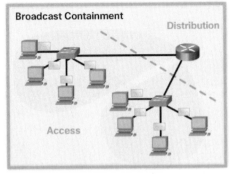

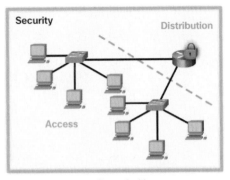

Routers limit broadcasts to the local network.

Routers can be configured with access control lists to filter unwanted traffic.

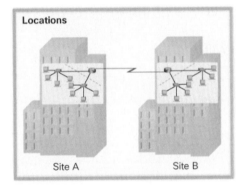

Routers can be used to interconnect geographically separated locations.

Routers logically group users who require access to the same resources.

**Figure 1-26**   Router Functions

## Cisco Routers (1.2.2.2)

As a network grows, it is important to select the proper routers to meet its requirements. As shown Figure 1-27, there are three categories of routers:

- *Branch router*—Branch routers optimize branch services on a single platform while delivering an optimal application experience across branch and WAN infrastructures. Maximizing service availability at the branch requires networks designed for 24x7x365 uptime. Highly available branch networks must ensure fast recovery from typical faults while minimizing or eliminating the impact on service, and they must provide simple network configuration and management.

**Figure 1-27**    Router Platforms

- *Network edge router*—Network edge routers enable the network edge to deliver high-performance, highly secure, and reliable services that unite campus, data center, and branch networks. Customers expect a high-quality media experience and more types of content than ever before. Customers want interactivity, personalization, mobility, and control for all content. Customers also want to access content anytime and anyplace they choose, over any device—whether at home, at work, or on the go. Network edge routers must deliver enhanced quality of service and nonstop video and mobile capabilities.

- *Service provider router*—Service provider routers differentiate the service portfolio and increase revenues by delivering end-to-end scalable solutions and subscriber-aware services. Operators must optimize operations, reduce expenses, and improve scalability and flexibility to deliver next-generation Internet experiences across all devices and locations. These systems are designed to simplify and enhance the operation and deployment of service-delivery networks.

## Router Hardware (1.2.2.3)

Routers are available in many form factors, as shown in Figure 1-28. Network administrators in an enterprise environment should be able to support a variety of routers, from a small desktop router to a rack-mounted or blade model.

**800 Series**
Small branch office routers

**2900 Series**
Large branch office routers

**2000 Series**
Industrial routers designed to operate in harsh, rugged environments

**ASR 1000 Series**
Aggregation Services Routers for the enterprise network edge

**Cisco CRS**
Cisco Carrier Routing System for data centers and service providers

**Figure 1-28**   A Sampling of Cisco Routers

Routers can also be categorized as fixed configuration or modular. With the fixed configuration, the desired router interfaces are built in. Modular routers come with multiple slots that allow a network administrator to change the interfaces on the router. For example, a Cisco 1941 router is a small modular router. It comes with two built-in Gigabit Ethernet RJ-45 interfaces, and it also has two slots that can accommodate many different network interface modules. Routers come with a variety of different interfaces, such as Fast Ethernet, Gigabit Ethernet, serial, and fiber-optic.

Visit www.cisco.com/c/en/us/products/routers/product-listing.html for a comprehensive list of Cisco routers.

**Interactive Graphic**

**Activity 1.2.2.4: Identify the Router Category**

Refer to the online course to complete this activity.

## Managing Devices (1.2.3)

Regardless of the form factor and the features each IOS device supports, it requires the *Cisco Internetwork Operating System (IOS)* to be operational.

The focus of this topic is on the Cisco IOS, how to manage it, and how to configure basic settings on Cisco IOS routers and switches.

## Managing IOS Files and Licensing (1.2.3.1)

With such a wide selection of network devices to choose from in the Cisco product line, an organization can carefully determine the ideal combination to meet the needs of employees and customers.

When selecting or upgrading a Cisco IOS device, it is important to choose the proper *IOS image* with the correct feature set and version. The IOS image refers to the package of routing, switching, security, and other internetworking technologies integrated into a single multitasking operating system. When a new device is shipped, it comes preinstalled with the software image and the corresponding permanent licenses for the customer-specified packages and features.

For routers, beginning with Cisco IOS Software Release 15.0, Cisco modified the process to enable new technologies within the IOS feature sets, as shown in Figure 1-29.

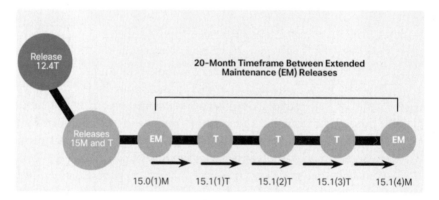

**Figure 1-29**   Cisco IOS Software Release 15 Family

In this figure, EM (or Extended Maintenance) releases are released approximately every 16 to 20 months. The T releases are between EM releases and are ideal for the very latest features and hardware support before the next EM release becomes available.

## In-Band versus Out-of-Band Management (1.2.3.2)

Regardless of the Cisco IOS network device being implemented, there are two methods for connecting a PC to that network device for configuration and monitoring tasks: *out-of-band management* and *in-band management* (see Figure 1-30).

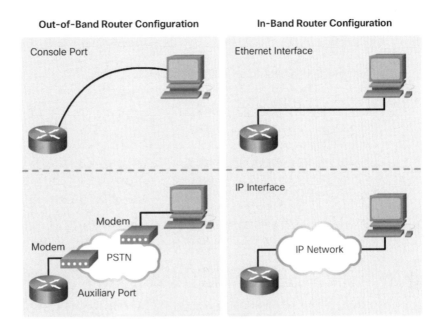

**Figure 1-30**   In-Band versus Out-of-Band Configuration Options

Out-of-band management is used for initial configuration or when a network connection is unavailable. Configuration using out-of-band management requires:

- A direct connection to a console or an AUX port

- A terminal emulation client (such as *PuTTY* or *TeraTerm*)

In-band management is used to monitor and make configuration changes to a network device over a network connection. Configuration using in-band management requires:

- At least one network interface on the device to be connected and operational

- Telnet, SSH, HTTP, or HTTPS to access a Cisco device

**Note**

Telnet and HTTP are less secure than the others listed here and are not recommended.

## Basic Router CLI Commands (1.2.3.3)

A basic router configuration includes the host name for identification, passwords for security, assignment of IP addresses to interfaces for connectivity, and basic routing.

Example 1-1 shows the commands entered to enable a router with RIPv2. Verify and save configuration changes by using the **copy running-config startup-config** command.

**Example 1-1**   Enabling a Router with RIPv2

```
Router# configure terminal
Router(config)# hostname R1
R1(config)# enable secret class
R1(config)# line con 0
R1(config-line)# password cisco
R1(config-line)# login
R1(config-line)# exec-timeout 0 0
R1(config-line)# line vty 0 4
R1(config-line)# password cisco
R1(config-line)# login
R1(config-line)# exit
R1(config)# service password-encryption
R1(config)# banner motd $ Authorized Access Only! $
R1(config)#
R1(config)# interface GigabitEthernet0/0
R1(config-if)# description Link to LAN 1
R1(config-if)# ip address 172.16.1.1 255.255.255.0
R1(config-if)# no shutdown
R1(config-if)# exit
R1(config)#
R1(config)# interface Serial0/0/0
R1(config-if)# description Link to R2
R1(config-if)# ip address 172.16.3.1 255.255.255.252
R1(config-if)# clock rate 128000
R1(config-if)# no shutdown
R1(config-if)# interface Serial0/0/1
R1(config-if)# description Link to R3
R1(config-if)# ip address 192.168.10.5 255.255.255.252
R1(config-if)# no shutdown
R1(config-if)# exit
R1(config)#
R1(config)# router rip
R1(config-router)# version 2
R1(config-router)# network 172.16.0.0
R1(config-router)# network 192.168.10.0
R1(config-router)# end
R1#
R1# copy running-config startup-config
```

Example 1-2 shows the results of the configuration commands entered in Example 1-1. To clear the router configuration, use the **erase startup-config** command and then the **reload** command.

**Example 1-2**   Router Running Configuration

```
R1# show running-config
Building configuration...

Current configuration : 1242 bytes
!
Version 15.1
Service timestamps debug datetime msec
Service timestamps log datetime msec
Service password-encryption
!
hostname R1
!
enable secret class
!
<output omitted>
!
interface GigabitEthernet0/0
 description Link to LAN 1
 ip address 172.16.1.1 255.255.255.0
 no shutdown
!
interface Serial0/0/0
 description Link to R2
 ip address 172.16.3.1 255.255.255.252
 clock rate 128000
 no shutdown
!
interface Serial0/0/1
 description Link to R3
 ip address 192.168.10.5 255.255.255.252
 no shutdown
!
router rip
 version 2
 network 172.16.1.0
 network 192.168.10.0
!
banner motd ^C Authorized Access Only! ^C
!
line console 0
 password cisco
 login
```

```
 exec-timeout 0 0
line aux 0
line vty 0 4
 password cisco
 login
```

## Basic Router Show Commands (1.2.3.4)

A variety of IOS commands are commonly used to display and verify the operational status of the router and related IPv4 network functionality. Similar commands are available for IPv6; they replace **ip** with **ipv6**.

The following list describes routing-related and interface-related IOS router commands:

- **show ip protocols**—Displays information about the routing protocols configured. If RIP is configured, this includes the version of RIP, networks the router is advertising, whether automatic summarization is in effect, the neighbors the router is receiving updates from, and the default administrative distance, which is 120 for RIP (see Example 1-3).

**Example 1-3**  The **show ip protocols** Command

```
R1# show ip protocols

Routing Protocol is "rip"
  Outgoing update filter list for all interfaces is not set
  Incoming update filter list for all interfaces is not set
  Sending updates every 30 seconds, next due in 26 seconds
  Invalid after 180 seconds, hold down 180, flushed after 240
  Redistributing: rip
  Default version control: send version 2, receive version 2
    Interface             Send  Recv  Triggered RIP  Key-chain
    GigabitEthernet0/0    2     2
    Serial0/0/0           2     2
    Serial0/0/1           2     2
    Interface             Send  Recv  Triggered RIP  Key-chain
  Automatic network summarization is in effect
  Maximum path: 4
  Routing for Networks:
   172.16.0.0
   192.168.10.0
  Routing Information Sources:
    Gateway         Distance      Last Update
    172.16.3.2           120      00:00:25
  Distance: (default is 120)
```

- **show ip route**—Displays routing table information, including routing codes, known networks, administrative distance and metrics, how routes were learned, next hop, static routes, and default routes (see Example 1-4).

**Example 1-4**   The **show ip route** Command

```
R1# show ip route | begin Gateway
Gateway of last resort is not set


      172.16.0.0/16 is variably subnetted, 5 subnets, 3 masks
C        172.16.1.0/24 is directly connected, GigabitEthernet0/0
L        172.16.1.1/32 is directly connected, GigabitEthernet0/0
C        172.16.3.0/30 is directly connected, Serial0/0/0
L        172.16.3.1/32 is directly connected, Serial0/0/0
R        172.16.5.0/24 [120/1] via 172.16.3.2, 00:00:25, Serial0/0/0
      192.168.10.0/24 is variably subnetted, 2 subnets, 2 masks
C        192.168.10.4/30 is directly connected, Serial0/0/1
L        192.168.10.5/32 is directly connected, Serial0/0/1
```

- **show interfaces**—Displays interface information and status, including the line (protocol) status, bandwidth, delay, reliability, encapsulation, duplex, and I/O statistics. If specified without a specific interface designation, all interfaces are displayed. If a specific interface is specified after the command, information about that interface only is displayed (see Example 1-5).

**Example 1-5**   The **show interfaces** Command

```
R1# show interfaces gigabitethernet 0/0
GigabitEthernet0/0 is up, line protocol is up (connected)
  Hardware is CN Gigabit Ethernet, address is 00e0.8fb2.de01 (bia 00e0.8fb2.de01)
  Description: Link to LAN 1
  Internet address is 172.16.1.1/24
  MTU 1500 bytes, BW 1000000 Kbit, DLY 10 usec,
     reliability 255/255, txload 1/255, rxload 1/255
  Encapsulation ARPA, loopback not set
  Keepalive set (10 sec)
  Full Duplex, 100Mbps, media type is RJ45
<output omitted>
Serial0/0/0 is up, line protocol is up (connected)
  Hardware is HD64570
  Description: Link to R2
```

```
   Internet address is 172.16.3.1/30
   MTU 1500 bytes, BW 1544 Kbit, DLY 20000 usec,
      reliability 255/255, txload 1/255, rxload 1/255
   Encapsulation HDLC, loopback not set, keepalive set (10 sec)
   Last input never, output never, output hang never
   Last clearing of "show interface" counters never
<output omitted>
Serial0/0/1 is up, line protocol is up (connected)
  Hardware is HD64570
  Description: Link to R3
  Internet address is 192.168.10.5/30
  MTU 1500 bytes, BW 1544 Kbit, DLY 20000 usec,
      reliability 255/255, txload 1/255, rxload 1/255
  Encapsulation HDLC, loopback not set, keepalive set (10 sec)
  Last input never, output never, output hang never
  Last clearing of "show interface" counters never
```

- **show ip interfaces**—Displays IP-related interface information, including protocol status, the IPv4 address, whether a helper address is configured, and whether an ACL is enabled on the interface. If specified without a specific interface designation, all interfaces are displayed. If a specific interface is specified after the command, information about that interface only is displayed (see Example 1-6).

**Example 1-6**  The **show ip interface** Command

```
R1# show ip interface gigabitEthernet 0/0
GigabitEthernet0/0 is up, line protocol is up
  Internet address is 172.16.1.1/24
  Broadcast address is 255.255.255.255
  Address determined by setup command
  MTU is 1500 bytes
  Helper address is not set
  Directed broadcast forwarding is disabled
  Multicast reserved groups joined: 224.0.0.5 224.0.0.6
  Outgoing access list is not set
  Inbound  access list is not set
  Proxy ARP is enabled
 Local Proxy ARP is disabled
  Security level is default
  Split horizon is enabled
  ICMP redirects are always sent
  ICMP unreachables are always sent
```

```
ICMP mask replies are never sent
IP fast switching is enabled
IP fast switching on the same interface is disabled
IP Flow switching is disabled
IP CEF switching is enabled
IP CEF switching turbo vector
IP multicast fast switching is enabled
IP multicast distributed fast switching is disabled
IP route-cache flags are Fast, CEF
Router Discovery is disabled
IP output packet accounting is disabled
IP access violation accounting is disabled
TCP/IP header compression is disabled
RTP/IP header compression is disabled
Policy routing is disabled
Network address translation is disabled
BGP Policy Mapping is disabled
Input features: MCI Check
IPv4 WCCP Redirect outbound is disabled
IPv4 WCCP Redirect inbound is disabled
IPv4 WCCP Redirect exclude is disabled
```

- **show ip interface brief**—Displays a summary status of all interfaces, including IPv4 addressing information and interface and line protocols status (see Example 1-7).

**Example 1-7**   The **show ip interface brief** Command

```
R1# show ip interface brief
Interface              IP-Address      OK? Method Status                Protocol
GigabitEthernet0/0     172.16.1.1      YES manual up                    up
GigabitEthernet0/1     unassigned      YES unset  administratively down down
Serial0/0/0            172.16.3.1      YES manual up                    up
Serial0/0/1            192.168.10.5    YES manual up                    up
Vlan1                  unassigned      YES unset  administratively down down
```

- **show protocols**—Displays information about the routed protocol that is enabled and the protocol status of interfaces (see Example 1-8).

**Example 1-8**   The **show protocols** Command

```
R1# show protocols
Global values:
    Internet Protocol routing is enabled
GigabitEthernet0/0 is up, line protocol is up
    Internet address is 172.16.1.1/24
GigabitEthernet0/1 is administratively down, line protocol is down
Serial0/0/0 is up, line protocol is up
    Internet address is 172.16.3.1/30
Serial0/0/1 is up, line protocol is up
    Internet address is 192.168.10.5/30
Vlan1 is administratively down, line protocol is down
```

- **show cdp neighbors**—Tests the Layer 2 connection and provides information about directly connected CDP enabled Cisco devices (see Example 1-9).

**Example 1-9**   The **show cdp neighbors** Command

```
R1# show cdp neighbors
Capability Codes: R - Router, T - Trans Bridge, B - Source Route Bridge
                  D - Remote, C - CVTA, M - Two-port MAC Relay
                  S - Switch, H - Host, I - IGMP, r - Repeater, P - Phone
Device ID     Local Intrfce    Holdtme    Capability    Platform    Port ID
R2            Ser 0/0/0        136        R             C1900       Ser 0/0/0
R3            Ser 0/0/1        133        R             C1900       Ser 0/0/0
```

This command tests the Layer 2 connection and displays information on directly connected Cisco devices. The information it provides includes the device ID, the local interface the device is connected to, capability (R = router, S = switch), the platform, and the port ID of the remote device. The **details** option includes IP addressing information and the IOS version.

## Basic Switch CLI Commands (1.2.3.5)

Basic switch configuration includes the host name for identification, passwords for security, and assignment of IP addresses for connectivity. In-band access requires the switch to have an IP address. Example 1-10 shows the commands entered to enable a switch.

Example 1-11 shows the results of the configuration commands that were entered in Example 1-10. Verify and save the switch configuration by using the **copy running-config startup-config** command. To clear the switch configuration, use the **erase startup-config** command and then the **reload** command. It may also be necessary to erase any VLAN information by using the command **delete flash:vlan.dat**. When switch configurations are in place, view the configurations by using the **show running-config** command.

**Example 1-10**  Enabling a Switch with a Basic Configuration

```
Switch# enable
Switch# configure terminal
Switch(config)# hostname S1
S1(config)# enable secret class
S1(config)# line con 0
S1(config-line)# password cisco
S1(config-line)# login
S1(config-line)# line vty 0 4
S1(config-line)# password cisco
S1(config-line)# login
S1(config-line)# service password-encryption
S1(config-line)# exit
S1(config)#
S1(config)# service password-encryption
S1(config)# banner motd $ Authorized Access Only! $
S1(config)#
S1(config)# interface vlan 1
S1(config-if)# ip address 192.168.1.5 255.255.255.0
S1(config-if)# no shutdown
S1(config-if)# exit
S1(config)# ip default-gateway 192.168.1.1
S1(config)#
S1(config)# interface fa0/2
S1(config-if)# switchport mode access
S1(config-if)# switchport port-security
S1(config-if)# end
S1#
S1# copy running-config startup-config
```

**Example 1-11**  Switch Running Configuration

```
S1# show running-config
<some output omitted>
version 15.0
service password-encryption
!
hostname S1
!
enable secret 4 06YFDUHH61wAE/kLkDq9BGho1QM5EnRtoyr8cHAUg.2
!
interface FastEthernet0/2
 switchport mode access
 switchport port-security
!
```

```
interface Vlan1
 ip address 192.168.1.5 255.255.255.0
!
ip default-gateway 192.168.1.1
!
banner motd ^C Authorized Access Only ^C
!
line con 0
 exec-timeout 0 0
 password 7 1511021F0725
 login
line vty 0 4
 password 7 1511021F0725
 login
line vty 5 15
 login
!
end

S1#
```

## Basic Switch Show Commands (1.2.3.6)

Switches make use of the following common IOS commands for configuration, to check for connectivity, and to display current switch status:

- **show port-security interface**—Displays any ports that have security activated. To examine a specific interface, include the interface ID. Information included in the output includes the maximum addresses allowed, the current count, the security violation count, and action to be taken (see Example 1-12).

**Example 1-12**   The **show port-security interface** Command

```
S1# show port-security interface fa0/2
Port Security              : Enabled
Port Status                : Secure-up
Violation Mode             : Shutdown
Aging Time                 : 0 mins
Aging Type                 : Absolute
SecureStatic Address Aging : Disabled
Maximum MAC Addresses      : 1
Total MAC Addresses        : 1
Configured MAC Addresses   : 0
Sticky MAC Addresses       : 0
Last Source Address:Vlan   : 0024.50d1.9902:1
Security Violation Count   : 0
```

- **show port-security address**—Displays all secure MAC addresses configured on all switch interfaces (see Example 1-13).

**Example 1-13**    The **show port-security address** Command

```
S1# show port-security address
Secure Mac Address Table
-------------------------------------------------------------------------------
Vlan    Mac Address       Type                           Ports    Remaining Age
                                                                   (mins)

----    -----------       ----                           -----    -------------
1       0024.50d1.9902    SecureDynamic                  Fa0/2        -
-------------------------------------------------------------------------------
Total Addresses in System (excluding one mac per port)     : 0
Max Addresses limit in System (excluding one mac per port) : 1536
```

- **show interfaces**—Displays one or all interfaces with line (protocol) status, bandwidth, delay, reliability, encapsulation, duplex, and I/O statistics (see Example 1-14).

**Example 1-14**    The **show interfaces** Command

```
S1# show interfaces fa0/2
FastEthernet0/2 is up, line protocol is up (connected)
  Hardware is Fast Ethernet, address is 001e.14cf.eb04 (bia 001e.14cf.eb04)
  MTU 1500 bytes, BW 100000 Kbit/sec, DLY 100 usec,
      reliability 255/255, txload 1/255, rxload 1/255
  Encapsulation ARPA, loopback not set
  Keepalive set (10 sec)
  Full-duplex, 100Mb/s, media type is 10/100BaseTX
  input flow-control is off, output flow-control is unsupported
  ARP type: ARPA, ARP Timeout 04:00:00
  Last input 00:00:08, output 00:00:00, output hang never
  Last clearing of "show interface" counters never
  Input queue: 0/75/0/0 (size/max/drops/flushes); Total output drops: 0
  Queueing strategy: fifo
  Output queue: 0/40 (size/max)
 5 minute input rate 0 bits/sec, 0 packets/sec
 5 minute output rate 2000 bits/sec, 3 packets/sec
     59 packets input, 11108 bytes, 0 no buffer
     Received 59 broadcasts (59 multicasts)
     0 runts, 0 giants, 0 throttles
     0 input errors, 0 CRC, 0 frame, 0 overrun, 0 ignored
     0 watchdog, 59 multicast, 0 pause input
```

```
   0 input packets with dribble condition detected
   886 packets output, 162982 bytes, 0 underruns
   0 output errors, 0 collisions, 1 interface resets
   0 unknown protocol drops
   0 babbles, 0 late collision, 0 deferred
   0 lost carrier, 0 no carrier, 0 pause output
   0 output buffer failures, 0 output buffers swapped out
```

- **show mac-address-table**—Displays all MAC addresses that the switch has learned, how those addresses were learned (dynamic/static), the port number, and the VLAN assigned to the port (see Example 1-15).

**Example 1-15**   The **show mac address-table** Command

```
S1# show mac address-table
          Mac Address Table
-------------------------------------------

Vlan    Mac Address       Type        Ports
----    -----------       --------    -----
 All    0100.0ccc.cccc    STATIC      CPU
 All    0100.0ccc.cccd    STATIC      CPU
 All    0180.c200.0000    STATIC      CPU
 All    0180.c200.0001    STATIC      CPU
  1     001e.4915.5405    DYNAMIC     Fa0/3
  1     001e.4915.5406    DYNAMIC     Fa0/4
  1     0024.50d1.9901    DYNAMIC     Fa0/1
  1     0024.50d1.9902    STATIC      Fa0/2
  1     0050.56be.0e67    DYNAMIC     Fa0/1
  1     0050.56be.c23d    DYNAMIC     Fa0/6
  1     0050.56be.df70    DYNAMIC     Fa0/
Total Mac Addresses for this criterion: 11
S1#
```

Like routers, switches also support the **show cdp neighbors** command.

The same in-band and out-of-band management techniques that apply to routers also apply to switch configuration.

# Summary (1.3)

**Class Activity 1.3.1.1: Layered Network Design Simulation**

Refer to *Scaling Networks v6 Labs & Study Guide* and the online course to complete this activity.

As the network administrator for a very small network, you want to prepare a simulated-network presentation for your branch manager to explain how the network currently operates.

The small network includes the following equipment:

- One 2911 Series router
- One 3560 switch
- One 2960 switch
- Four user workstations (PCs or laptops)
- One printer

**Interactive Graphic**

**Activity 1.3.1.2: Basic Switch Configurations**

Refer to the online course to complete this activity.

**Packet Tracer □ Activity**

**Packet Tracer 1.3.1.3: Skills Integration Challenge**

Background/Scenario

You are a recently hired LAN technician, and your network manager has asked you to demonstrate your ability to configure a small LAN. Your tasks include configuring initial settings on two switches using the Cisco IOS and configuring IP address parameters on host devices to provide end-to-end connectivity. You are to use two switches and two hosts/PCs on a cabled and powered network.

The hierarchical network design model divides network functionality into the access layer, the distribution layer, and the core layer. A campus wired LAN enables communications between devices in a building or group of buildings, as well as interconnection to the WAN and Internet edge at the network core.

A well-designed network controls traffic and limits the size of failure domains. Routers and switches can be deployed in pairs so that the failure of a single device does not cause service disruptions.

A network design should include an IP addressing strategy, scalable and fast-converging routing protocols, appropriate Layer 2 protocols, and modular or clustered devices that can be easily upgraded to increase capacity.

A mission-critical server should have connections to two different access layer switches. It should have redundant modules when possible, as well as a power backup source. It may be appropriate to provide multiple connections to one or more ISPs.

Security monitoring systems and IP telephony systems must have high availability and often require special design considerations.

It is important to deploy the appropriate type of routers and switches for a given set of requirements, features and specifications, and expected traffic flow.

## Practice

The following activities provide practice with the topics introduced in this chapter. The Labs and Class Activities are available in the companion *Scaling Networks v6 Labs & Study Guide* (ISBN 978-1-58713-433-3). The Packet Tracer activity instructions are also in the *Labs & Study Guide*. The PKA files are found in the online course.

**Class Activities**

Class Activity 1.0.1.2: Network by Design

Class Activity 1.3.1.1: Layered Network Design Simulation

**Packet Tracer Activities**

Packet Tracer 1.2.1.7: Comparing 2960 and 3560 Switches

Packet Tracer 1.3.1.3: Skills Integration Challenge

# Check Your Understanding Questions

Complete all the review questions listed here to test your understanding of the topics and concepts in this chapter. The appendix "Answers to 'Check Your Understanding' Questions" lists the answers.

1. In the Cisco Enterprise Architecture, which two functional parts of the network are combined to form a collapsed core design? (Choose two.)

    A. Access layer

    B. Core layer

    C. Distribution layer

    D. Enterprise edge

    E. Provider edge

2. Which design feature limits the impact of a distribution switch failure in an enterprise network?

    A. The installation of redundant power supplies

    B. The purchase of enterprise equipment that is designed for large traffic volume

    C. The use of a collapsed core design

    D. The use of the building switch block approach

3. What are two benefits of extending access layer connectivity to users through a wireless medium? (Choose two.)

    A. Decreased number of critical points of failure

    B. Increased bandwidth availability

    C. Increased flexibility

    D. Increased network management options

    E. Reduced costs

4. As the network administrator, you have been asked to implement EtherChannel on the corporate network. What does this configuration consist of?

    A. Grouping multiple physical ports to increase bandwidth between two switches

    B. Grouping two devices to share a virtual IP address

    C. Providing redundant devices to allow traffic to flow in the event of device failure

    D. Providing redundant links that dynamically block or forward traffic

5. Which statement describes a characteristic of Cisco Meraki switches?

   A. They are campus LAN switches that perform the same functions as Cisco 2960 switches.

   B. They are cloud-managed access switches that enable virtual stacking of switches.

   C. They are service provider switches that aggregate traffic at the edge of the network.

   D. They promote infrastructure scalability, operational continuity, and transport flexibility.

6. What term is used to express the thickness or height of a switch?

   A. Domain size

   B. Module size

   C. Port density

   D. Rack unit

7. What are two functions of a router? (Choose two.)

   A. It connects multiple IP networks.

   B. It controls the flow of data through the use of Layer 2 addresses.

   C. It determines the best path for sending packets.

   D. It increases the size of the broadcast domain.

   E. It manages the VLAN database.

8. Which two requirements must always be met to use in-band management to configure a network device? (Choose two.)

   A. A direct connection to the console port

   B. A direct connection to the auxiliary port

   C. A terminal emulation client

   D. At least one network interface that is connected and operational

   E. Telnet, SSH, or HTTP access to the device

9. What are two ways to access a Cisco switch for out-of-band management? (Choose two.)

   A. A connection that uses HTTP

   B. A connection that uses the AUX port

   C. A connection that uses the console port

   D. A connection that uses SSH

   E. A connection that uses Telnet

# CHAPTER 2

# Scaling VLANs

## Objectives

Upon completion of this chapter, you will be able to answer the following questions:

- How does VLAN Trunking Protocol (VTP) Version 1 compare with Version 2?

- How do you configure VTP Versions 1 and 2?

- How do you configure extended VLANs?

- How do you configure Dynamic Trunking Protocol (DTP)?

- How do you troubleshoot common inter-VLAN configuration issues?

- How do you troubleshoot common IP addressing issues in an inter-VLAN routed environment?

- How do you configure inter-VLAN routing using Layer 3 switching?

## Key Terms

This chapter uses the following key terms. You can find the definitions in the Glossary.

## Introduction (2.0.1.1)

As the number of switches increases on a small or medium-sized business network, the overall administration required to manage *virtual local area networks (VLANs)* and *trunks* in the network becomes challenging. This chapter examines some of the strategies and protocols that can be used to manage VLANs and trunks.

*VLAN Trunking Protocol (VTP)* reduces administration in a switched network. A switch in VTP server mode can manage additions, deletions, and renaming of VLANs across the domain. For example, when a new VLAN is added on the VTP server, the VLAN information is distributed to all switches in the domain. This eliminates the need to configure the new VLAN on every switch. VTP is a Cisco proprietary protocol that is available on most of the Cisco Catalyst Series products.

Using VLANs to segment a switched network provides improved performance, manageability, and security. Trunks are used to carry information from multiple VLANs between devices. *Dynamic Trunking Protocol (DTP)* provides the ability for ports to automatically negotiate trunking between switches.

Because VLANs segment a network, and each is on its own network or subnet, a Layer 3 process is required to allow traffic to move from one VLAN to another.

This chapter examines the implementation of inter-VLAN routing using a Layer 3 switch. It also describes issues encountered when implementing VTP, DTP, and inter-VLAN routing.

## VTP, Extended VLANs, and DTP (2.1)

Several technologies help simplify interswitch connectivity. VTP simplifies VLAN management in a switched network. VLANs are created and managed on VTP servers. Layer 2 access switches are typically configured as VTP clients that automatically update their VLAN database from VTP servers. Some Catalyst switches support the creation of *extended-range VLANs*. Extended-range VLANs, which are popular with service providers to segment their many clients, are numbered 1006 to 4094. Only transparent VTP mode switches can create extended VLANs. Finally, trunking must be enabled to transport VLAN frames between switches. DTP provides the ability for ports to automatically negotiate trunking between switches.

In this section, you will learn how to configure all of the enhanced interswitch connectivity technologies.

# VTP Concepts and Operation (2.1.1)

VTP propagates and synchronizes VLAN information to other switches in the VTP domain. There are currently three versions of VTP: VTP Version 1, VTP Version 2, and VTP Version 3. The focus of this topic is to compare VTP Versions 1 and 2.

## VTP Overview (2.1.1.1)

As the number of switches increases on a small or medium-sized business network, the overall administration required to manage VLANs and trunks in the network becomes challenging. In larger networks, VLAN management can become daunting. In Figure 2-1, assume that VLANs 10, 20, and 99 have already been implemented, and you must now add VLAN 30 to all switches. Manually adding the VLAN in this network would involve individually configuring 12 switches.

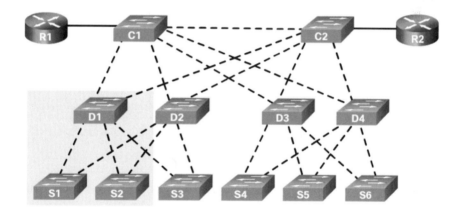

**Figure 2-1**   The VLAN Management Challenge

VTP allows a network administrator to manage VLANs on a master switch configured as a VTP server. The VTP server distributes and synchronizes VLAN information over trunk links to VTP-enabled client switches throughout the switched network. This minimizes problems caused by incorrect configurations and configuration inconsistencies.

### Note

VTP only learns about normal-range VLANs (VLAN IDs 1 to 1005). Extended-range VLANs (IDs greater than 1005) are not supported by VTP Version 1 or Version 2. VTP Version 3 does support extended VLANs but is beyond the scope of this course.

**Note**

VTP stores VLAN configurations in a database called *vlan.dat*.

Table 2-1 provides a brief description of important components of VTP.

**Table 2-1**   VTP Components

| VTP Components | Definition |
|---|---|
| *VTP domain* | A VTP domain consists of one or more interconnected switches. |
| | All switches in a domain share VLAN configuration details by using VTP advertisements. |
| | Switches that are in different VTP domains do not exchange VTP messages. |
| | A router or Layer 3 switch defines the boundary of a domain. |
| *VTP advertisements* | Each switch in a VTP domain sends periodic VTP advertisements from each trunk port to a reserved Layer 2 multicast address. |
| | Neighboring switches receive these advertisements and update their VTP and VLAN configurations as necessary. |
| *VTP modes* | A switch can be configured as a VTP server, client, or transparent. |
| VTP password | Switches in the VTP domain can also be configured with a password. |

**Note**

VTP advertisements are not exchanged if the trunk between switches is inactive.

## VTP Modes (2.1.1.2)

A switch can be configured in one of three VTP modes, as described in Table 2-2.

**Table 2-2**   VTP Modes

| VTP Mode | Definition |
|---|---|
| *VTP server* | VTP servers advertise the VTP domain VLAN information to other VTP-enabled switches in the same VTP domain. |
| | VTP servers store the VLAN information for the entire domain in NVRAM. |
| | The VTP server is where VLANs can be created, deleted, or renamed for the domain. |

| VTP Mode | Definition |
|----------|------------|
| *VTP client* | VTP clients function the same way as VTP servers, but you cannot create, change, or delete VLANs on a VTP client. |
| | A VTP client stores the VLAN information for the entire domain only while the switch is on. |
| | A switch reset deletes the VLAN information. |
| | You must configure VTP client mode on a switch. |
| *VTP transparent* | Transparent switches do not participate in VTP except to forward VTP advertisements to VTP clients and VTP servers. |
| | A VLAN that is created, renamed, or deleted on a transparent switch is local to that switch only. |
| | To create an extended VLAN, a switch must be configured as a VTP transparent switch when using VTP Version 1 or Version 2. |

Table 2-3 summarizes the operation of the three VTP modes.

**Table 2-3**   Comparing VTP Modes

| VTP Question | VTP Server | VTP Client | VTP Transparent |
|--------------|-----------|-----------|-----------------|
| What are the differences? | Manages domain and VLAN configuration. Multiple VTP servers can be configured. | Updates local VTP configurations. VTP client switches cannot change VLAN configurations. | Manages local VLAN configurations. VLAN configurations are not shared with the VTP network. |
| Does it respond to VTP advertisements? | Participates fully | Participates fully | Forwards only VTP advertisements |
| Is the global VLAN configuration preserved on restart? | Yes, global configurations are stored in NVRAM. | No, global configurations are stored in RAM only. | No, the local VLAN configuration is stored only in NVRAM. |
| Does it update other VTP-enabled switches? | Yes | Yes | No |

**Note**

A switch that is in server or client mode with a higher configuration revision number than the existing VTP server updates all VLAN information in the VTP domain. (Configuration revision numbers are discussed later in this chapter.) As a best practice, Cisco recommends deploying a new switch in VTP transparent mode and then configuring the VTP domain specifics.

## VTP Advertisements (2.1.1.3)

VTP includes three types of advertisements:

- *Summary advertisements*—These inform adjacent switches of the VTP domain name and configuration revision number.

- *Advertisement requests*—These are in response to a summary advertisement message when the summary advertisement contains a higher configuration revision number than the current value.

- *Subset advertisements*—These contain VLAN information, including any changes.

By default, Cisco switches issue summary advertisements every five minutes. Summary advertisements inform adjacent VTP switches of the current VTP domain name and the configuration revision number.

The configuration revision number is a 32-bit number that indicates the level of revision for a VTP packet. Each VTP device tracks the VTP configuration revision number that is assigned to it.

This information is used to determine whether the received information is more recent than the current version. The revision number increases by 1 each time you add a VLAN, delete a VLAN, or change a VLAN name. If the VTP domain name is changed or the switch is set to transparent mode, the revision number is reset to 0.

### Note

To reset a configuration revision on a switch, change the VTP domain name and then change the name back to the original name.

When the switch receives a summary advertisement packet, the switch compares the VTP domain name to its own VTP domain name. If the name is different, the switch simply ignores the packet. If the name is the same, the switch then compares the configuration revision to its own revision. If its own configuration revision number is higher or equal to the packet's configuration revision number, the packet is ignored. If its own configuration revision number is lower, an advertisement request is sent, asking for the subset advertisement message.

The subset advertisement message contains the VLAN information with any changes. When you add, delete, or change a VLAN on the VTP server, the VTP server increments the configuration revision and issues a summary advertisement. One or several subset advertisements follow the summary advertisement containing the VLAN information, including any changes. This process is shown in Figure 2-2.

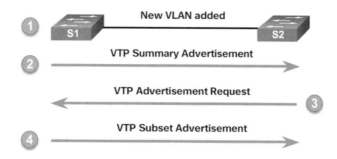

**Figure 2-2**   VTP Advertisements

## VTP Versions (2.1.1.4)

VTP Version 1 (VTPv1) and Version 2 (VTPv2) are described in Table 2-4. Switches in the same VTP domain must use the same VTP version.

**Table 2-4**   VTP Versions

| VTP Version | Definition |
|---|---|
| VTP Version 1 | Default VTP mode on all switches. |
|  | Supports *normal-range VLANs* only. |
| VTP Version 2 | Supports normal-range VLANs only. |
|  | Supports legacy Token Ring networks. |
|  | Supports advanced features, including unrecognized Type-Length-Value (TLV), version-dependent transparent mode, and consistency checks. |

**Note**

VTPv2 is not much different from VTPv1 and is generally configured only if legacy Token Ring support is required. The newest version is VTP Version 3 (VTPv3). VTPv3 is beyond the scope of this course.

## Default VTP Configuration (2.1.1.5)

The **show vtp status** privileged EXEC command displays the VTP status. Executing the command on a Cisco 2960 Plus Series switch generates the output shown in Example 2-1.

**Example 2-1** Verifying Default VTP Status

```
S1# show vtp status
VTP Version capable              : 1 to 3
VTP version running              : 1
VTP Domain Name                  :
VTP Pruning Mode                 : Disabled
VTP Traps Generation             : Disabled
Device ID                        : f078.167c.9900
Configuration last modified by 0.0.0.0 at 3-1-93 00:02:11


Feature VLAN:
--------------
VTP Operating Mode               : Transparent
Maximum VLANs supported locally  : 255
Number of existing VLANs         : 12
Configuration Revision           : 0
MD5 digest                       : 0x57 0xCD 0x40 0x65 0x63 0x59 0x47 0xBD
                                   0x56 0x9D 0x4A 0x3E 0xA5 0x69 0x35 0xBC
S1#
```

Table 2-5 briefly describes the command output for the **show vtp status** parameters.

**Table 2-5** Command Output Description

| Command Output | Description |
| --- | --- |
| VTP Version capable and VTP version running | Display the VTP version that the switch is capable of running and the version that it is currently running. |
| | Switches implement VTPv1 by default. |
| | Newer switches may support VTPv3. |
| VTP Domain Name | Name that identifies the administrative domain for the switch. |
| | VTP domain name is case sensitive. |
| | The VTP domain name is NULL by default. |
| VTP Pruning Mode | Displays whether pruning is enabled or disabled (default). |
| | VTP pruning prevents flooded traffic from propagating to switches that do not have members in specific VLANs. |
| VTP Traps Generation | Displays whether VTP traps are sent to a network management station. |
| | VTP traps are disabled by default. |
| Device ID | The switch MAC address. |

| Command Output | Description |
|---|---|
| Configuration last modified | Date and time of the last configuration modification and IP address of the switch that caused the configuration change to the database. |
| VTP Operating Mode | Can be server (default), client, or transparent. |
| Maximum VLANs supported locally | The number of VLANs supported varies across switch platforms. |
| Number of existing VLANs | Includes the number of default and configured VLANs. The default number of existing VLANs varies across switch platforms. |
| Configuration Revision | The current configuration revision number on this switch. The revision number is a 32-bit number that indicates the level of revision for a VTP frame. The default configuration number for a switch is 0. Each time a VLAN is added or removed, the configuration revision number is incremented. Each VTP device tracks the VTP configuration revision number that is assigned to it. |
| MD5 digest | A 16-byte checksum of the VTP configuration. |

## VTP Caveats (2.1.1.6)

Some network administrators avoid VTP because it could potentially introduce false VLAN information into the existing VTP domain. The configuration revision number is used when determining whether a switch should keep its existing VLAN database or overwrite it with the VTP update sent by another switch in the same domain with the same password.

Adding a VTP-enabled switch to an existing VTP domain wipes out the existing VLAN configurations in the domain if the new switch is configured with different VLANs and has a higher configuration revision number than the existing VTP server. The new switch can be either a VTP server or a client switch. This propagation can be difficult to correct.

To illustrate this problem, refer to the example in Figure 2-3. The S1 switch is the VTP server, and the S2 and S3 switches are VTP clients. All switches are in the **cisco1** domain, and the current VTP revision is **17**. In addition to the default VLAN 1, the VTP server (S1) has VLANs 10 and 20 configured. These VLANs have been propagated by VTP to the other two switches.

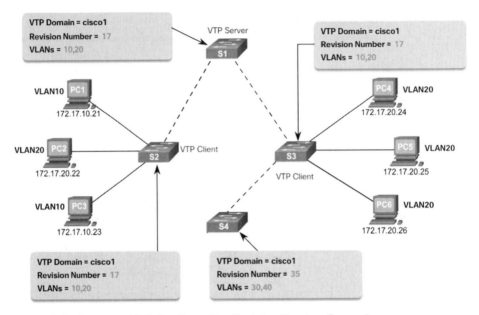

**Figure 2-3** Incorrect VTP Configuration Revision Number Scenario

A network technician adds S4 to the network to address the need for additional capacity. However, the technician has not erased the startup configuration or deleted the VLAN.DAT file on S4. S4 has the same VTP domain name configured as the other two switches, but its revision number is 35, which is higher than 17, the current revision number on the other two switches.

S4 has VLAN 1 and is configured with VLANs 30 and 40. But it does not have VLANs 10 and 20 in its database. Unfortunately, because S4 has a higher revision number, all the other switches in the domain will sync to S4's revision. The result is that VLANs 10 and 20 will no longer exist on the switches, leaving clients that are connected to ports belonging to those nonexistent VLANs without connectivity.

Therefore, when a switch is added to a network, ensure that it has a default VTP configuration. The VTP configuration revision number is stored in NVRAM (or flash memory, on some platforms) and is not reset if you erase the switch configuration and reload it. To reset the VTP configuration revision number to 0, you have two options:

- Change the switch's VTP domain to a nonexistent VTP domain and then change the domain back to the original name.

- Change the switch's VTP mode to transparent and then back to the previous VTP mode.

**Note**

The commands to reset the VTP configuration revision number are discussed in the next topic.

**Activity 2.1.1.7: Identify VTP Concepts and Operations**

Refer to the online course to complete this activity.

# VTP Configuration (2.1.2)

The focus of this topic is on how to configure VTP Versions 1 and 2.

## VTP Configuration Overview (2.1.2.1)

Complete the following steps to configure VTP:

**Step 1.** Configure the VTP server.

**Step 2.** Configure the VTP domain name and password.

**Step 3.** Configure the VTP clients.

**Step 4.** Configure VLANs on the VTP server.

**Step 5.** Verify that the VTP clients have received the new VLAN information.

Figure 2-4 shows the reference topology used in this section for configuring and verifying a VTP implementation. Switch S1 is the VTP server, and S2 and S3 are VTP clients.

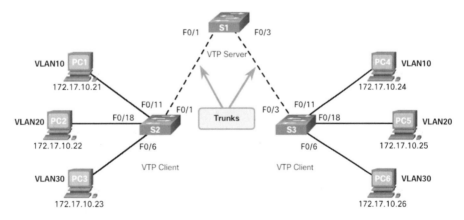

**Figure 2-4**   VTP Configuration Topology

## Step 1—Configure the VTP Server (2.1.2.2)

Confirm that all switches are configured with default settings to avoid any issues with configuration revision numbers. Configure S1 as the VTP server by using the **vtp mode server** global configuration command, as shown in Example 2-2.

**Example 2-2**   Configuring VTP Server Mode

```
S1# conf t
Enter configuration commands, one per line.  End with CNTL/Z.
S1(config)# vtp mode ?
  client      Set the device to client mode.
  off         Set the device to off mode.
  server      Set the device to server mode.
  transparent  Set the device to transparent mode.

S1(config)# vtp mode server
Setting device to VTP Server mode for VLANS.
S1(config)# end
S1#
```

Issue the **show vtp status** command to confirm that S1 is a VTP server, as shown in Example 2-3.

**Example 2-3**   Verifying VTP Mode

```
S1# show vtp status
VTP Version capable             : 1 to 3
VTP version running             : 1
VTP Domain Name                 :
VTP Pruning Mode                : Disabled
VTP Traps Generation            : Disabled
Device ID                       : f078.167c.9900
Configuration last modified by 0.0.0.0 at 3-1-93 00:02:11
Local updater ID is 0.0.0.0 (no valid interface found)


Feature VLAN:
--------------
VTP Operating Mode              : Server
Maximum VLANs supported locally : 255
Number of existing VLANs        : 5
Configuration Revision          : 0
MD5 digest                      : 0x57 0xCD 0x40 0x65 0x63 0x59 0x47 0xBD
                                  0x56 0x9D 0x4A 0x3E 0xA5 0x69 0x35 0xBC
S1#
```

Notice that the configuration revision number is still set to 0, and the number of existing VLANs is five. This is because no VLANs have yet been configured, and the switch does not belong to a VTP domain. The five VLANs are the default VLAN 1 and VLANs 1002 through 1005.

### Step 2—Configure the VTP Domain Name and Password (2.1.2.3)

The domain name is configured by using the **vtp domain** *domain-name* global configuration command. In Example 2-4, the domain name is configured as **CCNA** on S1. S1 then sends out a VTP advertisement to S2 and S3. If S2 and S3 have the default configuration with the NULL domain name, both switches accept CCNA as the new VTP domain name. A VTP client must have the same domain name as the VTP server before it will accept VTP advertisements.

**Example 2-4** Configuring the VTP Domain Name

```
S1(config)# vtp domain ?
  WORD  The ascii name for the VTP administrative domain.

S1(config)# vtp domain CCNA
Changing VTP domain name from NULL to CCNA
*Mar  1 02:55:42.768: %SW_VLAN-6-VTP_DOMAIN_NAME_CHG: VTP domain name changed to
  CCNA.
S1(config)#
```

For security reasons, a password should be configured using the **vtp password** *password* global configuration command. In Example 2-5, the VTP domain password is set to **cisco12345**. All switches in the VTP domain must use the same VTP domain password to successfully exchange VTP messages.

**Example 2-5** Configuring and Verifying the VTP Domain Password

```
S1(config)# vtp password cisco12345
Setting device VTP password to cisco12345
S1(config)# end
S1# show vtp password
VTP Password: cisco12345
S1#
```

Use the **show vtp password** command to verify the password entered, as shown in Example 2-5.

## Step 3—Configure the VTP Clients (2.1.2.4)

Configure S2 and S3 as VTP clients in the CCNA domain, using the VTP password cisco12345. The configuration for S2 is shown in Example 2-6. S3 has an identical configuration.

**Example 2-6**   Configuring the VTP Clients

```
S2(config)# vtp mode client
Setting device to VTP Client mode for VLANS.
S2(config)# vtp domain CCNA
Changing VTP domain name from NULL to CCNA
*Mar  1 00:12:22.484: %SW_VLAN-6-VTP_DOMAIN_NAME_CHG: VTP domain name changed to
  CCNA.
S2(config)# vtp password cisco12345
Setting device VTP password to cisco12345
S2(config)#
```

## Step 4—Configure VLANs on the VTP Server (2.1.2.5)

There are currently no VLANs configured on S1 except for the default VLANs. Configure three VLANs, as shown in Example 2-7.

**Example 2-7**   Configuring VLANs on the VTP Server

```
S1(config)# vlan 10
S1(config-vlan)# name SALES
S1(config-vlan)# vlan 20
S1(config-vlan)# name MARKETING
S1(config-vlan)# vlan 30
S1(config-vlan)# name ACCOUNTING
S1(config-vlan)# end
S1#
```

Verify the VLANs on S1, as shown in Example 2-8.

**Example 2-8**   Verifying the Configured VLANs

```
S1# show vlan brief

VLAN Name                             Status    Ports
---- -------------------------------- --------- -------------------------------
1    default                          active    Fa0/3, Fa0/4, Fa0/5, Fa0/6
                                                Fa0/7, Fa0/8, Fa0/9, Fa0/10
                                                Fa0/11, Fa0/12, Fa0/13, Fa0/14
                                                Fa0/15, Fa0/16, Fa0/17, Fa0/18
```

```
                                              Fa0/19, Fa0/20, Fa0/21, Fa0/22
                                              Fa0/23, Fa0/24, Gi0/1, Gi0/2
10    SALES                     active
20    MARKETING                 active
30    ACCOUNTING                active
1002  fddi-default              act/unsup
1003  token-ring-default        act/unsup
1004  fddinet-default           act/unsup
1005  trnet-default             act/unsup
S1#
```

Notice that the three VLANs are now in the VLAN database. Verify the VTP status, as shown in Example 2-9.

**Example 2-9**   Verifying the VTP Status

```
S1# show vtp status
VTP Version capable             : 1 to 3
VTP version running             : 1
VTP Domain Name                 : CCNA
VTP Pruning Mode                : Disabled
VTP Traps Generation            : Disabled
Device ID                       : f078.167c.9900
Configuration last modified by 0.0.0.0 at 3-1-93 02:02:45
Local updater ID is 0.0.0.0 (no valid interface found)


Feature VLAN:
--------------
VTP Operating Mode              : Server
Maximum VLANs supported locally : 255
Number of existing VLANs        : 8
Configuration Revision          : 6
MD5 digest                      : 0xFE 0x8D 0x2D 0x21 0x3A 0x30 0x99 0xC8
                                  0xDB 0x29 0xBD 0xE9 0x48 0x70 0xD6 0xB6
*** MD5 digest checksum mismatch on trunk: Fa0/2 ***
S1#
```

Notice that the configuration revision number incremented six times, from the default 0 to 6. This is because three new named VLANs were added. Each time the administrator makes a change to the VTP server's VLAN database, this number increases by 1. The number increased by 1 each time a VLAN was added or named.

### Step 5—Verify That the VTP Clients Have Received the New VLAN Information (2.1.2.6)

On S2, verify that the VLANs configured on S1 have been received and entered into the S2 VLAN database by using the **show vlan brief** command, as shown in Example 2-10.

**Example 2-10**  Verifying That the VTP Clients Have Received the New VLAN Information

```
S2# show vlan brief

VLAN Name                             Status    Ports
---- -------------------------------- --------- -------------------------------
1    default                          active    Fa0/2, Fa0/3, Fa0/4, Fa0/5
                                                Fa0/6, Fa0/7, Fa0/8, Fa0/9
                                                Fa0/10, Fa0/11, Fa0/12, Fa0/13
                                                Fa0/14, Fa0/15, Fa0/16, Fa0/17
                                                Fa0/18, Fa0/19, Fa0/20, Fa0/21
                                                Fa0/22, Fa0/23, Fa0/24, Gi0/1
                                                Gi0/2
10   SALES                            active
20   MARKETING                        active
30   ACCOUNTING                       active
1002 fddi-default                     act/unsup
1003 token-ring-default               act/unsup
1004 fddinet-default                  act/unsup
1005 trnet-default                    act/unsup
S2#
```

As expected, the VLANs configured on the VTP server have propagated to S2. Verify the VTP status on S2, as shown in Example 2-11.

**Example 2-11**  Verifying the VTP Status on S2

```
S2# show vtp status
VTP Version capable             : 1 to 3
VTP version running             : 1
VTP Domain Name                 : CCNA
VTP Pruning Mode                : Disabled
VTP Traps Generation            : Disabled
Device ID                       : b07d.4729.2400
Configuration last modified by 0.0.0.0 at 3-1-93 02:02:45
```

```
Feature VLAN:
--------------
VTP Operating Mode                    : Client
Maximum VLANs supported locally       : 255
Number of existing VLANs              : 8
Configuration Revision                : 6
MD5 digest                            : 0xFE 0x8D 0x2D 0x21 0x3A 0x30 0x99 0xC8
                                        0xDB 0x29 0xBD 0xE9 0x48 0x70 0xD6 0xB6
S2#
```

Notice that the configuration revision number on S2 is the same as the number on the VTP server.

Because S2 is operating in VTP client mode, attempts to configure VLANs are not allowed, as shown in Example 2-12.

**Example 2-12**   Attempting to Configure a VLAN on a Client

```
S2(config)# vlan 99
VTP VLAN configuration not allowed when device is in CLIENT mode.
S2(config)#
```

# Extended VLANs (2.1.3)

All Catalyst switches can create normal-range VLANs. Some switches can also use extended-range VLANs.

The focus of this topic is on how to configure extended VLANs.

## VLAN Ranges on Catalyst Switches (2.1.3.1)

Different Cisco Catalyst switches support various numbers of VLANs. The number of supported VLANs is typically large enough to accommodate the needs of most organizations. For example, the Catalyst 2960 and 3560 Series switches support more than 4000 VLANs. Normal-range VLANs on these switches are numbered 1 to 1005, and extended-range VLANs are numbered 1006 to 4094.

Example 2-13 displays the available VLANs on a Catalyst 2960 switch running Cisco IOS Release 15.x.

**Example 2-13**   Verifying VLANs on a Catalyst 2960 Switch

```
Switch# show vlan brief

VLAN Name                             Status    Ports
---- -------------------------------- --------- -------------------------------
1    default                          active    Fa0/2, Fa0/3, Fa0/4, Fa0/5
                                                Fa0/6, Fa0/7, Fa0/8, Fa0/9
                                                Fa0/10, Fa0/11, Fa0/12, Fa0/13
                                                Fa0/14, Fa0/15, Fa0/16, Fa0/17
                                                Fa0/18, Fa0/19, Fa0/20, Fa0/21
                                                Fa0/22, Fa0/23, Fa0/24, Gi0/1
                                                Gi0/2
1002 fddi-default                     act/unsup
1003 token-ring-default               act/unsup
1004 fddinet-default                  act/unsup
1005 trnet-default                    act/unsup
Switch#
```

Table 2-6 shows the features of normal-range and extended-range VLANs.

**Table 2-6**   Types of VLANs

| Type | Definition |
|---|---|
| Normal-range VLANs | Used in small and medium-sized business and enterprise networks. |
| | Identified by VLAN IDs between 1 and 1005. |
| | IDs 1 and 1002 to 1005 are automatically created and cannot be removed. (IDs 1002 through 1005 are reserved for Token Ring and Fiber Distributed Data Interface [FDDI] VLANs.) |
| | Configurations are stored within a VLAN database file called **vlan.dat**, which is stored in flash memory. |
| Extended-range VLANs | Used by service providers and large organizations to extend their infrastructure to a greater number of customers. |
| | Identified by VLAN IDs between 1006 and 4094. |
| | Support fewer VLAN features than normal-range VLANs. |
| | Configurations are saved in the running configuration file. |

VLAN Trunking Protocol (VTP), which helps manage VLAN configurations between switches, can learn and store only normal-range VLANs. VTP does not function with extended-range VLANs.

**Note**

4096 is the upper boundary for the number of VLANs available on Catalyst switches because there are 12 bits in the VLAN ID field of the IEEE 802.1Q header.

## Creating a VLAN (2.1.3.2)

When configuring normal-range VLANs, the configuration details are stored in flash memory on the switch, in a file called **vlan.dat**. Flash memory is persistent and does not require the **copy running-config startup-config** command. However, because other details are often configured on a Cisco switch at the same time that VLANs are created, it is good practice to save running configuration changes to the startup configuration file.

Table 2-7 shows the Cisco IOS command syntax used to add a VLAN to a switch and give it a name. Naming each VLAN is considered a best practice in switch configuration.

**Table 2-7**  Command Syntax for Creating a VLAN

| Command | Description |
|---------|-------------|
| S1(config)# **vlan** *vlan-id* | Create a VLAN with a valid ID number. |
| S1(config-vlan)# **name** *vlan-name* | Specify a unique name to identify the VLAN. |

Figure 2-5 shows how the student VLAN (VLAN 20) is configured on switch S1. In the topology example, notice that the student computer (PC2) has been an assigned an IP address that is appropriate for VLAN 20, but the port to which the PC attaches has not been associated with a VLAN yet.

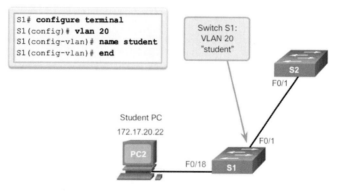

**Figure 2-5**  Sample VLAN Configuration

The **vlan** *vlan-id* command can be used to create several VLANs at once. To do so, enter a series of VLAN IDs separated by commas. You also can enter a range of VLAN IDs separated by hyphens. For example, the following command would create VLANs 100, 102, 105, 106, and 107.

```
S1(config)# vlan 100,102,105-107
```

### Assigning Ports to VLANs (2.1.3.3)

After creating a VLAN, the next step is to assign ports to the VLAN. An access port can belong to only one VLAN at a time; one exception to this rule is a port connected to an IP phone, in which case there are two VLANs associated with the port: one for voice and one for data.

Table 2-8 shows the syntax for defining a port to be an access port and assigning it to a VLAN. The **switchport mode access** command is optional but strongly recommended as a security best practice. With this command, the interface changes to permanent access mode.

**Table 2-8**   Command Syntax for Assigning Ports to VLANs

| Command | Description |
| --- | --- |
| S1(config)# **interface** *interface_id* | Enter interface configuration mode. |
| S1(config-if)# **switchport mode access** | Set the port to access mode. |
| S1(config-if)# **switchport access vlan** *vlan_id* | Assign the port to a VLAN. |

**Note**

Use the **interface range** command to simultaneously configure multiple interfaces.

In the example in Figure 2-6, VLAN 20 is assigned to port F0/18 on switch S1; therefore, the student computer (PC2) is in VLAN 20. When VLAN 20 is configured on other switches, the network administrator knows to configure the other student computers to be in the same subnet as PC2 (172.17.20.0/24).

The **switchport access vlan** command forces the creation of a VLAN if it does not already exist on the switch. For example, VLAN 30 is not present in the **show vlan brief** output of the switch. If the **switchport access vlan 30** command is entered on any interface with no previous configuration, the switch displays the following:

```
% Access VLAN does not exist. Creating vlan 30
```

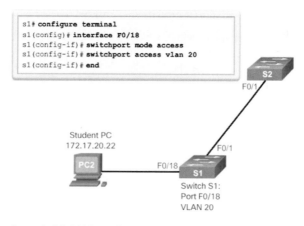

```
s1# configure terminal
s1(config)# interface F0/18
s1(config-if)# switchport mode access
s1(config-if)# switchport access vlan 20
s1(config-if)# end
```

**Figure 2-6**   Sample VLAN Port Assignment Configuration

## Verifying VLAN Information (2.1.3.4)

After a VLAN is configured, VLAN configurations can be validated using Cisco IOS **show** commands.

Table 2-9 shows the **show vlan** command options.

```
show vlan [brief | id vlan-id | name vlan-name | summary]
```

**Table 2-9**   The **show vlan** Command

| brief | Display one line for each VLAN with the VLAN name, status, and its ports. |
| --- | --- |
| **id** *vlan-id* | Display information about a single VLAN identified by VLAN ID number. For *vlan-id*, the range is 1 to 4094. |
| **name** *vlan-name* | Display information about a single VLAN identified by VLAN name. *vlan-name* is an ASCII string from 1 to 32 characters. |
| **summary** | Display VLAN summary information. |

Table 2-10 shows the **show interfaces** command options.

```
show interfaces [interface-id | vlan vlan-id] | switchport
```

**Table 2-10**   The **show interfaces** Command

| | |
|---|---|
| *interface-id* | Display information about a specific interface. Valid interfaces include physical ports (including type, module, and port number) and port channels. The port channel range is 1 to 6. |
| **vlan** *vlan-id* | Display information about a specific VLAN. The *vlan-id* range is 1 to 4094. |
| **switchport** | Display the administrative and operational status of a switching port, including port blocking and port protection settings. |

In Example 2-14, the **show vlan name student** command displays information that would also be found in the **show vlan brief** command, but only for VLAN 20, the student VLAN.

**Example 2-14**   Using the **show vlan** Command

```
S1# show vlan name student


VLAN Name                             Status    Ports
---- -------------------------------- --------- -------------------------------
20   student                          active    Fa0/11, Fa0/18


VLAN Type  SAID       MTU   Parent RingNo BridgeNo Stp  BrdgMode Trans1 Trans2
---- ----- ---------- ----- ------ ------ -------- ---- -------- ------ ------
20   enet  100020     1500  -      -      -        -    -        0      0


Remote SPAN VLAN
----------------
Disabled


Primary Secondary Type              Ports
------- --------- ----------------- -------------------------------------------


S1# show vlan summary
Number of existing VLANs              : 7
 Number of existing VTP VLANs         : 7
 Number of existing extended VLANS    : 0

S1#
```

Example 2-14 indicates that the status is active, and specifies which switch ports are assigned to the VLAN. The **show vlan summary** command displays the count of all configured VLANs. The output in Example 2-14 shows seven VLANs.

The **show interfaces vlan** *vlan-id* command displays details about the VLAN. In the second line, it indicates whether the VLAN is up or down, as shown in Example 2-15.

**Example 2-15**   Using the **show interfaces vlan** Command

```
S1# show interfaces vlan 99
Vlan99 is up, line protocol is up
  Hardware is EtherSVI, address is 0cd9.96e2.3d41 (bia 0cd9.96e2.3d41)
  Internet address is 192.168.99.1/24
  MTU 1500 bytes, BW 1000000 Kbit/sec, DLY 10 usec,
     reliability 255/255, txload 1/255, rxload 1/255
  Encapsulation ARPA, loopback not set
  Keepalive not supported
  ARP type: ARPA, ARP Timeout 04:00:00
  Last input 00:00:35, output 00:01:01, output hang never
  Last clearing of "show interface" counters never
  Input queue: 0/75/0/0 (size/max/drops/flushes); Total output drops: 0
  Queueing strategy: fifo
  Output queue: 0/40 (size/max)
  5 minute input rate 0 bits/sec, 0 packets/sec
  5 minute output rate 0 bits/sec, 0 packets/sec
     1 packets input, 60 bytes, 0 no buffer
     Received 0 broadcasts (0 IP multicasts)
     0 runts, 0 giants, 0 throttles
     0 input errors, 0 CRC, 0 frame, 0 overrun, 0 ignored
     1 packets output, 64 bytes, 0 underruns
     0 output errors, 1 interface resets
     0 unknown protocol drops
     0 output buffer failures, 0 output buffers swapped out
S1#
```

## Configuring Extended VLANs (2.1.3.5)

Extended-range VLANs are identified by a VLAN ID between 1006 and 4094. Example 2-16 shows that, by default, a Catalyst 2960 Plus Series switch does not support extended VLANs.

**Example 2-16**   Extended VLAN Failure

```
S1# conf t
Enter configuration commands, one per line.  End with CNTL/Z.
S1(config)# vlan 2000
S1(config-vlan)# exit
```

```
% Failed to create VLANs 2000
Extended VLAN(s) not allowed in current VTP mode.
%Failed to commit extended VLAN(s) changes.

S1(config)#
*Mar  1 00:51:48.893: %SW_VLAN-4-VLAN_CREATE_FAIL: Failed to create VLANs 2000:
  extended VLAN(s) not allowed in current VTP mode
```

In order to configure an extended VLAN on a 2960 switch, it must be set to VTP transparent mode. Example 2-17 shows how to create an extended-range VLAN on the Catalyst 2960 Plus Series switch.

**Example 2-17**    Configuring an Extended VLAN on a 2960 Switch

```
S1(config)# vtp mode transparent
Setting device to VTP Transparent mode for VLANS.
S1(config)# vlan 2000
S1(config-vlan)# end
S1#
```

The **show vlan brief** command is used to verify that a VLAN was created, as shown in Example 2-18. This output confirms that the extended VLAN 2000 has been configured and is active.

**Example 2-18**    Verifying an Extended VLAN Configuration

```
S1# show vlan brief

VLAN Name                             Status    Ports
---- -------------------------------- --------- -------------------------------
1    default                          active    Fa0/3, Fa0/4, Fa0/5, Fa0/6
                                                Fa0/7, Fa0/8, Fa0/9, Fa0/10
                                                Fa0/11, Fa0/12, Fa0/13, Fa0/14
                                                Fa0/15, Fa0/16, Fa0/17, Fa0/18
                                                Fa0/19, Fa0/20, Fa0/21, Fa0/22
                                                Fa0/23, Fa0/24, Gi0/1, Gi0/2
1002 fddi-default                     act/unsup
1003 token-ring-default               act/unsup
1004 fddinet-default                  act/unsup
1005 trnet-default                    act/unsup
2000 VLAN2000                         active
S1#
```

**Note**

A Cisco Catalyst 2960 switch can support up to 255 normal-range and extended-range VLANs. However, the number of VLANs configured affects the performance of the switch hardware.

# Dynamic Trunking Protocol (2.1.4)

DTP simplifies the negotiation of trunk links between two switches. The focus of this topic is on how to configure DTP.

## Introduction to DTP (2.1.4.1)

Ethernet trunk interfaces support different trunking modes. An interface can be set to trunking or non-trunking, or it can be set to negotiate trunking with the neighbor interface. Trunk negotiation is managed by DTP, which operates on a point-to-point basis only, between network devices.

DTP is a Cisco proprietary protocol that is automatically enabled on Catalyst 2960 and Catalyst 3560 Series switches. Switches from other vendors do not support DTP. DTP manages trunk negotiation only if the port on the neighbor switch is configured in a trunk mode that supports DTP.

**Caution**

Some internetworking devices might forward DTP frames improperly, which can cause mis-configurations. To avoid this, turn off DTP on interfaces on a Cisco switch connected to devices that do not support DTP.

The default DTP configuration for Cisco Catalyst 2960 and 3560 switches is dynamic auto, as shown in Figure 2-7 on interface F0/3 of switches S1 and S3.

To enable trunking from a Cisco switch to a device that does not support DTP, use the **switchport mode trunk** and **switchport nonegotiate** interface configuration mode commands. This causes the interface to become a trunk but not generate DTP frames.

In Figure 2-8, the link between switches S1 and S2 becomes a trunk because the F0/1 ports on switches S1 and S2 are configured to ignore all DTP advertisements and to come up in and stay in trunk port mode.

The F0/3 ports on switches S1 and S3 are set to dynamic auto, so the negotiation results in the access mode state. This creates an inactive trunk link. When configuring a port to be in trunk mode, use the **switchport mode trunk** command. Then there is no ambiguity about which state the trunk is in; it is always on.

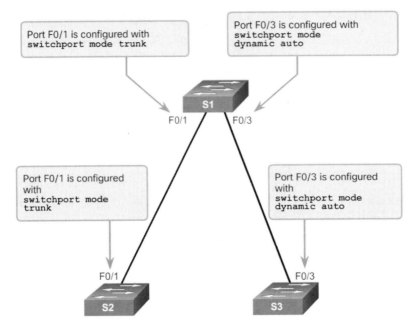

**Figure 2-7**   Initial DTP Configuration

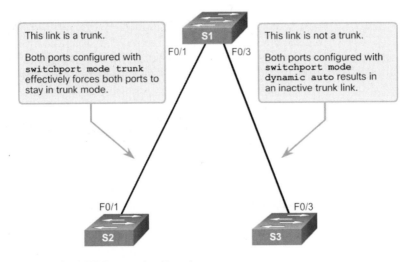

**Figure 2-8**   DTP Interaction Results

## Negotiated Interface Modes (2.1.4.2)

Ethernet interfaces on Catalyst 2960 and Catalyst 3560 Series switches support different trunking modes with the help of DTP:

- **switchport mode access**—Puts the interface (access port) into permanent non-trunking mode and negotiates to convert the link into a non-trunk link. The interface becomes an access port, regardless of whether the neighboring interface is a trunk port.

- **switchport mode dynamic auto**—This is the default switchport mode for all Ethernet interfaces. It makes the port able to convert the link to a trunk link. The port becomes a trunk if the neighboring interface is set to trunk or desirable mode. It does not trunk if the interface is also set to dynamic auto.

- **switchport mode dynamic desirable**—Makes the interface actively attempt to convert the link to a trunk link. The interface becomes a trunk interface if the neighboring interface is set to trunk, desirable, or dynamic auto mode. Note that this is the default switchport mode on older Catalyst switches, such as the Catalyst 2950 and 3550 Series switches.

- **switchport mode trunk**—Puts the interface into permanent trunking mode and negotiates to convert the neighboring link into a trunk link. The interface becomes a trunk interface even if the neighboring interface is not a trunk interface.

- **switchport nonegotiate**—Prevents the interface from generating DTP frames. You can use this command only when the interface switchport mode is access or trunk. You must manually configure the neighboring interface as a trunk interface to establish a trunk link.

Table 2-11 illustrates the results of the DTP configuration options on opposite ends of a trunk link connected to Catalyst 2960 switch ports.

**Table 2-11**   DTP–Negotiated Interface Modes

|  | dynamic auto | dynamic desirable | trunk | access |
|---|---|---|---|---|
| **dynamic auto** | Access | Trunk | Trunk | Access |
| **dynamic desirable** | Trunk | Trunk | Trunk | Access |
| **trunk** | Trunk | Trunk | Trunk | Limited connectivity |
| **access** | Access | Access | Limited connectivity | Access |

Configure trunk links statically whenever possible. The default DTP mode is dependent on the Cisco IOS Software version and on the platform. To determine the current DTP mode, issue the **show dtp interface** command, as shown in Example 2-19.

**Example 2-19**   Verifying DTP Mode

```
S1# show dtp interface f0/1
DTP information for FastEthernet0/1:
  TOS/TAS/TNS:                                    TRUNK/ON/TRUNK
  TOT/TAT/TNT:                                    802.1Q/802.1Q/802.1Q
  Neighbor address 1:                            0CD996D23F81
  Neighbor address 2:                            000000000000
  Hello timer expiration (sec/state):            12/RUNNING
  Access timer expiration (sec/state):           never/STOPPED
  Negotiation timer expiration (sec/state):      never/STOPPED
  Multidrop timer expiration (sec/state):        never/STOPPED
  FSM state:                                     S6:TRUNK
  # times multi & trunk                          0
  Enabled:                                       yes
  In STP:                                        no

<output omitted>
```

**Note**

A general best practice is to set the interface to **trunk** and **nonegotiate** when a trunk link is required. On links where trunking is not intended, DTP should be turned off.

Interactive
Graphic

**Activity 2.1.4.3: Predict DTP Behavior**

Refer to the online course to complete this activity.

Packet Tracer
☐ Activity

**Packet Tracer 2.1.4.4: Configure VTP and DTP**

In this activity, you will configure a switched environment in which trunks are negotiated and formed via DTP, and VLAN information is propagated automatically through a VTP domain.

**Lab 2.1.4.5: Configure Extended VLANs, VTP, and DTP**

Refer to *Scaling Networks v6 Labs & Study Guide* and the online course to complete this activity.

In this lab, you will complete the following objectives:

- Build the Network and Configure Basic Device Settings

- Use Dynamic Trunking Protocol (DTP) to Form Trunk Links

- Configure VLAN Trunking Activity 1.0.1.2: Do We Really Need a Map?

# Troubleshoot Multi-VLAN Issues (2.2)

VLANs are susceptible to specific types of problems in a campus LAN. Most of these problems are related to *inter-VLAN routing* configuration issues, IP addressing issues, VTP issues, and DTP issues.

In this section, you will learn how to troubleshoot issues in an inter-VLAN routing environment.

## Inter-VLAN Configuration Issues (2.2.1)

The focus of this topic is on how to troubleshoot common inter-VLAN configuration issues.

### Deleting VLANs (2.2.1.1)

On occasion, you have to remove a VLAN from the VLAN database. When deleting a VLAN from a switch that is in VTP server mode, the VLAN is removed from the VLAN database for all switches in the VTP domain. When you delete a VLAN from a switch that is in VTP transparent mode, the VLAN is deleted only on that specific switch or switch stack.

> **Note**
>
> You cannot delete the default VLANs (that is, VLANs 1 and 1002 through 1005).

The following scenario illustrates how to delete a VLAN. Assume that S1 has VLANs 10, 20, and 99 configured, as shown in Example 2-20. Notice that VLAN 99 is assigned to ports Fa0/18 through Fa0/24.

**Example 2-20**   Verifying the VLAN Configuration on S1

```
S1# show vlan brief

VLAN Name                             Status    Ports
---- -------------------------------- --------- -------------------------------
1    default                          active    Fa0/1, Fa0/2, Fa0/3, Fa0/4
                                                Fa0/5, Fa0/6, Fa0/7, Fa0/8
                                                Fa0/9, Fa0/10, Fa0/11, Fa0/12
                                                Fa0/13, Fa0/14, Fa0/15, Fa0/16
                                                Fa0/17, Gig0/1, Gig0/2
10   VLAN0010                         active
20   VLAN0020                         active
99   VLAN0099                         active    Fa0/18, Fa0/19, Fa0/20, Fa0/21
                                                Fa0/22, Fa0/23, Fa0/24
```

```
1002 fddi-default                   active
1003 token-ring-default             active
1004 fddinet-default                active
1005 trnet-default                  active
S1#
S1# show vlan id 99
VLAN Name                           Status    Ports
---- ------------------------------ --------- ------------------------------
99   VLAN0099                       active    Fa0/18, Fa0/19, Fa0/20, Fa0/21
                                              Fa0/22, Fa0/23, Fa0/24


VLAN Type  SAID       MTU   Parent RingNo BridgeNo Stp  BrdgMode Trans1 Trans2
---- ----- ---------- ----- ------ ------ -------- ---- -------- ------ ------
99   enet  100099     1500  -      -      -        -    -        0      0

S1#
```

To delete a VLAN, use the **no vlan** *vlan-id* global configuration mode command.

When you delete a VLAN, any ports assigned to that VLAN become inactive. They remain associated with the VLAN (and thus inactive) until you assign them to a new VLAN.

In Example 2-21 notice how interfaces Fa0/18 through 0/24 are no longer listed in the VLAN assignments. Any ports that are not moved to an active VLAN are unable to communicate with other stations after the VLAN is deleted. Therefore, before deleting a VLAN, reassign all member ports to a different VLAN.

**Example 2-21**   Deleting and Verifying a Deleted VLAN

```
S1# conf t
Enter configuration commands, one per line.  End with CNTL/Z.
S1(config)# no vlan 99
S1(config)# exit
S1# show vlan id 99
VLAN id 99 not found in current VLAN database
S1#
S1# show vlan brief

VLAN Name                           Status    Ports
---- ------------------------------ --------- ------------------------------
1    default                        active    Fa0/1, Fa0/2, Fa0/3, Fa0/4
                                              Fa0/5, Fa0/6, Fa0/7, Fa0/8
```

```
                                           Fa0/9, Fa0/10, Fa0/11, Fa0/12
                                           Fa0/13, Fa0/14, Fa0/15, Fa0/16
                                           Fa0/17, Gig0/1, Gig0/2
10    VLAN0010                 active
20    VLAN0020                 active
1002  fddi-default             active
1003  token-ring-default       active
1004  fddinet-default          active
1005  trnet-default            active
S1#
```

## Switch Port Issues (2.2.1.2)

Several common switch misconfigurations can arise when configuring routing
between multiple VLANs.

When configuring a *legacy inter-VLAN routing* solution (also referred to as traditional inter-VLAN routing), ensure that the switch ports that connect to the router
interfaces are configured with the correct VLANs. If a switch port is not configured
for the correct VLAN, devices on that VLAN are unable to send data to the other
VLANs.

For example, refer to the topology in Figure 2-9.

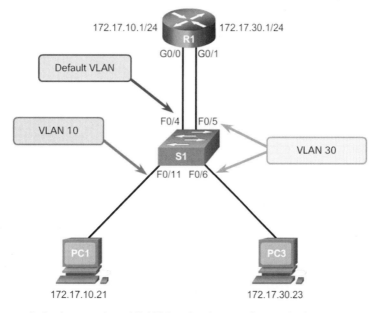

**Figure 2-9**  Legacy Inter-VLAN Routing Issue—Scenario 1

PC1 and router R1 interface G0/0 are configured to be on the same logical subnet, as indicated by their IPv4 address assignment. However, the S1 F0/4 port that connects to the R1 G0/0 interface has not been configured and therefore remains in the default VLAN. Because R1 is on a different VLAN than PC1, they are unable to communicate.

To correct this problem, port F0/4 on switch S1 must be in access mode (**switchport access mode**) and assigned to VLAN 20 (**switchport access vlan 20**). When this is configured, PC1 can communicate with the R1 G0/0 interface and be routed to other VLANs connected to R1.

When a *router-on-a-stick inter-VLAN routing* solution is implemented, ensure that interconnecting interfaces are configured properly as trunks. For example, refer to the topology in Figure 2-10. R1 has been configured with subinterfaces and trunking enabled. However, the F0/5 port on S1 has not been configured as a trunk and is left in the default VLAN. As a result, the router is unable to route between VLANs because each of its configured subinterfaces is unable to send or receive VLAN-tagged traffic.

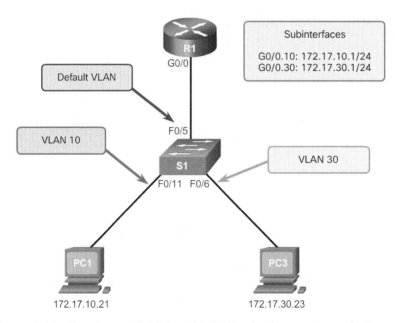

**Figure 2-10**   Router-on-a-Stick Inter-VLAN Routing Issue—Scenario 2

To correct this problem, issue the **switchport mode trunk** interface configuration mode command on the F0/5 interface of S1. This converts the interface to a trunk port, allowing a trunk to be established between R1 and S1. When the trunk is successfully established, devices connected to each of the VLANs are able to communicate with the subinterface assigned to their VLAN, thereby enabling inter-VLAN routing.

Another VLAN issue is if a link goes down or fails. A downed interswitch link disrupts the inter-VLAN routing process.

For example, refer to the topology in Figure 2-11. Notice that the trunk link between S1 and S2 is down. Because there is no redundant connection or path between the devices, all devices connected to S2 are unable to reach router R1. Therefore, all devices connected to S2 are unable to route to other VLANs through R1.

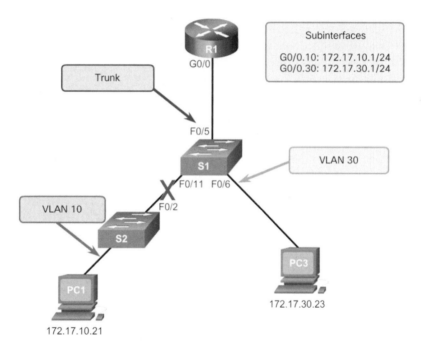

**Figure 2-11**   Failed Interswitch Link Issue—Scenario 3

The solution for this problem is not configuration related, but instead is a LAN design issue. The network design should include redundant links and alternate paths to reduce the risk of failed interswitch links.

## Verify Switch Configuration (2.2.1.3)

When an inter-VLAN problem is suspected with a switch configuration, use verification commands to examine the configuration and identify the problem. Knowing the right verification commands to use helps you quickly identify issues.

The **show interfaces** *interface-id* **switchport** command is useful for identifying VLAN assignment and port configuration issues.

For example, assume that the Fa0/4 port on switch S1 should be an access port configured in VLAN 10. To verify the correct port settings, use the **show interfaces** *interface-id* **switchport** command, as shown in Example 2-22.

**Example 2-22**   Verifying the Current Interface Settings

```
S1# show interfaces FastEthernet 0/4 switchport
Name: Fa0/4
Switchport: Enabled
Administrative Mode: static access
Operational Mode: up
Administrative Trunking Encapsulation: dot1q
Operational Trunking Encapsulation: native
Negotiation of Trunking: On
Access Mode VLAN: 1 (default)
Trunking Native Mode VLAN: 1 (default)
<output omitted>
S1#
```

The top highlighted area confirms that port F0/4 on switch S1 is in access mode. The bottom highlighted area confirms that port F0/4 is not set to VLAN 10 but instead is still set to the default VLAN. To correct this issue, the F0/4 port would have to be configured with the **switchport access vlan 10** command.

The **show running-config interface** is a useful command for identifying how an interface is configured. For example, assume that a device configuration changed, and the trunk link between R1 and S1 has stopped. Example 2-23 displays the output of the **show interfaces** *interface_id* **switchport** and **show running-config interface** verification commands.

**Example 2-23**   Switch IOS Commands

```
S1# show interface f0/4 switchport
Name: Fa0/4
Switchport: Enabled
Administrative Mode: static access
Operational Mode: down
Administrative Trunking Encapsulation: dot1q
Operational Trunking Encapsulation: native
<output omitted>
S1#
S1# show run interface fa0/4
interface FastEthernet0/4
 switchport mode access
S1#
```

The top highlighted area reveals that port F0/4 on switch S1 is in access mode. It should be in trunk mode. The bottom highlighted area also confirms that port F0/4 has been configured for access mode.

To correct this issue, the Fa0/4 port must be configured with the **switchport mode trunk** command.

### Interface Issues (2.2.1.4)

Many inter-VLAN issues are physical layer (Layer 1) errors. For example, one of the most common configuration errors is to connect the physical router interface to the wrong switch port.

Refer to the legacy inter-VLAN solution in Figure 2-12. The R1 G0/0 interface is connected to the S1 F0/9 port. However, the F0/9 port is configured for the default VLAN, not VLAN 10. This prevents PC1 from being able to communicate with its default gateway, the router interface. Therefore, the PC is unable to communicate with any other VLANs, such as VLAN 30.

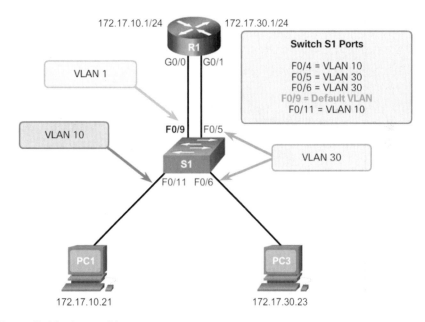

**Figure 2-12**   Layer 1 Issue

The port should have been connected to the Fa0/4 port on S1. Connecting the R1 interface G0/0 to switch S1 port F0/4 puts the interface in the correct VLAN and allows inter-VLAN routing.

Note that an alternative solution would be to change the VLAN assignment of port F0/9 to VLAN 10.

## Verify Routing Configuration (2.2.1.5)

With router-on-a-stick configurations, a common problem is assigning the wrong VLAN ID to the subinterface.

For example, as shown in Figure 2-13, router R1 subinterface G0/0.10 has been configured in VLAN 100 instead of VLAN 10. This prevents devices configured on VLAN 10 from communicating with subinterface G0/0.10 and from being able to send data to other VLANs on the network.

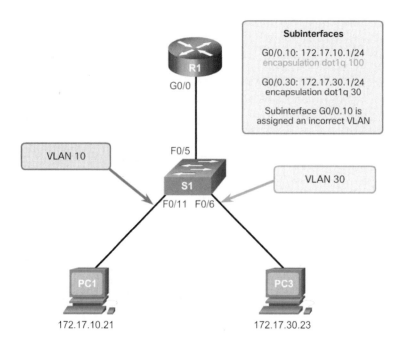

**Figure 2-13**   Router Configuration Issue

Using the **show interfaces** and the **show running-config interface** commands can be useful in troubleshooting this type of issue, as shown in Example 2-24.

**Example 2-24**   Verifying Router Configuration

```
R1# show interface G0/0.10
GigabitEthernet0/0.10 is up, line protocol is down (disabled)
  Encapsulation 802.1Q Virtual LAN, Vlan ID 100
  ARP type: ARPA, ARP Timeout 04:00:00,
  Last clearing of "show interface" counters never

<Output omitted>
```

```
R1#
R1# show run interface G0/0.10
interface GigabitEthernet0/0.10
encapsulation dot1Q 100
 ip address 172.17.10.1 255.255.255.0
R1#
```

The **show interfaces** command produces a lot of output, sometimes making it difficult to see the problem. However, the top highlighted section of Example 2-24 shows
that the subinterface G0/0.10 on router R1 uses VLAN 100.

The **show running-config** command confirms that subinterface G0/0.10 on router R1
has been configured to allow access to VLAN 100 traffic and not VLAN 10.

To correct this problem, configure subinterface G0/0.10 to be on the correct VLAN
by using the **encapsulation dot1q 10** subinterface configuration mode command.
Once this is configured, the subinterface performs inter-VLAN routing to users on
VLAN 10.

# IP Addressing Issues (2.2.2)

VLAN issues could also be caused by misconfigured network or IP address information. The focus of this topic is on how to troubleshoot common IP addressing issues
in an inter-VLAN routed environment.

## Errors with IP Addresses and Subnet Masks (2.2.2.1)

VLANs correspond to unique subnets on the network. For inter-VLAN routing to
operate, a router must be connected to all VLANs, either by separate physical interfaces or by subinterfaces.

Each interface or subinterface must be assigned an IP address that corresponds to the
subnet to which it is connected. This permits devices on the VLAN to communicate
with the router interface and enables the routing of traffic to other VLANs connected
to the router.

The following are examples of possible inter-VLAN routing problems related to IP
addressing errors.

In Figure 2-14, router R1 has been configured with an incorrect IPv4 address on
interface G0/0, preventing PC1 from being able to communicate with router R1 on
VLAN 10.

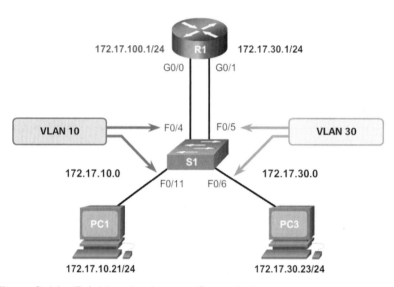

**Figure 2-14** IP Addressing Issues—Scenario 1

To correct this problem, configure the **ip address 172.17.10.1 255.255.255.0** command on the R1 G0/0 interface. Once this is configured, PC1 can use the router interface as a default gateway for accessing other VLANs.

Another problem is illustrated in Figure 2-15. In this example, PC1 has been configured with an incorrect IPv4 address for the subnet associated with VLAN 10, preventing it from being able to communicate with router R1 on VLAN 10.

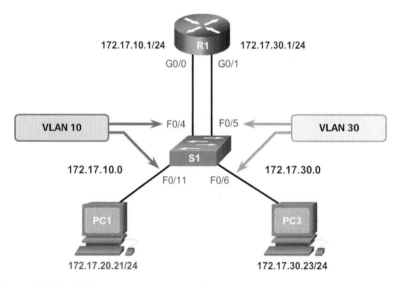

**Figure 2-15** IP Addressing Issues—Scenario 2

To correct this problem, assign the correct IPv4 address to PC1.

Another problem is shown in Figure 2-16. In this example, PC1 cannot send traffic to PC3. The reason is that PC1 has been configured with the incorrect subnet mask, /16, instead of the correct /24 mask. The /16 mask makes PC1 assume that PC3 is on the same subnet. Therefore, PC1 never forwards traffic destined to PC3 to its default gateway, R1.

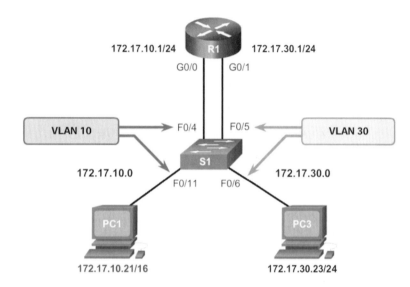

**Figure 2-16**   IP Addressing Issues—Scenario 3

To correct this problem, change the subnet mask on PC1 to 255.255.255.0.

### Verifying IP Address and Subnet Mask Configuration Issues (2.2.2.2)

When troubleshooting addressing issues, ensure that the subinterface is configured with the correct address for that VLAN. Each interface or subinterface must be assigned an IP address corresponding to the subnet to which it is connected. A common error is to incorrectly configure an IP address on a subinterface.

Example 2-25 displays the output of the **show running-config** and **show ip interface** commands. The highlighted areas show that subinterface G0/0.10 on router R1 has IPv4 address 172.17.20.1. However, this is the wrong IP address for this subinterface, and instead it should be configured for VLAN 10.

**Example 2-25**    Using Commands to Discover the Configuration Issues

```
R1# show run
Building configuration...
<output omitted>
!
interface GigabitEthernet0/0
 no ip address
 duplex auto
 speed auto
!
interface GigabitEthernet0/0.10
  encapsulation dot1Q 10
  ip address 172.17.20.1 255.255.255.0
!
interface GigabitEthernet0/0.30
<output omitted>
R1#
R1# show ip interface
<output omitted>
GigabitEthernet0/0.10 is up, line protocol is up
   Internet address is 172.17.20.1/24
   Broadcast address is 255.255.255.255
<output omitted>
R1#
```

To correct this problem, change the IP address of subinterface G0/0.10 to 172.17.10.1/24.

Sometimes it is the end-user device that is improperly configured. For example, Figure 2-17 displays the IPv4 configuration of PC1. The configured IPv4 address is 172.17.20.21/24. However, in this scenario, PC1 should be in VLAN 10, with address 172.17.10.21/24.

To correct this problem, correct the IP address of PC1.

**Note**

In the examples in this chapter, the subinterface numbers always match the VLAN assignment. This is not a configuration requirement but instead has been done intentionally to make it easier to manage inter-VLAN configuration.

**Interactive Graphic**

**Activity 2.2.2.3: Identify the Troubleshooting Command for an Inter-VLAN Routing Issue**

Refer to the online course to complete this activity.

```
Packet Tracer PC Command Line 1.0
PC1> ip config
Invalid Command.

PC1> ipconfig

IP Address.....................: 172.17.20.21
Subnet Mask....................: 255.255.255.0
Default Gateway................: 172.17.10.1

PC1>
```

This PC1 should be in the VLAN 10 subnet
So this should be: 172.17.10.21 with a subnet mask of
255.255.255.0

**Figure 2-17**   PC IP Addressing Issue

**Packet Tracer 2.2.2.4: Troubleshooting Inter-VLAN Routing**

In this activity, you will troubleshoot connectivity problems caused by improper configurations related to VLANs and inter-VLAN routing.

**Lab 2.2.2.5: Troubleshooting Inter-VLAN Routing**

Refer to *Scaling Networks v6 Labs & Study Guide* and the online course to complete this activity.

In this lab, you will complete the following objectives:

- Part 1: Build the Network and Load Device Configurations
- Part 2: Troubleshoot the Inter-VLAN Routing Configuration
- Part 3: Verify VLAN Configuration, Port Assignment, and Trunking
- Part 4: Test Layer 3 Connectivity

# VTP and DTP Issues (2.2.3)

The focus of this topic is on how to troubleshoot common VTP and DTP issues in an inter-VLAN routed environment.

## Troubleshoot VTP Issues (2.2.3.1)

Several issues can arise from an invalid VTP configuration. Common problems with VTP are listed in Table 2-12.

**Table 2-12**  Common VTP-Related Issues

| VTP Problem | Description |
| --- | --- |
| Incompatible VTP versions | VTP versions are incompatible with each other. |
| | Ensure that all switches are capable of supporting the required VTP version. |
| Incorrect VTP domain name | An improperly configured VTP domain affects VLAN synchronization between switches, and if a switch receives the wrong VTP advertisement, the switch discards the message. |
| | To avoid incorrectly configuring a VTP domain name, set the VTP domain name on only one VTP server switch. |
| | All other switches in the same VTP domain will accept and automatically configure their VTP domain name when they receive the first VTP summary advertisement. |
| Incorrect VTP mode | If all switches in the VTP domain are set to client mode, you cannot create, delete, or manage VLANs. |
| | To avoid losing all VLAN configurations in a VTP domain, configure two switches as VTP servers. |
| Invalid VTP authentication | If VTP authentication is enabled, switches must all have the same password configured to participate in VTP. |
| | Ensure that the password is manually configured on all switches in the VTP domain. |
| Incorrect configuration revision number | If a switch with the same VTP domain name but a higher configuration number is added to the domain, invalid VLANs can be propagated and/or valid VLANs can be deleted. |
| | The solution is to reset each switch to an earlier configuration and then reconfigure the correct VLANs. |
| | Before adding a switch to a VTP-enabled network, reset the revision number on the switch to 0 by assigning it to a false VTP domain and then reassigning it to the correct VTP domain name. |

### Troubleshoot DTP Issues (2.2.3.2)

Trunking issues are associated with incorrect configurations. As outlined Table 2-13, three common problems are associated with trunks.

**Table 2-13**  Common Trunk-Related Issues

| DTP Issues | Description |
|---|---|
| Trunk mode mismatches | One trunk port is configured with trunk mode "off" and the other with trunk mode "on." |
| | This configuration error causes the trunk link to stop working. |
| | Correct the situation by shutting down the interface, correcting the DTP mode settings, and re-enabling the interface. |
| Invalid allowed VLANs on trunks | The list of allowed VLANs on a trunk has not been updated with the current VLAN trunking requirements. |
| | In this situation, unexpected traffic or no traffic is being sent over the trunk. |
| | Configure the correct VLANs that are allowed on the trunk. |
| Native VLAN mismatches | When native VLANs do not match, the switches will generate informational messages letting you know about the problem. |
| | Ensure that both sides of a trunk link are using the same native VLAN. |

Packet Tracer
☐ Activity

**Packet Tracer 2.2.3.3: Troubleshoot VTP and DTP Issues**

In this activity, you will troubleshoot a switched environment where trunks are negotiated and formed via DTP and where VLAN information is propagated automatically through a VTP domain.

# Layer 3 Switching (2.3)

A router-on-a-stick inter-VLAN solution is relatively easy to configure and suitable in a smaller network. An alternative solution is to use Layer 3 switches to perform inter-VLAN routing.

In this section, you will learn how to implement inter-VLAN routing using Layer 3 switching to forward data in a small to medium-sized business LAN.

# Layer 3 Switching Operation and Configuration (2.3.1)

The focus of this topic is on how to configure inter-VLAN routing using Layer 3 switching.

## Introduction to Layer 3 Switching (2.3.1.1)

Inter-VLAN routing using the router-on-a-stick method was simple to implement because routers were usually available in every network. However, as shown in Figure 2-18, most modern enterprise networks use a *Layer 3 inter-VLAN routing* solution. This requires the use of multilayer switches to achieve high packet-processing rates using hardware-based switching.

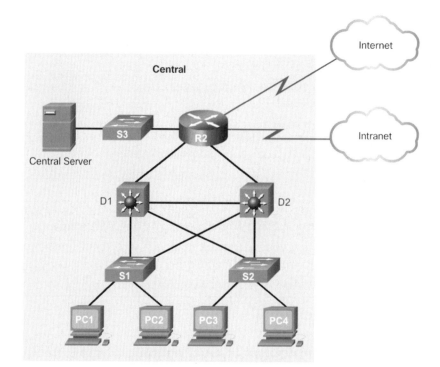

**Figure 2-18**   Layer 3 Switching Topology

Layer 3 switches usually have packet-switching throughputs in the millions of packets per second (pps), whereas traditional routers provide packet switching in the range of 100,000 pps to more than 1 million pps.

All Catalyst multilayer switches support the following types of Layer 3 interfaces:

- *Routed port*—A pure Layer 3 interface similar to a physical interface on a Cisco IOS router.

- *Switch virtual interface (SVI)*—A virtual VLAN interface for inter-VLAN routing. In other words, SVIs are virtual-routed VLAN interfaces.

High-performance switches, such as the Catalyst 6500 and Catalyst 4500, perform almost every function involving OSI Layer 3 and higher using hardware-based switching that is based on *Cisco Express Forwarding*.

All Layer 3 Cisco Catalyst switches support routing protocols, but several models of Catalyst switches require enhanced software for specific routing protocol features.

**Note**

Catalyst 2960 Series switches running IOS Release 12.2(55) or later support static routing.

Layer 3 Catalyst switches use different default settings for interfaces. For example:

- Catalyst 3560, 3650, and 4500 families of distribution layer switches use Layer 2 interfaces by default.

- Catalyst 6500 and 6800 families of core layer switches use Layer 3 interfaces by default.

Depending on which Catalyst family of switches is used, the **switchport** or **no switchport** interface configuration mode command might be present in the running config or startup configuration files.

## Inter-VLAN Routing with Switch Virtual Interfaces (2.3.1.2)

In the early days of switched networks, switching was fast (often at hardware speed, meaning the speed was equivalent to the time it took to physically receive and forward frames onto other ports), and routing was slow (because it had to be processed in software). This prompted network designers to extend the switched portion of the network as much as possible. Access, distribution, and core layers were often configured to communicate at Layer 2. This topology created loop issues. To solve these issues, spanning-tree technologies were used to prevent loops while still enabling flexibility and redundancy in interswitch connections.

However, as network technologies have evolved, routing has become faster and cheaper. Today, routing can be performed at wire speed. One consequence of this evolution is that routing can be transferred to the core and the distribution layers (and sometimes even the access layer) without impacting network performance.

Many users are in separate VLANs, and each VLAN is usually a separate subnet. Therefore, it is logical to configure the distribution switches as Layer 3 gateways for the users of each access switch VLAN. This implies that each distribution switch must have IP addresses matching each access switch VLAN. This can be achieved by SVIs and routed ports.

For example, refer to the topology in Figure 2-19.

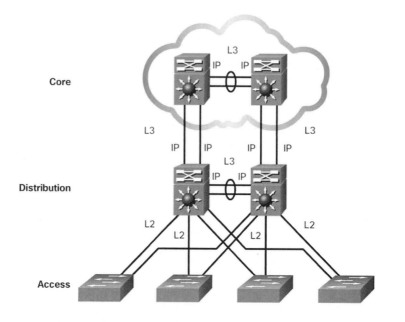

**Figure 2-19**   Switched Network Design

Layer 3 (routed) ports are normally implemented between the distribution layer and the core layer. Therefore, the core layer and distribution layer switches in the figure are interconnected using Layer 3 IP addressing.

The distribution layer switches are connected to the access layer switches using Layer 2 links. The network architecture depicted is not dependent on the spanning tree protocol (STP) because there are no physical loops in the Layer 2 portion of the topology.

### Inter-VLAN Routing with Switch Virtual Interfaces (Con't.) (2.3.1.3)

The topologies in Figure 2-20 compare configuring inter-VLAN routing on a router and on a Layer 3 switch.

An SVI is a virtual interface that is configured within a multilayer switch, as shown in the figure. An SVI can be created for any VLAN that exists on the switch. An SVI is considered to be virtual because there is no physical port dedicated to the interface. It can perform the same functions for the VLAN as a router interface would, and it can be configured in much the same way as a router interface (that is, IP address, inbound/outbound ACLs, and so on). The SVI for the VLAN provides Layer 3 processing for packets to or from all switch ports associated with that VLAN.

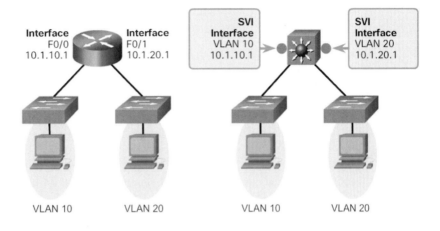

**Figure 2-20**    Switch Virtual Interface

By default, an SVI is created for the default VLAN (VLAN 1) to permit remote switch administration. Additional SVIs must be explicitly created. SVIs are created the first time the VLAN interface configuration mode is entered for a particular VLAN SVI, such as when the **interface vlan 10** command is entered. The VLAN number used corresponds to the VLAN tag associated with data frames on an 802.1Q encapsulated trunk or to the VLAN ID (VID) configured for an access port. When creating an SVI as a gateway for VLAN 10, name the SVI interface VLAN 10. Configure and assign an IP address to each VLAN SVI.

Whenever the SVI is created, ensure that the particular VLAN is present in the VLAN database. For the example shown in Figure 2-20, the switch should have VLAN 10 and VLAN 20 present in the VLAN database; otherwise, the SVI interface stays down.

The following are some of the reasons to configure SVI:

- To provide a gateway for a VLAN so that traffic can be routed into or out of that VLAN

- To provide Layer 3 IP connectivity to the switch

- To support routing protocol and bridging configurations

The only disadvantage of SVIs is that multilayer switches are expensive. The following are some of the advantages of SVIs:

- It is much faster than router-on-a-stick because everything is hardware switched and routed.

- There is no need for external links from the switch to the router for routing.

- It is not limited to one link. Layer 2 EtherChannels can be used between the switches to get more bandwidth.

- Latency is much lower because data does not need to leave the switch in order to be routed to a different network.

### Inter-VLAN Routing with Routed Ports (2.3.1.4)

#### Routed Ports and Access Ports on a Switch

A routed port is a physical port that acts similarly to an interface on a router. Unlike an access port, a routed port is not associated with a particular VLAN. A routed port behaves like a regular router interface. Also, because Layer 2 functionality has been removed, Layer 2 protocols, such as STP, do not function on a routed interface. However, some protocols, such as LACP and EtherChannel, do function at Layer 3.

Unlike Cisco IOS routers, routed ports on a Cisco IOS switch do not support subinterfaces.

Routed ports are used for point-to-point links. Routed ports can be used for connecting WAN routers and security devices, for example. In a switched network, routed ports are mostly configured between switches in the core and distribution layers. Figure 2-21 illustrates an example of routed ports in a campus switched network.

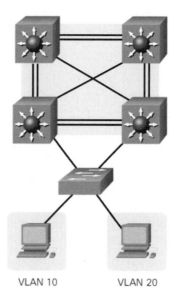

VLAN 10          VLAN 20

**Figure 2-21**   Routed Ports

To configure routed ports, use the **no switchport** interface configuration mode command on the appropriate ports. For example, the default configuration of the interfaces on Catalyst 3560 switches is as Layer 2 interfaces, so they must be manually configured as routed ports. In addition, assign an IP address and other Layer 3 parameters as necessary. After assigning the IP address, verify that IP routing is globally enabled and that applicable routing protocols are configured.

**Note**

Routed ports are not supported on Catalyst 2960 Series switches.

**Packet Tracer 2.3.1.5: Configure Layer 3 Switching and Inter-VLAN Routing**

In this activity, you will configure Layer 3 switching and inter-VLAN routing on a Cisco 3560 switch.

## Troubleshoot Layer 3 Switching (2.3.2)

The focus of this topic is on how to troubleshoot inter-VLAN routing in a Layer 3 switched environment.

### Layer 3 Switch Configuration Issues (2.3.2.1)

The issues common to legacy inter-VLAN routing and router-on-a-stick inter-VLAN routing also manifest in the context of Layer 3 switching.

Table 2-14 lists items that should be checked for accuracy when troubleshooting inter-VLAN routing issues.

**Table 2-14**   Common Layer 3 Switching Issues

| Check | Description |
| --- | --- |
| VLANs | VLANs must be defined across all the switches. |
| | VLANs must be enabled on the trunk ports. |
| | Ports must be in the right VLANs. |
| SVIs | SVIs must have the correct IP addresses or subnet masks. |
| | SVIs must be up. |
| | Each SVI must match the VLAN number. |

| Check | Description |
|-------|-------------|
| Routing | Routing must be enabled. |
|  | Each interface or network should be added to the routing protocol or static routes entered, where appropriate. |
| Hosts | Hosts must have the correct IP address or subnet mask. |
|  | Hosts must have a default gateway associated with an SVI or a routed port. |

To troubleshoot the Layer 3 switching problems, be familiar with the implementation and design layout of the topology, such as the one shown in Figure 2-22.

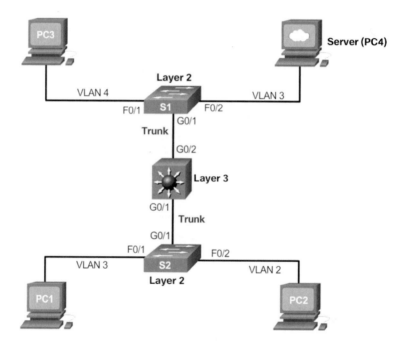

**Figure 2-22**   Layer 3 Switch Configuration Issues Topology

## Example: Troubleshooting Layer 3 Switching (2.3.2.2)

Company XYZ is adding a new floor, floor 5, to the network (see Figure 2-23).

The current requirement is to make sure the users on floor 5 can communicate with users on other floors. Currently, users on floor 5 cannot communicate with users on other floors. The following is an implementation plan to install a new VLAN for users on floor 5 and to ensure the VLAN is routing to other VLANs.

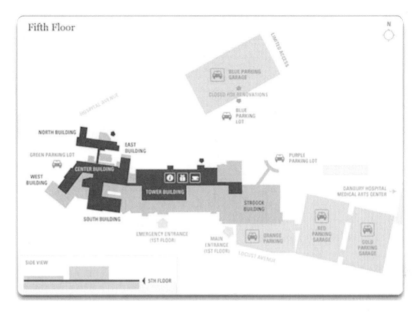

**Figure 2-23**   Company XYZ Floor Plan – Fifth Floor

There are four steps to implementing the new VLAN:

**Step 1.**   Create a new VLAN on the fifth floor switch and on the distribution switches. Name this VLAN 500.

**Step 2.**   Identify the ports needed for the users and switches. Set the **switchport access vlan** command to **500** and ensure that the trunk between the distribution switches is properly configured and that VLAN 500 is allowed on the trunk.

**Step 3.**   Create an SVI interface on the distribution switches and ensure that IP addresses are assigned.

**Step 4.**   Verify connectivity.

The troubleshooting plan checks for the following:

**Step 1.**   Verify that all VLANs have been created:

   ▪ Was the VLAN created on all the switches?

   ▪ Verify with the **show vlan** command.

**Step 2.**   Ensure that ports are in the right VLANs and that trunking is working as expected:

   ▪ Did all access ports have the **switchport access VLAN 500** command added?

- Should any other ports have been added? If so, make those changes.

- Were these ports previously used? If so, ensure that there are no extra commands enabled on these ports that can cause conflicts. If not, are the ports enabled?

- Are any user ports set to trunks? If so, issue the **switchport mode access** command.

- Are the trunk ports set to trunk mode?

- Is manual pruning of VLANs configured? VTP pruning prevents flooded traffic from propagating to switches that do not have members in specific VLANs. If manual pruning is enabled, ensure that the trunks necessary to carry VLAN 500 traffic have the VLAN in the allowed statements.

Step 3.   Verify SVI configurations (if necessary):

- Is the SVI already created with the correct IP address and subnet mask?

- Is it enabled?

- Is routing enabled?

**Interactive Graphic**

**Activity 2.3.2.3: Troubleshoot Layer 3 Switching Issues**

Refer to the online course to complete this activity.

# Summary (2.4)

VLAN Trunking Protocol (VTP) reduces administration of VLANs in a switched network. A switch configured as the VTP server distributes and synchronizes VLAN information over trunk links to VTP-enabled switches throughout the domain.

The three VTP modes are server, client, and transparent.

The configuration revision number is used when determining whether a VTP switch should keep or whether to update its existing VLAN database. A switch overwrites its existing VLAN database if it receives a VTP update from another switch in the same domain with a higher configuration revision number. Therefore, when a switch is being added to a VTP domain, it must have the default VTP configuration or a lower configuration revision number than the VTP server.

Troubleshooting VTP can involve dealing with errors caused by incompatible VTP versions and incorrectly configured domain names or passwords.

Trunk negotiation is managed by Dynamic Trunking Protocol (DTP), which operates on a point-to-point basis between network devices. DTP is a Cisco proprietary protocol that is automatically enabled on Catalyst 2960 and Catalyst 3560 Series switches. A general best practice when a trunk link is required is to set the interface to **trunk** and **nonegotiate**. On links where trunking is not intended, DTP should be turned off.

When troubleshooting DTP, problems can be related to trunk mode mismatches, allowed VLANS on a trunk, and native VLAN mismatches.

Layer 3 switching using switch virtual interfaces (SVI) is a method of inter-VLAN routing that can be configured on Catalyst 2960 switches. An SVI with appropriate IP addressing is configured for each VLAN, and provides Layer 3 processing for packets to or from all switch ports associated with those VLANs.

Another method of Layer 3 inter-VLAN routing is using routed ports. A routed port is a physical port that acts similarly to an interface on a router. Routed ports are mostly configured between switches in the core and distribution layers.

Troubleshooting inter-VLAN routing with a router and with a Layer 3 switch are similar. Common errors involve VLAN, trunk, Layer 3 interface, and IP address configurations.

# Practice

The following activities provide practice with the topics introduced in this chapter. The Labs and Class Activities are available in the companion *Scaling Networks v6 Labs & Study Guide* (ISBN 978-1-58713-433-3). The Packet Tracer activity instructions are also in the *Labs & Study Guide*. The PKA files are found in the online course.

**Labs**

Lab 2.1.4.5: Configure Extended VLANs, VTP, and DTP

Lab 2.2.2.5: Troubleshooting Inter-VLAN Routing

**Packet Tracer Activities**

Packet Tracer 2.1.4.4: Configure VTP and DTP

Packet Tracer 2.2.2.4: Troubleshooting Inter-VLAN Routing

Packet Tracer 2.2.3.3: Troubleshoot VTP and DTP Issues

Packet Tracer 2.3.1.5: Configure Layer 3 Switching and Inter-VLAN Routing

# Check Your Understanding Questions

Complete all the review questions listed here to test your understanding of the topics and concepts in this chapter. The appendix "Answers to 'Check Your Understanding' Questions" lists the answers.

1. Which statement is true when VTP is configured on a switched network that incorporates VLANs?

   A. VTP adds to the complexity of managing a switched network.

   B. VTP allows a switch to be configured to belong to more than one VTP domain.

   C. VTP dynamically communicates VLAN changes to all switches in the same VTP domain.

   D. VTP is only compatible with the 802.1Q standard.

2. What are two features of VTP client mode operation? (Choose two.)

   A. VTP clients can add VLANs of local significance.

   B. VTP clients can forward VLAN information to other switches in the same VTP domain.

   C. VTP clients can only pass VLAN management information without adopting changes.

   D. VTP clients can forward broadcasts out all ports with no respect to VLAN information.

   E. VTP clients are unable to add VLANs.

3. What does a client mode switch in a VTP management domain do when it receives a summary advertisement with a revision number higher than its current revision number?

   A. It deletes the VLANs not included in the summary advertisement.

   B. It increments the revision number and forwards it to other switches.

   C. It issues an advertisement request for new VLAN information.

   D. It issues summary advertisements to advise other switches of status changes.

   E. It suspends forwarding until a subset advertisement update arrives.

4. What causes a VTP-configured switch to issue a summary advertisement?

   A. A five-minute update timer has elapsed.

   B. A new host has been attached to a switch in the management domain.

   C. A port on the switch has been shut down.

   D. The switch is changed to transparent mode.

5. Which three VTP parameters must be identical on all switches to participate in the same VTP domain? (Choose three.)

   A. Domain name

   B. Domain password

   C. Mode

   D. Pruning

   E. Revision number

   F. Version number

6. Which two statements describe VTP transparent mode operation? (Choose two.)

   A. Transparent mode switches can add VLANs of local significance only.

   B. Transparent mode switches can adopt VLAN management changes that are received from other switches.

   C. Transparent mode switches can create VLAN management information.

   D. Transparent mode switches originate updates about the status of their VLANS and inform other switches about that status.

   E. Transparent mode switches pass any VLAN management information they receive to other switches.

7. Which two statements are true about the implementation of VTP? (Choose two.)

   A. Switches must be connected via trunks.

   B. Switches that use VTP must have the same switch name.

C.  The VTP domain name is case sensitive.

D.  The VTP password is mandatory and case sensitive.

E.  Transparent mode switches cannot be configured with new VLANs.

8.  A network administrator is replacing a failed switch with a switch that was previously on the network. What precautionary step should the administrator take on the replacement switch to avoid incorrect VLAN information from propagating through the network?

A.  Change all the interfaces on the switch to access ports.

B.  Change the VTP domain name.

C.  Change the VTP mode to client.

D.  Enable VTP pruning.

9.  Which two events cause the VTP revision number on a VTP server to change? (Choose two.)

A.  Adding VLANs

B.  Changing interface VLAN designations

C.  Changing the switch to a VTP client

D.  Changing the VTP domain name

E.  Rebooting the switch

10.  How are VTP messages sent between switches in a domain?

A.  Layer 2 broadcast

B.  Layer 2 multicast

C.  Layer 2 unicast

D.  Layer 3 broadcast

E.  Layer 3 multicast

F.  Layer 3 unicast

11.  A router has two FastEthernet interfaces and needs to connect to four VLANs in the local network. How can this be accomplished using the fewest number of physical interfaces without unnecessarily decreasing network performance?

A.  Add a second router to handle the inter-VLAN traffic.

B.  Implement a router-on-a-stick configuration.

C.  Interconnect the VLANs via the two additional FastEthernet interfaces.

D.  Use a hub to connect the four VLANS with a FastEthernet interface on the router.

12. What distinguishes traditional legacy inter-VLAN routing from router-on-a-stick?

    A. Traditional routing is only able to use a single switch interface, while router-on-a-stick can use multiple switch interfaces.

    B. Traditional routing requires a routing protocol, while router-on-a-stick needs to route only directly connected networks.

    C. Traditional routing uses one port per logical network, while router-on-a-stick uses subinterfaces to connect multiple logical networks to a single router port.

    D. Traditional routing uses multiple paths to the router and therefore requires STP, while router-on-a-stick does not provide multiple connections and therefore eliminates the need for STP.

13. What two statements are true regarding the use of subinterfaces for inter-VLAN routing? (Choose two.)

    A. Fewer router Ethernet ports are required than in traditional inter-VLAN routing.

    B. The physical connection is less complex than in traditional inter-VLAN routing.

    C. More switch ports are required than in traditional inter-VLAN routing.

    D. Layer 3 troubleshooting is simpler than with traditional inter-VLAN routing.

    E. Subinterfaces have no contention for bandwidth.

14. What is important to consider while configuring the subinterfaces of a router when implementing inter-VLAN routing?

    A. The IP address of each subinterface must be the default gateway address for each VLAN subnet.

    B. The **no shutdown** command must be run on each subinterface.

    C. The physical interface must have an IP address configured.

    D. The subinterface numbers must match the VLAN ID number.

15. What steps must be completed in order to enable inter-VLAN routing using router-on-a-stick?

    A. Configure the physical interfaces on the router and enable a routing protocol.

    B. Create the VLANs on the router and define the port membership assignments on the switch.

    C. Create the VLANs on the switch to include port membership assignment and enable a routing protocol on the router.

    D. Create the VLANs on the switch to include port membership assignment and configure subinterfaces on the router matching the VLANs.

# CHAPTER 3

# STP

## Objectives

Upon completion of this chapter, you will be able to answer the following questions:

- What are common problems in a redundant switched network?

- How do different varieties of spanning-tree protocols operate?

- How do you implement PVST+ and Rapid PVST+ in a switched LAN environment?

- How are switch stacking and chassis aggregation implemented in a small switched LAN?

## Key Terms

This chapter uses the following key terms. You can find the definitions in the Glossary.

*BPDU filter*    *Page 142*

*root guard*    *Page 142*

*loop guard*    *Page 142*

*listening state*    *Page 145*

*learning state*    *Page 145*

*forwarding state*    *Page 145*

*disabled state*    *Page 145*

*edge port*    *Page 150*

*point-to-point*    *Page 152*

*STP diameter*    *Page 171*

# Introduction (3.0.1.1)

Network redundancy is a key to maintaining network reliability. Multiple physical links between devices provide redundant paths. The network can then continue to operate when a single link or port has failed. Redundant links can also share the traffic load and increase capacity.

Multiple paths need to be managed so that *Layer 2 loops* are not created. The best paths are chosen, and an alternate path is immediately available in case a primary path fails. Spanning Tree Protocol (STP) is used to create one path through a Layer 2 network.

This chapter focuses on the protocols used to manage these forms of redundancy. It also covers some of the potential redundancy problems and their symptoms.

**Class Activity 3.0.1.2: Stormy Traffic**

Refer to *Scaling Networks v6 Labs & Study Guide* and the online course to complete this activity.

It is your first day on the job as a network administrator for a small to medium-sized business. The previous network administrator left suddenly after a network upgrade took place for the business.

During the upgrade, a new switch was added. Since the upgrade, many employees have complained that they are having trouble accessing the Internet and servers on the network. In fact, most of them cannot access the network at all. Your corporate manager asks you to immediately research what could be causing these connectivity problems and delays.

So you take a look at the equipment operating on the network at your main distribution facility in the building. You notice that the network topology seems to be visually correct and that cables have been connected correctly, routers and switches are powered on and operational, and switches are connected together to provide backup or redundancy.

However, you notice that all of your switches' status lights are constantly blinking at a very fast pace, to the point that they almost appear solid. You think you have found the problem with the connectivity issues your employees are experiencing.

Use the Internet to research STP. As you research, take notes and describe:

- Broadcast storm
- Switching loops
- The purpose of STP
- Variations of STP

Complete the reflection questions that accompany the PDF file for this activity. Save your work and be prepared to share your answers with the class.

# Spanning Tree Concepts (3.1)

In this section, you will learn how to build a simple switched network with redundant links.

## Purpose of Spanning Tree (3.1.1)

The focus of this topic is to describe how Spanning Tree Protocol can solve common looping problems in a redundant switched network.

### Redundancy at OSI Layers 1 and 2 (3.1.1.1)

The three-tier hierarchical network design that uses core, distribution, and access layers with redundancy attempts to eliminate single points of failure on the network. Multiple cabled paths between switches provide physical redundancy in a switched network. This improves the reliability and availability of the network. Having alternate physical paths for data to traverse the network makes it possible for users to access network resources, despite path disruption.

The following steps explain how redundancy works in the topology shown in Figure 3-1:

1. PC1 is communicating with PC4 over a redundant network topology.

2. When the network link between S1 and S2 is disrupted, the path between PC1 and PC4 is automatically adjusted by STP to compensate for the disruption.

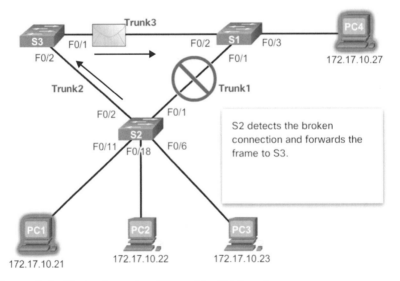

**Figure 3-1**  Redundancy in a Hierarchical Network

3. When the network connection between S1 and S2 is restored, the path is readjusted by STP to route traffic directly from S2 to S1 to get to PC4.

**Note**

To view an animation of these steps, refer to the online course.

For many organizations, the availability of the network is essential to supporting business needs. Therefore, the network infrastructure design is a critical business element. Path redundancy provides the necessary availability of multiple network services by eliminating the possibility of a single point of failure.

**Note**

OSI Layer 1 redundancy is illustrated using multiple links and devices, but more than just physical planning is required to complete the network setup. For the redundancy to work in a systematic way, the use of OSI Layer 2 protocols, such as STP, is also required.

Redundancy is an important part of the hierarchical design for preventing disruption of network services to users. Redundant networks require the addition of physical paths, but logical redundancy must also be part of the design. However, redundant paths in a switched Ethernet network may cause both physical and logical Layer 2 loops.

Logical Layer 2 loops may occur due to the natural operation of switches—specifically the learning and forwarding process. When multiple paths exist between two devices on a network, and there is no spanning-tree implementation on the switches, a Layer 2 loop occurs. A Layer 2 loop can result in three primary issues:

- **MAC database instability**—Instability in the content of the MAC address table results from copies of the same frame being received on different ports of the switch. Data forwarding can be impaired when the switch consumes the resources that are coping with instability in the MAC address table.

- *Broadcast storm*—Without some loop-avoidance process, each switch may flood broadcasts endlessly. This situation is commonly called a broadcast storm.

- **Multiple-frame transmission**—Multiple copies of unicast frames may be delivered to destination stations. Many protocols expect to receive only a single copy of each transmission. Multiple copies of the same frame can cause unrecoverable errors.

## Issues with Layer 1 Redundancy: MAC Database Instability (3.1.1.2)

Ethernet frames do not have a *time to live (TTL)* attribute. As a result, if there is no mechanism enabled to block continued propagation of these frames on a switched network, they continue to propagate between switches endlessly, or until a link is disrupted and breaks the loop. This continued propagation between switches can result in MAC database instability. This can occur due to broadcast frames forwarding.

Broadcast frames are forwarded out all switch ports except the original ingress port. This ensures that all devices in a broadcast domain are able to receive the frame. If there is more than one path through which the frame can be forwarded, an endless loop can result. When a loop occurs, it is possible for the MAC address table on a switch to constantly change with the updates from the broadcast frames, which results in MAC database instability.

The following sequence of events demonstrate the MAC database instability issue:

1. PC1 sends a broadcast frame to S2. S2 receives the broadcast frame on F0/11. When S2 receives the broadcast frame, it updates its MAC address table to record that PC1 is available on port F0/11.

2. Because it is a broadcast frame, S2 forwards the frame out all ports, including Trunk1 and Trunk2. When the broadcast frame arrives at S3 and S1, the switches update their MAC address tables to indicate that PC1 is available out port F0/1 on S1 and out port F0/2 on S3.

3. Because it is a broadcast frame, S3 and S1 forward the frame out all ports except the ingress port. S3 sends the broadcast frame from PC1 to S1. S1 sends the broadcast frame from PC1 to S3. Each switch updates its MAC address table with the incorrect port for PC1.

4. Each switch forwards the broadcast frame out all of its ports except the ingress port, which results in both switches forwarding the frame to S2.

5. When S2 receives the broadcast frames from S3 and S1, the MAC address table is updated with the last entry received from the other two switches.

6. S2 forwards the broadcast frame out all ports except the last received port. The cycle starts again.

**Note**

To view an animation of these sequence of events, refer to the online course.

Figure 3-2 shows a snapshot during sequence 6. Notice that S2 now thinks PC1 is reachable out the F0/1 interface.

This process repeats over and over again until the loop is broken by physically disconnecting the connections that are causing the loop or powering down one of the switches in the loop. This creates a high CPU load on all switches caught in the loop. Because the same frames are constantly being forwarded back and forth between all switches in the loop, the CPU of the switch must process a lot of data. This slows down performance on the switch when legitimate traffic arrives.

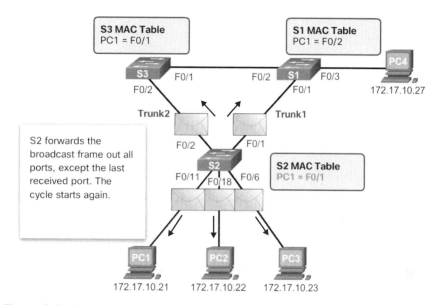

**Figure 3-2**  MAC Database Instability Example

A host caught in a network loop is not accessible to other hosts on the network. In addition, due to the constant changes in the MAC address table, the switch does not know which port to use to forward unicast frames. In this example just shown, the switches will have the incorrect ports listed for PC1. Any unicast frame destined for PC1 loops around the network, just as the broadcast frames do. More and more frames looping around the network eventually creates a broadcast storm.

## Issues with Layer 1 Redundancy: Broadcast Storms (3.1.1.3)

A broadcast storm occurs when there are so many broadcast frames caught in a Layer 2 loop that all available bandwidth is consumed. Consequently, no bandwidth is available for legitimate traffic, and the network becomes unavailable for data communication. This is an effective denial of service (DoS).

Broadcast storms are inevitable on a looped network. As more devices send broadcasts over the network, more traffic is caught in the loop, consuming resources. This eventually creates a broadcast storm that causes the network to fail.

There are other consequences of broadcast storms. Because broadcast traffic is forwarded out every port on a switch, all connected devices have to process all the broadcast traffic that is being flooded endlessly around the looped network. This can cause the end device to malfunction because of the processing requirements needed to sustain such a high traffic load on the NIC.

The following sequence of events demonstrate the broadcast storm issue:

1. PC1 sends a broadcast frame out onto the looped network.

2. The broadcast frame loops between all the interconnected switches on the network.

3. PC4 also sends a broadcast frame out onto the looped network.

4. The PC4 broadcast frame gets caught in the loop between all the interconnected switches, just like the PC1 broadcast frame.

5. As more devices send broadcasts over the network, more traffic is caught in the loop, consuming resources. This eventually creates a broadcast storm that causes the network to fail.

6. When the network is fully saturated with broadcast traffic that is looping between the switches, the switch discards new traffic because it is unable to process it. Figure 3-3 displays the resulting broadcast storm.

### Note

To view an animation of these sequence of events, refer to the online course.

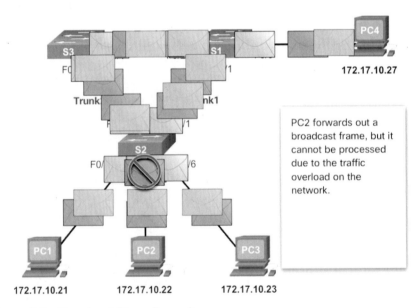

**Figure 3-3**   Broadcast Storm Example

A broadcast storm can develop in seconds because devices connected to a network regularly send out broadcast frames, such as ARP requests. As a result, when a loop is created, the switched network is quickly brought down.

## Issues with Layer 1 Redundancy: Duplicate Unicast Frames (3.1.1.4)

Broadcast frames are not the only type of frames that are affected by loops. Unknown unicast frames sent onto a looped network can result in duplicate frames arriving at the destination device. An unknown unicast frame occurs when the switch does not have the destination MAC address in its MAC address table and must forward the frame out all ports except the ingress port.

The following sequence of events demonstrate the duplicate unicast frames issue:

1. PC1 sends a unicast frame destined for PC4.

2. S2 does not have an entry for PC4 in its MAC table. In an attempt to find PC4, it floods the unknown unicast frame out all switch ports except the port that received the traffic.

3. The frame arrives at switches S1 and S3.

4. S1 has a MAC address entry for PC4, so it forwards the frame out to PC4.

5. S3 has an entry in its MAC address table for PC4, so it forwards the unicast frame out Trunk3 to S1.

6. S1 receives the duplicate frame and forwards the frame out to PC4.

7. PC4 has now received the same frame twice.

Figure 3-4 shows a snapshot during sequences 5 and 6.

**Note**

To view an animation of these sequence of events, refer to the online course.

Most upper-layer protocols are not designed to recognize duplicate transmissions. In general, protocols that make use of a sequence-numbering mechanism assume that the transmission has failed and that the sequence number has recycled for another communication session. Other protocols attempt to hand the duplicate transmission to the appropriate upper-layer protocol to be processed and possibly discarded.

Layer 2 LAN protocols, such as Ethernet, do not include a mechanism to recognize and eliminate endlessly looping frames. Some Layer 3 protocols implement a TTL mechanism that limits the number of times a Layer 3 networking device can retransmit a packet. Layer 2 devices do not have this mechanism, so they continue to retransmit looping traffic indefinitely. STP, a Layer 2 loop-avoidance mechanism, was developed to address these problems.

To prevent these issues from occurring in a redundant network, some type of spanning tree must be enabled on the switches. Spanning tree is enabled by default on Cisco switches to prevent Layer 2 loops from occurring.

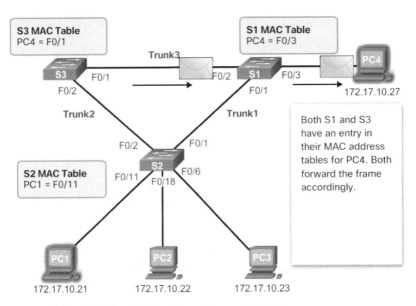

**Figure 3-4** S1 and S3 Send a Duplicate Frame to PC4

**Packet Tracer 3.1.1.5: Examining a Redundant Design**

Background/Scenario

In this activity, you will observe how STP operates by default, and how it reacts when faults occur. Switches have been added to the network "out of the box." Cisco switches can be connected to a network without any additional action required by the network administrator. For the purpose of this activity, the bridge priority (covered later in the chapter) was modified.

# STP Operation (3.1.2)

The focus of this topic is to learn how to build a simple switched network using STP.

## Spanning Tree Algorithm: Introduction (3.1.2.1)

Redundancy increases the availability of the network topology by protecting the network from a single point of failure, such as a failed network cable or switch. When physical redundancy is introduced into a design, loops and duplicate frames occur. Loops and duplicate frames have severe consequences for a switched network. Spanning Tree Protocol (STP) was developed to address these issues.

STP ensures that there is only one logical path between all destinations on the network by intentionally blocking redundant paths that could cause a loop. A port is considered blocked when user data is prevented from entering or leaving that port. This does not include *bridge protocol data unit (BPDU)* frames that are used by STP to prevent loops. Blocking the redundant paths is critical to preventing loops on the network. The physical paths still exist to provide redundancy, but these paths are disabled to prevent the loops from occurring. If the path is ever needed to compensate for a network cable or switch failure, STP recalculates the paths and unblocks the necessary ports to allow the redundant path to become active.

Figure 3-5 illustrates normal STP operation when all switches have STP enabled:

1. PC1 sends a broadcast out onto the network.

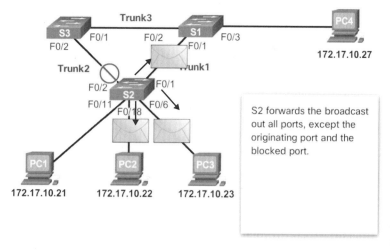

**Figure 3-5**   Normal STP Operation

2. S2 is configured with STP and has set the port for Trunk2 to a blocking state. The blocking state prevents ports from being used to forward user data, which prevents a loop from occurring. S2 forwards a broadcast frame out all switch ports except the originating port from PC1 and the port for Trunk2.

3. S1 receives the broadcast frame and forwards it out all of its switch ports, where it reaches PC4 and S3. S3 forwards the frame out the port for Trunk2, and S2 drops the frame. The Layer 2 loop is prevented.

**Note**

To view an animation of these steps, refer to the online course.

Figure 3-6 shows how STP recalculates the path when a failure occurs:

1. PC1 sends a broadcast out onto the network.

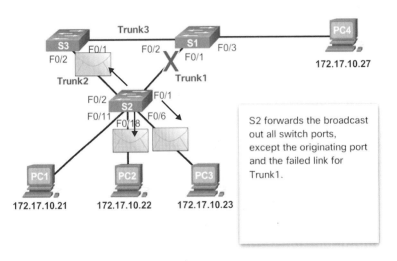

**Figure 3-6**   STP Compensates for Network Failure

2. The broadcast is then forwarded around the network.

3. As shown in the figure, the trunk link between S2 and S1 fails, resulting in the previous path being disrupted.

4. S2 unblocks the previously blocked port for Trunk2 and allows the broadcast traffic to traverse the alternate path around the network, permitting communication to continue. If this link comes back up, STP reconverges, and the port on S2 is again blocked.

**Note**

To view an animation of these sequence of events, refer to the online course.

STP prevents loops from occurring by configuring a loop-free path through the network using strategically placed "blocking-state" ports. The switches running STP are able to compensate for failures by dynamically unblocking the previously blocked ports and permitting traffic to traverse the alternate paths.

Up to now, we have used the terms *Spanning Tree Protocol* and *STP*. However, these terms can be misleading. Many professionals generically use these to refer to various implementations of spanning tree, such as Rapid Spanning Tree Protocol (RSTP) and Multiple Spanning Tree Protocol (MSTP).

To communicate spanning tree concepts correctly, it is important to refer to the particular implementation or standard in context. The latest IEEE documentation on spanning tree (IEEE-802-1D-2004) says, "STP has now been superseded by the

Rapid Spanning Tree Protocol (RSTP)." The IEEE uses "STP" to refer to the original implementation of spanning tree and "RSTP" to describe the version of spanning tree specified in IEEE-802.1D-2004. In this curriculum, when the original Spanning Tree Protocol is the context of a discussion, the phrase "original 802.1D spanning tree" is used to avoid confusion. Because the two protocols share much of the same terminology and methods for the loop-free path, the primary focus is on the current standard and the Cisco proprietary implementations of STP and RSTP.

**Note**

STP is based on an algorithm that Radia Perlman invented while working for Digital Equipment Corporation and published in the 1985 paper "An Algorithm for Distributed Computation of a Spanning Tree in an Extended LAN."

## Spanning Tree Algorithm: Port Roles (3.1.2.2)

IEEE 802.1D STP and RSTP use *Spanning Tree Algorithm (STA)* to determine which switch ports on a network must be put in blocking state to prevent loops from occurring. STA designates a single switch as the *root bridge* and uses it as the reference point for all path calculations. In Figure 3-7, the root bridge (switch S1) is chosen through an election process. All switches that are participating in STP exchange BPDU frames to determine which switch has the lowest *bridge ID (BID)* on the network. The switch with the lowest BID automatically becomes the root bridge for the STA calculations.

**Note**

For simplicity, assume until otherwise indicated that all ports on all switches are assigned to VLAN 1. Each switch has a unique MAC address associated with VLAN 1.

A BPDU is a messaging frame exchanged by switches for STP. Each BPDU contains a BID that identifies the switch that sent the BPDU. The BID contains a priority value, the MAC address of the sending switch, and an optional *extended system ID*. The lowest BID value is determined by the combination of these three fields.

After the root bridge has been determined, the STA calculates the shortest path to the root bridge. Each switch uses the STA to determine which ports to block. While the STA determines the best paths to the root bridge for all switch ports in the broadcast domain, traffic is prevented from being forwarded through the network. The STA considers both path and port costs when determining which ports to block. The path costs are calculated using port cost values associated with port speeds for each switch port along a given path. The sum of the port cost values determines the overall path cost to the root bridge. If there is more than one path to choose from, STA chooses the path with the lowest path cost.

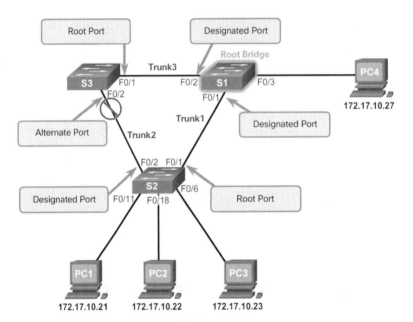

**Figure 3-7** STP Algorithm—RSTP Port Roles

When the STA has determined which paths are most desirable relative to each switch, it assigns port roles to the participating switch ports. The port roles describe their relationship in the network to the root bridge and whether they are allowed to forward traffic:

- *Root port*—A root port is selected on all non-root bridge switches on a per-switch basis. Root ports are the switch ports closest to the root bridge, based on the overall cost to the root bridge. There can be only one root port per non-root switch. Root ports could be single-link interfaces or an EtherChannel port channel interface.

- *Designated port*—A designated port is a non-root port that is permitted to forward traffic. Designated ports are selected on a per-segment basis, based on the cost of each port on either side of the segment and the total cost calculated by STP for that port to get back to the root bridge. If one end of a segment is a root port, then the other end is a designated port. All ports on the root bridge are designated ports.

- *Alternate port* and *backup port*—An alternate port and a backup port are in a *blocking state* (or discarding state) to prevent loops. Alternate ports are selected only on links where neither end is a root port. Only one end of the segment is blocked, while the other end remains in forwarding state, allowing for a faster transition to the forwarding state when necessary.

- **Disabled ports**—A disabled port is a switch port that is shut down.

**Note**

The port roles displayed are those defined by RSTP. The role originally defined by the 802.1D STP for alternate and backup ports was non-designated.

For example, on the link between S2 and the root bridge S1 in Figure 3-7, the root port selected by STP is the F0/1 port on S2. The root port selected by STP on the link between S3 and S1 is the F0/1 port on S3. Because S1 is the root bridge, all of its ports (that is, F0/1 and F0/2) become designated ports.

Next, the interconnecting link between S2 and S3 must negotiate to see which port will become the designated port and which port will transition to alternate. In this scenario, the F0/2 port on S2 transitioned to a designated port, and the F0/2 port on S3 transitioned to an alternate port and is therefore blocking traffic.

### Spanning Tree Algorithm: Root Bridge (3.1.2.3)

As shown in Figure 3-8, every *spanning-tree instance (STP instance)* has a switch designated as the root bridge. The root bridge serves as a reference point for all spanning-tree calculations to determine which redundant paths to block.

An election process determines which switch becomes the root bridge.

Figure 3-9 shows the BID fields. The BID is made up of a priority value, an extended system ID, and the MAC address of the switch. The *bridge priority* value is automatically assigned but can be modified. The extended system ID is used to specify a VLAN ID or a Multiple Spanning Tree Protocol (MSTP) instance ID. The MAC address field initially contains the MAC address of the sending switch.

All switches in the broadcast domain participate in the election process. After a switch boots, it begins to send out BPDU frames every two seconds. These BPDUs contain the switch BID and the root ID.

The switch with the lowest BID becomes the root bridge. At first, all switches declare themselves as the root bridge. But through the exchange of several BPDUs, the switches eventually agree on the root bridge.

Specifically, each switch forwards BPDU frames containing their BID and the root ID to adjacent switches in the broadcast domain. The receiving switch compares its current root ID with the received root ID identified in the received frames. If the received root ID is lower, the receiving switch updates its root ID with the lower root ID. It then forwards new BPDU frames containing the lower root ID to the other adjacent switches. Eventually, the switch with the lowest BID is identified as the root bridge for the spanning-tree instance.

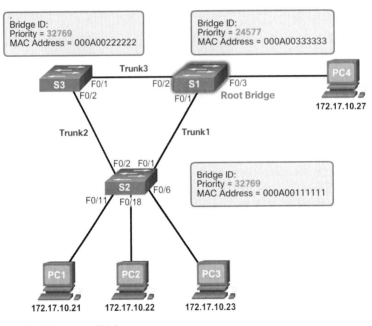

**Figure 3-8**    The Root Bridge

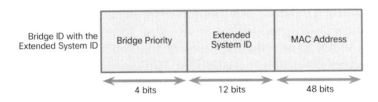

**Figure 3-9**    BID Fields

A root bridge is elected for each spanning-tree instance. It is possible to have multiple distinct root bridges for different sets of VLANs. If all ports on all switches are members of VLAN 1, then there is only one spanning-tree instance. The extended system ID includes the VLAN ID and plays a role in how spanning-tree instances are determined.

The BID consists of a configurable bridge priority number and a MAC address. Bridge priority is a value between 0 and 65,535. The default is 32,768. If two or more switches have the same priority, the switch with the lowest MAC address becomes the root bridge.

**Note**

The reason the bridge priority value in Figure 3-8 displays 32,769 instead of the default value 32,768 is that the STA also adds the default VLAN number (VLAN 1) to the priority value.

## Spanning Tree Algorithm: Root Path Cost (3.1.2.4)

When the root bridge has been elected for the spanning-tree instance, STA starts determining the best paths to the root bridge.

Switches send BPDUs, which include the *root path cost*. This is the cost of the path from the sending switch to the root bridge. It is calculated by adding the individual port costs along the path from the switch to the root bridge. When a switch receives the BPDU, it adds the ingress port cost of the segment to determine its internal root path cost. It then advertises the new root path cost to its adjacent peers.

The *default port cost* is defined by the speed at which the port operates. As shown in Table 3-1, 10 Gbps Ethernet ports have a port cost of 2, 1 Gbps Ethernet ports have a port cost of 4, 100 Mbps Fast Ethernet ports have a port cost of 19, and 10 Mbps Ethernet ports have a port cost of 100.

**Table 3-1**    Revised IEEE Cost Values

| Link Speed | Cost (Revised IEEE 802.1D-1998 Specification) |
| --- | --- |
| 10 Gbps | 2 |
| 1 Gbps | 4 |
| 100 Mbps | 19 |
| 10 Mbps | 100 |

**Note**

The original IEEE specification did not account for links faster than 1 Gbps. Specifically, 1 Gbps links were assigned a port cost of 1, 100 Mbps link a cost of 10, and 10 Mbps links a cost of 100. Any link faster than 1 Gbps (i.e., 10 GE) was automatically assigned the same port cost of 1 Gbps links (i.e., port cost of 1).

**Note**

Modular switches such as the Catalyst 4500 and 6500 switches support higher port costs—specifically, 10 Gbps = 2000, 100 Gbps = 200, and 1 Tbps = 20 port costs.

As Ethernet technologies evolve, the port cost values may change to accommodate the different speeds available. The nonlinear numbers in the table accommodate some improvements to the older Ethernet standard.

Although switch ports have a default port cost associated with them, the port cost is configurable. The ability to configure individual port costs gives the administrator the flexibility to manually control the spanning-tree paths to the root bridge.

To configure the port cost of an interface, enter the **spanning-tree cost** *value* command in interface configuration mode. The value can be between 1 and 200,000,000.

Example 3-1 displays how to change the port cost of F0/1 to 25 by using the **spanning-tree cost 25** interface configuration mode command.

**Example 3-1**    Changing the Default Port Cost

```
S2(config)# interface f0/1
S2(config-if)# spanning-tree cost 25
S2(config-if)# end
```

Example 3-2 shows how to restore the port cost to the default value, 19, by entering the **no spanning-tree cost** interface configuration mode command.

**Example 3-2**    Restoring the Default Port Cost

```
S2(config)# interface f0/1
S2(config-if)# no spanning-tree cost
S2(config-if)# end
S2#
```

The internal root path cost is equal to the sum of all the port costs along the path to the root bridge. Paths with the lowest cost become preferred, and all other redundant paths are blocked.

In Figure 3-10, the internal root path cost from S2 to the root bridge S1 using Path 1 is 19 (based on Table 3-1), while the internal root path cost using Path 2 is 38.

Path 1 has a lower overall path cost to the root bridge and therefore becomes the preferred path. STP configures the redundant path to be blocked, which prevents a loop from occurring.

Use the **show spanning-tree** command as shown in Example 3-3 to verify the root ID and internal root path cost to the root bridge.

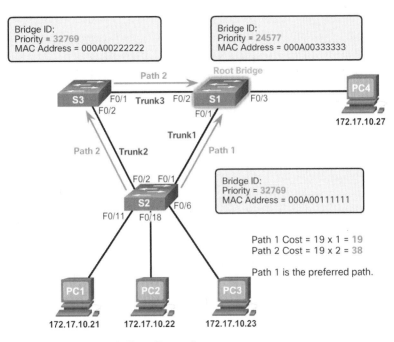

**Figure 3-10**    Root Path Cost Example

**Example 3-3**    Verifying the Root Bridge and Port Costs

```
S2# show spanning-tree
VLAN0001
  Spanning tree enabled protocol ieee
  Root ID    Priority    24577
             Address     000A.0033.0033
             Cost        19
             Port        1
             Hello Time 2 sec   Max Age 20 sec   Forward Delay 15 sec

  Bridge ID  Priority    32769   (priority 32768 sys-id-ext 1)
             Address     000A.0011.1111
             Hello Time  2 sec   Max Age 20 sec   Forward Delay 15 sec
             Aging Time 15 sec

Interface          Role Sts  Cost       Prio.Nbr Type
------------------ ---- ---  --------- -------- ------------------------
Fa0/1                   Root FWD  19         128.1    Edge P2p
Fa0/2                   Desg FWD  19         128.2    Edge P2p
```

The output generated identifies the root BID as 24577.000A0033003, with a root path cost of 19. The Cost field value changes depending on how many switch ports must be traversed to get to the root bridge. Also notice that each interface is assigned a port role and port cost of 19.

## Port Role Decisions for RSTP (3.1.2.5)

After the root bridge is elected, the STA determines port roles on interconnecting links. The next seven figures help illustrate this process.

In Figure 3-11, switch S1 is the root bridge.

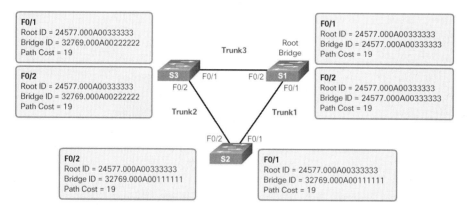

**Figure 3-11**   Port Role Decisions: Step 1

The root bridge always transitions its interconnecting links to designated port status. For example, in Figure 3-12, S1 configures both of its trunk ports connected to F0/1 and F0/2 as designated ports.

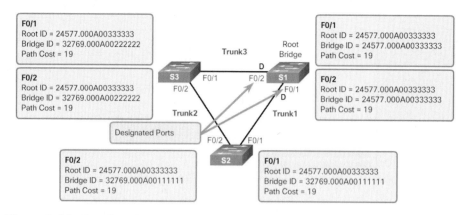

**Figure 3-12**   Port Role Decisions: Step 2

Non-root switches transition ports with the lowest root path cost to root ports. In Figure 3-13, S2 and S3 transition their F0/1 ports to root ports.

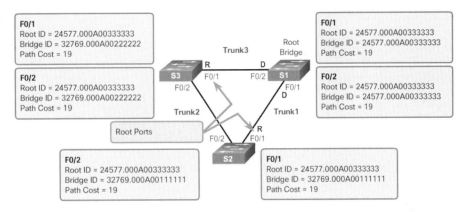

**Figure 3-13**   Port Role Decisions: Step 3

After the root ports are selected, the STA decides which ports will have the designated and alternate roles, as illustrated with the S2 to S3 link in Figure 3-14.

The root bridge already transitioned its ports to designated status. Non-root switches must transition their non-root ports to either designated or alternate port status.

The two non-root switches exchange BPDU frames, as illustrated in Figure 3-15.

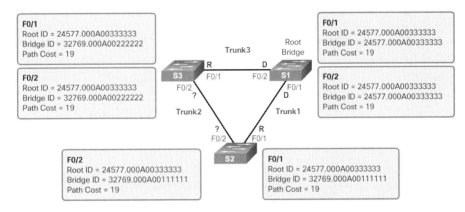

**Figure 3-14**   Port Role Decisions: Step 4

The incoming BPDU frames include the BID of the sending switch. When a switch receives a BPDU frame, it compares the BID in the BPDU with its BID to see which one is higher. The switch advertising the higher BID transitions its port to alternate status.

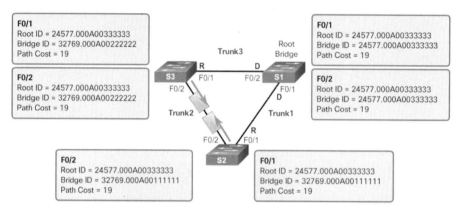

**Figure 3-15** Port Role Decisions: Step 5

As illustrated in Figure 3-16, S3 has a higher BID (32769.000A00222222) compared to the BID of S2 (32769.000A00111111). Therefore, S3 transitions its F0/2 port to alternate status.

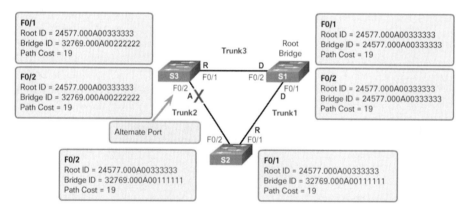

**Figure 3-16** Port Role Decisions: Step 6

S2 has the lower BID and therefore transitions its port to designated status, as shown in Figure 3-17.

Keep in mind that the first priority is the lowest-path cost to the root bridge and that the sender's BID is used only if the port costs are equal.

Each switch determines which port roles are assigned to each of its ports to create the loop-free spanning tree.

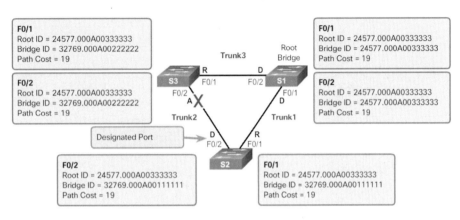

**Figure 3-17** Port Role Decisions: Step 7

## Designated and Alternate Ports (3.1.2.6)

When determining the root port on a switch, the switch compares the path costs on all switch ports participating in the spanning tree. The switch port with the lowest overall path cost to the root bridge is automatically assigned the root port role because it is closest to the root bridge. In a network topology of switches, all non-root bridge switches have a single root port chosen, and that port provides the lowest-cost path back to the root bridge.

A root bridge does not have any root ports. All ports on a root bridge are designated ports. A switch that is not the root bridge of a network topology has only one root port defined.

Figure 3-18 shows a topology with four switches.

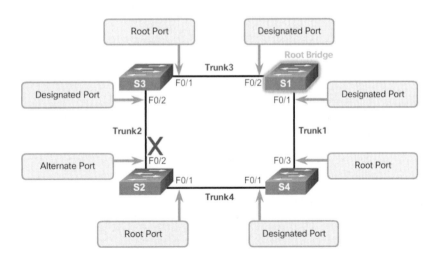

**Figure 3-18** Determining Designated and Alternate Ports

Examine the port roles, and you see that port F0/1 on switch S3 and port F0/3 on switch S4 have been selected as root ports because they have the lowest-cost path (root path cost) to the root bridge for their respective switches.

S2 has two ports, F0/1 and F0/2, with equal-cost paths to the root bridge. In this case, the bridge IDs of the neighboring switches, S3 and S4, will be used to break the tie. This is known as the sender's BID. S3 has a BID of 24577.5555.5555.5555, and S4 has a BID of 24577.1111.1111.1111. Because S4 has a lower BID, S2's F0/1 port, the port connected to S4, becomes the root port.

> **Note**
>
> The BIDs are not shown in Figure 3-18.

Next, designated ports need to be selected on shared segments. S2 and S3 connect to the same LAN segment, and therefore, they exchange BPDU frames. STP determines whether S2's F0/2 port or S3's F0/2 port is the designated port for the shared segment. The switch with the lower-cost path to the root bridge (root path cost) has its port selected as the designated port. S3's F0/2 port has a lower-cost path to the root bridge, so it is the designated port for that segment.

S2 and S4 go through a similar process for their shared segment. S4's F0/1 port has the lower-cost path to the root bridge and becomes the designated port on this shared segment.

All STP port roles have been assigned except for S2's F0/2 port. S2's F0/1 port has already been selected as the root port for that switch. Because S3's F0/2 port is the designated port for this segment, S2's F0/2 port becomes an alternate port.

The designated port is the port that sends and receives traffic to and from that segment to the root bridge. This is the best port on that segment toward the root bridge. The alternate port does not send or receive traffic on that segment; this is the loop prevention part of STP.

## 802.1D BPDU Frame Format (3.1.2.7)

The STA depends on the exchange of BPDUs to determine a root bridge. As shown in Table 3-2, a BPDU frame contains 12 distinct fields that convey the path and priority information used to determine the root bridge and the paths to the root bridge:

**Table 3-2**   The BPDU Fields

| Field Number | Bytes | Field | Description |
|---|---|---|---|
| 1 | 2 | Protocol ID | This field indicates the type of protocol being used. This field contains the value 0. |
| 2 | 1 | Version | This field indicates the version of the protocol. This field contains the value 0. |
| 3 | 1 | Message type | This field indicates the type of message. This field contains the value 0. |
| 4 | 1 | Flags | This field includes one of the following: <ul><li>*Topology change (TC) bit*, which signals a topology change in the event that a path to the root bridge has been disrupted</li><li>*Topology change acknowledgment (TCA) bit*, which is set to acknowledge receipt of a configuration message with the TC bit set</li></ul> |
| 5 | 8 | Root ID | This field indicates the root bridge by listing its 2-byte priority followed by its 6-byte MAC address ID. When a switch first boots, the root ID is the same as the bridge ID. However, as the election process occurs, the lowest bridge ID replaces the local root ID to identify the root bridge switch. |
| 6 | 4 | Root Path Cost | This field indicates the cost of the path from the bridge sending the configuration message to the root bridge. The path cost field is updated by each switch along the path to the root bridge. |
| 7 | 8 | Bridge ID | This field indicates the priority, extended system ID, and MAC address ID of the bridge sending the message. This label allows the root bridge to identify where the BPDU originated and to identify the multiple paths from the switch to the root bridge. When the root bridge receives more than one BPDU from a switch with different path costs, it knows that there are two distinct paths and uses the path with the lower cost. |
| 8 | 2 | Port ID | This field indicates the port number from which the configuration message was sent. This field allows loops created by multiple attached bridges to be detected and corrected. |

| Field Number | Bytes | Field | Description |
|---|---|---|---|
| 9 | 2 | Message age | This field indicates the amount of time that has elapsed since the root sent the configuration message on which the current configuration message is based. |
| 10 | 2 | Max age | This field indicates when the current configuration message should be deleted. When the message age reaches the maximum age, the switch expires the current configuration and initiates a new election to determine a new root bridge because it assumes that it has been disconnected from the root bridge. This is 20 seconds by default but can be tuned to be between 6 and 40 seconds. |
| 11 | 2 | Hello time | This field indicates the time between root bridge configuration messages. The interval defines how long the root bridge waits between sending configuration message BPDUs. This is equal to 2 seconds by default but can be tuned to be between 1 and 10 seconds. |
| 12 | 2 | Forward delay | This field indicates the length of time bridges should wait before transitioning to a new state after a topology change. If a bridge transitions too soon, it is possible that not all network links will be ready to change their state, and loops can result. This is, by default, equal to 15 seconds for each state but can be tuned to be between 4 and 30 seconds. |

The first four fields in the BPDU identify specifics about the type of BPDU message, including the protocol, version, message type, and status flags. The next four fields are used to identify the root bridge and the root path cost to the root bridge. The last four fields are all timer-related fields that determine how frequently BPDU messages are sent and how long the information received through the BPDU process is retained.

Figure 3-19 shows a BPDU frame that was captured using Wireshark. In this example, the BPDU frame contains more fields than previously described. The BPDU message is encapsulated in an Ethernet frame when it is transmitted across the network. The 802.3 header indicates the source and destination addresses of the BPDU frame. This frame has a destination MAC address of 01:80:C2:00:00:00, which is a multicast address for the spanning-tree group. When a frame is addressed with this MAC address, each switch that is configured for spanning tree accepts and reads the information from the frame. All other devices on the network disregard the frame.

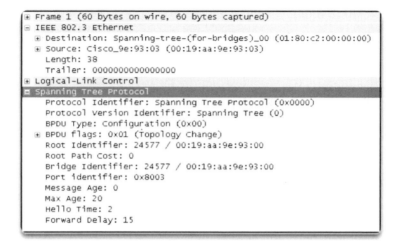

```
⊞ Frame 1 (60 bytes on wire, 60 bytes captured)
⊟ IEEE 802.3 Ethernet
  ⊞ Destination: Spanning-tree-(for-bridges)_00 (01:80:c2:00:00:00)
  ⊞ Source: Cisco_9e:93:03 (00:19:aa:9e:93:03)
    Length: 38
    Trailer: 0000000000000000
⊞ Logical-Link Control
⊟ Spanning Tree Protocol
    Protocol Identifier: Spanning Tree Protocol (0x0000)
    Protocol Version Identifier: Spanning Tree (0)
    BPDU Type: Configuration (0x00)
  ⊞ BPDU flags: 0x01 (Topology Change)
    Root Identifier: 24577 / 00:19:aa:9e:93:00
    Root Path Cost: 0
    Bridge Identifier: 24577 / 00:19:aa:9e:93:00
    Port Identifier: 0x8003
    Message Age: 0
    Max Age: 20
    Hello Time: 2
    Forward Delay: 15
```

**Figure 3-19**   The BPDU Example

In Figure 3-19, the root ID and the BID are the same in the captured BPDU frame. This indicates that the frame was captured from a root bridge. The timers are all set to the default values.

## 802.1D BPDU Propagation and Process (3.1.2.8)

Each switch in a broadcast domain initially assumes that it is the root bridge for a spanning-tree instance, so the BPDU frames that are sent contain the BID of the local switch as the root ID. By default, BPDU frames are sent every two seconds after a switch is booted. The default value of the hello timer specified in the BPDU frame is two seconds. Each switch maintains local information about its own BID, the root ID, and the root path cost.

When adjacent switches receive a BPDU frame, they compare the root ID from the BPDU frame with the local root ID. If the root ID in the received BPDU is lower than the local root ID, the switch updates the local root ID and the ID in its BPDU messages. These messages indicate the new root bridge on the network. If the local root ID is lower than the root ID received in the BPDU frame, the BPDU frame is discarded.

The distance to the root bridge is indicated by the root path cost in the BPDU. The ingress port cost is then added to the root path cost in the BPDU to determine the internal root path cost from this switch to the root bridge. For example, if the BPDU was received on a Fast Ethernet switch port, the root path cost in the BPDU would be added to the ingress port cost of 19, for a cumulative internal root path cost. This is the cost from this switch to the root bridge.

After a root ID has been updated to identify a new root bridge, all subsequent BPDU frames sent from that switch contain the new root ID and updated root path cost. That way, all other adjacent switches are able to see the lowest root ID identified at all times. As the BPDU frames pass between other adjacent switches, the path cost is continually updated to indicate the total path cost to the root bridge. Each switch in the spanning tree uses its path costs to identify the best possible path to the root bridge.

The following figures summarize the BPDU process.

**Note**

Bridge priority is the initial deciding factor when electing a root bridge. If the bridge priorities of all the switches are the same, the device with the lowest MAC address becomes the root bridge.

In Figure 3-20, S2 forwards BPDU frames identifying itself as the root bridge out all switch ports.

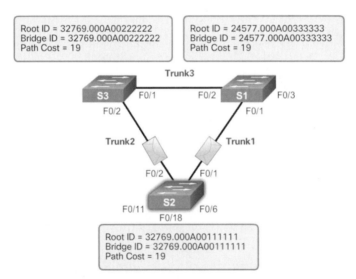

**Figure 3-20**   The BPDU Process: Step 1

In Figure 3-21, S3 receives the BPDU from S2 and compares its root ID with the BPDU frame it received. The priorities are equal, so S3 examines the MAC address portion. S2 has a lower MAC address value, so S3 updates its root ID with the S2 root ID. S3 now considers S2 the root bridge.

In Figure 3-22, S1 receives the BPDU from S2 and compares its root ID with the BPDU frame it received. S1 identifies its root ID as the lower value and discards the BPDU from S2.

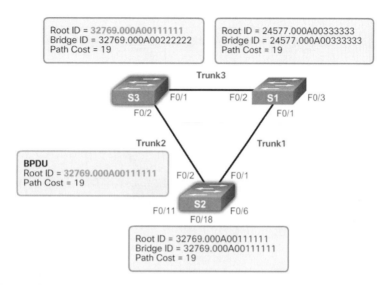

**Figure 3-21**   The BPDU Process: Step 2

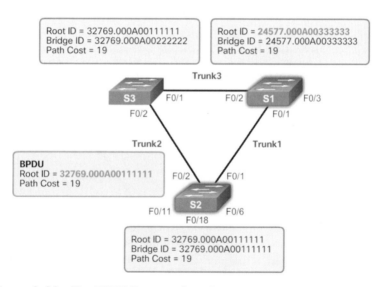

**Figure 3-22**   The BPDU Process: Step 3

In Figure 3-23, S3 sends out BPDU frames advertising its BID and the new root ID, which is that of S2.

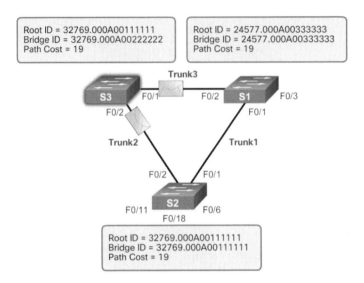

Figure 3-23   The BPDU Process: Step 4

In Figure 3-24, S2 receives the BPDU from S3 and discards it after verifying that the root ID in the BPDU matches its local root ID.

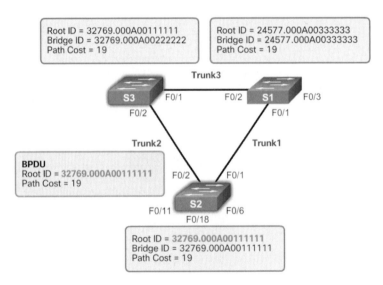

Figure 3-24   The BPDU Process: Step 5

In Figure 3-25, S1 receives the BPDU from S3 and discards it because S1 has a lower priority value in its root ID.

In Figure 3-26, S1 sends out BPDU frames advertising its BID and itself as the root ID.

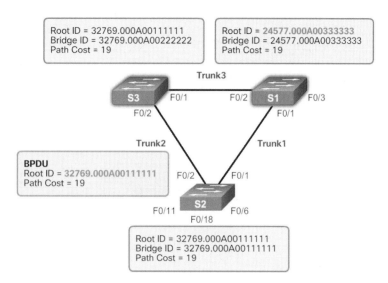

**Figure 3-25**   The BPDU Process: Step 6

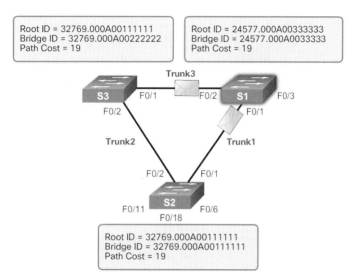

**Figure 3-26**   The BPDU Process: Step 7

In Figure 3-27, S3 receives the BPDU from S1 and compares its root ID with the BPDU frame it received. S3 identifies the received root ID to be the lower value. Therefore, S3 updates its root ID values to indicate that S1 is now the root bridge.

In Figure 3-28, S2 receives the BPDU from S1 and compares its root ID with the BPDU frame it received. S2 identifies the received root ID to be the lower value. Therefore, S2 updates its root ID values to indicate that S1 is now the root bridge.

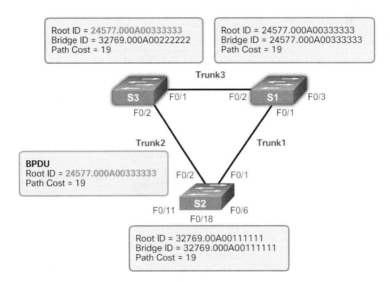

**Figure 3-27**   The BPDU Process: Step 8

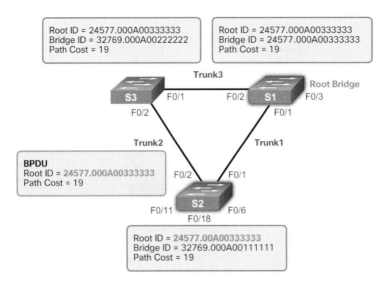

**Figure 3-28**   The BPDU Process: Step 9

## Extended System ID (3.1.2.9)

The bridge ID (BID) is used to determine the root bridge on a network. The BID field of a BPDU frame contains three separate fields:

- Bridge priority

- Extended system ID

- MAC address

Each of these fields is used during the root bridge election.

## Bridge Priority

The bridge priority is a customizable value that can be used to influence which switch becomes the root bridge. The switch with the lowest priority, which implies the lowest BID, becomes the root bridge because a lower priority value takes precedence. For example, to ensure that a specific switch is always the root bridge, set the priority to a lower value than the rest of the switches on the network.

The default priority value for all Cisco switches is the decimal value 32768. The range is 0 to 61440, in increments of 4096. Therefore, valid priority values are 0, 4096, 8192, 12288, 16384, 20480, 24576, 28672, 32768, 36864, 40960, 45056, 49152, 53248, 57344, and 61440. A bridge priority of 0 takes precedence over all other bridge priorities. All other values are rejected.

## Extended System ID

Early implementations of IEEE 802.1D were designed for networks that did not use VLANs. There was a single common spanning tree across all switches. For this reason, in older Cisco switches, the extended system ID could be omitted in BPDU frames.

As VLANs became common for network infrastructure segmentation, 802.1D was enhanced to include support for VLANs, which required that the VLAN ID be included in the BPDU frame. VLAN information is included in the BPDU frame through the use of the extended system ID. All newer switches include the use of the extended system ID by default.

As shown in Figure 3-29, the bridge priority field is 2 bytes, or 16 bits, in length. The first 4 bits identify the bridge priority, and the remaining 12 bits identify the VLAN participating in this particular STP process.

Using these 12 bits for the extended system ID reduces the bridge priority to 4 bits. This process reserves the rightmost 12 bits for the VLAN ID and the far-left 4 bits for the bridge priority. This explains why the bridge priority value can be configured only in multiples of 4096, or $2^{12}$. If the far-left bits are 0001, then the bridge priority is 4096. If the far-left bits are 1111, then the bridge priority is 61440 (= 15 × 4096). The Catalyst 2960 and 3560 Series switches do not allow the configuration of a bridge priority of 65536 (= 16 × 4096) because this priority assumes the use of a fifth bit that is unavailable due to the use of the extended system ID.

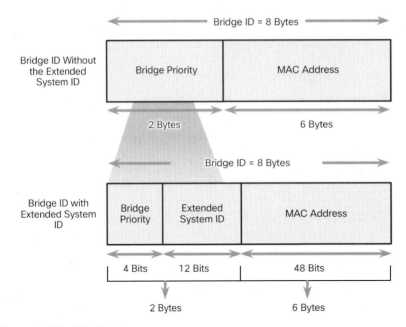

**Figure 3-29**   BID Fields

The extended system ID value is a decimal value added to the bridge priority value in the BID to identify the priority and VLAN of the BPDU frame.

When two switches are configured with the same priority and have the same extended system ID, the switch with the lowest MAC address has the lower BID. Initially, all switches are configured with the same default priority value. The MAC address is often the deciding factor in which switch becomes the root bridge.

To ensure that the root bridge decision best meets network requirements, it is recommended that the administrator configure the desired root bridge switch with a priority lower than 32768. This also ensures that the addition of new switches to the network does not trigger a new spanning-tree election, which can disrupt network communication while a new root bridge is being selected.

In Figure 3-30, S1 has been configured with a lower priority. Therefore, it is preferred as the root bridge for that spanning-tree instance.

What happens if all switches have the same priority, such as the default priority 32768? The lowest MAC address becomes the deciding factor in which switch becomes the root bridge.

In the scenario in Figure 3-31, S2 becomes the root bridge because it has the lowest MAC address.

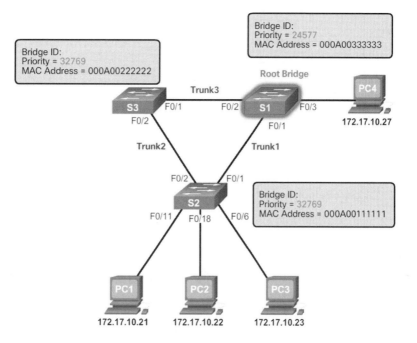

**Figure 3-30**    Priority-Based Decision

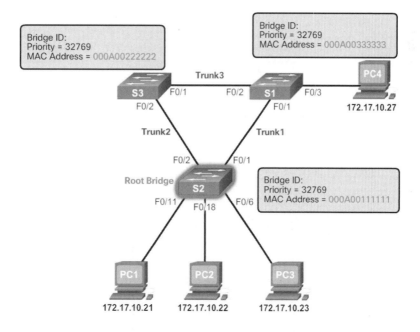

**Figure 3-31**    MAC Address–Based Decision

**Note**

In the example shown in Figure 3-31, the priority of all the switches is 32769. The value is based on the 32768 default priority and the VLAN 1 assignment associated with each switch (32768 + 1).

**Interactive Graphic**

**Activity 3.1.2.10: Identify 802.1D Port Rules**

Refer to the online course to complete this activity.

**Video**

**Video Demonstration 3.1.2.11: Observing Spanning Tree Protocol Operation**

Refer to the online course to view this video.

**Lab 3.1.2.12: Building a Switched Network with Redundant Links**

Refer to *Scaling Networks v6 Labs & Study Guide* and the online course to complete this activity.

In this lab, you will complete the following objectives:

- Part 1: Build the Network and Configure Basic Device Settings
- Part 2: Determine the Root Bridge
- Part 3: Observe STP Port Selection Based on Port Cost
- Part 4: Observe STP Port Selection Based on Port Priority

# Varieties of Spanning Tree Protocols (3.2)

There have been several implementations of STP. In this section, you will learn how different varieties of spanning-tree protocols operate.

## Overview (3.2.1)

The focus of this topic is on the different spanning-tree varieties.

## Types of Spanning Tree Protocols (3.2.1.1)

Several varieties of spanning-tree protocols have emerged since the original IEEE 802.1D.

The varieties of spanning-tree protocols include the following:

- *STP*—Defined in IEEE *802.1D*, this is the original standard that provided a loop-free topology in a network with redundant links. Also called *Common Spanning Tree (CST)*, it assumed one spanning-tree instance for the entire bridged network, regardless of the number of VLANs.

- *Per-VLAN Spanning Tree (PVST+)*—PVST+ is a Cisco enhancement of STP that provides a separate 802.1D spanning-tree instance for each VLAN configured in the network.

- *Rapid Spanning Tree Protocol (RSTP)*—RSTP is defined in *IEEE 802.1w*. It is an evolution of STP that provides faster convergence than STP.

- *Rapid Per-VLAN Spanning Tree (Rapid PVST+)*—Rapid PVST+ is a Cisco enhancement of RSTP that uses PVST+ and provides a separate instance of 802.1w for each VLAN.

- *Multiple Spanning Tree Protocol (MSTP)*—MSTP, defined in *IEEE 802.1s*, maps multiple VLANs into the same spanning-tree instance. The Cisco implementation of MSTP is often referred to as *Multiple Spanning Tree (MST)*.

A network professional whose duties include switch administration may be required to decide which type of spanning-tree protocol to implement.

## Characteristics of the Spanning Tree Protocols (3.2.1.2)

Table 3-3 lists the characteristics of the various STP versions.

**Table 3-3**    Spanning Tree Protocol Characteristics

| STP Version | Characteristics |
| --- | --- |
| STP | - IEEE 802.1D is the original standard.<br>- STP creates one spanning-tree instance for the entire bridged network, regardless of the number of VLANs.<br>- However, because there is only one root bridge, traffic for all VLANs flows over the same path, which can lead to suboptimal traffic flows.<br>- This version is slow to converge.<br>- The CPU and memory requirements are lower than for all other STP protocols. |

| STP Version | Characteristics |
| --- | --- |
| PVST+ | ■ This is a Cisco enhancement of STP that provides a separate STP instance for each VLAN.<br><br>■ Each instance supports *PortFast*, *BPDU guard*, *BPDU filter*, *root guard*, and *loop guard*.<br><br>■ This design allows the spanning tree to be optimized for the traffic of each VLAN.<br><br>■ However, CPU and memory requirements are high due to maintaining separate STP instances per VLAN.<br><br>■ Convergence is per-VLAN and is slow, like 802.1D. |
| RSTP | ■ 802.1w is an evolution of 802.1D that addresses many convergence issues.<br><br>■ Like STP, it provides only a single instance of STP and therefore does not address suboptimal traffic flow issues.<br><br>■ The CPU and memory requirements are less than for Rapid PVST+ but more than for 802.1D. |
| Rapid PVST+ | ■ This is a Cisco enhancement of RSTP.<br><br>■ Rapid PVST+ uses PVST+ and provides a separate instance of 802.1w for each VLAN.<br><br>■ Each instance supports PortFast, BPDU guard, BPDU filter, root guard, and loop guard.<br><br>■ This version addresses the convergence issues and the suboptimal traffic flow issues.<br><br>■ The CPU and memory requirements are the highest of all STP implementations. |
| MSTP | ■ IEEE 802.1s is based on the Cisco Multiple Instance Spanning-Tree Protocol (MISTP) which is often simply referred to as Multiple Spanning Tree (MST).<br><br>■ The Cisco implementation is often referred to as Multiple Spanning Tree (MST).<br><br>■ MSTP maps multiple VLANs into the same spanning-tree instance.<br><br>■ It supports up to 16 instances of RSTP.<br><br>■ Each instance supports PortFast, BPDU guard, BPDU filter, root guard, and loop guard.<br><br>■ The CPU and memory requirements are less than for Rapid PVST+ but more than for RSTP. |

Table 3-4 summarizes the STP characteristics.

**Table 3-4**  Comparing Spanning Tree Protocols

| Protocol | Standard | Resources Needed | Convergence | STP Tree Calculation |
|---|---|---|---|---|
| STP | IEEE 802.1D | Low | Slow | All VLANs |
| PVST+ | Cisco | High | Slow | Per VLAN |
| RSTP | IEEE 802.1w | Medium | Fast | All VLANs |
| Rapid PVST+ | Cisco | High | Fast | Per VLAN |
| MSTP (MST) | IEEE 802.1s, Cisco | Medium or high | Fast | Per instance |

Cisco switches running IOS 15.0 or later run PVST+ by default.

Cisco Catalyst switches support PVST+, Rapid PVST+, and MSTP. However, only one version can be active at any time.

**Activity 3.2.1.3: Identify Types of Spanning Tree Protocols**

Refer to the online course to complete this activity.

Interactive Graphic

# PVST+ (3.2.2)

The focus of this topic is on how the default mode of PVST+ on Cisco Catalyst switches operates.

## Overview of PVST+ (3.2.2.1)

The original IEEE 802.1D standard defines only one spanning-tree instance for the entire switched network, regardless of the number of VLANs. A network running 802.1D has these characteristics:

- No load sharing is possible. One uplink must block for all VLANs.
- The CPU is spared. Only one instance of spanning tree must be computed.

Cisco developed PVST+ so that a network can run an independent instance of the Cisco implementation of IEEE 802.1D for each VLAN in the network. A PVST+ topology is shown in Figure 3-32.

With PVST+, it is possible for one trunk port on a switch to block for a VLAN while forwarding for other VLANs. PVST+ can be used to manually implement Layer 2 load balancing. The switches in a PVST+ environment require greater CPU process and BPDU bandwidth consumption than a traditional STP because each VLAN runs a separate instance of STP.

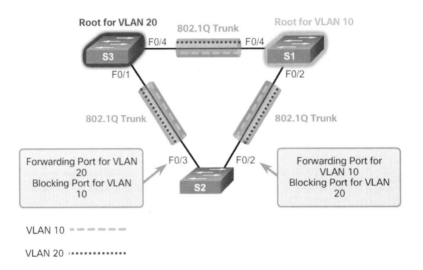

**Figure 3-32**   PVST+

In a PVST+ environment, spanning-tree parameters can be tuned so that half of the VLANs forward on each uplink trunk. In Figure 3-32, port F0/3 on S2 is the forwarding port for VLAN 20, and F0/2 on S2 is the forwarding port for VLAN 10. This is accomplished by configuring one switch to be elected the root bridge for half of the VLANs in the network and a second switch to be elected the root bridge for the other half of the VLANs. In the figure, S3 is the root bridge for VLAN 20, and S1 is the root bridge for VLAN 10. Having multiple STP root bridges per VLAN increases redundancy in the network.

Networks running PVST+ have these characteristics:

- Optimum load balancing can result.

- One spanning-tree instance for each VLAN maintained can mean a considerable waste of CPU cycles for all the switches in the network (in addition to the bandwidth that is used for each instance to send its own BPDU). This is problematic only if a large number of VLANs are configured.

## Port States and PVST+ Operation (3.2.2.2)

STP facilitates the logical loop-free path throughout the broadcast domain. The spanning tree is determined through the information learned by the exchange of the BPDU frames between the interconnected switches. To facilitate the learning of the logical spanning tree, each switch port transitions through five possible port states and three BPDU timers.

The spanning tree is determined immediately after a switch is finished booting up. If a switch port transitions directly from the blocking state to the forwarding state without information about the full topology during the transition, the port can temporarily create a data loop. For this reason, STP introduced five port states that PVST+ uses as well. Table 3-5 lists and explains the five port states.

**Table 3-5**  STP Port States

| Port State | Characteristics |
|---|---|
| Blocking state | ■ The port is an alternate port and does not participate in frame forwarding.<br>■ The port receives BPDU frames to determine the location and root ID of the root bridge switch and which port roles each switch port should assume in the final active STP topology. |
| *Listening state* | ■ Listens for the path to the root.<br>■ STP has determined that the port can participate in frame forwarding according to the BPDU frames that the switch has received.<br>■ The switch port receives BPDU frames, transmits its own BPDU frames, and informs adjacent switches that the switch port is preparing to participate in the active topology. |
| *Learning state* | ■ Learns the MAC addresses.<br>■ The port prepares to participate in frame forwarding and begins to populate the MAC address table. |
| *Forwarding state* | ■ The port is considered part of the active topology.<br>■ It forwards data frames and sends and receives BPDU frames. |
| *Disabled state* | ■ The Layer 2 port does not participate in spanning tree and does not forward frames.<br>■ The disabled state is set when the switch port is administratively disabled. |

Table 3-6 summarizes the port states which ensure that no loops are created during the creation of the logical spanning tree.

**Table 3-6**  Port States

| Operation Allowed | Port State | | | | |
|---|---|---|---|---|---|
| | **Blocking** | **Listening** | **Learning** | **Forwarding** | **Disabled** |
| Can receive and process BPDUs | Yes | Yes | Yes | No | No |
| Can forward data frames received on the interface | No | No | No | Yes | No |

| Operation Allowed | Port State | | | | |
|---|---|---|---|---|---|
| | **Blocking** | **Listening** | **Learning** | **Forwarding** | **Disabled** |
| Can forward data frames switched from another interface | No | No | No | Yes | No |
| Can learn MAC addresses | No | No | Yes | Yes | No |

Note that the number of ports in each of the various states (blocking, listening, learning, or forwarding) can be displayed with the **show spanning-tree summary** command.

For each VLAN in a switched network, PVST+ performs four steps to provide a loop-free logical network topology:

**Step 1.**    **It elects one root bridge.** Only one switch can act as the root bridge (for a given VLAN). The root bridge is the switch with the lowest bridge ID. On the root bridge, all ports are designated ports (no root ports).

**Step 2.**    **It selects the root port on each non-root bridge.** PVST+ establishes one root port on each non-root bridge for each VLAN. The root port is the lowest-cost path from the non-root bridge to the root bridge, which indicates the direction of the best path to the root bridge. Root ports are normally in the forwarding state.

**Step 3.**    **It selects the designated port on each segment.** On each link, PVST+ establishes one designated port for each VLAN. The designated port is selected on the switch that has the lowest-cost path to the root bridge. Designated ports are normally in the forwarding state and forwarding traffic for the segment.

**Step 4.**    **It makes the remaining ports in the switched network alternate ports.** Alternate ports normally remain in the blocking state to logically break the loop topology. When a port is in the blocking state, it does not forward traffic, but it can still process received BPDU messages.

### Extended System ID and PVST+ Operation (3.2.2.3)

In a PVST+ environment, the extended system ID (see Figure 3-33) ensures that each switch has a unique BID for each VLAN.

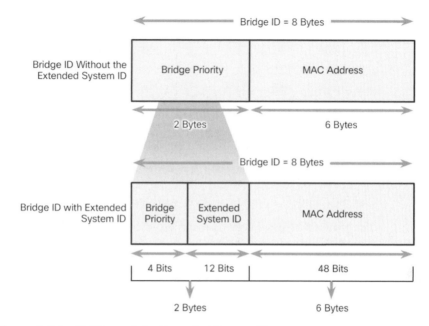

Figure 3-33   PVST+ and the Extended System ID

For example, the VLAN 2 default BID would be 32770 (priority 32768, plus the extended system ID 2). If no priority has been configured, every switch has the same default priority, and the election of the root bridge for each VLAN is based on the MAC address. Because the bridge ID is based on the lowest MAC address, the switch chosen to be root bridge might not be the most powerful or the most optimal switch.

In some situations, an administrator may want a specific switch to be selected as the root bridge. This may be for a variety of reasons, including the following:

■ The switch is more optimally located within the LAN design in regards to the majority of traffic flow patterns for a particular VLAN.

■ The switch has higher processing power.

■ The switch is simply easier to access and manage remotely.

To manipulate the root-bridge election, assign a lower priority to the switch that should be selected as the root bridge for the desired VLAN(s).

**Interactive Graphic**

**Activity 3.2.2.4: Identifying PVST+ Operation**

Refer to the online course to complete this activity.

# Rapid PVST+ (3.2.3)

The focus of this topic is on how Rapid PVST+ operates.

### Overview of Rapid PVST+ (3.2.3.1)

RSTP (IEEE 802.1w) is an evolution of the original 802.1D standard and is incorporated into the IEEE 802.1D-2004 standard. The 802.1w STP terminology remains primarily the same as the original IEEE 802.1D STP terminology. Most parameters have been left unchanged, so users who are familiar with STP can easily configure the new protocol. Rapid PVST+ is the Cisco implementation of RSTP on a per-VLAN basis. An independent instance of RSTP runs for each VLAN.

Figure 3-34 shows a network running RSTP. S1 is the root bridge, with two designated ports in a forwarding state. RSTP supports a new port type. Port F0/3 on S2 is an alternate port in discarding state. Notice that there are no blocking ports. RSTP does not have a blocking port state. RSTP defines port states as discarding, learning, or forwarding.

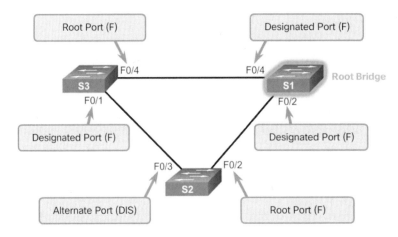

**Figure 3-34**   RSTP Topology

RSTP speeds the recalculation of the spanning tree when the Layer 2 network topology changes. RSTP can achieve much faster convergence in a properly configured network—sometimes in as little as a few hundred milliseconds.

RSTP redefines the types of ports and their states. If a port is configured to be an alternate port or a backup port, it can immediately change to a forwarding state without waiting for the network to converge.

The following is a brief description of RSTP characteristics:

- RSTP is the preferred protocol for preventing Layer 2 loops in a switched network environment. Many of the differences were established by Cisco proprietary enhancements to the original 802.1D. These enhancements, such as BPDUs carrying and sending information about port roles only to neighboring switches, require no additional configuration and generally perform better than the earlier Cisco proprietary versions. They are now transparent and integrated into the protocol's operation.

- RSTP (802.1w) supersedes the original 802.1D while retaining backward compatibility. Much of the original 802.1D terminology remains, and most parameters are unchanged. In addition, 802.1w is capable of reverting to legacy 802.1D to interoperate with legacy switches on a per-port basis. For example, the RSTP spanning-tree algorithm elects a root bridge in exactly the same way as the original 802.1D.

- RSTP keeps the same BPDU format as the original IEEE 802.1D, except that the version field is set to 2 to indicate RSTP, and the flags field uses all 8 bits.

- RSTP is able to actively confirm that a port can safely transition to the forwarding state without having to rely on a timer configuration.

## RSTP BPDUs (3.2.3.2)

RSTP uses type 2, Version 2 BPDUs. The original 802.1D STP uses type 0, Version 0 BPDUs. However, a switch running RSTP can communicate directly with a switch running the original 802.1D STP. RSTP sends BPDUs and populates the flags byte in a slightly different manner than in the original 802.1D:

- Protocol information can be immediately aged on a port if hello packets are not received for three consecutive hello times (six seconds, by default) or if the max age timer expires.

- BPDUs are used as a keepalive mechanism. Therefore, three consecutively missed BPDUs indicate lost connectivity between a bridge and its neighboring root or designated bridge. The fast aging of the information allows failures to be detected quickly.

**Note**

As with STP, an RSTP switch sends a BPDU with its current information every hello time period (two seconds, by default), even if the RSTP switch does not receive BPDUs from the root bridge.

As shown in Figure 3-35, RSTP uses the flags byte of a Version 2 BPDU:

**RSTP Version 2 BPDU**

| Field | Byte Length |
|---|---|
| Protocol ID=0x0000 | 2 |
| Protocol Version ID=0x02 | 1 |
| BPDU Type=0X02 | 1 |
| Flags | 1 |
| Root ID | 8 |
| Root Path Cost | 4 |
| Bridge ID | 8 |
| Port ID | 2 |
| Message Age | 2 |
| Max Age | 2 |
| Hello Time | 2 |
| Forward Delay | 2 |

**Flag Field**

| Field Bit | Bit |
|---|---|
| Topology Change | 0 |
| Proposal | 1 |
| Port Role | 2-3 |
| Unknown Port | 00 |
| Alternate or Backup Port | 01 |
| Root Port | 10 |
| Designated Port | 11 |
| Learning | 4 |
| Forwarding | 5 |
| Agreement | 6 |
| Topology Change Acknowledgment | 7 |

**Figure 3-35**   RSTP BPDU Fields

- Bits 0 and 7 are used for topology change and acknowledgment. They are in the original 802.1D.

- Bits 1 and 6 are used for the proposal agreement process (used for rapid convergence).

- Bits 2 to 5 encode the role and state of the port.

- Bits 4 and 5 are used to encode the port role using a 2-bit code.

## Edge Ports (3.2.3.3)

An RSTP *edge port* is a switch port that is never intended to be connected to another switch. It immediately transitions to the forwarding state when enabled.

The RSTP edge port concept corresponds to the PVST+ PortFast feature. An edge port is directly connected to an end station and assumes that no switch device is connected to it. RSTP edge ports should immediately transition to the forwarding state, thereby skipping the time-consuming original 802.1D listening and learning port states.

The Cisco RSTP implementation (Rapid PVST+) maintains the PortFast keyword, using the **spanning-tree portfast** command for edge port configuration. This makes the transition from STP to RSTP seamless.

Figure 3-36 shows examples of ports that can be configured as edge ports.

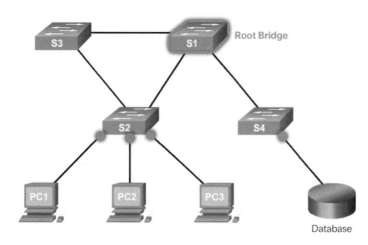

**Figure 3-36**    Edge Ports

Figure 3-37 shows examples of ports that are non-edge ports.

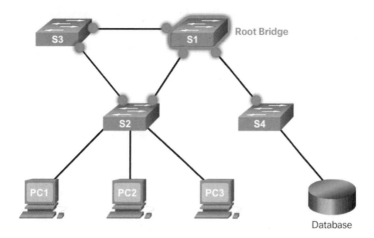

**Figure 3-37**    Non-Edge Ports

**Note**

Configuring an edge port to be attached to another switch is not recommended. It can have negative implications for RSTP because a temporary loop may result, possibly delaying the convergence of RSTP.

## Link Types (3.2.3.4)

The link type provides a categorization for each port participating in RSTP by using the duplex mode on the port. Depending on what is attached to each port, two different link types can be identified:

- *Point-to-point*—A port operating in full-duplex mode typically connects a switch to a switch and is a candidate for a rapid transition to a forwarding state.

- **Shared**—A port operating in half-duplex mode connects a switch to a hub that attaches multiple devices.

Figure 3-38 displays the various RSTP port assignments.

The link type can determine whether the port can immediately transition to a forwarding state, assuming that certain conditions are met. These conditions are different for edge ports and non-edge ports. Non-edge ports are categorized into two link types: point-to-point and shared.

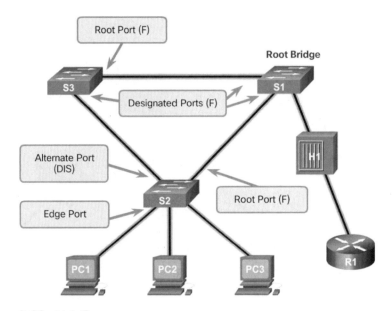

**Figure 3-38**  Link Types

The link type is automatically determined but can be overridden with an explicit port configuration, using the **spanning-tree link-type** { **point-to-point** | **shared** } command.

Characteristics of port roles, with regard to link types, include the following:

- Edge port connections and point-to-point connections are candidates for rapid transition to a forwarding state. However, before the **link-type** parameter is considered, RSTP must determine the port role.

- Root ports do not use the **link-type** parameter. Root ports are able to make a rapid transition to the forwarding state as soon as the port is in sync (that is, receives a BPDU from the root bridge).

- Alternate and backup ports do not use the **link-type** parameter in most cases.

- Designated ports make the most use of the **link-type** parameter. A rapid transition to the forwarding state for the designated port occurs only if the **link-type** parameter is set to **point-to-point**.

**Interactive Graphic**

**Activity 3.2.3.5: Identify Port Roles in Rapid PVST+**

Refer to the online course to complete this activity.

**Interactive Graphic**

**Activity 3.2.3.6: Compare PVST+ and Rapid PVST+**

Refer to the online course to complete this activity.

# Spanning Tree Configuration (3.3)

In this section, you will learn how to implement PVST+ and Rapid PVST+ in a switched LAN environment.

## PVST+ Configuration (3.3.1)

The focus of this topic is on how to configure PVST+ in a switched LAN environment.

### Catalyst 2960 Default Configuration (3.3.1.1)

Table 3-7 shows the default spanning-tree configuration for a Cisco Catalyst 2960 Series switch. Notice that the default spanning-tree mode is PVST+.

**Table 3-7**  Default Switch Configuration

| Feature | Default Setting |
| --- | --- |
| Enable state | Enabled on VLAN 1 |
| Spanning-tree mode | PVST+ (Rapid PVST+ and MSTP are disabled.) |
| Switch priority | 32768 |

| Feature | Default Setting |
|---------|-----------------|
| Spanning-tree port priority (configurable on a per-interface basis) | 128 |
| Spanning-tree port cost (configurable on a per-interface basis) | 1000 Mbps: 4 |
| | 100 Mbps: 19 |
| | 10 Mbps: 100 |
| Spanning-tree VLAN port priority (configurable on a per-VLAN basis) | 128 |
| Spanning-tree VLAN port cost (configurable on a per-VLAN basis) | 1000 Mbps: 4 |
| | 100 Mbps: 19 |
| | 10 Mbps: 100 |
| Spanning-tree timers | Hello time: 2 seconds |
| | Forward-delay time: 15 seconds |
| | Maximum-aging time: 20 seconds |
| | Transmit hold count: 6 BPDUs |

## Configuring and Verifying the Bridge ID (3.3.1.2)

When an administrator wants a specific switch to become a root bridge, the bridge priority value must be adjusted to ensure that it is lower than the bridge priority values of all the other switches on the network. There are two different methods to configure the bridge priority value on a Cisco Catalyst switch.

## Method 1

To ensure that a switch has the lowest bridge priority value, use the **spanning-tree vlan** *vlan-id* **root primary** command in global configuration mode. The priority for the switch is set to the predefined value of 24,576 or to the highest multiple of 4096 less than the lowest bridge priority detected on the network.

If an alternate root bridge is desired, use the **spanning-tree vlan** *vlan-id* **root secondary** global configuration mode command. This command sets the priority for the switch to the predefined value 28,672. This ensures that the alternate switch becomes the root bridge if the primary root bridge fails. This assumes that the rest of the switches in the network have the default 32,768 priority value defined.

In Figure 3-39, S1 has been assigned as the primary root bridge, using the **spanning-tree vlan 1 root primary** command, and S2 has been configured as the secondary root bridge, using the **spanning-tree vlan 1 root secondary** command.

## Method 2

Another method for configuring the bridge priority value is by using the **spanning-tree vlan** *vlan-id* **priority** *value* global configuration mode command. This command gives more granular control over the bridge priority value. The priority value is configured in increments of 4096 between 0 and 61,440.

In the example in Figure 3-39, S3 has been assigned a bridge priority value of 24,576, using the **spanning-tree vlan 1 priority 24576** command.

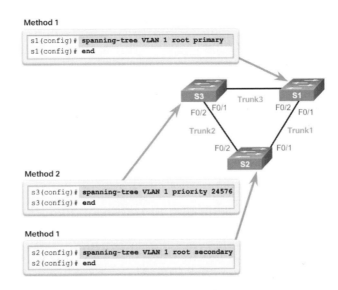

**Figure 3-39**   Configuring the Bridge ID

To verify the bridge priority of a switch, use the **show spanning-tree** command. In Example 3-4, the priority of the switch has been set to 24,576. Also notice that the switch is designated as the root bridge for the spanning-tree instance.

**Example 3-4**   Verifying the Root Bridge and BID

```
S3# show spanning-tree
VLAN0001
  Spanning tree enabled protocol ieee
  Root ID    Priority    24577
             Address     000A.0033.0033
             This bridge is the root
             Hello Time   2 sec  Max Age 20 sec  Forward Delay 15 sec
```

```
Bridge ID  Priority     24577   (priority 24576 sys-id-ext 1)
           Address       000A.0033.3333
           Hello Time   2 sec  Max Age 20 sec  Forward Delay 15 sec
           Aging Time   300
Interface           Role Sts Cost       Prio.Nbr Type
------------------- ---- --- --------- -------- ------------------------
Fa0/1               Desg FWD 4             128.1   P2p
Fa0/2               Desg FWD 4             128.2   P2p
```

## PortFast and BPDU Guard (3.3.1.3)

PortFast is a Cisco feature for PVST+ environments. When a switch port is config-ured with PortFast, that port transitions from blocking to forwarding state imme-diately, bypassing the usual 802.1D STP transition states (the listening and learning states). As shown in Figure 3-40, you can use PortFast on access ports to allow these devices to connect to the network immediately rather than wait for IEEE 802.1D STP to converge on each VLAN. Access ports are ports that are connected to a single workstation or to a server.

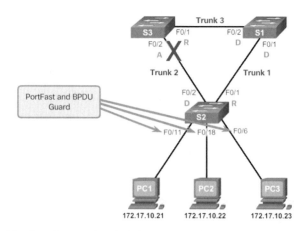

**Figure 3-40**  PortFast and BPDU Guard Topology

In a valid PortFast configuration, BPDUs should never be received because that would indicate that another bridge or switch is connected to the port, potentially causing a spanning-tree loop. Cisco switches support a feature called BPDU guard. When it is enabled, BPDU guard puts the port in an errdisabled (error-disabled) state on receipt of a BPDU. This effectively shuts down the port. The BPDU guard feature provides a secure response to invalid configurations because you must manually put the interface back into service.

Cisco PortFast technology is useful for DHCP. Without PortFast, a PC can send a DHCP request before the port is in forwarding state, denying the host from getting a usable IP address and other information. Because PortFast immediately changes the state to forwarding, the PC always gets a usable IP address (if the DHCP server has been configured correctly and communication with the DHCP server has occurred).

**Note**

Because the purpose of PortFast is to minimize the time that access ports must wait for spanning tree to converge, it should be used only on access ports. If you enable PortFast on a port connecting to another switch, you risk creating a spanning-tree loop.

To configure PortFast on a switch port, enter the **spanning-tree portfast** interface configuration mode command on each interface on which PortFast is to be enabled, as shown in Example 3-5.

**Example 3-5**   Configuring PortFast

```
S2(config)# interface FastEthernet 0/11
S2(config-if)# spanning-tree portfast
%Warning: portfast should only be enabled on ports connected to a single
  host. Connecting hubs, concentrators, switches, bridges, etc... to this
  interface when portfast is enabled, can cause temporary bridging loops.
  Use with CAUTION

%Portfast has been configured on FastEthernet0/11 but will only
  have effect when the interface is in a non-trunking mode.

S2(config-if)#
```

The **spanning-tree portfast default** global configuration mode command enables PortFast on all non-trunking interfaces.

To configure BPDU guard on a Layer 2 access port, use the **spanning-tree bpduguard enable** interface configuration mode command, as shown in Example 3-6.

**Example 3-6**   Configuring and Verifying BPDU Guard

```
S2(config-if)# spanning-tree bpduguard enable
S2(config-if)# end
S2#
S2# show running-config interface f0/11
interface FastEthernet0/11
spanning-tree portfast
spanning-tree bpduguard enable

S2#
```

The **spanning-tree portfast bpduguard default** global configuration command enables BPDU guard on all PortFast-enabled ports.

Notice in Example 3-6 how the **show running-config interface** command can be used to verify that PortFast and BPDU guard have been enabled for a switch port. PortFast and BPDU guard are disabled, by default, on all interfaces.

## PVST+ Load Balancing (3.3.1.4)

The topology in Figure 3-41 shows three switches with 802.1Q trunks connecting them.

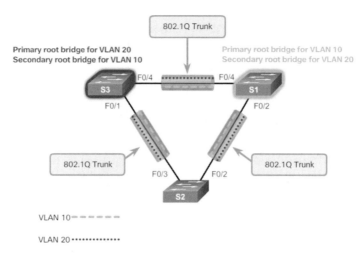

**Figure 3-41**   PVST+ Configuration Topology

Two VLANs, 10 and 20, are being trunked across these links. The goal is to configure S3 as the root bridge for VLAN 20 and S1 as the root bridge for VLAN 10. Port F0/3 on S2 is the forwarding port for VLAN 20 and the blocking port for VLAN 10. Port F0/2 on S2 is the forwarding port for VLAN 10 and the blocking port for VLAN 20.

In addition to establishing a root bridge, it is also possible to establish a secondary root bridge. A secondary root bridge is a switch that may become the root bridge for a VLAN if the primary root bridge fails. Assuming that the other bridges in the VLAN retain their default STP priority, this switch becomes the root bridge if the primary root bridge fails.

Configuring PVST+ on this topology involves the following steps:

**Step 1.**   Select the switches you want for the primary and secondary root bridges for each VLAN. For example, in Figure 3-41, S3 is the primary bridge for VLAN 20, and S1 is the secondary bridge for VLAN 20.

**Step 2.**    As shown in Example 3-7, configure S3 to be a primary bridge for VLAN 10 and the secondary bridge for VLAN 20 by using the **spanning-tree vlan** *number* **root** { **primary** | **secondary** } command.

**Example 3-7**    Configuring Primary and Secondary Root Bridges for Each VLAN on S3

```
S3(config)# spanning-tree vlan 20 root primary
S3(config)# spanning-tree vlan 10 root secondary
```

**Step 3.**    As shown in Example 3-8, configure S1 to be a primary bridge for VLAN 20 and the secondary bridge for VLAN 10.

**Example 3-8**    Configuring Primary and Secondary Root Bridges for Each VLAN on S1

```
S1(config)# spanning-tree vlan 10 root primary
S1(config)# spanning-tree vlan 20 root secondary
```

Another way to specify the root bridge is to set the spanning-tree priority on each switch to the lowest value so that the switch is selected as the primary bridge for its associated VLAN, as shown in Example 3-9.

**Example 3-9**    Configuring the Lowest Possible Priority to Ensure That a Switch Is Root

```
S3(config)# spanning-tree vlan 20 priority 4096
```

```
S1(config)# spanning-tree vlan 10 priority 4096
```

The switch priority can be set for any spanning-tree instance. This setting affects the likelihood that a switch is selected as the root bridge. A lower value increases the probability that the switch is selected. The range is 0 to 61,440, in increments of 4096; all other values are rejected. For example, a valid priority value is $4096 \times 2 = 8192$.

As shown in Example 3-10, the **show spanning-tree active** command displays spanning-tree configuration details for the active interfaces only.

The output shown is for S1 configured with PVST+. A number of Cisco IOS command parameters are associated with the **show spanning-tree** command.

In Example 3-11, the output shows that the priority for VLAN 10 is 4096, the lowest of the three respective VLAN priorities.

**Example 3-10**    Verifying STP Active Interfaces

```
S1# show spanning-tree active
<output omitted>
VLAN0010
  Spanning tree enabled protocol ieee
  Root ID    Priority    4106
             Address      ec44.7631.3880
             This bridge is the root
             Hello Time   2 sec  Max Age 20 sec   Forward Delay 15 sec

   Bridge ID  Priority    4106    (priority 4096 sys-id-ext 10)
             Address      ec44.7631.3880
             Hello Time   2 sec  Max Age 20 sec   Forward Delay 15 sec
             Aging Time   300 sec

Interface           Role Sts Cost      Prio.Nbr Type
------------------- ---- --- --------- -------- -------------------------------
Fa0/3               Desg FWD 19        128.5    P2p
Fa0/4               Desg FWD 19        128.6    P2p
```

**Example 3-11**    Verifying the S1 STP Configuration

```
S1# show running-config | include span
spanning-tree mode pvst
spanning-tree extend system-id
spanning-tree vlan 1 priority 24576
spanning-tree vlan 10 priority 4096
spanning-tree vlan 20 priority 28672
```

Packet Tracer
☐ Activity

**Packet Tracer 3.3.1.5: Configuring PVST+**

In this activity, you will configure VLANs and trunks and examine and configure the Spanning Tree Protocol primary and secondary root bridges. You will also optimize the switched topology by using PVST+, PortFast, and BPDU guard.

# Rapid PVST+ Configuration (3.3.2)

Rapid PVST+ is the Cisco implementation of RSTP. It supports RSTP on a per-VLAN basis. The focus of this topic is on how to configure Rapid PVST+ in a switched LAN environment.

## Spanning Tree Mode (3.3.2.1)

Rapid PVST+ commands control the configuration of VLAN spanning-tree instances. A spanning-tree instance is created when an interface is assigned to a VLAN, and is removed when the last interface is moved to another VLAN. In addition, you can configure STP switch and port parameters before a spanning-tree instance is created. These parameters are applied when a spanning-tree instance is created.

Use the **spanning-tree mode rapid-pvst** global configuration mode command to enable Rapid PVST+. Optionally, you can also identify interswitch links as point-to-point links by using the **spanning-tree link-type point-to-point** interface configuration command. When specifying an interface to configure, valid interfaces include physical ports, VLANs, and port channels.

To reset and reconverge STP, use the **clear spanning-tree detected-protocols** privileged EXEC mode command.

To illustrate how to configure Rapid PVST+, refer to the topology in Figure 3-42.

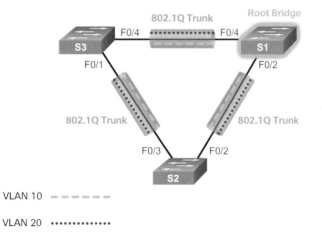

**Figure 3-42**   Rapid PVST+ Topology

> **Note**
>
> The default spanning-tree configuration on a Catalyst 2960 Series switch is PVST+. A Catalyst 2960 switch supports PVST+, Rapid PVST+, and MST, but only one version can be active for all VLANs at any time.

Example 3-12 displays the commands to configure Rapid PVST+ on S1.

**Example 3-12**   Configuring Rapid PVST+ on S1

```
S1# configure terminal
S1(config)# spanning-tree mode rapid-pvst
S1(config)# spanning-tree vlan 1 priority 24576
S1(config)# spanning-tree vlan 10 priority 4096
S1(config)# spanning-tree vlan 20 priority 28672
S1(config)# interface f0/2
S1(config-if)# spanning-tree link-type point-to-point
S1(config-if)# end
S1# clear spanning-tree detected-protocols
```

In Example 3-13, the **show spanning-tree vlan 10** command shows the spanning-tree configuration for VLAN 10 on switch S1.

**Example 3-13**   Verifying That VLAN 10 Is Using RSTP

```
S1# show spanning-tree vlan 10


VLAN0010
 Spanning tree enabled protocol rstp
  Root ID    Priority    4106
             Address     ec44.7631.3880
             This bridge is the root
             Hello Time  2 sec  Max Age 20 sec  Forward Delay 15 sec

  Bridge ID  Priority    4106    (priority 4096 sys-id-ext 10)
             Address     ec44.7631.3880
             Hello Time  2 sec  Max Age 20 sec  Forward Delay 15 sec
             Aging Time  300 sec
Interface           Role Sts Cost      Prio.Nbr Type
------------------- ---- --- --------- -------- --------------------------------
Fa0/3               Desg FWD 19          128.5   P2p Peer(STP)
Fa0/4               Desg FWD 19          128.6   P2p Peer(STP)
```

In the output, the statement "Spanning tree enabled protocol rstp" indicates that S1 is running Rapid PVST+. Notice that the BID priority is set to 4096. Because S1 is the root bridge for VLAN 10, all of its interfaces are designated ports.

In Example 3-14, the **show running-config** command is used to verify the Rapid PVST+ configuration on S1.

**Example 3-14**   Verifying the Rapid PVST+ Configuration

```
S1# show running-config | include span
spanning-tree mode rapid-pvst
spanning-tree extend system-id
spanning-tree vlan 1 priority 24576
spanning-tree vlan 10 priority 4096
spanning-tree vlan 20 priority 28672
spanning-tree link-type point-to-point
```

**Note**

Generally, it is unnecessary to configure the **point-to-point link-type** parameter for Rapid PVST+ because it is unusual to have a shared link type. In most cases, the only difference between configuring PVST+ and Rapid PVST+ is the **spanning-tree mode rapid-pvst** command.

**Packet Tracer 3.3.2.2: Configuring Rapid PVST+**

In this activity, you will configure VLANs and trunks and examine and configure the spanning-tree primary and secondary root bridges. You will also optimize it by using rapid PVST+, PortFast, and BPDU guard.

**Lab 3.3.2.3: Configuring Rapid PVST+, PortFast, and BPDU Guard**

Refer to *Scaling Networks v6 Labs & Study Guide* and the online course to complete this activity.

In this lab, you will complete the following objectives:

- Part 1: Build the Network and Configure Basic Device Settings

- Part 2: Configure VLANs, Native VLAN, and Trunks

- Part 3: Configure the Root Bridge and Examine PVST+ Convergence

- Part 4: Configure Rapid PVST+, PortFast, BPDU Guard, and Examine Convergence

# STP Configuration Issues (3.3.3)

The focus of this topic is on how to analyze common STP configuration issues.

## Analyzing the STP Topology (3.3.3.1)

To analyze the STP topology, follow these steps, as shown in the logic diagram in Figure 3-43:

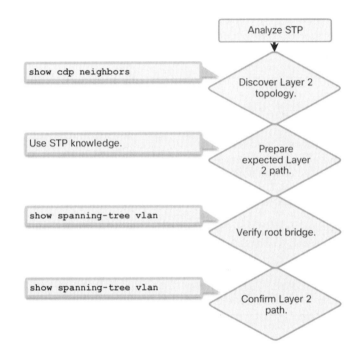

**Figure 3-43**    Analyzing the STP Topology

**Step 1.**    Discover the Layer 2 topology. Use network documentation if it exists or use the **show cdp neighbors** command to discover the Layer 2 topology.

**Step 2.**    After discovering the Layer 2 topology, use STP knowledge to determine the expected Layer 2 path. It is necessary to know which switch is the root bridge.

**Step 3.**    Use the **show spanning-tree vlan** command to determine which switch is the root bridge.

**Step 4.**    Use the **show spanning-tree vlan** command on all switches to find out which ports are in blocking or forwarding state and confirm your expected Layer 2 path.

## Expected Topology versus Actual Topology (3.3.3.2)

In many networks, the optimal STP topology is determined as part of the network design and then implemented through manipulation of STP priority and cost values, as shown in Figure 3-44.

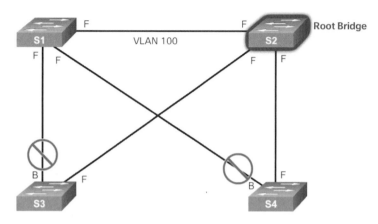

**Figure 3-44**   Verifying That Actual Topology Matches Expected Topology

Situations may occur in which STP was not considered in the network design and implementation, or in which it was considered or implemented before the network underwent significant growth and change. In such situations, it is important to know how to analyze the STP topology in the operational network.

A big part of troubleshooting consists of comparing the actual state of the network against the expected state of the network and spotting the differences to gather clues about the troubleshooting problem. A network professional should be able to examine the switches and determine the actual topology, as well as understand what the underlying spanning-tree topology should be.

### Overview of Spanning Tree Status (3.3.3.3)

Using the **show spanning-tree** command without specifying any additional options provides a quick overview of the status of STP for all VLANs that are defined on a switch.

Use the **show spanning-tree vlan** *vlan_id* command to get STP information for a particular VLAN. Use this command to get information about the role and status of each port on the switch. If you are interested only in a particular VLAN, limit the scope of this command by specifying that VLAN as an option, as shown for VLAN 100 in Figure 3-45.

The output on switch S1 in this example shows all three ports in the forwarding (FWD) state and the roles of the three ports as either designated ports or root ports. Any ports being blocked display the output status as "BLK."

The output also gives information about the BID of the local switch and the root ID, which is the BID of the root bridge.

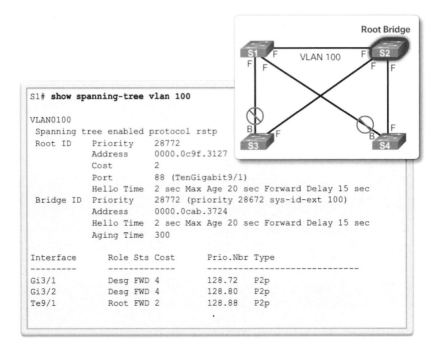

```
S1# show spanning-tree vlan 100

VLAN0100
  Spanning tree enabled protocol rstp
  Root ID    Priority    28772
             Address     0000.0c9f.3127
             Cost        2
             Port        88 (TenGigabit9/1)
             Hello Time  2 sec Max Age 20 sec Forward Delay 15 sec
  Bridge ID  Priority    28772 (priority 28672 sys-id-ext 100)
             Address     0000.0cab.3724
             Hello Time  2 sec Max Age 20 sec Forward Delay 15 sec
             Aging Time  300

Interface       Role Sts Cost      Prio.Nbr Type
-----------     -------------      ----------------------------
Gi3/1           Desg FWD 4         128.72   P2p
Gi3/2           Desg FWD 4         128.80   P2p
Te9/1           Root FWD 2         128.88   P2p
                                   .
```

**Figure 3-45** Overview of STP Status

## Spanning Tree Failure Consequences (3.3.3.4)

Figure 3-46 shows a functional STP network. But what happens when there is an STP failure?

There are two types of STP failure. First, STP might erroneously block ports that should have gone into the forwarding state. Connectivity might be lost for traffic that would normally pass through this switch, but the rest of the network remains unaffected. Second, STP might erroneously move one or more ports into the forwarding state, as shown for S4 in Figure 3-47.

Remember that an Ethernet frame header does not include a TTL field, which means that any frame that enters a bridging loop continues to be forwarded by the switches indefinitely. The only exceptions are frames that have their destination address recorded in the MAC address table of the switches. These frames are simply forwarded to the port that is associated with the MAC address and do not enter a loop. However, any frame that is flooded by a switch enters the loop. This may include broadcasts, multicasts, and unicasts with a globally unknown destination MAC address.

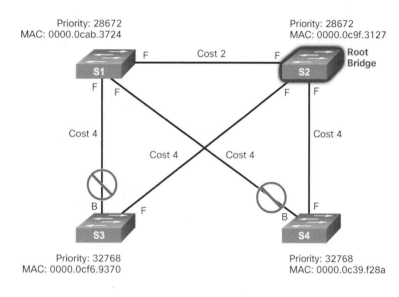

**Figure 3-46**   STP Switch Topology

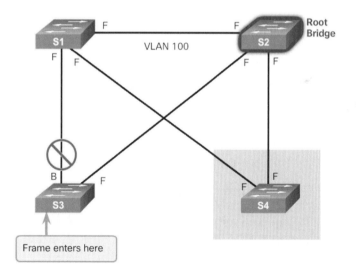

**Figure 3-47**   Erroneous Transition to Forwarding

Figure 3-48 shows the consequences and corresponding symptoms of STP failure.

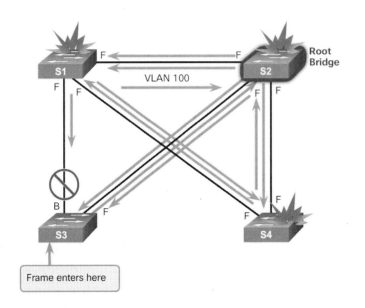

**Figure 3-48**    Consequences of STP Failure Are Severe

The load on all links in the switched LAN quickly starts increasing as more and more frames enter the loop. This problem is not limited to the links that form the loop but also affects any other links in the switched domain because the frames are flooded on all links. When the spanning-tree failure is limited to a single VLAN only, links in that VLAN are affected. Switches and trunks that do not carry that VLAN operate normally.

If the spanning-tree failure has created a bridging loop, traffic increases exponentially. The switches then flood the broadcasts out multiple ports. This creates copies of the frames every time the switches forward them.

When control plane traffic (for example, routing messages) starts entering the loop, the devices that are running these protocols quickly start getting overloaded. Their CPUs approach 100 percent utilization while they are trying to process an ever-increasing load of control plane traffic. In many cases, the earliest indication of this broadcast storm in progress is that routers or Layer 3 switches report control plane failures and that they are running at a high CPU load.

The switches experience frequent MAC address table changes. If a loop exists, a switch may see a frame with a certain source MAC address coming in on one port and then see another frame with the same source MAC address coming in on a different port a fraction of a second later. This causes the switch to update the MAC address table twice for the same MAC address.

## Repairing a Spanning Tree Problem (3.3.3.5)

One way to correct spanning-tree failure is to manually remove redundant links in the switched network, either physically or through configuration, until all loops are eliminated from the topology. When the loops are broken, the traffic and CPU loads should quickly drop to normal levels, and connectivity to devices should be restored.

Although this intervention restores connectivity to the network, it is not the end of the troubleshooting process. All redundancy from the switched network has been removed, and now the redundant links must be restored.

If the underlying cause of the spanning-tree failure has not been fixed, chances are that restoring the redundant links will trigger a new broadcast storm. Before restoring the redundant links, determine and correct the cause of the spanning-tree failure. Carefully monitor the network to ensure that the problem is fixed.

**Interactive Graphic**

**Activity 3.3.3.6: Troubleshoot STP Configuration Issues**

Refer to the online course to complete this activity.

# Switch Stacking and Chassis Aggregation (3.3.4)

The focus of this topic is to explain the value of switch stacking and chassis aggregation in a small switched LAN.

## Switch Stacking Concepts (3.3.4.1)

A switch stack can consist of up to nine Catalyst 3750 switches connected through their StackWise ports. One of the switches controls the operation of the stack and is called the *stack master*. The stack master and the other switches in the stack are stack members.

Figure 3-49 shows the backplane of four Catalyst 3750 switches and how they are connected in a stack.

Every member is uniquely identified by its own stack member number. All members are eligible masters. If the master becomes unavailable, there is an automatic process to elect a new master from the remaining stack members. One of the factors is the stack member priority value. The switch with the highest stack member priority value becomes the master.

Layer 2 and Layer 3 protocols present the entire switch stack as a single entity to the network. One of the primary benefits of switch stacks is that you manage the stack through a single IP address. The IP address is a system-level setting and is not specific to the master or to any other member. You can manage the stack through the same IP address even if you remove the master or any other member from the stack.

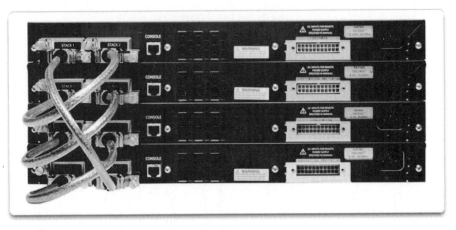

**Figure 3-49**   Cisco Catalyst 3750 Switch Stack

The master contains the saved and running configuration files for the stack. Therefore, there is only one configuration file to manage and maintain. The configuration files include the system-level settings for the stack and the interface-level settings for each member. Each member has a current copy of these files for backup purposes.

The switch is managed as a single switch, including passwords, VLANs, and interfaces. Example 3-15 shows the interfaces on a switch stack with four 52-port switches. Notice that the first number after the interface type is the stack member number.

**Example 3-15**   Switch Stack Interfaces

```
Switch# show running-config | begin interface
interface GigabitEthernet1/0/1
!
interface GigabitEthernet1/0/2
!
interface GigabitEthernet1/0/3
!
<output omitted>
!
interface GigabitEthernet1/0/52
!
interface GigabitEthernet2/0/1
!
interface GigabitEthernet2/0/2
!
<output omitted>
!
interface GigabitEthernet2/0/52
!
```

```
interface GigabitEthernet3/0/1
!
interface GigabitEthernet3/0/2
!
<output omitted>
!
interface GigabitEthernet3/0/52
!
interface GigabitEthernet4/0/1
!
interface GigabitEthernet4/0/2
!
<output omitted>
!
interface GigabitEthernet4/0/52
!
Switch#
```

## Spanning Tree and Switch Stacks (3.3.4.2)

Another benefit to switch stacking is the ability to add more switches to a single STP instance without increasing the *STP diameter*. The diameter is the maximum number of switches that data must cross to connect any two switches. The IEEE recommends a maximum diameter of seven switches for the default STP timers. For example, in Figure 3-50, the diameter from S1-4 to S3-4 is nine switches. This design violates the IEEE recommendation.

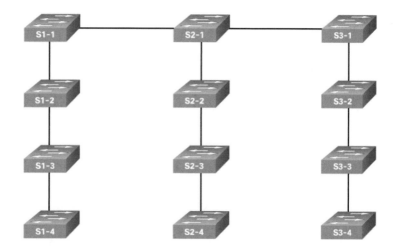

**Figure 3-50**   Diameter Greater Than 7

The recommended diameter is based on default STP timer values, which are as follows:

- **Hello Timer (2 seconds)**—The interval between BPDU updates.

- **Max Age Timer (20 seconds)**—The maximum length of time a switch saves BPDU information.

- **Forward Delay Timer (15 seconds)**—The time spent in the listening and learning states.

**Note**

The formulas used to calculate the diameter are beyond the scope of this course. Refer to the following Cisco document for more information: www.cisco.com/c/en/us/support/docs/lan-switching/spanning-tree-protocol/19120-122.html.

Switch stacks help maintain or reduce the impact of diameter on STP reconvergence. In a switch stack, all switches use the same bridge ID for a given spanning-tree instance. This means that, if the switches are stacked, as shown in Figure 3-51, the maximum diameter becomes 3 instead of 9.

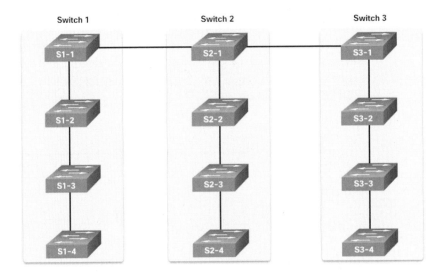

**Figure 3-51**   Switch Stacking Reduces STP Diameter

**Activity 3.3.4.3: Identify Switch Stacking Concepts**

Refer to the online course to complete this activity.

# Summary (3.4)

**Class Activity 3.4.1.1: Documentation Tree**

Refer to *Scaling Networks v6 Labs & Study Guide* and the online course to complete this activity.

The employees in your building are having difficulty accessing a web server on the network. You look for the network documentation that the previous network engineer used before he transitioned to a new job; however, you cannot find any network documentation whatsoever.

Therefore, you decide to create your own network record-keeping system. You decide to start at the access layer of your network hierarchy. This is where redundant switches are located, as well as the company servers, printers, and local hosts.

You create a matrix to record your documentation and include access layer switches on the list. You also decide to document switch names, ports in use, cabling connections, root ports, designated ports, and alternate ports.

---

Problems that can result from a redundant Layer 2 network include broadcast storms, MAC database instability, and duplicate unicast frames. STP is a Layer 2 protocol, which ensures that there is only one logical path between all destinations on the network by intentionally blocking redundant paths that could cause a loop.

STP sends BPDU frames for communication between switches. One switch is elected as the root bridge for each instance of spanning tree. An administrator can control this election by changing the bridge priority. Root bridges can be configured to enable spanning-tree load balancing by a VLAN or by a group of VLANs, depending on the spanning-tree protocol used. STP then assigns a port role to each participating port, using a path cost. The root path cost is equal to the sum of all the port costs along the path to the root bridge. A port cost is automatically assigned to each port; however, it can also be manually configured. Paths with the lowest cost become preferred, and all other redundant paths are blocked.

PVST+ is the default configuration of IEEE 802.1D on Cisco switches. It runs one instance of STP for each VLAN. A newer, faster-converging spanning-tree protocol, RSTP, can be implemented on Cisco switches on a per-VLAN basis in the form of Rapid PVST+. Multiple Spanning Tree (MST) is the Cisco implementation of Multiple Spanning Tree Protocol (MSTP), where one instance of spanning tree runs for a defined group of VLANs. Features such as PortFast and BPDU guard ensure that hosts in the switched environment are provided immediate access to the network without interfering with spanning-tree operation.

Switch stacking allows connection of up to nine Catalyst 3750 switches to be configured and presented to the network as a single entity. STP views the switch stack as a single switch. This additional benefit helps ensure the IEEE recommended maximum diameter of seven switches.

## Practice

The following activities provide practice with the topics introduced in this chapter. The Labs and Class Activities are available in the companion *Scaling Networks v6 Labs & Study Guide* (ISBN 9781587134333). The Packet Tracer activity instructions are also in the *Labs & Study Guide*. The PKA files are found in the online course.

**Class Activities**

Class Activity 3.0.1.2: Stormy Traffic

Class Activity 3.4.1.1: Documentation Tree

**Labs**

Lab 3.1.2.12: Building a Switched Network with Redundant Links

Lab 3.3.2.3: Configuring Rapid PVST+, PortFast, and BPDU Guard

**Packet Tracer Activities**

Packet Tracer 3.1.1.5: Examining a Redundant Design

Packet Tracer 3.3.1.5: Configuring PVST+

Packet Tracer 3.3.2.2: Configuring Rapid PVST+

## Check Your Understanding Questions

Complete all the review questions listed here to test your understanding of the topics and concepts in this chapter. The appendix "Answers to 'Check Your Understanding' Questions" lists the answers.

1. What could be the effect of duplicate unicast frames arriving at a destination device due to multiple active alternative physical paths?

   A. Application protocols malfunction.

   B. Frame collisions increase.

C. The number of broadcast domains increases.

D. The number of collision domains increases.

2. What additional information is contained in the 12-bit extended system ID of a BPDU?

A. IP address

B. MAC address

C. Port ID

D. VLAN ID

3. Which three components are combined to form a bridge ID? (Choose three.)

A. Bridge priority

B. Cost

C. Extended system ID

D. IP address

E. MAC address

F. Port ID

4. Which STP port role is adopted by a switch port if there is no other port with a lower cost to the root bridge?

A. Alternate port

B. Designated port

C. Disabled port

D. Root port

5. Which is the default STP operation mode on Cisco Catalyst switches?

A. MST

B. MSTP

C. PVST+

D. Rapid PVST+

E. RSTP

6. What is an advantage of PVST+?

A. PVST+ optimizes performance on the network through autoselection of the root bridge.

B. PVST+ optimizes performance on the network through load sharing.

C.  PVST+ reduces bandwidth consumption compared to traditional implementations of STP that use CST.

D.  PVST+ requires fewer CPU cycles for all the switches in the network.

7.  In which two port states does a switch learn MAC addresses and process BPDUs in a PVST network? (Choose two.)

A.  Blocking

B.  Disabled

C.  Forwarding

D.  Learning

E.  Listening

8.  Which STP priority configuration would ensure that a switch would always be the root switch?

A.  **spanning-tree vlan 10 priority 0**

B.  **spanning-tree vlan 10 priority 4096**

C.  **spanning-tree vlan 10 priority 61440**

D.  **spanning-tree vlan 10 root primary**

9.  To obtain an overview of the spanning-tree status of a switched network, a network engineer issues the **show spanning-tree** command on a switch. Which two items of information does this command display? (Choose two.)

A.  The IP address of the management VLAN interface

B.  The number of broadcasts received on each root port

C.  The role of the ports in all VLANs

D.  The root bridge BID

E.  The status of native VLAN ports

10.  Which two network design features require Spanning Tree Protocol (STP) to ensure correct network operation? (Choose two.)

A.  Implementing VLANs to contain broadcasts

B.  Link-state dynamic routing that provides redundant routes

C.  Redundant links between Layer 2 switches

D.  Removing single points of failure with multiple Layer 2 switches

E.  Static default routes

11. What value determines the root bridge when all switches connected by trunk links have default STP configurations?

  A. Bridge priority

  B. Extended system ID

  C. MAC address

  D. VLAN ID

12. Which two concepts relate to a switch port that is intended to have only end devices attached and intended never to be used to connect to another switch? (Choose two.)

  A. Bridge ID

  B. Edge port

  C. Extended system ID

  D. PortFast

  E. PVST+

13. Which Cisco switch feature ensures that configured switch edge ports do not cause Layer 2 loops if a port is mistakenly connected to another switch?

  A. BPDU guard

  B. Extended system ID

  C. PortFast

  D. PVST+

# CHAPTER 4

# EtherChannel and HSRP

## Objectives

Upon completion of this chapter, you will be able to answer the following questions:

- What is the purpose of link aggregation operation in a switched LAN environment?

- How do you implement link aggregation to improve performance on high-traffic switch links?

- How do first-hop redundancy protocols operate?

- How does HSRP work?

- How do you configure HSRP using Cisco IOS commands?

- How do you troubleshoot HSRP?

## Key Terms

This chapter uses the following key terms. You can find the definitions in the Glossary.

# Introduction (4.0.1.1)

Link aggregation is the ability to create one logical link using multiple physical links between two devices. This allows load sharing among the physical links rather than having STP block one or more of the links. EtherChannel is a form of link aggregation used in switched networks.

EtherChannel can be manually configured or can be negotiated by using the Cisco proprietary protocol *Port Aggregation Protocol (PAgP)* or the *IEEE 802.3ad-*defined protocol *Link Aggregation Control Protocol (LACP)*. The configuration, verification, and troubleshooting of EtherChannel are discussed.

Redundant devices, such as multilayer switches or routers, provide the capability for a client to use an alternate default gateway if the primary default gateway fails. A client may have multiple paths to more than one default gateway. *First-hop redundancy protocols (FHRP)* are used to manage multiple Layer 3 devices that serve as a default gateway or alternate default gateway and influence the IP address a client is assigned as a default gateway.

This chapter describes EtherChannel and the methods used to create an EtherChannel. It also focuses on the operations and configuration of *Hot Standby Router Protocol (HSRP)*, a first-hop redundancy protocol. Finally, the chapter examines a few potential redundancy problems and their symptoms.

**Class Activity 4.0.1.2: Imagine This**

Refer to *Scaling Networks v6 Labs & Study Guide* and the online course to complete this activity.

It is the end of the work day. In your small to medium-sized business, you are trying to explain EtherChannel to the network engineers and help them understand what it looks like when it is physically set up. The network engineers have difficulty envisioning how two switches could possibly be connected via several links that collectively act as one channel or connection. Your company is definitely considering implementing an EtherChannel network.

You end the meeting with an assignment for the engineers. To prepare for the next day's meeting, they are to each perform some research and bring to the meeting one graphic representation of an EtherChannel network connection. They are tasked with explaining how an EtherChannel network operates to the other engineers.

When researching EtherChannel, a good question to search for is "What does EtherChannel look like?" Prepare a few slides to demonstrate your research that will be presented to the network engineering group. These slides should provide a solid grasp of how EtherChannels are physically created within a network topology. Your goal is to ensure that everyone leaving the next meeting will have a good idea about why they would consider moving to a network topology that uses EtherChannel as an option.

# Link Aggregation Concepts (4.1)

Link aggregation is commonly implemented between access layer and distribution layer switches to increase the uplink bandwidth. In this section you will learn about the link aggregation operation in a switched LAN environment.

## Link Aggregation (4.1.1)

This topic describes link aggregation.

### Introduction to Link Aggregation (4.1.1.1)

In Figure 4-1, traffic coming from several links (usually 100 or 1000 Mbps links) aggregates on the access switch and must be sent to distribution switches. Because of the traffic aggregation, links with higher bandwidth must be available between the access and distribution switches.

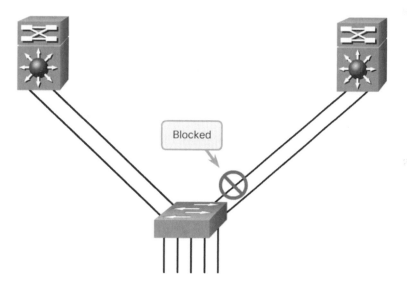

**Figure 4-1**    Redundant Links with STP

It might be possible to use faster links, such as 10 Gbps, on the aggregated link between the access and distribution layer switches. However, adding faster links is expensive. In addition, as the speed increases on the access links, even the fastest possible port on the aggregated link is no longer fast enough to aggregate the traffic coming from all access links.

It is also possible to combine the number of physical links between the switches to increase the overall speed of switch-to-switch communication. However, by default, STP is enabled on Layer 2 switches and therefore blocks redundant links to prevent routing loops as shown in the figure.

For these reasons, the best solution is to implement an EtherChannel configuration.

## Advantages of EtherChannel (4.1.1.2)

As illustrated in Figure 4-2, EtherChannel technology was originally developed by Cisco as a LAN switch-to-switch technique of grouping several Fast Ethernet or Gigabit Ethernet ports into one logical channel.

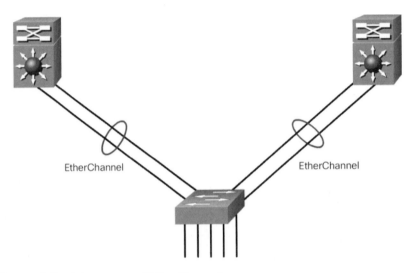

**Figure 4-2**   Advantages of EtherChannel

When EtherChannel is configured, the resulting virtual interface is called a *port channel interface*. The physical interfaces are bundled together into a virtual port channel interface.

Table 4-1 lists some of the technology advantages of EtherChannel.

**Table 4-1**   EtherChannel Advantages

| EtherChannel Advantage | Description |
| --- | --- |
| Most configurations are done on the port channel interface. | ■ Most configuration tasks can be done on the Ether-Channel interface instead of on individual ports.<br>■ This ensures configuration consistency throughout the links. |
| EtherChannel relies on existing switch ports. | ■ There is no need to upgrade to faster and more expensive connection options. |
| EtherChannel bundled links appear as one logical link. | ■ When there is only one EtherChannel link, all physical links in the EtherChannel are active because STP sees only one (logical) link.<br>■ STP may block all the ports belonging to one Ether-Channel link to prevent switching loops. |

| EtherChannel Advantage | Description |
|---|---|
| Load balancing automatically occurs between the same EtherChannel bundled links. | ■ Load-balancing methods vary between switch platforms.<br><br>■ Load-balancing methods include *source MAC to destination MAC load balancing* and *source IP to destination IP load balancing*. |
| EtherChannel provides redundancy because the overall link is seen as one logical connection. | ■ The EtherChannel continues to operate even if one of its bundled links fails.<br><br>■ The loss of one physical link within the channel does not create a change in the topology; therefore, an STP recalculation is not required. |

# EtherChannel Operation (4.1.2)

In this topic you will learn about Cisco EtherChannel technology.

## Implementation Restrictions (4.1.2.1)

An EtherChannel can be implemented by grouping up to eight compatibly-configured Ethernet ports into one port channel. Therefore, EtherChannel can provide full-duplex bandwidth up to 800 Mbps (Fast EtherChannel) or 8 Gbps (Gigabit EtherChannel) between one switch and another switch or host. However, interface types cannot be mixed. For example, Fast Ethernet and Gigabit Ethernet cannot be mixed within a single EtherChannel.

Cisco IOS switches currently support up to six EtherChannels per switch. However, as new IOSs are developed and platforms change, some cards and platforms may support increased numbers of ports within an EtherChannel link, as well as an increased number of Gigabit EtherChannels. The concept is the same no matter the speeds or number of links involved.

**Note**

When configuring EtherChannel on switches, be aware of the hardware platform boundaries and specifications.

The original purpose of EtherChannel was to increase speed capability on aggregated links between switches. However, this concept was extended as EtherChannel technology became more popular, and now many servers also support link aggregation with EtherChannel. EtherChannel creates a one-to-one relationship—that is, one EtherChannel link connects only two devices. An EtherChannel link can be created between two switches or an EtherChannel link can be created between an Ether-Channel-enabled server and a switch.

The individual EtherChannel group member port configuration must be consistent on both devices. If the physical ports of one side are configured as trunks, the physical ports of the other side must also be configured as trunks with the same native VLAN. In addition, all ports in each EtherChannel link must be configured as Layer 2 ports.

Each EtherChannel has a logical port channel interface, as illustrated in Figure 4-3. A configuration applied to the port channel interface affects all physical interfaces that are assigned to that interface.

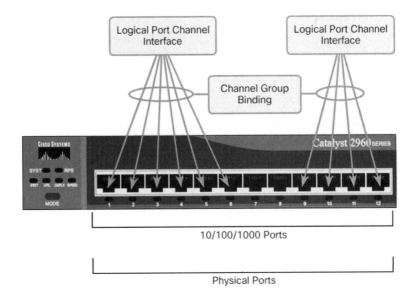

**Figure 4-3**   Implementation Restrictions

---

**Note**

Layer 3 EtherChannels can be configured on Cisco Catalyst multilayer switches, such as the Catalyst 3560 or 3650. A Layer 3 EtherChannel has a single IP address associated with the logical aggregation of switch ports in the EtherChannel. Configuring Layer 3 EtherChannels is beyond the scope in this course.

---

EtherChannels can be negotiated dynamically using PAgP or LACP. These protocols allow adjoining switch ports with similar characteristics to form a channel through dynamic negotiation.

---

**Note**

An EtherChannel can also be statically configured without using PAgP or LACP.

---

## Port Aggregation Protocol (4.1.2.2)

PAgP (pronounced "Pag–P") is a Cisco proprietary protocol that simplifies the automatic creation of EtherChannel links between interconnecting switches.

When a PAgP EtherChannel link is enabled, PAgP packets are exchanged between interconnecting links to negotiate the forming of an EtherChannel. If the PAgP parameters are compatible, EtherChannel groups the links into a port channel interface. The port channel interface is then added to the spanning tree as a single port.

**Note**

In EtherChannel, it is mandatory that all ports have the same speed, duplex setting, and VLAN information. Any port modification after the creation of the channel also changes all other channel ports.

Once the EtherChannel is successfully established, as shown in Figure 4-4, each switch continues to send PAgP packets every 30 seconds. These packets are to keep checking for configuration consistency and to manage link additions and failures between the two switches.

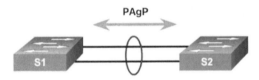

**Figure 4-4**   PAgP Topology

PAgP can be configured in one of two modes:

- **PAgP desirable**—This PAgP mode places an interface in an active negotiating state and sends PAgP packets.

- **PAgP auto**—This PAgP mode places an interface in a passive negotiating state, in which the interface responds to the PAgP packets it receives. However, PAgP auto does not initiate PAgP negotiation. Therefore, interconnecting ports configured as PAgP auto do not create an EtherChannel.

An EtherChannel can also be created without using PAgP or LACP. This is referred to as *on mode*. This mode forces the interface to create an EtherChannel channel without PAgP or LACP. The on mode manually places the interface in an EtherChannel, without any negotiation. It works only if the other side is also set to on. If the other side is set to negotiate parameters through PAgP, no EtherChannel forms because the side that is set to on mode does not negotiate.

The modes must be compatible on each side. If one side is configured to be in PAgP auto mode, it is placed in a passive state, waiting for the other side to initiate the

EtherChannel negotiation. If the other side is also set to PAgP auto, the negotiation never starts, and the EtherChannel does not form.

Table 4-2 summarizes whether a PAgP EtherChannel is established with various configuration settings on switch *x* and switch *y*.

**Table 4-2**    PAgP Channel Establishment

| Switch *x* Port Configured As | Switch *y* Configured As | EtherChannel Established? |
|---|---|---|
| Desirable | Auto/desirable | Yes |
| Desirable | On | No |
| Auto | Auto/on | No |
| Not configured | On/auto/desirable | No |
| On | On | Yes |

If all modes are disabled by using the **no** command, or if no mode is configured, the EtherChannel is disabled. No negotiation between the two switches means there is no checking to make sure that all the links in the EtherChannel are terminating on the other side or that there is PAgP compatibility on the other switch.

## Link Aggregation Control Protocol (4.1.2.3)

LACP is part of an IEEE specification (802.3ad) that allows several physical ports to be bundled to form a single logical channel. LACP allows a switch to negotiate an automatic bundle by sending LACP packets to the peer. It performs a function similar to PAgP with Cisco EtherChannel, but it can be used to facilitate EtherChannels in multivendor environments. Cisco devices support both PAgP and LACP configurations.

**Note**

LACP was originally defined as IEEE 802.3ad. However, LACP is now defined in the newer IEEE 802.1AX standard for local and metropolitan area networks.

LACP, shown in Figure 4-5, provides the same negotiation benefits as PAgP.

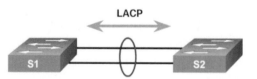

**Figure 4-5**    LACP Topology

LACP helps create the EtherChannel link by detecting the configuration of each side and making sure that the two sides are compatible so that the EtherChannel link can be enabled when needed. LACP can be configured in one of two modes:

- **LACP active**—This LACP mode places a port in an active negotiating state. In this state, the port initiates negotiations with other ports by sending LACP packets.

- **LACP passive**—This LACP mode places a port in a passive negotiating state. In this state, the port responds to the LACP packets it receives, but it does not initiate LACP packet negotiation.

**Note**

LACP active mode is similar to PAgP auto mode, and LACP passive mode is similar to PAgP desirable mode.

Table 4-3 summarizes whether a LACP EtherChannel is established with various configuration settings on switch *x* and switch *y*.

**Table 4-3**   LACP Channel Establishment

| Switch *x* Port Configured As | Switch *y* Configured As | EtherChannel Established? |
|---|---|---|
| Active | Active/passive | Yes |
| Active | On | No |
| Passive | Passive/on | No |
| Not configured | On/active/passive | No |
| On | On | Yes |

Just as with PAgP, modes must be compatible on both sides for an EtherChannel link to form. The on mode is repeated because it creates the EtherChannel configuration unconditionally, without PAgP or LACP dynamic negotiation.

LACP allows for eight active links and also eight standby links. A standby link becomes active if one of the currently active links fails.

**Interactive
Graphic**

**Activity 4.1.2.4: Identify the PAgP and LACP Modes**

Refer to the online course to complete this activity.

# Link Aggregation Configuration (4.2)

PAgP and LACP EtherChannels are commonly deployed in enterprise networks. In this section you will learn how to implement link aggregation to improve performance on high-traffic switch links.

## Configuring EtherChannel (4.2.1)

In this topic you will learn how to configure link aggregation.

### Configuration Guidelines (4.2.1.1)

The following guidelines and restrictions are useful for configuring EtherChannel:

- **EtherChannel support**—All Ethernet interfaces on all modules must support EtherChannel, with no requirement that interfaces be physically contiguous or on the same module.

- **Speed and duplex**—All interfaces in an EtherChannel are configured to operate at the same speed and in the same duplex mode.

- **VLAN match**—All interfaces in the EtherChannel bundle must be assigned to the same VLAN or must be configured as a trunk.

- **Range of VLANs**—An EtherChannel supports the same allowed range of VLANs on all the interfaces in a trunking EtherChannel. If the allowed range of VLANs is not the same, the interfaces do not form an EtherChannel, even when set to auto or desirable mode.

Figure 4-6 shows a configuration that allows an EtherChannel to form between S1 and S2.

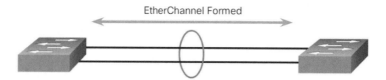

| S1 Port Configurations | | S2 Port Configurations | |
| --- | --- | --- | --- |
| Speed | 1 Gb/s | Speed | 1 Gb/s |
| Duplex | Full | Duplex | Full |
| VLAN | 10 | VLAN | 10 |

**Figure 4-6**    Configuration Settings Match on Both Switches

In Figure 4-7, the S1 ports are configured as half duplex. Therefore, an EtherChannel will not form between S1 and S2.

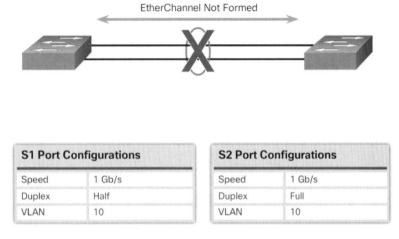

EtherChannel Not Formed

| S1 Port Configurations | | | S2 Port Configurations | |
| --- | --- | --- | --- | --- |
| Speed | 1 Gb/s | | Speed | 1 Gb/s |
| Duplex | Half | | Duplex | Full |
| VLAN | 10 | | VLAN | 10 |

**Figure 4-7**  Configuration Settings Do Not Match on the Switches

If these settings must be changed, configure them in port channel interface configuration mode. Any configuration that is applied to the port channel interface also affects individual interfaces. However, configurations that are applied to the individual interfaces do not affect the port channel interface. Therefore, making configuration changes to an interface that is part of an EtherChannel link may cause interface compatibility issues.

The port channel can be configured in access mode or trunk mode (most common) or on a routed port.

## Configuring Interfaces (4.2.1.2)

Figure 4-8 shows a topology example that is used to configure an LACP EtherChannel between S1 and S2.

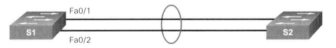

Fa0/1

S1    Fa0/2    S2

**Figure 4-8**  EtherChannel Configuration Topology

Configuring EtherChannel with LACP requires two steps:

**Step 1.**   Simultaneously configure the interfaces to be bundled in the EtherChannel group by using the **interface range** *interface* global configuration mode command. A good practice is to start by shutting down those interfaces so that any incomplete configuration does not create activity on the link. It is also suggested that the duplex and speed settings be manually configured.

**Step 2.**    Assign the interfaces to a port channel interface by using the **channel-group** *identifier* **mode active** interface configuration command. *identifier* specifies a channel group number. The **active** keyword in this example enables LACP to actively negotiate an EtherChannel configuration. Re-enable the physical interfaces.

**Note**

The **channel-group** command automatically creates a port channel interface in the running configuration.

Example 4-1 shows how to configure the F0/1 and F0/2 on switch S1 to be LACP links in port channel number 1.

**Example 4-1**    Configuring EtherChannel with LACP

```
S1(config)# interface range FastEthernet 0/1 - 2
S1(config-if-range)# shutdown
S1(config-if-range)# duplex auto
S1(config-if-range)# speed 100
S1(config-if-range)# channel-group 1 mode active
S1(config-if-range)# no shutdown
S1(config-if-range)# exit
S1(config)#
```

In the example, FastEthernet0/1 and FastEthernet0/2 are disabled and duplex and speed settings are manually set, bundled into EtherChannel interface Port Channel 1, and finally re-enabled.

The port channel interface is used to change LACP EtherChannel settings. To change Layer 2 settings on the port channel interface, enter port channel interface configuration mode by using the **interface port-channel** command, followed by the *interface* identifier.

In Example 4-2, the LACP port channel is configured as a trunk interface that allows traffic from VLANs 1, 2, and 20.

**Example 4-2**   Configuring the LACP Port Channel Settings

```
S1(config)# interface port-channel 1
S1(config-if)# switchport mode trunk
S1(config-if)# switchport trunk allowed vlan 1,2,20
S1(config-if)#
```

**Packet Tracer 4.2.1.3: Configuring EtherChannel**

Background/Scenario

Three switches have just been installed. There are redundant uplinks between the switches. Usually, only one of these links can be used to prevent a bridging loop from occurring. However, using only one link utilizes only half of the available bandwidth. EtherChannel allows up to eight redundant links to be bundled together into one logical link. In this lab, you will configure Port Aggregation Protocol (PAgP), a Cisco EtherChannel protocol, and Link Aggregation Control Protocol (LACP), an IEEE 802.3ad open standard version of EtherChannel.

**Lab 4.2.1.4: Configuring EtherChannel**

Refer to *Scaling Networks v6 Labs & Study Guide* and the online course to complete this activity.

In this lab, you will complete the following objectives:

- Part 1: Configure Basic Switch Settings

- Part 2: Configure PAgP

- Part 3: Configure LACP

# Verifying and Troubleshooting EtherChannel (4.2.2)

In this topic you will learn how to troubleshoot a link aggregation implementation.

## Verifying EtherChannel (4.2.2.1)

There are a number of commands to verify an EtherChannel configuration. First, the **show interfaces port-channel** command displays the general status of the port channel interface.

In Example 4-3, the Port Channel 1 interface is up.

**Example 4-3**  The **show interface port-channel** Command

```
S1# show interface Port-channel1
Port-channel1 is up, line protocol is up (connected)
  Hardware is EtherChannel, address is 0cd9.96e8.8a01 (bia 0cd9.96e8.8a01)
  MTU 1500 bytes, BW 200000 Kbit/sec, DLY 100 usec,
     reliability 255/255, txload 1/255, rxload 1/255
  Encapsulation ARPA, loopback not set
<output omitted>
```

When several port channel interfaces are configured on the same device, use the **show etherchannel summary** command to simply display one line of information per port channel.

In Example 4-4, the switch has one EtherChannel configured; group 1 uses LACP.

**Example 4-4**  The **show etherchannel summary** Command

```
S1# show etherchannel summary
Flags:  D - down         P - bundled in port-channel
        I - stand-alone  s - suspended
        H - Hot-standby (LACP only)
        R - Layer3        S - Layer2
        U - in use        f - failed to allocate aggregator

        M - not in use, minimum links not met
        u - unsuitable for bundling
        w - waiting to be aggregated
        d - default port


Number of channel-groups in use:  1
Number of aggregators:           1

Group  Port-channel  Protocol    Ports
------+-------------+-----------+------------------------------------------------
1      Po1(SU)          LACP      Fa0/1(P)    Fa0/2(P)
```

The interface bundle consists of the FastEthernet0/1 and FastEthernet0/2 interfaces. The group is a Layer 2 EtherChannel, and it is in use, as indicated by the letters SU next to the port channel number.

Use the **show etherchannel port-channel** command to display information about a specific port channel interface, as shown in Example 4-5.

**Example 4-5**    The **show etherchannel port-channel** Command

```
S1# show etherchannel Port-channel
            Channel-group listing:
            ----------------------
Group: 1
----------
            Port-channels in the group:
            --------------------------


Port-channel: Po1     (Primary Aggregator)


------------

Age of the Port-channel   = 0d:00h:25m:17s
Logical slot/port    = 2/1              Number of ports = 2
HotStandBy port = null
Port state              = Port-channel Ag-Inuse
Protocol                = LACP
Port security           = Disabled
 Ports in the Port-channel:

Index    Load    Port     EC state         No of bits
------+------+------+------------------+-----------
   0      00    Fa0/1     Active                0
   0      00    Fa0/2     Active                0

Time since last port bundled:    0d:00h:05m:41s    Fa0/2
Time since last port Un-bundled: 0d:00h:05m:48s    Fa0/2
```

In Example 4-5, the Port Channel 1 interface consists of two physical interfaces, FastEthernet0/1 and FastEthernet0/2. It uses LACP in active mode. It is properly connected to another switch with a compatible configuration, which is why the port channel is said to be in use.

On any physical interface member of an EtherChannel bundle, the **show interfaces etherchannel** command can provide information about the role of the interface in the EtherChannel.

Example 4-6 confirms that interface FastEthernet0/1 is part of the EtherChannel bundle 1 using LACP.

**Example 4-6**   The **show interfaces f0/1 etherchannel** Command

```
S1# show interfaces f0/1 etherchannel
Port state      = Up Mstr Assoc In-Bndl
Channel group = 1              Mode = Active         Gcchange = -
Port-channel  = Po1            GC   =   -            Pseudo port-channel = Po1
Port index    = 0              Load = 0x00           Protocol =    LACP


Flags:   S - Device is sending Slow LACPDUs   F - Device is sending fast LACPDUs.
         A - Device is in active mode.         P - Device is in passive mode.
Local information:
                              LACP port     Admin    Oper    Port      Port
Port       Flags    State     Priority      Key      Key     Number    State
Fa0/1      SA       bndl      32768         0x1      0x1     0x102     0x3D


Partner's information:

                              LACP port                 Admin  Oper  Port    Port
Port       Flags    Priority  Dev ID          Age       key    Key   Number  State
Fa0/1      SA       32768     0cd9.96d2.4000  4s        0x0    0x1   0x102   0x3D
```

## Troubleshooting EtherChannel (4.2.2.2)

All interfaces within an EtherChannel must have the same configuration of speed and duplex mode, native and allowed VLANs on trunks, and access VLAN on access ports:

- Assign all ports in the EtherChannel to the same VLAN or configure them as trunks. Ports with different native VLANs cannot form an EtherChannel.

- When configuring a trunk on an EtherChannel, verify the trunking mode on the EtherChannel. It is not recommended that you configure trunking mode on individual ports that make up the EtherChannel. But if it is done, verify that the trunking configuration is the same on all interfaces.

- An EtherChannel supports the same allowed range of VLANs on all the ports. If the allowed range of VLANs is not the same, the ports do not form an EtherChannel, even when PAgP is set to the auto or desirable mode.

- The dynamic negotiation options for PAgP and LACP must be compatibly configured on both ends of the EtherChannel.

> **Note**
>
> It is easy to confuse PAgP or LACP with DTP because these protocols are used to automate behavior on trunk links. PAgP and LACP are used for link aggregation (EtherChannel). DTP is used for automating the creation of trunk links. When an EtherChannel trunk is configured, typically EtherChannel (PAgP or LACP) is configured first and then DTP.

Example 4-7 shows that F0/1 and F0/2 on S1 are connected with an EtherChannel, but the EtherChannel is down.

**Example 4-7**    Verifying EtherChannel Status on S1

```
S1# show etherchannel summary
Flags:    D - down          P - bundled in port-channel
          I - stand-alone   s - suspended
          H - Hot-standby   (LACP only)
          R - Layer3        S - Layer2
          U - in use        f - failed to allocate aggregator
          M - not in use, minimum links not met
          u - unsuitable for bundling
          w - waiting to be aggregated
          d - default port


Number of channel-groups in use:  1
Number of aggregators:             1


Group  Port-channel  Protocol     Ports
------+-------------+-----------+-----------------------------------------------
1      Po1(SD)          -         Fa0/1(D)    Fa0/2(D)
```

Example 4-8 shows more detailed output for the F0/1 and F0/2 interfaces on S1.

**Example 4-8**    Verifying Interfaces on S1

```
S1# show run | begin interface Port-channel
interface Port-channel1
 switchport mode trunk
!
interface FastEthernet0/1
 switchport mode trunk
 channel-group 1 mode on
!
interface FastEthernet0/2
 switchport mode trunk
 channel-group 1 mode on
!
<output omitted>
```

S1 is configured to enable a static EtherChannel. Next, verify the S2 interfaces.

Example 4-9 shows more detailed output for the F0/1 and F0/2 interfaces on S2.

**Example 4-9**   Verifying Interfaces on S2

```
S2# show run | begin interface Port-channel
interface Port-channel1
 switchport mode trunk
!
interface FastEthernet0/1
 switchport mode trunk
 channel-group 1 mode desirable
!
interface FastEthernet0/2
 switchport mode trunk
 channel-group 1 mode desirable
!
<output omitted>
```

EtherChannel is down in Example 4-7 because the interconnecting interfaces are configured with incompatible EtherChannel settings. Example 4-8 shows that S1 is configured to statically enable an EtherChannel using the "mode on" option, while Example 4-9 shows that S2 is configured to dynamically enable a PAgP EtherChannel using the "mode desirable" option.

In Example 4-10, Port Channel 1 is removed on S1, the F0/1 and F0/2 interfaces of S1 are configured for PAgP desirable mode, and the port channel is reconfigured as a trunk.

**Example 4-10**   Configuring PAgP Settings on S1

```
S1(config)# no interface Port-channel 1
S1(config)#
S1(config)# interface range f0/1 - 2
S1(config-if-range)# channel-group 1 mode desirable
Creating a port-channel interface Port-channel 1
S1(config-if-range)# no shutdown
S1(config-if-range)# exit
S1(config)#
S1(config)# interface Port-channel 1
S1(config-if)# switchport mode trunk
S1(config-if)# end
S1#
```

**Note**

EtherChannel and spanning tree must interoperate. For this reason, the order in which EtherChannel-related commands are entered is important, which is why Port Channel 1 was removed and then re-added with the **channel-group** command, as opposed to being directly changed. If you try to change the configuration directly, spanning-tree errors cause the associated ports to go into blocking or errdisabled state.

Example 4-11 confirms that the PAgP EtherChannel is operational after the configuration change.

**Example 4-11**    Re-verifying EtherChannel Status on S1

```
S1# show etherchannel summary
Flags:   D - down        P - bundled in port-channel
         I - stand-alone  s - suspended
         H - Hot-standby (LACP only)
         R - Layer3       S - Layer2
         U - in use       f - failed to allocate aggregator
         M - not in use, minimum links not met
         u - unsuitable for bundling
         w - waiting to be aggregated
         d - default port


Number of channel-groups in use:  1
Number of aggregators:            1


Group  Port-channel  Protocol     Ports
------+-------------+-----------+--------------------------------------------
1       Po1(SU)       PAgP        Fa0/1(P)    Fa0/2(P)
```

**Packet Tracer 4.2.2.3: Troubleshooting EtherChannel**

Background/Scenario

Four switches were recently configured by a junior technician. Users are complaining that the network is running slowly and would like you to investigate.

**Lab 4.2.2.4: Troubleshooting EtherChannel**

Refer to *Scaling Networks v6 Labs & Study Guide* and the online course to complete this activity.

In this lab, you will complete the following objectives:

- Part 1: Build the Network and Load Device Configurations
- Part 2: Troubleshoot EtherChannel

# First Hop Redundancy Protocols (4.3)

If a router or router interface (which serves as a default gateway) fails, the hosts configured with that default gateway are isolated from outside networks. A mechanism is needed to provide alternate default gateways in switched networks where two or more routers are connected to the same VLANs.

In this section you will learn how to implement HSRP.

## Concept of First Hop Redundancy Protocols (4.3.1)

In this topic you will learn about the purpose and operation of first-hop redundancy protocols.

### Default Gateway Limitations (4.3.1.1)

In a switched network, each client receives only one default gateway. There is no way to use a secondary gateway, even if a second path exists to carry packets off the local segment.

End devices are typically configured with a single IP address for a default gateway. This address does not change when the network topology changes. If that default gateway IP address cannot be reached, the local device is unable to send packets off the local network segment, effectively disconnecting it from other networks. Even if a redundant router exists that could serve as a default gateway for that segment, there is no dynamic method by which these devices can determine the address of a new default gateway.

In Figure 4-9, R1 is responsible for routing packets from PC1. If R1 becomes unavailable, the routing protocols can dynamically converge, and R2 then routes packets from outside networks that would have gone through R1.

However, traffic from the inside network associated with R1, including traffic from workstations, servers, and printers configured with R1 as their default gateway, are still sent to R1 and therefore are dropped.

> **Note**
>
> For the purposes of the discussion on router redundancy, there is no functional difference between a multilayer switch and a router at the distribution layer. In practice, it is common for a multilayer switch to act as the default gateway for each VLAN in a switched network. This discussion focuses on the functionality of routing, regardless of the physical device used.

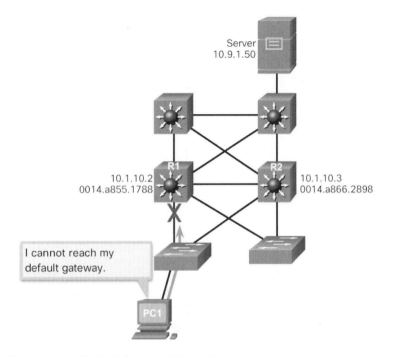

**Figure 4-9**   Default Gateway Limitations

## Router Redundancy (4.3.1.2)

One way to prevent a single point of failure at the default gateway is to implement a virtual router. To implement this type of router redundancy, multiple routers are configured to work together to present the illusion of a single router to the hosts on the LAN. By sharing an IP address and a MAC address, two or more routers can act as a single virtual router.

The example in Figure 4-10 shows PC2 sending a packet destined to the Internet.

Notice how PC2 forwards the packet to its default gateway, 192.0.2.100. This is the IP address of the virtual router.

The IPv4 address of the virtual router is configured as the default gateway for the workstations on a specific IPv4 segment. When frames are sent from host devices to the default gateway, the hosts use ARP to resolve the MAC address that is associated with the IPv4 address of the default gateway. The ARP resolution returns the MAC address of the virtual router. Frames that are sent to the MAC address of the virtual router can then be physically processed by the currently *active router* within the virtual router group.

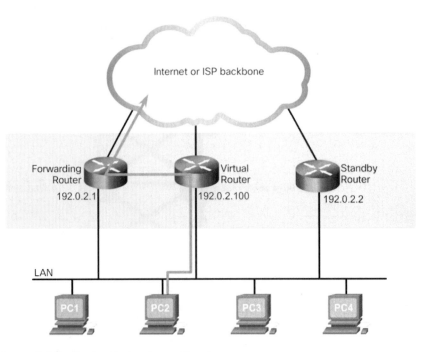

**Figure 4-10**  Router Redundancy Topology

An FHRP is used to identify two or more routers as the devices that are responsible for processing frames that are sent to the MAC or IP address of a single virtual router. Host devices send traffic to the address of the virtual router. The physical router that forwards this traffic is transparent to the host devices.

A redundancy protocol provides the mechanism for determining which router should take the active role in forwarding traffic. It also determines when the forwarding role must be taken over by a *standby router*. The transition from one forwarding router to another is transparent to the end devices.

The ability of a network to dynamically recover from the failure of a device acting as a default gateway is known as first-hop redundancy.

## Steps for Router Failover (4.3.1.3)

When the active router fails, the redundancy protocol transitions the standby router to the new active router role, as shown in Figure 4-11.

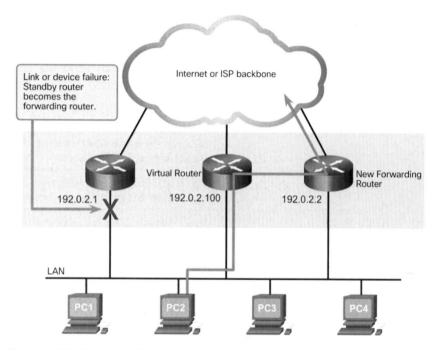

**Figure 4-11**   Steps for Router Failover

These are the steps that take place when the active router fails:

1. The standby router stops receiving hello messages from the forwarding router.

2. The standby router sends a coup message, indicating that it is assuming the role of the forwarding router.

3. Because the new forwarding router assumes both the IPv4 and MAC addresses of the virtual router, the host devices suffer no disruption in service.

**Interactive Graphic**

**Activity 4.3.1.4: Identify FHRP Terminology**

Refer to the online course to complete this activity.

## First Hop Redundancy Protocols (4.3.1.5)

Table 4-4 defines the options available for FHRPs.

**Table 4-4** FHRP Options

| FHRP | Description |
|---|---|
| Hot Standby Router Protocol (HSRP) | ▪ This Cisco proprietary FHRP provides high network availability.<br><br>▪ HSRP selects an active router and a standby router.<br><br>▪ The standby HSRP router actively monitors the operational status of the active HSRP router and quickly assumes packet-forwarding responsibility if the active router fails. |
| HSRP for IPv6 | ▪ This Cisco proprietary FHRP provides the same functionality as HSRP but in an IPv6 environment. |
| *Virtual Router Redundancy Protocol (VRRP)* | ▪ VRRP Version 2 is a nonproprietary FHRP that provides high network availability.<br><br>▪ VRRP selects a *master router* and one or more other routers as *backup routers*.<br><br>▪ VRRP backup routers monitor the VRRP master router. |
| VRRPv3 | ▪ VRRPv3 provides the capability to support IPv4 and IPv6 addresses in multivendor environments. |
| *Gateway Load Balancing Protocol (GLBP)* | ▪ This Cisco proprietary FHRP protects data traffic from a failed router or circuit, like HSRP and VRRP, while also allowing load balancing (also called load sharing) between a group of redundant routers. |
| GLBP for IPv6 | ▪ This Cisco proprietary FHRP provides the same functionality as GLBP but in an IPv6 environment. |
| *ICMP Router Discovery Protocol (IRDP)* | ▪ Specified in RFC 1256, IRDP is a legacy FHRP solution.<br><br>▪ IRDP allows IPv4 hosts to locate routers that provide IPv4 connectivity to other (nonlocal) IP networks. |

**Interactive Graphic**

**Activity 4.3.1.6: Identify the Type of FHRP**

Refer to the online course to complete this activity.

# HSRP Operations (4.3.2)

In this topic you will learn how HSRP operates.

## HSRP Overview (4.3.2.1)

Hot Standby Router Protocol (HSRP) was designed by Cisco to allow for gateway redundancy without any additional configuration on end devices. Routers configured with HSRP work together to present themselves as a single virtual default gateway (router) to end devices, as shown in Figure 4-12.

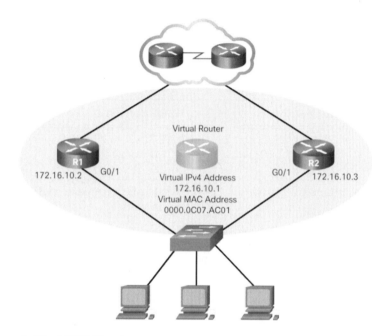

**Figure 4-12**   HSRP Topology

HSRP selects one of the routers to be the active router. The active router will act as the default gateway for end devices. The other router will become the standby router. If the active router fails, the standby router will automatically assume the role of the active router. It will assume the role of default gateway for end devices. This does not require any configuration changes on the end devices.

Hosts are configured with a single default gateway address that is recognizable by both the active and standby routers. The default gateway address is a virtual IPv4 address, along with a virtual MAC address that is shared by both HSRP routers. End devices use this virtual IPv4 address as their default gateway address. The HSRP virtual IPv4 address is configured by the network administrator. The virtual MAC address is created automatically. Regardless of which physical router is used, the virtual IPv4 and MAC addresses provide consistent default gateway addressing for the end devices.

Only the active router will receive and forward traffic sent to the default gateway. If the active router fails, or if communication to the active router fails, the standby router will assume the role of the active router.

## HSRP Versions (4.3.2.2)

The default HSRP version for Cisco IOS 15 is Version 1. However, HSRP Version 2 can also be enabled.

Table 4-5 identifies the differences between HSRPv1 and HSRPv2.

**Table 4-5**  Differences in HSRP Versions

| HSRP Version 1 | HSRP Version 2 |
|---|---|
| ■ HSRPv1 supports group numbers from 0 to 255. | ■ HSRPv2 expands the number of supported group numbers from 0 to 4095. |
| ■ HSRPv1 uses the multicast address 224.0.0.2.<br><br>■ HSRPv1 uses the virtual MAC address range 0000.0C07.AC00 to 0000.0C07.ACFF, where the last two hexadecimal digits indicate the HSRP group number. | ■ HSRP 2 uses the IPv4 multicast address 224.0.0.102 or the IPv6 multicast address FF02::66 to send hello packets.<br><br>■ HSRPv2 uses the virtual MAC address range from 0000.0C9F.F000 to 0000.0C9F.FFFF for IPv4 and 0005.73A0.0000 through 0005.73A0.0FFF for IPv6 addresses.<br><br>■ For both IPv4 and IPv6, the last three hexadecimal digits in the MAC address indicate the HSRP group number. |

**Note**

Group numbers are used for more advanced HSRP configurations that are beyond the scope of this course. For our purposes, we use group number 1.

## HSRP Priority and Preemption (4.3.2.3)

The roles of the active and standby routers are determined during the HSRP election process. By default, the router with the numerically highest IPv4 address is elected as the active router. However, it is always better to control how your network will operate under normal conditions than to leave it to chance.

### HSRP Priority

HSRP priority can be used to determine the active router. The router with the highest HSRP priority becomes the active router. By default, the HSRP priority is 100. If the priorities are equal, the router with the numerically highest IPv4 address is elected the active router.

To configure a router to be the active router, use the **standby priority** interface command. The range of the HSRP priority is 0 to 255.

## HSRP Preemption

By default, after a router becomes the active router, it remains the active router even if another router comes online with a higher HSRP priority.

To force a new HSRP election process, preemption must be enabled, using the **standby preempt** interface command. Preemption is the ability of an HSRP router to trigger the re-election process. With preemption enabled, a router that comes online with a higher HSRP priority assumes the role of the active router.

Preemption allows a router to become the active router only if it has a higher priority. A router enabled for preemption with equal priority but a higher IPv4 address cannot preempt an active router.

In the topology in Figure 4-12, R1 has been configured with the HSRP priority 150, and R2 has the default HSRP priority 100. Preemption has been enabled on R1. With a higher priority, R1 is the active router, and R2 is the standby router. When a power failure affects only R1, the active router is no longer available, and the standby router, R2, assumes the role of the active router. After power is restored, R1 comes back online. Because R1 has a higher priority and preemption is enabled, it forces a new election process. R1 re-assumes the role of the active router, and R2 falls back to the role of standby router.

**Note**

With preemption disabled, the router that boots up first becomes the active router if there are no other routers online during the election process.

## HSRP States and Timers (4.3.2.4)

A router can either be the active HSRP router responsible for forwarding traffic for the segment, or it can be a passive HSRP router on standby, ready to assume the active role if the active router fails. When an interface is configured with HSRP or is first activated with an existing HSRP configuration, the router sends and receives HSRP hello packets to begin the process of determining which state it will assume in the HSRP group.

Table 4-6 summarizes the HSRP states.

**Table 4-6**   HSRP States

| State | Definition |
| --- | --- |
| Initial | ■ This state is entered through a configuration change or when an interface first becomes available. |
| Learn | ■ The router has not determined the virtual IP address and has not yet seen a hello message from the active router.<br>■ In this state, the router waits to hear from the active router. |
| Listen | ■ The router knows the virtual IP address, but the router is neither the active router nor the standby router.<br>■ It listens for hello messages from those routers. |
| Speak | ■ The router sends periodic hello messages and actively participates in the election of the active and/or standby router. |
| Standby | ■ The router is a candidate to become the next active router and sends periodic hello messages. |
| Active | ■ The router currently forwards packets that are sent to the group virtual MAC address.<br>■ The router sends periodic hello messages. |

The active and standby HSRP routers send hello packets to the HSRP group multicast address every 3 seconds, by default. The standby router becomes active if it does not receive a hello message from the active router after 10 seconds. You can lower these timer settings to speed up the failover or preemption. However, to avoid increased CPU usage and unnecessary standby state changes, do not set the hello timer below 1 second or the hold timer below 4 seconds.

**Interactive Graphic**

**Activity 4.3.2.5: Identify HSRP Terminology and States**

Refer to the online course to complete this activity.

# HSRP Configuration (4.3.3)

In this topic you will learn how to configure HSRP by using Cisco IOS commands.

## HSRP Configuration Commands (4.3.3.1)

Complete the following steps to configure HSRP:

Step 1.   Configure HSRP Version 2.

Step 2.   Configure the virtual IP address for the group.

**Step 3.**   Configure the priority for the desired active router to be greater than 100.

**Step 4.**   Configure the active router to preempt the standby router in cases where the active router comes online after the standby router.

Table 4-7 shows the command syntax used to complete the configuration steps.

**Table 4-7**   HSRP Command Syntax

| HSRP Interface Configuration Command | Description |
|---|---|
| standby version 2 | ■ Enables HSRPv2 instead of the default HSRPv1. |
| standby [*group-#*] ip-address | ■ Configures the HSRP virtual IP address.<br>■ If no group is configured, then group 0 is used. |
| standby [*group-#*] priority [*value*] | ■ Configures a higher or lower priority (in the range 0 to 255) value.<br>■ The default priority value is 100.<br>■ If no priority is configured or if priority is equal, then the router with the highest IP address wins. |
| standby [*group-#*] preempt | ■ Enables a router to preempt the currently active router. |

## HSRP Sample Configuration (4.3.3.2)

In Example 4-12, R1 is configured to provide HSRP services for virtual IP address 172.16.10.1 for HSRP group 1. R1 is also configured with high priority and the ability to preempt existing HSRP configurations.

**Example 4-12**   HSRP Configuration for Active Router R1

```
R1(config)# interface g0/1
R1(config-if)# ip address 172.16.10.2 255.255.255.0
R1(config-if)# standby version 2
R1(config-if)# standby 1 ip 172.16.10.1
R1(config-if)# standby 1 priority 150
R1(config-if)# standby 1 preempt
R1(config-if)# no shutdown
```

In Example 4-13, R2 is configured to provide HSRP services for virtual IP address 172.16.10.1 for HSRP group 1. However, R2 is left with the default priority of 100, with no preemption ability.

**Example 4-13**   HSRP Configuration for Standby Router R2

```
R2(config)# interface g0/1
R2(config-if)# ip address 172.16.10.3 255.255.255.0
R2(config-if)# standby version 2
R2(config-if)# standby 1 ip 172.16.10.1
R2(config-if)# no shutdown
```

Because R1 has the higher priority, it becomes the HSRP active router, and R2 becomes the standby router.

## HSRP Verification (4.3.3.3)

Use the **show standby** commands to verify the configuration of R1 and R2.

Example 4-14 shows how to verify the HSRP configuration and the HSRP status on R1 by using the **show standby** and **show standby brief** commands.

**Example 4-14**   HSRP Configuration Verification on R1

```
R1# show standby
GigabitEthernet0/1 - Group 1 (version 2)
  State is Active
    5 state changes, last state change 01:02:18
  Virtual IP address is 172.16.10.1
  Active virtual MAC address is 0000.0c9f.f001
    Local virtual MAC address is 0000.0c9f.f001 (v2 default)
  Hello time 3 sec, hold time 10 sec
    Next hello sent in 1.120 secs
  Preemption enabled
  Active router is local
  Standby router is 172.16.10.3, priority 100 (expires in 9.392 sec)
  Priority 150 (configured 150)
  Group name is "hsrp-Gi0/1-1" (default)
R1#
R1# show standby brief
                     P indicates configured to preempt.
                     |
Interface   Grp  Pri  P State   Active       Standby        Virtual IP
Gi0/1        1   150  P Active  local        172.16.10.3    172.16.10.1
R1#
```

Example 4-15 shows how to verify the configuration and the HSRP status on R2 by using the **show standby** and **show standby brief** commands.

**Example 4-15**   HSRP Configuration Verification on R2

```
R2# show standby
GigabitEthernet0/1 - Group 1 (version 2)
  State is Standby
    5 state changes, last state change 01:03:59
  Virtual IP address is 172.16.10.1
  Active virtual MAC address is 0000.0c9f.f001
    Local virtual MAC address is 0000.0c9f.f001 (v2 default)
  Hello time 3 sec, hold time 10 sec
    Next hello sent in 0.944 secs
  Preemption disabled
  Active router is 172.16.10.2, priority 150 (expires in 8.160 sec)
    MAC address is fc99.4775.c3e1
  Standby router is local
  Priority 100 (default 100)
  Group name is "hsrp-Gi0/1-1" (default)
R2#
R2# show standby brief
                     P indicates configured to preempt.
                     |
Interface   Grp  Pri  P State    Active        Standby      Virtual IP
Gi0/1       1    100    Standby  172.16.10.2   local        172.16.10.1
R2#
```

**Lab 4.3.3.4: Configure HSRP**

Refer to *Scaling Networks v6 Labs & Study Guide* and the online course to complete this activity.

In this lab, you will complete the following objectives:

- Part 1: Build the Network and Verify Connectivity
- Part 2: Configure First Hop Redundancy Using HSRP

# HSRP Troubleshooting (4.3.4)

In this topic you will learn how to troubleshoot HSRP.

## HSRP Failure (4.3.4.1)

To troubleshoot HSRP, you need to understand the basic operation. Most issues arise during one of the following HSRP functions:

- Failing to successfully elect the active router that controls the virtual IP for the group.

- Failure of the standby router to successfully keep track of the active router.

- Failing to determine when control of the virtual IP for the group should be handed over to another router.

- Failure of end devices to successfully configure the virtual IP address as the default gateway.

## HSRP Debug Commands (4.3.4.2)

The HSRP **debug** commands allow you to view the operation of HSRP when a router fails or is administratively shut down. The available HSRP **debug** commands can be viewed by entering the **debug standby ?** command, as shown in Example 4-16.

**Example 4-16**   HSRP **debug** Commands

```
R2# debug standby ?
  errors    HSRP errors
  events    HSRP events
  packets   HSRP packets
  terse     Display limited range of HSRP errors, events and packets
  <cr>
```

Use **debug standby packets** to view the receiving and sending of hello packets every three seconds, as shown in Example 4-17 for R2.

**Example 4-17**   Viewing the HSRP Hello Packets on a Standby Router

```
R2# debug standby packets
*Dec  2 15:20:12.347: HSRP: Gi0/1 Grp 1 Hello in  172.16.10.2 Active  pri 150 vIP
  172.16.10.1
*Dec  2 15:20:12.643: HSRP: Gi0/1 Grp 1 Hello out 172.16.10.3 Standby pri 100 vIP
  172.16.10.1
```

HSRP routers monitor these hello packets and initiate a state change after 10 seconds if no hellos are heard from an HSRP neighbor.

HSRP behaves differently when the active router fails than when it is manually shut down by the administrator. For instance, assume that **debug standby terse** has been configured on the standby router, R2. Next, the active router R1 has been powered off. Example 4-18 shows HSRP-related messages as R2 assumes the role of active HSRP router for the 172.16.10.0/24 network.

**Example 4-18**   R1 Fails, and R2 Is Elected Active HSRP Router

```
R2# debug standby terse
HSRP:
  HSRP Errors debugging is on
  HSRP Events debugging is on
    (protocol, neighbor, redundancy, track, arp, interface)
  HSRP Packets debugging is on
    (Coup, Resign)
R2#
*Dec  2 16:11:31.855: HSRP: Gi0/1 Grp 1 Standby: c/Active timer expired
  (172.16.10.2)
*Dec  2 16:11:31.855: HSRP: Gi0/1 Grp 1 Active router is local, was 172.16.10.2
*Dec  2 16:11:31.855: HSRP: Gi0/1 Nbr 172.16.10.2 no longer active for group 1
  (Standby)
*Dec  2 16:11:31.855: HSRP: Gi0/1 Nbr 172.16.10.2 Was active or standby - start
  passive holddown
*Dec  2 16:11:31.855: HSRP: Gi0/1 Grp 1 Standby router is unknown, was local
*Dec  2 16:11:31.855: HSRP: Gi0/1 Grp 1 Standby -> Active
<output omitted>
R2#
```

Example 4-19 shows what happens on R2 when R1 is powered back on.

**Example 4-19**   R1 Initiates Coup to Become Active HSRP Router

```
R2#
*Dec  2 18:01:30.183: HSRP: Gi0/1 Nbr 172.16.10.2 Adv in, active 0 passive 1
*Dec  2 18:01:30.183: HSRP: Gi0/1 Nbr 172.16.10.2 created
*Dec  2 18:01:30.183: HSRP: Gi0/1 Nbr 172.16.10.2 is passive
*Dec  2 18:01:32.443: HSRP: Gi0/1 Nbr 172.16.10.2 Adv in, active 1 passive 1
*Dec  2 18:01:32.443: HSRP: Gi0/1 Nbr 172.16.10.2 is no longer passive
*Dec  2 18:01:32.443: HSRP: Gi0/1 Nbr 172.16.10.2 destroyed
*Dec  2 18:01:32.443: HSRP: Gi0/1 Grp 1 Coup   in  172.16.10.2 Listen  pri 150 vIP
  172.16.10.1
*Dec  2 18:01:32.443: HSRP: Gi0/1 Grp 1 Active: j/Coup rcvd from higher pri router
  (150/172.16.10.2)
*Dec  2 18:01:32.443: HSRP: Gi0/1 Grp 1 Active router is 172.16.10.2, was local
*Dec  2 18:01:32.443: HSRP: Gi0/1 Nbr 172.16.10.2 created
*Dec  2 18:01:32.443: HSRP: Gi0/1 Nbr 172.16.10.2 active for group 1
*Dec  2 18:01:32.443: HSRP: Gi0/1 Grp 1 Active -> Speak
*Dec  2 18:01:32.443: %HSRP-5-STATECHANGE: GigabitEthernet0/1 Grp 1 state Active ->
  Speak
*Dec  2 18:01:32.443: HSRP: Gi0/1 Grp 1 Redundancy "hsrp-Gi0/1-1" state Active ->
  Speak
*Dec  2 18:01:32.443: HSRP: Gi0/1 Grp 1 Removed 172.16.10.1 from ARP
```

```
*Dec  2 18:01:32.443: HSRP: Gi0/1 IP Redundancy "hsrp-Gi0/1-1" update, Active ->
   Speak
*Dec  2 18:01:43.771: HSRP: Gi0/1 Grp 1 Speak: d/Standby timer expired (unknown)
*Dec  2 18:01:43.771: HSRP: Gi0/1 Grp 1 Standby router is local
*Dec  2 18:01:43.771: HSRP: Gi0/1 Grp 1 Speak -> Standby
```

Because R1 is configured with the **standby 1 preempt** command, it initiates a coup and assumes the role of active router, as highlighted at the bottom of Example 4-19. The rest of the output in this listing shows that R2 actively listens to hello messages during the speak state until it confirms that R1 is the new active router and R2 is the new standby router.

If the R1 G0/1 interface is administratively shut down, R1 sends an Init message indicating to all HSRP routers on the link that it is resigning the role of active router. As shown in Example 4-20, 10 seconds later, R2 assumes the role of active HSRP router.

**Example 4-20**   R1 Is Administratively Shut Down and Resigns as Active HSRP Router

```
R1(config)# interface g0/1
R1(config-if)# shutdown
R1(config-if)#
*Dec  2 17:36:20.275: %HSRP-5-STATECHANGE: GigabitEthernet0/1 Grp 1 state Active ->
   Init
*Dec  2 17:36:22.275: %LINK-5-CHANGED: Interface GigabitEthernet0/1, changed state
   to administratively down
*Dec  2 17:36:23.275: %LINEPROTO-5-UPDOWN: Line protocol on Interface GigabitEther-
   net0/1, changed state to down
R1(config-if)#

R2#
*Dec  2 17:36:30.699: HSRP: Gi0/1 Grp 1 Resign in  172.16.10.2 Active  pri 150 vIP
   172.16.10.1
*Dec  2 17:36:30.699: HSRP: Gi0/1 Grp 1 Standby: i/Resign rcvd (150/172.16.10.2)
*Dec  2 17:36:30.699: HSRP: Gi0/1 Grp 1 Active router is local, was 172.16.10.2
*Dec  2 17:36:30.699: HSRP: Gi0/1 Nbr 172.16.10.2 no longer active for group 1
   (Standby)
*Dec  2 17:36:30.699: HSRP: Gi0/1 Nbr 172.16.10.2 Was active or standby - start
   passive holddown
*Dec  2 17:36:30.699: HSRP: Gi0/1 Grp 1 Standby router is unknown, was local
*Dec  2 17:36:30.699: HSRP: Gi0/1 Grp 1 Standby -> Active
*Dec  2 17:36:30.699: %HSRP-5-STATECHANGE: GigabitEthernet0/1 Grp 1 state Standby
   -> Active
*Dec  2 17:36:30.699: HSRP: Gi0/1 Grp 1 Redundancy "hsrp-Gi0/1-1" state Standby ->
   Active
*Dec  2 17:36:30.699: HSRP: Gi0/1 Grp 1 Added 172.16.10.1 to ARP (0000.0c9f.f001)
```

```
*Dec  2 17:36:30.699: HSRP: Gi0/1 IP Redundancy "hsrp-Gi0/1-1" standby, local ->
      unknown
*Dec  2 17:36:30.699: HSRP: Gi0/1 IP Redundancy "hsrp-Gi0/1-1" update, Standby ->
      Active
*Dec  2 17:36:33.707: HSRP: Gi0/1 IP Redundancy "hsrp-Gi0/1-1" update, Active ->
      Active
*Dec  2 17:39:30.743: HSRP: Gi0/1 Nbr 172.16.10.2 Passive timer expired
*Dec  2 17:39:30.743: HSRP: Gi0/1 Nbr 172.16.10.2 is no longer passive
*Dec  2 17:39:30.743: HSRP: Gi0/1 Nbr 172.16.10.2 destroyed
R2#
```

Notice that R2 starts a passive holddown timer for R1. After three minutes, this passive holddown timer expires, and R1 (172.16.10.2) is destroyed, meaning it is removed from the HSRP database.

## Common HSRP Configuration Issues (4.3.4.3)

The **debug** examples in the previous section illustrate the expected operation of HSRP. You can also use the **debug** commands to detect common configuration issues such as the following:

- The HSRP routers are not connected to the same network segment. Although this could be a physical layer issue, it could also be a VLAN subinterface configuration issue.

- The HSRP routers are not configured with IPv4 addresses from the same subnet. HSRP hello packets are local. They are not routed beyond the network segment. Therefore, a standby router would not know when the active router fails.

- The HSRP routers are not configured with the same virtual IPv4 address. The virtual IPv4 address is the default gateway for end devices.

- The HSRP routers are not configured with the same HSRP group number, which causes each router to assume the active role.

- End devices are not configured with the correct default gateway address. Although not directly related to HSRP, configuring the DHCP server with one of the HSRP router's real IP addresses would mean that end devices would only have connectivity to remote networks when that HSRP router is active.

Packet Tracer
☐ Activity

**Packet Tracer 4.3.4.4: Troubleshoot HSRP**

In this activity, you will troubleshoot and resolve the HSRP issues in the network. You will also verify that all the HSRP configurations meet the network requirement.

# Summary (4.4)

**Class Activity 4.4.1.1: Linking Up**

Refer to *Scaling Networks v6 Labs & Study Guide* and the online course to complete this activity.

Many bottlenecks can occur on your small to medium-sized business network, even though you have configured VLANs, STP, and other network traffic options on the company's switches.

Instead of keeping the switches as they are currently configured, you would like to try EtherChannel as an option for at least part of the network to see if it will decrease traffic congestion between your access and distribution layer switches.

Your company uses Catalyst 3560 switches at the distribution layer and Catalyst 2960 and 2950 switches at the access layer of the network. To verify whether these switches can perform EtherChannel, you visit the System Requirements to Implement EtherChannel on Catalyst Switches site. This site allows you to gather more information to determine whether EtherChannel is a good option for the equipment and network currently in place.

After researching the models, you decide to use a simulation software program to practice configuring EtherChannel before implementing it live on your network. As part of this procedure, you ensure that the equipment simulated in a packet tracer will support these practice configurations.

---

**Packet Tracer 4.4.1.2: Skills Integration Challenge**

Background/Scenario

In this activity, two routers are configured to communicate with each other. You are responsible for configuring subinterfaces to communicate with the switches. You will configure VLANs, trunking, and EtherChannel with PVST. The Internet devices are all preconfigured.

---

EtherChannel aggregates multiple switched links together to do load balancing over redundant paths between two devices. All ports in one EtherChannel must have the same speed, duplex setting, and VLAN information on all interfaces on the devices at both ends. Settings configured in the port channel interface configuration mode are also applied to the individual interfaces in that EtherChannel. Settings configured on individual interfaces are not applied to the EtherChannel or to the other interfaces in the EtherChannel.

PAgP is a Cisco proprietary protocol that aids in the automatic creation of Ether-Channel links. PAgP modes are on, PAgP desirable, and PAgP auto. LACP is part of an IEEE specification that also allows multiple physical ports to be bundled into one logical channel. The LACP modes are on, LACP active, and LACP passive. PAgP and LACP do not interoperate. The on mode is repeated in both PAgP and LACP because it creates an EtherChannel unconditionally, without the use of PAgP or LACP. The default for EtherChannel is that no mode is configured.

FHRPs, such as HSRP, VRRP, and GLBP, provide alternate default gateways for hosts in the redundant router or multilayer switched environment. Multiple routers share a virtual IP address and MAC address that is used as the default gateway on a client. This ensures that hosts maintain connectivity in the event of the failure of one device serving as a default gateway for a VLAN or a set of VLANs. When using HSRP or VRRP, one router is active, or forwarding, for a particular group while others are in standby mode. GLBP allows the simultaneous use of multiple gateways in addition to providing automatic failover.

# Practice

The following activities provide practice with the topics introduced in this chapter. The Labs and Class Activities are available in the companion *Scaling Networks v6 Labs & Study Guide* (ISBN 9781587134333). The Packet Tracer activity instructions are also in the Labs & Study Guide. The PKA files are found in the online course.

**Class Activities**

Class Activity 4.0.1.2: Imagine This

Class Activity 4.4.1.1: Linking Up

**Labs**

Lab 4.2.1.4: Configuring EtherChannel

Lab 4.2.2.4: Troubleshooting EtherChannel

Lab 4.3.3.4: Configure HSRP

**Packet Tracer Activities**

Packet Tracer 4.2.1.3: Configuring EtherChannel

Packet Tracer 4.2.2.3: Troubleshooting EtherChannel

Packet Tracer 4.3.4.4: Troubleshoot HSRP

Packet Tracer 4.4.1.2: Skills Integration Challenge

# Check Your Understanding Questions

Complete all the review questions listed here to test your understanding of the topics and concepts in this chapter. The appendix "Answers to 'Check Your Understanding' Questions" lists the answers.

1. The trunk link between two 2960 switches has reached its capacity. How can you address this in the most economical way?

   A. Add routers between the switches to create additional broadcast domains.

   B. Bundle physical ports using EtherChannel.

   C. Configure smaller VLANs to decrease the size of the collision domain.

   D. Increase the speed of the ports by using the **bandwidth** command.

2. Which two load-balancing methods can be implemented with EtherChannel technology? (Choose two.)

   A. Destination IP to destination MAC

   B. Destination IP to source IP

   C. Destination MAC to destination IP

   D. Destination MAC to source MAC

   E. Source IP to destination IP

   F. Source MAC to destination MAC

3. Which statement is true regarding the use of PAgP to create EtherChannels?

   A. It increases the number of ports that are participating in spanning tree.

   B. It is Cisco proprietary.

   C. It mandates that an even number of ports (2, 4, 6, etc.) be used for aggregation.

   D. It requires full duplex.

   E. It requires more physical links than LACP does.

4. Which two protocols are link aggregation protocols? (Choose two.)

   A. 802.3ad

   B. EtherChannel

   C. PAgP

   D. RSTP

   E. STP

5. Which combination of modes establishes an EtherChannel?

   A. Switch 1 set to auto; switch 2 set to auto.

   B. Switch 1 set to auto; switch 2 set to on.

   C. Switch 1 set to desirable; switch 2 set to desirable.

   D. Switch 1 set to on; switch 2 set to desirable

6. Which interface configuration command enables a port to initiate an LACP EtherChannel?

   A. **channel-group mode active**

   B. **channel-group mode auto**

   C. **channel-group mode desirable**

   D. **channel-group mode on**

   E. **channel-group mode passive**

7. Which interface configuration command enables a port to establish an EtherChannel only if it receives PAgP packets from the other switch?

   A. **channel-group mode active**

   B. **channel-group mode auto**

   C. **channel-group mode desirable**

   D. **channel-group mode on**

   E. **channel-group mode passive**

8. Which statement describes a characteristic of EtherChannel?

   A. It can combine up to a maximum of four physical links.

   B. It can bundle mixed types of 100 Mbps and 1 Gbps Ethernet links.

   C. It consists of multiple parallel links between a switch and a router.

   D. It is made by combining multiple physical links that are seen as one link between two switches.

9. What are two advantages of using LACP? (Choose two.)

   A. LACP allows automatic formation of EtherChannel links.

   B. LACP allows the use of multivendor devices.

   C. LACP decreases the amount of configuration that is needed on a switch for EtherChannel.

   D. LACP eliminates the need for a spanning-tree protocol.

   E. LACP increases redundancy to Layer 3 devices.

   F. LACP provides a simulated environment for testing link aggregation.

10. Which three settings must match in order for switch ports to form an EtherChannel? (Choose three.)

    A. Non-trunk ports must belong to the same VLAN.

    B. Port security violation settings on interconnecting ports must match.

    C. The duplex settings on interconnecting ports must match.

    D. The port channel group number on interconnecting switches must match.

    E. The SNMP community strings must match.

    F. The speed settings on interconnecting ports must match.

11. Which statement about HSRP operation is true?

    A. HSRP supports only clear-text authentication.

    B. The active router responds to requests to the virtual MAC address and virtual IP address.

    C. The AVF responds to default gateway ARP requests.

    D. The HSRP virtual IP address must be the same as one of the router's interface addresses on the LAN.

12. Which statement regarding VRRP is true?

    A. VRRP elects a master router and one or more other routers as backup routers.

    B. VRRP elects a master router and one backup routers, and all other routers are standby routers.

    C. VRRP elects an active router and a standby router, and all other routers are backup routers.

    D. VRRP is a Cisco proprietary protocol.

13. A network administrator is overseeing the implementation of first-hop redundancy protocols. Which protocol is a Cisco proprietary protocol?

    A. HSRP

    B. IRDP

    C. Proxy ARP

    D. VRRP

14. What is the purpose of HSRP?

    A. It enables an access port to immediately transition to the forwarding state.

    B. It prevents a rogue switch from becoming the STP root.

    C. It prevents malicious hosts from connecting to trunk ports.

    D. It provides a continuous network connection when a default gateway fails.

# CHAPTER 5

# Dynamic Routing

## Objectives

Upon completion of this chapter, you will be able to answer the following questions:

- What are the features and characteristics of dynamic routing protocols?

- How do distance vector routing protocols operate?

- How do link-state routing protocols operate?

## Key Terms

This chapter uses the following key terms. You can find the definitions in the Glossary.

*best path*   Page 221

*Interior Gateway Protocol (IGP)*   Page 223

*Exterior Gateway Protocol (EGP)*   Page 223

*path-vector routing protocol*   Page 223

*classless*   Page 223

*Routing Information Protocol Version 1 (RIPv1)*   Page 223

*Interior Gateway Routing Protocol (IGRP)*   Page 223

*Routing Information Protocol Version 2 (RIPv2)*   Page 223

*Enhanced Interior Gateway Routing Protocol (EIGRP)*   Page 223

*Open Shortest Path First (OSPF)*   Page 223

*Intermediate System-to-Intermediate System (IS-IS)*   Page 223

*Border Gateway Protocol (BGP)*   Page 223

*classless routing protocols*   Page 223

*autonomous system (AS)*   Page 224

*multihomed*   Page 225

*single-homed*   Page 225

*distance*   Page 226

*metric*   Page 226

*cost*   Page 226

*periodic update*   Page 227

*neighbor*   Page 227

*variable-length subnet mask (VLSM)*   Page 228

*classless interdomain routing (CIDR)*   Page 228

*parent route*   Page 232

*child route*   Page 232

*ultimate route*   Page 232

*convergence*   Page 233

*route summarization*   Page 233

# Introduction (5.0.1.1)

The data networks that we use in our everyday lives to learn, play, and work range from small, local networks to large, global internetworks. A home network may have a router and two or more computers. At work, an organization may have multiple routers and switches servicing the data communication needs of hundreds, or even thousands, of end devices.

Routers forward packets by using information in the routing table. Routes to remote networks can be learned by the router in two ways: static routing and dynamic routing.

In a large network with numerous networks and subnets, configuring and maintaining static routes between these networks requires a great deal of administrative and operational overhead. This operational overhead is especially cumbersome when changes to the network occur, such as a failed link or a newly implemented subnet. The use of dynamic routing protocols can ease the burden of configuration and maintenance tasks, and it can give the network infrastructure scalability.

This chapter introduces dynamic routing protocols. It explores the benefits of using dynamic routing protocols, how different routing protocols are classified, and the metrics routing protocols use to determine the *best path* for network traffic. In addition, this chapter examines the characteristics of dynamic routing protocols and the differences between the various routing protocols. Network professionals must understand the different routing protocols available in order to make informed decisions about when to use static routing, dynamic routing, or both. They also need to know which dynamic routing protocol is most appropriate in a particular network environment.

### Class Activity 5.0.1.2: How Much Does This Cost

Refer to *Scaling Networks v6 Labs & Study Guide* and the online course to complete this activity.

This modeling activity illustrates the network concept of routing cost.

You will be a member of a team of five students who travel routes to complete the activity scenarios. Each group will be required to have one digital camera or any device that has a camera, a stopwatch, and the provided student file for this activity. One person will function as the photographer and event recorder, as selected by each group. The remaining four team members will actively participate in the scenarios below.

A school or university classroom, hallway, outdoor track area, school parking lot, or any other location can serve as the venue for these activities.

### Activity 1

The tallest person in the group establishes a start and finish line by marking 15 steps from start to finish, indicating the distance of the team route. Each student will take 15 steps from the start line toward the finish line and then stop on the 15th step. No further steps are allowed.

**Note:** Not all of the students may reach the same distance from the start line due to their height and stride differences. The photographer will take a group picture of the entire team's final locations after taking the 15 steps required.

### Activity 2

A new start and finish line will be established; however, this time, a longer distance for the route will be established than the distance specified in Activity 1. No maximum steps are to be used as a basis for creating this particular route. One at a time, students will walk the new route from beginning to end twice.

Each team member will count the steps taken to complete the route. The recorder will time each student and at the end of each team member's route, record the time that it took to complete the full route and how many steps were taken, as recounted by each team member and recorded on the team's student file.

After both activities have been completed, teams will use the digital picture taken for Activity 1 and their recorded data from Activity 2 file to answer the reflection questions.

Group answers can be discussed as a class, time permitting.

# Dynamic Routing Protocols (5.1)

Routers can learn about remote network by using static routing or dynamic routing. In this section you will learn about the features and characteristics of dynamic routing protocols.

## Types of Routing Protocols (5.1.1)

In this topic you will learn about the different types of routing protocols.

### Classifying Routing Protocols (5.1.1.1)

Dynamic routing protocols are used to facilitate the exchange of routing information between routers. A routing protocol is a set of processes, algorithms, and messages that are used to exchange routing information and populate the routing table with the routing protocol's choice of best paths. The purpose of dynamic routing protocols includes:

- Discovery of remote networks
- Maintaining up-to-date routing information
- Choosing the best paths to destination networks
- Finding a new best path if the current path is no longer available

Routing protocols can be classified into different groups according to their characteristics. Specifically, routing protocols can be classified by their:

- **Purpose**—*Interior Gateway Protocol (IGP)* or *Exterior Gateway Protocol (EGP)*
- **Operation**—Distance vector routing protocol, link-state routing protocol, or *path-vector routing protocol*
- **Behavior**—Classful (legacy) or *classless* protocol

Table 5-1 lists common IPv4 routing protocols and their characteristics.

**Table 5-1**   Comparing Routing Protocols

| Routing Protocol | Characteristics |
|---|---|
| *Routing Information Protocol Version 1 (RIPv1)* | Classful legacy distance vector IGP. Use RIPv2 instead of RIPv1. |
| *Interior Gateway Routing Protocol (IGRP)* | Classful legacy distance vector IGP. Deprecated since IOS 12.2. Replaced by EIGRP. |
| *Routing Information Protocol Version 2 (RIPv2)* | Classless distance vector IGP |
| *Enhanced Interior Gateway Routing Protocol (EIGRP)* | Classless distance vector IGP |
| *Open Shortest Path First (OSPF)* | Classless link-state IGP |
| *Intermediate System-to-Intermediate System (IS-IS)* | Classless link-state IGP |
| *Border Gateway Protocol (BGP)* | Classless path-vector EGP |

The classful routing protocols, RIPv1 and IGRP, are legacy protocols and no longer used. These routing protocols have evolved into the *classless routing protocols* RIPv2 and EIGRP, respectively. Link-state routing protocols are classless by nature.

Figure 5-1 shows a hierarchical view of dynamic routing protocol classification.

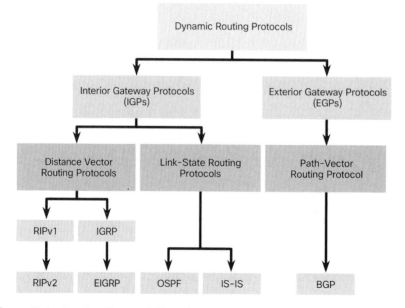

**Figure 5-1**    Routing Protocol Classification

## IGP and EGP Routing Protocols (5.1.1.2)

An *autonomous system (AS)*, also known as a routing domain, is a collection of routers under a common administration, such as a company or an organization. Typical examples of an AS are a company's internal network and an ISP's network.

The Internet is based on the AS concept; therefore, two types of routing protocols are required:

- **Interior Gateway Protocols (IGP)**—Used for routing within an AS. It is also referred to as intra-AS routing. Companies, organizations, and even service providers use an IGP on their internal networks. IGPs include RIP, EIGRP, OSPF, and IS-IS.

- **Exterior Gateway Protocols (EGP)**—Used for routing between ASes. It is also referred to as inter-AS routing. Service providers and large companies may interconnect using an EGP. BGP is the only currently viable EGP and is the official routing protocol used on the Internet.

**Note**

Because BGP is the only EGP available, the term EGP is rarely used; instead, most engineers simply refer to BGP.

The example in Figure 5-2 provides simple scenarios highlighting the deployment of IGPs, BGP, and static routing:

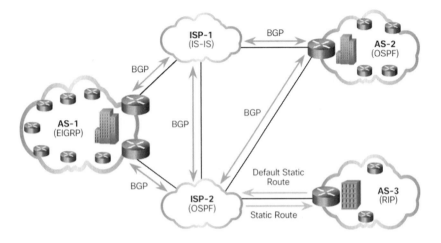

**Figure 5-2**   IGP versus EGP Routing Protocols

- **ISP-1**—This is an AS, and it uses IS-IS as the IGP. It interconnects with other autonomous systems and service providers, using BGP, to explicitly control how traffic is routed.

- **ISP-2**—This is an AS, and it uses OSPF as the IGP. It interconnects with other autonomous systems and service providers, using BGP, to explicitly control how traffic is routed.

- **AS-1**—This is a large organization, and it uses EIGRP as the IGP. Because it is *multihomed* (i.e., connects to two different service providers), it uses BGP to explicitly control how traffic enters and leaves the AS.

- **AS-2**—This is a medium-sized organization, and it uses OSPF as the IGP. It is also multihomed; therefore, it uses BGP to explicitly control how traffic enters and leaves the AS.

- **AS-3**—This is a small organization with older routers within the AS; it uses RIP as the IGP. BGP is not required because it is *single-homed* (that is, connects to one service provider). Instead, static routing is implemented between the AS and the service provider.

**Note**

BGP is beyond the scope of this course and is not discussed in detail.

## Distance Vector Routing Protocols (5.1.1.3)

*Distance vector* means that routes are advertised by providing two characteristics:

- *Distance*—Identifies how far it is to the destination network and is based on a *metric* such as the hop count, *cost*, bandwidth, or delay.

- **Vector**—Specifies the direction of the next-hop router or exit interface to reach the destination.

For example, in Figure 5-3, R1 knows that the distance to reach network 172.16.3.0/24 is one hop and that the direction is out of interface S0/0/0 toward R2.

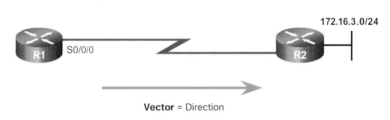

**Figure 5-3**   The Meaning of Distance Vector

A router using a distance vector routing protocol does not have the knowledge of the entire path to a destination network. Distance vector protocols use routers as sign posts along the path to the final destination. The only information a router knows about a remote network is the distance or metric to reach that network and which path or interface to use to get there.

There are four distance vector IPv4 IGPs:

- **RIPv1**—First-generation legacy protocol

- **RIPv2**—Simple distance vector routing protocol

- **IGRP**—First-generation Cisco proprietary protocol (obsolete and replaced by EIGRP)

- **EIGRP**—Advanced version of distance vector routing

## Link-State Routing Protocols (5.1.1.4)

In contrast to distance vector routing protocol operation, a router configured with a link-state routing protocol gathers information from all the other routers to create a complete view of the network topology.

To continue our analogy of sign posts, using a link-state routing protocol is like having a complete map of the network topology. The sign posts along the way from source to destination are not necessary because all link-state routers are using an identical map of the network. A link-state router uses the link-state information to create a topology map and to select the best path to all destination networks in the topology.

**Note**

Distance vector routing protocols do not have a map of the network topology as link-state routing protocols do.

Link-state routing protocols do not use *periodic updates*. In contrast, RIP-enabled routers send periodic updates of their routing information to their *neighbors*. After the routers have learned about all the required networks (achieved convergence), a link-state update is sent only when there is a change in the topology.

For example, the link-state update in Figure 5-4 is not sent until the 172.16.3.0 network goes down.

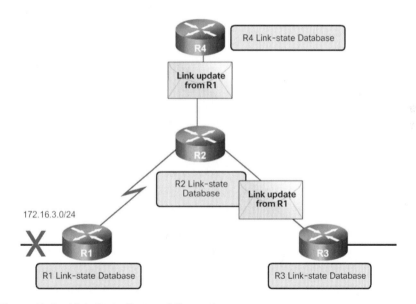

**Figure 5-4**   Link-State Protocol Operation

In the figure, the LAN link on R1 goes down. Immediately, R1 sent an LSU to its peer, R2. As illustrated in the figure, as soon as R2 received the LSU from R1, it immediately sent LSUs to R4 and R3. Each router then runs it SPF algorithm to determine whether any changes to their routing tables are required.

Link-state protocols work best in situations where:

- The network design is hierarchical, usually in large networks
- Fast adaptation to network changes is crucial
- The administrators are knowledgeable about the implementation and maintenance of a link-state routing protocol

There are two link-state IPv4 IGPs:

- OSPF—Popular standards-based routing protocol
- IS-IS—Popular in provider networks

## Classful Routing Protocols (5.1.1.5)

The biggest distinction between classful and classless routing protocols is in regard to the subnet mask. Classful routing protocols do not include subnet mask information in routing updates, whereas classless routing protocols do include subnet mask information.

The two IPv4 routing protocols originally developed are RIPv1 and IGRP. They were created when network addresses were allocated based on classes (that is, class A, B, or C). At that time, a routing protocol update did not include the subnet mask because the network mask could be determined based on the first octet of the network address.

> **Note**
>
> Only RIPv1 and IGRP are classful. All other IPv4 and IPv6 routing protocols are classless. There is no concept of classful addressing in IPv6.

The fact that RIPv1 and IGRP do not include subnet mask information in their updates means that they do not support *variable-length subnet mask (VLSM)* and *classless interdomain routing (CIDR)*.

Classful routing protocols also create problems in discontiguous networks. A *discontiguous network* (sometimes referred to as a noncontiguous network) is a network in which subnets from the same classful major network address are separated by a different classful network address.

To illustrate the shortcoming of classful routing, refer to the topology in Figure 5-5.

Notice that the LANs of R1 (172.16.1.0/24) and R3 (172.16.2.0/24) are both subnets of the same class B network (172.16.0.0/16). They are separated by different classful subnets (192.168.1.0/30 and 192.168.2.0/30) of the same class C networks (192.168.1.0/24 and 192.168.2.0/24).

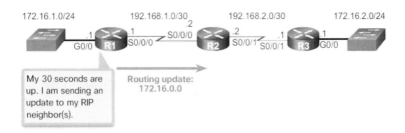

**Figure 5-5**   R1 Forwards a Classful Update to R2

When R1 forwards an update to R2, RIPv1 does not include the subnet mask information with the update; it only forwards the class B network address 172.16.0.0.

R2 receives and processes the update. It then creates and adds an entry for the class B 172.16.0.0/16 network in the routing table, as shown in Example 5-1.

**Example 5-1**   R2 Adds the Entry for 172.16.0.0 by Using R1

```
R2# show ip route | begin Gateway
Gateway of last resort is not set

R       172.16.0.0/16 [120/1] via 192.168.1.1, 00:00:11, Serial0/0/0
        192.168.1.0/24 is variably subnetted, 2 subnets, 2 masks
C          192.168.1.0/30 is directly connected, Serial0/0/0
L          192.168.1.2/32 is directly connected, Serial0/0/0
        192.168.2.0/24 is variably subnetted, 2 subnets, 2 masks
C          192.168.2.0/30 is directly connected, Serial0/0/1
L          192.168.2.2/32 is directly connected, Serial0/0/1
R2#
```

Figure 5-6 shows R3 forwarding an update to R2.

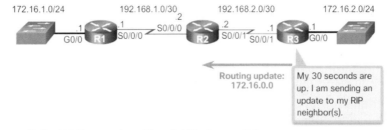

**Figure 5-6**   R3 Forwards a Classful Update to R2

The update also does not include the subnet mask information and therefore only forwards the classful network address 172.16.0.0.

R2 receives and processes the update and adds another entry for the classful network address 172.16.0.0/16 to its routing table. Example 5-2 displays the resulting routing table.

**Example 5-2**   R2 Adds the Entry for 172.16.0.0 by Using R3

```
R2# show ip route | begin Gateway
Gateway of last resort is not set

R        172.16.0.0/16 [120/1] via 192.168.2.1, 00:00:14, Serial0/0/1
                       [120/1] via 192.168.1.1, 00:00:16, Serial0/0/0
         192.168.1.0/24 is variably subnetted, 2 subnets, 2 masks
C           192.168.1.0/30 is directly connected, Serial0/0/0
L           192.168.1.2/32 is directly connected, Serial0/0/0
         192.168.2.0/24 is variably subnetted, 2 subnets, 2 masks
C           192.168.2.0/30 is directly connected, Serial0/0/1
L           192.168.2.2/32 is directly connected, Serial0/0/1
R2#
```

When there are two entries with identical metrics in the routing table, the router load balances between the two links. Load balancing is usually a good thing. However, because of the discontiguous 172.16.0.0/16 networks, load balancing has a negative effect.

Example 5-3 displays the result of connectivity tests using the **ping** and **traceroute** commands.

**Example 5-3**   Connectivity Fails

```
R2# ping 172.16.1.1
Type escape sequence to abort.
Sending 5, 100-byte ICMP Echos to 172.16.1.1, timeout is 2 seconds:
U.U.U
Success rate is 0 percent (0/5)
R2#
R2# traceroute 172.16.1.1
Type escape sequence to abort.
Tracing the route to 172.16.1.1
VRF info: (vrf in name/id, vrf out name/id)
  1 192.168.1.1 4 msec
    192.168.2.1 4 msec
    192.168.1.1 4 msec
R2#
```

The reason connectivity fails is because R2 sends one packet to R1 and the next pack to R3.

To correct the discontiguous network problem, configure a classless routing protocol.

## Classless Routing Protocols (5.1.1.6)

Modern networks use classless IPv4 routing protocols such as RIPv2, EIGRP, OSPF, and IS-IS. All these protocols include network addresses with subnet mask information in their routing updates. Classless routing protocols therefore support VLSM and CIDR.

IPv6 routing protocols are classless. All IPv6 routing protocols are considered classless because they include the prefix length with the IPv6 address. The distinction of being classful or classless only applies to IPv4 routing protocols.

Figure 5-7 shows how classless routing solves the discontiguous network issues.

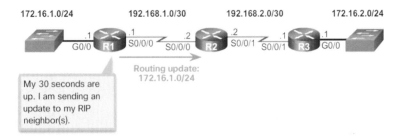

**Figure 5-7**    R1 Forwards a Classless Update to R2

In the figure, the classless protocol RIPv2 has been implemented on all three routers. When R1 forwards an update to R2, RIPv2 includes the subnet mask information with the update 172.16.1.0/24.

R2 receives, processes, and adds two entries in the routing table. Example 5-4 verifies the routing table of R2.

**Example 5-4**    R2 Adds the Entry for 172.16.0.0 by Using R1

```
R2# show ip route | begin Gateway
Gateway of last resort is not set
        172.16.0.0/24 is subnetted, 1 subnets
R         172.16.1.0 [120/1] via 192.168.1.1, 00:00:06, Serial0/0/0
      192.168.1.0/24 is variably subnetted, 2 subnets, 2 masks
C         192.168.1.0/30 is directly connected, Serial0/0/0
L         192.168.1.2/32 is directly connected, Serial0/0/0
R2#
```

The first line displays the classful network address 172.16.0.0 *parent route* with the /24 subnet mask of the update. The second entry displays the VLSM network address 172.16.1.0 *child route* with the exit and next-hop address. A route that includes an exit interface or next-hop IP address is called an *ultimate route*. Parent routes are never ultimate routes.

When R3 forwards an update to R2, RIPv2 includes the subnet mask information with the update 172.16.2.0/24, as shown in Figure 5-8.

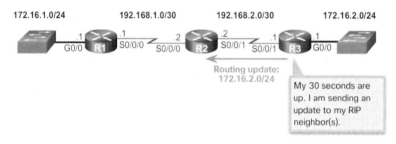

**Figure 5-8**   R3 Forwards a Classless Update to R2

R2 receives, processes, and adds the child route entry 172.16.2.0/24 under the parent route entry 172.16.0.0. Example 5-5 verifies the routing table of R2.

**Example 5-5**   R2 Adds the Entry for 172.16.0.0 by Using R3

```
R2# show ip route | begin Gateway
Gateway of last resort is not set

      172.16.0.0/24 is subnetted, 2 subnets
R         172.16.1.0 [120/1] via 192.168.1.1, 00:00:03, Serial0/0/0
R         172.16.2.0 [120/1] via 192.168.2.1, 00:00:03, Serial0/0/1
      192.168.1.0/24 is variably subnetted, 2 subnets, 2 masks
C         192.168.1.0/30 is directly connected, Serial0/0/0
L         192.168.1.2/32 is directly connected, Serial0/0/0
      192.168.2.0/24 is variably subnetted, 2 subnets, 2 masks
C         192.168.2.0/30 is directly connected, Serial0/0/1
L         192.168.2.2/32 is directly connected, Serial0/0/1
R2#
```

R2 is now aware of the subnetted networks.

Example 5-6 verifies connectivity to the R1 LAN interface.

**Example 5-6**   Connectivity Success

```
R2# ping 172.16.1.1
Type escape sequence to abort.
Sending 5, 100-byte ICMP Echos to 172.16.1.1, timeout is 2 seconds:
!!!!!
Success rate is 100 percent (5/5), round-trip min/avg/max = 12/14/16 ms
R2#
R2# traceroute 172.16.1.1
Type escape sequence to abort.
Tracing the route to 172.16.1.1
VRF info: (vrf in name/id, vrf out name/id)
  1 192.168.1.1 4 msec 4 msec *
R2#
```

## Routing Protocol Characteristics (5.1.1.7)

Table 5-2 lists characteristics of routing protocols.

**Table 5-2**   Routing Protocol Characteristics

| Routing Protocol Characteristics | Description |
| --- | --- |
| Speed of convergence | ■ Defines how quickly the routers exchange routing information and reach a state of consistent knowledge. <br> ■ The faster the convergence, the more preferable the protocol. <br> ■ Routing loops can occur when inconsistent routing tables are not updated due to slow *convergence* in a changing network. |
| Scalability | ■ Defines the size of a network that the routing protocol can support. <br> ■ A large network requires a scalable routing protocol. |
| Support VLSM | ■ Classful routing protocols cannot support VLSM. <br> ■ Classless routing protocols support VLSM and better *route summarization*. |
| Resource usage | ■ Defines the amount of memory space (RAM), CPU utilization, and link bandwidth utilization the routing protocol consumes. |
| Implementation and maintenance | ■ Describes the level of knowledge that is required to implement and maintain the network, based on the routing protocol deployed. |

Table 5-3 summarizes the characteristics of the routing protocols.

**Table 5-3**    Comparing Routing Protocols

| Characteristic | Distance Vector | | | Link State | | |
|---|---|---|---|---|---|---|
| | RIPv1 | RIPv2 | IGRP | EIGRP | OSPF | IS-IS |
| Speed of convergence | Slow | Slow | Slow | Fast | Fast | Fast |
| Scalability—size of network | Small | Small | Small | Large | Large | Large |
| Use of VLSM | No | Yes | No | Yes | Yes | Yes |
| Resource usage | Low | Low | Low | Medium | High | High |
| Implementation and maintenance | Simple | Simple | Simple | Complex | Complex | Complex |

## Routing Protocol Metrics (5.1.1.8)

There are cases when a routing protocol learns of more than one route to the same destination. To select the best path, the routing protocol must be able to evaluate and decide between the available paths. This is accomplished through the use of routing metrics.

A metric is a measurable value that is assigned by the routing protocol to different routes, based on the usefulness of that route. In situations where there are multiple paths to the same remote network, the routing metrics are used to determine the overall "cost" of a path, from source to destination. Routing protocols determine the best path based on the route with the lowest cost.

Different routing protocols use different metrics. Table 5-4 lists some dynamic protocols and the metrics they use.

**Table 5-4**    Routing Protocol Metrics

| Routing Protocol | Metric |
|---|---|
| RIP | ■ The metric is based on hop count. <br> ■ Hop count identifies the number of routers to the destination network. <br> ■ It does not take bandwidth into consideration. <br> ■ RIP uses the *Bellman-Ford algorithm* to determine the best paths. |

| Routing Protocol | Metric |
|---|---|
| OSPF | ■ The metric is based on cost.<br><br>■ OSPF uses *Dijkstra's algorithm* or the *shortest path first (SPF) algorithm* to determine best paths. |
| EIGRP | ■ The metric is based on a composite metric consisting of minimum bandwidth and delays.<br><br>■ Optionally, load and reliability can also be included.<br><br>■ EIGRP uses the *Diffusing Update Algorithm (DUAL)* to determine the best path. |

The metric used by one routing protocol is not comparable to the metric used by another. As a result, two different routing protocols might choose different paths to the same destination.

For example, PC1 is pinging PC2 in the example in Figure 5-9. How would the packets be routed if RIP were configured? How would the packets be routed if OSPF were configured?

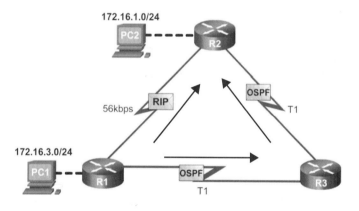

RIP chooses best path based on hop count.
OSPF chooses best path based on bandwidth.

**Figure 5-9**  Comparing RIP and OSPF Updates

The metric for RIP is the lowest hop count. Therefore, RIP would choose the path with the smallest number of hops. In this example, packets would flow from R1 directly to R2. However, this is a very slow link of 56 kbps. RIP cannot take into account bandwidth link.

The metric for OSPF is the lowest cost, which is based on accumulated bandwidth. Higher-bandwidth links are assigned a low cost value, while slower links are assigned a high cost value. Therefore, in this example, OSPF would choose the path with the lowest cost. Packets from PC1 would flow to R3 and then to R2 because the T1 links provide bandwidth up to 1.546 Mbps.

**Interactive Graphic**

**Activity 5.1.1.9: Classify Dynamic Routing Protocols**

Refer to the online course to complete this activity.

**Interactive Graphic**

**Activity 5.1.1.10: Compare Routing Protocols**

Refer to the online course to complete this activity.

**Interactive Graphic**

**Activity 5.1.1.11: Match the Metric to the Protocol**

Refer to the online course to complete this activity.

# Distance Vector Dynamic Routing (5.2)

The first routing protocols to be developed were distance vector routing protocols. RIPv1 and IGRP were created to provide routing functions for classful networks. However, as classful gave way to classless routing, newer protocols such as RIPv2 and EIGRP were developed.

In this section you will learn how distance vector routing protocols operate.

## Distance Vector Fundamentals (5.2.1)

In this topic you will learn how dynamic routing protocols achieve convergence.

### Dynamic Routing Protocol Operation (5.2.1.1)

All routing protocols are designed to learn about remote networks and to quickly adapt whenever there is a change in the topology. The method that a routing protocol uses to accomplish this depends upon the algorithm it uses and the operational characteristics of that protocol.

In general, the operations of a dynamic routing protocol can be described as follows:

1. The router sends and receives routing messages on its interfaces.

2. The router shares routing messages and routing information with other routers that are using the same routing protocol.

3. Routers exchange routing information to learn about remote networks.

4. When a router detects a topology change, the routing protocol can advertise this change to other routers.

## Cold Start (5.2.1.2)

All routing protocols follow the same patterns of operation. To help illustrate this, consider a scenario in which three interconnected routers are all running RIPv2.

When a router powers up, it knows nothing about the network topology. It does not even know that there are devices on the other end of its links. The only information a router has is from its own saved configuration file, stored in NVRAM. After a router boots successfully, the router discovers its own *directly connected networks*.

Figure 5-10 shows simplified routing tables after the initial discovery of connected networks for each router.

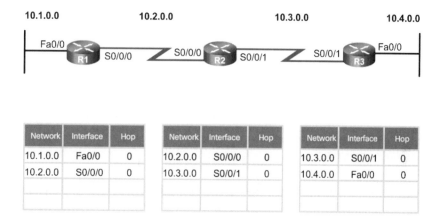

**Figure 5-10**   Directly Connected Networks Detected

Notice how the routers proceed through the bootup process and then discover any directly connected networks and subnet masks. This information is added to their routing tables as follows:

- R1 adds the 10.1.0.0 network available through interface FastEthernet 0/0, and 10.2.0.0 is available through interface Serial 0/0/0.

- R2 adds the 10.2.0.0 network available through interface Serial 0/0/0, and 10.3.0.0 is available through interface Serial 0/0/1.

- R3 adds the 10.3.0.0 network available through interface Serial 0/0/1, and 10.4.0.0 is available through interface FastEthernet 0/0.

With this initial information, the routers then proceed to find additional route sources for their routing tables.

## Network Discovery (5.2.1.3)

After initial bootup and discovery, the routing table is updated with all directly connected networks and the interfaces those networks reside on.

Because RIPv2 is configured, the router begins exchanging routing updates to learn about any other remote routes. Updates contain the entries in each router's routing table. The initial updates contain only each router's directly connected networks.

Upon receiving an update, a router checks it for new network information. It adds all network entries that are not currently listed in its routing table.

Table 5-5 summarizes the updates exchanged by R1, R2, and R3 during initial convergence.

**Table 5-5**   Initial RIPv2 Updates Between R1, R2, and R3

| Router | Update Information |
| --- | --- |
| R1 | ■ Sends an update about network 10.1.0.0 out the Serial 0/0/0 interface. |
| | ■ Sends an update about network 10.2.0.0 out the FastEthernet 0/0 interface. |
| | ■ Receives an update from R2 about network 10.3.0.0 and increments the hop count by 1. |
| | ■ Stores network 10.3.0.0 in the routing table with a metric of 1. |
| R2 | ■ Sends an update about network 10.3.0.0 out the Serial 0/0/0 interface. |
| | ■ Sends an update about network 10.2.0.0 out the Serial 0/0/1 interface. |
| | ■ Receives an update from R1 about network 10.1.0.0 and increments the hop count by 1. |
| | ■ Stores network 10.1.0.0 in the routing table with a metric of 1. |
| | ■ Receives an update from R3 about network 10.4.0.0 and increments the hop count by 1. |
| | ■ Stores network 10.4.0.0 in the routing table with a metric of 1. |
| R3 | ■ Sends an update about network 10.4.0.0 out the Serial 0/0/1 interface. |
| | ■ Sends an update about network 10.3.0.0 out the FastEthernet 0/0 interface. |
| | ■ Receives an update from R2 about network 10.2.0.0 and increments the hop count by 1. |
| | ■ Stores network 10.2.0.0 in the routing table with a metric of 1. |

Figure 5-11 shows the routing tables after the initial exchange of RIPv2 updates for each router.

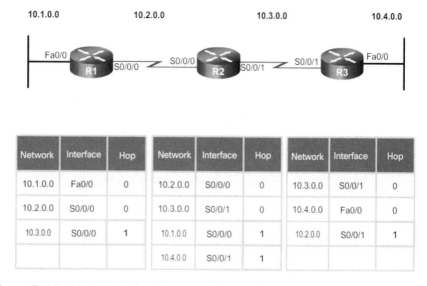

**Figure 5-11**   Initial Exchange Between Directly Connected Routers

After this first round of update exchanges, each router knows about the connected networks of its directly connected neighbors.

However, notice that R1 does not yet know about 10.4.0.0 and that R3 does not yet know about 10.1.0.0. Full knowledge and a converged network do not take place until there is another exchange of routing information.

## Exchanging the Routing Information (5.2.1.4)

At this point the routers have knowledge about their own directly connected networks and about the connected networks of their immediate neighbors. Continuing the journey toward convergence, the routers exchange the next round of periodic updates. Each router again checks the updates for new information.

Based on the topology in Figure 5-11, each router continues the convergence process by sending and receiving updates.

Table 5-6 summarize the next updates exchanged by R1, R2, and R3 during convergence.

**Table 5-6**   RIPv2 Updates Between R1, R2, and R3

| Router | Update Information |
| --- | --- |
| R1 | ■ Sends an update about network 10.1.0.0 out the Serial 0/0/0 interface. |
| | ■ Sends an update about networks 10.2.0.0 and 10.3.0.0 out the FastEthernet 0/0 interface. |
| | ■ Receives an update from R2 about network 10.4.0.0 and increments the hop count by 1. |
| | ■ Stores network 10.4.0.0 in the routing table with a metric of 2. |
| | ■ The same update from R2 contains information about network 10.3.0.0, with a metric of 1. There is no change; therefore, the routing information remains the same. |
| R2 | ■ Sends an update about networks 10.3.0.0 and 10.4.0.0 out the Serial 0/0/0 interface. |
| | ■ Sends an update about networks 10.1.0.0 and 10.2.0.0 out the Serial 0/0/1 interface. |
| | ■ Receives an update from R1 about network 10.1.0.0. There is no change; therefore, the routing information remains the same. |
| | ■ Receives an update from R3 about network 10.4.0.0. There is no change; therefore, the routing information remains the same. |
| R3 | ■ Sends an update about network 10.4.0.0 out the Serial 0/0/1 interface. |
| | ■ Sends an update about networks 10.2.0.0 and 10.3.0.0 out the FastEthernet 0/0 interface. |
| | ■ Receives an update from R2 about network 10.1.0.0 and increments the hop count by 1. |
| | ■ Stores network 10.1.0.0 in the routing table with a metric of 2. |
| | ■ The same update from R2 contains information about network 10.2.0.0, with a metric of 1. There is no change; therefore, the routing information remains the same. |

Figure 5-12 shows the routing tables after R1, R2, and R3 send the latest RIPv2 updates to their neighbors.

Distance vector routing protocols typically implement a routing loop-prevention technique known as *split horizon*. Split horizon prevents information from being sent out the same interface from which it was received. For example, R2 does not send an update containing the network 10.1.0.0 out of Serial 0/0/0 because R2 learned about network 10.1.0.0 through Serial 0/0/0.

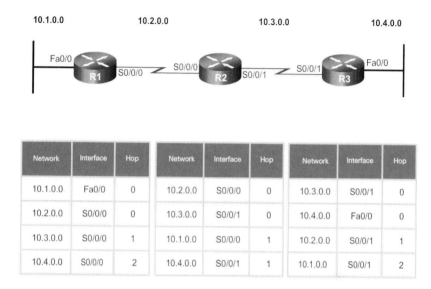

**Figure 5-12**    Next Update—All Routing Tables Converged

After routers within a network have converged, a router can then use the information within the routing table to determine the best path to reach a destination. Different routing protocols have different ways of calculating the best path. However, it is always based on the lower metric value.

## Achieving Convergence (5.2.1.5)

Figure 5-12 displays the routing tables after convergence, which means all routers have complete and accurate information about the entire network.

Convergence is both collaborative and independent. The routers share information with each other but must independently calculate the impacts of the topology change on their own routes. Because they develop an agreement with the new topology independently, they are said to *converge* on this consensus.

Convergence properties include the speed of propagation of routing information and the calculation of optimal paths. The speed of propagation refers to the amount of time it takes for routers in the network to forward routing information.

*Convergence time* is the time it takes routers to share information, calculate best paths, and update their routing tables. A network is not completely operable until the network has converged; therefore, most networks require short convergence times.

Routing protocols are often rated based on the speed to convergence. The faster the convergence, the better the routing protocol. RIP is an older protocol and slow to converge. EIGRP and OSPF are more modern routing protocols that converge more quickly.

**Packet Tracer 5.2.1.6: Investigating Convergence**

This activity will help you identify important information in routing tables and witness the process of network convergence.

# Distance Vector Routing Protocol Operation (5.2.2)

In this topic you will learn about the algorithm used by distance vector routing protocols to determine the best path.

## Distance Vector Technologies (5.2.2.1)

Distance vector routing protocols share updates between neighbors. Neighbors, or peers as they are often called, are routers that share a link and are configured to use the same routing protocol.

A router is only aware of the network addresses of its own interfaces and the remote network addresses it can reach through its neighbors. Routers using distance vector routing are not aware of the network topology.

Older routing protocols are not as efficient as the newer protocols. For instance, RIPv1 broadcasts periodic updates to the all-IPv4 address 255.255.255.255 every 30 seconds—even if the topology has not changed.

The broadcasting of periodic updates is very inefficient because the updates consume bandwidth and network router CPU resources. These updates also consume the resources of connected switches and hosts because they also have to process these broadcast message.

RIPv2 and EIGRP address this inefficiency by using *multicast addresses* to reach only specific neighbor routers. EIGRP can also use a unicast message to reach one specific neighbor router. In addition, EIGRP sends updates only when needed instead of periodically.

The two modern IPv4 distance vector routing protocols are RIPv2 and EIGRP. RIPv1 and IGRP are listed only for historical accuracy.

## Distance Vector Algorithm (5.2.2.2)

At the core of the distance vector protocol is the routing algorithm. The algorithm is used to calculate the best paths and then send that information to the neighbors.

The algorithm used for the routing protocols defines the following processes:

- A mechanism for sending and receiving routing information

- A mechanism for calculating the best paths and installing routes in the routing table

- A mechanism for detecting and reacting to topology changes

In Figure 5-13, R1 and R2 are configured with the RIP routing protocol. The algorithm sends and receives updates.

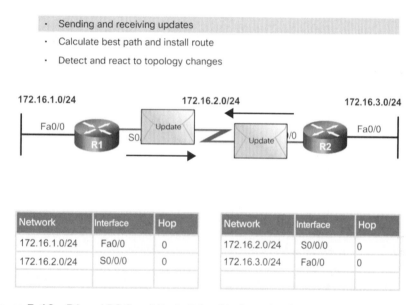

**Figure 5-13**   R1 and R2 Send Each Other Updates for Connected LANs

Both R1 and R2 then glean new information from the update. In this case, each router learns about a new network. The algorithm on each router makes its calculations independently and updates the routing table with the new information, as shown in Figure 5-14.

When the LAN on R2 goes down, the algorithm constructs a triggered update and sends it to R1. R1 then removes the network from the routing table, as shown in Figure 5-15.

Different routing protocols use different algorithms to install routes in the routing table, send updates to neighbors, and make path determination decisions.

- Sending and receiving updates
- Calculate best path and install route
- Detect and react to topology changes

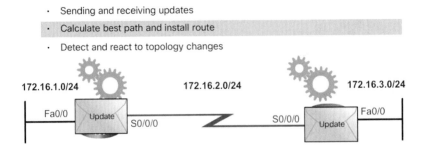

| Network | Interface | Hop |
|---|---|---|
| 172.16.1.0/24 | Fa0/0 | 0 |
| 172.16.2.0/24 | S0/0/0 | 0 |
| | | |

| Network | Interface | Hop |
|---|---|---|
| 172.16.2.0/24 | S0/0/0 | 0 |
| 172.16.3.0/24 | Fa0/0 | 0 |
| **172.16.1.0/24** | S0/0/0 | 1 |

**Figure 5-14**    R1 and R2 Install a Route in the Routing Table

- Sending and receiving updates
- Calculate best path and install route
- Detect and react to topology changes

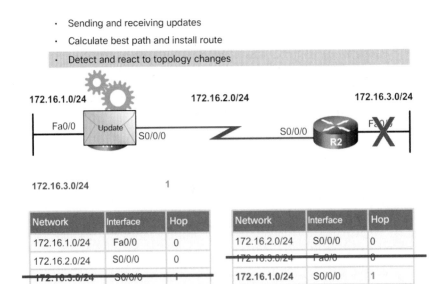

172.16.3.0/24                    1

| Network | Interface | Hop |
|---|---|---|
| 172.16.1.0/24 | Fa0/0 | 0 |
| 172.16.2.0/24 | S0/0/0 | 0 |
| ~~172.16.3.0/24~~ | ~~S0/0/0~~ | ~~1~~ |

| Network | Interface | Hop |
|---|---|---|
| 172.16.2.0/24 | S0/0/0 | 0 |
| ~~172.16.3.0/24~~ | ~~Fa0/0~~ | ~~0~~ |
| 172.16.1.0/24 | S0/0/0 | 1 |

**Figure 5-15**    R2 Sends an Update to R1 to Remove a Route from the Routing Table

Table 5-7 summarizes the two algorithms used by distance vector routing protocols.

**Table 5-7**   Distance Vector Routing Algorithms

| Algorithm | Description |
|---|---|
| Bellman-Ford algorithm | ■ Used by RIPv1 and RIPv2.<br>■ It is based on two algorithms developed in 1958 and 1956 by Richard Bellman and Lester Ford, Jr. |
| Diffusing Update Algorithm (DUAL) routing algorithm | ■ Used by IGRP and EIGRP.<br>■ Developed by Dr. J.J. Garcia-Luna-Aceves at SRI International. |

**Interactive Graphic**

**Activity 5.2.2.3: Identify Distance Vector Terminology**

Refer to the online course to complete this activity.

# Types of Distance Vector Routing Protocols (5.2.3)

In this topic you will learn about the types of distance-vector routing protocols.

## Routing Information Protocol (5.2.3.1)

Routing Information Protocol Version 1 (RIPv1) was a first-generation routing protocol for IPv4. Originally specified in RFC 1058, it is a classful routing protocol that is easy to configure, making it a good choice for small networks. Its disadvantages include the fact that it is classful, and it broadcasts routing updates to all hosts every 30 seconds.

In 1993, RIPv1 was updated to RIP Version 2 (RIPv2), which added the improvements listed in Table 5-8.

**Table 5-8**   RIPv2 Improvements

| Improvement | Description |
|---|---|
| Classless routing protocol | ■ Supports VLSM and CIDR because it includes the subnet mask in the routing updates. |
| Increased efficiency | ■ Forwards updates to multicast address 224.0.0.9 instead of the broadcast address 255.255.255.255. |
| Reduced routing entries | ■ Supports manual route summarization on any interface. |
| Secure | ■ Supports an authentication mechanism to secure routing table updates between neighbors. |

Both RIPv1 and RIPv2 use hop count as the metric for path selection. Also, both deem a hop count greater than 15 hops as infinite. An infinite route is considered too far, and the 15th hop router does not propagate the routing update to the next router.

Table 5-9 summarizes the differences between RIPv1 and RIPv2.

**Table 5-9**   RIPv1 versus RIPv2

| Characteristics and Features | RIPv1 | RIPv2 |
|---|---|---|
| Metric | Both use hop count as a simple metric. The maximum number of hops is 15. | |
| Updates forwarded to address | 255.255.255.255 | 224.0.0.9 |
| Supports VLSM | No | Yes |
| Supports CIDR | No | Yes |
| Supports summarization | No | Yes |
| Supports authentication | No | Yes |

RIP updates are encapsulated into a UDP segment, with both source and destination port numbers set to UDP port 520.

In 1997, an IPv6-enabled version of RIP was released. *RIPng* is based on RIPv2. It still has a 15-hop limitation, and the *administrative distance* is 120.

## Enhanced Interior-Gateway Routing Protocol (5.2.3.2)

Interior Gateway Routing Protocol (IGRP), developed in 1984, was the first proprietary IPv4 routing protocol developed by Cisco. It had the following design characteristics:

- Bandwidth, delay, load, and reliability are used to create a composite metric.

- Routing updates are broadcast every 90 seconds, by default.

- It has a maximum limit of 255 hops.

In 1992, IGRP was replaced by Enhanced IGRP (EIGRP). Like RIPv2, EIGRP also introduced support for VLSM and CIDR. EIGRP increases efficiency, reduces routing updates, and supports secure message exchange.

Table 5-10 summarizes the differences between IGRP and EIGRP.

**Table 5-10**   IGRP versus EIGRP

| Characteristics and Features | IGRP | EIGRP |
|---|---|---|
| Metric | Both use a composite metric consisting of bandwidth and delay. Reliability and load can also be included in the metric calculation. | |
| Updates forwarded to address | 255.255.255.255 | 224.0.0.10 |
| Supports VLSM | No | Yes |
| Supports CIDR | No | Yes |
| Supports summarization | No | Yes |
| Supports authentication | No | Yes |

EIGRP also introduced the following:

- *Bounded triggered updates*—EIGRP does not send periodic updates. Whenever a change occurs, only routing table changes are propagated. This reduces the amount of load the routing protocol places on the network. *Bounded triggered updates* means that EIGRP only sends to the neighbors that need it. It uses less bandwidth, especially in large networks with many routes.

- *Hello keepalive mechanism*—A small hello message is periodically exchanged to maintain adjacencies with neighboring routers. This requires a very low usage of network resources during normal operation compared to periodic updates.

- **Maintains a topology table**—EIGRP maintains all the routes received from neighbors (not only the best paths) in a topology table. DUAL can insert backup routes into the EIGRP topology table.

- **Rapid convergence**—In most cases, EIGRP is the fastest IGP to converge because it maintains alternate routes, enabling almost instantaneous convergence. If a primary route fails, the router can use the already identified alternate route. The switchover to the alternate route is immediate and does not involve interaction with other routers.

- **Multiple network layer protocol support**—EIGRP uses protocol-dependent modules (PDM), which means it is the only protocol to include support for protocols other than IPv4 and IPv6, such as legacy IPX and AppleTalk.

**Interactive Graphic**

**Activity 5.2.3.3: Compare RIP and EIGRP**

Refer to the online course to complete this activity.

**Packet Tracer 5.2.3.4: Comparing RIP and EIGRP Path Selection**

PCA and PCB need to communicate. The path that the data takes between these end devices can travel through R1, R2, and R3, or it can travel through R4 and R5. The process by which routers select the best path depends on the routing protocol. In this packet tracer, you will examine the behavior of two distance vector routing protocols, EIGRP and RIPv2.

# Link-State Dynamic Routing (5.3)

Link-state routing protocols such as OSPF and IS-IS were developed as classless and faster-converging routing alternatives to RIP.

In this section you will learn how link-state protocols operate.

## Link-State Routing Protocol Operation (5.3.1)

In this topic you will learn about the algorithm used by link-state routing protocols to determine the best path.

### Shortest Path First Protocols (5.3.1.1)

Link-state routing protocols are also known as shortest path first protocols and are built around Edsger Dijkstra's shortest path first (SPF) algorithm. The SPF algorithm is discussed in more detail in a later section.

The IPv4 link-state routing protocols include the very popular OSPF and the less popular IS-IS routing protocol.

> **Note**
>
> Although both OSPF and IS-IS are link-state routing protocols, most of the discussion and examples are based on OSPF.

Link-state routing protocols appear to be more complex than their distance vector counterparts. However, their basic functionality and configuration are comparable.

### Dijkstra's Algorithm (5.3.1.2)

All link-state routing protocols apply Dijkstra's algorithm, commonly referred to as the shortest path first (SPF) algorithm, to calculate the best path route. This algorithm uses accumulated costs along each path, from source to destination, to determine the total cost of a route.

For example, in Figure 5-16, each path is labeled with an arbitrary value for cost. The cost of the shortest path for R2 to send packets to the LAN attached to R3 is 27.

Each router determines its own cost to each destination in the topology. In other words, each router calculates the SPF algorithm and determines the cost from its own perspective.

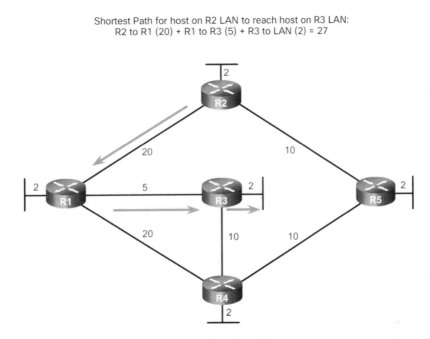

Shortest Path for host on R2 LAN to reach host on R3 LAN:
R2 to R1 (20) + R1 to R3 (5) + R3 to LAN (2) = 27

**Figure 5-16**   Dijkstra's Shortest Path First Algorithm

---

**Note**

The focus of this section is on cost, which is determined by the *SPF tree*. For this reason, the graphics throughout this section show the connections of the SPF tree, not the topology. All links are represented with solid black lines.

---

## SPF Example (5.3.1.3)

Refer to the link-state topology in Figure 5-17 to determine how different routers would calculate the SPF routes.

Table 5-11 displays the shortest path and the accumulated cost to reach the identified destination networks from the perspective of R1.

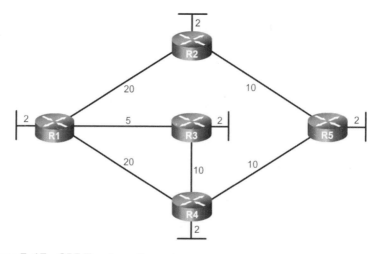

**Figure 5-17**   SPF Topology Example

**Table 5-11**   R1 SPF Tree

| Destination | Shortest Path | Cost |
|---|---|---|
| R2 LAN | R1 → R2 | 22 |
| R3 LAN | R1 → R3 | 7 |
| R4 LAN | R1 → R3 → R4 | 17 |
| R5 LAN | R1 → R3 → R4 → R5 | 27 |

The shortest path is not necessarily the path with the smallest number of hops. For example, look at the path to the R5 LAN. It might be assumed that R1 would send directly to R4 instead of to R3. However, the cost to reach R4 directly (22) is higher than the cost to reach R4 through R3 (17).

The shortest paths for the other routers to reach each of the LANs are shown in Tables 5-12 through 5-15.

**Table 5-12**   R2 SPF Tree

| Destination | Shortest Path | Cost |
|---|---|---|
| ■ R1 LAN | ■ R2 → R1 | ■ 22 |
| ■ R3 LAN | ■ R2 → R1 → R3 | ■ 27 |
| ■ R4 LAN | ■ R2 → R5 → R4 | ■ 22 |
| ■ R5 LAN | ■ R2 → R5 | ■ 12 |

**Table 5-13**   R3 SPF Tree

| Destination | Shortest Path | Cost |
|---|---|---|
| ▪ R1 LAN | ▪ R3 → R1 | ▪ 7 |
| ▪ R2 LAN | ▪ R3 → R1 → R2 | ▪ 27 |
| ▪ R4 LAN | ▪ R3 → R4 | ▪ 12 |
| ▪ R5 LAN | ▪ R3 → R4 → R5 | ▪ 22 |

**Table 5-14**   R4 SPF Tree

| Destination | Shortest Path | Cost |
|---|---|---|
| ▪ R1 LAN | ▪ R4 → R3 → R1 | ▪ 17 |
| ▪ R2 LAN | ▪ R4 → R5 → R2 | ▪ 22 |
| ▪ R3 LAN | ▪ R4 → R3 | ▪ 12 |
| ▪ R5 LAN | ▪ R4 → R5 | ▪ 12 |

**Table 5-15**   R5 SPF Tree

| Destination | Shortest Path | Cost |
|---|---|---|
| ▪ R1 LAN | ▪ R5 → R4 → R3 → R1 | ▪ 27 |
| ▪ R2 LAN | ▪ R5 → R2 | ▪ 12 |
| ▪ R3 LAN | ▪ R5 → R4 → R3 | ▪ 22 |
| ▪ R4 LAN | ▪ R5 → R4 | ▪ 12 |

# Link-State Updates (5.3.2)

In this topic you will learn how the link-state routing protocol uses information sent in a link-state update.

## Link-State Routing Process (5.3.2.1)

So exactly how does a link-state routing protocol work? With link-state routing protocols, a link is an interface on a router. Information about the state of such links is known as *link-state information*.

All routers in an *OSPF area* complete the following generic link-state routing process to reach a state of convergence:

1. An OSPF router first learns about its directly connected networks by detecting interfaces in the "up" state.

2. The router attempts to connect to other *link-state routers* by exchanging *hello packets*.

3. When a neighbor is detected, the router builds a *link-state packet (LSP)* containing the state of each directly connected link, including its *router ID*, link type, and bandwidth.

4. The router floods the LSPs to all neighbors using the *all OSPF routers* multicast address 224.0.0.5. Neighbors receive and store the LSPs in a *link-state database (LSDB)*. Neighbors then flood the LSPs to their neighbors. The process continues until all routers in the area have received the LSPs.

5. Each router uses the LSDB to build its SPF tree. The SPF algorithm is used to construct the map of the topology and to determine the best path to each network. With the resulting SPF tree, each router has a complete map of all destinations in the topology and the routes to reach them.

> **Note**
>
> This process is the same for both OSPF for IPv4 and OSPF for IPv6. The examples in this section refer to OSPF for IPv4.

## Link and Link-State (5.3.2.2)

Let's examine the link-state routing process in more detail. The first step in the link-state routing process is that each router discovers its own directly connected networks. When a router interface is configured with an IP address and subnet mask, the interface becomes part of that network.

Refer to the topology in Figure 5-18.

For purposes of this discussion, assume that R1 was previously configured and had full connectivity to all neighbors. However, R1 lost power briefly and had to restart. During bootup, R1 loads the saved startup configuration file. As the previously configured interfaces become active, R1 learns about its own directly connected networks. Regardless of the routing protocols used, these directly connected networks are now entries in the routing table.

As with distance vector protocols and static routes, the interface must be properly configured with an IPv4 address and subnet mask, and the link must be in the up state before the link-state routing protocol can learn about a link.

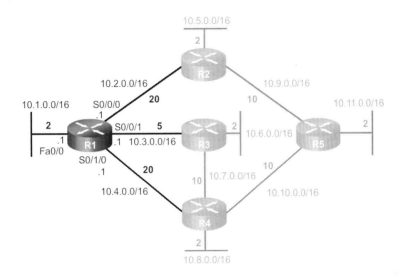

**Figure 5-18**   R1 Links

Figure 5-18 shows R1 linked to four directly connected networks:

■ FastEthernet 0/0—10.1.0.0/16

■ Serial 0/0/0—10.2.0.0/16

■ Serial 0/0/1—10.3.0.0/16

■ Serial 0/1/0—10.4.0.0/16

Figure 5-19 shows the link-state information for Fa0/0.

Notice that the link-state information includes the following:

■ The interface's IPv4 address and subnet mask

■ The type of network, such as Ethernet (broadcast) or serial point-to-point link

■ The cost of the link

■ Any neighbor routers on the link

Figure 5-20 shows the link information for S0/0/0.

Figure 5-21 shows the link information for S0/0/1.

Figure 5-22 shows the link information for S0/1/0.

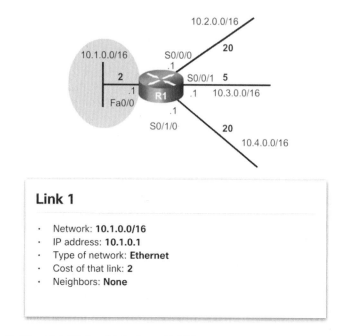

### Link 1

- · Network: **10.1.0.0/16**
- · IP address: **10.1.0.1**
- · Type of network: **Ethernet**
- · Cost of that link: **2**
- · Neighbors: **None**

**Figure 5-19**   Link State of Interface Fa0/0

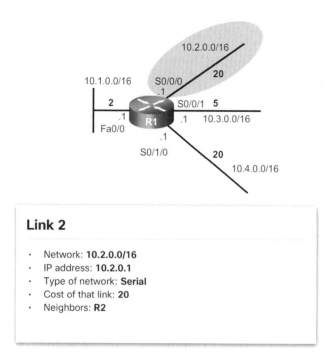

### Link 2

- · Network: **10.2.0.0/16**
- · IP address: **10.2.0.1**
- · Type of network: **Serial**
- · Cost of that link: **20**
- · Neighbors: **R2**

**Figure 5-20**   Link State of Interface S0/0/0

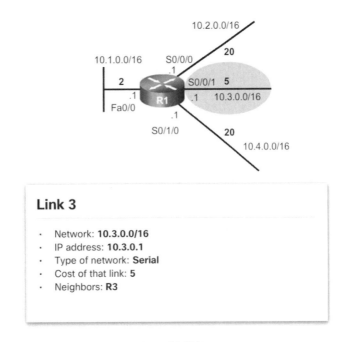

Figure 5-21   Link State of Interface S0/0/1

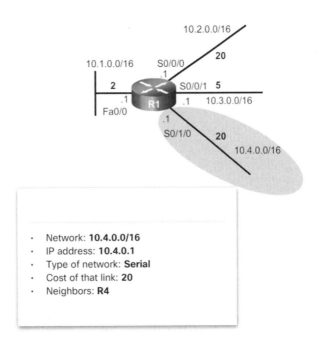

Figure 5-22   Link State of Interface S0/1/0

> **Note**
>
> Cisco's implementation of OSPF specifies the OSPF routing metric as the cost of the link based on the bandwidth of the outgoing interface. For the purposes of this chapter, we use arbitrary cost values to simplify the demonstration.

## Say Hello (5.3.2.3)

In the second step in the link-state routing process, each router is responsible for meeting its neighbors on directly connected networks. For example, OSPF-enabled routers use hello packets to discover any other OSPF-enabled neighbors on their links.

Figure 5-23 shows R1 beginning the link-state neighbor discovery process with hello packets.

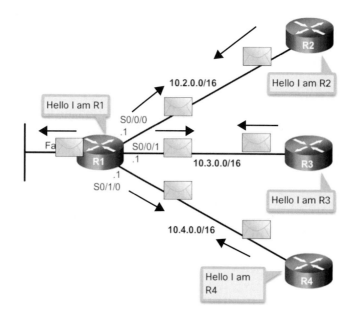

**Figure 5-23**   Neighbor Discovery—Hello Packets

R1 sends hello packets out its links (interfaces) to discover any neighbors. R2, R3, and R4 are OSPF-enabled routers and therefore reply to these hello packet with their own hello packets.

There are no neighbors connected to FastEthernet 0/0 interface. Therefore, R1 does not continue with the link-state routing process steps for this link.

When two link-state routers learn that they are neighbors, they form an *adjacency*. These small hello packets continue to be exchanged between two adjacent neighbors and serve as a keepalive function to monitor the state of the neighbor. If a router stops receiving hello packets from a neighbor, that neighbor is considered unreachable, and the adjacency is broken.

## Building the Link-State Packet (5.3.2.4)

In the third step in the link-state routing process, each router builds a link-state packet (LSP) that contains the state of each directly connected link.

After a router has established its adjacencies, it can build its LSP, which contains the link-state information about its links. A simplified version of the LSP from R1 displayed in Figure 5-24 would contain the following:

- R1, Ethernet network 10.1.0.0/16, cost = 2

- R1 → R2, serial point-to-point network; 10.2.0.0/16, cost = 20

- R1 → R3, serial point-to-point network; 10.3.0.0/16, cost = 5

- R1 → R4, serial point-to-point network; 10.4.0.0/16, cost = 20

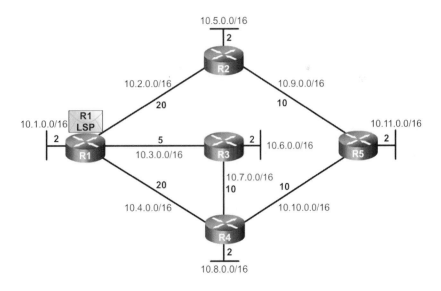

**Figure 5-24**   Building the LSP

## Flooding the LSP (5.3.2.5)

In the fourth step in the link-state routing process, each router floods the LSP to all neighbors, which then store all LSPs received in a database. Figure 5-25 shows R1 flooding its LSPs.

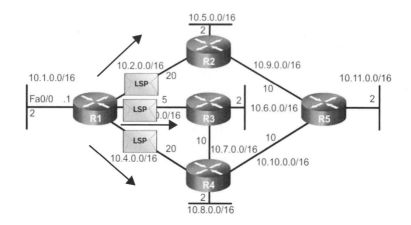

**Figure 5-25**   R1 Flooding LSPs

The other routers also send their link-state information to all other link-state routers in the routing area.

Whenever a router receives an LSP from a neighboring router, it immediately sends that LSP out all other interfaces except the interface that received the LSP. LSPs are flooded almost immediately after being received without any intermediate calculations. Link-state routing protocols calculate the SPF algorithm after the flooding is complete.

This process creates a flooding effect of LSPs from all routers throughout the routing area. As a result, link-state routing protocols reach convergence very quickly.

Unlike RIP sending periodic updates every 30 seconds, LSPs do not need to be sent periodically. An LSP only needs to be sent:

- During initial startup of the routing protocol process on that router (for example, router restart).

- Whenever there is a change in the topology (for example, a link going down or coming up, a neighbor adjacency being established or broken).

In addition to the link-state information, other information is included in the LSP, such as sequence numbers and aging information, to help manage the flooding process. This information is used by each router to determine whether it has already received the LSP from another router or whether the LSP has newer information than what is already contained in the link-state database. This process allows a router to keep only the most current information in its link-state database.

## Building the Link-State Database (5.3.2.6)

The fifth and final step in the link-state routing process is for each router to use the database to construct a complete map of the topology and compute the best path to each destination network.

Eventually, every router receives an LSP from every other link-state router in the routing area. These LSPs are stored in the link-state database.

Table 5-16 displays the link-state database contents for R1.

**Table 5-16**   Contents of the Link-State Database of R1

| R1 LSDB Contains... | Link-State Entries |
|---|---|
| R1 entries | ■ Connected to network 10.1.0.0/16, cost = 2<br>■ Connected to R2 on network 10.2.0.0/16, cost = 20<br>■ Connected to R3 on network 10.2.0.0/16, cost = 5<br>■ Connected to R4 on network 10.3.0.0/16, cost = 20 |
| R2 entries | ■ Connected to network 10.5.0.0/16, cost = 2<br>■ Connected to R1 on network 10.2.0.0/16, cost = 20<br>■ Connected to R5 on network 10.9.0.0/16, cost = 10 |
| R3 entries | ■ Connected to network 10.6.0.0/16, cost = 2<br>■ Connected to R1 on network 10.3.0.0/16, cost = 5<br>■ Connected to R4 on network 10.7.0.0/16, cost = 10 |
| R4 entries | ■ Connected to network 10.8.0.0/16, cost = 2<br>■ Connected to R1 on network 10.4.0.0/16, cost = 20<br>■ Connected to R3 on network 10.7.0.0/16, cost = 10<br>■ Connected to R5 on network 10.10.0.0/16, cost = 10 |
| R5 entries | ■ Connected to network 10.11.0.0/16, cost = 2<br>■ Connected to R2 on network 10.9.0.0/16, cost = 10<br>■ Connected to R4 on network 10.10.0.0/16, cost = 10 |

As a result of the flooding process, R1 has learned the link-state information for each router in its routing area. Notice that R1 also includes its own link-state information in the link-state database.

With a complete link-state database, R1 can now use the database and the SPF algorithm to calculate the preferred path or shortest path to each network, which results in the construction of the SPF tree.

### Building the SPF Tree (5.3.2.7)

Each router in the routing area uses the LSDB and SPF algorithm to construct the SPF tree.

Using the link-state information in its LSDB, R1 begins to build an SPF tree of the network. The SPF algorithm interprets each router's LSP to identify networks and associated costs.

In Figure 5-26, R1 first identifies its directly connected networks and costs.

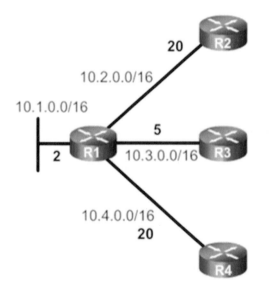

**Figure 5-26**   R1 Identifies the Directly Connected Networks

In Figures 5-27 through 5-31, R1 keeps adding any unknown network and associated costs to the SPF tree.

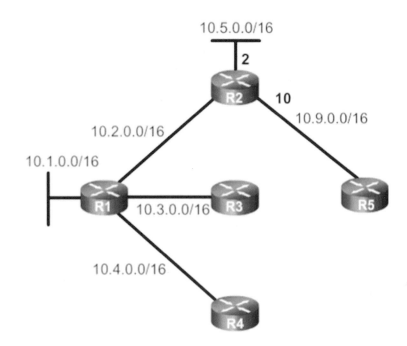

**Figure 5-27**   Adding Links from R2 to the SPF Tree

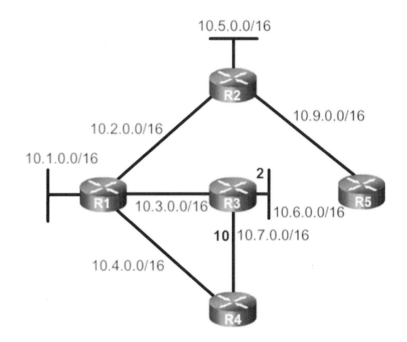

**Figure 5-28**   Adding Links from R3 to the SPF Tree

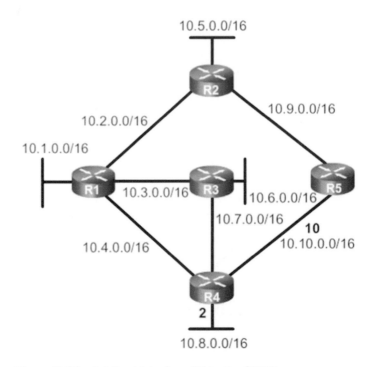

**Figure 5-29** Adding Links from R4 to the SPF Tree

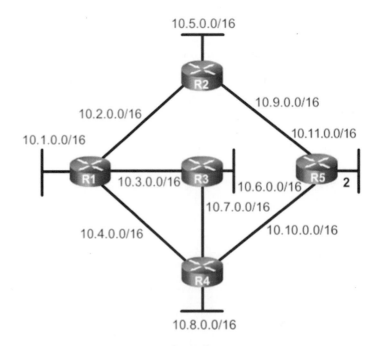

**Figure 5-30** Adding Links from R5 to the SPF Tree

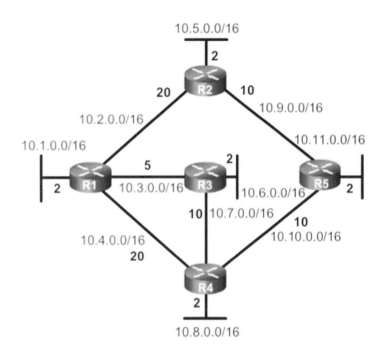

**Figure 5-31** The Resulting SFP Tree for R1

The SPF algorithm then calculates the shortest paths to reach each individual network, which results in the construction of the SPF tree, as shown in Figure 5-31. R1 now has a complete topology view of the link-state area, as shown in Table 5-17.

**Table 5-17** The Complete SPF Database for R1

| Destination | Shortest Path | Cost |
|---|---|---|
| 10.5.0.0/16 | R1 → R2 | 22 |
| 10.6.0.0/16 | R1 → R3 | 7 |
| 10.7.0.0/16 | R1 → R3 | 15 |
| 10.8.0.0/16 | R1 → R3 → R4 | 17 |
| 10.9.0.0/16 | R1 → R2 | 30 |
| 10.10.0.0/16 | R1 → R3 → R4 | 25 |
| 10.11.0.0/16 | R1 → R3 → R4 → R5 | 27 |

Each router constructs its own SPF tree independently from all other routers. To ensure proper routing, the link-state databases used to construct those trees must be identical on all routers.

## Adding OSPF Routes to the Routing Table (5.3.2.8)

Using the shortest-path information determined by the SPF algorithm, these paths can now be added to the routing table. Table 5-18 displays the routes that are added to R1 routing table.

**Table 5-18**    Resulting R1 Routing Table Entries

| Networks | Routing Table Entries |
| --- | --- |
| R1 entries | ■ 10.1.0.0/16 directly connected network |
| | ■ 10.2.0.0/16 directly connected network |
| | ■ 10.3.0.0/16 directly connected network |
| | ■ 10.4.0.0/16 directly connected network |
| Remote networks | ■ 10.5.0.0/16 via R2 serial 0/0/0, cost = 22 |
| | ■ 10.6.0.0/16 via R3 serial 0/0/1, cost = 7 |
| | ■ 10.7.0.0/16 via R3 serial 0/0/1, cost = 15 |
| | ■ 10.8.0.0/16 via R3 serial 0/0/1, cost = 17 |
| | ■ 10.9.0.0/16 via R2 serial 0/0/0, cost = 30 |
| | ■ 10.10.0.0/16 via R3 serial 0/0/1, cost = 25 |
| | ■ 10.11.0.0/16 via R3 serial 0/0/1, cost = 27 |

The routing table also includes all directly connected networks and routes from any other sources, such as static routes. Packets are now forwarded according to these entries in the routing table.

**Interactive Graphic**

**Activity 5.3.2.9: Building the Link-State Database and SPF Tree**

Refer to the online course to complete this activity.

# Link-State Routing Protocol Benefits (5.3.3)

In this topic you will learn about the advantages and disadvantages of using link-state routing protocols.

## Why Use Link-State Protocols? (5.3.3.1)

There are several advantages of link-state routing protocols compared to distance vector routing protocols. Table 5-19 lists the advantages of link-state routing protocols.

**Table 5-19**   Link-State Routing Protocol Advantages

| Advantage | Description |
|---|---|
| Builds a topological map | ■ Link-state routing protocols create a topological map, or SPF tree, of the network topology.<br><br>■ Because link-state routing protocols exchange link states, the SPF algorithm can build an SPF tree of the network.<br><br>■ Using the SPF tree, each router can independently determine the shortest path to every network.<br><br>■ Link-state routing protocols support VLSM and CIDR, because they include the subnet mask in the routing updates. |
| Fast convergence | ■ When receiving an LSP, link-state routing protocols immediately flood the LSP out all interfaces except for the interface from which the LSP was received.<br><br>■ In contrast, RIP needs to process each routing update and update its routing table before flooding them out other interfaces. |
| Event-driven updates | ■ After the initial flooding of LSPs, link-state routing protocols send out an LSP only when there is a change in the topology.<br><br>■ The LSP contains only the information regarding the affected link.<br><br>■ Unlike some distance vector routing protocols, link-state routing protocols do not send periodic updates. |
| Hierarchical design | ■ Link-state routing protocols use the concept of areas.<br><br>■ Multiple areas create a hierarchical design to networks, allowing for better route aggregation (summarization) and isolation of routing issues within an area. |

## Disadvantages of Link-State Protocols (5.3.3.2)

Link-state protocols also have a few disadvantages compared to distance vector routing protocols. Table 5-20 lists the disadvantages of link-state routing protocols.

**Table 5-20**   Link-State Routing Protocol Disadvantages

| Disadvantage | Description |
|---|---|
| Increased memory requirements | ■ Link-state protocols require additional memory to create and maintain the link-state database and SPF tree. |
| Increased processing requirements | ■ Link-state protocols can require more CPU processing than distance vector routing protocols.<br><br>■ The SPF algorithm requires more CPU time than distance vector algorithms such as Bellman-Ford because link-state protocols build a complete map of the topology. |

| Disadvantage | Description |
|---|---|
| Increased bandwidth requirements | ■ The flooding of link-state packets can adversely affect the available bandwidth on a network. |
| | ■ This should only occur during initial startup of routers but can also be an issue on unstable networks. |

Modern link-state routing protocols are designed to minimize the effects on memory, CPU, and bandwidth.

For example, the use and configuration of multiple areas can reduce the size of the link-state databases. Multiple areas can limit the amount of link-state information flooding in a routing domain and can send LSPs only to the routers that need them. When there is a change in the topology, only the routers in the affected area receive the LSP and run the SPF algorithm. This can help isolate an unstable link to a specific area in the routing domain.

For example, in Figure 5-32, there are three separate routing domains: area 1, area 0, and area 51. If a network in area 51 goes down, the LSP with the information about this downed link is only flooded to other routers in that area. Only the routers in area 51 need to update their link-state databases, rerun the SPF algorithm, create a new SPF tree, and update their routing tables. Routers in other areas learn that this route is down, but this is done with a type of LSP that does not cause them to rerun their SPF algorithm. Routers in other areas can update their routing tables directly.

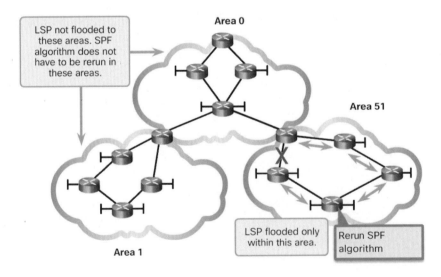

**Figure 5-32**    Creating Areas to Minimize Router Resource Usage

## Protocols That Use Link-State (5.3.3.3)

There are only two link-state routing protocols: OSPF and IS-IS.

OSPF is the most popular implementation. It was designed by the Internet Engineering Task Force (IETF) OSPF Working Group. The development of OSPF began in 1987, and there are currently two versions in use:

- *OSPFv2*—OSPF for IPv4 networks (RFC 1247 and RFC 2328)
- *OSPFv3*—OSPF for IPv6 networks (RFC 2740)

**Note**

With the OSPFv3 Address Families feature, OSPFv3 includes support for both IPv4 and IPv6.

IS-IS was designed by the International Organization for Standardization (ISO) and is described in ISO 10589. The first incarnation of this routing protocol was developed at Digital Equipment Corporation (DEC) and is known as DECnet Phase V. Radia Perlman was the chief designer of the IS-IS routing protocol.

IS-IS was originally designed for the OSI protocol suite and not the TCP/IP protocol suite. Later, Integrated IS-IS, or Dual IS-IS, included support for IP networks. Although IS-IS has been a routing protocol used mainly by ISPs and carriers, more enterprise networks are beginning to use IS-IS.

OSPF and IS-IS share many similarities but also have several differences. There are pro-OSPF and pro-IS-IS factions that discuss and debate the advantages of one routing protocol over the other. However, both routing protocols provide the necessary routing functionality for a large enterprise or ISP.

**Note**

Further study of IS-IS is beyond the scope of this course.

# Summary (5.4)

Dynamic routing protocols are used by routers to facilitate the exchange of routing information between routers. The purposes of dynamic routing protocols include discovering of remote networks, maintaining up-to-date routing information, choosing the best paths to destination networks, and finding a new best path if the current path is no longer available. While dynamic routing protocols require less administrative overhead than static routing protocols, they do require dedicating part of a router's resources for protocol operation, including CPU time and network link bandwidth.

Networks typically use a combination of both static and dynamic routing. Dynamic routing is the best choice for large networks, and static routing is better for *stub networks*.

When there is a change in the topology, routing protocols propagate that information throughout the routing domain. The process of bringing all routing tables to a state of consistency, where all the routers in the same routing domain or area have complete and accurate information about the network, is called convergence. Some routing protocols converge faster than others.

Routing protocols use metrics to determine the best path or shortest path to reach a destination network. Different routing protocols may use different metrics. Typically, a lower metric means a better path. Metrics used by dynamic routing protocols include hops, bandwidth, delay, reliability, and load.

Routing protocols can be classified as either classful or classless, distance vector or link state, and either interior gateway or exterior gateway.

Distance vector protocols use routers as "sign posts" along the path to the final destination. The only information a router knows about a remote network is the distance or metric to reach that network and which path or interface to use to get there. Distance vector routing protocols do not have an actual map of the network topology. Modern distance vector protocols are RIPv2, RIPng, and EIGRP.

A router configured with a link-state routing protocol can create a complete view or topology of the network by gathering information from all the other routers. This information is collected by using link-state packets (LSP).

Link-state routing protocols apply Dijkstra's algorithm to calculate the best path route. The algorithm is commonly referred to as the shortest path first (SPF) algorithm. This algorithm uses accumulated costs along each path, from source to destination, to determine the total cost of a route. The link-state routing protocols are IS-IS and OSPF.

# Practice

The following activities provide practice with the topics introduced in this chapter. The Labs and Class Activities are available in the companion *Scaling Networks v6 Labs & Study Guide* (ISBN 9781587134333). The Packet Tracer activity instructions are also in the Labs & Study Guide. The PKA files are found in the online course.

### Class Activities

Class Activity 5.0.1.2: How Much Does This Cost?

### Packet Tracer Activities

Packet Tracer 5.2.1.6: Investigating Convergence

Packet Tracer 5.2.3.4: Comparing RIP and EIGRP Path Selection

# Check Your Understanding Questions

Complete all the review questions listed here to test your understanding of the topics and concepts in this chapter. The appendix "Answers to 'Check Your Understanding' Questions" lists the answers.

1. Which dynamic routing protocol was developed to interconnect different Internet service providers?

   A. BGP

   B. EIGRP

   C. OSPF

   D. RIP

2. Which routing protocol is limited to smaller network implementations because it does not accommodate growth for larger networks?

   A. EIGRP

   B. IS-IS

   C. RIP

   D. OSPF

3. What two tasks do dynamic routing protocols perform? (Choose two.)

   A. Assigning IP addressing

   B. Discovering hosts

   C. Doing network discovery

   D. Propagating host default gateways

   E. Updating and maintaining routing tables

4. Which two statements are true regarding classless routing protocols? (Choose two.)

   A. Classless routing protocols reduce the amount of address space available in an organization.

   B. Classless routing protocols send complete routing table updates to all neighbors.

   C. Classless routing protocols support VLSM and CIDR.

   D. Classless routing protocols send subnet mask information in routing updates.

   E. RIPv1 is a classless routing protocols.

5. In the context of routing protocols, what is convergence time?

   A. A measure of protocol configuration complexity

   B. The amount of time a network administrator needs to configure a routing protocol in a small to medium-sized network

   C. The amount of time for the routing tables to achieve a consistent state after a topology change

   D. The capability to transport data, video, and voice over the same media

6. Which two events will trigger the sending of a link-state packet by a link-state routing protocol? (Choose two.)

   A. A change in the topology

   B. A link to a neighbor router becoming congested

   C. The initial startup of the routing protocol process

   D. The requirement to periodically flood link-state packets to all neighbors

   E. The router update timer expiring

7. Which two requirements are necessary before a router configured with a link-state routing protocol can build and send its link-state packets? (Choose two.)

   A. The router has built its link-state database.

   B. The router has constructed an SPF tree.

   C. The router has determined the costs associated with its active links.

D.   The router has established its adjacencies.

E.   The routing table has been refreshed.

8.   Which two statements describe the OSPF routing protocol? (Choose two.)

A.   It automatically summarizes networks at the classful boundaries.

B.   It calculates its metric by using bandwidth.

C.   It has an administrative distance of 120.

D.   It uses Dijkstra's algorithm to build the SPF tree.

E.   It is used primarily as an EGP.

9.   How do EIGRP routers establish and maintain neighbor relationships?

A.   They compare known routes to information received in updates.

B.   They dynamically learn new routes from neighbors.

C.   They exchange hello packets with neighboring routers.

D.   They exchange neighbor tables with directly attached routers.

E.   They exchange routing tables with directly attached routers.

10.   Which OSPF component is identical in all routers in an OSPF area after convergence?

A.   Adjacency database

B.   Link-state database

C.   Routing table

D.   SPF tree

11.   Which of the following is a function of OSPF hello packets?

A.   To discover neighbors and build adjacencies between them

B.   To ensure database synchronization between routers

C.   To request specific link-state records from neighbor routers

D.   To send specifically requested link-state records

12.   Which two parameters does EIGRP use as metrics to select the best path to reach a network? (Choose two.)

A.   Bandwidth

B.   Confidentiality

C.   Delay

D.   Hop count

E.   Jitter

F.   Resiliency

13. Which statement describes a route that has been learned dynamically?

    A. It has an administrative distance of 1.

    B. It is automatically updated and maintained by routing protocols.

    C. It is identified by the prefix C in the routing table.

    D. It is unaffected by changes in the topology of the network.

14. Which two factors are important when deciding which interior gateway routing protocol to use? (Choose two.)

    A. Campus backbone architecture

    B. ISP selection

    C. Scalability

    D. Speed of convergence

    E. The autonomous system that is used

## Objectives

Upon completion of this chapter, you will be able to answer the following questions:

- What are the features and characteristics of EIGRP?

- How do you implement EIGRP for IPv4 in a small to medium-sized business network?

- How does EIGRP operate in a small to medium-sized business network?

- How do you implement EIGRP for IPv6 in a small to medium-sized business network?

## Key Terms

This chapter uses the following key terms. You can find the definitions in the Glossary.

# Introduction (6.0.1.1)

Enhanced Interior Gateway Routing Protocol (EIGRP) is an advanced distance vector routing protocol developed by Cisco Systems. As the name suggests, EIGRP is an enhancement of another protocol, IGRP (Interior Gateway Routing Protocol), which is also a Cisco routing protocol. IGRP is an older classful, distance vector routing protocol, which has been obsolete since IOS 12.3.

EIGRP includes features found in link-state routing protocols. EIGRP is suited for many different topologies and media. In a well-designed network, EIGRP can scale to include multiple topologies and can provide extremely quick convergence times with minimal network traffic.

This chapter introduces EIGRP and provides basic configuration commands to enable it on a Cisco IOS router. It also explores the operation of the routing protocol and provides more detail on how EIGRP determines best path.

**Class Activity 6.0.1.2: Classless EIGRP**

Refer to *Scaling Networks v6 Labs & Study Guide* and the online course to complete this activity.

EIGRP was introduced as a distance vector routing protocol in 1992. It was originally designed to work as a proprietary protocol on Cisco devices only. In 2013, EIGRP became a multivendor routing protocol, meaning that it can be used by other device vendors in addition to Cisco devices.

Complete the reflection questions that accompany the PDF file for this activity. Save your work and be prepared to share your answers with the class.

# EIGRP Characteristics (6.1)

EIGRP is an advanced distance vector routing protocol developed by Cisco. In this section, you will learn about the features and characteristics of EIGRP.

## EIGRP Basic Features (6.1.1)

In this topic, you will learn about the basic features of EIGRP.

### Features of EIGRP (6.1.1.1)

EIGRP was initially released in 1992 as a proprietary protocol available only on Cisco devices. However, in 2013, Cisco released a basic functionality of EIGRP as an open standard in an informational RFC to the IETF. This means that other networking vendors can now implement EIGRP on their equipment to interoperate with both Cisco and non-Cisco routers running EIGRP. However, Cisco does not plan to release advanced features of EIGRP to the IETF but will continue to maintain control of EIGRP as an informational RFC.

EIGRP includes features of both link-state and distance vector routing protocols. However, EIGRP is based on the key distance vector routing protocol principle: It learns information about the rest of the network from directly connected neighbors.

Figure 6-1 shows the classification of routing protocols. EIGRP is an advanced distance vector routing protocol that includes features not found in other distance vector routing protocols, such as RIP and IGRP.

| | Interior Gateway Protocols | | | | Exterior Gateway Protocols |
|---|---|---|---|---|---|
| | Distance Vector Routing Protocols | | Link State Routing Protocols | | Path Vector |
| IPv4 | RIPv2 | EIGRP | OSPFv2 | IS-IS | BGP-4 |
| IPv6 | RIPng | EIGRP for IPv6 | OSPFv3 | IS-IS for IPv6 | BGP-4 for IPv6 |

**Figure 6-1**    Types of Routing Protocols

In Cisco IOS Release 15.0(1)M, Cisco introduced the new EIGRP configuration option *named EIGRP*. Named EIGRP enables the configuration of EIGRP for both IPv4 and IPv6 under a single configuration mode. This helps eliminate configuration complexity that occurs when configuring EIGRP for both IPv4 and IPv6. Named EIGRP is beyond the scope of this course.

Features of EIGRP are listed in Table 6-1.

**Table 6-1**    EIGRP Features

| Feature | Description |
|---|---|
| Diffusing Update Algorithm | ▪ DUAL is the computational algorithm of EIGRP. <br> ▪ DUAL guarantees loop-free and backup paths throughout the routing domain. <br> ▪ Using DUAL, EIGRP stores all available backup routes for destinations so that it can quickly adapt to alternate routes when necessary. |

| Feature | Description |
|---|---|
| Establishing neighbor adjacencies | ■ EIGRP establishes relationships with directly connected EIGRP-enabled routers.<br>■ Neighbor adjacencies are used to track the status of these neighbors. |
| Reliable Transport Protocol | ■ The *Reliable Transport Protocol (RTP)* is unique to EIGRP and provides reliable delivery of EIGRP packets to neighbors.<br>■ RTP and the tracking of neighbor adjacencies set the stage for DUAL. |
| Partial and bounded updates | ■ EIGRP uses partial updates and bounded updates to minimize the bandwidth that is required to send EIGRP updates.<br>■ A *partial update* includes only information about the route changes, such as a new link or a link becoming unavailable.<br>■ A *bounded update* is sent only to the routers that the changes affect. |
| Equal- and unequal-cost load balancing | ■ EIGRP supports *equal-cost load balancing* and *unequal-cost load balancing*, which allows administrators to better distribute traffic flow in their networks. |

**Note**

The term *hybrid routing protocol* may be used in some older documentation to define EIGRP. However, this term is misleading because EIGRP is not a hybrid between distance vector and link-state routing protocols. EIGRP is solely a distance vector routing protocol; therefore, Cisco no longer uses this term to refer to it.

## Protocol Dependent Modules (6.1.1.2)

EIGRP has the capability for routing different protocols, including IPv4 and IPv6. EIGRP does so by using protocol-dependent modules (PDM), as shown in Figure 6-2.

**Note**

PDMs were also used to support the now obsolete Novell IPX and Apple Computer's Apple-Talk network layer protocols.

PDMs are responsible for network layer protocol–specific tasks. For example, an EIGRP module is responsible for sending and receiving EIGRP packets that are encapsulated in IPv4. This module is also responsible for parsing EIGRP packets and informing DUAL of the new information that is received. EIGRP asks DUAL to make routing decisions, but the results are stored in the IPv4 routing table.

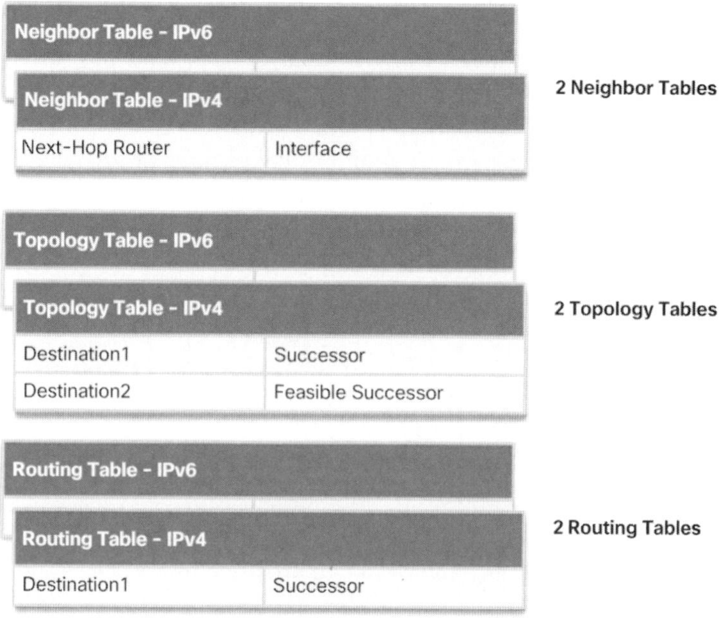

**Figure 6-2**  EIGRP Protocol-Dependent Modules (PDM)

PDMs are responsible for the specific routing tasks for each network layer protocol, including the following:

- Maintaining the neighbor and topology tables of EIGRP routers that belong to that protocol suite
- Building and translating protocol-specific packets for DUAL
- Interfacing DUAL to the protocol-specific routing table
- Computing the metric and passing this information to DUAL
- Implementing filtering and access lists
- Performing redistribution functions to and from other routing protocols
- Redistributing routes that are learned by other routing protocols

When a router discovers a new neighbor, it records the neighbor's address and interface as an entry in the neighbor table. One *neighbor table* exists for each protocol-dependent module, such as IPv4. EIGRP also maintains a *topology table*. The topology table contains all destinations that are advertised by neighboring routers. There is also a separate topology table for each PDM.

## Reliable Transport Protocol (6.1.1.3)

EIGRP was designed as a network layer–independent routing protocol. Because of this design, EIGRP cannot use the services of UDP or TCP. Instead, EIGRP uses Reliable Transport Protocol (RTP) for the delivery and reception of EIGRP packets. This allows EIGRP to be flexible and to be used for protocols other than those from the TCP/IP protocol suite, such as the now obsolete IPX and AppleTalk protocols.

Figure 6-3 shows conceptually where RTP operates.

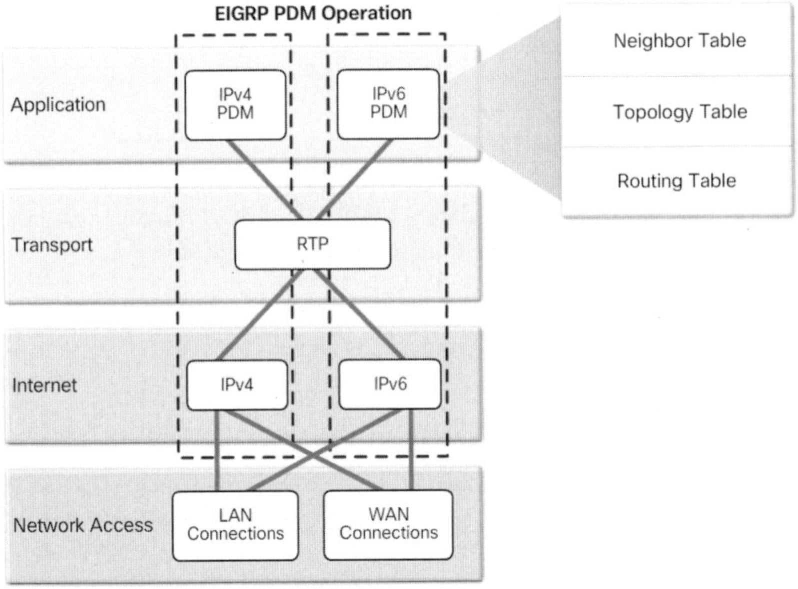

**Figure 6-3**    EIGRP Replaces TCP with RTP

Although "reliable" is part of its name, RTP includes both reliable delivery and unreliable delivery of EIGRP packets, making it similar to both TCP and UDP. Reliable RTP requires an acknowledgment to be returned from the receiver to the sender. An unreliable RTP packet does not require an acknowledgment. For example, an EIGRP *Update packet* is sent reliably over RTP and requires an acknowledgment. An EIGRP Hello packet is also sent over RTP, but unreliably—that is, without requiring an acknowledgment.

RTP can send EIGRP packets as unicast or multicast:

- Multicast EIGRP packets for IPv4 use the reserved IPv4 multicast address 224.0.0.10.

- Multicast EIGRP packets for IPv6 are sent to the reserved IPv6 multicast address FF02::A.

### Authentication (6.1.1.4)

Like other routing protocols, EIGRP can be configured for authentication. RIPv2, EIGRP, OSPF, IS-IS, and BGP can each be configured to authenticate their routing information.

It is a good practice to authenticate transmitted routing information. Doing so ensures that routers accept routing information only from other routers that have been configured with the same password or authentication information.

**Note**

Authentication does not encrypt the EIGRP routing updates.

# EIGRP Packet Types (6.1.2)

In this topic, you will learn about the types of packets used to establish and maintain an EIGRP neighbor adjacency.

### EIGRP Packet Types (6.1.2.1)

EIGRP uses five different packet types, as described in Table 6-2. EIGRP packets are sent using either RTP reliable or unreliable delivery and can be sent as unicast, multicast, or sometimes both. EIGRP packet types are also called *EIGRP packet formats* or *EIGRP messages*.

**Table 6-2**   EIGRP Packet Types

| Packet Type | Description |
| --- | --- |
| Hello packet | ▪ Used for neighbor discovery and to maintain neighbor adjacencies. <br> ▪ Sent unreliably. <br> ▪ Multicast packet. |
| Update packet | ▪ Propagates routing information to EIGRP neighbors. <br> ▪ Sent as a unicast or multicast packet. <br> ▪ Sent reliably and expects an Acknowledgment packet in return. |
| *Acknowledgment packet* | ▪ Used to acknowledge the receipt of an Update, Query, or Reply packet. <br> ▪ Sent as a unicast packet. <br> ▪ Sent unreliably. |

| Packet Type | Description |
| --- | --- |
| *Query packet* | ■ Used to ask a neighbor about a missing route.<br>■ Sent as a unicast or multicast packet.<br>■ Sent reliably and expects an Acknowledgment packet in return. |
| *Reply packet* | ■ Generated in response to an EIGRP query.<br>■ Sent as a unicast packet.<br>■ Sent reliably and expects an Acknowledgment packet in return. |

Figure 6-4 shows that EIGRP messages are typically encapsulated in IPv4 or IPv6 packets.

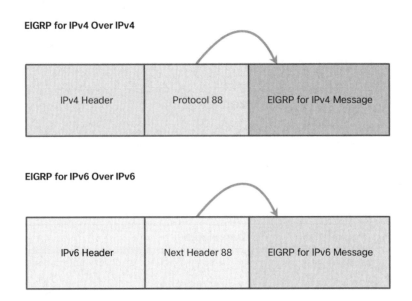

**Figure 6-4**   EIGRP Messages Are Sent Over IP

EIGRP for IPv4 messages are identified with the number 88 in the IPv4 protocol field. This value indicates that the data portion of the packet is an EIGRP for an IPv4 message. EIGRP for IPv6 messages are encapsulated in IPv6 packets, using the next header field, 88. Much like to the protocol field for IPv4, the IPv6 next header field indicates the type of data carried in the IPv6 packet.

## EIGRP Hello Packets (6.1.2.2)

EIGRP uses small Hello packets to discover other EIGRP-enabled routers on directly connected links. Routers use Hello packets to form EIGRP neighbor adjacencies, also known as neighbor relationships.

EIGRP Hello packets are sent as IPv4 or IPv6 multicasts and use RTP unreliable delivery. This means that the receiver does not reply with an Acknowledgment packet.

EIGRP routers discover neighbors and establish adjacencies with neighbor routers using the Hello packet. On most modern networks, EIGRP Hello packets are sent as multicast packets every five seconds. However, on multipoint, *non-broadcast multiple access (NBMA)* networks with access links of T1 (1.544 Mbps) or slower, Hello packets are sent as unicast packets every 60 seconds.

**Note**

Legacy NBMA networks using slower interfaces include Frame Relay, Asynchronous Transfer Mode (ATM), and X.25.

EIGRP also uses Hello packets to maintain established adjacencies. An EIGRP router assumes that as long as it receives Hello packets from a neighbor, the neighbor and its routes remain viable.

EIGRP uses a hold timer to determine the maximum time the router should wait to receive the next Hello before declaring that neighbor as unreachable.

By default, the hold time is three times the *Hello interval*, or 15 seconds on most networks and 180 seconds on low-speed NBMA networks. If the hold time expires, EIGRP declares the route to be down, and DUAL searches for a new path by sending out queries.

Table 6-3 summarizes the default EIGRP Hello intervals and timers.

**Table 6-3**  Default Hello Intervals and Hold Timers for EIGRP

| Bandwidth | Example Link | Default Hello Interval | Default Hold Time |
| --- | --- | --- | --- |
| Greater than 1.544 Mbps | T1, Ethernet | 5 seconds | 15 seconds |
| 1.544 Mbps | Multipoint Frame Relay | 60 seconds | 180 seconds |

**Note**

Most links today provide T1 or better bandwidth.

## EIGRP Update and Acknowledgment Packets (6.1.2.3)

EIGRP Update and Acknowledgment packets are often discussed together because of their symbiotic relationship. Update packets require Acknowledgment packets.

EIGRP sends Update packets to propagate routing information:

- Update packets contain only the routing information needed and not the entire routing table.

- They are sent only when necessary, such as when the state of a destination changes.

- They are sent only to the routers that require them.

Unlike RIP, which sends periodic updates, EIGRP sends incremental updates only when the state of a destination changes. This may include when a new network becomes available, when an existing network becomes unavailable, or when a change occurs in the routing metric for an existing network.

EIGRP uses two terms when referring to its updates:

- **Partial update**—This update includes only information about route changes.

- **Bounded update**—EIGRP sends partial updates only to the routers that are affected by the changes, which helps EIGRP minimize bandwidth.

EIGRP Update packets are sent reliably, which means the sending router requires an acknowledgment.

An EIGRP acknowledgment is an EIGRP Hello packet without any data. RTP uses reliable delivery for Update, Query, and Reply packets. EIGRP Acknowledgment packets are always sent as unreliable unicast messages. Unreliable delivery is understandable in this case, because without it, there would be an endless loop of acknowledgments.

Update packets are sent as multicast messages when required by multiple routers or as a unicast when required by only a single router.

In Figure 6-5, for example, R2 has lost connectivity to the LAN attached to its Gigabit Ethernet interface. R2 immediately sends an update to R1 and R3, noting the downed route.

The updates are sent by R2 as unicasts because the links are point-to-point links. If the links were Ethernet links, the updates would be sent using the EIGRP all routers multicast address, 224.0.0.10.

R1 and R3 respond with unicast acknowledgments to let R2 know that they have received the update.

---

**Note**

Some documentation refers to Hello and Acknowledgment as a single type of EIGRP packet.

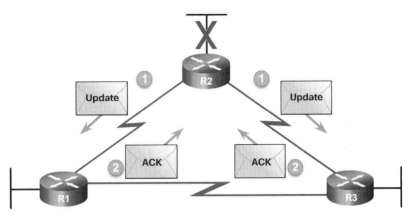

**Figure 6-5**   EIGRP Update and Acknowledgment Messages

## EIGRP Query and Reply Packets (6.1.2.4)

EIGRP Query and Reply packets are also often discussed together because of their symbiotic relationship. A Query packet requires a Reply packet. Both Query and Reply packets also requires Acknowledgment packets.

DUAL uses Query and Reply packets when searching for networks and other tasks. Queries and replies use reliable delivery, which means they require acknowledgments. Queries can use multicast or unicast, whereas replies are always sent as unicast.

In Figure 6-6, R2 has lost connectivity to the LAN, and it sends out queries to all EIGRP neighbors, searching for any possible routes to the LAN.

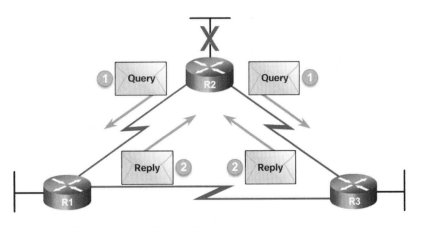

**Figure 6-6**   EIGRP Query and Reply Messages

Queries are always sent reliably, and therefore R1 and R3 must acknowledge receipt of the query.

> **Note**
>
> When EIGRP sends Query or Reply packets, each packet requires EIGRP Acknowledgment packets. In this example, only the Query and Reply packets are shown; the Acknowledgment packets were omitted to simplify the graphic.

A Query packet must get a Reply packet in return. Therefore, R1 and R3 must send a Reply packet to inform R2 if they have a route to the downed network.

Replies are always sent reliably, and therefore R2 must acknowledge receipt of the R1 and R3 Reply packets.

It may not be obvious why R2 would send out a query for a network it knows is down. Actually, only R2's interface that is attached to the network is down. Another router could be attached to the same LAN and have an alternate path to the same network. Therefore, R2 queries for such a router before completely removing the network from its topology table.

**Interactive Graphic**

**Activity 6.1.2.5: Identify the EIGRP Packet Type**

Refer to the online course to complete this activity.

**Video**

**Video Demonstration 6.1.2.6: Observing EIGRP Protocol Communications**

Refer to the online course to view this video.

# EIGRP Messages (6.1.3)

In this topic, you will learn how EIGRP messages are encapsulated.

## Encapsulating EIGRP Messages (6.1.3.1)

The data portion of an EIGRP message is encapsulated in a packet. This data field is called *type, length, value (TLV)*. The types of TLVs relevant to this course are EIGRP parameters, IP internal routes, and IP external routes.

The EIGRP packet header is included with every EIGRP packet, regardless of its type. The EIGRP packet header and TLV are encapsulated in an IPv4 packet.

Figure 6-7 shows the data link Ethernet frame. EIGRP for IPv4 is encapsulated in an IPv4 packet.

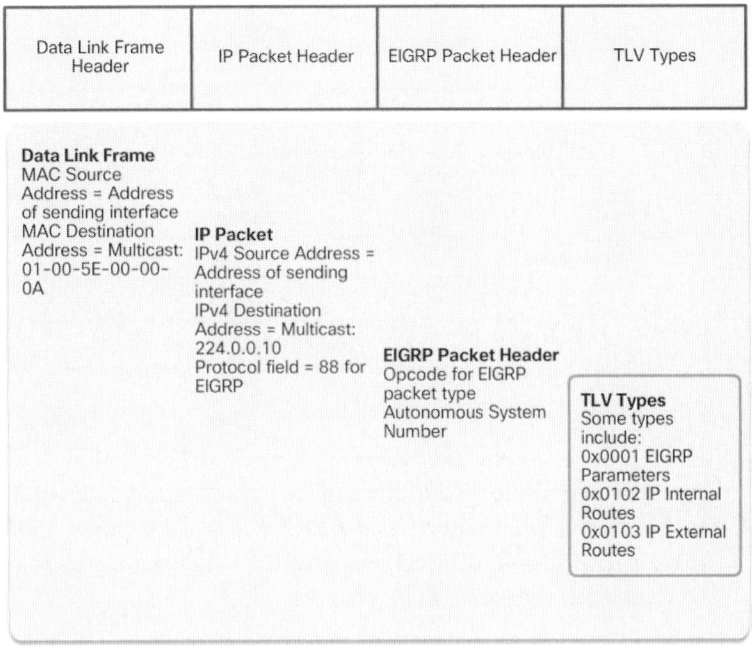

| Data Link Frame Header | IP Packet Header | EIGRP Packet Header | TLV Types |
|---|---|---|---|

**Data Link Frame**
MAC Source
Address = Address
of sending interface
MAC Destination
Address = Multicast:
01-00-5E-00-00-
0A

**IP Packet**
IPv4 Source Address =
Address of sending
interface
IPv4 Destination
Address = Multicast:
224.0.0.10
Protocol field = 88 for
EIGRP

**EIGRP Packet Header**
Opcode for EIGRP
packet type
Autonomous System
Number

**TLV Types**
Some types
include:
0x0001 EIGRP
Parameters
0x0102 IP Internal
Routes
0x0103 IP External
Routes

**Figure 6-7**    Encapsulated EIGRP Message

In this example, the EIGRP packet is encapsulated in an Ethernet frame. Therefore, the destination MAC address is set to the multicast MAC address 01-00-5E-00-00-0A.

In the IPv4 packet header, the protocol field is set to 88 to indicate that the next portion of the header is the EIGRP packet header. It also includes the sending device IP address and the destination IPv4 destination address set to the IPv4 multicast address 224.0.0.10. If this packet were sent on a point-to-point link, the destination would be the IP address of the peer.

EIGRP for IPv6 would be encapsulated using an IPv6 header with the next header field set to 88 and the destination multicast IPv6 address FF02::A.

The TLV fields vary depending on the type of EIGRP message being sent.

## EIGRP Packet Header and TLV (6.1.3.2)

Every EIGRP packet header includes the fields shown in Figure 6-8.

An important field is the opcode field, which specifies what type of EIGRP packet is being sent. Specifically, it identifies the EIGRP message as either type 1 = Update, type 3 = Query, type 4 = Reply, or type 5 = Hello. Other types of messages are also possible but beyond the scope of this course.

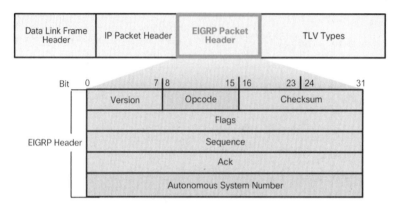

**Figure 6-8** EIGRP Packet Header

Another important field in the EIGRP packet header is the autonomous system number field, which specifies the EIGRP routing process. Unlike with RIP, multiple instances of EIGRP can run on a network. The *autonomous system number* is used to track each running EIGRP process.

TLV fields identify the following:

- **Type**—A binary number indicating the kind of fields included in the message. Common types include 0x0001 for EIGRP parameters, 0x0102 to advertise IP Internal routes, and 0x0103 to advertise IP External routes.

- **Length**—Identifies the size, in bytes, of the value field.

- **Value**—This contains data for the EIGRP message and varies in size, depending on the type of message.

Figure 6-9 displays the EIGRP parameters TLV fields.

The EIGRP parameters include the weights that EIGRP uses for its *composite metric*. By default, only bandwidth and delay are weighted equally. Therefore, the K1 field for bandwidth and the K3 field for delay are both set to 1, and the other K values are set to 0.

The hold time is the amount of time the EIGRP neighbor receiving this message should wait before considering the advertising router to be down.

Every Update, Query, and Reply packet contains at least one routes TLV. Each IP internal routes and IP external routes TLV contains one route entry and includes the metric information for the route.

Figure 6-10 displays the IP internal routes TLV fields.

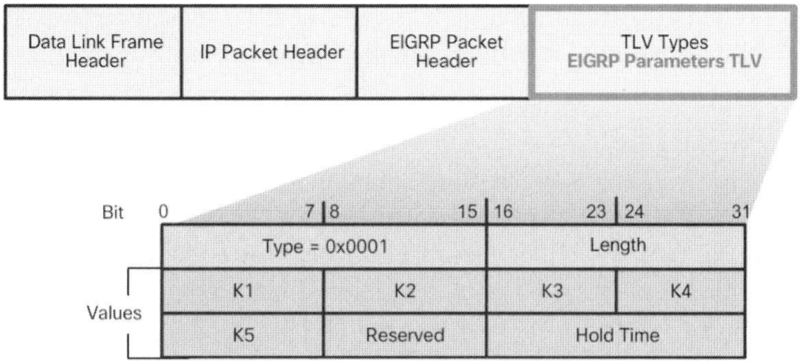

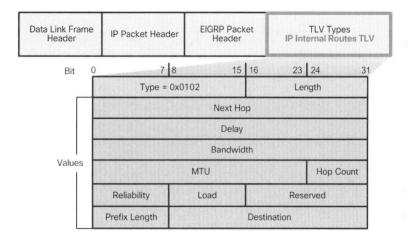

**Figure 6-9**    EIGRP Parameters TLV Fields

**Figure 6-10**    EIGRP IP Internal Routes TLV Fields

The Update packet parameters identify IP internal routes. The IP internal message is used to advertise EIGRP routes within an autonomous system. Important fields include the following:

- **Metric fields**—Delay and bandwidth are the most important. Delay is calculated as the sum of delays from source to destination in units of 10 microseconds. Bandwidth is the lowest configured bandwidth of any interface along the route.

- **Prefix length field**—This is the subnet mask of the destination network specified as the prefix length or the number of network bits in the subnet mask. For example, the prefix length for 255.255.255.0 is 24 because 24 is the number of network bits.

- **Destination field**—The destination field stores the address of the destination network.

The destination field varies in number of bits based on the value of the network portion of the 32-bit network address. However, the minimum field length is 24 bits.

For example, assume that the destination network of 10.1.0.0/16 is being advertised. In this case, the network portion would be 10.1, and the destination field would store the first 16 bits. Because the minimum length of this field is 24 bits, the remainder of the field is padded with zeros. If a network address is longer than 24 bits (192.168.1.32/27, for example), the destination field is extended for another 32 bits (for a total of 56 bits), and the unused bits are padded with zeros.

Figure 6-11 displays the IP external routes TLV fields.

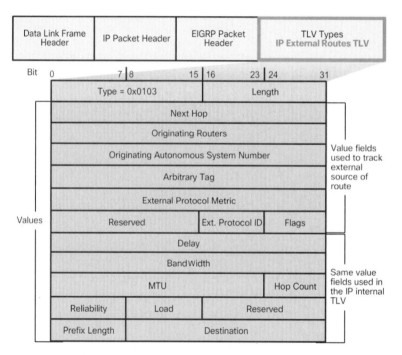

**Figure 6-11**  EIGRP IP External Routes TLV Fields

The IP external message is used when external routes are imported into the EIGRP routing process. In this chapter, you will import or redistribute a default static route into EIGRP. Notice that the bottom half of the IP external routes TLV includes all the fields used by the IP internal TLV.

**Note**

The maximum transmission unit (MTU) is not a metric used by EIGRP. The MTU is included in the routing updates, but it is not used to determine the routing metric.

# Implement EIGRP for IPv4 (6.2)

In this section, you will learn how to implement EIGRP for IPv4 in a small to medium-sized business network.

## Configure EIGRP with IPv4 (6.2.1)

In this topic, you will learn how to configure EIGRP for IPv4 in a small routed network.

### EIGRP Network Topology (6.2.1.1)

Figure 6-12 shows the reference topology that is used in this chapter to configure EIGRP for IPv4.

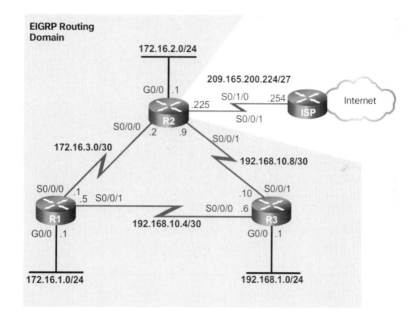

**Figure 6-12**   EIGRP for IPv4 Topology

The routers in the topology have a starting configuration that includes addresses on the interfaces. There is currently no static routing or dynamic routing configured on any of the routers.

Example 6-1 shows the interface configurations for the three EIGRP routers in the topology. Only routers R1, R2, and R3 are part of the EIGRP routing domain. The ISP router is used as the routing domain's gateway to the Internet.

**Example 6-1**  Interface Configurations

```
R1# show running-config
<Output omitted>
!
interface GigabitEthernet0/0
 ip address 172.16.1.1 255.255.255.0
!
interface Serial0/0/0
 ip address 172.16.3.1 255.255.255.252
 clock rate 64000
!
interface Serial0/0/1
 ip address 192.168.10.5 255.255.255.252
!
```

```
R2# show running-config
<Output omitted>
!
interface GigabitEthernet0/0
 ip address 172.16.2.1 255.255.255.0
!
interface Serial0/0/0
 ip address 172.16.3.2 255.255.255.252
!
interface Serial0/0/1
 ip address 192.168.10.9 255.255.255.252
 clock rate 64000
!
interface Serial0/1/0
 ip address 209.165.200.225 255.255.255.224
!
```

```
R3# show running-config
<Output omitted>
!
interface GigabitEthernet0/0
 ip address 192.168.1.1 255.255.255.0
!
interface Serial0/0/0
 ip address 192.168.10.6 255.255.255.252
 clock rate 64000
!
interface Serial0/0/1
 ip address 192.168.10.10 255.255.255.252
!
```

## Autonomous System Numbers (6.2.1.2)

EIGRP uses the **router eigrp** *autonomous-system* command to enable the EIGRP process. The autonomous system number referred to in the EIGRP configuration is not associated with the *Internet Assigned Numbers Authority (IANA)* globally assigned autonomous system numbers used by external routing protocols.

So what is the difference between the IANA globally assigned autonomous system number and the EIGRP autonomous system number?

An IANA globally assigned autonomous system is a collection of networks under the administrative control of a single entity that presents a common routing policy to the Internet.

Figure 6-13 shows companies A, B, C, and D, which are all under the administrative control of ISP1 identified as AS 64515. ISP1 presents a common routing policy for all these companies when advertising routes to ISP2.

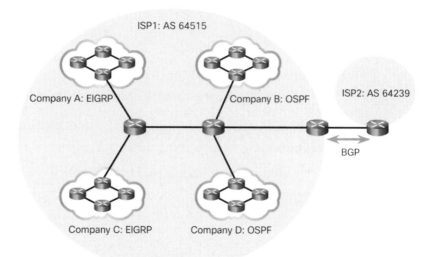

**Figure 6-13**  Autonomous Systems

The guidelines for the creation, selection, and registration of an autonomous system are described in RFC 1930. Global autonomous system numbers are assigned by IANA, the same authority that assigns IP address space. The local *regional Internet registry (RIR)* is responsible for assigning an autonomous system number to an entity from its block of assigned autonomous system numbers. Prior to 2007, assigned autonomous system numbers were 16-bit numbers ranging from 0 to 65,535. Today, 32-bit autonomous system numbers are assigned, thereby increasing the number of available autonomous system numbers to over 4 billion.

Usually, only Internet service providers (ISP), Internet backbone providers, and large institutions connecting to other entities require an autonomous system number. These ISPs and large institutions use the BGP exterior gateway routing protocol to propagate routing information. BGP is the only routing protocol that uses an autonomous system number in its configuration.

The vast majority of companies and institutions with IP networks do not need an autonomous system number because they are controlled by a larger entity, such as an ISP. These companies use interior gateway protocols, such as RIP, EIGRP, OSPF, and IS-IS, to route packets within their own networks. Each of them is one of many independent and separate networks within the autonomous system of the ISP. The ISP is responsible for the routing of packets within its autonomous system and between other autonomous systems.

The autonomous system number used for EIGRP configuration is only significant to the EIGRP routing domain. It functions as a process ID to help routers keep track of multiple running instances of EIGRP. This is required because it is possible to have more than one instance of EIGRP running on a network. Each instance of EIGRP can be configured to support and exchange routing updates for different networks.

### The **router eigrp** Command (6.2.1.3)

The Cisco IOS includes the processes to enable and configure several different types of dynamic routing protocols. The **router** global configuration mode command is used to begin the configuration of any dynamic routing protocol. The topology shown in Figure 6-12 is used to demonstrate this command.

As shown in Example 6-2, when followed by a question mark (**?**), the **router** global configuration mode command lists all the available routing protocols supported by this specific IOS release running on the router.

**Example 6-2**   Router Configuration Command

```
R1(config)# router ?
  bgp        Border Gateway Protocol (BGP)
  eigrp      Enhanced Interior Gateway Routing Protocol (EIGRP)
  isis       ISO IS-IS
  iso-igrp   IGRP for OSI networks
  lisp       Locator/ID Separation Protocol
  mobile     Mobile routes
  odr        On Demand stub Routes
  ospf       Open Shortest Path First (OSPF)
  rip        Routing Information Protocol (RIP)

R1(config)# router ?
```

Use the **router eigrp** *autonomous-system* global configuration mode command to enter the router configuration mode for EIGRP and begin the configuration of the EIGRP process.

The *autonomous-system* argument can be assigned to any 16-bit value between 1 and 65,535. However, all routers within the EIGRP routing domain must use the same autonomous system number.

Example 6-3 shows the configuration of the EIGRP process on routers R1, R2, and R3. Notice that the prompt changes from a global configuration mode prompt to router configuration mode.

**Example 6-3**   Router Configuration Command for All Three Routers

```
R1(config)# router eigrp 1
R1(config-router)#
```

```
R2(config)# router eigrp 1
R2(config-router)#
```

```
R3(config)# router eigrp 1
R3(config-router)#
```

In this example, **1** identifies this particular EIGRP process running on this router. To establish neighbor adjacencies, EIGRP requires all routers in the same routing domain to be configured with the same autonomous system number.

**Note**

EIGRP and OSPF can support multiple instances of the routing protocol. However, this multiple–routing protocol implementation is not usually needed or recommended.

The **router eigrp** *autonomous-system* command does not start the EIGRP process itself. The router does not start sending updates. Rather, this command only provides access to configure the EIGRP settings.

To completely remove the EIGRP routing process from a device, use the **no router eigrp** *autonomous-system* global configuration mode command, which stops the EIGRP process and removes all existing EIGRP router configurations.

## EIGRP Router ID (6.2.1.4)

The EIGRP router ID is used to uniquely identify each router in an EIGRP routing domain.

The router ID is used with both EIGRP and OSPF routing protocols. However, the role of the router ID is more significant in OSPF. In EIGRP IPv4 implementations, the use of the router ID is not that apparent. EIGRP for IPv4 uses the 32-bit router ID to identify the originating router for redistribution of external routes. The need for a router ID becomes more evident in the discussion of EIGRP for IPv6. While the router ID is necessary for redistribution, the details of EIGRP redistribution are beyond the scope of this course. For purposes of this course, it is only necessary to understand what the router ID is and how it is determined.

To determine its router ID, a Cisco IOS router uses the following three criteria, in order:

1. Use the address configured with the **eigrp router-id** *ipv4-address* router configuration mode command.

2. If the router ID is not configured, choose the highest *loopback interface* IPv4 address.

3. If no loopback interfaces are configured, choose the highest active IPv4 address of any of the router's physical interfaces.

If the network administrator does not explicitly configure a router ID using the **eigrp router-id** command, EIGRP generates its own router ID, using either a loopback or physical IPv4 address. A loopback address is a virtual interface and is automatically in the up state when configured. The interface does not need to be enabled for EIGRP, meaning that it does not need to be included in one of the EIGRP **network** commands. However, the interface must be in the up/up state.

Using the criteria just described, Figure 6-14 displays the default EIGRP router IDs that are determined by the highest active IPv4 addresses of these routers.

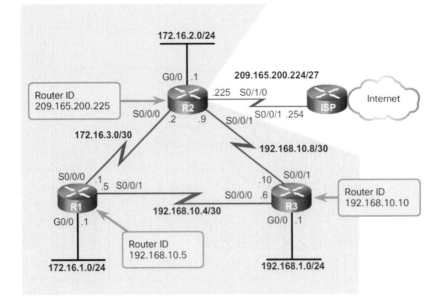

**Figure 6-14** Topology with Default EIGRP Router IDs

> **Note**
>
> The **eigrp router-id** command is used to configure the router ID for EIGRP. Some versions of IOS accept the command **router-id**, without first specifying **eigrp**. The running config, however, displays **eigrp router-id**, regardless of which command is used.

## Configuring the EIGRP Router ID (6.2.1.5)

Using the **eigrp router-id** *ipv4-address* router configuration command is the preferred method of configuring the EIGRP router ID. This method takes precedence over any configured loopback or physical interface IPv4 addresses.

> **Note**
>
> The IPv4 address used to indicate the router ID is actually any 32-bit number displayed in dotted-decimal notation.

The *ipv4-address* router ID can be configured with any IPv4 address except 0.0.0.0 and 255.255.255.255. The router ID should be a unique 32-bit number in the EIGRP routing domain; otherwise, routing inconsistencies can occur.

Example 6-4 shows the configuration of the EIGRP router ID for routers R1 and R2.

**Example 6-4**   Configuring and Verifying the EIGRP Router ID

```
R1(config)# router eigrp 1
R1(config-router)# eigrp router-id 1.1.1.1
R1(config-router)#

R2(config)# router eigrp 1
R2(config-router)# eigrp router-id 2.2.2.2
R2(config-router)#
```

If a router ID is not explicitly configured, the router uses its highest IPv4 address configured on a loopback interface. The advantage of using a loopback interface is that unlike physical interfaces, loopbacks cannot fail. There are no actual cables or adjacent devices on which the loopback interface depends for being in the up state. Therefore, using a loopback address for the router ID can provide a more consistent router ID than using an interface address.

If the **eigrp router-id** command is not used and loopback interfaces are configured, EIGRP chooses the highest IPv4 address of any of its loopback interfaces. The following commands are used to enable and configure a loopback interface:

```
Router(config)# interface loopback number
Router(config-if)# ip address ipv4-address subnet-mask
```

## Verifying the EIGRP Process

Example 6-5 shows the **show ip protocols** output for R2, including its router ID.

**Example 6-5**   Verifying Router ID on R2

```
R2# show ip protocols
*** IP Routing is NSF aware ***
Routing Protocol is "eigrp 1"
<Output omitted>
  EIGRP-IPv4 Protocol for AS(1)
    Metric weight K1=1, K2=0, K3=1, K4=0, K5=0
    NSF-aware route hold timer is 240
    Router-ID: 2.2.2.2
    Topology : 0 (base)
      Active Timer: 3 min
      Distance: internal 90 external 170
      Maximum path: 4
      Maximum hopcount 100
      Maximum metric variance 1

  Automatic Summarization: disabled
  Maximum path: 4
  Routing for Networks:
  Routing Information Sources:
    Gateway         Distance      Last Update
  Distance: internal 90 external 170

R1#
```

The **show ip protocols** command displays the parameters and current state of any active routing protocol processes, including both EIGRP and OSPF.

## The **network** Command (6.2.1.6)

EIGRP router configuration mode allows for the configuration of the EIGRP routing protocol. Notice in Figure 6-12 that R1, R2, and R3 all have networks that should be included within a single EIGRP routing domain. To enable EIGRP routing on an interface, use the **network** *ipv4-network-address* router configuration mode command. *ipv4-network-address* is the classful network address for each directly connected network.

The **network** command has the same function in all IGP routing protocols. With EIGRP the **network** command does the following:

- It enables any interface on this router that matches the network address in the **network** router configuration mode command to send and receive EIGRP updates.

- It includes the network of the interfaces in EIGRP routing updates.

Figure 6-15 shows the **network** commands required to configure EIGRP on R1. A single classful **network** statement, **network 172.16.0.0**, is used on R1 to include both interfaces in subnets 172.16.1.0/24 and 172.16.3.0/30. Notice that only the classful network address is used.

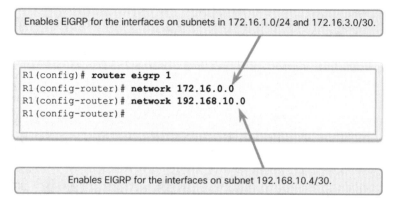

**Figure 6-15**   EIGRP Network Commands for R1

Example 6-6 shows the **network** command used to enable EIGRP on R2's interfaces for subnets 172.16.1.0/24 and 172.16.2.0/24.

**Example 6-6**   EIGRP Neighbor Adjacency Message

```
R2(config)# router eigrp 1
R2(config-router)# network 172.16.0.0
R2(config-router)#
*Feb 28 17:51:42.543: %DUAL-5-NBRCHANGE: EIGRP-IPv4 1: Neighbor 172.16.3.1
  (Serial0/0/0) is up: new adjacency
R2(config-router)#
```

When EIGRP is configured on R2's S0/0/0 interface, DUAL sends a notification message to the console, stating that a neighbor adjacency with another EIGRP router on that interface has been established. This new adjacency happens automatically because both R1 and R2 use the same autonomous system number (that is, **1**), and both routers now send updates on their interfaces in the 172.16.0.0 network.

DUAL automatically generates the notification message because the **eigrp log-neighbor-changes** router configuration mode command is enabled by default. Specifically, the command helps verify neighbor adjacencies during configuration of EIGRP and displays any changes in EIGRP neighbor adjacencies, such as when an EIGRP adjacency has been added or removed.

### The **network** Command and Wildcard Mask (6.2.1.7)

By default, when using the **network** command and an IPv4 network address, such as 172.16.0.0, all interfaces on the router that belong to that classful network address are enabled for EIGRP. However, there may be times when a network administrator does not want to include all interfaces within a network when enabling EIGRP.

For example, in Figure 6-16, assume that an administrator wants to enable EIGRP on R2, but only for the subnet 192.168.10.8 255.255.255.252 on the S0/0/1 interface.

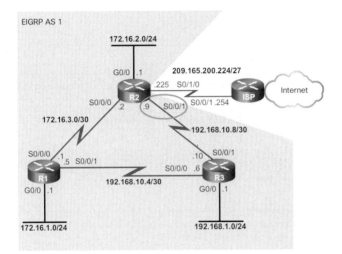

**Figure 6-16**   EIGRP for IPv4 Topology

To configure EIGRP to advertise specific subnets only, use the *wildcard-mask* option with the **network** *network-address* [*wildcard-mask*] router configuration command.

A *wildcard mask*, also called an *inverse mask*, is similar to the inverse of a subnet mask. In a subnet mask, binary 1s are significant, and binary 0s are not. In a wildcard mask, binary 0s are significant, and binary 1s are not. For example, the inverse of subnet mask 255.255.255.252 is 0.0.0.3.

Calculating a wildcard mask may seem daunting at first, but it's actually pretty easy to do. To calculate the inverse of the subnet mask, subtract the subnet mask from 255.255.255.255, as follows:

$$255.255.255.255$$

$$- 255.255.255.252$$

-------------------------

$$\begin{array}{ccccc} 0. & 0. & 0. & 3 & \text{Wildcard mask} \end{array}$$

Figure 6-17 continues the EIGRP network configuration of R2. The **network 192.168.10.8 0.0.0.3** command specifically enables EIGRP on the S0/0/1 interface, a member of the 192.168.10.8 255.255.255.252 subnet.

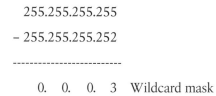

Enables EIGRP for a specific interface, using 192.168.10.8/30 subnet.

```
R2(config)# router eigrp 1
R2(config-router)# network 192.168.10.8 0.0.0.3
R2(config-router)
```

**Figure 6-17**    **network** Command with Wildcard Mask

A wildcard mask is part of the official command syntax of the EIGRP **network** command. However, the Cisco IOS version also accepts a subnet mask to be used instead. For example, Example 6-7 configures the same S0/0/1 interface on R2 but this time using a subnet mask in the **network** command. Notice in the output of the **show running-config** command that the IOS converted the subnet mask to its wildcard mask.

**Example 6-7**    Alternative Network Command Configuration Using a Subnet Mask

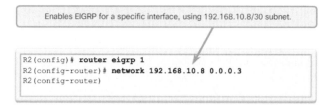

```
R2(config)# router eigrp 1
R2(config-router)# network 192.168.10.8 255.255.255.252
R2(config-router)# end
R2# show running-config | section eigrp 1
router eigrp 1
 network 172.16.0.0
 network 192.168.10.8 0.0.0.3
 eigrp router-id 2.2.2.2
R2#
```

Example 6-8 shows the configuration of R3 using just a network address for 192.168.1.0 and using a wildcard mask configuration for 192.168.10.4/30 and 192.168.10.8/30.

**Example 6-8**   Configuring the Network Command and Wildcard Mask on R3

```
R3(config)# router eigrp 1
R3(config-router)# network 192.168.1.0
R3(config-router)# network 192.168.10.4 0.0.0.3
*Feb 28 20:47:22.695: %DUAL-5-NBRCHANGE: EIGRP-IPv4 1: Neighbor 192.168.10.5
  (Serial0/0/0) is up: new adjacency
R3(config-router)# network 192.168.10.8 0.0.0.3
*Feb 28 20:47:06.555: %DUAL-5-NBRCHANGE: EIGRP-IPv4 1: Neighbor 192.168.10.9
  (Serial0/0/1) is up: new adjacency
R3(config-router)#
```

## Passive Interface (6.2.1.8)

As soon as a new interface is enabled in an EIGRP network, EIGRP attempts to form a neighbor adjacency with any neighboring routers to send and receive EIGRP updates.

At times it may be necessary, or advantageous, to include a directly connected network in the EIGRP routing update but not allow any neighbor adjacencies off that interface to form. The **passive-interface** command can be used to prevent the neighbor adjacencies. There are two primary reasons for enabling the **passive-interface** command:

- To suppress unnecessary update traffic, such as when an interface is a LAN interface, with no other routers connected

- To increase security controls, such as preventing unknown rogue routing devices from receiving EIGRP updates

Figure 6-18 illustrates how R1, R2, and R3 do not have neighbors on their GigabitEthernet 0/0 interfaces.

The **passive-interface** *interface-type interface-number* router configuration mode command disables the transmission and receipt of EIGRP Hello packets on these interfaces.

Example 6-9 shows the **passive-interface** command configured to suppress Hello packets on the LANs for R1, R2, and R3.

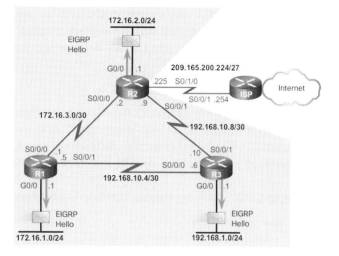

**Figure 6-18**   EIGRP for IPv4 Topology

**Example 6-9**   Configuring and Verifying EIGRP Passive Interfaces

```
R1(config)# router eigrp 1
R1(config-router)# passive-interface gigabitethernet 0/0

R2(config)# router eigrp 1
R2(config-router)# passive-interface gigabitethernet 0/0

R3(config)# router eigrp 1
R3(config-router)# passive-interface gigabitethernet 0/0
```

Without a neighbor adjacency, EIGRP cannot exchange routes with a neighbor. Therefore, the **passive-interface** command prevents the exchange of routes on the interface. Although EIGRP does not send or receive routing updates on an interface configured with the **passive-interface** command, it still includes the address of the interface in routing updates sent out other nonpassive interfaces.

**Note**

To configure all interfaces as passive, use the **passive-interface default** command. To disable an interface as passive, use the **no passive-interface** *interface-type interface-number* command.

An example of using the passive interface to increase security controls is when a network must connect to a third-party organization of which the local administrator has no control, such as when connecting to an ISP network. In this case, the local network administrator would need to advertise the interface link through the company's own network but would not want the third-party organization to receive or send routing updates to the local routing device because that would be a security risk.

### Verifying the Passive Interface

To verify whether any interface on a router is configured as passive, use the **show ip protocols** privileged EXEC mode command, as shown in Example 6-10. Notice that although R2's GigabitEthernet 0/0 interface is a passive interface, EIGRP still includes the interface's network address, 172.16.0.0, in its routing updates.

**Example 6-10**   Verifying Passive Interface Configuration

```
R2# show ip protocols
*** IP Routing is NSF aware ***


Routing Protocol is "eigrp 1"
<output omitted>
  Routing for Networks:
    172.16.0.0
    192.168.10.8/30
  Passive Interface(s):
    GigabitEthernet0/0
  Routing Information Sources:
    Gateway         Distance      Last Update
    192.168.10.10          90      02:14:28
    172.16.3.1             90      02:14:28
  Distance: internal 90 external 170


R2#
```

# Verify EIGRP with IPv4 (6.2.2)

In this topic, you will learn about the EIGRP for IPv4 operation in a small routed network.

## Verifying EIGRP: Examining Neighbors (6.2.2.1)

Before EIGRP can send or receive any updates, routers must establish adjacencies with their neighbors. EIGRP routers establish adjacencies with neighbor routers by exchanging EIGRP Hello packets.

Use the **show ip eigrp neighbors** command to view the neighbor table and verify that EIGRP has established an adjacency with its neighbors. For each router, you should be able to see the IPv4 address of the adjacent router and the interface that this router uses to reach that EIGRP neighbor.

Based on the topology in Figure 6-18, each router has two neighbors listed in the neighbor table. R1's neighbor table is shown in Figure 6-19.

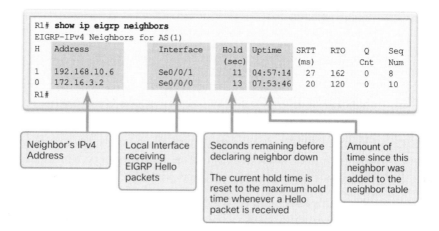

**Figure 6-19**    The **show ip eigrp neighbors** Command

The column headers in the **show ip eigrp neighbors** command output identify the following:

- **H**—The neighbors, listed in the order in which they were learned.

- **Address**—The IPv4 address of the neighbor.

- **Interface**—The local interface on which this Hello packet was received.

- **Hold**—The current hold time. When a Hello packet is received, this value is reset to the maximum hold time for that interface and then counts down to zero. If zero is reached, the neighbor is considered down.

- **Uptime**—The amount of time since this neighbor was added to the neighbor table.

- **Smooth Round Trip Timer (SRTT) and Retransmission Timeout (RTO)**—Used by RTP to manage reliable EIGRP packets.

- **Queue Count**—Should always be zero. If it is more than zero, EIGRP packets wait to be sent.

- **Sequence Number**—Used to track Update, Query, and Reply packets.

The **show ip eigrp neighbors** command is very useful for verifying and troubleshooting EIGRP.

If a neighbor is not listed after adjacencies have been established with a router's neighbors, check the local interface by using the **show ip interface brief** command to ensure that it is activated. If the interface is active, try to **ping** the IPv4 address of the neighbor. If the **ping** fails, it means that the neighbor interface is down and needs to be activated. If the **ping** is successful and EIGRP still does not see the router as a neighbor, examine the following configurations:

■ Are both routers configured with the same EIGRP autonomous system number?

■ Is the directly connected network included in the EIGRP **network** statements?

## Verifying EIGRP: show ip protocols Command (6.2.2.2)

The **show ip protocols** command is useful for identifying the parameters and other information about the current state of any active IPv4 routing protocol processes configured on the router. The **show ip protocols** command displays different types of output specific to each routing protocol.

The output in Figure 6-20 indicates several EIGRP parameters. Details of the numbering in the figure are as follows:

1. EIGRP is an active dynamic routing protocol on R1, configured with the autonomous system number 1.

2. The EIGRP router ID of R1 is 1.1.1.1.

3. The EIGRP administrative distances on R1 are internal AD of 90 and external of 170 (default values).

4. By default, EIGRP does not automatically summarize networks. Subnets are included in the routing updates.

5. The output shows the EIGRP neighbor adjacencies that R1 has with other routers used to receive EIGRP routing updates.

**Note**

Prior to IOS 15, EIGRP automatic summarization was enabled by default.

The output from the **show ip protocols** command is useful in debugging routing operations. Information in the routing information sources field can help identify a router suspected of delivering bad routing information. The field lists all the EIGRP routing sources the Cisco IOS software uses to build its IPv4 routing table. For each source, note the following:

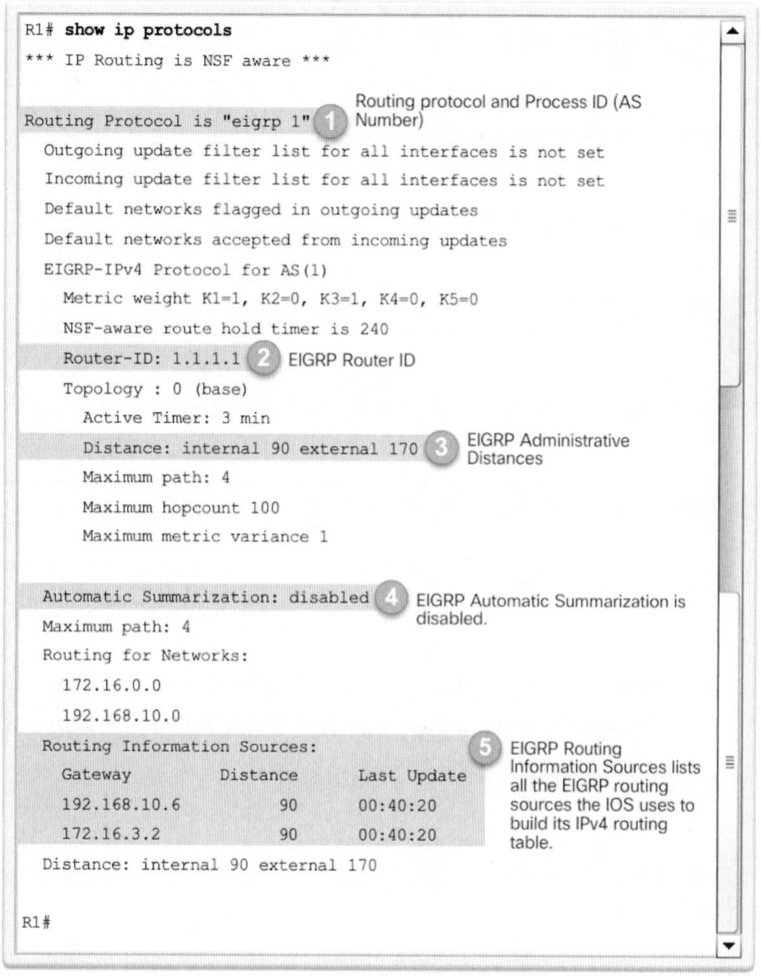

```
R1# show ip protocols
*** IP Routing is NSF aware ***

                                          Routing protocol and Process ID (AS
Routing Protocol is "eigrp 1"  1   Number)
  Outgoing update filter list for all interfaces is not set
  Incoming update filter list for all interfaces is not set
  Default networks flagged in outgoing updates
  Default networks accepted from incoming updates
  EIGRP-IPv4 Protocol for AS(1)
    Metric weight K1=1, K2=0, K3=1, K4=0, K5=0
    NSF-aware route hold timer is 240
    Router-ID: 1.1.1.1  2   EIGRP Router ID
    Topology : 0 (base)
      Active Timer: 3 min
      Distance: internal 90 external 170  3   EIGRP Administrative
                                              Distances
      Maximum path: 4
      Maximum hopcount 100
      Maximum metric variance 1


  Automatic Summarization: disabled  4   EIGRP Automatic Summarization is
  Maximum path: 4                        disabled.
  Routing for Networks:
    172.16.0.0
    192.168.10.0
  Routing Information Sources:             5   EIGRP Routing
    Gateway         Distance               Information Sources lists
                               Last Update all the EIGRP routing
    192.168.10.6         90    00:40:20    sources the IOS uses to
    172.16.3.2          90    00:40:20     build its IPv4 routing
                                           table.
  Distance: internal 90 external 170

R1#
```

**Figure 6-20**   The **show ip protocols** Command

- IPv4 address

- Administrative distance

- Time the last update was received from this source

The Cisco IOS prefers EIGRP to other IGPs because it has the lowest administrative distance. As shown in Table 6-4, EIGRP has a default AD of 90 for internal routes and 170 for routes imported from an external source, such as default routes. EIGRP has a third AD value of 5 for summary routes.

**Table 6-4**    Default Administrative Distances

| Route Source | Administrative Distance |
| --- | --- |
| Connected | 0 |
| Static | 1 |
| EIGRP summary route | 5 |
| External BGP | 20 |
| Internal EIGRP | 90 |
| IGRP | 100 |
| OSPF | 110 |
| IS-IS | 115 |
| RIP | 120 |
| External EIGRP | 170 |
| Internal BGP | 200 |

## Verifying EIGRP: Examine the IPv4 Routing Table (6.2.2.3)

Another way to verify that EIGRP and other functions of the router are configured properly is to examine the IPv4 routing tables by using the **show ip route** command. As with any other dynamic routing protocol, the network administrator must verify the information in the routing table to ensure that it is populated as expected, based on configurations entered. For this reason, it is important to have a good understanding of the routing protocol configuration commands, as well as the routing protocol operations and the processes used by the routing protocol to build the IP routing table.

Notice that the outputs used throughout this course are from Cisco IOS 15. Prior to IOS 15, EIGRP *automatic summarization* was enabled by default. The state of automatic summarization can make a difference in the information displayed in the IPv4 routing table. If a previous version of the IOS is used, automatic summarization can be disabled by using the **no auto-summary** router configuration mode command.

In Example 6-11, the IPv4 routing table is examined by using the **show ip route** command. EIGRP routes are denoted in the routing table with a **D**. The letter D was used to represent EIGRP because the protocol is based on the DUAL algorithm.

**Example 6-11**    R1's IPv4 Routing Tables

```
R1# show ip route
Codes: L - local, C - connected, S - static, R - RIP, M - mobile, B - BGP
       D - EIGRP, EX - EIGRP external, O - OSPF, IA - OSPF inter area
       <Output omitted>


Gateway of last resort is not set


     172.16.0.0/16 is variably subnetted, 5 subnets, 3 masks
C       172.16.1.0/24 is directly connected, GigabitEthernet0/0
L       172.16.1.1/32 is directly connected, GigabitEthernet0/0
D         172.16.2.0/24 [90/2170112] via 172.16.3.2, 00:14:35, Serial0/0/0
C       172.16.3.0/30 is directly connected, Serial0/0/0
L       172.16.3.1/32 is directly connected, Serial0/0/0
D     192.168.1.0/24 [90/2170112] via 192.168.10.6, 00:13:57, Serial0/0/1
     192.168.10.0/24 is variably subnetted, 3 subnets, 2 masks
C       192.168.10.4/30 is directly connected, Serial0/0/1
L       192.168.10.5/32 is directly connected, Serial0/0/1
D         192.168.10.8/30 [90/2681856] via 192.168.10.6, 00:50:42, Serial0/0/1
                          [90/2681856] via 172.16.3.2, 00:50:42, Serial0/0/0
R1#
```

The **show ip route** command verifies that routes received by EIGRP neighbors are installed in the IPv4 routing table. The **show ip route** command displays the entire routing table, including remote networks learned dynamically, as well as directly connected and static routes. For this reason, it is normally the first command used to check for convergence. When routing is correctly configured on all routers, the **show ip route** command reflects that each router has a full routing table, with a route to each network in the topology.

Notice that R1 has installed routes to three IPv4 remote networks in its IPv4 routing table:

- The 172.16.2.0/24 network, received from router R2 on the Serial 0/0/0 interface

- The 192.168.1.0/24 network, received from router R2 on the Serial 0/0/1 interface

- The 192.168.10.8/30 network, received from both R2 on the Serial 0/0/0 interface and R3 on the Serial0/0/1 interface

R1 has two paths to the 192.168.10.8/30 network because its cost or metric to reach that network is the same or equal using both routers. These are known as *equal-cost routes*. R1 uses both paths to reach this network, which is known as *load balancing*. The EIGRP metric is discussed later in this chapter.

Example 6-12 displays the routing table for R2. Notice that the results are similar to those displayed for R1 in Example 6-11, including an equal-cost route for the 192.168.10.4/30 network.

**Example 6-12**   R2's IPv4 Routing Tables

```
R2# show ip route | begin Gateway
Gateway of last resort is not set

  172.16.0.0/16 is variably subnetted, 5 subnets, 3 masks
D        172.16.1.0/24 [90/2170112] via 172.16.3.1, 00:11:05, Serial0/0/0
C        172.16.2.0/24 is directly connected, GigabitEthernet0/0
L        172.16.2.1/32 is directly connected, GigabitEthernet0/0
C        172.16.3.0/30 is directly connected, Serial0/0/0
L        172.16.3.2/32 is directly connected, Serial0/0/0
D     192.168.1.0/24 [90/2170112] via 192.168.10.10, 00:15:16, Serial0/0/1
      192.168.10.0/24 is variably subnetted, 3 subnets, 2 masks
D        192.168.10.4/30 [90/2681856] via 192.168.10.10, 00:52:00, Serial0/0/1
                         [90/2681856] via 172.16.3.1, 00:52:00, Serial0/0/0
C        192.168.10.8/30 is directly connected, Serial0/0/1
L        192.168.10.9/32 is directly connected, Serial0/0/1
      209.165.200.0/24 is variably subnetted, 2 subnets, 2 masks
C        209.165.200.224/27 is directly connected, Loopback209
L        209.165.200.225/32 is directly connected, Loopback209
R2#
```

Example 6-13 displays the routing table for R3. Much as with the results for R1 and R2, remote networks are learned using EIGRP, including an equal-cost route for the 172.16.3.0/30 network.

**Example 6-13**   R3's IPv4 Routing Tables

```
R3# show ip route | begin Gateway
Gateway of last resort is not set

  172.16.0.0/16 is variably subnetted, 3 subnets, 2 masks
D        172.16.1.0/24 [90/2170112] via 192.168.10.5, 00:12:00, Serial0/0/0
D        172.16.2.0/24 [90/2170112] via 192.168.10.9, 00:16:49, Serial0/0/1
D        172.16.3.0/30 [90/2681856] via 192.168.10.9, 00:52:55, Serial0/0/1
                        [90/2681856] via 192.168.10.5, 00:52:55, Serial0/0/0
      192.168.1.0/24 is variably subnetted, 2 subnets, 2 masks
C        192.168.1.0/24 is directly connected, GigabitEthernet0/0
```

```
L          192.168.1.1/32 is directly connected, GigabitEthernet0/0
        192.168.10.0/24 is variably subnetted, 4 subnets, 2 masks
C          192.168.10.4/30 is directly connected, Serial0/0/0
L          192.168.10.6/32 is directly connected, Serial0/0/0
C          192.168.10.8/30 is directly connected, Serial0/0/1
L          192.168.10.10/32 is directly connected, Serial0/0/1
R3#
```

**Packet Tracer 6.2.2.4: Configuring Basic EIGRP with IPv4**

Background/Scenario

In this activity, you will implement basic EIGRP configurations, including using network commands, configuring passive interfaces, and disabling automatic summarization. You will then verify your EIGRP configuration by using a variety of **show** commands and testing end-to-end connectivity.

**Lab 6.2.2.5: Configuring Basic EIGRP with IPv4**

Refer to *Scaling Networks v6 Labs & Study Guide* and the online course to complete this activity.

In this lab, you will complete the following objectives:

- Part 1: Build the Network and Verify Connectivity
- Part 2: Configure EIGRP Routing
- Part 3: Verify EIGRP Routing
- Part 4: Configure Bandwidth and Passive Interfaces

# EIGRP Operation (6.3)

In this section, you will learn how EIGRP operates in a small to medium-sized business network.

## EIGRP Initial Route Discovery (6.3.1)

In this topic, you will learn how EIGRP forms neighbor relationships.

## EIGRP Neighbor Adjacency (6.3.1.1)

The goal of any dynamic routing protocol is to learn about remote networks from other routers and to reach convergence in the routing domain. Before any EIGRP Update packets can be exchanged between routers, EIGRP must first discover its neighbors. EIGRP neighbors are other routers running EIGRP on directly connected networks.

EIGRP uses Hello packets to establish and maintain neighbor adjacencies. For two EIGRP routers to become neighbors, several parameters between the two routers must match. For example, two EIGRP routers must use the same EIGRP metric parameters, and both must be configured using the same autonomous system number.

Each EIGRP router maintains a neighbor table, which contains a list of routers on shared links that have an EIGRP adjacency with this router. The neighbor table is used to track the status of these EIGRP neighbors.

Figure 6-21 displays two EIGRP-enabled routers exchanging initial EIGRP Hello packets.

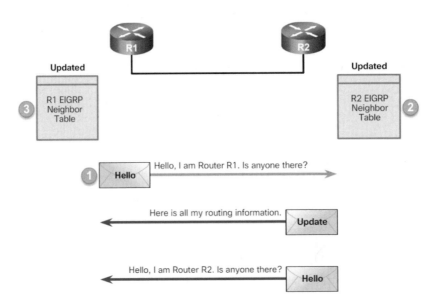

**Figure 6-21**   Discovering Neighbors

As illustrated in the figure, these are the steps in discovering neighbors:

1. A new router (R1) comes up on the link and sends an EIGRP Hello packet through all its EIGRP-configured interfaces.

2. R2 receives the Hello packet on an EIGRP-enabled interface and adds R1 to its neighbor table. R2 replies with an EIGRP Update packet that contains all the routes it has in its routing table, except those learned through that interface (split horizon).

3. R2 sends a Hello packet to R1, and R1 adds R2 to its neighbor table.

## EIGRP Topology Table (6.3.1.2)

EIGRP updates contain networks that are reachable from the router sending the update. As EIGRP updates are exchanged between neighbors, the receiving router adds these entries to its EIGRP topology table.

Each EIGRP router maintains a topology table for each routed protocol configured, such as IPv4 and IPv6. The topology table includes route entries for every destination that the router learns from its directly connected EIGRP neighbors.

Figure 6-22 displays the continuation of the initial route discovery process just described and illustrates how the routers update the topology table.

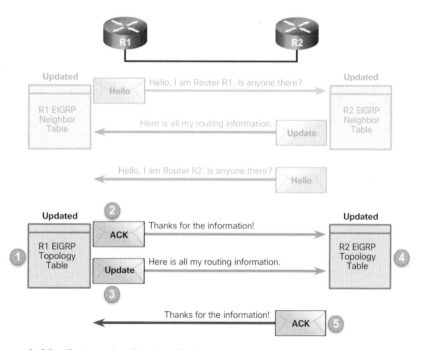

**Figure 6-22**   Exchanging Routing Updates

As illustrated in the figure, these are the steps in exchanging routing updates:

1. In the neighbor discovery process just described, R1 had received an update from R2. The Update packet included information about the routes and their metrics that the neighbor was advertising. R1 adds all update entries to its topology table. The topology table includes all destinations advertised by neighboring (adjacent) routers and the cost (metric) to reach each network.

2. EIGRP Update packets use reliable delivery; therefore, R1 replies with an EIGRP Acknowledgment packet, informing R2 that it has received the update.

3. R1 sends an EIGRP update to R2, advertising the routes that it is aware of, except those learned from R2 (split horizon).

4. R2 receives the EIGRP update from neighbor R1 and adds this information to its own topology table.

5. R2 responds to R1's EIGRP Update packet with an EIGRP acknowledgment.

## EIGRP Convergence (6.3.1.3)

Figure 6-23 displays the final steps of the initial route discovery process.

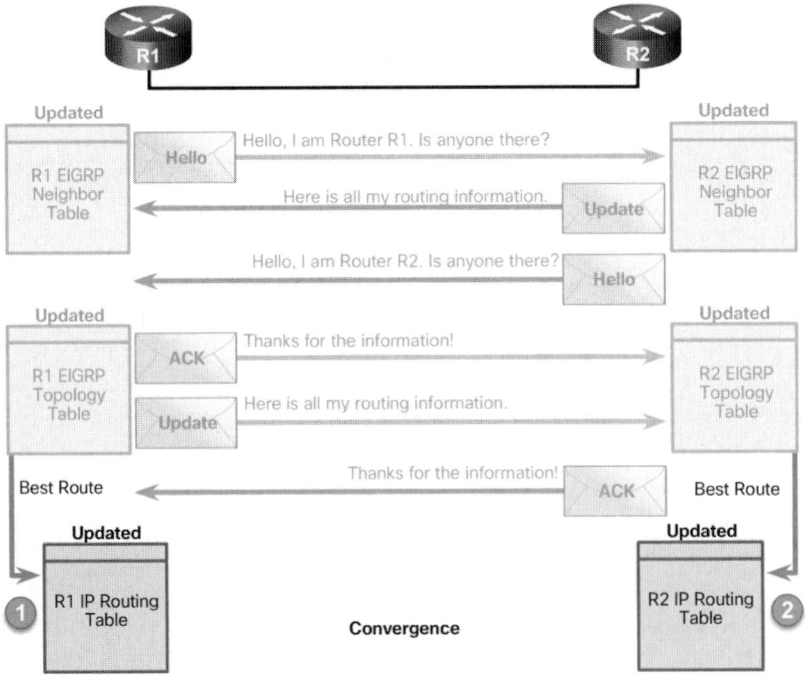

**Figure 6-23**   Updating the IPv4 Routing Table

As illustrated in the figure, these are the steps in updating the IPv4 routing table:

1. After receiving the EIGRP Update packets from R2, using the information in the topology table, R1 updates its IP routing table with the best path to each destination, including the metric and the next-hop router.

2. Similarly to R1, R2 updates its IP routing table with the best path routes to each network.

At this point, EIGRP on both routers is considered to be in the converged state.

**Interactive Graphic**

**Activity 6.3.1.4: Identify the Steps in Establishing EIGRP Neighbor Adjacencies**

Refer to the online course to complete this activity.

# EIGRP Metrics (6.3.2)

In this topic, you will learn about the EIGRP metric.

## EIGRP Composite Metric (6.3.2.1)

By default, EIGRP uses the following values in its composite metric to calculate the preferred path to a network:

- **Bandwidth**—The slowest bandwidth among all the outgoing interfaces, along the path from source to destination.

- **Delay**—The cumulative (sum) of all interface delay along the path (in tens of microseconds).

The following values can be used but are not recommended because they typically result in frequent recalculation of the topology table:

- **Reliability**—Represents the worst reliability between the source and destination, which is based on keepalives.

- **Load**—Represents the worst load on a link between the source and destination, which is computed based on the packet rate and the configured bandwidth of the interface.

**Note** .

Although the MTU is included in the routing table updates, it is not a routing metric used by EIGRP.

Figure 6-24 displays the composite metric formula used by EIGRP.

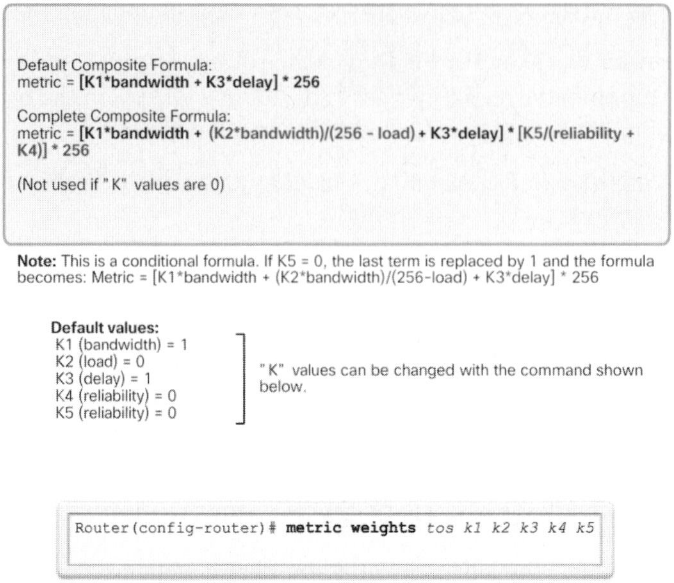

Default Composite Formula:
metric = **[K1\*bandwidth + K3\*delay]** \* 256

Complete Composite Formula:
metric = **[K1\*bandwidth** + (K2\*bandwidth)/(256 − load) + **K3\*delay]** \* **[K5/(reliability +
K4)]** \* 256

(Not used if "K" values are 0)

**Note:** This is a conditional formula. If K5 = 0, the last term is replaced by 1 and the formula
becomes: Metric = [K1\*bandwidth + (K2\*bandwidth)/(256−load) + K3\*delay] \* 256

**Default values:**
K1 (bandwidth) = 1
K2 (load) = 0
K3 (delay) = 1        "K" values can be changed with the command shown
K4 (reliability) = 0   below.
K5 (reliability) = 0

```
Router(config-router)# metric weights tos k1 k2 k3 k4 k5
```

**Figure 6-24**    EIGRP Composite Metric

The formula consists of values K1 to K5, known as EIGRP metric weights. K1 and
K3 represent bandwidth and delay, respectively. K2 represents load, and K4 and
K5 represent reliability. By default, K1 and K3 are set to 1, and K2, K4, and K5
are set to 0. The result is that only the bandwidth and delay values are used in the
computation of the default composite metric. EIGRP for IPv4 and EIGRP for IPv6
use the same formula for the composite metric.

The metric calculation method (*K* values) and the EIGRP autonomous system number
must match between EIGRP neighbors. If they do not match, the routers do not form
an adjacency.

The default *K* values can be changed with the **metric weights** router configuration
mode command:

```
Router(config-router)# metric weights tos k1 k2 k3 k4 k5
```

> **Note**
>
> Modifying the **metric weights** value is generally not recommended and is beyond the scope
> of this course. However, its relevance is important in establishing neighbor adjacencies. If
> one router has modified the metric weights and another router has not, an adjacency does
> not form.

The **show ip protocols** command is used to verify the *k* values. The command output
for R1 is shown in Example 6-14. Notice that the *k* values on R1 are set to the default.

**Example 6-14**  Verifying Metric K Values

```
R1# show ip protocols
*** IP Routing is NSF aware ***

Routing Protocol is "eigrp 1"
  Outgoing update filter list for all interfaces is not set
  Incoming update filter list for all interfaces is not set
  Default networks flagged in outgoing updates
  Default networks accepted from incoming updates
  EIGRP-IPv4 Protocol for AS(1)
    Metric weight K1=1, K2=0, K3=1, K4=0, K5=0
    NSF-aware route hold timer is 240
    Router-ID: 1.1.1.1
<Output omitted>
R1#
```

## Examining Interface Metric Values (6.3.2.2)

The **show interfaces** command displays interface information, including the parameters used to compute the EIGRP metric.

Example 6-15 shows the **show interfaces** command for the Serial 0/0/0 interface on R1.

**Example 6-15**  Verifying Metrics with the **show interface** Command

```
R1# show interface serial 0/0/0
Serial0/0/0 is up, line protocol is up
  Hardware is WIC MBRD Serial
  Internet address is 172.16.3.1/30
  MTU 1500 bytes, BW 1544 Kbit/sec, DLY 20000 usec,
     reliability 255/255, txload 1/255, rxload 1/255
  Encapsulation HDLC, loopback not set

<Output omitted>

R1# show interface gigabitethernet 0/0
GigabitEthernet0/0 is up, line protocol is up
  Hardware is CN Gigabit Ethernet, address is fc99.4775.c3e0 (bia fc99.4775.c3e0)
  Internet address is 172.16.1.1/24
  MTU 1500 bytes, BW 100000 Kbit/sec, DLY 100 usec,
     reliability 255/255, txload 1/255, rxload 1/255
  Encapsulation ARPA, loopback not set
<Output omitted>
R1#
```

Table 6-5 explains the significance of the highlighted output in Example 6-15.

**Table 6-5    show interface** Output Explained

| Field in Output | Description |
|---|---|
| BW | ■ Bandwidth of the interface (in kilobits per second). |
| DLY | ■ Delay of the interface (in microseconds). |
| reliability | ■ Reliability of the interface as a fraction of 255 (255 / 255 is 100% reliability), calculated as an exponential average over five minutes. |
| | ■ By default, EIGRP does not include this value in the computing of the metric. |
| txload, rxload | ■ Transmit and receive load on the interface as a fraction of 255 (255 / 255 is completely saturated), calculated as an exponential average over five minutes. |
| | ■ By default, EIGRP does not include its value in the computing of the metric. |

**Note**

Throughout this course, bandwidth is indicated in Kbps. However, router output displays bandwidth by using the Kbit/sec abbreviation. Router output also displays delay in *usec*. In this course, delay is referenced in *microseconds*.

## Bandwidth Metric (6.3.2.3)

The bandwidth metric is a static value that EIGRP and OSPF use to calculate their routing metric. The bandwidth is displayed in kilobits per second (Kbps).

On older routers, the serial link bandwidth metric defaults to 1544 Kbps. This is the bandwidth of a T1 connection. On newer routers, such as the Cisco 4321, serial link bandwidth defaults to the clock rate used on the link.

The serial links in the topology in Figure 6-25 will be configured with the bandwidths used in this section.

**Note**

The bandwidths used in this topology were chosen to help explain the calculation of the routing protocol metrics and the process of best path selection. These bandwidth values do not reflect the common types of connections found in today's networks.

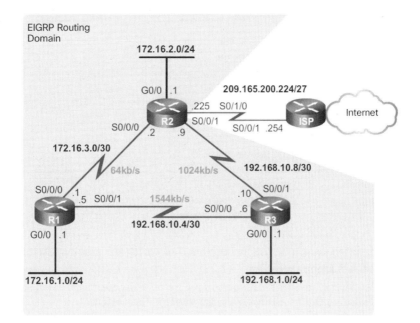

**Figure 6-25**   EIGRP for IPv4 Topology with Bandwidth Values

Always verify bandwidth with the **show interfaces** command. The default value of the bandwidth may or may not reflect the actual physical bandwidth of the interface. If actual bandwidth of the link differs from the default bandwidth value, the bandwidth value should be modified.

Because both EIGRP and OSPF use bandwidth in default metric calculations, a correct value for bandwidth is very important to the accuracy of routing information.

Use the **bandwidth** *kilobits-bandwidth-value* interface configuration mode command to modify the bandwidth metric. Use the **no bandwidth** command to restore the default value. This command must be configured on both interconnecting links to ensure proper routing in both directions.

For example, the link between R1 and R2 has a bandwidth of 64 Kbps, and the link between R2 and R3 has a bandwidth of 1024 Kbps.

Example 6-16 shows the configurations used on all three routers to modify the bandwidth on the appropriate serial interfaces.

**Example 6-16**    Bandwidth Configuration on All Three Routers

```
R1(config)# interface s 0/0/0
R1(config-if)# bandwidth 64
```

```
R2(config)# interface s 0/0/0
R2(config-if)# bandwidth 64
R2(config-if)# exit
R2(config)# interface s 0/0/1
R2(config-if)# bandwidth 1024
```

```
R3(config)# interface s 0/0/1
R3(config-if)# bandwidth 1024
```

Use the **show interfaces** command to verify the new bandwidth parameters, as shown Example 6-17.

**Example 6-17**    Verifying the Bandwidth Parameters

```
R1# show interface s 0/0/0
Serial0/0/0 is up, line protocol is up
  Hardware is WIC MBRD Serial
  Internet address is 172.16.3.1/30
 MTU 1500 bytes, BW 64 Kbit/sec, DLY 20000 usec,
      reliability 255/255, txload 1/255, rxload 1/255
<Output omitted>
R1#
```

```
R2# show interface s 0/0/0
Serial0/0/0 is up, line protocol is up
  Hardware is WIC MBRD Serial
  Internet address is 172.16.3.2/30
  MTU 1500 bytes, BW 64 Kbit/sec, DLY 20000 usec,
      reliability 255/255, txload 1/255, rxload 1/255
<Output omitted>
R2#
```

Modifying the bandwidth value does not change the actual bandwidth of the link. The **bandwidth** command only modifies the bandwidth metric used by EIGRP and OSPF.

## Delay Metric (6.3.2.4)

Delay is a measure of the time it takes for a packet to traverse a route. The delay (DLY) metric is a static value based on the type of link to which the interface is connected; it is expressed in microseconds.

Delay is not measured dynamically. In other words, the router does not actually track how long packets take to reach the destination. The delay value, much like the bandwidth value, is a default value that can be changed by the network administrator.

When used to determine the EIGRP metric, delay is the cumulative (sum) of all interface delays along the path (measured in tens of microseconds).

Table 6-6 shows the default delay values for various interfaces. Notice that the default value is 20,000 microseconds for serial interfaces and 10 microseconds for GigabitEthernet interfaces.

**Table 6-6**   Interface Delay Values

| Medium | Delay (Microseconds) |
| --- | --- |
| Gigabit Ethernet | 10 |
| Fast Ethernet | 100 |
| FDDI | 100 |
| Ethernet | 1000 |
| T1 (serial default) | 20,000 |
| DS0 (64 Kbps) | 20,000 |
| 1024 Kbps | 20,000 |
| 56 Kbps | 20,000 |

Use the **show interfaces** command to verify the delay value on an interface, as shown in Example 6-18.

**Example 6-18**   Verifying the Delay Value

```
R1# show interface s 0/0/0
Serial0/0/0 is up, line protocol is up
  Hardware is WIC MBRD Serial
  Internet address is 172.16.3.1/30
  MTU 1500 bytes, BW 64 Kbit/sec, DLY 20000 usec,
     reliability 255/255, txload 1/255, rxload 1/255
<Output omitted>
```

```
R1# show interface g 0/0
GigabitEthernet0/0 is up, line protocol is up
 Hardware is CN Gigabit Ethernet, address is fc99.4775.c3e0 (bia fc99.4775.c3e0)
  Internet address is 172.16.1.1/24
  MTU 1500 bytes, BW 1000000 Kbit/sec, DLY 10 usec,
     reliability 255/255, txload 1/255, rxload 1/255
<Output omitted>
R1#
```

Although an interface with various bandwidths can have the same delay value, Cisco recommends not modifying the delay parameter unless the network administrator has a specific reason to do so.

## How to Calculate the EIGRP Metric (6.3.2.5)

Although EIGRP automatically calculates the routing table metric used to choose the best path, it is important for a network administrator to understand how these metrics were determined.

Figure 6-26 shows the composite metric used by EIGRP.

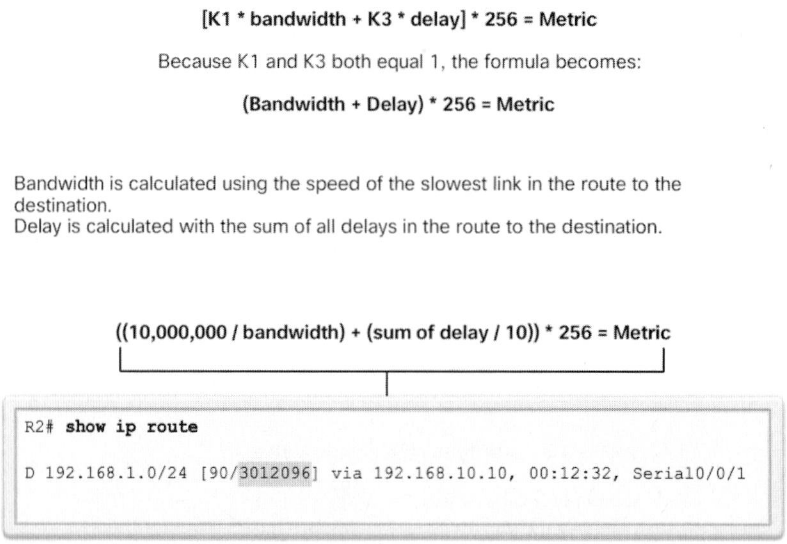

**[K1 * bandwidth + K3 * delay] * 256 = Metric**

Because K1 and K3 both equal 1, the formula becomes:

**(Bandwidth + Delay) * 256 = Metric**

Bandwidth is calculated using the speed of the slowest link in the route to the destination.
Delay is calculated with the sum of all delays in the route to the destination.

**((10,000,000 / bandwidth) + (sum of delay / 10)) * 256 = Metric**

```
R2# show ip route

D 192.168.1.0/24 [90/3012096] via 192.168.10.10, 00:12:32, Serial0/0/1
```

**Figure 6-26**   EIGRP Metric Calculation

Using the default values for K1 and K3, the calculation can be simplified to the slowest bandwidth (or minimum bandwidth) plus the sum of all of the delays. In other words, by examining the bandwidth and delay values for all of the outgoing interfaces of the route, you can determine the EIGRP metric as follows:

**Step 1.** Determine the link with the slowest bandwidth. Use that value to calculate bandwidth (10,000,000/bandwidth).

**Step 2.** Determine the delay value for each outgoing interface on the way to the destination. Add the delay values and divide by 10 (sum of delay/10).

**Step 3.** This composite metric produces a 24-bit value; however, EIGRP uses a 32-bit value. Multiplying the 24-bit value by 256 extends the composite metric into 32 bits. Therefore, add the computed values for bandwidth and delay and then multiply the sum by 256 to obtain the EIGRP metric.

The routing table output for R2 shows that the route to 192.168.1.0/24 has an EIGRP metric of 3,012,096.

## Calculating the EIGRP Metric (6.3.2.6)

This example illustrates how EIGRP determines the metric displayed in R2's routing table for the 192.168.1.0/24 network.

EIGRP uses the slowest bandwidth in its metric calculation. The slowest bandwidth can be determined by examining each interface between R2 and the destination network, 192.168.1.0. The Serial 0/0/1 interface on R2 has a bandwidth of 1024 Kbps. The GigabitEthernet 0/0 interface on R3 has a bandwidth of 1,000,000 Kbps. Therefore, the slowest bandwidth is 1024 Kbps, and this is used in the calculation of the metric.

EIGRP divides a reference bandwidth value of 10,000,000 by the interface bandwidth value in Kbps. This results in higher bandwidth values receiving a lower metric and lower bandwidth values receiving a higher metric. 10,000,000 is divided by 1024. If the result is not a whole number, the value is rounded down. In this case, 10,000,000 divided by 1024 equals 9,765.625. The .625 is dropped to yield 9765 for the bandwidth portion of the composite metric, as shown in Figure 6-27.

The same outgoing interfaces are used to determine the delay value, as shown in Figure 6-28.

EIGRP uses the sum of all delays to the destination. The Serial 0/0/1 interface on R2 has a delay of 20,000 microseconds. The Gigabit 0/0 interface on R3 has a delay of 10 microseconds. The sum of these delays is divided by 10. In the example, (20,000 + 10) / 10 results in a value of 2001 for the delay portion of the composite metric.

Use the calculated values for bandwidth and delay in the metric formula. This results in a metric of 3,012,096, as shown in Figure 6-29. This value matches the value shown in the routing table for R2.

```
R2# show interface s 0/0/1
Serial0/0/1 is up, line protocol is up
  Hardware is WIC MBRD Serial
  Internet address is 192.168.10.9/30
  MTU 1500 bytes, BW 1024 Kbit/sec, DLY 20000 usec,
     reliability 255/255, txload 1/255, rxload 1/255
<output omitted>
R2#
```

```
R3# show interface g 0/0
GigabitEthernet0/0 is up, line protocol is up
  Hardware is CN Gigabit Ethernet, address is fc99.4771.7a20
(bia fc99.4771.7a20)
  Internet address is 192.168.1.1/24
  MTU 1500 bytes, BW 1000000 Kbit/sec, DLY 10 usec,
     reliability 255/255, txload 1/255, rxload 1/255
<output omitted>
R3#
```

Calculate bandwidth using the slowest bandwidth to the destination: **1024**

$(10,000,000 \div \mathbf{1024}) = 9,765$

Note: 9765.625 is rounded down to 9765.

**Figure 6-27**   Calculating the Bandwidth

```
R2# show interface s 0/0/1
Serial0/0/1 is up, line protocol is up
  Hardware is WIC MBRD Serial
  Internet address is 192.168.10.9/30
  MTU 1500 bytes, BW 1024 Kbit/sec, DLY 20000 usec,
     reliability 255/255, txload 1/255, rxload 1/255
<output omitted>
R2#
```

```
R3# show interface g 0/0
GigabitEthernet0/0 is up, line protocol is up
  Hardware is CN Gigabit Ethernet, address is fc99.4771.7a20
(bia fc99.4771.7a20)
  Internet address is 192.168.1.1/24
  MTU 1500 bytes, BW 1000000 Kbit/sec, DLY 10 usec,
     reliability 255/255, txload 1/255, rxload 1/255
<output omitted>
R3#
```

Calculate delay using the sum of all delays to the destination: **20,000 + 10**

$(\mathbf{20,000 + 10}) \div 10 = 2001$

**Figure 6-28**   Examining the Delay Values

```
R2# show ip route
<output omitted>

D 192.168.1.0/24 [90/3012096] via 192.168.10.10, 00:12:32,
   Serial0/0/1
```

Use the results in the default metric formula:

**(Bandwidth + Delay)** * 256 = **Metric**

**(9765 + 2001)** * 256 = **3,012,096**

**Figure 6-29**    Verifying the EIGRP Metric

Interactive
Graphic

**Activity 6.3.2.7: Calculate the EIGRP Metric**

Refer to the online course to complete this Activity.

# DUAL and the Topology Table (6.3.3)

In this topic, you will learn how EIGRP uses the Diffusing Update Algorithm (DUAL) and the topology table to identify the best routes.

## DUAL Concepts (6.3.3.1)

EIGRP uses DUAL to provide the best loop-free path and loop-free backup paths.

Several terms and concepts that are at the center of the loop-avoidance mechanism of DUAL are discussed in more detail throughout this section:

- *Successor*
- *Feasible distance (FD)*
- *Feasible successor (FS)*
- *Reported distance (RD)* or *advertised distance (AD)*
- *Feasible condition (FC)*

## Introduction to DUAL (6.3.3.2)

EIGRP uses the DUAL convergence algorithm. Convergence is critical in a network to avoid routing loops because even temporary routing loops can be detrimental to network performance.

Distance vector routing protocols, such as RIP, prevent routing loops using hold-down timers and split horizon. Although EIGRP uses both of these techniques, it uses them somewhat differently, and the primary way that EIGRP prevents routing loops is by using the DUAL algorithm.

The DUAL algorithm is used to obtain loop-free paths at every instance throughout a route computation. This allows all routers involved in a topology change to synchronize at the same time. Routers that are not affected by the topology changes are not involved in the recomputation. DUAL enables EIGRP to have faster convergence times than other distance vector routing protocols.

The decision process for all route computations is done by the DUAL *finite state machine (FSM)*. An FSM is a workflow model, similar to a flowchart, that is composed of the following:

- A finite number of stages (states)
- Transitions between those stages
- Operations

The DUAL FSM tracks all routes and uses EIGRP metrics to select efficient, loop-free paths and to identify the routes with the least-cost path to be inserted into the routing table.

Recomputation of the DUAL algorithm can be processor intensive. For this reason, EIGRP maintains a list of backup routes that DUAL has already determined to be loop free. If the primary route in the routing table fails, the best backup route is immediately added to the routing table.

## Successor and Feasible Distance (6.3.3.3)

Figure 6-30 shows the reference topology for this topic.

In the example, R2 has two possible ways to get to network 192.168.1.0/24: It can go via R1 and then R3, or it can go directly to R3. R2 must choose a successor and possibly choose a feasible successor.

A successor is a neighboring router that is used for packet forwarding and is the least-cost route to the destination network. The IP address of a successor is displayed in a routing table entry right after the word *via*.

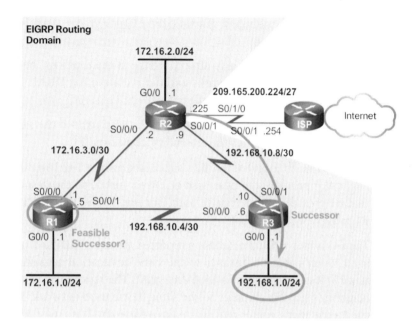

**Figure 6-30**   EIGRP for IPv4 Topology: Successor Example

The feasible distance (FD) is the lowest calculated metric to reach the destination network. In the routing table, FD is the metric listed as the second number inside the brackets.

For example, in the routing table in Figure 6-31, the best path to reach 192.168.1.0/24 is through R3. Therefore, R3 is the successor, and the feasible distance to 192.168.1.0/24 is 3,012,096.

```
R2# show ip route
<output omitted>
D 192.168.1.0/24 [90/3012096] via 192.168.10.10, 00:12:32,
Serial0/0/1
```

Feasible Distance                     Successor

**Figure 6-31**   Feasible Distance to the Successor

## Feasible Successors, Feasibility Condition, and Reported Distance (6.3.3.4)

DUAL can converge quickly after a change in the topology because it can use backup paths to other networks without recomputing DUAL. These backup paths are known as feasible successors (FS).

An FS is a neighbor that has a loop-free backup path to the same network as the successor, and it satisfies the feasibility condition (FC).

For example, in Figure 6-30, R2's successor for the 192.168.1.0/24 network is R3 because it provides the best path or lowest metric to the destination network. Notice that R1 provides an alternative path, but is it an FS? Before R1 can be an FS for R2, R1 must first meet the FC.

The FC is met when a neighbor's reported distance (RD) to a network is less than the local router's feasible distance to the same destination network. If the reported distance is less, it represents a loop-free path. The reported distance is simply an EIGRP neighbor's feasible distance to the same destination network. The reported distance is the metric that a router reports to a neighbor about its own cost to that network.

In Figure 6-32, the routing table entry to network 192.168.1.0/24 on R1 has a feasible distance of 2,170,112.

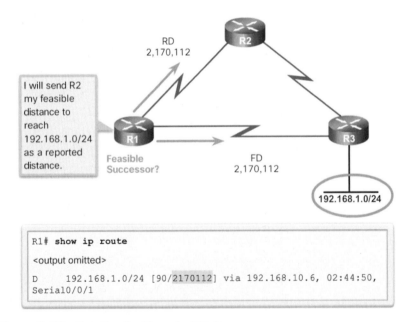

**Figure 6-32**   Sending the Reported Distance

R1 reports to R2 that its FD to 192.168.1.0/24 is 2,170,112. Therefore, from R2's perspective, 2,170,112 is R1's RD. R2 uses this information to determine whether R1 meets the FC and, therefore, can be an FS.

Figure 6-33 compares the R1 and R2 routing table entries to network 192.168.1.0/24.

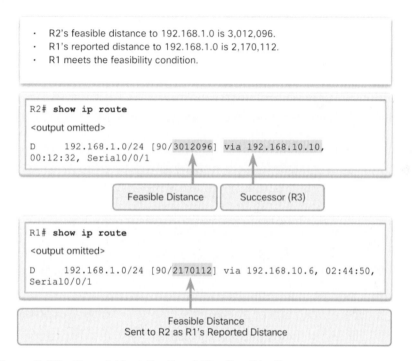

**Figure 6-33**   Does It Meet the Feasibility Condition?

In this scenario, R1 meets the FC because the RD of R1 (2,170,112) is less than R2's own FD (3,012,096). R1 is now an FS for R2 to the 192.168.1.0/24 network.

For example, in Figure 6-34, there is a failure in R2's path to 192.168.1.0/24 via R3 (successor).

Therefore, R2 immediately installs the path via R1 (FS) in its routing table, and R1 becomes the new successor for R2's path to this network.

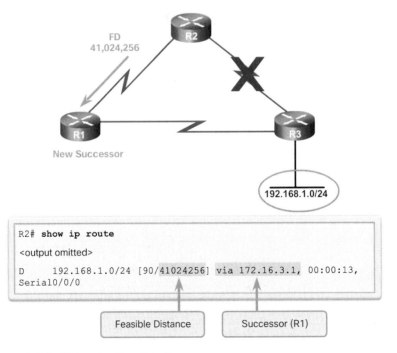

**Figure 6-34**   Using the Feasible Successor

## Topology Table: show ip eigrp topology Command (6.3.3.5)

The EIGRP topology table contains all the routes that are known to each EIGRP neighbor. As an EIGRP router learns routes from its neighbors, those routes are installed in its EIGRP topology table.

To view the topology table, use the **show ip eigrp topology** command. Example 6-19 displays the topology table for R2.

**Example 6-19**   Topology Table for R2

```
R2# show ip eigrp topology
EIGRP-IPv4 Topology Table for AS(1)/ID(2.2.2.2)
Codes: P - Passive, A - Active, U - Update, Q - Query, R - Reply,
       r - reply Status, s - sia Status

P 172.16.2.0/24, 1 successors, FD is 2816
        via Connected, GigabitEthernet0/0
P 192.168.10.4/30, 1 successors, FD is 3523840
        via 192.168.10.10 (3523840/2169856), Serial0/0/1
        via 172.16.3.1 (41024000/2169856), Serial0/0/0
```

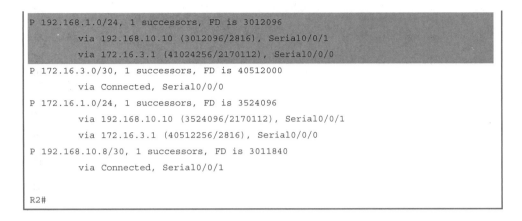

```
P 192.168.1.0/24, 1 successors, FD is 3012096
        via 192.168.10.10 (3012096/2816), Serial0/0/1
        via 172.16.3.1 (41024256/2170112), Serial0/0/0
P 172.16.3.0/30, 1 successors, FD is 40512000
        via Connected, Serial0/0/0
P 172.16.1.0/24, 1 successors, FD is 3524096
        via 192.168.10.10 (3524096/2170112), Serial0/0/1
        via 172.16.3.1 (40512256/2816), Serial0/0/0
P 192.168.10.8/30, 1 successors, FD is 3011840
        via Connected, Serial0/0/1

R2#
```

### Topology Table: show ip eigrp topology Command (Cont.) (6.3.3.6)

The EIGRP topology table contains all the networks advertised by neighboring EIGRP routers. The topology table lists all successors and FSs that DUAL has calculated to destination networks. Only the successor is installed into the IP routing table. Also, not every route has an FS.

Figure 6-35 focuses on the entry for the 192.168.1.0/24 network in the output of the **show ip eigrp topology** command on R2.

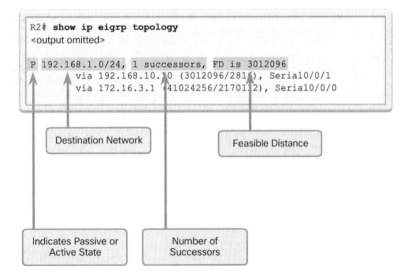

**Figure 6-35**  Examining an Entry in the Topology Table: First Line

Table 6-7 explains the significance of the highlighted output for the first line in the output.

**Table 6-7**  First Line of the **show ip eigrp topology** Output Explained

| Field in Output | Description |
| --- | --- |
| P | ■ The route is in a stable *passive state*, and DUAL is not performing its diffusing computations.<br><br>■ If DUAL were performing computations, the route would be in an *active state* (A).<br><br>■ All routes in the topology table should be in the passive state for a stable routing domain. |
| 192.168.1.0/24 | ■ This is the destination network that is also found in the routing table. |
| 1 successors | ■ This is the number of successors for this network.<br><br>■ There could be multiple successors if there were multiple equal-cost paths to this network. |
| FD is 3012096 | ■ FD is the EIGRP metric to reach the destination network.<br><br>■ This is the metric displayed in the IP routing table. |

Figure 6-36 displays the second line in the entry for the 192.168.1.0/24 network.

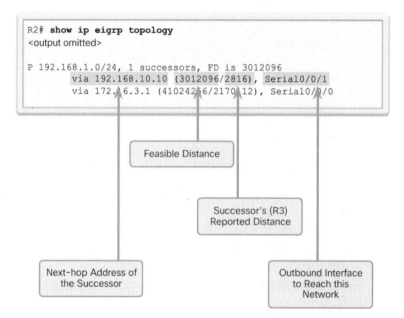

**Figure 6-36**  Examining an Entry in the Topology Table: First Subentry

Table 6-8 explains the significance of the highlighted output for the first subentry in the output.

**Table 6-8**   First Subentry of the **show ip eigrp topology** Output Explained

| Field in Output | Description |
|---|---|
| via 192.168.10.10 | ■ This is the next-hop address of the successor, R3.<br>■ This address is shown in the routing table |
| 3012096 | ■ This is the FD to 192.168.1.0/24.<br>■ It is the metric shown in the IP routing table. |
| 2816 | ■ This is the RD of the successor and is R3's cost to reach this network. |
| Serial 0/0/1 | ■ This is the outbound interface used to reach this network, also shown in the routing table. |

Figure 6-37 displays the third line in the entry for the 192.168.1.0/24 network.

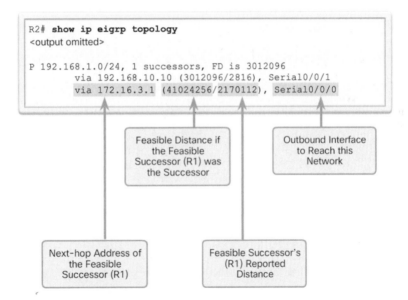

**Figure 6-37**   Examining an Entry in the Topology Table: Second Subentry

Table 6-9 explains the significance of the highlighted output for the second subentry in the output. The second subentry shows the FS, R1. If there is not a second entry, then there are no FSs.

**Table 6-9**  Second Subentry of the **show ip eigrp topology** Output Explained

| Field in Output | Description |
|---|---|
| via 172.16.3.1 | ■ This is the next-hop address of the FS, R1. |
| 41024256 | ■ This would be R2's new FD to 192.168.1.0/24 if R1 became the new successor, and it would be the new metric displayed in the IP routing table. |
| 2170112 | ■ This is the RD of the FS, or R1's metric to reach this network. |
| | ■ The RD must be less than the current FD of 3,012,096 to meet the FC. |
| Serial 0/0/0 | ■ This is the outbound interface used to reach FS if this router becomes the successor. |

## Topology Table: No Feasible Successor (6.3.3.7)

To see how DUAL uses successors and FSs, let's examine the partial routing table of R1 displayed in Figure 6-38.

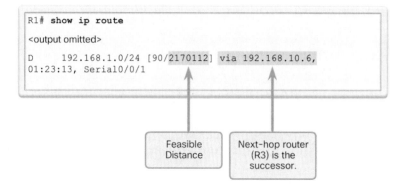

**Figure 6-38**  R1's Routing Table Entry for 192.168.1.0/24

The route to 192.168.1.0/24 shows that the successor is R3 via 192.168.10.6 with an FD of 2,170,112.

The IP routing table includes only the best path, the successor. To see if there are any FSs, you must examine the EIGRP topology table. The topology table in Figure 6-39 shows only the successor 192.168.10.6, which is R3. Notice that there are no FSs.

By looking at the physical topology or network diagram, you see that there is a backup route to 192.168.1.0/24 through R2. However, R2 is not an FS because it does not meet the FC.

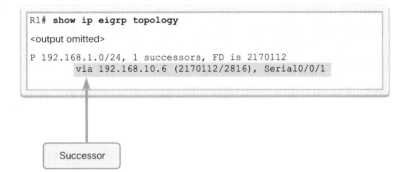

**Figure 6-39**    R1's Topology Table Entry for 192.168.1.0/24

DUAL does not store the route through R2 in the topology table. All links can be displayed using the **show ip eigrp topology all-links** command. This command displays links whether they satisfy the FC or not.

As shown in Figure 6-40, the **show ip eigrp topology all-links** command shows all possible paths to a network, including successors, FSs, and even routes that are not FSs.

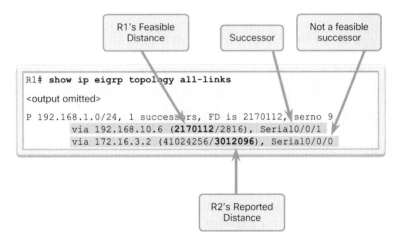

**Figure 6-40**    R1's All-Links Topology Table Entry for 192.168.1.0/24

R1's FD to 192.168.1.0/24 is 2,170,112 via the successor R3.

For R2 to be considered an FS, it must meet the FC. R2's RD to R1 to reach 192.168.1.0/24 must be less than R1's current FD. Per Figure 6-40, R2's RD is 3,012,096, which is higher than R1's current FD of 2,170,112.

Even though R2 looks like a viable backup path to 192.168.1.0/24, R1 cannot guarantee that the path is not a potential loop back through itself. EIGRP is a distance vector routing protocol, so it does not have the ability to see a complete, loop-free topological map of the network. DUAL's method of guaranteeing that a neighbor has a loop-free path is that the neighbor's metric must satisfy the FC. By ensuring that the RD of the neighbor is less than its own FD, the router can assume that this neighboring router is not part of its own advertised route—thus always avoiding the potential for a loop.

R2 can be used as a successor if R3 fails. However, there is a longer delay before adding it to the routing table. Before R2 can be used as a successor, DUAL must do further processing.

**Interactive Graphic**

### Activity 6.3.3.8: Determine the Feasible Successor

Refer to the online course to complete this activity.

## DUAL and Convergence (6.3.4)

In this topic, you will learn about events that trigger EIGRP updates.

### DUAL Finite State Machine (FSM) (6.3.4.1)

The centerpiece of EIGRP is DUAL and its EIGRP route-calculation engine. The actual name of this technology is the DUAL finite state machine (FSM). This FSM contains all the logic used to calculate and compare routes in an EIGRP network.

Figure 6-41 shows a simplified version of the DUAL FSM.

Use the **debug eigrp fsm** command to examine what DUAL does when a route is removed from the routing table.

An FSM is an abstract machine, not a mechanical device with moving parts. An FSM defines a set of possible states that something can go through, what events cause those states, and what events result from those states. Designers use FSMs to describe how a device, computer program, or routing algorithm reacts to a set of input events.

**Note**

FSMs are beyond the scope of this course.

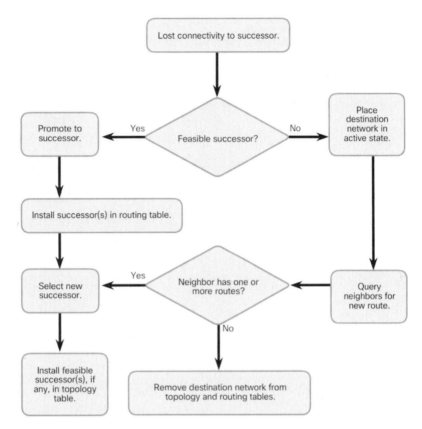

**Figure 6-41**    DUAL Finite State Machine

## DUAL: Feasible Successor (6.3.4.2)

Figure 6-42 illustrates how DUAL reacts when a route is no longer available.

In the example, R2 is currently using R3 as the successor to 192.168.1.0/24. In addition, R2 currently lists R1 as an FS.

The **show ip eigrp topology** output for R2 in Figure 6-43 verifies that R3 is the successor and R1 is the FS for the 192.168.1.0/24 network.

To understand how DUAL can use an FS when the path using the successor is no longer available, a link failure is simulated between R2 and R3. Before simulating the failure, DUAL debugging needs to be enabled. Example 6-20 shows how to enable the **debug eigrp fsm** command on R2 and then simulate a link failure by using the **shutdown** command on the Serial 0/0/1 interface.

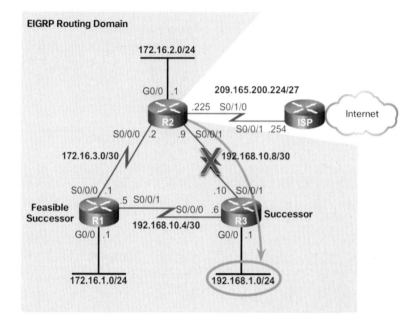

**Figure 6-42**   EIGRP for IPv4 Topology with Simulated Link Failure

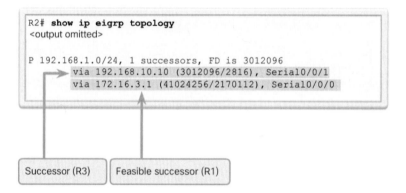

**Figure 6-43**   R2 Topology Table Entry for 192.168.1.0/24

**Example 6-20**   Debugging the EIGRP Finite State Machine on R2

```
R2# debug eigrp fsm
EIGRP Finite State Machine debugging is on
R2# conf t
Enter configuration commands, one per line.   End with CNTL/Z.
R2(config)# interface s 0/0/1
R2(config-if)# shutdown
```

```
<Output omitted>

EIGRP-IPv4(1):Find FS for dest 192.168.1.0/24. FD is 3012096, RD is 3012096 on tid 0
DUAL: AS(1) Removing dest 172.16.1.0/24, nexthop 192.168.10.10
DUAL: AS(1) RT installed 172.16.1.0/24 via 172.16.3.1

<Output omitted>

R2(config-if)# end
R2# undebug all
```

In Example 6-20, the highlighted **debug** output displays the activity generated by DUAL when a link goes down. R2 must inform all EIGRP neighbors of the lost link, as well as update its own routing and topology tables. This example shows only selected **debug** output. In particular, notice that the DUAL FSM searches for and finds an FS for the route in the EIGRP topology table.

The FS R1 now becomes the successor and is installed in the routing table as the new best path to 192.168.1.0/24, as shown in Figure 6-44.

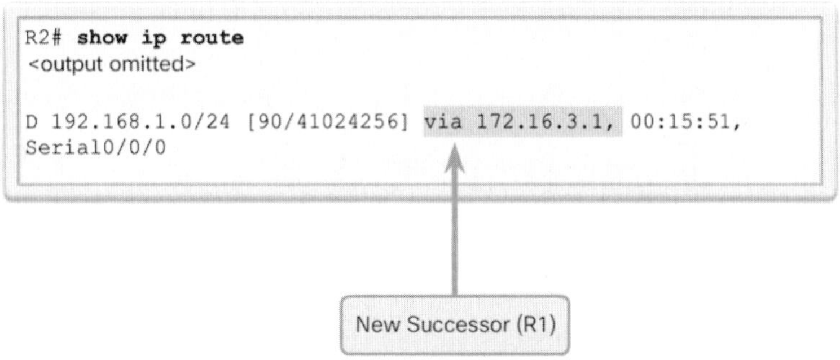

```
R2# show ip route
<output omitted>

D 192.168.1.0/24 [90/41024256] via 172.16.3.1, 00:15:51,
Serial0/0/0
```

New Successor (R1)

**Figure 6-44**   R2 Routing Table Entry for 192.168.1.0/24

With an FS, this change in the routing table happens almost immediately.

As shown in Figure 6-45, the topology table for R2 now shows R1 as the successor, and there are no new FSs.

If the link between R2 and R3 is made active again, R3 returns as the successor, and R1 once again becomes the FS.

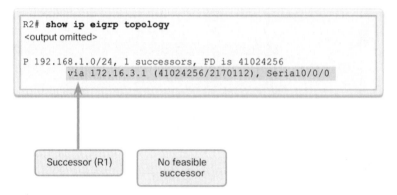

**Figure 6-45**  R2 Topology Table Entry for 192.168.1.0/24

## DUAL: No Feasible Successor (6.3.4.3)

Occasionally, the path to the successor fails, and there are no FSs. In such an instance, DUAL does not have a guaranteed loop-free backup path to the network, so the path is not in the topology table as an FS. If there are no FSs in the topology table, DUAL transitions to active state and actively queries its neighbors for a new successor.

In Figure 6-46, R1 is currently using R3 as the successor to 192.168.1.0/24.

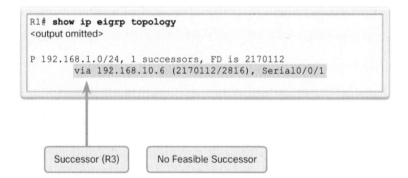

**Figure 6-46**  R1 Topology Table Entry for 192.168.1.0/24

However, R1 does not have R2 listed as an FS because R2 does not satisfy the FC. When the successor is no longer available and there is no feasible successor, DUAL puts the route into an active state. DUAL sends EIGRP queries, asking other routers for a path to the network. Other routers return EIGRP replies, letting the sender of the EIGRP query know whether they have a path to the requested network. If none of the EIGRP replies have a path to this network, the sender of the query does not have a route to this network.

To understand how DUAL searches for a new successor when there is no FS, a link failure is simulated between R1 and R3.

As shown in Example 6-21, DUAL debugging is enabled with the **debug eigrp fsm** command on R1, and a link failure is simulated using the **shutdown** command on the Serial 0/0/1 interface.

**Example 6-21**  Debugging the EIGRP Finite State Machine on R1

```
R1# debug eigrp fsm
EIGRP Finite State Machine debugging is on
R1# conf t
Enter configuration commands, one per line.  End with CNTL/Z.
R1(config)# interface s 0/0/1
R1(config-if)# shutdown

<Output omitted>

EIGRP-IPv4(1): Find FS for dest 192.168.1.0/24. FD is 2170112, RD is 2170112
DUAL: AS(1) Dest 192.168.1.0/24 entering active state for tid 0.
EIGRP-IPv4(1): dest(192.168.1.0/24) active
EIGRP-IPv4(1): rcvreply: 192.168.1.0/24 via 172.16.3.2 metric 41024256/3012096
  EIGRP-IPv4(1): reply count is 1
EIGRP-IPv4(1): Find FS for dest 192.168.1.0/24. FD is 72057594037927935, RD is
  72057594037927935
DUAL: AS(1) Removing dest 192.168.1.0/24, nexthop 192.168.10.6
DUAL: AS(1) RT installed 192.168.1.0/24 via 172.16.3.2

<Output omitted>

R1(config-if)# end
R1# undebug all
```

The highlighted **debug** output in Example 6-21 shows the 192.168.1.0/24 network transitioning to the active state and EIGRP queries sent to other neighbors. R2 replies with a path to this network, which becomes the new successor and is installed into the routing table.

If the sender of the EIGRP queries receives EIGRP replies that include a path to the requested network, the preferred path is added as the new successor and is added to the routing table. This process takes longer than if DUAL had an FS in its topology table and were able to quickly add the new route to the routing table.

In Figure 6-47, notice that R1 has a new route to the 192.168.1.0/24 network, and the new EIGRP successor is router R2.

```
R1# show ip route
<output omitted>

D      192.168.1.0/24 [90/41024256] via 172.16.3.2, 00:05:25,
       Serial0/0/0
```

New Successor (R2)

**Figure 6-47**   R1 Routing Table Entry for 192.168.1.0/24

Figure 6-48 shows that the R1 topology table identifies R2 as the successor, and there are no new FSs.

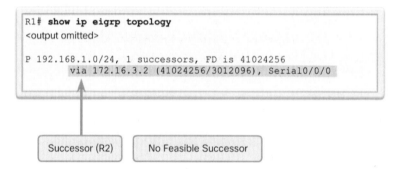

```
R1# show ip eigrp topology
<output omitted>

P 192.168.1.0/24, 1 successors, FD is 41024256
        via 172.16.3.2 (41024256/3012096), Serial0/0/0
```

Successor (R2)        No Feasible Successor

**Figure 6-48**   R1 Topology Table Entry for 192.168.1.0/24

If the link between R1 and R3 is made active again, R3 returns as the successor. However, R2 is still not the FS because it does not meet the FC.

**Packet Tracer**
☐ **Activity**

**Packet Tracer 6.3.4.4: Investigating DUAL FSM**

Background/Scenario

In this activity, you will modify the EIGRP metric formula to cause a change in the topology so you can see how EIGRP reacts when a neighbor goes down due to unforeseen circumstances. You will then use the **debug** command to view topology changes and how the DUAL finite state machine determines successor and feasible successor paths to reconverge the network.

# Implement EIGRP for IPv6 (6.4)

In this section, you will learn how to implement EIGRP for IPv6 in a small to medium-sized business network.

## EIGRP for IPv6 (6.4.1)

In this topic, you will learn the differences in the characteristics and operation of EIGRP for IPv4 and EIGRP for IPv6.

### EIGRP for IPv6 (6.4.1.1)

Much like its IPv4 counterpart, EIGRP for IPv6 exchanges routing information to populate the IPv6 routing table with remote prefixes. EIGRP for IPv6 was made available in Cisco IOS Release 12.4(6)T.

**Note**

In IPv6, the network address is referred to as the *prefix*, and the subnet mask is called the *prefix length*.

EIGRP for IPv4 runs over the IPv4 network layer, communicating with other EIGRP IPv4 peers and advertising only IPv4 routes. EIGRP for IPv6 has the same functionality as EIGRP for IPv4 but uses IPv6 as the network layer transport, communicating with EIGRP for IPv6 peers and advertising IPv6 routes.

EIGRP for IPv6 also uses DUAL as the computation engine to guarantee loop-free paths and backup paths throughout the routing domain.

As with all other IPv6 routing protocols, EIGRP for IPv6 has separate processes from its IPv4 counterpart. The processes and operations are basically the same as in the IPv4 routing protocol. However, they run independently.

EIGRP for IPv4 and EIGRP for IPv6 each have separate EIGRP neighbor tables, EIGRP topology tables, and IP routing tables, as shown in Figure 6-49. EIGRP for IPv6 is a separate protocol-dependent module (PDM).

The EIGRP for IPv6 configuration and verification commands are very similar to those used in EIGRP for IPv4. These commands are described later in this section.

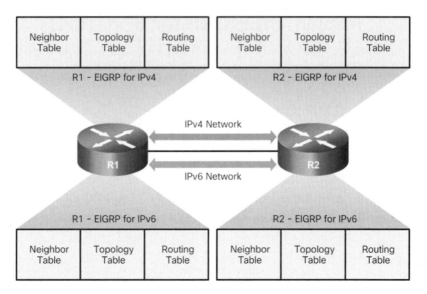

**Figure 6-49**   Comparing EIGRP for IPv4 and EIGRP for IPv6

## Compare EIGRP for IPv4 and IPv6 (6.4.1.2)

Table 6-10 lists similarities between EIGRP for IPv4 and EIGRP for IPv6.

**Table 6-10**   Similarities Between EIGRP for IPv4 and EIGRP for IPv6

| Similarity | Description |
|---|---|
| Distance vector | ■ Both protocols are advanced distance vector routing protocols.<br>■ The two protocols use the same administrative distances. |
| Convergence technology | ■ Both protocols use DUAL techniques and processes, including successor, FS, FD, and RD. |
| Metric | ■ Both protocols use bandwidth and delay for their composite metric and can be configured to also use reliability and load. |
| Transport protocol | ■ Both protocols use RTP for guaranteed delivery of EIGRP packets to all neighbors. |
| Update messages | ■ Both EIGRP for IPv4 and IPv6 send incremental updates when the state of a destination changes.<br>■ Both protocols use the terms *partial updates* and *bounded updates*. |
| Neighbor discovery mechanism | ■ Both protocols use Hello packets to discover neighboring routers and form adjacencies. |

| Similarity | Description |
|---|---|
| Authentication | ■ Both protocols use Message Digest 5 (MD5) authentication.<br><br>■ Named EIGRP for IPv4 and IPv6 address families also supports the stronger SHA256 algorithm. |
| Router ID | ■ Both protocols use a 32-bit IP address for the EIGRP router ID.<br><br>■ Both protocols use the same process for determining the router ID. |

Table 6-11 lists differences between EIGRP for IPv4 and EIGRP for IPv6.

**Table 6-11**    Differences Between EIGRP for IPv4 and EIGRP for IPv6

| Difference | EIGRP for IPv4 | EIGRP for IPv6 |
|---|---|---|
| Advertised routes | ■ EIGRP for IPv4 advertises IPv4 networks. | ■ EIGRP for IPv6 advertises IPv6 prefixes. |
| Source and destination addresses | ■ EIGRP for IPv4 sends messages to the multicast address 224.0.0.10.<br><br>■ These messages use the source IPv4 address of the outbound interface. | ■ EIGRP for IPv6 sends messages to the multicast address FF02::A.<br><br>■ EIGRP for IPv6 messages are sourced using the IPv6 link-local address of the exit interface. |
| Command to advertise networks | ■ EIGRP for IPv4 advertises networks using the network router configuration command. | ■ EIGRP for IPv6 advertises networks using the **ipv6 eigrp** *autonomous-system* interface configuration command. |
| Starting EIGRP | ■ EIGRP for IPv4 requires no command to be enabled. | ■ EIGRP for IPv6 requires that IPv6 unicast routing be enabled, using the **ipv6 unicast-routing** global configuration command.<br><br>■ EIGRP also requires that EIGRP be enabled by using the **no shutdown** router configuration command. |
| Router ID | ■ EIGRP for IPv4 creates its own router ID if none are configured. | ■ EIGRP for IPv6 uses either an explicitly configure IPv4 router ID or the highest IPv4 address configured on an interface (if one is configured). |

## IPv6 Link-local Addresses (6.4.1.3)

Routers running EIGRP for IPv6 exchange messages between neighbors on the same subnet or link, as shown in Figure 6-50.

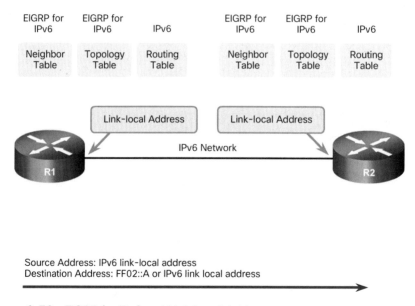

Figure 6-50    EIGRP for IPv6 and Link-Local Addresses

Routers only need to send and receive routing protocol messages with their directly connected neighbors. These messages are always sent from the source IP address of the router that is doing the forwarding.

IPv6 link-local addresses are ideal for this purpose. An IPv6 link-local address enables a device to communicate with other IPv6-enabled devices on the same link and only on that link (subnet). Packets with a source or destination link-local address cannot be routed beyond the link from which the packet originated.

EIGRP for IPv6 messages are sent using the following:

- **Source IPv6 address**—This is the IPv6 link-local address of the exit interface.

- **Destination IPv6 address**—When a packet needs to be sent to a multicast address, it is sent to the IPv6 multicast address FF02::A, the address for all EIGRP routers with link-local scope. If the packet can be sent as a unicast address, it is sent to the link-local address of the neighboring router.

> **Note**
>
> IPv6 link-local addresses are in the FE80::/10 range. The /10 indicates that the first 10 bits are 1111 1110 10xx xxxx, which results in the first hextet having a range of 1111 1110 1000 0000 (FE80) to 1111 1110 1011 1111 (FEBF).

**Activity 6.4.1.4: Compare EIGRPv4 and EIGRPv6**

Refer to the online course to complete this activity.

# Configure EIGRP for IPv6 (6.4.2)

In this topic, you will learn how to configure EIGRP for IPv6 in a small routed network.

## EIGRP for IPv6 Network Topology (6.4.2.1)

Figure 6-51 shows the network topology that is used here for configuring EIGRP for IPv6.

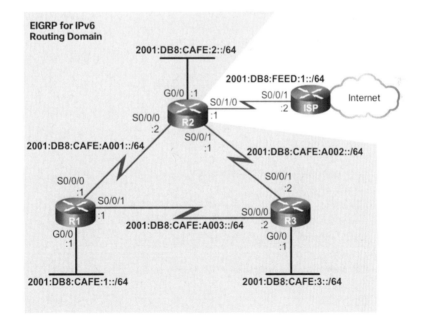

**Figure 6-51**   EIGRP for IPv6 Topology

If the network is running dual-stack, using both IPv4 and IPv6 on all devices, EIGRP for both IPv4 and IPv6 can be configured on all the routers. However, in this section, the focus is on EIGRP for IPv6.

In this example, only the IPv6 global unicast addresses have been configured on each router. Example 6-22 displays the starting interface configurations on each router.

**Example 6-22**   IPv6 Interface Configurations

```
R1# show running-config
<Output omitted>
!
interface GigabitEthernet0/0
 ipv6 address 2001:DB8:CAFE:1::1/64
!
interface Serial0/0/0
 ipv6 address 2001:DB8:CAFE:A001::1/64
 clock rate 64000
!
interface Serial0/0/1
 ipv6 address 2001:DB8:CAFE:A003::1/64
```

```
R2# show running-config
<Output omitted>
!
interface GigabitEthernet0/0
 ipv6 address 2001:DB8:CAFE:2::1/64
!
interface Serial0/0/0
 ipv6 address 2001:DB8:CAFE:A001::2/64
!
interface Serial0/0/1
 ipv6 address 2001:DB8:CAFE:A002::1/64
 clock rate 64000
!
interface Serial0/1/0
 ipv6 address 2001:DB8:FEED:1::1/64
```

```
R3# show running-config
<Output omitted>
!
interface GigabitEthernet0/0
 ipv6 address 2001:DB8:CAFE:3::1/64
!
```

```
interface Serial0/0/0
 ipv6 address 2001:DB8:CAFE:A003::2/64
 clock rate 64000
!
interface Serial0/0/1
 ipv6 address 2001:DB8:CAFE:A002::2/64
```

Notice the interface bandwidth values from the previous EIGRP for IPv4 configuration. Because EIGRP for IPv4 and IPv6 use the same metrics, modifying the bandwidth parameters influences both routing protocols.

## Configuring IPv6 Link-local Addresses (6.4.2.2)

Link-local addresses are automatically created when an IPv6 global unicast address is assigned to the interface. Global unicast addresses are not required on an interface. However, IPv6 link-local addresses are required.

Unless configured manually, Cisco routers create the link-local address by using FE80::/10 prefix and the EUI-64 process. EUI-64 involves using the 48-bit Ethernet MAC address, inserting FFFE in the middle, and flipping the seventh bit. For serial interfaces, Cisco uses the MAC address of an Ethernet interface. A router with several serial interfaces can assign the same link-local address to each IPv6 interface because link-local addresses only need to be local on the link.

Link-local addresses created using the EUI-64 format, or in some cases random interface IDs, make it difficult to recognize and remember those addresses. Because IPv6 routing protocols use IPv6 link-local addresses for unicast addressing and next-hop address information in the routing table, it is common practice to make it an easily recognizable address. Configuring the link-local address manually provides the ability to create an address that is recognizable and easier to remember.

Link-local addresses can be configured manually using the **ipv6 address** *link-local-address* **link-local** interface configuration mode command.

A link-local address has a prefix in the range FE80 to FEBF. When an address begins with this hextet (16-bit segment), the **link-local** keyword must follow the address.

Example 6-23 shows the configuration of a link-local address using the **ipv6 address** interface configuration mode command for each of the three routers.

**Example 6-23**   Configuring Link-Local Addresses

```
R1(config)# interface s 0/0/0
R1(config-if)# ipv6 address fe80::1 ?
  link-local  Use link-local address

R1(config-if)# ipv6 address fe80::1 link-local
R1(config-if)# interface s 0/0/1
R1(config-if)# ipv6 address fe80::1 link-local
R1(config-if)# interface g 0/0
R1(config-if)# ipv6 address fe80::1 link-local
R1(config-if)#
```

```
R2(config)# interface s 0/0/0
R2(config-if)# ipv6 address fe80::2 link-local
R2(config-if)# interface s 0/0/1
R2(config-if)# ipv6 address fe80::2 link-local
R2(config-if)# interface s 0/1/0
R2(config-if)# ipv6 address fe80::2 link-local
R2(config-if)# interface g 0/0
R2(config-if)# ipv6 address fe80::2 link-local
R2(config-if)#
```

```
R3(config)# interface serial 0/0/0
R3(config-if)# ipv6 address fe80::3 link-local
R3(config-if)# interface serial 0/0/1
R3(config-if)# ipv6 address fe80::3 link-local
R3(config-if)# interface gigabitethernet 0/0
R3(config-if)# ipv6 address fe80::3 link-local
R3(config-if)#
```

For R1, the link-local address FE80::1 is used to make it easily recognizable as belonging to router R1. The same IPv6 link-local address is configured on all of R1's interfaces. FE80::1 can be configured on each link because it has to be unique only on that link.

Similarly to R1, R2 is configured with FE80::2 as the IPv6 link-local address on all its interfaces. R3 is configured with FE80::3.

As shown in Figure 6-52, the **show ipv6 interface brief** command is used to verify the IPv6 link-local and global unicast addresses on all interfaces.

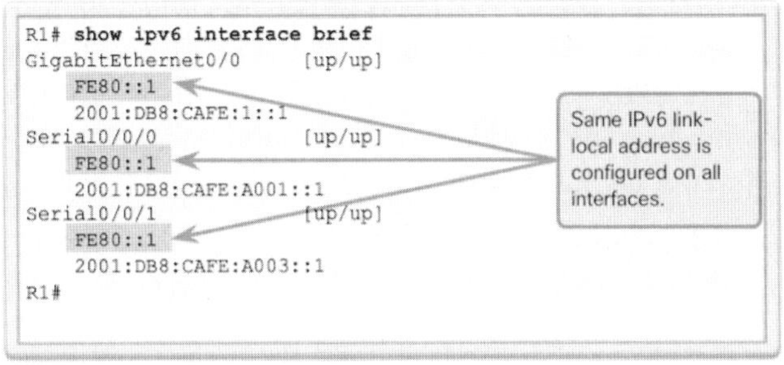

```
R1# show ipv6 interface brief
GigabitEthernet0/0      [up/up]
    FE80::1
    2001:DB8:CAFE:1::1
Serial0/0/0             [up/up]
    FE80::1
    2001:DB8:CAFE:A001::1
Serial0/0/1             [up/up]
    FE80::1
    2001:DB8:CAFE:A003::1
R1#
```

Same IPv6 link-local address is configured on all interfaces.

**Figure 6-52**   Verifying Link-Local Addresses on R1

## Configuring the EIGRP for IPv6 Routing Process (6.4.2.3)

The **ipv6 unicast-routing** global configuration mode command enables IPv6 routing on the router. This command is required before any IPv6 routing protocol can be configured. This command is not required to configure IPv6 addresses on the interfaces but is necessary for the router to be enabled as an IPv6 router.

**Note**

The EIGRP for IPv6 routing process cannot be configured until IPv6 routing is enabled with the **ipv6 unicast-routing** global configuration mode command.

The **ipv6 router eigrp** *autonomous-system* global configuration mode command is used to enter router configuration mode for EIGRP for IPv6. As with EIGRP for IPv4, the *autonomous-system* value must be the same on all routers in the routing domain.

The **eigrp router-id** command is used to configure the router ID. EIGRP for IPv6 uses a 32-bit value for the router ID. To obtain that value, EIGRP for IPv6 uses the same process as EIGRP for IPv4. The **eigrp router-id** command takes precedence over any loopback or physical interface IPv4 addresses. If an EIGRP for IPv6 router does not have any active interfaces with an IPv4 address, the **eigrp router-id** command is required.

The router ID should be a unique 32-bit number in the EIGRP for IP routing domain; otherwise, routing inconsistencies can occur.

**Note**

The **eigrp router-id** command is used to configure the router ID for EIGRP. Some versions of IOS accept the command **router-id**, without first specifying **eigrp**. The running config, however, displays **eigrp router-id**, regardless of which command is used.

By default, the EIGRP for IPv6 process is in a shutdown state. The **no shutdown** command is required to activate the EIGRP for IPv6 process. This command is not required for EIGRP for IPv4. Although EIGRP for IPv6 is enabled, neighbor adjacencies and routing updates cannot be sent and received until EIGRP is activated on the appropriate interfaces.

Both the **no shutdown** command and a router ID are required for the router to form neighbor adjacencies.

Example 6-24 shows the EIGRP for IPv6 configuration for R1, R2, and R3.

**Example 6-24**   Configuring the EIGRP for IPv6 Routing Process

```
#R1(config)# ipv6 router eigrp 2
% IPv6 routing not enabled
R1(config)# ipv6 unicast-routing
R1(config)# ipv6 router eigrp 2
R1(config-rtr)# eigrp router-id 1.0.0.0
R1(config-rtr)# no shutdown


R2(config)# ipv6 unicast-routing
R2(config)# ipv6 router eigrp 2
R2(config-rtr)# eigrp router-id 2.0.0.0
R2(config-rtr)# no shutdown
R2(config-rtr)#


R3(config)# ipv6 unicast-routing
R3(config)# ipv6 router eigrp 2
R3(config-rtr)# eigrp router-id 3.0.0.0
R3(config-rtr)# no shutdown
R3(config-rtr)#
```

## The ipv6 eigrp Interface Command (6.4.2.4)

EIGRP for IPv6 uses a different method to enable an interface for EIGRP. Instead of using the **network** router configuration mode command to specify matching interface addresses, EIGRP for IPv6 is configured directly on the interface.

Use the **ipv6 eigrp** *autonomous-system* interface configuration mode command to enable EIGRP for IPv6 on an interface. The *autonomous-system* value must be the same as the autonomous system number used to enable the EIGRP routing process.

Much like the **network** command used in EIGRP for IPv4, the **ipv6 eigrp** interface command:

- Enables the interface to form adjacencies and send or receive EIGRP for IPv6 updates.

- Includes the prefix (network) of this interface in EIGRP for IPv6 routing updates.

Example 6-25 shows the configuration to enable EIGRP for IPv6 on the R1, R2, and R3 interfaces.

**Example 6-25**    Enabling EIGRP for IPv6 on the Interfaces

```
R1(config)# interface g0/0
R1(config-if)# ipv6 eigrp 2
R1(config-if)# interface s 0/0/0
R1(config-if)# ipv6 eigrp 2
R1(config-if)# interface s 0/0/1
R1(config-if)# ipv6 eigrp 2
R1(config-if)#


R2(config)# interface g 0/0
R2(config-if)# ipv6 eigrp 2
R2(config-if)# interface s 0/0/0
R2(config-if)# ipv6 eigrp 2
%DUAL-5-NBRCHANGE: EIGRP-IPv6 2: Neighbor FE80::1 (Serial0/0/0) is up: new
  adjacency
R2(config-if)# interface s 0/0/1
R2(config-if)# ipv6 eigrp 2
R2(config-if)#


R3(config)# interface g 0/0
R3(config-if)# ipv6 eigrp 2
R3(config-if)# interface s 0/0/0
R3(config-if)# ipv6 eigrp 2
*Mar  4 03:02:00.696: %DUAL-5-NBRCHANGE: EIGRP-IPv6 2: Neighbor FE80::1
  (Serial0/0/0) is up: new adjacency
R3(config-if)# interface s 0/0/1
R3(config-if)# ipv6 eigrp 2
*Mar  4 03:02:17.264: %DUAL-5-NBRCHANGE: EIGRP-IPv6 2: Neighbor FE80::2
  (Serial0/0/1) is up: new adjacency
R3(config-if)#
```

In Example 6-25, notice the highlighted message, which indicates that R2 has now formed an EIGRP–IPv6 adjacency with the neighbor at link-local address FE80::1.

Because static link-local addresses were configured on all three routers, it is easy to determine that this adjacency is with router R1 (FE80::1).

The same **passive-interface** command used for IPv4 is used to configure an interface as passive with EIGRP for IPv6. In Example 6-26, the **show ipv6 protocols** command is used to verify the configuration.

**Example 6-26**   Configuring and Verifying EIGRP for IPv6 Passive Interfaces

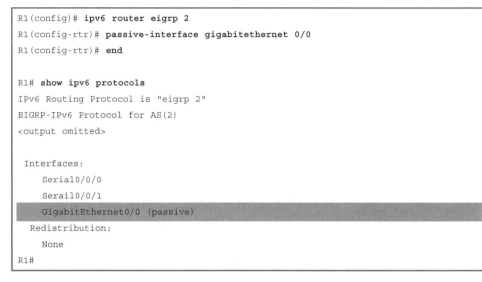

```
R1(config)# ipv6 router eigrp 2
R1(config-rtr)# passive-interface gigabitethernet 0/0
R1(config-rtr)# end

R1# show ipv6 protocols
IPv6 Routing Protocol is "eigrp 2"
EIGRP-IPv6 Protocol for AS(2)
<output omitted>

  Interfaces:
      Serial0/0/0
      Serail0/0/1
      GigabitEthernet0/0 (passive)
  Redistribution:
      None
R1#
```

# Verifying EIGRP for IPv6 (6.4.3)

In this topic, you will learn how to verify an EIGRP for IPv6 implementation in a small routed network.

### IPv6 Neighbor Table (6.4.3.1)

As with EIGRP for IPv4, before any EIGRP for IPv6 updates can be sent or received, routers must establish adjacencies with their neighbors.

Use the **show ipv6 eigrp neighbors** command to view the neighbor table and verify that EIGRP for IPv6 has established an adjacency with its neighbors.

The output shown in Figure 6-53 displays the IPv6 link-local address of the adjacent neighbor and the interface that this router uses to reach that EIGRP neighbor.

Using meaningful link-local addresses makes it easy to recognize the neighbors R2 at FE80::2 and R3 at FE80::3.

```
R1# show ipv6 eigrp neighbors
EIGRP-IPv6 Neighbors for AS(2)
H  Address                  Interface   Hold   Uptime    SRTT   RTO   Q   Seq
                                        (sec)            (ms)         Cnt  Num
1  Link-local address:      Se0/0/1     13     00:37:17  45     270   0   8
   FE80::3
0  Link-local address:      Se0/0/0     14     00:53:16  32     2370  0   8
   FE80::2
R1#
```

Neighbor's IPv6 Link-local Address.

Local Interface receiving EIGRP for IPv6 Hello packets.

Amount of time since this neighbor was added to the neighbor table.

Seconds remaining before declaring neighbor down.

The current hold time and is reset to the maximum hold time whenever a Hello packet is received.

**Figure 6-53**   The **show ipv6 eigrp neighbors** Command

Table 6-12 explains the significance of the highlighted output in Figure 6-53.

**Table 6-12**   **show ipv6 eigrp neighbors** Output Explained

| Field in Output | Description |
|---|---|
| H | ▪ Lists the neighbors in the order in which they were learned. |
| Address | ▪ The IPv6 link-local address of the neighbor. |
| Interface | ▪ The local interface on which this Hello packet was received. |
| Hold | ▪ Current hold time.<br>▪ When a Hello packet is received, this value is reset to the maximum hold time for that interface and then counts down to zero.<br>▪ If zero is reached, the neighbor is considered down. |
| Uptime | ▪ The amount of time since this neighbor was added to the neighbor table. |
| SRTT and RTO | ▪ Used by RTP to manage reliable EIGRP packets. |
| Queue Count | ▪ Should always be zero.<br>▪ If it is more than zero, EIGRP packets are waiting to be sent. |
| Sequence Number | ▪ Used to track Update, Query, and Reply packets. |

The **show ipv6 eigrp neighbors** command is useful for verifying and troubleshooting EIGRP for IPv6. If an expected neighbor is not listed, ensure that both ends of the link are up/up by using the **show ipv6 interface brief** command. The same requirements exist for establishing neighbor adjacencies with EIGRP for IPv6 as for IPv4. If both sides of the link have active interfaces, check the following:

- Are both routers configured with the same EIGRP autonomous system number?

- Is the interface enabled for EIGRP for IPv6 with the correct autonomous system number?

### The show ip protocols Command (6.4.3.2)

The **show ipv6 protocols** command displays the parameters and other information about the state of any active IPv6 routing protocol processes currently configured on the router. The **show ipv6 protocols** command displays different types of output specific to each IPv6 routing protocol.

Figure 6-54 indicates several EIGRP for IPv6 parameters previously discussed.

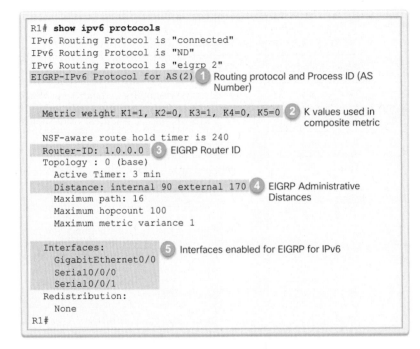

**Figure 6-54**   The **show ipv6 protocols** Command

Details of the numbering in the figure are as follows:

1. EIGRP for IPv6 is an active dynamic routing protocol on R1, configured with the autonomous system number 2.

2. These are the *K* values used to calculate the EIGRP composite metric. K1 and K3 are 1 by default, and K2, K4, and K5 are 0 by default.

3. The EIGRP for IPv6 router ID of R1 is 1.0.0.0.

4. As with EIGRP for IPv4, EIGRP for IPv6 administrative distances have internal AD of 90 and external of 170 (default values).

5. These interfaces are enabled for EIGRP for IPv6.

The output from the **show ipv6 protocols** command is useful in debugging routing operations. The Interfaces section identifies on which interfaces EIGRP for IPv6 has been enabled. This is useful in verifying that EIGRP is enabled on all the appropriate interfaces with the correct autonomous system number.

## The EIGRP for IPv6 Routing Table (6.4.3.3)

As with any other routing protocol, the goal with EIGRP for IPv6 is to populate the IP routing table with routes to remote networks and the best paths for reaching those networks. As with IPv4, it is important to examine the IPv6 routing table and determine whether it is populated with the correct routes.

You can examine the IPv6 routing table by using the **show ipv6 route** command. EIGRP for IPv6 routes are denoted in the routing table with a D, as are EIGRP for IPv4 routes in the IPv4 routing table.

Example 6-27 shows the EIGRP routes for R1, R2, and R3.

**Example 6-27**  The IPv6 EIGRP Routes

```
R1# show ipv6 route eigrp
<Output omitted>

D    2001:DB8:CAFE:2::/64 [90/3524096]
       via FE80::3, Serial0/0/1
D    2001:DB8:CAFE:3::/64 [90/2170112]
       via FE80::3, Serial0/0/1
D    2001:DB8:CAFE:A002::/64 [90/3523840]
       via FE80::3, Serial0/0/1
R1#
```

```
R2# show ipv6 route eigrp
<Output omitted>

D    2001:DB8:CAFE:1::/64 [90/3524096]
       via FE80::3, Serial0/0/1
D    2001:DB8:CAFE:3::/64 [90/3012096]
       via FE80::3, Serial0/0/1
D    2001:DB8:CAFE:A003::/64 [90/3523840]
       via FE80::3, Serial0/0/1
R2#
```

```
R3# show ipv6 route eigrp
<Output omitted>

D    2001:DB8:CAFE:1::/64 [90/2170112]
       via FE80::1, Serial0/0/0
D    2001:DB8:CAFE:2::/64 [90/3012096]
       via FE80::2, Serial0/0/1
D    2001:DB8:CAFE:A001::/64 [90/41024000]
       via FE80::1, Serial0/0/0
       via FE80::2, Serial0/0/1
R3#
```

R1 has installed three EIGRP routes to remote IPv6 networks in its IPv6 routing table:

- 2001:DB8:CAFE:2::/64 via R3 (FE80::3) using its Serial 0/0/1 interface
- 2001:DB8:CAFE:3::/64 via R3 (FE80::3) using its Serial 0/0/1 interface
- 2001:DB8:CAFE:A002::/64 via R3 (FE80::3) using its Serial 0/0/1 interface

All three routes are using router R3 as the next-hop router (successor). Notice that the routing table uses the link-local address as the next-hop address. Because each router has had all its interfaces configured with a unique and distinguishable link-local address, it is easy to recognize that the next-hop router via FE80::3 is router R3.

Notice that R3 has two equal-cost paths to 2001:DB8:CAFE:A001::/64. One path is via R1 at FE80::1, and the other path is via R2 at FE80::2.

<table>
<tr><td>Packet Tracer<br />☐ Activity</td></tr>
</table>

### Packet Tracer 6.4.3.4: Configuring Basic EIGRP with IPv6

Background/Scenario

In this activity, you will configure the network with EIGRP routing for IPv6. You will also assign router IDs, configure passive interfaces, verify that the network is fully converged, and display routing information by using **show** commands.

EIGRP for IPv6 has the same overall operation and features as EIGRP for IPv4, but there are a few major differences between them:

- EIGRP for IPv6 is configured directly on the router interfaces.

- With EIGRP for IPv6, a router ID is required on each router, or the routing process does not start.

- The EIGRP for IPv6 routing process uses a shutdown feature.

**Lab 6.4.3.5: Configuring Basic EIGRP for IPv6**

Refer to *Scaling Networks v6 Labs & Study Guide* and the online course to complete this activity.

In this lab, you will complete the following objectives:

- Part 1: Build the Network and Verify Connectivity

- Part 2: Configure EIGRP for IPv6 Routing

- Part 3: Verify EIGRP for IPv6 Routing

- Part 4: Configure and Verify Passive Interfaces

# Summary (6.5)

**Class Activity 6.5.1.1: Portfolio RIP and EIGRP**

Refer to *Scaling Networks v6 Labs & Study Guide* and the online course to complete this activity.

You are preparing a portfolio file for comparison of RIP and EIGRP routing protocols.

Consider a network with three interconnected routers. R1 is connected to R2 and R2 is connected to R3. Each router also has a LAN consisting of PCs, printers, and other end devices.

In this modeling activity scenario, you will be creating, addressing, and configuring a topology, using verification commands, and comparing/contrasting RIP and EIGRP routing protocol outputs.

Complete the PDF reflection questions accompanying this activity. Save your work and be prepared to share your answers with the class. Also save a copy of your work for later use in this course or for portfolio reference.

---

EIGRP (Enhanced Interior Gateway Routing Protocol) is a classless distance vector routing protocol. EIGRP is an enhancement of another Cisco routing protocol, IGRP (Interior Gateway Routing Protocol), which is now obsolete. EIGRP was initially released in 1992 as a Cisco proprietary protocol available only on Cisco devices. In 2013, Cisco released a basic functionality of EIGRP as an open standard to the IETF.

EIGRP uses the source code D for DUAL in the routing table. EIGRP has a default administrative distance of 90 for internal routes and 170 for routes imported from an external source, such as default routes.

EIGRP is an advanced distance vector routing protocol that includes features not found in other distance vector routing protocols, such as RIP. These features include Diffusing Update Algorithm (DUAL), neighbor adjacency establishment, Reliable Transport Protocol (RTP), partial and bounded updates, and equal- and unequal-cost load balancing.

EIGRP uses PDMs (protocol-dependent modules), which give it the capability to support different Layer 3 protocols, including IPv4 and IPv6. EIGRP uses RTP (Reliable Transport Protocol) as the transport layer protocol for the delivery of EIGRP packets. EIGRP uses reliable delivery for EIGRP updates, queries, and replies; it uses unreliable delivery for EIGRP hellos and acknowledgments. Reliable RTP means an EIGRP acknowledgment must be returned.

Before any EIGRP updates are sent, a router must first discover its neighbors. This is done with EIGRP Hello packets. The Hello and hold-down values do not need to match for two routers to become neighbors. The **show ip eigrp neighbors** command is used to view the neighbor table and verify that EIGRP has established an adjacency with its neighbors.

Unlike RIP, EIGRP does not send periodic updates. EIGRP sends partial or bounded updates, which include only route changes. Updates are sent only to the routers that are affected by a change. The EIGRP composite metric uses bandwidth, delay, reliability, and load to determine the best path. By default only bandwidth and delay are used.

At the center of EIGRP is DUAL. The DUAL finite state machine is used to determine the best path and potential backup paths to every destination network. The successor is a neighboring router that is used to forward a packet using the least-cost route to the destination network. Feasible distance (FD) is the lowest calculated metric to reach the destination network through the successor. A feasible successor (FS) is a neighbor who has a loop-free backup path to the same network as the successor and also meets the feasibility condition. The feasibility condition (FC) is met when a neighbor's reported distance (RD) to a network is less than the local router's feasible distance to the same destination network. The reported distance is simply an EIGRP neighbor's feasible distance to the destination network.

EIGRP is configured with the **router eigrp** *autonomous-system* command. The *autonomous-system* value is actually a process ID and must be the same on all routers in the EIGRP routing domain. The **network** command is similar to the **network** command used with RIP. The network is the classful network address of the directly connected interfaces on the router. A wildcard mask is an optional parameter that can be used to include only specific interfaces.

EIGRP for IPv6 shares many similarities with EIGRP for IPv4. However, whereas EIGRP for IPv4 uses the **network** command, IPv6 is enabled on the interface using the **ipv6 eigrp** *autonomous-system* interface configuration command.

# Practice

The following activities provide practice with the topics introduced in this chapter. The Labs and Class Activities are available in the companion *Scaling Networks v6 Labs & Study Guide* (ISBN 9781587134333). The Packet Tracer activity instructions are also in the Labs & Study Guide. The PKA files are found in the online course.

**Class Activities**

Class Activity 6.0.1.2: Classless EIGRP

Class Activity 6.5.1.1: Portfolio RIP and EIGRP

**Labs**

Lab 6.2.2.5: Configuring Basic EIGRP with IPv4

Lab 6.4.3.5: Configuring Basic EIGRP for IPv6

Packet Tracer
☐ **Activity**

**Packet Tracer Activities**

Packet Tracer 6.2.2.4: Configuring Basic EIGRP with IPv4

Packet Tracer 6.3.4.4: Investigating DUAL FSM

Packet Tracer 6.4.3.4: Configuring Basic EIGRP with IPv6

# Check Your Understanding Questions

Complete all the review questions listed here to test your understanding of the topics and concepts in this chapter. The appendix "Answers to 'Check Your Understanding' Questions" lists the answers.

1. What is the purpose of using protocol-dependent modules in EIGRP?

   A. To accommodate routing of different network layer protocols

   B. To describe different routing processes

   C. To identify different application layer protocols

   D. To use different transport protocols for different packets

2. If all router Ethernet interfaces in an EIGRP network are configured with the default EIGRP timers, how long will a router wait by default to receive an EIGRP packet from its neighbor before declaring the neighbor unreachable?

   A. 5 seconds

   B. 10 seconds

   C. 15 seconds

   D. 30 seconds

3. Which two EIGRP packet types are sent with unreliable delivery? (Choose two.)

   A. Acknowledgment packet

   B. Hello packet

   C. Query packet

   D. Reply packet

   E. Update packet

4. Which destination MAC address is used when a multicast EIGRP packet is encapsulated into an Ethernet frame?

    A. 01-00-5E-00-00-09

    B. 01-00-5E-00-00-10

    C. 01-00-5E-00-00-0A

    D. 01-00-5E-00-00-0B

5. What is identified within the opcode of an EIGRP packet header?

    A. The EIGRP autonomous system metrics

    B. The EIGRP hold timer agreed upon with a neighbor

    C. The EIGRP message type that is being sent to or received from a neighbor

    D. The EIGRP sum of delays from source to destination

6. Why would a network administrator use a wildcard mask in the **network** command when configuring a router to use EIGRP?

    A. To exclude some interfaces from the EIGRP process

    B. To reduce the router overhead

    C. To send a manual summarization

    D. To subnet at the time of the configuration

7. An administrator issues the **router eigrp 100** command on a router. What is the number 100 used for?

    A. As the autonomous system number

    B. As the length of time this router will wait to hear Hello packets from a neighbor

    C. As the maximum bandwidth of the fastest interface on the router

    D. As the number of neighbors supported by this router

8. What information does EIGRP maintain within the routing table?

    A. Adjacent neighbors

    B. All routes known to the router

    C. Both successors and feasible successors

    D. Only feasible successors

    E. Only successors

9. Which table does EIGRP use to store all routes that are learned from EIGRP neighbors?

    A. The adjacency table

    B. The neighbor table

    C. The routing table

    D. The topology table

10. Which command is used to display the bandwidth of an interface on an EIGRP-enabled router?

    A. **show ip route**

    B. **show interfaces**

    C. **show ip interface brief**

    D. **show ip protocols**

11. A new network administrator has been asked to verify the metrics that are used by EIGRP on a Cisco device. Which two EIGRP metrics are measured by using static values on a Cisco device? (Choose two.)

    A. Bandwidth

    B. Delay

    C. Load

    D. MTU

    E. Reliability

12. How do EIGRP routers establish and maintain neighbor adjacencies?

    A. By comparing known routes to information received in updates

    B. By dynamically learning new routes from neighbors

    C. By exchanging Hello packets with neighboring routers

    D. By exchanging neighbor tables with directly attached routers

    E. By exchanging routing tables with directly attached routers

13. What is indicated when an EIGRP route is in the passive state?

    A. The route has the highest path cost of all routes to that destination network.

    B. The route is a feasible successor and will be used if the active route fails.

    C. The route is viable and can be used to forward traffic.

    D. The route must be confirmed by neighboring routers before it is put in the active state.

    E. There is no activity on the route to that network.

14. What is the multicast address used by an EIGRP-enabled router operating with IPv6?

    A. FF02::1

    B. FF02::A

    C. FF02::B

    D. FFFF:FFFF:FFFF:FFFF:FFFF:FFFF:FFFF:FFFF

15. Which configuration is necessary to ensure successful operation of EIGRP for IPv6?

    A. The **eigrp router-id** command requires an IPv6 address in the router configuration mode.

    B. The **network** command is required in the router configuration mode.

    C. The **no shutdown** command is required in the router configuration mode.

    D. The **router eigrp** *autonomous-system* command is required in the router configuration mode.

# CHAPTER 7

# EIGRP Tuning and Troubleshooting

## Objectives

Upon completion of this chapter, you will be able to answer the following questions:

- How do you configure EIGRP to improve network performance?

- How do you troubleshoot common EIGRP configuration issues in a small to medium-sized business network?

## Key Terms

This chapter uses the following key terms. You can find the definitions in the Glossary.

*Null0*   *Page 377*

*quad zero*   *Page 380*

# Introduction (7.0.1.1)

EIGRP is a versatile routing protocol that can be fine-tuned in many ways. Two of the most important tuning capabilities are the ability to summarize routes and the ability to implement load balancing. Other tuning capabilities include being able to propagate a default route, fine-tune timers, and implement authentication between EIGRP neighbors to increase security.

This chapter discusses these additional tuning features and the configuration mode commands to implement these features for both IPv4 and IPv6.

**Class Activity 7.0.1.2: EIGRP—Back to the Future**

Refer to *Scaling Networks v6 Labs & Study Guide* and the online course to complete this activity.

This chapter teaches you how to maintain your EIGRP networks and to influence them to do what you want them to do. EIGRP concepts from this chapter include:

- Auto-summarization
- Load balancing
- Default routes
- Hold-down timers
- Authentication

With a partner, write 10 EIGRP review questions based on Chapter 6's curriculum content. Three of the questions must focus on the bulleted items above. Ideally, you will design multiple-choice, true/false, or fill-in-the-blank question types. As you design questions, ensure that you record the curriculum section and page numbers of the supporting content in case you need to refer back for answer verification.

Save your work and then meet with another group, or the entire class, and quiz them using the questions you developed.

# Tune EIGRP (7.1)

In this section, you will learn how to configure EIGRP to improve network performance.

## Automatic Summarization (7.1.1)

In this topic, you will learn how to configure EIGRP summarization.

## Network Topology (7.1.1.1)

Before fine-tuning EIGRP features, start with a basic implementation of EIGRP.

Figure 7-1 shows the reference network topology used for this chapter.

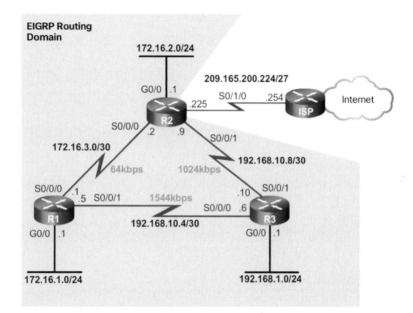

**Figure 7-1**   EIGRP for IPv4 Topology

Examples 7-1, 7-2, and 7-3 show the IPv4 interface configurations and the EIGRP implementations on R1, R2, and R3, respectively.

**Example 7-1**   Starting IPv4 Interface and EIGRP for IPv4 Configuration for R1

```
R1# show running-config
<Output omitted>
version 15.2
!
interface GigabitEthernet0/0
 ip address 172.16.1.1 255.255.255.0
!
interface Serial0/0/0
 bandwidth 64
 ip address 172.16.3.1 255.255.255.252
 clock rate 64000
!
```

```
interface Serial0/0/1
 ip address 192.168.10.5 255.255.255.252
!
router eigrp 1
 network 172.16.0.0
 network 192.168.10.0
 eigrp router-id 1.1.1.1
```

**Example 7-2**    Starting IPv4 Interface and EIGRP for IPv4 Configuration for R2

```
R2# show running-config
<Output omitted>
version 15.2
!
interface GigabitEthernet0/0
 ip address 172.16.2.1 255.255.255.0
!
interface Serial0/0/0
 bandwidth 64
 ip address 172.16.3.2 255.255.255.252
!
interface Serial0/0/1
 bandwidth 1024
 ip address 192.168.10.9 255.255.255.252
 clock rate 64000
!
interface Serial0/1/0
 ip address 209.165.200.225 255.255.255.224
!
router eigrp 1
 network 172.16.0.0
 network 192.168.10.8 0.0.0.3
 eigrp router-id 2.2.2.2
```

**Example 7-3**    Starting IPv4 Interface and EIGRP for IPv4 Configuration for R3

```
R3# show running-config
<Output omitted>
version 15.2
!
interface GigabitEthernet0/0
 ip address 192.168.1.1 255.255.255.0
!
```

```
interface Serial0/0/0
 ip address 192.168.10.6 255.255.255.252
 clock rate 64000
!
interface Serial0/0/1
 bandwidth 1024
 ip address 192.168.10.10 255.255.255.252
!
router eigrp 1
 network 192.168.1.0
 network 192.168.10.4 0.0.0.3
 network 192.168.10.8 0.0.0.3
 eigrp router-id 3.3.3.3
```

The types of serial interfaces and their associated bandwidths may not necessarily reflect the most common types of connections found in networks today. The bandwidths of the serial links used in this topology help explain the calculation of the routing protocol metrics and the process of best path selection.

Notice that the **bandwidth** command on the serial interfaces were used to modify the default bandwidth of 1544 Kbps.

In this chapter, the ISP router is used as the routing domain's gateway to the Internet. All three routers are running Cisco IOS Release 15.2.

## EIGRP Automatic Summarization (7.1.1.2)

One of the most common tuning methods with EIGRP is enabling and disabling automatic route summarization. Route summarization allows a router to group networks together and advertise them as one large group using a single, summarized route. The rapid growth of networks makes it necessary to be able to summarize routes.

A border router is a router that sits at the edge of a network. This router must be able to advertise all of the known networks within its routing table to a directly connected network router or ISP router. This convergence can potentially result in very large routing tables. Imagine if a single router had 10 different networks and had to advertise all 10 route entries to a connecting router. What if that connecting router also had 10 networks and had to advertise all 20 routes to an ISP router? If every enterprise router followed this pattern, the routing table of the ISP router would be huge.

To limit the number of routing advertisements and the size of routing tables, EIGRP provides route summarization features. Summarization decreases the number of entries in routing updates and lowers the number of entries in local routing tables. It also reduces bandwidth utilization for routing updates and results in faster routing table lookups.

EIGRP can be enabled to perform automatic summarization at classful boundaries. This means that EIGRP automatically recognizes subnets as a single Class A, B, or C network, and it creates only one entry in the routing table for the summary route. As a result, all traffic destined for the subnets travels across that one path.

Figure 7-2 shows an example of how automatic summarization works.

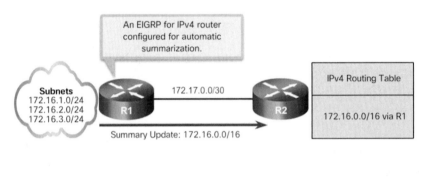

| Classful Networks | |
| --- | --- |
| Class A: 0.0.0.0 to 127.255.255.255 | Default Mask: 255.0.0.0 or /8 |
| Class B: 128.0.0.0 to 191.255.255.255 | Default Mask: 255.255.0.0 or /16 |
| Class C: 192.0.0.0 to 223.255.255.255 | Default Mask: 255.255.255.0 or /24 |

**Figure 7-2**   Automatic Summarization at a Classful Network Boundary

Routers R1 and R2 are both configured using EIGRP for IPv4 with automatic summarization. R1 has three subnets in its routing table: 172.16.1.0/24, 172.16.2.0/24, and 172.16.3.0/24. In the classful network addressing architecture, these subnets are all considered part of a larger class B network, 172.16.0.0/16. EIGRP on router R1 is configured for automatic summarization. Therefore, when it sends its routing update to R2, it summarizes the three /24 subnets as a single network of 172.16.0.0/16. This reduces the number of routing updates sent and the number of entries in R2's IPv4 routing table.

All traffic destined for the three subnets travels across the one path. R2 does not maintain routes to individual subnets, and no subnet information is learned.

In an enterprise network, the path chosen to reach the summary route may not be the best choice for the traffic that is trying to reach each individual subnet. The only way that all routers can find the best routes for each individual subnet is for neighbors to send subnet information. In this situation, automatic summarization should be disabled. When automatic summarization is disabled, updates are classless and include subnet information.

## Configuring EIGRP Automatic Summarization (7.1.1.3)

EIGRP for IPv4 automatic summarization is disabled by default beginning with Cisco IOS Release 15.0(1)M and 12.2(33). Prior to this, automatic summarization was enabled by default, which means EIGRP performed automatic summarization each time the EIGRP topology crossed a border between two different major class networks.

In Example 7-4, the output from the **show ip protocols** command on R1 indicates that EIGRP automatic summarization is disabled.

**Example 7-4**  Verifying that Automatic Summarization Is Disabled

```
R1# show ip protocols
*** IP Routing is NSF aware ***

Routing Protocol is "eigrp 1"
  Outgoing update filter list for all interfaces is not set
  Incoming update filter list for all interfaces is not set
  Default networks flagged in outgoing updates
  Default networks accepted from incoming updates
  EIGRP-IPv4 Protocol for AS(1)
    Metric weight K1=1, K2=0, K3=1, K4=0, K5=0
<Output omitted>

  Automatic Summarization: disabled
  Maximum path: 4
  Routing for Networks:
    172.16.0.0
    192.168.10.0
<Output omitted>
```

R1 is running IOS 15.2, and therefore EIGRP automatic summarization is disabled by default.

Example 7-5 shows the current routing table for R3.

**Example 7-5**  Verifying that Routes Are Not Automatically Summarized

```
R3# show ip route eigrp
<Output omitted>

  172.16.0.0/16 is variably subnetted, 3 subnets, 2 masks
D      172.16.1.0/24 [90/2170112]  via 192.168.10.5, 02:21:10, Serial0/0/0
D      172.16.2.0/24 [90/3012096]  via 192.168.10.9, 02:21:10, Serial0/0/1
D      172.16.3.0/30 [90/41024000] via 192.168.10.9, 02:21:10, Serial0/0/1
                     [90/41024000] via 192.168.10.5, 02:21:10, Serial0/0/0
R3#
```

Notice that the IPv4 routing table for R3 contains all the networks and subnets within the EIGRP routing domain.

To enable automatic summarization for EIGRP, enter the **auto-summary** router configuration command on all three routers, as shown in Example 7-6. The **no** form of this command is used to disable automatic summarization.

**Example 7-6**   Configuring Automatic Summarization

```
R1(config)# router eigrp 1
R1(config-router)# auto-summary
R1(config-router)#
*Mar  9 19:40:19.342: %DUAL-5-NBRCHANGE: EIGRP-IPv4 1: Neighbor 192.168.10.6
   (Serial0/0/1) is resync: summary configured
*Mar  9 19:40:19.342: %DUAL-5-NBRCHANGE: EIGRP-IPv4 1: Neighbor 192.168.10.6
   (Serial0/0/1) is resync: summary up, remove components
*Mar  9 19:41:03.630: %DUAL-5-NBRCHANGE: EIGRP-IPv4 1: Neighbor 192.168.10.6
   (Serial0/0/1) is resync: peer graceful-restart
```

```
R2(config)# router eigrp 1
R2(config-router)# auto-summary
R2(config-router)#
```

```
R3(config)# router eigrp 1
R3(config-router)# auto-summary
R3(config-router)#
```

## Verifying Auto-Summary: show ip protocols (7.1.1.4)

In Figure 7-1, notice that the EIGRP routing domain has three classful networks:

- 172.16.0.0/16 class B network consisting of the 172.16.1.0/24, 172.16.2.0/24, and 172.16.3.0/30 subnets

- 192.168.10.0/24 class C network consisting of the 192.168.10.4/30 and 192.168.10.8/30 subnets

- 192.168.1.0/24 class C network, which is not subnetted

The output from R1's **show ip protocols** command in Example 7-7 shows that automatic summarization is now enabled.

**Example 7-7**    Verifying that Automatic Summarization Is Enabled

```
R1# show ip protocols
*** IP Routing is NSF aware ***

Routing Protocol is "eigrp 1"
  Outgoing update filter list for all interfaces is not set
  Incoming update filter list for all interfaces is not set
  Default networks flagged in outgoing updates
  Default networks accepted from incoming updates
  EIGRP-IPv4 Protocol for AS(1)
    Metric weight K1=1, K2=0, K3=1, K4=0, K5=0
<Output omitted>

Automatic Summarization: enabled
    192.168.10.0/24 for Gi0/0, Se0/0/0
       Summarizing 2 components with metric 2169856
    172.16.0.0/16 for Se0/0/1
       Summarizing 3 components with metric 2816
<Output omitted>
```

The output in Example 7-7 also indicates the networks that are summarized and on which interfaces. Notice that R1 summarizes two networks in its EIGRP routing updates:

- 192.168.10.0/24 sent out the GigabitEthernet 0/0 and Serial 0/0/0 interfaces.

- 172.16.0.0/16 sent out the Serial 0/0/1 interface.

R1 has the 192.168.10.4/30 and 192.168.10.8/30 subnets in its IPv4 routing table. As illustrated in Figure 7-3, R1 summarizes the two highlighted subnets as 192.168.10.0/24.

R1 then forwards the summarized address 192.168.10.0/24 to its neighbors out its Serial 0/0/0 and GigabitEthernet 0/0 interfaces. Because R1 does not have any EIGRP neighbors connected on its GigabitEthernet 0/0 interface, the summarized routing update is received only by R2.

R1 also has the 172.16.1.0/24, 172.16.2.0/24, and 172.16.3.0/30 subnets in its IPv4 routing table. As illustrated in Figure 7-4, R1 summarizes these three highlighted subnets as 172.16.0.0/16.

R1 then forwards the summarized address 172.16.0.0/16 out its Serial 0/0/1 interface to R3. R2 is also configured for automatic summarization and advertises the same summary address 172.16.0.0/16 to R3. In this example, R3 would select R1 as the successor to 172.16.0.0/16 because it has a lower feasible distance due to the higher bandwidth of the R3-to-R1 serial interface link.

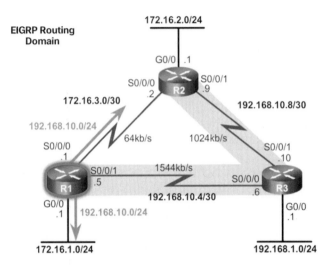

**Figure 7-3** R1 192.168.10.0/24 Summary

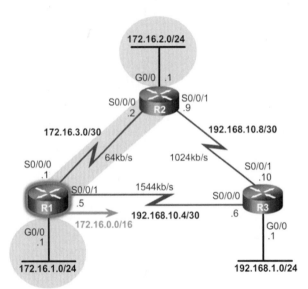

**Figure 7-4** R1 172.16.0.0/16 Summary

Notice that the 172.16.0.0/16 summarized update is not sent out R1's GigabitEthernet 0/0 and Serial 0/0/0 interfaces. This is because these two interfaces are members of the same 172.16.0.0/16 class B network. The 172.16.1.0/24 nonsummarized routing update is sent by R1 to R2.

Summarized updates are only sent out interfaces on different major classful networks. In this example, R1 was advertising the 172.16.0.0/16 network to R3 because the R1-to-R3 link is on a different classful network (that is, 192.168.10.0/24).

## Verifying Auto-Summary: Topology Table (7.1.1.5)

The routing tables of R1 and R2 contain subnets of the 172.16.0.0/16 network. Therefore, as illustrated in Figure 7-5, both routers advertise the summary route of 172.16.0.0/16 to R3.

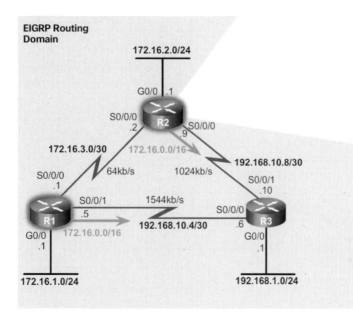

**Figure 7-5**   R3 Sources for 172.16.0.0/16

Use the **show ip eigrp topology all-links** command to view all incoming EIGRP routes, as shown in Example 7-8.

**Example 7-8**   Verifying the Summary Route in the Topology Table

```
R3# show ip eigrp topology all-links

P 172.16.0.0/16, 1 successors, FD is 2170112, serno 9
        via 192.168.10.5 (2170112/2816), Serial0/0/0
        via 192.168.10.9 (3012096/2816), Serial0/0/1

<Output omitted>
```

The output verifies that R3 has received the 172.16.0.0/16 summary route from both R1 (that is, 192.168.10.5) and R2 (that is, 192.168.10.9). Notice that only one successor has been chosen. This is the link to R1 due to its faster interface bandwidth.

The **all-links** option shows all received updates, including routes from the feasible successor (FS). In this instance, R2 qualifies as an FS because its reported distance (RD) of 2816 is less than the feasible distance (FD) of 2,170,112 via R1.

### Verifying Auto-Summary: Routing Table (7.1.1.6)

Example 7-9 displays the routing table when automatic summarization is not enabled, which has been the default since IOS 15.0(1)M.

**Example 7-9**   Verifying the Routing Table When Automatic Summarization Is Disabled

```
R3# show ip route eigrp

<Output omitted>

 172.16.0.0/16 is variably subnetted, 3 subnets, 2 masks
D        172.16.1.0/24 [90/2170112]   via 192.168.10.5, 02:21:10, Serial0/0/0
D        172.16.2.0/24 [90/3012096]   via 192.168.10.9, 02:21:10, Serial0/0/1
D        172.16.3.0/30 [90/41024000] via 192.168.10.9, 02:21:10, Serial0/0/1
                       [90/41024000] via 192.168.10.5, 02:21:10, Serial0/0/0
R3#
```

As shown in Example 7-9, all subnets appear in the routing table when automatic summarization is enabled.

Example 7-10 shows how to display the routing table after summarization is enabled by using the **auto-summary** command.

**Example 7-10**   Verifying the Routing Table When Automatic Summarization Is Enabled

```
R3# show ip route eigrp

<Output omitted>

D        172.16.0.0/16 [90/2170112] via 192.168.10.5, 00:12:05, Serial0/0/0
         192.168.10.0/24 is variably subnetted, 5 subnets, 3 masks
D            192.168.10.0/24 is a summary, 00:11:43, Null0
R3#
```

Notice that with automatic summarization enabled, R3's routing table now contains only the single class B network address 172.16.0.0/16. The successor or next-hop router is R1, via 192.168.10.5.

**Note**

Automatic summarization is only an option with EIGRP for IPv4. Classful addressing does not exist in IPv6; therefore, there is no need for automatic summarization with EIGRP for IPv6.

A problem associated with automatic route summarization is that a summary address also advertises networks that are not available on the advertising router. For instance, R1 is advertising the summary address 172.16.0.0/16, but it is really only connected to the 172.16.1.0/24, 172.16.2.0/24, and 172.16.3.0/30 subnets. Therefore, R1 may receive incoming packets to destinations that do not exist. This could be a problem if R1 had a default gateway configured, as it would in turn forward a request to a destination that does not exist.

EIGRP avoids this problem by adding a network route for the classful network route to the routing table. This network entry routes packets to a Null interface. The *Null0* interface, commonly known as "the bit bucket," is a virtual IOS interface that is a route to nowhere. Packets that match a route with a Null0 exit interface are discarded.

Example 7-11 displays the routing table of R1. Notice that the two highlighted entries are summary routes for 172.16.0.0/16 and 192.168.10.0/24 to Null0. If R1 receives a packet destined for a network that is advertised by the classful mask but does not exist, it discards the packet and sends a notification message back to the source.

**Example 7-11**   Null0 Summary Routes on R1

```
R1# show ip route

      172.16.0.0/16 is variably subnetted, 6 subnets, 4 masks
D        172.16.0.0/16 is a summary, 00:03:06, Null0
C        172.16.1.0/24 is directly connected, GigabitEthernet0/0
L        172.16.1.1/32 is directly connected, GigabitEthernet0/0
D        172.16.2.0/24 [90/40512256] via 172.16.3.2, 00:02:52, Serial0/0/0
C        172.16.3.0/30 is directly connected, Serial0/0/0
L        172.16.3.1/32 is directly connected, Serial0/0/0
D     192.168.1.0/24 [90/2170112] via 192.168.10.6, 00:02:51, Serial0/0/1
      192.168.10.0/24 is variably subnetted, 4 subnets, 3 masks
D        192.168.10.0/24 is a summary, 00:02:52, Null0
C        192.168.10.4/30 is directly connected, Serial0/0/1
L        192.168.10.5/32 is directly connected, Serial0/0/1
D        192.168.10.8/30 [90/3523840] via 192.168.10.6, 00:02:59, Serial0/0/1
R1#
```

EIGRP for IPv4 automatically includes a Null0 summary route whenever the following conditions exist:

■ Automatic summarization is enabled.

■ There is at least one subnet that was learned via EIGRP.

■ There are two or more **network** EIGRP router configuration mode commands.

### Summary Route (7.1.1.7)

The topology in Figure 7-6 provides a scenario that explains how automatic summarization could cause a routing loop.

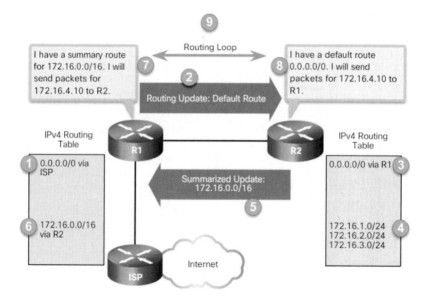

**Figure 7-6**   Example of a Routing Loop

Details of the numbering in the figure are as follows:

1. R1 has a default route, 0.0.0.0/0, via the ISP router.

2. R1 sends to R2 a routing update that contains the default route.

3. R2 installs the default route from R1 in its IPv4 routing table.

4. R2's routing table contains the 172.16.1.0/24, 172.16.2.0/24, and 172.16.3.0/24 subnets in its routing table.

5. R2 sends a summarized update to R1 for the 172.16.0.0/16 network.

6. R1 installs the summarized route for 172.16.0.0/16 via R2.

7.  R1 receives a packet for 172.16.4.10. Because R1 has a route for 172.16.0.0/16 via R2, it forwards the packet to R2.

8.  R2 receives the packet with the destination address 172.16.4.10 from R1. The packet does not match any specific route, so using the default route in its routing table, R2 forwards the packet back to R1.

9.  The packet for 172.16.4.10 loops between R1 and R2 until the TTL expires and the packet is dropped.

## Summary Route (Cont.) (7.1.1.8)

EIGRP uses the Null0 interface to prevent the types of routing loops just described. The topology in Figure 7-7 provides a scenario that explains how the Null0 route prevents the routing loop illustrated in the previous scenario.

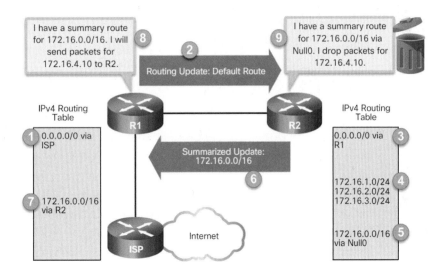

**Figure 7-7**    Null0 Route Is Used for Loop Prevention

Details of the numbering in the figure are as follows:

1.  R1 has a default route, 0.0.0.0/0, via the ISP router.

2.  R1 sends to R2 a routing update that contains the default route.

3.  R2 installs the default route from R1 in its IPv4 routing table.

4.  R2's routing table contains the 172.16.1.0/24, 172.16.2.0/24, and 172.16.3.0/24 subnets in its routing table.

5.  R2 installs the 172.16.0.0/16 summary route to Null0 in its routing table.

6. R2 sends a summarized update to R1 for the 172.16.0.0/16 network.

7. R1 installs the summarized route for 172.16.0.0/16 via R2.

8. R1 receives a packet for 172.16.4.10. Because R1 has a route for 172.16.0.0/16 via R2, it forwards the packet to R2.

9. R2 receives the packet with the destination address 172.16.4.10 from R1. The packet does not match any specific subnet of 172.16.0.0 but does match the 172.16.0.0/16 summary route to Null0. Using the Null0 route, the packet is discarded.

A summary route on R2 for 172.16.0.0/16 to the Null0 interface discards any packets that begin with 172.16.x.x and that do not have a longer match with any of the subnets 172.16.1.0/24, 172.16.2.0/24, or 172.16.3.0/24.

Even if R2 has a default route of 0.0.0.0/0 in its routing table, the Null0 route is a longer match.

**Note**

The Null0 summary route is removed when autosummarization is disabled by using the **no auto-summary** router configuration mode command.

**Interactive Graphic**

**Activity 7.1.1.9: Determine the Classful Summarization**

Refer to the online course to complete this activity.

**Interactive Graphic**

**Activity 7.1.1.10: Determine the Exit Interface for a Given Packet**

Refer to the online course to complete this activity.

# Default Route Propagation (7.1.2)

In this topic, you will learn how to propagate a default route in EIGRP.

## Propagating a Default Static Route (7.1.2.1)

Using a static route to 0.0.0.0/0 as a default route is not routing protocol dependent. The *quad zero* default static route can be used with any currently supported routing protocols. The default static route is usually configured on the router that has a connection to a network outside the EIGRP routing domain (for example, an ISP).

As shown in Figure 7-8, R2 is a gateway router connecting the EIGRP routing domain to the Internet.

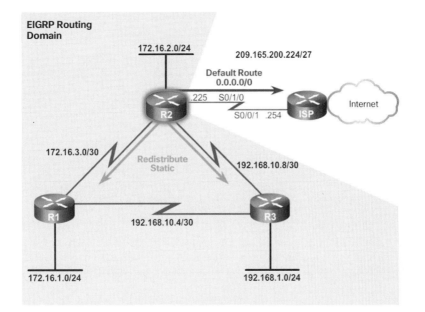

**Figure 7-8**   EIGRP for IPv4 Topology: Default Route Propagation

When the default static route is configured on the edge router, it is necessary to propagate that route throughout the EIGRP domain.

One method of propagating a default static route within the EIGRP routing domain is by using the **redistribute static** command. The **redistribute static** command tells EIGRP to include static routes in its EIGRP updates to other routers.

Example 7-12 shows the configuration of the default static route and the **redistribute static** command on router R2.

**Example 7-12**   R2 Static Default Route Configuration and Propagation

```
R2(config)# ip route 0.0.0.0 0.0.0.0 serial 0/1/0
R2(config)# router eigrp 1
R2(config-router)# redistribute static
```

Example 7-13 verifies that the default route has been received by router R2 and installed in its IPv4 routing table.

**Example 7-13**   Verifying the Default Route on R2

```
R2# show ip route | include 0.0.0.0
Gateway of last resort is 0.0.0.0 to network 0.0.0.0
S*      0.0.0.0/0 is directly connected, Serial0/1/0
R2#
```

In Example 7-14, the **show ip protocols** command verifies that R2 is redistributing static routes within the EIGRP routing domain.

**Example 7-14**   Verifying Redistribution on R2

```
R2# show ip protocols
*** IP Routing is NSF aware ***

Routing Protocol is "eigrp 1"
  Outgoing update filter list for all interfaces is not set
  Incoming update filter list for all interfaces is not set
  Default networks flagged in outgoing updates
  Default networks accepted from incoming updates
  Redistributing: static
  EIGRP-IPv4 Protocol for AS(1)

<Output omitted>
```

## Verifying the Propagated Default Route (7.1.2.2)

In this scenario, R2 is the edge router that has been configured to propagate a default static route to other EIGRP routers.

Example 7-15 shows a portion of the IPv4 routing tables for R1 and R3.

**Example 7-15**   Verifying the Default Route on R1 and R3

```
R1# show ip route | include 0.0.0.0
Gateway of last resort is 192.168.10.6 to network 0.0.0.0
D*EX  0.0.0.0/0 [170/3651840] via 192.168.10.6, 00:25:23, Serial0/0/1
R1#
```

```
R3# show ip route | include 0.0.0.0
Gateway of last resort is 192.168.10.9 to network 0.0.0.0
D*EX  0.0.0.0/0 [170/3139840] via 192.168.10.9, 00:27:17, Serial0/0/1
R3#
```

In the routing tables for R1 and R3, notice the routing source and administrative distance for the new default route learned using EIGRP. The entry for the EIGRP-learned default route is identified by the following:

- **D**—This route was learned from an EIGRP routing update.

- *****—The route is a candidate for a default route.

- **EX**—The route is an external EIGRP route, in this case a static route outside the EIGRP routing domain.

- **170**—This is the administrative distance of an external EIGRP route.

Notice that R1 selects R3 as the successor to the default route because it has a lower feasible distance. Default routes provide a default path to outside the routing domain and, like summary routes, minimize the number of entries in the routing table.

## EIGRP for IPv6: Default Route (7.1.2.3)

Recall that EIGRP maintains separate tables for IPv4 and IPv6. Therefore, an IPv6 default route must be propagated separately, as shown in Figure 7-9.

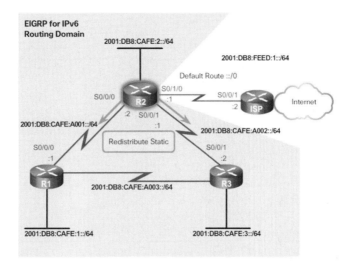

**Figure 7-9**   EIGRP for IPv6 Topology: Default Route Propagation

As with EIGRP for IPv4, with EIGRP for IPv6, a default static route is configured on the gateway router (R2), as shown in Example 7-16.

**Example 7-16**   R2 IPv6 Static Default Route Configuration and Propagation

```
R2(config)# ipv6 route ::/0 serial 0/1/0
R2(config)# ipv6 router eigrp 2
R2(config-router)# redistribute static
```

The ::/0 prefix and prefix length are equivalent to the 0.0.0.0 0.0.0.0 address and subnet mask used in IPv4. Both are all-zero addresses with a /0 prefix length.

There is no specific IPv6 command to redistribute the IPv6 default static route. The IPv6 default static route is redistributed into the EIGRP for the IPv6 domain by using the same **redistribute static** command that is used in EIGRP for IPv4.

> **Note**
>
> Some IOSs may require that the **redistribute static** command include the EIGRP metric parameters before the static route can be redistributed.

You can verify the propagation of the IPv6 static default route by examining R1's IPv6 routing table using the **show ipv6 route** command, as shown in Example 7-17. Notice that the successor or next-hop address is not R2 but R3. This is because R3 provides a better path to R2 at a lower cost metric than R1.

**Example 7-17**    Verifying the Default Route on R1

```
R1# show ipv6 route
IPv6 Routing Table - default - 12 entries
Codes: C - Connected, L - Local, S - Static, U - Per-user Static route
       B - BGP, R - RIP, I1 - ISIS L1, I2 - ISIS L2
       IA - ISIS interarea, IS - ISIS summary, D - EIGRP, EX - EIGRP external
       ND - ND Default, NDp - ND Prefix, DCE - Destination, NDr - Redirect
       O - OSPF Intra, OI - OSPF Inter, OE1 - OSPF ext 1, OE2 - OSPF ext 2
       ON1 - OSPF NSSA ext 1, ON2 - OSPF NSSA ext 2
EX  ::/0 [170/3523840]
     via FE80::3, Serial0/0/1
<output omitted>
```

**Packet Tracer ☐ Activity**

**Packet Tracer 7.1.2.4: Propagating a Default Route in EIGRP for IPv4 and IPv6**

Background/Scenario

In this activity, you will configure and propagate a default route in EIGRP for IPv4 and IPv6 networks. EIGRP is already configured. However, you are required to configure an IPv4 default route and an IPv6 default route. Then you will configure the EIGRP routing process to propagate the default route to downstream EIGRP neighbors. Finally, you will verify the default routes by pinging hosts outside the EIGRP routing domain.

# Fine-tuning EIGRP Interfaces (7.1.3)

In this topic, you will learn how to configure EIGRP interface settings to improve network performance.

## EIGRP Bandwidth Utilization (7.1.3.1)

By default, EIGRP uses only up to 50 percent of an interface's bandwidth for EIGRP information. This prevents the EIGRP process from over-utilizing a link and not allowing enough bandwidth for the routing of normal traffic.

Use the **ip bandwidth-percent eigrp** *as-number percent* interface configuration command to configure the percentage of bandwidth that EIGRP can use on an interface. The command uses the amount of configured bandwidth (or the default bandwidth) when calculating the percentage that EIGRP can use.

In Figure 7-10, R1 and R2 share a very slow 64 Kbps link.

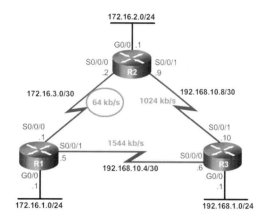

**Figure 7-10**   EIGRP for IPv4 Topology: Bandwidth

Example 7-18 configures EIGRP to use no more than 50 percent of the bandwidth on the link between R2 and R1 and no more than 75 percent of the bandwidth on the link between R2 and R3.

**Example 7-18**   Configuring Bandwidth Utilization with EIGRP for IPv4

```
R1(config)# interface serial 0/0/0
R1(config-if)# ip bandwidth-percent eigrp 1 50
```

```
R2(config)# interface serial 0/0/0
R2(config-if)# ip bandwidth-percent eigrp 1 50
R2(config-if)# interface serial 0/0/1
R2(config-if)# ip bandwidth-percent eigrp 1 75
```

```
R3(config)# interface serial 0/0/1
R3(config-if)# ip bandwidth-percent eigrp 1 75
```

In this example, EIGRP never uses more the 32 Kbps of the link's bandwidth for EIGRP packet traffic between R2 and R1.

To restore the default value, use the **no** form of this command.

To configure the percentage of bandwidth that EIGRP can use for IPv6 on an interface, use the **ipv6 bandwidth-percent eigrp** *as-number percent* interface configuration command. To restore the default value, use the **no** form of this command.

Example 7-19 shows the configuration of the interfaces between R1 and R2 to limit the bandwidth used by EIGRP for IPv6.

**Example 7-19**   Configuring Bandwidth Utilization with EIGRP for IPv6

```
R1(config)# interface serial 0/0/0
R1(config-if)# ipv6 bandwidth-percent eigrp 2 50
R1(config-if)#

R2(config)# interface serial 0/0/0
R2(config-if)# ipv6 bandwidth-percent eigrp 2 50
R2(config-if)#
```

## Hello and Hold Timers (7.1.3.2)

EIGRP uses Hello packets to establish and monitor the connection status of its neighbor. The hold time tells the router the maximum time that the router should wait to receive the next Hello packet before declaring that neighbor unreachable.

Hello intervals and hold times are configurable on a per-interface basis and do not have to match with other EIGRP routers to establish or maintain adjacencies.

Use the **ip hello-interval eigrp** *as-number seconds* interface configuration command to configure a different hello interval.

If the hello interval is changed, ensure that the hold time value is equal to or greater than the hello interval. Otherwise, neighbor adjacency goes down after the hold time expires and before the next hello interval.

Use the **ip hold-time eigrp** *as-number seconds* interface configuration command to configure a different hold time. The seconds value for both hello and hold time intervals can range from 1 to 65,535.

Table 7-1 shows the default hello intervals and hold timers for EIGRP.

**Table 7-1**  Default Hello Intervals and Hold Timers for EIGRP

| Bandwidth | Link Example | Default Hello Interval | Default Hold Time |
|---|---|---|---|
| 1.544 Mbps | Multipoint Frame Relay | 60 seconds | ■ 180 seconds |
| Greater than 1.544 Mbps | T1, Ethernet | 5 seconds | ■ 15 seconds |

Example 7-20 shows the configuration of R1 to use a 50-second hello interval and 150-second hold time. The **no** form can be used on both of these commands to restore the default values.

**Example 7-20**  Configuring EIGRP for IPv4 Hello and Hold Timers

```
R1(config)# interface serial 0/0/0
R1(config-if)# ip hello-interval eigrp 1 50
R1(config-if)# ip hold-time eigrp 1 150
```

The hello interval time and hold time do not need to match for two routers to form an EIGRP adjacency.

EIGRP for IPv6 uses the same hello interval and hold times as EIGRP for IPv4. The interface configuration mode commands are similar to those for IPv4.

Use the **ipv6 hello-interval eigrp** *as-number seconds* interface configuration command to change the hello interval and use the **ipv6 hold-time eigrp** *as-number seconds* command to change the hold time.

Example 7-21 shows the hello interval and hold time configurations for R1 and R2 with EIGRP for IPv6.

**Example 7-21**  Configuring EIGRP for IPv6 Hello and Hold Timers

```
R1(config)# inter serial 0/0/0
R1(config-if)# ipv6 hello-interval eigrp 2 50
R1(config-if)# ipv6 hold-time eigrp 2 150

R2(config)# inter serial 0/0/0
R2(config-if)# ipv6 hello-interval eigrp 2 50
R2(config-if)# ipv6 hold-time eigrp 2 150
```

## Load Balancing IPv4 (7.1.3.3)

Equal-cost load balancing is the ability of a router to distribute outbound traffic using all interfaces that have the same metric from the destination address. Load balancing uses network segments and bandwidth more efficiently. For IP, Cisco IOS Software applies load balancing using up to four equal-cost paths by default.

For example, the topology in Figure 7-11 shows that R3 has two EIGRP equal-cost routes for the 172.16.3.0/30 network between R1 and R2. One route is via R1 at 192.168.10.4/30, and the other route is via R2 at 192.168.10.8/30.

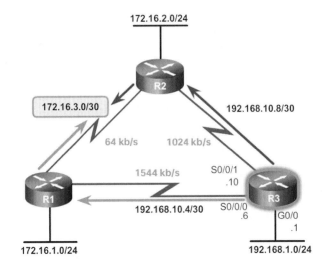

**Figure 7-11**   EIGRP for IPv4 Topology: Load Balancing

The **show ip protocols** command can be used to verify the number of equal-cost paths currently configured on the router. Example 7-22 shows the result of the **show ip protocols** command on R3.

**Example 7-22**   Maximum Paths for R3

```
R3# show ip protocols
*** IP Routing is NSF aware ***

Routing Protocol is "eigrp 1"
  Outgoing update filter list for all interfaces is not set
  Incoming update filter list for all interfaces is not set
  Default networks flagged in outgoing updates
  Default networks accepted from incoming updates
  EIGRP-IPv4 Protocol for AS(1)
    Metric weight K1=1, K2=0, K3=1, K4=0, K5=0
    NSF-aware route hold timer is 240
```

```
        Router-ID: 3.3.3.3
        Topology : 0 (base)
          Active Timer: 3 min
          Distance: internal 90 external 170
          Maximum path: 4
          Maximum hopcount 100
          Maximum metric variance 1
    Automatic Summarization: disabled
    Address Summarization:
      192.168.0.0/22 for Se0/0/0, Se0/0/1
        Summarizing 3 components with metric 2816
  Maximum path: 4

<Output omitted>
```

The output in Example 7-22 shows that R3 can use up to the default of four equal-cost paths.

Example 7-23 shows that R3 has two EIGRP equal-cost routes for the 172.16.3.0/30 network. One route is via R1 at 192.168.10.5, and the other route is via R2 at 192.168.10.9.

**Example 7-23**   IPv4 Routing Table for R3

```
R3# show ip route eigrp

<Output omitted>

Gateway of last resort is 192.168.10.9 to network 0.0.0.0

D*EX   0.0.0.0/0 [170/3139840] via 192.168.10.9, 00:14:24, Serial0/0/1
        172.16.0.0/16 is variably subnetted, 3 subnets, 2 masks
D          172.16.1.0/24 [90/2170112]  via 192.168.10.5, 00:14:28, Serial0/0/0
D          172.16.2.0/24 [90/3012096]  via 192.168.10.9, 00:14:24, Serial0/0/1
D          172.16.3.0/30 [90/41024000] via 192.168.10.9, 00:14:24, Serial0/0/1
                         [90/41024000] via 192.168.10.5, 00:14:24, Serial0/0/0
D      192.168.0.0/22 is a summary, 00:14:40, Null0
R3#
```

In the topology in Figure 7-11, it may seem as if the path via R1 is the better route because there is a 1544 Kbps link between R3 and R1, whereas the link to R2 is only a 1024 Kbps link. However, EIGRP only uses the slowest bandwidth in its composite metric, which is the 64 Kbps link between R1 and R2. Both paths have the same 64 Kbps link as the slowest bandwidth, resulting in both paths being equal, as shown in Example 7-23.

When a packet is process switched, load balancing over equal-cost paths occurs on a per-packet basis. When packets are fast switched, load balancing over equal-cost paths occurs on a per-destination basis. Cisco Express Forwarding can perform both per-packet and per-destination load balancing.

Cisco IOS, by default, allows load balancing using up to four equal-cost paths; however, this can be modified. By using the **maximum-paths** *value* router configuration mode command, you can keep up to 32 equal-cost routes in the routing table. The *value* argument refers to the number of paths that should be maintained for load balancing. If the value is set to **1**, load balancing is disabled.

## Load Balancing IPv6 (7.1.3.4)

Figure 7-12 shows the EIGRP for IPv6 network topology.

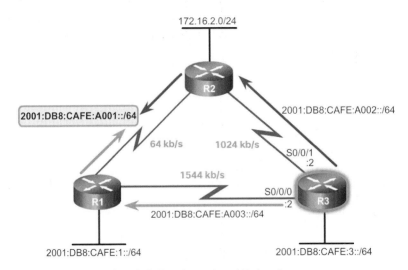

**Figure 7-12**   EIGRP for IPv6 Topology: Load Balancing

The serial links in the topology have the same bandwidth that is used in the EIGRP for IPv4 topology.

As in the previous scenario for IPv4, R3 has two EIGRP equal-cost routes for the network between R1 and R2, 2001:DB8:CAFE:A001::/64. One route is via R1 at FE80::1, and the other route is via R2 at FE80::2.

Example 7-24 shows that the EIGRP metrics are the same in the IPv6 routing table and in the IPv4 routing table for the 2001:DB8:CAFE:A001::/64 and 172.16.3.0/30 networks. This is because the EIGRP composite metric is the same for both EIGRP for IPv6 and EIGRP for IPv4.

**Example 7-24**   IPv6 Routing Table for R3

```
R3# show ipv6 route eigrp

<Output omitted>

EX   ::/0 [170/3011840]
     via FE80::2, Serial0/0/1
D    2001:DB8:ACAD::/48 [5/128256]
     via Null0, directly connected
D    2001:DB8:CAFE:1::/64 [90/2170112]
     via FE80::1, Serial0/0/0
D    2001:DB8:CAFE:2::/64 [90/3012096]
     via FE80::2, Serial0/0/1
D    2001:DB8:CAFE:A001::/64 [90/41024000]
     via FE80::2, Serial0/0/1
     via FE80::1, Serial0/0/0
R3#
```

## Unequal-Cost Load Balancing

EIGRP for IPv4 and EIGRP for IPv6 can also balance traffic across multiple routes that have different metrics. This type of balancing is called unequal-cost load balancing. Setting a value by using the **variance** router configuration command enables EIGRP to install multiple loop-free routes with unequal cost in a local routing table.

A route learned through EIGRP must meet two criteria to be installed in the local routing table:

- The route must be loop free, being either a feasible successor or having a reported distance that is less than the total distance.

- The metric of the route must be lower than the metric of the best route (the successor) multiplied by the variance configured on the router.

For example, if the variance is set to 1, only routes with the same metric as the successor are installed in the local routing table. If the variance is set to 2, any EIGRP-learned route with a metric less than 2 times the successor metric is installed in the local routing table.

To control how traffic is distributed among routes when there are multiple routes for the same destination network that have different costs, use the **traffic-share balanced** command. Traffic is then distributed proportionately to the ratio of the costs.

Interactive
Graphic

**Activity 7.1.3.5: Determine the EIGRP Fine Tuning Commands**

Refer to the online course to complete this activity.

**Lab 7.1.3.6: Configuring Advanced EIGRP for IPv4 Features**

Refer to *Scaling Networks v6 Labs & Study Guide* and the online course to complete this activity.

Upon completing this activity, you will be able to:

- Build the network and configure basic device settings
- Configure EIGRP and verify connectivity
- Configure EIGRP for automatic summarization
- Configure and propagate a default static route
- Fine-tune EIGRP

# Troubleshoot EIGRP (7.2)

In this section, you will learn how to troubleshoot common EIGRP configuration issues in a small to medium-sized business network.

## Components of Troubleshooting EIGRP (7.2.1)

In this topic, you will learn about the process and tools used to troubleshoot an EIGRP network.

### Basic EIGRP Troubleshooting Commands (7.2.1.1)

EIGRP is commonly used in large enterprise networks. Troubleshooting problems related to the exchange of routing information is an essential skill for a network administrator. This is particularly true for administrators who are involved in the implementation and maintenance of large, routed enterprise networks that use EIGRP as the interior gateway protocol (IGP). Several commands are useful when troubleshooting an EIGRP network.

The **show ip eigrp neighbors** command verifies that the router recognizes its neighbors. The output in Example 7-25 indicates two successful EIGRP neighbor adjacencies on R1.

**Example 7-25**   R1 EIGRP Neighbor Table

```
R1# show ip eigrp neighbors
EIGRP-IPv4 Neighbors for AS(1)
H   Address           Interface    Hold Uptime    SRTT    RTO   Q    Seq
                                   (sec)          (ms)          Cnt  Num
1   172.16.3.2        Se0/0/0      140 03:28:12   96      2340  0    23
0   192.168.10.6      Se0/0/1      14 03:28:27    49      294   0    24
R1#
```

In Example 7-26, the **show ip route** command verifies that the router learned the route to a remote network through EIGRP. The output shows that R1 has learned about four remote networks through EIGRP.

**Example 7-26**   R1 IPv4 Routing Table

```
R1# show ip route eigrp

Gateway of last resort is 192.168.10.6 to network 0.0.0.0

D*EX   0.0.0.0/0 [170/3651840] via 192.168.10.6, 05:32:02, Serial0/0/1
        172.16.0.0/16 is variably subnetted, 5 subnets, 3 masks
D          172.16.2.0/24 [90/3524096] via 192.168.10.6, 05:32:02, Serial0/0/1
D       192.168.0.0/22 [90/2170112] via 192.168.10.6, 05:32:02, Serial0/0/1
        192.168.10.0/24 is variably subnetted, 3 subnets, 2 masks
D          192.168.10.8/30 [90/3523840] via 192.168.10.6, 05:32:02, Serial0/0/1
R1#
```

Example 7-27 shows the output from the **show ip protocols** command, which displays various EIGRP settings.

**Example 7-27**   R1 Routing Protocol Processes

```
R1# show ip protocols
*** IP Routing is NSF aware ***

Routing Protocol is "eigrp 1"
  Outgoing update filter list for all interfaces is not set
  Incoming update filter list for all interfaces is not set
  Default networks flagged in outgoing updates
  Default networks accepted from incoming updates
  EIGRP-IPv4 Protocol for AS(1)
    Metric weight K1=1, K2=0, K3=1, K4=0, K5=0
    NSF-aware route hold timer is 240
```

```
        Router-ID: 1.1.1.1
        Topology : 0 (base)
           Active Timer: 3 min
           Distance: internal 90 external 170
           Maximum path: 4
           Maximum hopcount 100
           Maximum metric variance 1

   Automatic Summarization: disabled
   Maximum path: 4
   Routing for Networks:
     172.16.0.0
     192.168.10.0
   Passive Interface(s):
     GigabitEthernet0/0
   Routing Information Sources:
     Gateway          Distance       Last Update
     192.168.10.6           90       05:43:44
     172.16.3.2             90       05:43:44
   Distance: internal 90 external 170

R1#
```

Similar commands and troubleshooting criteria also apply to EIGRP for IPv6. The following are the equivalent commands used with EIGRP for IPv6:

- **show ipv6 eigrp neighbors**

- **show ipv6 route**

- **show ipv6 protocols**

## Components (7.2.1.2)

A systematic approach to troubleshooting is recommended. After configuring EIGRP, the first step is to test connectivity to the remote network. If the **ping** fails, confirm the EIGRP neighbor adjacencies, as shown in Figure 7-13.

EIGRP neighbors must first establish adjacencies with each other before they can exchange routes. There are a number of common reasons an EIGRP neighbor adjacency might fail, including the following:

- The interface between the devices is down.

- The two routers have mismatched EIGRP autonomous system numbers.

- Proper interfaces are not enabled for the EIGRP process.

- An interface is configured as passive.

Other reasons that affect neighbor adjacencies include misconfigured $K$ values, incompatible hello and hold interval times, and misconfigured EIGRP authentication.

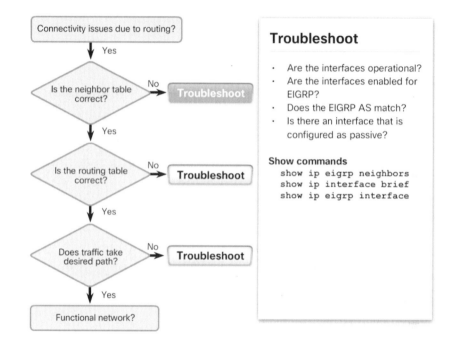

**Figure 7-13**   Troubleshooting Neighbor Issues

After a neighbor adjacency is established, EIGRP begins the process of exchanging routing information. If two routers are EIGRP neighbors, but there is still a connection issue, there may be a routing problem, as shown in Figure 7-14.

Several issues, including the following, may cause connectivity problems for EIGRP:

- Proper networks are not being advertised on remote routers.

- An incorrectly configured passive interface, or an ACL, is blocking advertisements of remote networks.

- Automatic summarization is causing inconsistent routing in a discontiguous network.

If all the required routes are in the routing table, but the path that traffic takes is not correct, verify the interface bandwidth values, as shown in Figure 7-15.

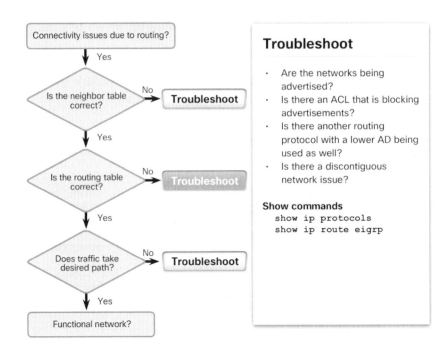

**Figure 7-14**   Troubleshooting Routing Table Issues

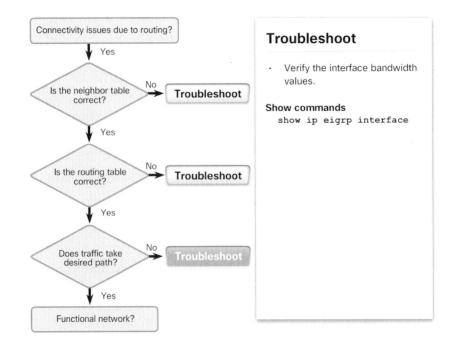

**Figure 7-15**   Troubleshooting Path Selection Issues

**Activity 7.2.1.3: Identify the Troubleshooting Command**

Refer to the online course to complete this activity.

# Troubleshoot EIGRP Neighbor Issues (7.2.2)

In this topic, you will learn how to troubleshoot neighbor adjacency issues in an EIGRP network.

## Layer 3 Connectivity (7.2.2.1)

A prerequisite for a neighbor adjacency to form between two directly connected routers is Layer 3 connectivity. By examining the output of the **show ip interface brief** command, a network administrator can verify that the status and protocol of connecting interfaces are up. A **ping** from one router to another directly connected router should confirm IPv4 connectivity between the devices.

Example 7-28 displays the **show ip interface brief** command output for R1 and the result of a connectivity test to R2.

**Example 7-28**   Testing Connectivity from R1 to R2

```
R1# show ip interface brief
Interface               Address         OK? Method Status        Protocol
GigabitEthernet0/0      172.16.1.1      YES manual up            up
Serial0/0/0             172.16.3.1      YES manual up            up
Serial0/0/1             192.168.10.5    YES manual up            up
R1#
R1# ping 172.16.3.2
Type escape sequence to abort.
Sending 5, 100-byte ICMP Echos to 172.16.3.2, timeout is 2 seconds:
!!!!!
Success rate is 100 percent (5/5), round-trip min/avg/max = 28/28/28 ms
R1#
```

If the **ping** is unsuccessful, use the **show cdp neighbor** command to verify the Layer 1 and 2 connections to the neighbor. If the output does not display the neighboring router, then verify Layer 1 and check the cabling, connections, and interfaces.

If you see the neighbor in the output of the **show cdp neighbor** command, then Layer 1 and 2 are verified, and we can assume that the problem is with Layer 3.

Layer 3 problems include misconfigured IP addresses, subnets, network addresses, and more. For example, interfaces on connected devices must be on a common subnet. A log message which states that EIGRP neighbors are not on a common subnet indicates that there is an incorrect IPv4 address on one of the two EIGRP neighbor interfaces.

Similar commands and troubleshooting criteria also apply to EIGRP for IPv6.

The equivalent command used with EIGRP for IPv6 is **show ipv6 interface brief**.

## EIGRP Parameters (7.2.2.2)

When troubleshooting an EIGRP network, one of the first things to verify is that all routers that are participating in the EIGRP network are configured with the same autonomous system number. The **router eigrp** *as-number* command starts the EIGRP process and is followed by a number that is the autonomous system number. The value of the *as-number* argument must be the same in all routers in the EIGRP routing domain.

In Example 7-29, the **show ip protocols** command verifies that R1, R2, and R3 all use the same autonomous system number.

**Example 7-29**   Verifying the Autonomous System Number

```
R1# show ip protocols
*** IP Routing is NSF aware ***


Routing Protocol is "eigrp 1"


<Output omitted>
```

```
R2# show ip protocols
*** IP Routing is NSF aware ***


Routing Protocol is "eigrp 1"


<Output omitted>
```

```
R3# show ip protocols
*** IP Routing is NSF aware ***


Routing Protocol is "eigrp 1"


<Output omitted>
```

> **Note**
>
> At the top of the output, "IP Routing is NSF aware" refers to Nonstop Forwarding (NSF). This is a route redundancy feature available on modular Catalyst switches such as Catalyst 4500 and 6500 switches. It enables modular switches with dual supervisory modules to retain the routing information advertised and to continue using this information until the failed supervisory module resumes normal operation and is able to exchange routing information. For more information, refer to www.cisco.com/en/US/docs/ios-xml/ios/iproute_eigrp/configuration/15-mt/eigrp-nsf-awa.html.

Similar commands and troubleshooting criteria also apply to EIGRP for IPv6. The following are the equivalent commands used with EIGRP for IPv6:

- **ipv6 router eigrp** *as-number*
- **show ipv6 protocols**

## EIGRP Interfaces (7.2.2.3)

In addition to verifying the autonomous system number, it is necessary to verify that all interfaces are participating in the EIGRP network. The **network** command that is configured in the EIGRP routing process indicates which router interface participates in EIGRP. This command is applied to the classful network address of the interface or to a subnet when the wildcard mask is included.

In Example 7-30, the **show ip eigrp interfaces** command displays which interfaces are enabled for EIGRP on R1.

**Example 7-30**   Verifying EIGRP for IPv4 Interfaces

```
R1# show ip eigrp interfaces
EIGRP-IPv4 Interfaces for AS(1)
                Xmit Queue    PeerQ        Mean  Pacing Time   Multicast     Pending
Interface  Peers Un/Reliable  Un/Reliable  SRTT  Un/Reliable   Flow Timer    Routes
Gi0/1      0     0/0          0/0          0     0/0           0             0
Se0/0/0    1     0/0          0/0          1295  0/23          6459          0
Se0/0/1    1     0/0          0/0          1044  0/15          5195          0
R1#
```

If connected interfaces are not enabled for EIGRP, neighbors do not form an adjacency.

Example 7-31 verifies which networks on R1 are being advertised.

**Example 7-31**   Verifying EIGRP for IPv4 Networks

```
R1# show ip protocols
*** IP Routing is NSF aware ***

Routing Protocol is "eigrp 1"

<Output omitted>

Routing for Networks:
    172.16.0.0
    192.168.10.0
  Passive Interface(s):
    GigabitEthernet0/0
  Routing Information Sources:
    Gateway          Distance       Last Update
    192.168.10.6            90       00:42:31
    172.16.3.2              90       00:42:31
  Distance: internal 90 external 170

R1#
```

Notice that the "Routing for Networks" section indicates which networks have been configured. Any interfaces in those networks participate in EIGRP.

If the network is not present in this section, use **show running-config** to ensure that the proper **network** command was configured.

In Example 7-32, the output from the **show running-config | section eigrp 1** command confirms that any interfaces with these addresses, or a subnet of these addresses, are enabled for EIGRP.

**Example 7-32**   Verifying the EIGRP for IPv4 Configuration

```
R1# show running-config | section eigrp 1
router eigrp 1
 network 172.16.0.0
 network 192.168.10.0
 passive-interface GigabitEthernet0/0
 eigrp router-id 1.1.1.1
R1#
```

Similar commands and troubleshooting criteria also apply to EIGRP for IPv6. The following are the equivalent commands used with EIGRP for IPv6:

- show ipv6 protocols

- show ipv6 eigrp interfaces

**Interactive Graphic**

**Activity 7.2.2.4: Troubleshoot EIGRP Neighbor Issues**

Refer to the online course to complete this activity.

# Troubleshoot EIGRP Routing Table Issues (7.2.3)

In this topic, you will troubleshoot missing route entries in an EIGRP routing table.

## Passive Interface (7.2.3.1)

One reason that routing tables may not reflect the correct routes is due to the **passive-interface** command. With EIGRP running on a network, the **passive-interface** command stops both outgoing and incoming routing updates, and routers do not become neighbors.

To verify whether any interface on a router is configured as passive, use the **show ip protocols** privileged EXEC mode command.

Example 7-33 shows that R2's GigabitEthernet 0/0 interface is configured as a passive interface because there are no neighbors on that link.

**Example 7-33**   Verifying Passive Interfaces

```
R2# show ip protocols
*** IP Routing is NSF aware ***

Routing Protocol is "eigrp 1"
<Output omitted>

Routing for Networks:
    172.16.0.0
    192.168.10.8/30
  Passive Interface(s):
    GigabitEthernet0/0
  Routing Information Sources:
    Gateway         Distance      Last Update
    192.168.10.10        90        00:08:59
    172.16.3.1           90        00:08:59
  Distance: internal 90 external 170
R2#
```

In addition to being configured on interfaces that have no neighbors, an interface can be made passive for security purposes. In Figure 7-16, notice that the shading for the EIGRP routing domain is different than in previous topologies.

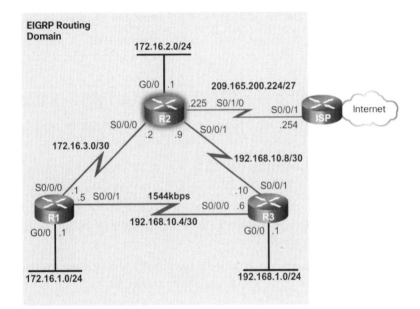

**Figure 7-16** EIGRP for IPv4 Topology

The 209.165.200.224/27 network must now also be included in R2's EIGRP updates. However, for security reasons, the network administrator does not want R2 to form an EIGRP neighbor adjacency with the ISP router.

Example 7-34 advertises network 209.165.200.224/27 and makes the link to the ISP passive.

**Example 7-34** Configuring the Network to the ISP as a Passive Interface

```
R2(config)# router eigrp 1
R2(config-router)# network 209.165.200.0
R2(config-router)# passive-interface serial 0/1/0
R2(config-router)# end
R2#
```

The **passive-interface** router configuration mode command is configured on Serial 0/1/0 to prevent R2's EIGRP updates from being sent to the ISP router.

Example 7-35 verifies the EIGRP neighbor relationships on R2.

**Example 7-35**   Verifying the EIGRP Neighbor Relationship on R2

```
R2# show ip eigrp neighbors
EIGRP-IPv4 Neighbors for AS(1)
H   Address         Interface        Hold Uptime     SRTT   RTO  Q   Seq
                                     (sec)           (ms)        Cnt Num
1   172.16.3.1      Se0/0/0          175 01:09:18     80   2340  0   16
0   192.168.10.10   Se0/0/1          11 01:09:33     1037  5000  0   17
R2#
```

The command verifies that R2 has not established a neighbor adjacency with ISP.

Example 7-36 shows that R1 has an EIGRP route to the 209.165.200.224/27 network in its IPv4 routing table because R2 is now advertising it. (R3 will also have an EIGRP route to that network in its IPv4 routing table.)

**Example 7-36**   Verifying a Network Propagated as an EIGRP Route

```
R1# show ip route | include 209.165.200.224
D        209.165.200.224 [90/3651840] via 192.168.10.6, 00:06:02, Serial0/0/1
R1#
```

Similar commands and troubleshooting criteria also apply to EIGRP for IPv6. The following are the equivalent commands used with EIGRP for IPv6:

- **show ipv6 protocols**
- **passive-interface** *type number*

## Missing Network Statement (7.2.3.2)

In Figure 7-17, R1's GigabitEthernet 0/1 interface has just been configured with the 10.10.10.1/24 address and is active.

R1 and R3 have an established EIGRP neighbor adjacency and are exchanging routing information. However, as shown in Example 7-37, a **ping** test from the R3 router to a R1's G0/1 interface of 10.10.10.1 is unsuccessful.

**Example 7-37**   10.10.10.0/24 Unreachable from R3

```
R3# ping 10.10.10.1
Type escape sequence to abort.
Sending 5, 100-byte ICMP Echos to 10.10.10.1, timeout is 2 seconds:
.....
Success rate is 0 percent (0/5)
R3#
```

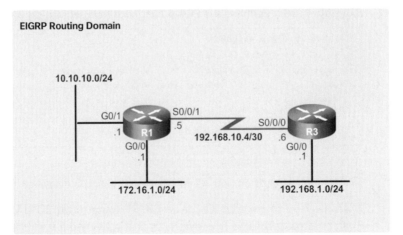

**Figure 7-17**    Topology for Troubleshooting a Missing Network Statement

Example 7-38 verifies which networks are being advertised.

**Example 7-38**    Checking for 10.10.10.0/24 R1 Updates

```
R1# show ip protocols | begin Routing for Networks
  Routing for Networks:
    172.16.0.0
    192.168.10.0
  Passive Interface(s):
    GigabitEthernet0/0
  Routing Information Sources:
    Gateway          Distance        Last Update
    192.168.10.6           90        01:34:19
    172.16.3.2             90        01:34:19
  Distance: internal 90 external 170

R1#
```

The output of the command in Example 7-38 confirms that the 10.10.10.0/24 network is not being advertised to EIGRP neighbors. Therefore, network 10.10.10.0 must be advertised.

In Example 7-39, R1's EIGRP process is configured to include the advertisement of the classful 10.0.0.0 network.

**Example 7-39**    Configuring the Missing Network

```
R1(config)# router eigrp 1
R1(config-router)# network 10.0.0.0
```

Example 7-40 confirms the addition of the 10.10.10.0/24 route in R3's routing table, and reachability is verified and confirmed with a **ping** to R1's GigabitEthernet 0/1 interface.

**Example 7-40**    Verifying a Network Propagated as an EIGRP Route

```
R3# show ip route | include 10.10.10.0
D       10.10.10.0 [90/2172416] via 192.168.10.5, 00:04:14, Serial0/0/0
R3#
R3# ping 10.10.10.1
Type escape sequence to abort.
Sending 5, 100-byte ICMP Echos to 10.10.10.1, timeout is 2 seconds:
!!!!!
Success rate is 100 percent (5/5), round-trip min/avg/max = 24/27/28 ms
R3#
```

Similar commands and troubleshooting criteria also apply to EIGRP for IPv6. The following are the equivalent commands used with EIGRP for IPv6:

- **show ipv6 protocols**

- **show ipv6 route**

To add a missing network statement with IPv6, use the **ipv6 eigrp** *autonomous-system* interface configuration command.

**Note**

Another form of missing route may result from the router filtering inbound or outbound routing updates. ACLs provide filtering for different protocols, and these ACLs may affect the exchange of routing protocol messages. This can cause routes to be absent from the routing table. Use the **show ip protocols** command to see if there are any ACLs that are applied to EIGRP. Applying filters to routing updates is beyond the scope of this course.

## Autosummarization (7.2.3.3)

Another issue that may create EIGRP routing problems is EIGRP automatic summarization.

Figure 7-18 shows a network topology that is different from the other topologies used throughout this chapter.

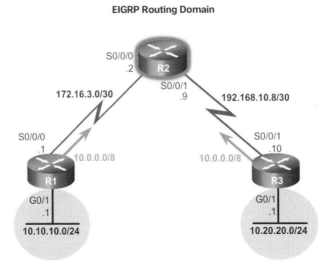

**EIGRP Routing Domain**

**Figure 7-18**    Topology for Troubleshooting Automatic Summarization

There is no connection between R1 and R3. R1's LAN has the network address 10.10.10.0/24, and R3's LAN is 10.20.20.0/24.

R1 and R3 have their LAN and serial interfaces enabled for EIGRP, as shown in Example 7-41.

**Example 7-41**    EIGRP Configurations for R1 and R3

```
R1(config)# router eigrp 1
R1(config-router)# network 10.0.0.0
R1(config-router)# network 172.16.0.0
R1(config-router)# auto-summary

R3(config)# router eigrp 1
R3(config-router)# network 10.0.0.0
R3(config-router)# network 192.168.10.0
R3(config-router)# auto-summary
```

Both routers perform EIGRP automatic summarization.

**Note**

EIGRP for IPv4 can be configured to automatically summarize routes at classful boundaries. However, if there are discontiguous networks, automatic summarization causes inconsistent routing.

In Example 7-42, R2's routing table shows that R2 does not receive individual routes for the 10.10.10.0/24 and 10.20.20.0/24 subnets.

**Example 7-42** Inconsistent Forwarding From R2

```
R2# show ip route

<Output omitted>

      10.0.0.0/8 is subnetted, 1 subnets
D        10.0.0.0 [90/3014400] via 192.168.10.10, 00:02:06, Serial0/0/1
                  [90/3014400] via 172.16.3.1, 00:02:06, Serial0/0/0
```

Both R1 and R3 automatically summarized those subnets to the 10.0.0.0/8 classful boundary when sending EIGRP update packets to R2. The result is that R2 has two equal-cost routes to 10.0.0.0/8 in the routing table, which can result in inaccurate routing and packet loss. Depending on whether per-packet, per-destination, or Cisco Express Forwarding load balancing is being used, packets may or may not be forwarded out the proper interface.

In Example 7-43, the **show ip protocols** command verifies that automatic summarization is performed on both R1 and R3. Notice that both routers summarize the 10.0.0.0/8 network using the same metric.

**Example 7-43** Verifying Automatic Summarization Status

```
R1# show ip protocols
*** IP Routing is NSF aware ***

Routing Protocol is "eigrp 1"

  Automatic Summarization: enabled
    10.0.0.0/8 for Se0/0/0
      Summarizing 1 component with metric 28160

<Output omitted>

R3# show ip protocols
*** IP Routing is NSF aware ***

Routing Protocol is "eigrp 1"

  Automatic Summarization: enabled
    10.0.0.0/8 for Se0/0/1
      Summarizing 1 component with metric 28160
<Output omitted>
```

Autosummarization is disabled by default in IOS 12.2(33) and IOS 15. To enable automatic summarization, use the **auto-summary** EIGRP router configuration mode command.

Before IOS 12.2(33) and IOS 15, autosummarization was enabled by default. To disable automatic summarization, enter the **no auto-summary** command in router EIGRP configuration mode.

The cause of inconsistent routing may be due to the autosummarization feature being enabled. To correct this problem, disable the feature on R1 and R3 as shown in Example 7-44.

**Example 7-44**   Disabling Automatic Summarization

```
R1(config)# router eigrp 1
R1(config-router)# no auto-summary


R3(config)# router eigrp 1
R3(config-router)# no auto-summary
```

Example 7-45 displays the routing table on R2 after automatic summarization has been disabled on R1 and R3.

**Example 7-45**   All Networks Are Reachable from R2

```
R2# show ip route
<Output omitted>


 10.0.0.0/24 is subnetted, 2 subnets
D        10.10.10.0 [90/3014400] via 172.16.3.1, 00:00:27, Serial0/0/0
D        10.20.20.0 [90/3014400] via 192.168.10.10, 00:00:11, Serial0/0/1
```

Notice that R2 now receives the individual 10.10.10.0/24 and 10.20.20.0/24 subnets from R1 and R3, respectively. Accurate routing and connectivity to both subnets has been restored.

Classful networks do not exist in IPv6; therefore, EIGRP for IPv6 does not support automatic summarization. All summarization must be accomplished using EIGRP manual summary routes.

Interactive
Graphic

**Activity 7.2.3.4: Troubleshoot EIGRP Routing Table Issues**

Refer to the online course to complete this activity.

**Packet Tracer 7.2.3.5: Troubleshooting EIGRP for IPv4**

Packet Tracer
☐ **Activity**

Background/Scenario

In this activity, you will troubleshoot EIGRP neighbor issues. You will use **show** commands to identify errors in the network configuration. Then you will document the errors you discover and implement an appropriate solution. Finally, you will verify that full end-to-end connectivity is restored.

---

**Lab 7.2.3.6: Troubleshooting Basic EIGRP for IPv4 and IPv6**

Refer to *Scaling Networks v6 Labs & Study Guide* and the online course to complete this activity.

In this lab, you will complete the following objectives:

- Part 1: Build the Network and Load Device Configurations
- Part 2: Troubleshoot Layer 3 Connectivity
- Part 3: Troubleshoot EIGRP for IPv4
- Part 4: Troubleshoot EIGRP for IPv6

---

**Lab 7.2.3.7: Troubleshooting Advanced EIGRP**

Refer to *Scaling Networks v6 Labs & Study Guide* and the online course to complete this activity.

In this lab, you will complete the following objectives:

- Part 1: Build the Network and Load Device Configurations
- Part 2: Troubleshoot EIGRP

# Summary (7.3)

### Class Activity 7.3.1.1: Tuning EIGRP

Refer to *Scaling Networks v6 Labs & Study Guide* and the online course to complete this activity.

The purpose of this activity is to review EIGRP routing protocol tuning concepts.

You will work with a partner to design an EIGRP topology. This topology will be the basis for two parts of the activity. The first will use default settings for all configurations, and the second will incorporate at least three of the following EIGRP tuning options:

- Default routes
- Default route propagation
- Hello interval timer settings
- EIGRP bandwidth percentage utilization

Refer to the labs, Packet Tracer activities, and interactive activities as you progress through this modeling activity.

Directions are listed on the PDF file for this activity. Share your completed work with another group. You may wish to save a copy of this activity to a portfolio.

Packet Tracer
☐ Activity

### Packet Tracer 7.3.1.2: Skills Integration Challenge

#### Background/Scenario

In this activity, you are tasked with implementing EIGRP for IPv4 and IPv6 on two separate networks. You must enable EIGRP, assign router IDs, change the hello timers, configure EIGRP summary routes, and limit EIGRP advertisements.

EIGRP is one of the routing protocols commonly used in large enterprise networks. Modifying EIGRP features and troubleshooting problems is one of the most essential skills for a network engineer involved in the implementation and maintenance of large routed enterprise networks that use EIGRP.

Summarization decreases the number of entries in routing updates and reduces the number of entries in local routing tables. It also reduces bandwidth utilization for routing updates and results in faster routing table lookups. EIGRP for IPv4 automatic summarization has been disabled by default since Cisco IOS Release 15.0(1)M and 12.2(33). Prior to those releases, automatic summarization was enabled by default. To enable automatic summarization for EIGRP, use the **auto-summary** command in router configuration mode. Use the **show ip protocols** command to verify the status of automatic summarization. Examine the routing table to verify that automatic summarization is working.

EIGRP automatically includes summary routes to Null0 to prevent routing loops that are included in the summary but do not actually exist in the routing table. The Null0 interface is a virtual IOS interface that is a route to nowhere, commonly known as "the bit bucket." Packets that match a route with a Null0 exit interface are discarded.

One method of propagating a default route within the EIGRP routing domain is to use the **redistribute static** command. This command tells EIGRP to include this static route in its EIGRP updates to other routers. The **show ip protocols** command verifies that static routes in the EIGRP routing domain are being redistributed.

Use the **ip bandwidth-percent eigrp** *as-number percent* interface configuration mode command to configure the percentage of bandwidth that EIGRP can use on an interface.

To configure the percentage of bandwidth that can be used by EIGRP for IPv6 on an interface, use the **ipv6 bandwidth-percent eigrp** command in interface configuration mode. To restore the default value, use the **no** form of this command.

Hello intervals and hold times are configurable on a per-interface basis in EIGRP and do not have to match with other EIGRP routers to establish or maintain adjacencies.

For IP in EIGRP, Cisco IOS Software applies load balancing using up to four equal-cost paths by default. With the **maximum-paths** router configuration mode command, up to 32 equal-cost routes can be kept in the routing table.

The **show ip route** command verifies that the router learned EIGRP routes. The **show ip protocols** command is used to verify that EIGRP displays the currently configured values.

# Practice

The following activities provide practice with the topics introduced in this chapter. The Labs and Class Activities are available in the companion *Scaling Networks v6 Labs & Study Guide* (ISBN 9781587134333). The Packet Tracer activity instructions are also in the Labs & Study Guide. The PKA files are found in the online course.

**Class Activities**

Class Activity 7.0.1.2: EIGRP—Back to the Future

Class Activity 7.3.1.1: Tuning EIGRP

**Labs**

Lab 7.1.3.6: Configuring Advanced EIGRP for IPv4 Features

Lab 7.2.3.6: Troubleshooting Basic EIGRP for IPv4 and IPv6

Lab 7.2.3.7: Troubleshooting Advanced EIGRP

Packet Tracer
☐ Activity

**Packet Tracer Activities**

Packet Tracer 7.1.2.4: Propagating a Default Route in EIGRP for IPv4 and IPv6

Packet Tracer 7.2.3.5: Troubleshooting EIGRP for IPv4

Packet Tracer 7.3.1.2: Skills Integration Challenge

# Check Your Understanding Questions

Complete all the review questions listed here to test your understanding of the topics
and concepts in this chapter. The appendix "Answers to 'Check Your Understanding'
Questions" lists the answers.

1. What is the purpose of a Null0 route in the routing table?

    A.  To act as a gateway of last resort

    B.  To prevent routing loops when summarizing routes

    C.  To prevent the router from sending EIGRP packets

    D.  To redistribute external routes into EIGRP

2. Which administrative distance is used to advertise routes learned from other
   protocols that are redistributed into EIGRP?

    A.  5

    B.  90

    C.  115

    D.  170

3. Which command would limit the amount of bandwidth that is used by EIGRP
   for protocol control traffic to approximately 128 Kbps on a 1.544 Mbps link?

    A.  **ip bandwidth-percent eigrp 100 8**

    B.  **maximum-paths 8**

    C.  **traffic-share balanced**

    D.  **variance 8**

4. By default, how many equal-cost routes to the same destination network will EIGRP install in the routing table?

   A. 2

   B. 4

   C. 6

   D. 8

5. Which EIGRP parameter must match between all routers forming an EIGRP adjacency?

   A. Administrative distance

   B. Autonomous system number

   C. Hello timer

   D. Hold timer

   E. Variance

6. In which scenario will the use of EIGRP automatic summarization cause inconsistent routing in a network?

   A. When the routers in an IPv4 network are connected to discontiguous networks with automatic summarization enabled

   B. When the routers in an IPv4 network have mismatching EIGRP AS numbers

   C. When there is no adjacency that is established between neighboring routers

   D. When there is no common subnet that exists between neighboring routers

7. Which command can be issued on a router to verify that automatic summarization is enabled?

   A. **show ip eigrp interfaces**

   B. **show ip eigrp neighbors**

   C. **show ip interface brief**

   D. **show ip protocols**

8. Which address is used by an IPv6 EIGRP router as the source for hello messages?

   A. The 32-bit router ID

   B. The all-EIGRP-routers multicast address

   C. The interface IPv6 link-local address

   D. The IPv6 global unicast address that is configured on the interface

9. When will a router that is running EIGRP put a destination network in the active state?

   A. When the connection to the successor of the destination network fails and there is no feasible successor available

   B. When the EIGRP domain is converged

   C. When there is an EIGRP message from the successor of the destination network

   D. When there is outgoing traffic toward the destination network

10. Which two parameters does EIGRP use by default to calculate the best path? (Choose two.)

    A. Bandwidth

    B. Delay

    C. MTU

    D. Reliability

    E. Transmit and receive load

11. A network administrator wants to verify the default delay values for the interfaces on an EIGRP-enabled router. Which command will display these values?

    A. **show interfaces**

    B. **show ip protocols**

    C. **show ip route**

    D. **show running-config**

12. An administrator issues the **router eigrp 100** command on a router. What is the number 100 used for?

    A. The autonomous system number

    B. The length of time this router will wait to hear hello packets from a neighbor

    C. The maximum bandwidth of the fastest interface on the router

    D. The number of neighbors supported by this router

# CHAPTER 8

# Single-Area OSPF

## Objectives

Upon completion of this chapter, you will be able to answer the following questions:

- How does single-area OSPF operate?

- How does single-area OSPFv2 operate in a small to medium-sized business network?

- How does single-area OSPFv3 operate in a small to medium-sized business network?

## Key Terms

This chapter uses the following key terms. You can find the definitions in the Glossary.

# Introduction (8.0.1.1)

Open Shortest Path First (OSPF) is a link-state routing protocol that was developed as an alternative for the distance vector routing protocol RIP. RIP was an acceptable routing protocol in the early days of networking and the Internet. However, RIP's reliance on hop count as the only metric for determining the best route quickly became problematic. Using hop count does not scale well in larger networks with multiple paths of varying speeds. OSPF has significant advantages over RIP in that it offers faster convergence, and it scales to much larger network implementations.

OSPF is a classless routing protocol that uses the concept of areas for scalability. This chapter covers basic, single-area OSPF implementations and configurations.

**Class Activity 8.0.1.2: Can Submarines Swim?**

Refer to *Scaling Networks v6 Labs & Study Guide* and the online course to complete this activity.

Scenario

Edsger Wybe Dijkstra was a famous computer programmer and theoretical physicist. One of his most notable quotes was, "The question of whether computers can think is like the question of whether submarines can swim." Dijkstra's work has been applied, among other things, to routing protocols. He created the shortest path first (SPF) algorithm for network routing.

Open the PDF provided with this activity and answer the reflection questions. Save your work.

Get together with two of your classmates and compare your answers.

After completing this activity, do you have an idea about how the OSPF protocol may work?

# OSPF Characteristics (8.1)

OSPF is a popular multivendor, open-standard, classless link-state routing protocol. In this section, you will learn how OSPF operates.

# Open Shortest Path First (8.1.1)

In this topic, you will learn about the features and characteristics of OSPF.

## Evolution of OSPF (8.1.1.1)

As shown in Figure 8-1, OSPF Version 2 (OSPFv2) is available for IPv4, and OSPF Version 3 (OSPFv3) is available for IPv6.

| | Interior Gateway Protocols | | | | Exterior Gateway Protocols |
|---|---|---|---|---|---|
| | Distance Vector | | Link-State | | Path Vector |
| IPv4 | RIPv2 | EIGRP | OSPFv2 | IS-IS | BGP-4 |
| IPv6 | RIPng | EIGRP for IPv6 | OSPFv3 | IS-IS for IPv6 | BGP-MP |

**Figure 8-1**   Types of Routing Protocols

Internet Engineering Task Force (IETF) OSPF Working Group initially began developing OSPF in 1987. At that time, the Internet was largely an academic and research network funded by the U.S. government.

In 1989, the specification for OSPFv1 was published in RFC 1131. Two implementations were written. One implementation was developed to run on routers, and the other was developed to run on UNIX workstations. The latter implementation became a widespread UNIX process known as GATED. OSPFv1 was an experimental routing protocol that was never deployed.

In 1991, OSPFv2 was introduced in RFC 1247 by John Moy. OSPFv2 offered significant technical improvements over OSPFv1. It is classless by design; therefore, it supports VLSM and CIDR.

At the same time that OSPF was introduced, The *International Organization for Standardization (ISO)* was working on a link-state routing protocol of its own, Intermediate System-to-Intermediate System (IS-IS). IETF chose OSPF as its recommended IGP.

In 1998, the OSPFv2 specification was updated in RFC 2328, which remains the current RFC for OSPF.

In 1999, OSPFv3 for IPv6 was published in RFC 2740. OSPF for IPv6, created by John Moy, Rob Coltun, and Dennis Ferguson, is not only a new protocol implementation for IPv6 but also a major rewrite of the operation of the protocol.

In 2008, OSPFv3 was updated in RFC 5340 as OSPF for IPv6.

In 2010, the support of the Address Families (AF) feature in OSPFv3 was introduced with RFC 5838. The AF feature allows a routing protocol to support both IPv4 and IPv6 in a single unified configuration process. OSPFv3 with AF is beyond the scope of this course.

> **Note**
>
> In this chapter, unless explicitly identified as OSPFv2 or OSPFv3, the term *OSPF* is used to indicate concepts that are shared by both.

## Features of OSPF (8.1.1.2)

Table 8-1 lists some of the features of OSPF.

**Table 8-1**  OSPF Features

| Feature | Description |
|---|---|
| Classless | ■ OSPFv2 is classless by design and supports IPv4 VLSM and CIDR. |
| Efficient | ■ Routing changes trigger routing updates (no periodic updates).<br>■ It uses the SPF algorithm to choose the best path. |
| Fast convergence | ■ It quickly propagates network changes. |
| Scalable | ■ It works well in small and large networks.<br>■ Routers can be grouped into areas to support a hierarchical system. |
| Secure | ■ When authentication is enabled, OSPF routers only accept encrypted routing updates from peers with the same preshared password.<br>■ OSPFv2 supports *MD5 authentication* and *SHA authentication*.<br>■ OSPFv3 uses *Internet Protocol Security (IPsec)* to add authentication for OSPFv3 packets. |

Administrative distance (AD) is the trustworthiness (or preference) of the route source. OSPF has a default administrative distance of 110. As shown in Table 8-2, OSPF has a lower number (making it a preferred routing protocol over IS-IS and RIP) on Cisco devices.

**Table 8-2**  OSPF Administrative Distance

| Router Source | Administrative Distance |
|---|---|
| Connected | 0 |
| Static | 1 |
| EIGRP summary route | 5 |
| External BGP | 20 |
| Internal EIGRP | 90 |

| Router Source | Administrative Distance |
|---------------|------------------------|
| IGRP | 100 |
| **OSPF** | **110** |
| IS-IS | 115 |
| RIP | 120 |
| External EIGRP | 170 |
| Internal BGP | 200 |

## Components of OSPF (8.1.1.3)

All routing protocols share similar components. They all use routing protocol messages to exchange route information. The messages help build data structures, which are then processed using a routing algorithm.

The OSPF routing protocol has three main components:

- Data structures
- Routing protocol messages
- Algorithm

Data structures are the tables or databases that OSPF builds in order to operate. OSPF creates and maintains three databases. These databases contain lists of neighboring routers to exchange routing information with and are kept and maintained in RAM.

Table 8-3 describes these three OSPF data structures.

**Table 8-3**   OSPF Data Structures

| Database | Table | Description |
|----------|-------|-------------|
| Adjacency database | Neighbor table | ■ List of all neighbor routers with which a router has established bidirectional communication.<br>■ This table is unique for each router.<br>■ Can be viewed using the **show ip ospf neighbor** command. |
| Link-state database (LSDB) | Topology table | ■ List of information about all other routers in the network.<br>■ The database shows the network topology.<br>■ All routers in an area have identical link-state databases.<br>■ Can be viewed using the **show ip ospf database** command. |

| Database | Table | Description |
|---|---|---|
| Forwarding database | Routing table | ■ List of routes generated when an algorithm is run on the link-state database.<br><br>■ Each router's routing table is unique and contains information on how and where to send packets to other routers.<br><br>■ Can be viewed using the **show ip route** command. |

OSPF uses routing protocol messages to convey routing information. These packets are used to discover neighboring routers and also to exchange routing information to maintain accurate information about the network.

OSPF uses five types of packets:

- Hello packet
- *Database Description (DBD)* packet
- *Link-State Request (LSR)* packet
- *Link-State Update (LSU)* packet
- *Link-State Acknowledgment (LSAck)* packet

The algorithm that OSPF uses to build the topology table is based on the Dijkstra SPF algorithm, which is based on the cumulative cost to reach a destination.

The SPF algorithm creates an SPF tree by placing each router at the root of the tree and calculating the shortest path to each node. The SPF tree is then used to calculate the best routes. OSPF places the best routes in the forwarding database, which is used to make the routing table.

## Link-State Operation (8.1.1.4)

To maintain routing information, OSPF routers complete the following generic link-state routing process to reach a state of convergence:

1. **Establish neighbor adjacencies (see Figure 8-2).** OSPF-enabled routers must recognize each other on the network before they can share information. An OSPF-enabled router sends Hello packets out all OSPF-enabled interfaces to determine whether neighbors are present on those links. If a neighbor is present, the OSPF-enabled router attempts to establish a neighbor adjacency with that neighbor.

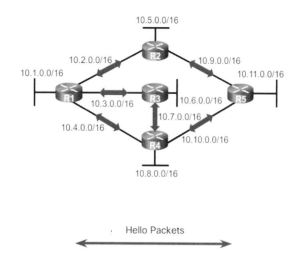

**Figure 8-2**   Routers Exchange Hello Packets

2. **Exchange link-state advertisements (see Figure 8-3).** After adjacencies are established, routers exchange link-state advertisements (LSAs). An LSA contains the state and cost of each directly connected link. Routers flood their LSAs to adjacent neighbors. Adjacent neighbors receiving the LSA immediately flood the LSA to other directly connected neighbors, until all routers in the area have all LSAs.

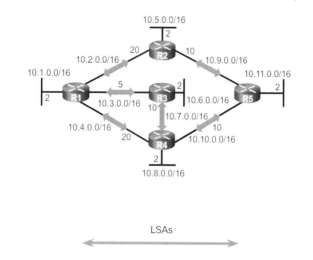

**Figure 8-3**   Routers Exchange LSAs

3. **Build the topology table (see Figure 8-4).** After LSAs are received, OSPF-enabled routers build the topology table (LSDB) based on the received LSAs. This database eventually holds all the information about the topology of the network.

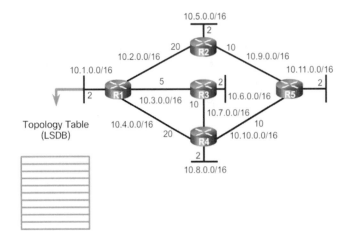

**Figure 8-4**   R1 Creates Its Topological Database

4. **Execute the SPF algorithm (see Figure 8-5 and Figure 8-6).** Routers execute the SPF algorithm. The gears in the figures indicate the execution of the SPF algorithm. The SPF algorithm creates the SPF tree.

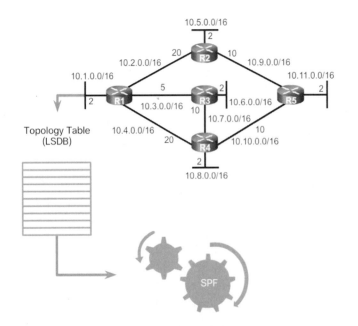

**Figure 8-5**   R1 Executes the SPF Algorithm

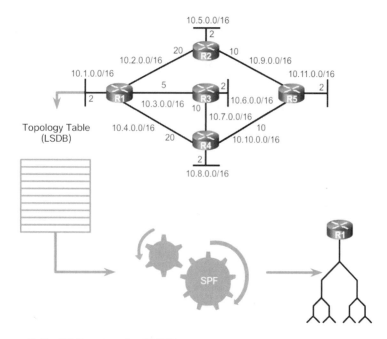

**Figure 8-6**   R1 Creates the SFP Tree

The contents of the R1 SPF tree are shown in Figure 8-7.

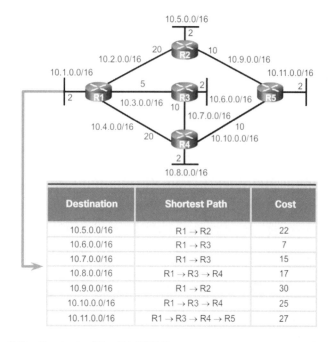

| Destination | Shortest Path | Cost |
|-------------|---------------|------|
| 10.5.0.0/16 | R1 → R2 | 22 |
| 10.6.0.0/16 | R1 → R3 | 7 |
| 10.7.0.0/16 | R1 → R3 | 15 |
| 10.8.0.0/16 | R1 → R3 → R4 | 17 |
| 10.9.0.0/16 | R1 → R2 | 30 |
| 10.10.0.0/16 | R1 → R3 → R4 | 25 |
| 10.11.0.0/16 | R1 → R3 → R4 → R5 | 27 |

**Figure 8-7**   Content of the R1 SPF Tree

From the SPF tree, the best paths are offered to the IP routing table. The route will be inserted into the routing table unless there is a route source to the same network with a lower administrative distance, such as a static route. Routing decisions are made based on the entries in the routing table.

## Single-Area and Multiarea OSPF (8.1.1.5)

To make OSPF more efficient and scalable, OSPF supports hierarchical routing using areas. An OSPF area is a group of routers that share the same link-state information in their LSDBs.

OSPF can be implemented in a single area or with multiple areas. These two implementation methods are simply referred to as *single-area OSPF* and *multiarea OSPF*.

When deployed as a single-area OSPF, all routers in one area are called the *backbone area* (area 0), as shown in Figure 8-8.

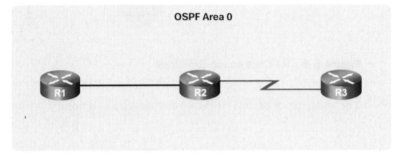

**Figure 8-8**   Single-Area OSPF

Single-area OSPF is useful in small networks with few routers.

When deployed with multiple areas, multiarea OSPF is implemented in a hierarchal fashion, as shown in Figure 8-9.

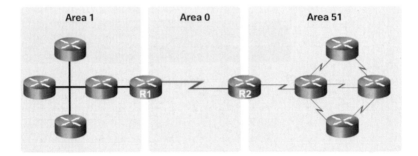

**Figure 8-9**   Multiarea OSPF

All areas must connect to the backbone area (area 0). Routers interconnecting the areas are referred to as *area border routers (ABR)*. Multiarea OSPF is useful for reducing processing and memory overhead in larger network deployments.

With multiarea OSPF, OSPF can divide one large routing domain into smaller areas to support hierarchical routing. With hierarchical routing, routing still occurs between the areas (*interarea routing*), while many of the processor-intensive routing operations, such as recalculating the database, are kept within an area.

For instance, any time a router receives new information about a topology change within the area (including the addition, deletion, or modification of a link), the router must rerun the SPF algorithm, create a new SPF tree, and update the routing table. The SPF algorithm is CPU intensive, and the time it takes for calculation depends on the size of the area.

**Note**

Routers in other areas receive messages regarding topology changes, but these routers only update the routing table; they do not rerun the SPF algorithm.

Having too many routers in one area makes the link-state database (LSDB) very large and increases the load on the CPU. Therefore, arranging routers into areas effectively partitions a potentially large database into smaller and more manageable databases.

Table 8-4 lists advantages of using a multiarea OSPF hierarchical topology design.

**Table 8-4**  Multiarea OSPF Advantages

| Advantage | Description |
|---|---|
| Smaller routing tables | ■ There are fewer routing table entries because network addresses can be summarized between areas.<br>■ Route summarization is not enabled by default. |
| Reduced link-state update overhead | ■ Designing multiarea OSPF with smaller areas minimizes processing and memory requirements. |
| Reduced frequency of SPF calculations | ■ Multiarea OSPF localizes the impact of a topology change within an area.<br>■ For instance, it minimizes routing update impact because LSA flooding stops at the area boundary. |

In Figure 8-10, for example, R2 is an ABR connecting area 51 to the backbone area 0.

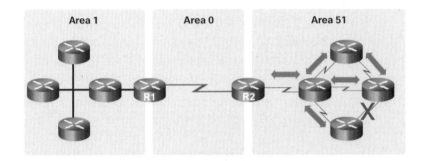

**Figure 8-10**   Link Change Impacts Local Area Only

As ABR, R2 summarizes the area 51 routes into area 0. When one of the summarized links fails, as illustrated in Figure 8-10, LSAs are exchanged within area 51 only. Routers in area 51 must rerun the SPF algorithm to identify the best routes.

The ABR (R2) isolates the fault to area 51, and therefore routers in areas 0 and 1 do not need to run the SPF algorithm. This reduces the link-state update overhead and also keeps the routing tables smaller.

The focus of this chapter is on single-area OSPF.

**Interactive Graphic**

**Activity 8.1.1.6: Identify OSPF Features and Terminology**

Refer to the online course to complete this activity.

## OSPF Messages (8.1.2)

In this topic, you will learn about the types of packets used to establish and maintain an OSPF neighbor relationship.

### Encapsulating OSPF Messages (8.1.2.1)

Figure 8-11 shows the OSPFv2 IPv4 header fields.

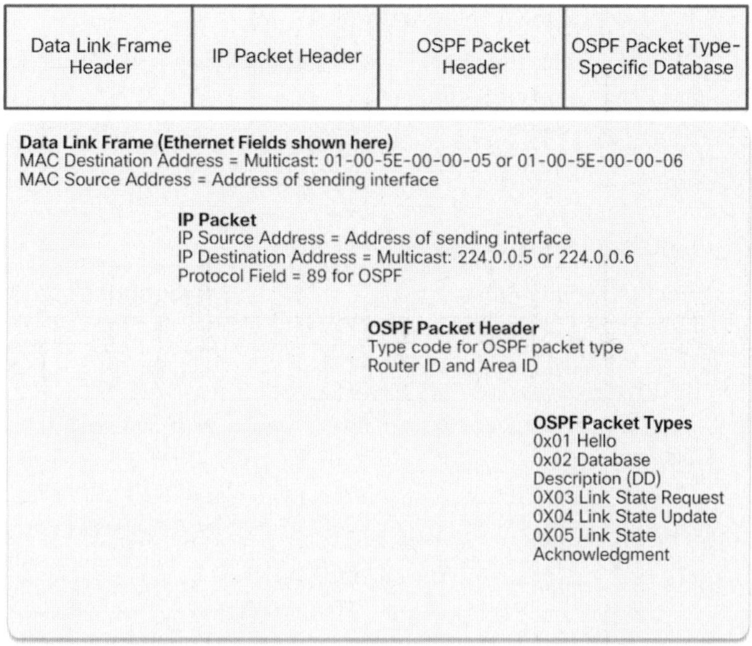

**Figure 8-11**   OSPF IPv4 Header Fields

Table 8-5 lists the fields contained in an OSPFv2 packet transmitted over an Ethernet link.

**Table 8-5**   OSPFv2 Header Fields

| Field | Description |
|---|---|
| Data link Ethernet frame header | ■ Identifies the destination multicast MAC addresses 01-00-5E-00-00-05 or 01-00-5E-00-00-06 when encapsulating an OSPFv2 message. |
| IPv4 packet header | ■ Identifies the IP source address and destination address. |
| | ■ The destination address is one of two OSPFv2 multicast addresses, 224.0.0.5 or 224.0.0.6. |
| | ■ The header also contains a protocol field, which contains the code 89 for OSPF. |
| OSPF packet header | ■ Identifies the OSPF packet type, the router ID, and the area ID. |
| OSPF packet type specific data | ■ Contains the OSPF packet type information. |
| | ■ The content differs depending on the packet type. |

## Types of OSPF Packets (8.1.2.2)

OSPF uses link-state packets (LSPs) to establish and maintain neighbor adjacencies and exchange routing updates.

OSPFv2 uses five different types of LSPs (see Table 8-6). OSPFv3 has similar packet types.

**Table 8-6**  OSPFv2 Packet Types

| Packet Type | Description |
| --- | --- |
| Type 1: Hello packet | ■ Used to establish and maintain adjacency with other OSPF routers. |
| Type 2: Database Description (DBD) packet | ■ Contains an abbreviated list of the sending router's LSDB and used by receiving routers to check against the local LSDB. <br> ■ The LSDB must be identical on all link-state routers within an area to construct an accurate SPF tree. |
| Type 3: Link-State Request (LSR) packet | ■ Receiving routers can request more information about any entry in the DBD by sending an LSR. |
| Type 4: Link-State Update (LSU) packet | ■ Used to reply to LSRs and to announce new information. <br> ■ LSUs contain seven different types of LSAs. |
| Type 5: Link-State Acknowledgment (LSAck) packet | ■ When an LSU is received, the router sends an LSAck to confirm receipt of the LSU. <br> ■ The LSAck data field is empty. |

## Hello Packet (8.1.2.3)

The OSPF type 1 packet is the Hello packet:

- Hello packets are used to discover OSPF neighbors and establish neighbor adjacencies.

- They advertise parameters on which two routers must agree to become neighbors.

- They elect the *designated router (DR)* and *backup designated router (BDR)* on multiaccess networks such as Ethernet and Frame Relay. Point-to-point links do not require DR or BDR.

Figure 8-12 displays the fields contained in the OSPFv2 type 1 Hello packet.

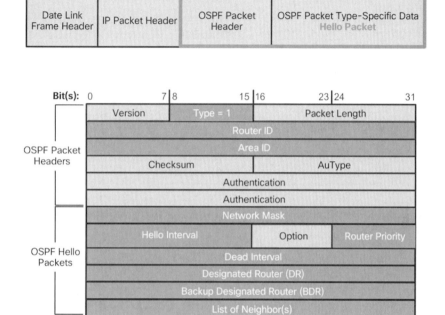

**Figure 8-12**    OSPF Hello Packet Content

Table 8-7 lists important fields shown in an OSPF Hello packet.

**Table 8-7**    Hello Packet Fields

| Packet Field | Description |
|---|---|
| Type | ■ Identifies the type of packet. |
| | ■ 1 indicates a Hello packet, 2 a DBD packet, 3 an LSR packet, 4 an LSU packet, and 5 an LSAck packet. |
| Router ID | ■ A 32-bit IPv4 address used to uniquely identify the originating router. |
| Area ID | ■ The number of the area from which the packet originated. |
| Network mask | ■ The subnet mask associated with the sending interface. |
| Hello interval | ■ Specifies the frequency, in seconds, at which a router sends Hello packets. |
| | ■ The default hello interval on multiaccess networks is 10 seconds. |
| | ■ The timer must be identical on peer routers; otherwise, there is no adjacency. |

| Packet Field | Description |
|---|---|
| *Router priority* | ■ Used in a DR/BDR election.<br><br>■ The default priority for all OSPF routers is 1, but this can be manually altered to anywhere from 0 to 255.<br><br>■ The higher the value, the more likely the router is to become the DR on the link. |
| *Dead interval* | ■ This is the time in seconds that a router waits to hear from a neighbor before declaring it down.<br><br>■ By default, the dead interval is four times the hello interval.<br><br>■ The timer must be identical on peer routers; otherwise, there is no adjacency. |
| Designated router (DR) | ■ The router ID of the DR. |
| Backup designated router (BDR) | ■ The router ID of the BDR. |
| List of neighbors | ■ A list that identifies the router IDs of all adjacent routers. |

## Hello Packet Intervals (8.1.2.4)

OSPF Hello packets are transmitted to multicast address 224.0.0.5 in IPv4 and FF02::5 in IPv6 (all OSPF routers) every

- 10 seconds (default on multiaccess and point-to-point networks)
- 30 seconds (default on nonbroadcast multiple access [NBMA] networks, such as Frame Relay)

The dead interval is the period that the router waits to receive a Hello packet before declaring the neighbor down. If the dead interval expires before the router receives a Hello packet, OSPF removes that neighbor from its LSDB. The router floods the LSDB with information about the down neighbor out all OSPF-enabled interfaces.

Cisco uses a default of four times the hello interval for the dead interval:

- 40 seconds (default on multiaccess and point-to-point networks)
- 120 seconds (default on NBMA networks, such as Frame Relay)

## Link-State Updates (8.1.2.5)

Routers initially exchange type 2 DBD packets, which is an abbreviated list of the sending router's LSDB and is used by receiving routers to check against the local LSDB.

A type 3 LSR packet is used by the receiving routers to request more information about an entry in the DBD, and a type 4 LSU packet is used to reply to an LSR packet. A type 5 packet is used to acknowledge the receipt of a type 4 LSU.

LSUs are also used to forward OSPF routing updates, such as link changes. Specifically, an LSU packet can contain 11 different types of OSPFv2 LSAs, as shown in Figure 8-13. OSPFv3 renamed several of these LSAs and also contains two additional LSAs.

| Type | Packet Name | Description |
| --- | --- | --- |
| 1 | Hello | Discovers neighbors and builds adjacencies between them |
| 2 | DBD | Checks for database synchronization between routers |
| 3 | LSR | Requests specific link-state records from router to router |
| 4 | LSU | Sends specifically requested link-state records |
| 5 | LSAck | Acknowledges the other packet types |

- An LSU contains one or more LSAs.
- LSAs contain route information for destination networks.

| LSA Type | Description |
| --- | --- |
| 1 | Router LSAs |
| 2 | Network LSAs |
| 3 or 4 | Summary LSAs |
| 5 | Autonomous System External LSAs |
| 6 | Multicast OSPF LSAs |
| 7 | Defined for Not-So-Stubby Areas |
| 8 | External Attributes LSA for Border Gateway Protocol (BGP) |
| 9, 10, 11 | Opaque LSAs |

**Figure 8-13**   LSUs Contain LSAs

**Note**

The use of the terms LSU and LSA can sometimes be confusing because these terms are often used interchangeably. However, they are different: An LSU contains one or more LSAs.

**Interactive Graphic**

**Activity 8.1.2.6: Identify the OSPF Packet Types**

Refer to the online course to complete this activity.

# OSPF Operation (8.1.3)

In this topic, you will learn how OSPF achieves convergence.

## OSPF Operational States (8.1.3.1)

When an OSPF router is initially connected to a network, it attempts to

- Create adjacencies with neighbors
- Exchange routing information
- Calculate the best routes
- Reach convergence

Figure 8-14 displays the states OSPF progresses through to reach convergence.

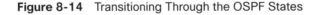

**Figure 8-14**   Transitioning Through the OSPF States

Table 8-8 lists the details of these states.

**Table 8-8**   OSPF State Descriptions

| OSPF State | Description |
| --- | --- |
| Down state | <ul><li>No Hello packets received = Down.</li><li>Router sends Hello packets.</li><li>Transition to Init state.</li></ul> |
| *Init state* | <ul><li>Hello packets are received from the neighbor.</li><li>They contain the sending router's router ID.</li><li>Transition to Two-Way state.</li></ul> |

| OSPF State | Description |
|------------|-------------|
| Two-Way state | <ul><li>On Ethernet links, elect a DR and a BDR.</li><li>Transition to ExStart state.</li></ul> |
| *ExStart state* | <ul><li>Negotiate the master/slave relationship and DBD packet sequence number.</li><li>The master initiates the DBD packet exchange.</li></ul> |
| *Exchange state* | <ul><li>Routers exchange DBD packets.</li><li>If additional router information is required, transition to Loading; otherwise, transition to the Full state.</li></ul> |
| *Loading state* | <ul><li>LSRs and LSUs are used to gain additional route information.</li><li>Routes are processed using the SPF algorithm.</li><li>Transition to the Full state.</li></ul> |
| *Full state* | <ul><li>Routers have converged.</li></ul> |

## Establish Neighbor Adjacencies (8.1.3.2)

When OSPF is enabled on an interface, the router must determine whether there is another OSPF neighbor on the link. To accomplish this, the router forwards a Hello packet that contains its router ID out all OSPF-enabled interfaces. The OSPF router ID is used by the OSPF process to uniquely identify each router in the OSPF area. A router ID is a 32-bit number formatted like an IP address and assigned to uniquely identify a router among OSPF peers.

When a neighboring OSPF-enabled router receives a Hello packet with a router ID that is not within its neighbor list, the receiving router attempts to establish an adjacency with the initiating router.

Refer to R1 in Figure 8-15.

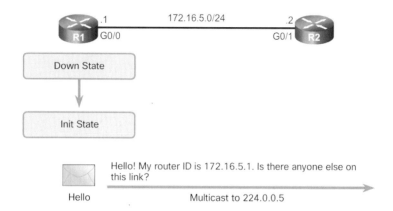

**Figure 8-15**    Down State to Init State

When OSPFv2 is enabled, the enabled GigabitEthernet 0/0 interface transitions from the Down state to the Init state. R1 starts sending Hello packets out all OSPF-enabled interfaces to discover OSPF neighbors with which to develop adjacencies.

In Figure 8-16, R2 receives the Hello packet from R1 and adds the R1 router ID to its neighbor list.

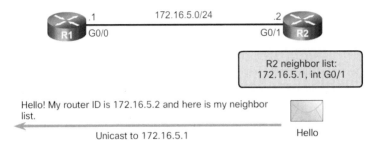

**Figure 8-16**   The Init State

R2 then sends a Hello packet to R1. The packet contains the R2 router ID and the R1 router ID in its list of neighbors on the same interface.

In Figure 8-17, R1 receives the Hello packet and adds the R2 router ID in its list of OSPF neighbors.

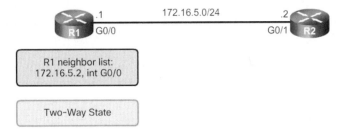

**Figure 8-17**   Two-Way State

R2 also notices its own router ID in the Hello packet's list of neighbors and therefore transitions to Two-Way state. When a router receives a Hello packet with its router ID listed in the list of neighbors, the router transitions from the Init state to the Two-Way state.

The action performed in Two-Way state depends on the type of interconnection between the adjacent routers:

- If the two adjacent neighbors are interconnected over a point-to-point link, they immediately transition from the Two-Way state to the database synchronization phase.

- If the routers are interconnected over a common Ethernet network, a DR and a BDR must be elected.

Because R1 and R2 are interconnected over an Ethernet network, a DR and BDR election takes place.

As shown in Figure 8-18, R2 becomes the DR, and R1 is the BDR.

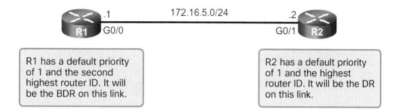

**Figure 8-18**   Electing the DR and BDR

## OSPF DR and BDR (8.1.3.3)

Why is a DR and BDR election necessary?

Multiaccess networks can create two challenges for OSPF regarding the flooding of LSAs:

- **Creation of multiple adjacencies**—Ethernet networks could potentially interconnect many OSPF routers over a common link. Creating adjacencies with every router is unnecessary and undesirable. It would lead to an excessive number of LSAs exchanged between routers on the same network.

- **Extensive flooding of LSAs**—Link-state routers flood their LSAs any time OSPF is initialized or when there is a change in the topology. This flooding can become excessive.

To understand the problem with multiple adjacencies, we must use this formula:

$n \ (n - 1) \ / \ 2$

Specifically, for any number of routers (designated as $n$) on a multiaccess network, there are $n \ (n - 1) \ / \ 2$ adjacencies.

To illustrate this, refer to the simple multiaccess five-router Ethernet topology in Figure 8-19.

Without some type of mechanism to reduce the number of adjacencies, collectively these routers would form 10 adjacencies. This may not seem like much, but as routers are added to the network, the number of adjacencies increases dramatically, as shown in Table 8-9.

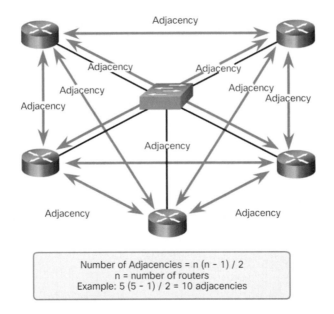

Number of Adjacencies = n (n - 1) / 2
n = number of routers
Example: 5 (5 - 1) / 2 = 10 adjacencies

**Figure 8-19**   Creating Adjacencies with Every Neighbor

**Table 8-9**   Calculating Adjacencies in a Full Mesh

| Routers: *n* | Adjacencies: *n* (*n* − 1) / 2 |
| --- | --- |
| 5 | 10 |
| 10 | 45 |
| 20 | 190 |
| 100 | 4950 |

In Figure 8-20, R2 sends out an LSA, which triggers every other router to also send out an LSA.

Not shown in the figure are the required acknowledgments sent for every LSA received. If every router in a multiaccess network had to flood and acknowledge all received LSAs to all other routers on that same multiaccess network, the network traffic would become quite chaotic.

The solution to managing the number of adjacencies and the flooding of LSAs on a multiaccess network is to identify a designated router (DR). On multiaccess networks, OSPF elects a DR to be the collection and distribution point for LSAs sent and received. The DR reduces the number of adjacencies required on a multiaccess network, which in turn reduces the amount of routing protocol traffic and the size of the topological database.

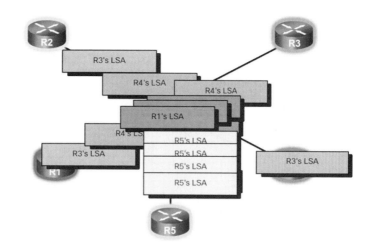

**Figure 8-20** Flooding LSAs

A backup designated router (BDR) is also elected, to take over if the DR fails. All other routers become *DROTHERs*—routers that are neither the DR nor the BDR.

Only the DR and the BDR listen for LSAs, as shown when R1 sends an LSA in Figure 8-21.

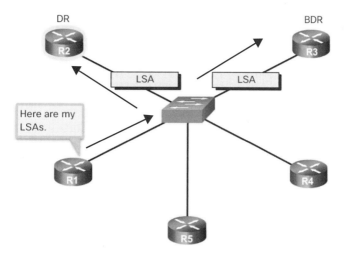

**Figure 8-21** R1 Sends LSAs to DR and BDR

R2, the DR, then forwards the LSA to the BDR and DROTHERs, as shown in Figure 8-22.

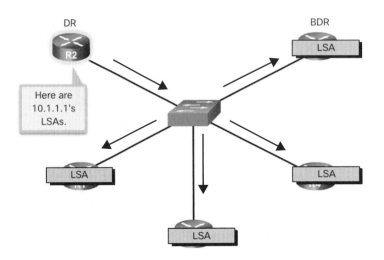

**Figure 8-22**   The DR, R2, Sends the LSA to Other Routers

**Note**

The DR is only used for the dissemination of LSAs. The router still uses the best next-hop router indicated in the routing table for the forwarding of all other packets.

## Synchronizing OSPF Databases (8.1.3.4)

After the Two-Way state, routers transition to database synchronization states. Whereas the Hello packet was used to establish neighbor adjacencies, the other four types of OSPF packets are used during the process of exchanging and synchronizing LSDBs.

In the ExStart state, the two routers decide which router will send the DBD packets first. The router with the higher router ID will be the first router to send DBD packets during the Exchange state.

In Figure 8-23, R2 has the higher router ID and therefore sends its DBD packets first.

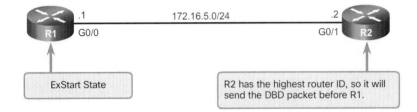

**Figure 8-23**   Deciding Which Router Sends the First DBD

In the Exchange state, the two routers exchange one or more DBD packets. A DBD packet includes information about the LSA entry header that appears in the router's LSDB. The entries can be about a link or about a network. Each LSA entry header includes information about the link-state type, the address of the advertising router, the link's cost, and the sequence number. The router uses the sequence number to determine the newness of the received link-state information.

In Figure 8-24, R2 sends a DBD packet to R1. This is what happens in this example:

1. When R1 receives the DBD, it acknowledges the receipt of the DBD, using the LSAck packet.

2. R1 sends DBD packets to R2.

3. R2 acknowledges R1.

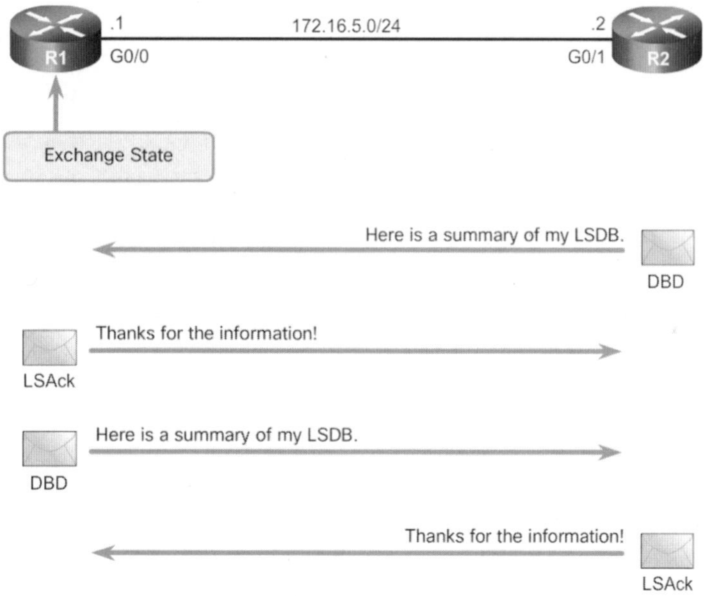

**Figure 8-24**  Exchanging DBD Packets

R1 compares the information received with the information it has in its own LSDB. If the DBD packet has a more current link-state entry, the router transitions to the Loading state.

For example, in Figure 8-25, R1 sends an LSR regarding network 172.16.6.0 to R2. R2 responds with the complete information about 172.16.6.0 in an LSU packet.

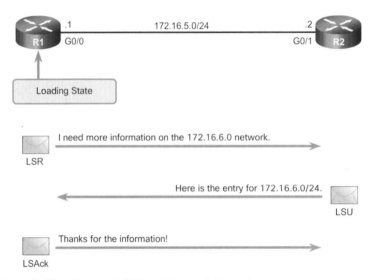

**Figure 8-25**   Getting Additional Route Information

Again, when R1 receives an LSU, it sends an LSAck. R1 then adds the new link-state entries to its LSDB. After all LSRs have been satisfied for a given router, the adjacent routers are considered synchronized and in a Full state.

As long as the neighboring routers continue receiving Hello packets, the network in the transmitted LSAs remain in the topology database. After the topology databases are synchronized, updates (LSUs) are sent only to neighbors:

- When a change is perceived (incremental updates)
- Every 30 minutes

**Activity 8.1.3.5: Identify the OSPF States for Establishing Adjacency**

Refer to the online course to complete this activity.

**Video Demonstration 8.1.3.6: Observing OSPF Protocol Communications**

Refer to the online course to view this video.

# Single-Area OSPFv2 (8.2)

In this section, you will learn how to implement single-area OSPFv2.

# OSPF Router ID (8.2.1)

In this topic, you will configure the OSPF router ID.

## OSPF Network Topology (8.2.1.1)

Introduced in 1991, OSPFv2 is a link-state routing protocol for IPv4. OSPF was designed as an alternative to another IPv4 routing protocol, RIP.

Figure 8-26 shows the reference topology used for configuring OSPFv2 in this section.

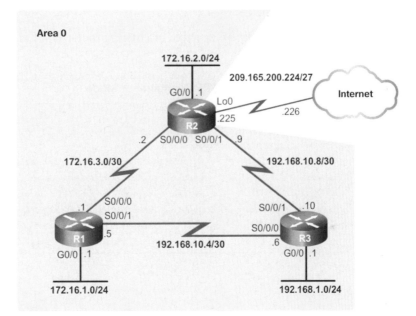

**Figure 8-26**   OSPF Reference Topology

The types of serial interfaces and their associated bandwidths may not necessarily reflect the most common types of connections found in networks today. The bandwidths of the serial links used in this topology were chosen to help explain the calculation of the routing protocol metrics and the process of best path selection.

The routers in the topology have a starting configuration, including interface addresses. There is currently no static routing or dynamic routing configured on any of the routers. All interfaces on routers R1, R2, and R3 (except the loopback on R2) are within the OSPF backbone area. The ISP router is used as the routing domain's gateway to the Internet.

> **Note**
>
> In the topology in Figure 8-26, the loopback interface is used to simulate the WAN link to the Internet.

## Router OSPF Configuration Mode (8.2.1.2)

OSPFv2 is enabled using the **router ospf** *process-id* global configuration mode command. The *process-id* value is set to a number between 1 and 65,535, as selected by the network administrator. The *process-id* value is locally significant, which means it does not have to be the same value on the other OSPF routers to establish adjacencies with those neighbors.

Example 8-1 provides an example of entering router OSPFv2 configuration mode on R1.

**Example 8-1**   Entering OSPF Configuration Mode

```
R1(config)# router ospf 10
R1(config-router)# ?
Router configuration commands:
  auto-cost             Calculate OSPF interface cost according to bandwidth
  network               Enable routing on an IP network
  no                    Negate a command or set its defaults
  passive-interface     Suppress routing updates on an interface
  priority              OSPF topology priority
  router-id             router-id for this OSPF process
```

> **Note**
>
> The list of commands in the output in Example 8-1 has been altered to display only the commands that are used in this chapter.

## Router IDs (8.2.1.3)

Every router requires a router ID to participate in an OSPF domain. The router ID can be defined by an administrator or automatically assigned by the router. The router ID is used by the OSPF-enabled router to:

- **Uniquely identify the router**—The router ID is used by other routers to uniquely identify each router within the OSPF domain and all packets that originate from them.

- **Participate in the election of the DR**—In a multiaccess LAN environment, the election of the DR occurs during initial establishment of the OSPF network.

When OSPF links become active, the routing device configured with the highest priority is elected the DR. Assuming that there is no priority configured, or there is a tie, the router with the highest router ID is elected the DR. The routing device with the second-highest router ID is elected the BDR.

But how does the router determine the router ID? The process is illustrated in Figure 8-27.

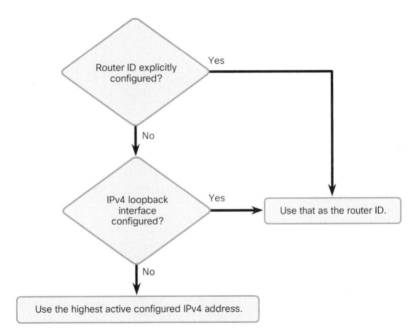

**Figure 8-27**   Router ID Order of Precedence

As presented in the figure, Cisco routers derive the router ID based on one of three criteria, in the following preferential order:

- The router ID is explicitly configured using the OSPF **router-id** *rid* router configuration mode command. The *rid* value is any 32-bit value expressed as an IPv4 address. This is the recommended method to assign a router ID.

- If no router ID is explicitly configured, the router chooses the highest IPv4 address of any of configured loopback interfaces. This is the next best alternative to assigning a router ID.

- If no loopback interfaces are configured, the router chooses the highest active IPv4 address of any of its physical interfaces. This is the least recommended method because it makes it more difficult for administrators to distinguish between specific routers.

If the router uses the highest IPv4 address for the router ID, the interface does not need to be OSPF enabled. This means that the interface address does not need to be included in the OSPF **network** command for the router to use that IPv4 address as the router ID. The only requirement is that the interface must be active and in the up state.

---

**Note**

The router ID looks like an IPv4 address, but it is not routable and, therefore, is not included in the routing table, unless the OSPF routing process chooses an interface (physical or loop-back) that is appropriately defined by the **network** command.

---

## Configuring an OSPF Router ID (8.2.1.4)

Use the **router-id** *rid* router configuration mode command to manually assign a 32-bit value expressed as an IPv4 address to a router. An OSPF router identifies itself to other routers using this router ID.

As shown in Figure 8-28, R1 is configured with a router ID of 1.1.1.1, R2 with 2.2.2.2, and R3 with 3.3.3.3.

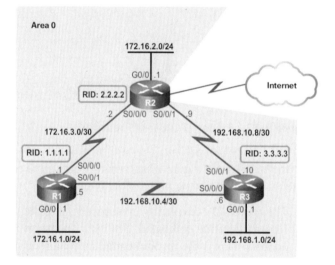

**Figure 8-28**   OSPF Reference Topology with Router IDs

In Example 8-2, the router ID 1.1.1.1 is assigned to R1, and the **show ip protocols** command is used to verify the router ID.

**Example 8-2**   Assigning a Router ID to R1

```
R1(config)# router ospf 10
R1(config-router)# router-id 1.1.1.1
R1(config-router)# end
R1#
*Mar 25 19:50:36.595: %SYS-5-CONFIG_I: Configured from console by console
R1#
R1# show ip protocols
*** IP Routing is NSF aware ***

Routing Protocol is "ospf 10"
  Outgoing update filter list for all interfaces is not set
  Incoming update filter list for all interfaces is not set
  Router ID 1.1.1.1
  Number of areas in this router is 0. 0 normal 0 stub 0 nssa
  Maximum path: 4
  Routing for Networks:
  Routing Information Sources:
    Gateway         Distance      Last Update
  Distance: (default is 110)

R1#
```

**Note**

In Example 8-2 R1 had never been configured with an OSPF router ID. If it had been, the router ID would have needed to be modified.

The error message "%OSPF-4-DUP_RTRID1: Detected router with duplicate router ID" would be displayed if the router ID were configured the same between two neighboring routers. To correct this problem, configure all routers so that they have unique OSPF router IDs.

## Modifying a Router ID (8.2.1.5)

Sometimes a router ID needs to be changed, such as when a network administrator establishes a new router ID scheme for the network. However, after a router selects a router ID, an active OSPFv2 router does not allow the router ID to be changed until the router is reloaded or the OSPFv2 process is cleared.

In Example 8-3, notice that the current router ID is 192.168.10.5.

**Example 8-3**  Verifying the Router ID

```
R1# show ip protocols
*** IP Routing is NSF aware ***

Routing Protocol is "ospf 10"
  Outgoing update filter list for all interfaces is not set
  Incoming update filter list for all interfaces is not set
  Router ID 192.168.10.5
  Number of areas in this router is 1. 1 normal 0 stub 0 nssa
  Maximum path: 4
  Routing for Networks:
    172.16.1.0 0.0.0.255 area 0
    172.16.3.0 0.0.0.3 area 0
    192.168.10.4 0.0.0.3 area 0
  Routing Information Sources:
    Gateway          Distance      Last Update
    209.165.200.225      110       00:07:02
    192.168.10.10        110       00:07:02
  Distance: (default is 110)

R1#
```

The router ID here should be 1.1.1.1.

In Example 8-4, the router ID 1.1.1.1 is being assigned to R1.

**Example 8-4**  Changing the Router ID

```
R1(config)# router ospf 10
R1(config-router)# router-id 1.1.1.1
% OSPF: Reload or use "clear ip ospf process" command, for this to take effect
R1(config-router)# end
R1#
*Mar 25 19:46:09.711: %SYS-5-CONFIG_I: Configured from console by console
```

Notice in Example 8-4 that an informational message appears, stating that the OSPFv2 process must be cleared or that the router must be reloaded. The reason is because R1 already has adjacencies with other neighbors using the router ID 192.168.10.5. Those adjacencies must be renegotiated using the new router ID 1.1.1.1.

Clearing the OSPF process is the preferred method to reset the router ID.

In Example 8-5, the OSPFv2 routing process is cleared using the **clear ip ospf process** privileged EXEC mode command, and the **show ip protocols** command verifies that the router ID has changed.

**Example 8-5**  Clearing the OSPF Process

```
R1# clear ip ospf process
Reset ALL OSPF processes? [no]: y
R1#
*Mar 25 19:46:22.423: %OSPF-5-ADJCHG: Process 10, Nbr 3.3.3.3 on Serial0/0/1 from
   FULL to DOWN, Neighbor Down: Interface down or detached
*Mar 25 19:46:22.423: %OSPF-5-ADJCHG: Process 10, Nbr 2.2.2.2 on Serial0/0/0 from
   FULL to DOWN, Neighbor Down: Interface down or detached
*Mar 25 19:46:22.475: %OSPF-5-ADJCHG: Process 10, Nbr 3.3.3.3 on Serial0/0/1 from
   LOADING to FULL, Loading Done
*Mar 25 19:46:22.475: %OSPF-5-ADJCHG: Process 10, Nbr 2.2.2.2 on Serial0/0/0 from
   LOADING to FULL, Loading Done
R1#
R1# show ip protocols | section Router ID
Router ID 1.1.1.1
R1#
```

This **clear ip ospf process** command forces OSPFv2 on R1 to transition to the Down
and Init states. Notice that the adjacency change messages go from full to down and
then from loading to full.

## Using a Loopback Interface as the Router ID (8.2.1.6)

Assigning the router ID manually with the **router-id** command is the preferred
method of setting the router ID. An alternative method of assigning the router ID is
to use a loopback interface.

The IPv4 address of the loopback interface should be configured using a 32-bit subnet mask (255.255.255.255). This effectively creates a host route. A 32-bit host route
does not get advertised as a route to other OSPF routers.

Example 8-6 displays how to configure a loopback interface with a host route on R1.

**Example 8-6**  Configuring a Host Route on a Loopback Interface

```
R1(config)# interface loopback 0
R1(config-if)# ip address 1.1.1.1 255.255.255.255
R1(config-if)# end
R1#
```

R1 uses the host route as its router ID, assuming that there is no router ID explicitly
configured or previously learned.

**Note**

Using the **router-id** command is the preferred method for setting the OSPF router ID.

## Configure Single-Area OSPFv2 (8.2.2)

In this topic, you will configure single-area OSPF.

### Enabling OSPF on Interfaces (8.2.2.1)

The **network** command determines which interfaces participate in the routing process for an OSPFv2 area. Any interfaces on a router that match the network address in the **network** command are enabled to send and receive OSPF packets. The **network** command also indicates the network (or subnet) address for the interface that is included in OSPF routing updates.

The basic command syntax is **network** *network-address wildcard-mask* **area** *area-id*. The **area** *area-id* syntax refers to the OSPF area. When configuring single-area OSPFv2, the **network** command must be configured with the same *area-id* value on all routers. Although any area ID can be used, it is good practice to use area ID 0 with single-area OSPFv2. This convention makes it easier if the network is later altered to support multiarea OSPFv2.

### Wildcard Mask (8.2.2.2)

OSPFv2 uses the argument combination *network-address wildcard-mask* to enable OSPF on interfaces. OSPF is classless by design; therefore, the wildcard mask is always required. When identifying interfaces that are participating in a routing process, the wildcard mask is typically the inverse of the subnet mask configured on that interface.

A wildcard mask is a string of 32 binary digits used by the router to determine which bits of the address to examine for a match. In a subnet mask, binary 1 is equal to a match, and binary 0 is not a match. In a wildcard mask, the reverse is true:

- **Wildcard mask bit 0**—Matches the corresponding bit value in the address.
- **Wildcard mask bit 1**—Ignores the corresponding bit value in the address.

The easiest method for calculating a wildcard mask is to subtract the network subnet mask from 255.255.255.255.

The example in Figure 8-29 calculates the wildcard mask from the network address 192.168.10.0/24.

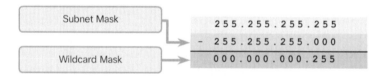

**Figure 8-29**   Calculating a Wildcard Mask for /24

The subnet mask 255.255.255.0 is subtracted from 255.255.255.255, providing a result of 0.0.0.255. Therefore, 192.168.10.0/24 is 192.168.10.0 with a wildcard mask of 0.0.0.255.

The example in Figure 8-30 calculates the wildcard mask from the network address 192.168.10.64/26. Again, the subnet mask 255.255.255.192 is subtracted from 255.255.255.255, providing a result of 0.0.0.63. Therefore, 192.168.10.0/26 is 192.168.10.0 with a wildcard mask of 0.0.0.63.

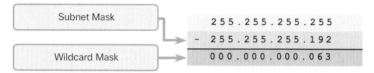

**Figure 8-30**   Calculating a Wildcard Mask for /26

## The network Command (8.2.2.3)

There are several ways to identify the interfaces that will participate in the OSPFv2 routing process. Example 8-7 shows the commands used to determine which interfaces on R1 and R2 will participate in the OSPFv2 routing process for an area.

**Example 8-7**   Enabling OSPF on R1 and R2

```
R1(config)# router ospf 10
R1(config-router)# network 172.16.1.0 0.0.0.255 area 0
R1(config-router)# network 172.16.3.0 0.0.0.3 area 0
R1(config-router)# network 192.168.10.4 0.0.0.3 area 0
R1(config-router)# end
R1#

R2(config)# router ospf 10
R2(config-router)# network 172.16.2.0 0.0.0.255 area 0
R2(config-router)# network 172.16.3.0 0.0.0.3 area 0
R2(config-router)# network 192.168.10.8 0.0.0.3 area 0
R2(config-router)#
*Mar 25 21:19:21.938: %OSPF-5-ADJCHG: Process 10, Nbr 1.1.1.1 on Serial0/0/0 from
   LOADING to FULL, Loading Done
R2(config-router)# end
R2#
```

Notice the use of wildcard masks to identify the interfaces based on their network addresses. Because this is a single-area OSPF network, all area IDs are set to 0.

As an alternative, OSPFv2 can be enabled using the **network** *intf-ip-address* **0.0.0.0** *area area-id* router configuration mode command.

Example 8-8 shows how to specify the interface IPv4 address with a quad 0 wildcard mask.

**Example 8-8**    Enabling OSPF by Specifying the IPv4 Interface Addresses on R3

```
R3(config)# router ospf 10
R3(config-router)# router-id 3.3.3.3
R3(config-router)# network 192.168.1.1 0.0.0.0 area 0
R3(config-router)# network 192.168.10.6 0.0.0.0 area 0
R3(config-router)# network 192.168.10.10 0.0.0.0 area 0
R3(config-router)#
*Mar 26 14:00:55.183: %OSPF-5-ADJCHG: Process 10, Nbr 1.1.1.1 on Serial0/0/0 from
   LOADING to FULL, Loading Done
*Mar 26 14:00:55.243: %OSPF-5-ADJCHG: Process 10, Nbr 2.2.2.2 on Serial0/0/1 from
   LOADING to FULL, Loading Done
R3(config-router)# end
R3#
```

Entering **network 192.168.10.6 0.0.0.0 area 0** on R3 tells the router to enable interface Serial 0/0/0 for the routing process. As a result, the OSPFv2 process will advertise the network that is on this interface (192.168.10.4/30).

The advantage of specifying the interface is that the wildcard mask calculation is not necessary. OSPFv2 uses the interface address and subnet mask to determine the network to advertise.

Some IOS versions allow the subnet mask to be entered instead of the wildcard mask. The IOS then converts the subnet mask to the wildcard mask format.

## Passive Interface (8.2.2.4)

By default, OSPF messages are forwarded out all OSPF-enabled interfaces. However, these messages really only need to be sent out interfaces connecting to other OSPF-enabled routers.

Refer to the topology in the Figure 8-26. OSPFv2 messages are forwarded out all three routers' G0/0 interface, even though no OSPFv2 neighbor exists on that LAN. Sending out unneeded messages on a LAN affects the network in three ways:

■ **Inefficient use of bandwidth**—Available bandwidth is consumed transporting unnecessary messages. Messages are multicasted; therefore, switches are also forwarding the messages out all ports.

■ **Inefficient use of resources**—All devices on the LAN must process the message and eventually discard the message.

■ **Increased security risk**—Advertising updates on a broadcast network is a security risk. OSPF messages can be intercepted with packet sniffing software.

Routing updates can be modified and sent back to the router, corrupting the routing table with false metrics that misdirect traffic.

## Configuring Passive Interfaces (8.2.2.5)

Use the **passive-interface** router configuration mode command to prevent the transmission of routing messages through a router interface but still allow that network to be advertised to other routers, as shown in Example 8-9 for R1.

**Example 8-9**   Configuring a Passive Interface

```
R1(config)# router ospf 10
R1(config-router)# passive-interface GigabitEthernet 0/0
R1(config-router)# end
R1#
```

Specifically, the **passive-interface** command stops routing messages from being sent out the specified interface. However, the network that the specified interface belongs to is still advertised in routing messages that are sent out other interfaces.

For instance, there is no need for R1, R2, and R3 to forward OSPF messages out their LAN interfaces. The configuration identifies the R1 G0/0 interface as passive.

It is important to know that a neighbor adjacency cannot be formed over a passive interface. This is because link-state packets cannot be sent or acknowledged.

The **show ip protocols** command is then used to verify that the Gigabit Ethernet interface was passive, as shown in Example 8-10.

**Example 8-10**   Verifying Passive Interfaces on R1

```
R1# show ip protocols
*** IP Routing is NSF aware ***

Routing Protocol is "ospf 10"
  Outgoing update filter list for all interfaces is not set
  Incoming update filter list for all interfaces is not set
  Router ID 1.1.1.1
  Number of areas in this router is 1. 1 normal 0 stub 0 nssa
  Maximum path: 4
  Routing for Networks:
    172.16.1.1 0.0.0.0 area 0
    172.16.3.1 0.0.0.0 area 0
    192.168.10.5 0.0.0.0 area 0
```

```
 Passive Interface(s):
    GigabitEthernet0/0
 Routing Information Sources:
    Gateway          Distance      Last Update
    3.3.3.3               110      00:08:35
    2.2.2.2               110      00:08:35
 Distance: (default is 110)

R1#
```

Notice that the G0/0 interface is now listed under the "Passive Interface(s)" section. The network 172.16.1.0 is still listed under "Routing for Networks," which means this network is still included as a route entry in OSPFv2 updates that are sent to R2 and R3.

### Note

OSPFv2 and OSPFv3 both support the **passive-interface** command.

As an alternative, all interfaces can be made passive by using the **passive-interface default** command. Interfaces that should not be passive can be re-enabled by using the **no passive-interface** command.

In Example 8-11, R3 is configured using this method.

**Example 8-11**   Configuring a Passive Interface as the Default on R3

```
R3(config)# router ospf 10
R3(config-router)# passive-interface default
R3(config-router)#
*Mar 26 16:22:58.090: %OSPF-5-ADJCHG: Process 10, Nbr 1.1.1.1 on Serial0/0/0 from
   FULL to DOWN, Neighbor Down: Interface down or detached
*Mar 26 16:22:58.090: %OSPF-5-ADJCHG: Process 10, Nbr 2.2.2.2 on Serial0/0/1 from
   FULL to DOWN, Neighbor Down: Interface down or detached
R3(config-router)# no passive-interface serial 0/0/0
*Mar 26 16:23:18.590: %OSPF-5-ADJCHG: Process 10, Nbr 1.1.1.1 on Serial0/0/0 from
   LOADING to FULL, Loading Done
R3(config-router)# no passive-interface serial 0/0/1
*Mar 26 16:23:24.462: %OSPF-5-ADJCHG: Process 10, Nbr 2.2.2.2 on Serial0/0/1 from
   LOADING to FULL, Loading Done
R3(config-router)# end
R3#
*Mar 26 16:23:30.522: %SYS-5-CONFIG_I: Configured from console by console
R3# show ip protocols
*** IP Routing is NSF aware ***
```

```
Routing Protocol is "ospf 10"
  Outgoing update filter list for all interfaces is not set
  Incoming update filter list for all interfaces is not set
  Router ID 3.3.3.3
  Number of areas in this router is 1. 1 normal 0 stub 0 nssa
  Maximum path: 4
  Routing for Networks:
    192.168.1.0 0.0.0.255 area 0
    192.168.10.4 0.0.0.3 area 0
    192.168.10.8 0.0.0.3 area 0
  Passive Interface(s):
    Embedded-Service-Engine0/0
    GigabitEthernet0/0
    GigabitEthernet0/1
    GigabitEthernet0/3
    RG-AR-IF-INPUT1
  Routing Information Sources:
    Gateway         Distance    Last Update
    2.2.2.2              110      00:00:06
    1.1.1.1              110      00:00:11
  Distance: (default is 110)

R3#
```

**Note**

Notice the OSPFv2 informational state messages as the interfaces are all rendered passive and then the two serial interfaces are made nonpassive.

**Interactive Graphic**

**Activity 8.2.2.6: Calculate the Subnet and Wildcard Masks**

Refer to the online course to complete this activity.

**Packet Tracer 8.2.2.7: Configuring OSPFv2 in a Single-area**

In this activity, the IPv4 addressing is already configured. You are responsible for configuring the three-router topology with basic single-area OSPFv2 and then verifying connectivity between end devices.

# OSPF Cost (8.2.3)

In this topic, you will learn how OSPF uses cost to determine the best path.

## OSPF Metric = Cost (8.2.3.1)

Recall that a routing protocol uses a metric to determine the best path of a packet across a network. A metric gives an indication of the overhead that is required to send packets across a certain interface. OSPF uses cost as a metric, where a lower cost indicates a better path than a higher cost.

The cost of an interface is inversely proportional to the bandwidth of the interface. Therefore, a higher bandwidth indicates a lower cost. More overhead and time delays equal a higher cost. Therefore, a 10 Mbps Ethernet line has a higher cost than a 100 Mbps Ethernet line.

This is the formula used to calculate the OSPF cost:

Cost = *Reference bandwidth* / Interface bandwidth

The default reference bandwidth is 10^8 (100,000,000); therefore, the formula is

Cost = 100,000,000 bps / interface bandwidth in bps

Figure 8-31 shows a breakdown of the cost calculation.

| Interface Type | Reference Bandwidth in bps | Default Bandwidth in bps | Cost |
|---|---|---|---|
| 10 Gigabit Ethernet 10 Gbps | 100,000,000 ÷ | 10,000,000,000 | 1 |
| Gigabit Ethernet 1 Gbps | 100,000,000 ÷ | 1,000,000,000 | 1 |
| Fast Ethernet 100 Mbps | 100,000,000 ÷ | 100,000,000 | 1 |
| Ethernet 10 Mbps | 100,000,000 ÷ | 10,000,000 | 10 |
| Serial 1.544 Mbps | 100,000,000 ÷ | 1,544,000 | 64 |
| Serial 128 kbps | 100,000,000 ÷ | 128,000 | 781 |
| Serial 64 kbps | 100,000,000 ÷ | 64,000 | 1562 |

Same Cost due to reference bandwidth

**Figure 8-31**   Default Cisco OSPF Cost Values

Notice that Fast Ethernet, Gigabit Ethernet, and 10 GigE interfaces share the same cost because the OSPF cost value must be an integer. Consequently, because the default reference bandwidth is set to 100 Mbps, all links that are faster than Fast Ethernet also have a cost of 1.

## OSPF Accumulates Costs (8.2.3.2)

The cost of an OSPF route is the accumulated value from one router to the destination network.

For example, in Figure 8-32, the cost to reach the R2 LAN 172.16.2.0/24 from R1 should be as follows:

- Serial link from R1 to R2 cost = 64

- Gigabit Ethernet link on R2 cost = 1

- Total cost to reach 172.16.2.0/24 = **65**

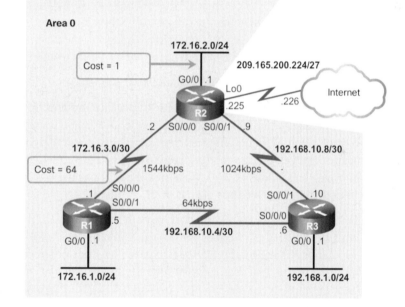

**Figure 8-32**   OSPF Reference Topology with Costs Labeled

The routing table of R1 in Example 8-12 confirms that the metric to reach the R2 LAN is a cost of 65.

**Example 8-12**   Verifying the Cost

```
R1# show ip route | include 172.16.2.0
O         172.16.2.0/24 [110/65] via 172.16.3.2, 03:39:07, Serial0/0/0
R1#
R1# show ip route 172.16.2.0
Routing entry for 172.16.2.0/24
  Known via "ospf 10", distance 110, metric 65, type intra area
  Last update from 172.16.3.2 on Serial0/0/0, 03:39:15 ago
  Routing Descriptor Blocks:
  * 172.16.3.2, from 2.2.2.2, 03:39:15 ago, via Serial0/0/0
      Route metric is 65, traffic share count is 1
R1#
```

## Adjusting the Reference Bandwidth (8.2.3.3)

OSPF uses a reference bandwidth of 100 Mbps for any links that are equal to or faster than a Fast Ethernet connection. Therefore, the cost assigned to a Fast Ethernet interface with an interface bandwidth of 100 Mbps would equal 1.

Cost = 100,000,000 bps / 100,000,000 = 1

While this calculation works for Fast Ethernet interfaces, it is problematic for links that are faster than 100 Mbps because the OSPF metric only uses integers as its final cost of a link. If something less than an integer is calculated, OSPF rounds up to the nearest integer. For this reason, from the perspective of OSPF, an interface with an interface bandwidth of 100 Mbps (a cost of 1) has the same cost as an interface with a bandwidth of 100 Gbps (a cost of 1).

To assist OSPF in making the correct path determination, the reference bandwidth must be changed to a higher value to accommodate networks with links faster than 100 Mbps. Changing the reference bandwidth does not actually affect the bandwidth capacity on the link. Rather, it simply affects the calculation used to determine the metric.

To adjust the reference bandwidth, use the **auto-cost reference-bandwidth** *Mbps* router configuration command. This command must be configured on every router in the OSPF domain. Notice that the value is expressed in Mbps.

- Therefore, to adjust the costs for Gigabit Ethernet (GE), use **auto-cost reference-bandwidth 1000**.

- To adjust the costs for 10 Gigabit Ethernet (10GE), use **auto-cost reference-bandwidth 10000**. To return to the default reference bandwidth, use the **auto-cost reference-bandwidth 100** command.

The table in Figure 8-33 displays the OSPF cost if the reference bandwidth is set to accommodate Gigabit Ethernet links. Although the metric values increase, OSPF makes better choices because it can now distinguish between Fast Ethernet and Gigabit Ethernet links.

| Interface Type | Reference Bandwidth in bps | Default Bandwidth in bps | Cost |
|---|---|---|---|
| **10 Gigabit Ethernet** 10 Gbps | 1,000,000,000 ÷ 10,000,000,000 | | 1 |
| **Gigabit Ethernet** 1 Gbps | 1,000,000,000 ÷ 1,000,000,000 | | 1 |
| **Fast Ethernet** 100 Mbps | 1,000,000,000 ÷ 100,000,000 | | 10 |
| **Ethernet** 10 Mbps | 1,000,000,000 ÷ 10,000,000 | | 100 |
| **Serial** 1.544 Mbps | 1,000,000,000 ÷ 1,544,000 | | 647 |
| **Serial** 128 kbps | 1,000,000,000 ÷ 128,000 | | 7812 |
| **Serial** 64 kbps | 1,000,000,000 ÷ 64,000 | | 15625 |

**Figure 8-33**    Changing the Reference Bandwidth to 1000

The table in Figure 8-34 displays the OSPF cost if the reference bandwidth is set to accommodate 10 Gigabit Ethernet links.

The reference bandwidth should always be adjusted on all OSPF routers any time there are links faster than Fast Ethernet (100 Mbps).

**Note**

The costs in the figures in this section are whole numbers that have been rounded down.

In Figure 8-35, all routers have been configured to accommodate the Gigabit Ethernet link with the **auto-cost reference-bandwidth 1000** router configuration command.

| Interface Type | Reference Bandwidth in bps | | Default Bandwidth in bps | Cost |
|---|---|---|---|---|
| **10 Gigabit Ethernet**<br>10 Gbps | 10,000,000,000 | ÷ | 10,000,000,000 | 1 |
| **Gigabit Ethernet**<br>1 Gbps | 10,000,000,000 | ÷ | 1,000,000,000 | 10 |
| **Fast Ethernet**<br>100 Mbps | 10,000,000,000 | ÷ | 100,000,000 | 100 |
| **Ethernet**<br>10 Mbps | 10,000,000,000 | ÷ | 10,000,000 | 1000 |
| **Serial**<br>1.544 Mbps | 10,000,000,000 | ÷ | 1,544,000 | 6477 |
| **Serial**<br>128 kbps | 10,000,000,000 | ÷ | 128,000 | 78125 |
| **Serial**<br>64 kbps | 10,000,000,000 | ÷ | 64,000 | 156250 |

**Figure 8-34**   Changing the Reference Bandwidth to 10000

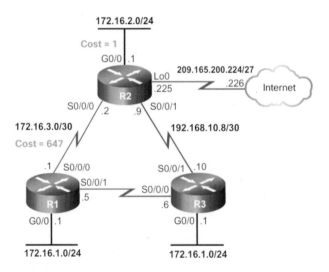

**Figure 8-35**   OSPF Reference Topology with Costs Labeled

Using the costs listed in the table in Figure 8-33, the new accumulated cost to reach the R2 LAN 172.16.2.0/24 from R1 should be as follows:

- Serial link from R1 to R2 cost = 647

- Gigabit Ethernet link on R2 cost = 1

- Total cost to reach 172.16.2.0/24 = **648**

Use the **show ip ospf interface s0/0/0** command to verify the current OSPFv2 cost assigned to the R1 Serial 0/0/0 interface, as shown in Example 8-13. Notice that it displays a cost of 647.

**Example 8-13**    Verifying the OSPF Cost of a Link

```
R1# show ip ospf interface serial 0/0/0
Serial0/0/0 is up, line protocol is up
  Internet Address 172.16.3.1/30, Area 0, Attached via Network Statement
  Process ID 10, Router ID 1.1.1.1, Network Type POINT_TO_POINT, Cost: 647
  Topology-MTID    Cost    Disabled    Shutdown      Topology Name
        0           647       no          no            Base
  Transmit Delay is 1 sec, State POINT_TO_POINT
  Timer intervals configured, Hello 10, Dead 40, Wait 40, Retransmit 5
    oob-resync timeout 40
    Hello due in 00:00:01
  Supports Link-local Signaling (LLS)
  Cisco NSF helper support enabled
  IETF NSF helper support enabled
  Index 3/3, flood queue length 0
  Next 0x0(0)/0x0(0)
  Last flood scan length is 1, maximum is 1
  Last flood scan time is 0 msec, maximum is 0 msec
  Neighbor Count is 1, Adjacent neighbor count is 1
    Adjacent with neighbor 2.2.2.2
  Suppress hello for 0 neighbor(s)
R1#
```

The routing table of R1 in Example 8-14 confirms that the metric to reach the R2 LAN is a cost of 648.

**Example 8-14**    Verifying the Route Metric

```
R1# show ip route | include 172.16.2.0
O        172.16.2.0/24 [110/648] via 172.16.3.2, 00:06:03, Serial0/0/0
R1#
R1# show ip route 172.16.2.0
```

```
Routing entry for 172.16.2.0/24
  Known via "ospf 10", distance 110, metric 648, type intra area
  Last update from 172.16.3.2 on Serial0/0/0, 00:06:17 ago
  Routing Descriptor Blocks:
  * 172.16.3.2, from 2.2.2.2, 00:06:17 ago, via Serial0/0/0
      Route metric is 648, traffic share count is 1
R1#
```

## Default Interface Bandwidths (8.2.3.4)

All interfaces have default bandwidth values assigned to them. As with reference bandwidth, interface bandwidth values do not actually affect the speed or capacity of the link. Instead, they are used by some routing protocols, such as OSPF, to compute the routing metric. Therefore, it is important that the bandwidth value reflect the actual speed of the link so that the routing table has accurate best path information.

Although the bandwidth values of Ethernet interfaces usually match the link speed, this may not be the case for some other interfaces. For instance, the actual speed of serial interfaces is often different from the default bandwidth. On Cisco routers, the default bandwidth on most serial interfaces is set to 1.544 Mbps.

### Note

Older serial interfaces may default to 128 Kbps.

Refer to the topology in Figure 8-32. Notice the following:

- The link between R1 and R2 should be set to 1544 Kbps (default value).
- The link between R2 and R3 should be set to 1024 Kbps.
- The link between R1 and R3 should be set to 64 Kbps.

Use the **show interfaces** command to view the interface bandwidth setting. Example 8-15 displays the Serial 0/0/0 settings for R1.

**Example 8-15**    Verifying the Default Bandwidth of the R1 Serial 0/0/0

```
R1# show interfaces serial 0/0/0
Serial0/0/0 is up, line protocol is up
  Hardware is WIC MBRD Serial
  Description: Link to R2
  Internet address is 172.16.3.1/30
  MTU 1500 bytes, BW 1544 Kbit/sec, DLY 20000 usec,
     reliability 255/255, txload 1/255, rxload 1/255
```

```
    Encapsulation HDLC, loopback not set
    Keepalive set (10 sec)
    Last input 00:00:05, output 00:00:03, output hang never
    Last clearing of "show interface" counters never
    Input queue: 0/75/0/0 (size/max/drops/flushes); Total output drops: 0
    Queueing strategy: fifo
    Output queue: 0/40 (size/max)
    5 minute input rate 0 bits/sec, 0 packets/sec
    5 minute output rate 0 bits/sec, 0 packets/sec
       215 packets input, 17786 bytes, 0 no buffer
       Received 109 broadcasts (0 IP multicasts)
       0 runts, 0 giants, 0 throttles
       0 input errors, 0 CRC, 0 frame, 0 overrun, 0 ignored, 0 abort
       216 packets output, 17712 bytes, 0 underruns
       0 output errors, 0 collisions, 5 interface resets
       3 unknown protocol drops
       0 output buffer failures, 0 output buffers swapped out
       0 carrier transitions
       DCD=up  DSR=up  DTR=up  RTS=up  CTS=up

R1#
```

The bandwidth setting is accurate, and therefore the serial interface does not have to be adjusted.

Example 8-16 displays the Serial 0/0/1 settings for R1.

**Example 8-16**   R1 Serial 0/0/1 Bandwidth

```
R1# show interfaces serial 0/0/1 | include BW
  MTU 1500 bytes, BW 1544 Kbit/sec, DLY 20000 usec,
R1#
```

Example 8-16 also confirms that the interface is using the default interface bandwidth 1544 Kbps. According to the reference topology, this should be set to 64 Kbps. Therefore, the R1 Serial 0/0/1 interface must be adjusted.

Example 8-17 displays the resulting cost metric of 647, which is based on the reference bandwidth set to 1,000,000,000 bps and the default interface bandwidth of 1544 Kbps (1,000,000,000 / 1,544,000).

**Example 8-17**   R1 Serial 0/0/1 Cost

```
R1# show ip ospf interface serial 0/0/1
Serial0/0/1 is up, line protocol is up
  Internet Address 192.168.10.5/30, Area 0, Attached via Network Statement
  Process ID 10, Router ID 1.1.1.1, Network Type POINT_TO_POINT, Cost: 647
  Topology-MTID    Cost    Disabled    Shutdown       Topology Name
        0           647        no          no              Base
  Transmit Delay is 1 sec, State POINT_TO_POINT
  Timer intervals configured, Hello 10, Dead 40, Wait 40, Retransmit 5
    oob-resync timeout 40
    Hello due in 00:00:04
  Supports Link-local Signaling (LLS)
  Cisco NSF helper support enabled
  IETF NSF helper support enabled
  Index 3/3, flood queue length 0
  Next 0x0(0)/0x0(0)
  Last flood scan length is 1, maximum is 1
  Last flood scan time is 0 msec, maximum is 0 msec
  Neighbor Count is 1, Adjacent neighbor count is 1
    Adjacent with neighbor 3.3.3.3
  Suppress hello for 0 neighbor(s)
R1#
R1# show ip ospf interface serial 0/0/1 | include Cost:
  Process ID 10, Router ID 1.1.1.1, Network Type POINT_TO_POINT, Cost: 647
R1#
```

## Adjusting the Interface Bandwidth (8.2.3.5)

To adjust the interface bandwidth, use the **bandwidth** *kilobits* interface configuration command. Use the **no bandwidth** command to restore the default value.

Example 8-18 adjusts the R1 Serial 0/0/1 interface bandwidth to 64 Kbps and verifies that the interface bandwidth setting is now 64 Kbps.

**Example 8-18**   Adjusting Interface Bandwidths

```
R1(config)# int s0/0/1
R1(config-if)# bandwidth 64
R1(config-if)# end
R1#
*Mar 27 10:10:07.735: %SYS-5-CONFIG_I: Configured from console by c
R1#
```

```
R1# show interfaces serial 0/0/1 | include BW
  MTU 1500 bytes, BW 64 Kbit/sec, DLY 20000 usec,
R1#
R1# show ip ospf interface serial 0/0/1 | include Cost:
  Process ID 10, Router ID 1.1.1.1, Network Type POINT_TO_POINT, Cost: 15625
R1#
```

The bandwidth must be adjusted at each end of the serial links:

- R2 requires its S0/0/1 interface to be adjusted to 1024 Kbps.

- R3 requires its Serial 0/0/0 to be adjusted to 64 Kbps and its Serial 0/0/1 to be adjusted to 1024 Kbps.

**Note**

A common misconception for students who are new to networking and the Cisco IOS is to assume that the **bandwidth** command changes the physical bandwidth of the link. The command only modifies the bandwidth metric used by EIGRP and OSPF. The command does not modify the actual bandwidth on the link.

## Manually Setting the OSPF Cost (8.2.3.6)

As an alternative to setting the default interface bandwidth, the cost can be manually configured on an interface by using the **ip ospf cost** *value* interface configuration command.

An advantage of configuring a cost over setting the interface bandwidth is that the router does not have to calculate the metric when the cost is manually configured. In contrast, when the interface bandwidth is configured, the router must calculate the OSPF cost based on the bandwidth. The **ip ospf cost** command is useful in multivendor environments where non-Cisco routers may use a metric other than bandwidth to calculate the OSPFv2 costs.

The **bandwidth** interface command and the **ip ospf cost** interface command achieve the same result, which is to provide an accurate value for use by OSPFv2 in determining the best route.

For instance, in the example in Example 8-19, the interface bandwidth of Serial 0/0/1 is reset to the default value, and the OSPF cost is manually set to 15,625. Although the interface bandwidth is reset to the default value, the OSPFv2 cost is set as if the bandwidth were still calculated.

**Example 8-19**   Adjusting Interface OSPF Cost

```
R1(config)# int s0/0/1
R1(config-if)# no bandwidth 64
R1(config-if)# ip ospf cost 15625
R1(config-if)# end
R1#
R1# show interface serial 0/0/1 | include BW
  MTU 1500 bytes, BW 1544 Kbit/sec, DLY 20000 usec,
R1#
R1# show ip ospf interface serial 0/0/1 | include Cost:
  Process ID 10, Router ID 1.1.1.1, Network Type POINT_TO_POINT, Cost: 15625
R1#
```

Figure 8-36 shows the two alternatives that can be used in modifying the costs of the serial links in the topology. The right side of the figure shows the **ip ospf cost** command equivalents of the **bandwidth** commands on the left.

| Adjusting the Interface Bandwidth | = | Manually Setting the OSPF Cost |
|---|---|---|
| R1(config)# **interface S0/0/1**<br>R1(config-if)# **bandwidth 64** | = | R1(config)# **interface S0/0/1**<br>R1(config-if)# **ip ospf cost 15625** |
| R2(config)# **interface S0/0/1**<br>R2(config-if)# **bandwidth 1024** | = | R2(config)# **interface S0/0/1**<br>R2(config-if)# **ip ospf cost 976** |
| R3(config)# **interface S0/0/0**<br>R3(config-if)# **bandwidth 64** | = | R3(config)# **interface S0/0/0**<br>R3(config-if)# **ip ospf cost 15625** |
| R3(config)# **interface S0/0/1**<br>R3(config-if)# **bandwidth 1024** | = | R3(config)# **interface S0/0/1**<br>R3(config-if)# **ip ospf cost 976** |

**Figure 8-36**   Bandwidth versus OSPF Cost

# Verify OSPF (8.2.4)

In this topic, you will verify single-area OSPFv2.

## Verify OSPF Neighbors (8.2.4.1)

Use the **show ip ospf neighbor** command to verify that a router has formed an adjacency with its neighboring routers. If the router ID of the neighboring router is not displayed, or if it does not show as being in the Full state, the two routers have not formed an OSPFv2 adjacency.

If two routers do not establish adjacency, link-state information is not exchanged. Incomplete LSDBs can cause inaccurate SPF trees and routing tables. Routes to destination networks may not exist, or they may not be the most optimum paths.

Example 8-20 displays the neighbor adjacency of R1.

**Example 8-20**   Verifying R1's OSPF Neighbors

```
R1# show ip ospf neighbor

Neighbor ID     Pri   State         Dead Time   Address        Interface
3.3.3.3          0    FULL/  -      00:00:37    192.168.10.6   Serial0/0/1
2.2.2.2          0    FULL/  -      00:00:30    172.16.3.2     Serial0/0/0
R1#
```

Table 8-10 explains the fields in the output in Example 8-20.

**Table 8-10**   Fields in the **show ip ospf neighbor** Command

| Field in Output | Description |
| --- | --- |
| Neighbor ID | ■ The router ID of the neighboring router. |
| Pri | ■ The OSPFv2 priority of the interface. |
| | ■ This value is used in the DR and BDR election. |
| State | ■ The OSPFv2 state of the interface. |
| | ■ Full state means that the router and its neighbor have identical OSPFv2 LSDBs. On multiaccess networks, such as Ethernet, two routers that are adjacent may have their states displayed as 2WAY. |
| | ■ The dash indicates that no DR or BDR is required because of the network type. |
| Dead time | ■ The amount of time remaining that the router waits to receive an OSPFv2 Hello packet from the neighbor before declaring the neighbor down. |
| | ■ This value is reset when the interface receives a Hello packet. |
| Address | ■ The IPv4 address of the neighbor's interface to which this router is directly connected. |
| Interface | ■ The interface on which this router has formed adjacency with the neighbor. |

Two routers may not form an OSPFv2 adjacency if:

- The subnet masks do not match, causing the routers to be on separate networks.

- OSPFv2 hello or dead timers do not match.

- OSPFv2 network types do not match.

- There is a missing or incorrect OSPFv2 **network** command.

## Verify OSPF Protocol Settings (8.2.4.2)

As shown in Example 8-21, using the **show ip protocols** command is a quick way to verify vital OSPF configuration information.

**Example 8-21**    Verifying R1's OSPF Neighbors

```
R1# show ip protocols
*** IP Routing is NSF aware ***

Routing Protocol is "ospf 10"
  Outgoing update filter list for all interfaces is not set
  Incoming update filter list for all interfaces is not set
  Router ID 1.1.1.1
  Number of areas in this router is 1. 1 normal 0 stub 0 nssa
  Maximum path: 4
  Routing for Networks:
    172.16.1.0 0.0.0.255 area 0
    172.16.3.0 0.0.0.3 area 0
    192.168.10.4 0.0.0.3 area 0
  Routing Information Sources:
    Gateway         Distance      Last Update
    2.2.2.2              110       00:17:18
    3.3.3.3              110       00:14:49
  Distance: (default is 110)

R1#
```

The command displays the OSPFv2 process ID, the router ID, the networks the router is advertising, the neighbors the router is receiving updates from, and the default administrative distance, which is 110 for OSPF.

## Verify OSPF Process Information (8.2.4.3)

The **show ip ospf** command can also be used to examine the OSPFv2 process ID and router ID, as shown in Example 8-22.

**Example 8-22**    Verifying R1's OSPF Process

```
R1# show ip ospf
 Routing Process "ospf 10" with ID 1.1.1.1
 Start time: 01:37:15.156, Time elapsed: 01:32:57.776
 Supports only single TOS(TOS0) routes
 Supports opaque LSA
 Supports Link-local Signaling (LLS)
 Supports area transit capability
 Supports NSSA (compatible with RFC 3101)
 Event-log enabled, Maximum number of events: 1000, Mode: cyclic
 Router is not originating router-LSAs with maximum metric
 Initial SPF schedule delay 5000 msecs
 Minimum hold time between two consecutive SPFs 10000 msecs
 Maximum wait time between two consecutive SPFs 10000 msecs
 Incremental-SPF disabled
 Minimum LSA interval 5 secs
 Minimum LSA arrival 1000 msecs
 LSA group pacing timer 240 secs
 Interface flood pacing timer 33 msecs
 Retransmission pacing timer 66 msecs
 Number of external LSA 0. Checksum Sum 0x000000
 Number of opaque AS LSA 0. Checksum Sum 0x000000
 Number of DCbitless external and opaque AS LSA 0
 Number of DoNotAge external and opaque AS LSA 0
 Number of areas in this router is 1. 1 normal 0 stub 0 nssa
 Number of areas transit capable is 0
 External flood list length 0
 IETF NSF helper support enabled
 Cisco NSF helper support enabled
 Reference bandwidth unit is 1000 mbps
    Area BACKBONE(0)
        Number of interfaces in this area is 3
        Area has no authentication
       SPF algorithm last executed 01:30:45.364 ago
        SPF algorithm executed 3 times
        Area ranges are
        Number of LSA 3. Checksum Sum 0x02033A
        Number of opaque link LSA 0. Checksum Sum 0x000000
        Number of DCbitless LSA 0
        Number of indication LSA 0
        Number of DoNotAge LSA 0
        Flood list length 0

R1#
```

The command displays the OSPFv2 area information and the last time the SPF algorithm was calculated.

## Verify OSPF Interface Settings (8.2.4.4)

The quickest way to verify OSPFv2 interface settings is to use the **show ip ospf interface** command. This command provides a detailed list for every OSPFv2-enabled interface. The command is useful in determining whether the **network** statements were correctly composed.

To get a summary of OSPFv2-enabled interfaces, use the **show ip ospf interface brief** command, as shown in Example 8-23.

**Example 8-23**   Verifying R1's OSPF Interfaces

```
R1# show ip ospf interface brief
Interface    PID   Area         IP Address/Mask      Cost   State Nbrs F/C
Se0/0/1      10    0            192.168.10.5/30      15625  P2P   1/1
Se0/0/0      10    0            172.16.3.1/30        647    P2P   1/1
Gi0/0        10    0            172.16.1.1/24        1      DR    0/0
R1#
```

Example 8-24 shows that specifying the interface name provides detailed OSPFv2 information for Serial 0/0/1 on R2.

**Example 8-24**   Verifying the OSPFv2 Interface Details

```
R2# show ip ospf interface serial 0/0/1
Serial0/0/1 is up, line protocol is up
  Internet Address 192.168.10.9/30, Area 0, Attached via Network Statement
  Process ID 10, Router ID 2.2.2.2, Network Type POINT_TO_POINT, Cost: 976
  Topology-MTID    Cost     Disabled     Shutdown        Topology Name
        0          976        no            no              Base
  Transmit Delay is 1 sec, State POINT_TO_POINT
  Timer intervals configured, Hello 10, Dead 40, Wait 40, Retransmit 5
    oob-resync timeout 40
    Hello due in 00:00:03
  Supports Link-local Signaling (LLS)
  Cisco NSF helper support enabled
  IETF NSF helper support enabled
  Index 3/3, flood queue length 0
  Next 0x0(0)/0x0(0)
```

```
    Last flood scan length is 1, maximum is 1
    Last flood scan time is 0 msec, maximum is 0 msec
    Neighbor Count is 1, Adjacent neighbor count is 1
      Adjacent with neighbor 3.3.3.3
    Suppress hello for 0 neighbor(s)
R2#
```

**Lab 8.2.4.5: Configuring Basic Single-Area OSPFv2**

Refer to *Scaling Networks v6 Labs & Study Guide* and the online course to complete this activity.

In this lab, you will complete the following objectives:

- Part 1: Build the Network and Configure Basic Device Settings
- Part 2: Configure and Verify OSPFv2 Routing
- Part 3: Change Router ID Assignments
- Part 4: Configure OSPFv2 Passive Interfaces
- Part 5: Change OSPFv2 Metrics

# Single-Area OSPFv3 (8.3)

In this section, you will configure, verify, and troubleshoot single-area and multiarea OSPFv3 for IPv6.

## OSPFv2 vs. OSPFv3 (8.3.1)

In this topic, you will compare the characteristics and operations of OSPFv2 and OSPFv3.

### OSPFv3 (8.3.1.1)

OSPFv3 is the version of OSPF for exchanging IPv6 prefixes. Recall that in IPv6, the network address is referred to as the *prefix*, and the subnet mask is called the *prefix length*.

Similarly to its IPv4 counterpart, OSPFv3 exchanges routing information to populate the IPv6 routing table with remote prefixes, as shown in Figure 8-37.

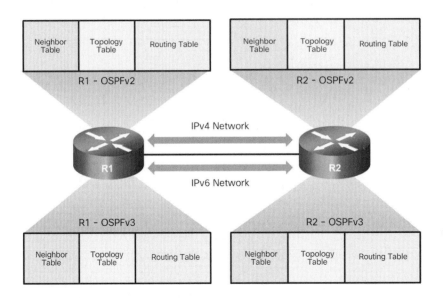

**Figure 8-37**   OSPFv2 and OSPFv3 Data Structures

OSPFv2 runs over the IPv4 network layer, communicating with other OSPF IPv4 peers and advertising only IPv4 routes.

OSPFv3 has the same functionality as OSPFv2 but uses IPv6 as the network layer transport, communicating with OSPFv3 peers and advertising IPv6 routes. OSPFv3 also uses the SPF algorithm as the computation engine to determine the best paths throughout the routing domain.

Like all other IPv6 routing protocols, OSPFv3 has separate processes from its IPv4 counterpart. The processes and operations are basically the same as in the IPv4 routing protocol, but they run independently. OSPFv2 and OSPFv3 each have separate adjacency tables, OSPF topology tables, and IP routing tables, as shown in Figure 8-37.

The OSPFv3 configuration and verification commands are similar to those used in OSPFv2.

## Similarities Between OSPFv2 and OSPFv3 (8.3.1.2)

Table 8-11 lists similarities between OSPFv2 and OSPFv3.

**Table 8-11**    Similarities Between OSPFv2 and OSPFv3

| Similarities | Description |
|---|---|
| Link-state routing protocol | ■ OSPFv2 and OSPFv3 are both classless link-state routing protocols. |
| Metric | ■ OSPFv2 and OSPFv3 RFCs define *metric* as the cost of sending packets out the interface. |
| | ■ OSPFv2 and OSPFv3 reference bandwidth can be modified by using the **auto-cost reference-bandwidth** *ref-bw* router configuration mode command. |
| OSPF packet types | ■ OSPFv3 uses the same five basic packet types as OSPFv2: Hello, DBD, LSR, LSU, and LSAck. |
| Neighbor discovery mechanism | ■ Neighbor states and events are the same in both protocols. |
| | ■ OSPFv2 and OSPFv3 use Hello packets to learn and form adjacencies. |
| Router ID | ■ OSPFv2 and OSPFv3 both use a 32-bit IP address for the router ID. |
| | ■ The process of determining the 32-bit router ID is the same in both protocols (using an explicitly configured router ID; otherwise, the highest loopback or configured active IPv4 address becomes the router ID). |
| Areas | ■ The concept of multiple areas is the same in both protocols. |
| DR/BDR election process | ■ The DR/BDR election process is the same in both protocols. |

## Differences Between OSPFv2 and OSPFv3 (8.3.1.3)

Table 8-12 highlights similarities and differences between OSPFv2 nd OSPFv3.

**Table 8-12**    Similarities and Differences Between OSPFv2 and OSPFv3

| Specifics | OSPFv2 | OSPFv3 |
|---|---|---|
| Advertising | Advertises IPv4 networks | Advertises IPv6 prefixes |
| Source address | OSPFv2 messages are sourced from the IPv4 address of the exit interface. | OSPFv3 messages are sourced using the IPv6 link-local address of the exit interface. |

| Specifics | OSPFv2 | OSPFv3 |
|---|---|---|
| Destination address | OSPFv2 messages are sent to:<br>■ Neighbor IPv4 unicast address<br>■ 224.0.0.5 all-OSPF-routers multicast address<br>■ 224.0.0.6 DR/BDR multicast address | OSPFv3 messages are sent to:<br>■ Neighbor IPv6 link-local address<br>■ FF02::5 all-OSPFv3-routers multicast address<br>■ FF02::6 DR/BDR multicast address |
| Advertise networks | OSPFv2 advertises networks configured using the **network** router configuration command | OSPFv3 advertises networks configured using the **ipv6 ospf** *process-id* **area** *area-id* interface configuration command |
| IP unicast routing | IPv4 unicast routing is enabled by default. | IPv6 unicast routing must be enabled using the **ipv6 unicast-routing** global configuration command. |
| Authentication | OSPFv2 uses either plaintext authentication, MD5, or HMAC-SHA authentication. | OSPFv3 uses IPsec to add authentication for OSPFv3 packets. |

## Link-Local Addresses (8.3.1.4)

Routers running a dynamic routing protocol, such as OSPF, exchange messages between neighbors on the same subnet or link. Routers need to send and receive routing protocol messages only with their directly connected neighbors. These messages are always sent from the source IP address of the router doing the forwarding.

IPv6 link-local addresses are ideal for this purpose. An IPv6 link-local address enables a device to communicate with other IPv6-enabled devices on the same link and only on that link (subnet). Packets with a source or destination link-local address cannot be routed beyond the link from which the packet originated.

As shown in Figure 8-38, OSPFv3 messages are sent using the following:

- **Source IPv6 address**—This is the IPv6 link-local address of the exit interface.

- **Destination IPv6 address**—OSPFv3 packets can be sent to a unicast address using the neighbor IPv6 link-local address. They can also be sent using a multicast address. FF02::5 address is the all-OSPF-routers address, and FF02::6 is the DR/BDR multicast address.

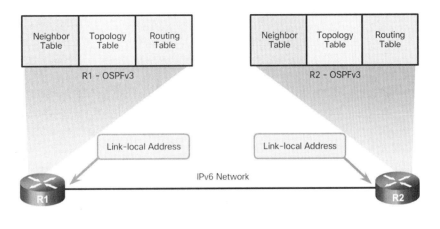

**Figure 8-38**   OSPFv3 Packet Destination

**Activity 8.3.1.5: Compare and Contrast OSPFv2 and OSPFv3**

Refer to the online course to complete this activity.

# Configuring OSPFv3 (8.3.2)

In this topic, you will configure single-area OSPFv3.

## OSPFv3 Network Topology (8.3.2.1)

Figure 8-39 shows the network topology that is used to configure OSPFv3 in this section.

Example 8-25 shows IPv6 unicast routing and the configuration of the global unicast addresses of R1, as identified in the reference topology.

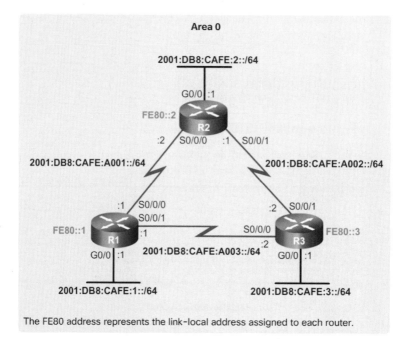

**Figure 8-39**    OSPFv3 Topology

**Example 8-25**    Configuring Global Unicast Addresses on R1

```
R1(config)# ipv6 unicast-routing
R1(config)# interface GigabitEthernet 0/0
R1(config-if)# description R1 LAN
R1(config-if)# ipv6 address 2001:DB8:CAFE:1::1/64
R1(config-if)# no shut
R1(config-if)# interface Serial0/0/0
R1(config-if)# description Link to R2
R1(config-if)# ipv6 address 2001:DB8:CAFE:A001::1/64
R1(config-if)# clock rate 128000
R1(config-if)# no shut
R1(config-if)# interface Serial0/0/1
R1(config-if)# description Link to R3
R1(config-if)# ipv6 address 2001:DB8:CAFE:A003::1/64
R1(config-if)# no shut
R1(config-if)# end
R1#
```

Assume that the interfaces of R2 and R3 have also been configured with their global unicast addresses, as identified in the reference topology.

In this topology, the routers do not have IPv4 addresses configured. Routers with IPv4 and IPv6 addresses configured are referred to as dual-stacked, and a dual-stacked network can have OSPFv2 and OSPFv3 simultaneously enabled.

The steps to configure basic OSPFv3 in a single area are as follows:

**Step 1.** Enable IPv6 unicast routing by using the **ipv6 unicast-routing** command.

**Step 2.** (Optional) Configure link-local addresses.

**Step 3.** Configure a 32-bit router ID in OSPFv3 router configuration mode by using the **router-id** *rid* command.

**Step 4.** Configure optional routing specifics such as adjusting the reference bandwidth.

**Step 5.** (Optional) Configure OSPFv3 interface-specific settings. For example, adjust the interface bandwidth.

**Step 6.** Enable IPv6 routing by using the **ipv6 ospf area** command.

## Link-Local Addresses (8.3.2.2)

Example 8-26 shows the output of the **show ipv6 interface brief** command.

**Example 8-26**   Verifying the IPv6-Enabled Interfaces on R1

```
R1# show ipv6 interface brief
Em0/0                   [administratively down/down]
    unassigned
GigabitEthernet0/0      [up/up]
    FE80::32F7:DFF:FEA3:DA0
    2001:DB8:CAFE:1::1
GigabitEthernet0/1      [administratively down/down]
    unassigned
Serial0/0/0             [up/up]
    FE80::32F7:DFF:FEA3:DA0
    2001:DB8:CAFE:A001::1
Serial0/0/1             [up/up]
    FE80::32F7:DFF:FEA3:DA0
    2001:DB8:CAFE:A003::1
R1#
```

The output in Example 8-26 confirms that the correct global IPv6 addresses have been successfully configured and that the interfaces are enabled. Notice that each interface automatically generated a link-local address.

Link-local addresses are automatically created when an IPv6 global unicast address is assigned to the interface. Global unicast addresses are not required on an interface. However, IPv6 link-local addresses are required on interfaces.

Unless link-local addresses are configured manually, Cisco routers create link-local addresses using FE80::/10 prefix and the EUI-64 process. EUI-64 involves using the 48-bit Ethernet MAC address, inserting FFFE in the middle, and flipping the seventh bit. For serial interfaces, Cisco uses the MAC address of an Ethernet interface. Notice in Figure 8-39 that all three interfaces are using the same link-local address.

## Assigning Link-Local Addresses (8.3.2.3)

Link-local addresses created using the EUI-64 format or, in some cases, random interface IDs can be difficult to recognize and remember. Because IPv6 routing protocols use IPv6 link-local addresses for unicast addressing and next-hop address information in the routing table, it is common practice to make these addresses easily recognizable.

Configuring a link-local address manually provides the ability to create an address that is recognizable and easier to remember. In addition, a router with several interfaces can assign the same link-local address to each IPv6 interface because the link-local address is only required for local communications.

Link-local addresses can be configured manually using the same interface command used to create IPv6 global unicast addresses, **ipv6 address**, but with the **link-local** keyword appended.

A link-local address has a prefix in the range FE80 to FEBF. When an address begins with this hextet (16-bit segment), the **link-local** keyword must follow the address.

Example 8-27 configures the same link-local address FE80::1 on the three R1 interfaces. FE80::1 was chosen to make it easy to remember the link-local addresses of R1.

**Example 8-27**  Configuring Link-Local Addresses on R1

```
R1(config)# interface GigabitEthernet 0/0
R1(config-if)# ipv6 address fe80::1 link-local
R1(config-if)# interface Serial0/0/0
R1(config-if)# ipv6 address fe80::1 link-local
R1(config-if)# interface Serial0/0/1
R1(config-if)# ipv6 address fe80::1 link-local
R1(config-if)#
```

A quick look at the interfaces, as shown in Example 8-28, confirms that the R1 interface link-local addresses have been changed to FE80::1.

**Example 8-28**    Verifying the Link-Local Addresses on R1

```
R1# show ipv6 interface brief
Em0/0                      [administratively down/down]
    unassigned
GigabitEthernet0/0         [up/up]
    FE80::1
    2001:DB8:CAFE:1::1
GigabitEthernet0/1         [administratively down/down]
    unassigned
Serial0/0/0                [up/up]
    FE80::1
    2001:DB8:CAFE:A001::1
Serial0/0/1                [up/up]
    FE80::1
    2001:DB8:CAFE:A003::1
R1#
```

Notice how much easier it is to "read" the link-local addresses in Example 8-28 than in Example 8-27. Assume that R2 and R3 have been configured with FE80::2 and FE80::3, respectively.

## Configuring the OSPFv3 Router ID (8.3.2.4)

The OSPF router ID is assigned in router configuration mode. From this mode, you can configure global OSPFv3 parameters, such as assigning a 32-bit OSPFv3 router ID and reference bandwidth.

Use the **ipv6 router ospf** *process-id* global configuration mode command to enter router configuration mode. As with OSPFv2, the *process-id* value is a number between 1 and 65,535 that is chosen by the network administrator. The *process-id* value is locally significant, which means it does not have to match other OSPF routers to establish adjacencies with those neighbors.

OSPFv3 requires a 32-bit router ID to be assigned before OSPF can be enabled on an interface. The logic diagram in Figure 8-40 displays how a router ID is chosen:

1. Like OSPFv2, OSPFv3 uses an explicitly configured router ID first, using the **router-id** *rid* command.

2. If none are configured, the router uses the highest configured IPv4 address of a loopback interface.

3. If none are configured, the router uses the highest configured IPv4 address of an active interface.

4. If there are no sources of IPv4 addresses on a router, the router displays a console message that requires the configuration of the router ID manually.

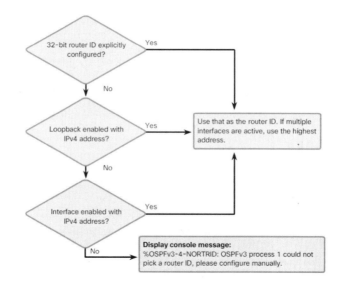

**Figure 8-40** Router ID Order of Precedence

Routers R1, R2, and R3 are to be assigned the router IDs indicated in the topology in Figure 8-41.

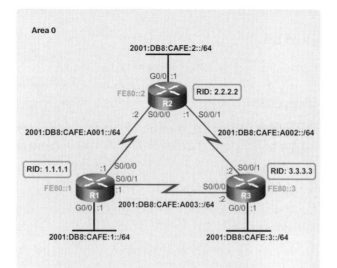

**Figure 8-41** OSPFv3 Topology with Router IDs

The **router-id** *rid* router configuration mode command used to assign a router ID in OSPFv2 is the same command used in OSPFv3.

Example 8-29 assigns the OSPFv3 router ID and adjusts the reference bandwidth on R1.

**Example 8-29**  Assigning a Router ID to R1

```
R1(config)# ipv6 router ospf 10
R1(config-rtr)#
*Mar 29 11:21:53.739: %OSPFv3-4-NORTRID: Process OSPFv3-1-IPv6 could not pick a
  router-id, please configure manually
R1(config-rtr)# router-id 1.1.1.1
R1(config-rtr)# auto-cost reference-bandwidth 1000
% OSPFv3-1-IPv6:  Reference bandwidth is changed.
        Please ensure reference bandwidth is consistent across all routers.
R1(config-rtr)# end
R1# show ipv6 protocols
IPv6 Routing Protocol is "connected"
IPv6 Routing Protocol is "ND"
IPv6 Routing Protocol is "ospf 10"
  Router ID 1.1.1.1
  Number of areas: 0 normal, 0 stub, 0 nssa
  Redistribution:
    None
R1#
```

Notice the informational console message generated when the **ipv6 router ospf** command is entered. Next, R1 is assigned the router ID 1.1.1.1 and the reference bandwidth has been adjusted to account for the GigabitEthernet interfaces. Again, an information message is generated stating that same **auto-cost reference-bandwidth** command must be configured on all routers in the routing domain.

The **show ipv6 protocols** command is used to verify that the OSPFv3 process ID 10 is using the router ID 1.1.1.1.

Assume that R2 and R3 have been configured with router IDs 2.2.2.2 and 3.3.3.3, respectively. Their reference bandwidth has also been adjusted accordingly.

## Modifying an OSPFv3 Router ID (8.3.2.5)

Router IDs sometimes must be changed, such as if the network administrator has established a new router ID scheme. However, after an OSPFv3 router establishes a router ID, that router ID cannot be changed until the router is reloaded or the OSPFv3 process is cleared.

In Example 8-30, notice that the current router ID is 10.1.1.1. The OSPFv3 router ID should be 1.1.1.1.

**Example 8-30**   Verifying the Router ID

```
R1# show ipv6 protocols
IPv6 Routing Protocol is "connected"
IPv6 Routing Protocol is "ND"
IPv6 Routing Protocol is "ospf 10"
  Router ID 10.1.1.1
  Number of areas: 0 normal, 0 stub, 0 nssa
  Redistribution:
    None
R1#
```

In Example 8-31, the router ID 1.1.1.1 is being assigned to R1.

**Example 8-31**   Change the Router ID on R1

```
R1(config)# ipv6 router ospf 10
R1(config-rtr)# router-id 1.1.1.1
R1(config-rtr)# end
R1#
```

**Note**

Clearing the OSPF process is the preferred method for resetting the router ID.

In Example 8-32, the OSPFv3 routing process is cleared using the **clear ipv6 ospf process** privileged EXEC mode command. Doing this forces OSPF on R1 to renegotiate neighbor adjacencies using the new router ID.

The **show ipv6 protocols** command verifies that the router ID has changed.

**Example 8-32**   Clearing the OSPF Process

```
R1# clear ipv6 ospf process
Reset selected OSPFv3 processes? [no]: y
R1#
R1# show ipv6 protocols
IPv6 Routing Protocol is "connected"
IPv6 Routing Protocol is "ND"
IPv6 Routing Protocol is "ospf 10"
  Router ID 1.1.1.1
  Number of areas: 0 normal, 0 stub, 0 nssa
  Redistribution:
    None
R1#
```

### Enabling OSPFv3 on Interfaces (8.3.2.6)

OSPFv3 uses a different method than OSPFv2 to enable an interface for OSPF. OSPFv3 is enabled on an interface rather than from router configuration mode, as with OSPFv2. Therefore, the **network** router configuration mode command is not available in OSPFv3.

To enable OSPFv3 on an interface, use the **ipv6 ospf** *process-id* **area** *area-id* interface configuration mode command. The *process-id* value identifies the specific routing process and must be the same as the process ID used to create the routing process in the **ipv6 router ospf** *process-id* command.

The *area-id* value is the area to be associated with the OSPFv3 interface. Although any value could be configured for the area, 0 was selected here because area 0 is the backbone area to which all other areas must attach, as shown in Figure 8-41. This helps in the migration to multiarea OSPF, if the need arises.

In Example 8-33, OSPFv3 is enabled on the R1 interfaces by using the **ipv6 ospf 10 area 0** command, and the **show ipv6 ospf interface brief** command is used to verify the status of OSPFv3 interfaces.

**Example 8-33**   Enabling OSPFv3 on the R1 Interfaces

```
R1(config)# interface GigabitEthernet 0/0
R1(config-if)# ipv6 ospf 10 area 0
R1(config-if)# interface Serial0/0/0
R1(config-if)# ipv6 ospf 10 area 0
R1(config-if)# interface Serial0/0/1
R1(config-if)# ipv6 ospf 10 area 0
R1(config-if)# end
R1#
R1# show ipv6 ospf interfaces brief
Interface    PID   Area            Intf ID    Cost   State Nbrs F/C
Se0/0/1      10    0               7          15625  P2P    0/0
Se0/0/0      10    0               6          647    P2P    0/0
Gi0/0        10    0               3          1      WAIT   0/0
R1#
```

The output in Example 8-33 confirms that the three interfaces have OSPFv3 configured. However, notice that the Nbrs field is displaying 0/0. This indicates that R2 and R3 have not yet been configured for OSPFv3.

After R2 and R3 are configured for OSPFv3, the Nbrs field increases accordingly.

## Verify OSPFv3 (8.3.3)

In this topic, you will verify single-area OSPFv3.

## Verify OSPFv3 Neighbors (8.3.3.1)

Use the **show ipv6 ospf neighbor** command to verify that the router has formed an adjacency with its neighboring routers.

Two routers have not formed an OSPFv3 adjacency if the router ID of the neighboring router is not displayed or if it does not show as being in the Full state.

If two routers do not establish a neighbor adjacency, link-state information is not exchanged. Incomplete LSDBs can cause inaccurate SPF trees and routing tables. Routes to destination networks may not exist or may not be the most optimum path.

Example 8-34 displays the neighbor adjacency of R1.

**Example 8-34**   Verifying R1 OSPFv3 Neighbors

```
R1# show ipv6 ospf neighbor


          OSPFv3 Router with ID (1.1.1.1) (Process ID 10)


Neighbor ID     Pri   State           Dead Time    Interface ID    Interface
3.3.3.3          0    FULL/  -        00:00:39     6               Serial0/0/1
2.2.2.2          0    FULL/  -        00:00:36     6               Serial0/0/0
R1#
```

Table 8-13 explains the significance of field names in the output in Example 8-34.

**Table 8-13    show ip ospf neighbor** Output Explained

| Field in Output | Description |
|---|---|
| Neighbor ID | ■ The router ID of the neighboring router. |
| Pri | ■ The OSPFv3 priority value of the interface that is used in the DR and BDR election. |
| State | ■ The OSPFv3 state of the interface.<br>■ Full state means that the router and its neighbor have identical OSPFv3 LSDBs. |
| Dead Time | ■ The amount of time remaining that the router waits to receive an OSPFv3 Hello packet from the neighbor before declaring the neighbor down.<br>■ This value is reset when the interface receives a Hello packet. |
| Interface ID | ■ The interface ID or link ID. |
| Interface | ■ The interface on which this router has formed an adjacency with the neighbor. |

## Verify OSPFv3 Protocol Settings (8.3.3.2)

As shown in Example 8-35, using the **show ipv6 protocols** command is a quick way to verify vital OSPFv3 configuration information, including the OSPFv3 process ID, the router ID, and the interfaces enabled for OSPFv3.

**Example 8-35**  Verifying OSPFv3 Protocol Setting for R1

```
R1# show ipv6 protocols
IPv6 Routing Protocol is "connected"
IPv6 Routing Protocol is "ND"
IPv6 Routing Protocol is "ospf 10"
  Router ID 1.1.1.1
  Number of areas: 1 normal, 0 stub, 0 nssa
  Interfaces (Area 0):
    Serial0/0/1
    Serial0/0/0
    GigabitEthernet0/0
  Redistribution:
    None
R1#
```

You can also use the **show ipv6 ospf** command to examine the OSPFv3 process ID and router ID. This command displays the OSPFv3 area information and the last time the SPF algorithm was calculated.

## Verify OSPFv3 Interfaces (8.3.3.3)

To view a status summary of OSPFv3-enabled interfaces on R1, use the **show ipv6 ospf interface brief** command, as shown in Example 8-36.

**Example 8-36**  Verifying R1's OSPF Interfaces

```
R1# show ipv6 ospf interface brief
Interface    PID    Area           Intf ID    Cost   State Nbrs F/C
Se0/0/1      10     0              7          15625  P2P   1/1
Se0/0/0      10     0              6          647    P2P   1/1
Gi0/0        10     0              3          1      DR    0/0
R1#
```

Notice how the serial interfaces have each identified an adjacent OSPFv3 neighbor.

To verify OSPFv3 interface settings, use the **show ipv6 ospf interface** command. This command provides a detailed list for every OSPFv3-enabled interface.

Example 8-37 shows that specifying the interface name provides detailed OSPFv3 information for Serial 0/0/1 on R2.

**Example 8-37**    Verifying the OSPFv3 Interface Details

```
R2# show ipv6 ospf interface serial0/0/1
Serial0/0/1 is up, line protocol is up
  Link Local Address FE80::2, Interface ID 7
  Area 0, Process ID 10, Instance ID 0, Router ID 2.2.2.2
  Network Type POINT_TO_POINT, Cost: 647
  Transmit Delay is 1 sec, State POINT_TO_POINT
  Timer intervals configured, Hello 10, Dead 40, Wait 40, Retransmit 5
    Hello due in 00:00:01
  Graceful restart helper support enabled
  Index 1/3/3, flood queue length 0
  Next 0x0(0)/0x0(0)/0x0(0)
  Last flood scan length is 2, maximum is 4
  Last flood scan time is 0 msec, maximum is 0 msec
  Neighbor Count is 1, Adjacent neighbor count is 1
    Adjacent with neighbor 3.3.3.3
  Suppress hello for 0 neighbor(s)
R2#
```

## Verify the IPv6 Routing Table (8.3.3.4)

In Example 8-38, the **show ipv6 route ospf** command provides specifics about OSPFv3 routes in the routing table.

**Example 8-38**    Verifying the IPv6 Routing Table of R1

```
R1# show ipv6 route ospf
IPv6 Routing Table - default - 10 entries
Codes: C - Connected, L - Local, S - Static, U - Per-user Static route
       B - BGP, R - RIP, H - NHRP, I1 - ISIS L1
       I2 - ISIS L2, IA - ISIS interarea, IS - ISIS summary, D - EIGRP
       EX - EIGRP external, ND - ND Default, NDp - ND Prefix, DCE - Destination
       NDr - Redirect, O - OSPF Intra, OI - OSPF Inter, OE1 - OSPF ext 1
       OE2 - OSPF ext 2, ON1 - OSPF NSSA ext 1, ON2 - OSPF NSSA ext 2
O    2001:DB8:CAFE:2::/64 [110/657]
     via FE80::2, Serial0/0/0
O    2001:DB8:CAFE:3::/64 [110/1304]
     via FE80::2, Serial0/0/0
O    2001:DB8:CAFE:A002::/64 [110/1294]
     via FE80::2, Serial0/0/0
R1#
```

**Packet Tracer 8.3.3.5: Configuring Basic OSPFv3**

In this activity, the IPv6 addressing is already configured. You are responsible for configuring the three-router topology with a basic single-area OSPFv3 and then verifying connectivity between the end devices.

**Lab 8.3.3.6: Configuring Basic Single-Area OSPFv3**

Refer to *Scaling Networks v6 Labs & Study Guide* and the online course to complete this activity.

In this lab, you will complete the following objectives:

- Part 1: Build the Network and Configure Basic Device Settings
- Part 2: Configure OSPFv3 Routing
- Part 3: Configure OSPFv3 Passive Interfaces

# Summary (8.4)

**Activity 8.4.1.1: Stepping Through OSPFv3**

Refer to *Scaling Networks v6 Labs & Study Guide* and the online course to complete this activity.

**Scenario**

This class activity is designed for groups of three students. The objective is to review the shortest path first (SPF) routing process.

You will design and address a network, communicate the network address scheme and operation of network links to your group members, and compute the SPF.

Complete the steps shown on the PDF for this class activity.

If you have time, share your network design and the SPF process with another group.

Packet Tracer
☐ Challenge

**Packet Tracer 8.4.1.2: Skills Integration Challenge**

In this skills integration challenge, your focus is OSPFv2 and OSPFv3 configurations. You will configure IP addressing for all devices. Then you will configure OSPFv2 routing for the IPv4 portion of the network and OSPFv3 routing for the IPv6 portion of the network. One router will be configured with both IPv4 and IPv6 configurations. Finally, you will verify your configurations and test connectivity between end devices.

The current version of OSPF for IPv4 is OSPFv2, introduced in RFC 1247 and updated in RFC 2328 by John Moy. In 1999, OSPFv3 for IPv6 was published in RFC 2740.

OSPF is a link-state routing protocol with a default administrative distance of 110, and it is denoted in the routing table with the route source code **O**.

OSPFv2 is enabled with the **router ospf** *process-id* global configuration mode command. The *process-id* value is locally significant, which means it does not need to match other OSPFv2 routers to establish adjacencies with those neighbors.

The **network** command used with OSPFv2 has the same function as when used with other IGP routing protocols but with slightly different syntax. The *wildcard-mask* value is the inverse of the subnet mask, and the *area-id* value should be set to 0.

By default, OSPF Hello packets are sent every 10 seconds on multiaccess and point-to-point segments and every 30 seconds on NBMA segments (Frame Relay, X.25, ATM), and OSPF uses these packets to establish neighbor adjacencies. The dead interval is four times the hello interval, by default.

For routers to become adjacent, their hello intervals, dead intervals, network types, and subnet masks must match. Use the **show ip ospf neighbors** command to verify OSPFv2 adjacencies.

OSPF elects a DR to act as a collection and distribution point for LSAs sent and received in the multiaccess network. A BDR is elected to assume the role of the DR if the DR fails. All other routers are known as DROTHERs. All routers send their LSAs to the DR, which then floods the LSA to all other routers in the multiaccess network.

The **show ip protocols** command is used to verify important OSPFv2 configuration information, including the OSPF process ID, the router ID, and the networks the router is advertising.

OSPFv3 is enabled on an interface and not under router configuration mode. OSPFv3 needs link-local addresses to be configured. IPv6 unicast routing must be enabled for OSPFv3. A 32-bit router ID is required before an interface can be enabled for OSPFv3. Verification commands similar to those used for OSPFv2 are used for OSPFv3.

# Practice

The following activities provide practice with the topics introduced in this chapter. The Labs and Class Activities are available in the companion *Scaling Networks v6 Labs & Study Guide* (ISBN 978-1-58713-433-3). The Packet Tracer activity instructions are also in the Labs & Study Guide. The PKA files are found in the online course.

**Class Activities**

Class Activity 8.0.1.2: Can Submarines Swim?

Class Activity 8.4.1.1: Stepping Through OSPFv3

**Labs**

Lab 8.2.4.5: Configuring Basic Single-Area OSPFv2

Lab 8.3.3.6: Configuring Basic Single-Area OSPFv3

Packet Tracer
☐ Activity

**Packet Tracer Activities**

Packet Tracer 8.2.2.7: Configuring OSPFv2 in a Single-area

Packet Tracer 8.3.3.5: Configuring Basic OSPFv3

Packet Tracer 8.4.1.2: Skills Integration Challenge

# Check Your Understanding Questions

Complete all the review questions listed here to test your understanding of the topics and concepts in this chapter. The appendix "Answers to 'Check Your Understanding' Questions" lists the answers.

1. A router is participating in an OSPFv2 domain. What will always happen if the dead interval expires before the router receives a Hello packet from an adjacent DROTHER OSPF router?

   A. A new dead interval timer of four times the hello interval will start.

   B. OSPF will remove that neighbor from the router link-state database.

   C. OSPF will run a new DR/BDR election.

   D. SPF will run and determine which neighbor router is down.

2. Which three statements describe the similarities between OSPFv2 and OSPFv3? (Choose three.)

   A. They both are link-state protocols.

   B. They both have unicast routing enabled by default.

   C. They both share the concept of multiple areas.

   D. They both support IPsec for authentication.

   E. They both use the global address as the source address when sending OSPF messages.

   F. They both use the same DR/BDR election process.

3. Which OSPF component is identical in all routers in an OSPF area after convergence?

   A. adjacency database

   B. link-state database

   C. routing table

   D. SPF tree

4. Which three statements describe features of the OSPF topology table? (Choose three.)

   A. After convergence, the table contains only the lowest-cost route entries for all known networks.

   B. It is a link-state database that represents the network topology.

   C. Its contents are the result of running the SPF algorithm.

   D. The table can be viewed via the **show ip ospf database** command.

   E. The topology table contains feasible successor routes.

   F. When converged, all routers in an area have identical topology tables.

5. Which of the following is used to create the OSPF neighbor table?

   A. Adjacency database

   B. Link-state database

   C. Forwarding database

   D. Routing table

6. What is a function of OSPF Hello packets?

   A. to discover neighbors and build adjacencies between them

   B. to ensure database synchronization between routers

   C. to request specific link-state records from neighbor routers

   D. to send specifically requested link-state records

7. Which OSPF packet contains the different types of link-state advertisements?

   A. Hello

   B. DBD

   C. LSAck

   D. LSR

   E. LSU

8. What are the two purposes of an OSPF router ID? (Choose two.)

   A. To enable the SPF algorithm to determine the lowest-cost path to remote networks

   B. To facilitate router participation in the election of the designated router

   C. To facilitate the establishment of network convergence

   D. To facilitate the transition of the OSPF neighbor state to Full

   E. To uniquely identify the router within the OSPF domain

9. What is the first criterion used by OSPF routers to elect a DR?

   A. Highest priority

   B. Highest IP address

   C. Highest router ID

   D. Highest MAC address

**10.** Which wildcard mask would be used to advertise the 192.168.5.96/27 network as part of an OSPF configuration?

A. 0.0.0.31

B. 0.0.0.32

C. 255.255.255.223

D. 255.255.255.224

**11.** What are two factors that will prevent two routers from forming an OSPFv2 adjacency? (Choose two.)

A. Mismatched Cisco IOS versions are used

B. Mismatched Ethernet interface (for example, Fa0/0 to G0/0)

C. Mismatched OSPF hello or dead timers

D. Mismatched subnet masks on the link interfaces

E. Use of private IP addresses on the link interfaces

**12.** What command would be used to determine whether a routing protocol–initiated relationship had been made with an adjacent router?

A. **ping**

B. **show ip interface brief**

C. **show ip ospf neighbor**

D. **show ip protocols**

**13.** Which function works differently in OSPFv3 than in OSPFv2?

A. Authentication

B. Election process

C. Hello mechanism

D. Metric calculation

E. OSPF packet types

**14.** Which three addresses could be used as the destination address for OSPFv3 messages? (Choose three.)

A. FE80::1

B. FF02::5

C. FF02::6

D. FF02::A

E. FF02::1:2

F. 2001:db8:cafe::1

15. What does a Cisco router use automatically to create link-local addresses on serial interfaces when OSPFv3 is implemented?

    A. An Ethernet interface MAC address available on the router, the FE80::/10 prefix, and the EUI-64 process

    B. The FE80::/10 prefix and the EUI-48 process

    C. The highest MAC address available on the router, the FE80::/10 prefix, and the EUI-48 process

    D. The MAC address of the serial interface, the FE80::/10 prefix, and the EUI-64 process

16. A network administrator enters the command **ipv6 router ospf 64** in global configuration mode. What is the result of this command?

    A. The router is assigned an autonomous system number of 64.

    B. The router is assigned a router ID of 64.

    C. The reference bandwidth is set to 64 Mbps.

    D. The OSPFv3 process is assigned an ID of 64.

17. Single-area OSPFv3 has been enabled on a router via the **ipv6 router ospf 20** command. Which command enables this OSPFv3 process on an interface of that router?

    A. **ipv6 ospf 0 area 0**

    B. **ipv6 ospf 0 area 20**

    C. **ipv6 ospf 20 area 0**

    D. **ipv6 ospf 20 area 20**

18. Which command verifies that a router that is running OSPFv3 has formed an adjacency with other routers in its OSPF area?

    A. **show ipv6 interface brief**

    B. **show ipv6 ospf neighbor**

    C. **show ipv6 route ospf**

    D. **show running-configuration**

19. Which command provides information specific to OSPFv3 routes in the routing table?

    A. **show ip route**

    B. **show ip route ospf**

    C. **show ipv6 route**

    D. **show ipv6 route ospf**

# CHAPTER 9

# Multiarea OSPF

## Objectives

Upon completion of this chapter, you will be able to answer the following questions:

- How does multiarea OSPF operate in a small to medium-sized business network?

- How do you implement multiarea OSPFv2 and OSPFv3?

## Key Terms

This chapter uses the following key terms. You can find the definitions in the Glossary.

# Introduction (9.0.1.1)

Multiarea OSPF is used to divide a large OSPF network. Having too many routers in one area increases the load on the CPU and creates a large link-state database. In this chapter, directions are provided to effectively partition a large single area into multiple areas. Area 0, used in a single-area OSPF, is known as the backbone area.

Discussion in this chapter is focused on the LSAs exchanged between areas. In addition, activities for configuring OSPFv2 and OSPFv3 are provided. The chapter concludes with the **show** commands used to verify OSPF configurations.

**Class Activity 9.0.1.2: Leaving on a Jet Plane**

Refer to *Scaling Networks v6 Labs & Study Guide* and the online course to complete this activity.

You and a classmate are starting a new airline to serve your continent.

In addition to your core area or headquarters airport, you will locate and map four intra-continental airport service areas and one transcontinental airport service area that can be used for additional source and destination travel.

Use the blank world map provided to design your airport locations. Additional instructions for completing this activity can be found in the accompanying PDF.

# Multiarea OSPF Operation (9.1)

In this section, you will learn how multiarea OSPF operates in a small to medium-sized business network.

## Why Multiarea OSPF? (9.1.1)

In this topic, you will learn why multiarea OSPF is used.

### Single-Area OSPF (9.1.1.1)

Single-area OSPF is useful in smaller networks where the web of router links is not complex, and paths to individual destinations are easily deduced. However, as illustrated in Figure 9-1, several issues can occur if an area becomes too big. Table 9-1 describes these issues.

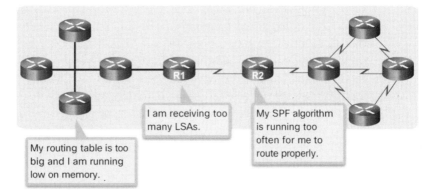

**Figure 9-1**   Issues in a Large OSPF Single Area

**Table 9-1**   Large Single-Area OSPF Issues

| Issue | Description |
|---|---|
| Large routing tables | ■ OSPF does not perform route summarization by default. |
| | ■ Therefore, routing tables can become very large in big networks. |
| Large link-state database | ■ Each router maintains detailed information about every network in the area. |
| | ■ The LSDB can become very big. |
| Frequent SPF calculations | ■ In a large network with many network changes, each router spends many CPU cycles recalculating the SPF algorithm and updating the routing table. |

To make OSPF more efficient and scalable, OSPF supports hierarchical routing using areas. An OSPF area is a group of routers that share the same link-state information in their link-state databases.

**Note**

OSPF route summarization is beyond the scope of this course.

## Multiarea OSPF (9.1.1.2)

Dividing a large OSPF area into smaller areas is called multiarea OSPF. Multiarea OSPF is useful in large network deployments to reduce processing and memory overhead.

For instance, any time a router receives new information about the topology—for example, with additions, deletions, or modifications of a link—the router must rerun the SPF algorithm, create a new SPF tree, and update the routing table. The SPF algorithm is CPU intensive, and the time it takes for calculation depends on the size of the area. Having many routers in one area makes the LSDB larger and increases the load on the CPU. Therefore, arranging routers into areas effectively partitions one potentially large database into smaller and more manageable databases.

### Note

It is often stated that there should be no more than 50 routers per OSPF area. However, the maximum number of routers to use in an area depends on several factors, including the network design, type of area, type of router platform, and media available. It is recommended to consult with Cisco certified partners for specific network design assistance.

Multiarea OSPF requires a hierarchical network design. The main area is called the backbone area (area 0), and all other areas must connect to the backbone area. With hierarchical routing, routing occurs between the areas (interarea routing). However, the CPU-intensive routing operation of recalculating the SPF algorithm is done only for routes within an area. A change in one area does not cause an SPF algorithm recalculation in other areas.

As shown in Figure 9-2, the hierarchical topology possibilities of multiarea OSPF have multiple advantages:

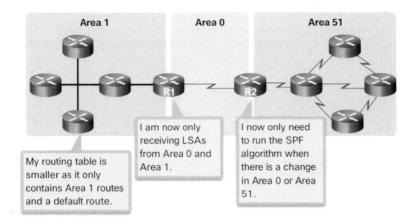

**Figure 9-2**   Multiarea OSPF Advantages

- **Smaller routing tables**—There are fewer routing table entries because network addresses can be summarized between areas. Also, routers in an area may receive default routes only for destinations outside their area. For example, R1 summarizes the routes from area 1 to area 0, and R2 summarizes the routes from area 51 to area 0. R1 and R2 also propagate default static routes to area 1 and area 51.

- **Reduced link-state update overhead**—Multiarea OSPF minimizes processing and memory requirements because there are fewer routers exchanging LSAs with detailed topology information.

- **Reduced frequency of SPF calculations**—Multiarea OSPF localizes the impact of a topology change within an area. For instance, it minimizes routing update impact because LSA flooding stops at the area boundary.

Table 9-2 lists advantages of using a multiarea OSPF hierarchical topology design.

**Table 9-2**  Multiarea OSPF Advantages

| Advantage | Description |
|---|---|
| Smaller routing tables | <ul><li>There are fewer routing table entries because network addresses can be summarized between areas.</li><li>Route summarization is not enabled by default.</li></ul> |
| Reduced link-state update overhead | <ul><li>Designing multiarea OSPF with smaller areas minimizes processing and memory requirements.</li></ul> |
| Reduced frequency of SPF calculations | <ul><li>Multiarea OSPF localizes the impact of a topology change within an area.</li><li>For instance, it minimizes routing update impact because LSA flooding stops at the area boundary.</li></ul> |

As illustrated in Figure 9-3, if a link fails between two internal routers in area 51, only the routers in area 51 exchange LSAs and run the SPF algorithm for this event.

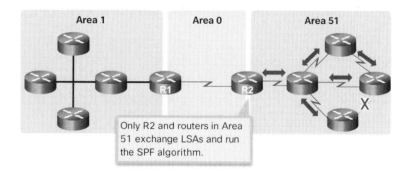

Only R2 and routers in Area 51 exchange LSAs and run the SPF algorithm.

**Figure 9-3**  Multiarea Link Failure Example

R1 receives a different type of LSA from area 51 and does not recalculate the SPF algorithm. The different types of LSAs are discussed later in this chapter.

## OSPF Two-Layer Area Hierarchy (9.1.1.3)

Multiarea OSPF is implemented in a two-layer area hierarchy:

■ **Backbone (transit) area**—The primary function of this OSPF area is the fast and efficient movement of IP packets. Backbone areas interconnect with other OSPF area types. Generally, end users are not found within a backbone area. The backbone area is also called OSPF area 0. Hierarchical networking defines area 0 as the core to which all other areas directly connect (see Figure 9-4).

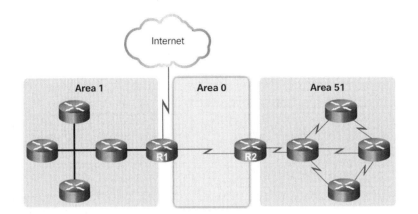

**Figure 9-4**   Backbone (Transit) Area

■ **Regular (non-backbone) area**—This area connects users and resources. Regular areas are usually set up along functional or geographic groupings. By default, a regular area does not allow traffic from another area to use its links to reach other areas. All traffic from other areas must cross a transit area (see Figure 9-5).

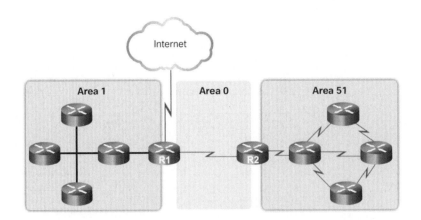

**Figure 9-5**   Regular (Non-backbone) Area

**Note**

A regular area can have a number of subtypes, including a standard area, stub area, totally stubby area, and not-so-stubby area (NSSA). Stub areas, totally stubby areas, and NSSAs are beyond the scope of this chapter.

OSPF enforces this rigid two-layer area hierarchy. The underlying physical connectivity of the network must map to the two-layer area structure, with all non-backbone areas attaching directly to area 0. All traffic moving from one area to another area must traverse the backbone area. This traffic is referred to as *interarea traffic*.

The optimal number of routers per area varies based on factors such as network stability, but Cisco recommends the following guidelines:

- An area should have no more than 50 routers.

- A router should not be in more than three areas.

- Any single router should not have more than 60 neighbors.

## Types of OSPF Routers (9.1.1.4)

OSPF routers of different types control the traffic that goes into and out of areas. The OSPF routers are categorized based on the function they perform in the routing domain.

There are four different types of OSPF routers:

- *Internal router*—This type of router has all its interfaces in the same area. All internal routers in an area have identical LSDBs (see Figure 9-6).

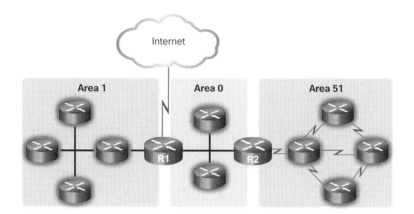

**Figure 9-6**  Internal Routers

- *Backbone router*—This type of router is used in the backbone area, area 0 (see Figure 9-7).

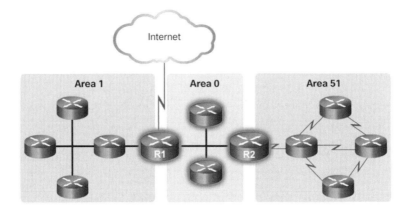

**Figure 9-7**    Backbone Routers

- **Area border router (ABR)**—This type of router has interfaces attached to multiple areas. It must maintain separate LSDBs for each area it is connected to and can route between areas. ABRs are exit points for the area, which means routing information destined for another area can get there only via the ABR of the local area. ABRs can be configured to summarize the routing information from the LSDBs of their attached areas. ABRs distribute the routing information into the backbone. The backbone routers then forward the information to the other ABRs. In a multiarea network, an area can have one or more ABRs (see Figure 9-8).

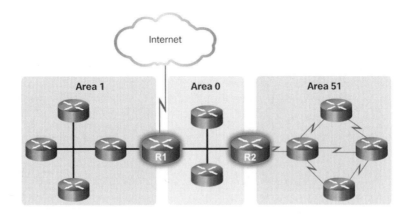

**Figure 9-8**    Area Border Routers (ABRs)

■ *Autonomous System Boundary Router (ASBR)*—This type of router has at least one interface attached to an external internetwork. An external network is a network that is not part of this OSPF routing domain (for example, a network connection to an ISP). An ASBR can import external network information to the OSPF network, and vice versa, using a process called *route redistribution* (see Figure 9-9).

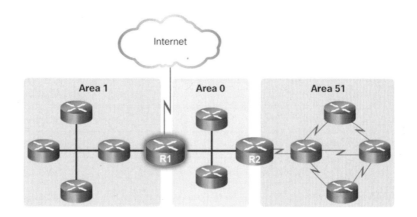

**Figure 9-9**   Autonomous System Boundary Router (ASBR)

Redistribution in multiarea OSPF occurs when an ASBR connects different routing domains (for example, EIGRP and RIP) and configures them to exchange and advertise routing information between those routing domains. A static route, including a default route, can also be redistributed as an external route into the OSPF routing domain.

A router can be classified as more than one router type. For example, if a router connects to area 0 and area 1, and in addition maintains routing information for external networks, it falls under three different classifications: a backbone router, an ABR, and an ASBR.

Interactive
Graphic

**Activity 9.1.1.5: Identify the Multiarea OSPF Terminology**

Refer to the online course to complete this activity.

## Multiarea OSPF LSA Operation (9.1.2)

In this topic, you will learn how multiarea OSPFv2 uses link-state advertisements (LSAs).

## OSPF LSA Types (9.1.2.1)

LSAs are the building blocks of the OSPF LSDB. Individually, they act as database records and provide specific OSPF network details. In combination, they describe the entire topology of an OSPF network or area.

The RFCs for OSPF currently specify up to 11 different LSA types. However, any implementation of multiarea OSPF must support LSA type 1 to LSA type 5.

Although all 11 LSA types are shown in Table 9-3, the focus of this topic is on the first five types.

**Table 9-3**   OSPF LSA Types

| LSA Type | Description |
| --- | --- |
| *LSA Type 1* | Router LSA |
| *LSA Type 2* | Network LSA |
| *LSA Type 3* and *LSA Type 4* | Summary LSAs |
| *LSA Type 5* | AS external LSA |
| LSA Type 6 | Multicast OSPF LSA |
| LSA Type 7 | Defined for NSSAs |
| LSA Type 8 | External attributes LSA for Border Gateway Protocol (BGP) |
| LSA Type 9, LSA Type 10, and LSA Type 11 | Opaque LSAs |

Each router link is defined as an LSA type. The LSA includes a link ID field that identifies, by network number and mask, the object to which the link connects. Depending on the type, the link ID has different meanings. LSAs differ in terms of how they are generated and propagated within the routing domain.

**Note**

OSPFv3 includes additional LSA types.

## OSPF LSA Type 1 (9.1.2.2)

As shown in Figure 9-10, all routers advertise their directly connected OSPF-enabled links in a type 1 LSA and forward their network information to OSPF neighbors. The

LSA contains a list of the directly connected interfaces, link types, neighbors, and link states.

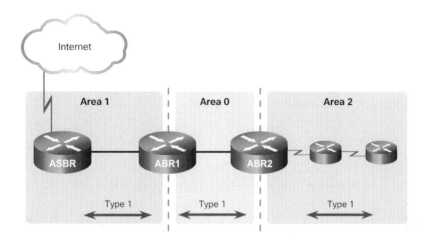

**Figure 9-10**    Type 1 LSA Message Propagation

Type 1 LSAs are also referred to as *router link entries*.

Type 1 LSAs are flooded only within the area in which they originated. ABRs subsequently advertise the networks learned from the type 1 LSAs to other areas as type 3 LSAs.

The type 1 LSA link ID is identified by the router ID of the originating router.

## OSPF LSA Type 2 (9.1.2.3)

A type 2 LSA exists only for multiaccess and nonbroadcast multiaccess (NBMA) networks that have a DR elected and at least two routers on the multiaccess segment. A type 2 LSA contains the router ID and IP address of the DR, along with the router IDs of all other routers on the multiaccess segment. A type 2 LSA is created for every multiaccess network in the area.

The purpose of a type 2 LSA is to give other routers information about multiaccess networks within the same area.

The DR floods type 2 LSAs only within the area in which they originated. Type 2 LSAs are not forwarded outside an area.

Type 2 LSAs are also referred to as *network link entries*.

In Figure 9-11, ABR1 is the DR for the Ethernet network in area 1.

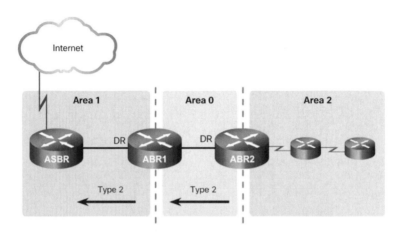

**Figure 9-11**   Type 2 LSA Message Propagation

ABR1 generates the type 2 LSA and forwards it into area 1. ABR2 is the DR for the multiaccess network in area 0. There are no multiaccess networks in area 2, and therefore no type 2 LSAs are ever propagated in that area.

The link-state ID for a network LSA is the IP interface address of the DR that advertises it.

## OSPF LSA Type 3 (9.1.2.4)

ABRs use type 3 LSAs to advertise networks from other areas. ABRs collect type 1 LSAs in the LSDB. After an OSPF area has converged, the ABR creates a type 3 LSA for each of its learned OSPF networks. Therefore, an ABR with many OSPF routes must create type 3 LSAs for each network.

In Figure 9-12, ABR1 and ABR2 flood type 3 LSAs from one area to other areas.

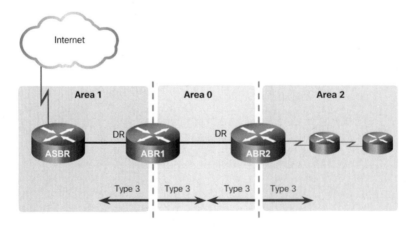

**Figure 9-12**   Type 3 LSA Message Propagation

ABR1 propagates the area 1 information into area 0, using type 3 LSAs. ABR1 also propagates the area 0 information into area 1, using type 3 LSAs. ABR2 does the same thing for area 2 and area 0. In a large OSPF deployment with many networks, propagating type 3 LSAs can cause significant flooding problems. For this reason, it is strongly recommended that manual route summarization be configured on the ABR.

The link-state ID is set to the network number, and the mask is also advertised.

Receiving a type 3 LSA into an area does not cause a router to run the SPF algorithm. The routes being advertised in the type 3 LSAs are appropriately added to or deleted from the router's routing table, but a full SPF calculation is not necessary.

## OSPF LSA Type 4 (9.1.2.5)

Type 4 and type 5 LSAs are used collectively to identify an ASBR and advertise external networks into an OSPF routing domain.

A type 4 summary LSA is generated by an ABR only when an ASBR exists within an area. A type 4 LSA identifies the ASBR and provides a route to it. All traffic destined to an external network requires routing table knowledge of the ASBR that originated the external routes.

In Figure 9-13, the ASBR sends a type 1 LSA, identifying itself as an ASBR.

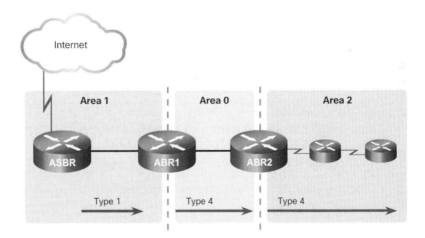

**Figure 9-13**    Type 4 LSA Message Propagation

The LSA includes a special bit known as the external bit (e bit) that is used to identify the router as an ASBR. When ABR1 receives the type 1 LSA, it notices the e bit, builds a type 4 LSA, and then floods the type 4 LSA to the backbone (area 0). Subsequent ABRs flood the type 4 LSA into other areas.

The link-state ID is set to the ASBR's router ID.

### OSPF LSA Type 5 (9.1.2.6)

Type 5 external LSAs describe routes to networks outside the OSPF routing domain. Type 5 LSAs are originated by the ASBR and are flooded to the entire routing domain.

Type 5 LSAs are also referred to as *external LSA entries*.

In Figure 9-14, the ASBR generates type 5 LSAs for each external route and floods them into the area.

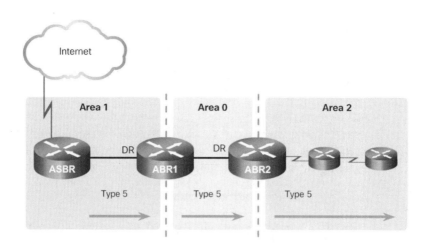

**Figure 9-14**   Type 5 LSA Message Propagation

Subsequent ABRs also flood the type 5 LSA into other areas. Routers in other areas use the information from the type 5 LSA to reach the external routes.

In a large OSPF deployment with many networks, propagating multiple type 5 LSAs can cause significant flooding problems. For this reason, it is strongly recommended that manual route summarization be configured on the ASBR.

The link-state ID is the external network number.

**Interactive Graphic**

**Activity 9.1.2.7: Identify the OSPF LSA Type**

Refer to the online course to complete this activity.

## OSPF Routing Table and Types of Routes (9.1.3)

In this topic, you will explain how multiarea OSPF establishes neighbor adjacencies.

## OSPF Routing Table Entries (9.1.3.1)

Example 9-1 provides a sample IPv4 routing table for a multiarea OSPF topology with a link to an external non-OSPF network, a default route provided by the type 5 LSA from the ASBR.

**Example 9-1** OSPFv2 Routing Table Entries

```
R1# show ip route | begin Gateway

Gateway of last resort is 192.168.10.2 to network 0.0.0.0

O*E2   0.0.0.0/0 [110/1] via 192.168.10.2, 00:00:19, Serial0/0/0
       10.0.0.0/8 is variably subnetted, 5 subnets, 2 masks
C         10.1.1.0/24 is directly connected, GigabitEthernet0/0
L         10.1.1.1/32 is directly connected, GigabitEthernet0/0
C         10.1.2.0/24 is directly connected, GigabitEthernet0/1
L         10.1.2.1/32 is directly connected, GigabitEthernet0/1
O         10.2.1.0/24 [110/648] via 192.168.10.2, 00:04:34, Serial0/0/0
O IA   192.168.1.0/24 [110/1295] via 192.168.10.2, 00:01:48, Serial0/0/0
O IA   192.168.2.0/24 [110/1295] via 192.168.10.2, 00:01:48, Serial0/0/0
       192.168.10.0/24 is variably subnetted, 3 subnets, 2 masks
C         192.168.10.0/30 is directly connected, Serial0/0/0
L         192.168.10.1/32 is directly connected, Serial0/0/0
O         192.168.10.4/30 [110/1294] via 192.168.10.2, 00:01:55, Serial0/0/0
R1#
```

OSPF routes in an IPv4 routing table are identified as O, O IA, O E1, and O E2. Table 9-4 summarizes the meaning of these route source designators.

**Table 9-4** OSPF Routing Table Entries

| Routing Table Code | Description |
| --- | --- |
| O | ■ Router (type 1) and network (type 2) LSAs describe the details within an area. <br> ■ The routing table reflects this link-state information with a designation of O, meaning that the route is intra-area. |
| O IA | ■ When an ABR receives a router LSA (type 1) in one area, it sends a summary LSA (type 3) into the adjacent area. <br> ■ Summary LSAs appear in the routing table as IA (interarea routes). Summary LSAs received in one area are also forwarded to other areas. |
| O E1 or O E2 | ■ External LSAs appear in the routing table marked as external type 1 (E1) or external type 2 (E2) routes. <br> ■ Type 2 (E2) is the default. The differences between type 1 (E1) and type 2 (E2) are beyond the scope of this course. |

Example 9-2 shows an IPv6 routing table with OSPF intra-area, interarea, and external routing table entries.

**Example 9-2**   OSPFv3 Routing Table Entries

```
R1# show ipv6 route
IPv6 Routing Table - default - 9 entries
Codes: C - Connected, L - Local, S - Static, U - Per-user Static route
       B - BGP, R - RIP, H - NHRP, I1 - ISIS L1
       I2 - ISIS L2, IA - ISIS interarea, IS - ISIS summary, D - EIGRP
       EX - EIGRP external, ND - ND Default, NDp - ND Prefix, DCE - Destination
       NDr - Redirect, O - OSPF Intra, OI - OSPF Inter, OE1 - OSPF ext 1
       OE2 - OSPF ext 2, ON1 - OSPF NSSA ext 1, ON2 - OSPF NSSA ext 2
OE2 ::/0 [110/1], tag 10
     via FE80::2, Serial0/0/0
C    2001:DB8:CAFE:1::/64 [0/0]
     via GigabitEthernet0/0, directly connected
L    2001:DB8:CAFE:1::1/128 [0/0]
     via GigabitEthernet0/0, receive
O    2001:DB8:CAFE:2::/64 [110/648]
     via FE80::2, Serial0/0/0
OI   2001:DB8:CAFE:3::/64 [110/1295]
     via FE80::2, Serial0/0/0
C    2001:DB8:CAFE:A001::/64 [0/0]
     via Serial0/0/0, directly connected
L    2001:DB8:CAFE:A001::1/128 [0/0]
     via Serial0/0/0, receive
O    2001:DB8:CAFE:A002::/64 [110/1294]
     via FE80::2, Serial0/0/0
L    FF00::/8 [0/0]
     via Null0, receive
R1#
```

## OSPF Route Calculation (9.1.3.2)

Each router uses the SPF algorithm against the LSDB to build the SPF tree. The SPF tree is used to determine the best path(s).

As shown in Figure 9-15, the order in which the best paths are calculated is as follows:

```
R1# show ip route | begin Gateway
Gateway of last resort is 192.168.10.2 to network 0.0.0.0
O*E2 0.0.0.0/0 [110/1] via 192.168.10.2, 00:00:19, Serial0/0/0
      10.0.0.0/8 is variably subnetted, 5 subnets, 2 masks
C        10.1.1.0/24 is directly connected, GigabitEthernet0/0
L        10.1.1.1/32 is directly connected, GigabitEthernet0/0
C        10.1.2.0/24 is directly connected, GigabitEthernet0/1
L        10.1.2.1/32 is directly connected, GigabitEthernet0/1
O        10.2.1.0/24 [110/648] via 192.168.10.2, 00:04:34,Serial0/0/0
O IA 192.168.1.0/24 [110/1295] via 192.168.10.2, 00:01:48,Serial0/0/0
O IA 192.168.2.0/24 [110/1295] via 192.168.10.2, 00:01:48,Serial0/0/0
      192.168.10.0/24 is variably subnetted, 3 subnets, 2 masks
C        192.168.10.0/30 is directly connected, Serial0/0/0
L        192.168.10.1/32 is directly connected, Serial0/0/0
O        192.168.10.4/30 [110/1294] via 192.168.10.2, 00:01:55,Serial0/0/0
R1#
```

**Figure 9-15**   Steps to OSPF Convergence

1. **Calculate intra-area OSPF routes.** All routers calculate the best path(s) to destinations within their area (intra-area) and add these entries to the routing table. These are the type 1 and type 2 LSAs, which are noted in the routing table with the routing designator O.

2. **Calculate best path to interarea OSPF routes.** All routers calculate the best path(s) to the other areas within the internetwork. These best paths are the interarea route entries, or type 3 LSAs, and are noted with the routing designator O IA.

3. **Calculate best path route to external non-OSPF networks.** All routers (except those that are in a form of stub area) calculate the best path(s) to the external autonomous system (type 5) destinations. These are noted with either an O E1 or an O E2 route designator, depending on the configuration.

When converged, a router can communicate with any network within or outside the OSPF routing domain.

**Interactive Graphic**

**Activity 9.1.3.3: Order the Steps for OSPF Best Path Calculations**

Refer to the online course to complete this activity.

# Configuring Multiarea OSPF (9.2)

In this section, you will learn how to implement multiarea OSPFv2 and OSPFv3.

# Configuring Multiarea OSPF (9.2.1)

In this topic, you will configure multiarea OSPFv2 and OSPFv3 in a routed network.

## Implementing Multiarea OSPF (9.2.1.1)

OSPF can be implemented as single-area or multiarea. The type of OSPF implementation chosen depends on the specific network design requirements and existing topology.

There are four steps to implementing multiarea OSPF. Steps 1 and 2 are part of the planning process:

**Step 1.**    **Gather the network requirements and parameters.** Gathering the network requirements and parameters includes determining the number of host and network devices, the IP addressing scheme (if already implemented), the size of the routing domain, the size of the routing tables, the risk of topology changes, whether existing routers can support OSPF, and other network characteristics.

**Step 2.**    **Define the OSPF parameters.** Based on information gathered during step 1, the network administrator must determine whether single-area or multiarea OSPF is the preferred implementation. If multiarea OSPF is selected, the network administrator must take into account several considerations while determining the OSPF parameters to include:

- **IP addressing plan**—The IP addressing plan governs how OSPF can be deployed and how well the OSPF deployment might scale. A detailed IP addressing plan, including IP subnetting information, must be created. A good IP addressing plan should enable the usage of OSPF multiarea design and summarization. This plan helps the network scale more easily  and optimizes OSPF behavior and the propagation of LSA.

- **OSPF areas**—Dividing an OSPF network into areas decreases the LSDB size and limits the propagation of link-state updates when the topology changes. The routers that are to be ABRs and ASBRs must be identified, as are the ABRs or ASBRs that are to perform any summarization or redistribution.

- **Network topology**—This consists of links that connect the network equipment and belong to different OSPF areas in a multiarea OSPF design. Network topology is important for determining primary and backup links. Primary and backup links are defined by the changing OSPF cost on interfaces. A detailed network topology plan should also be used to determine the different OSPF areas, ABR, and ASBR, as well as summarization and redistribution points, if multiarea OSPF is used.

**Step 3.** Configure the multiarea OSPF implementation based on the parameters.

**Step 4.** Verify the multiarea OSPF implementation based on the parameters.

## Configuring Multiarea OSPFv2 (9.2.1.2)

Figure 9-16 shows the reference multiarea OSPF topology used in this section.

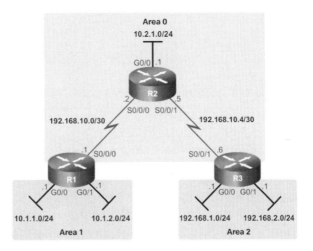

**Figure 9-16** OSPFv2 Multiarea Topology

Note the following in this topology:

- R1 is an ABR because it has interfaces in area 1 and an interface in area 0.

- R2 is an internal backbone router because all its interfaces are in area 0.

- R3 is an ABR because it has interfaces in area 2 and an interface in area 0.

> **Note**
>
> This topology is not a typical multiarea OSPF routing domain but is used to provide a configuration example.

There are no special commands required to implement this multiarea OSPF network. A router simply becomes an ABR when it has two **network** statements in different areas.

As shown in Example 9-3, R1 is assigned the router ID 1.1.1.1. This example enables OSPF on the two LAN interfaces in area 1. The serial interface is configured as part of OSPF area 0. Because R1 has interfaces connected to two different areas, it is an ABR.

**Example 9-3** Configuring Multiarea OSPFv2 on R1

```
R1(config)# router ospf 10
R1(config-router)# router-id 1.1.1.1
R1(config-router)# network 10.1.1.1 0.0.0.0 area 1
R1(config-router)# network 10.1.2.1 0.0.0.0 area 1
R1(config-router)# network 192.168.10.1 0.0.0.0 area 0
R1(config-router)# end
R1#
```

Example 9-4 is the multiarea OSPF configuration for R2 and R3.

**Example 9-4** Configuring Multiarea OSPFv2 on R2 and R3

```
R2(config)# router ospf 10
R2(config-router)# router-id 2.2.2.2
R2(config-router)# network 192.168.10.0 0.0.0.3 area 0
R2(config-router)# network 192.168.10.4 0.0.0.3 area 0
R2(config-router)# network 10.2.1.0 0.0.0.255 area 0
R2(config-router)# end
*Apr 19 18:11:04.029: %OSPF-5-ADJCHG: Process 10, Nbr 1.1.1.1 on Serial0/0/0 from
  LOADING to FULL, Loading Done
*Apr 19 18:11:06.781: %SYS-5-CONFIG_I: Configured from console by console
R2#
```

```
R3(config)# router ospf 10
R3(config-router)# router-id 3.3.3.3
R3(config-router)# network 192.168.10.6 0.0.0.0 area 0
R3(config-router)# network 192.168.1.1 0.0.0.0 area 2
R3(config-router)# network 192.168.2.1 0.0.0.0 area 2
R3(config-router)# end
*Apr 19 18:12:55.881: %OSPF-5-ADJCHG: Process 10, Nbr 2.2.2.2 on Serial0/0/1 from
  LOADING to FULL, Loading Done
```

R2 uses the wildcard mask of the interface network address. R3 uses the 0.0.0.0 wildcard mask for all networks.

Upon completion of the R2 configuration, notice the messages informing of the adjacency with R1 (1.1.1.1).

Upon completion of the R3 configuration, notice the messages informing of an adjacency with R2 (2.2.2.2). Also notice that the IPv4 addressing scheme used for the router ID makes it easy to identify the neighbor.

**Note**

The inverse wildcard masks used to configure R2 and R3 purposely differ to demonstrate the two alternatives to entering **network** statements. The interface method used for R3 is simpler because the wildcard mask is always **0.0.0.0** and does not need to be calculated.

## Configuring Multiarea OSPFv3 (9.2.1.3)

Implementing the multiarea OSPFv3 topology in Figure 9-17 is as simple as implementing the OSPFv2 topology in the preceding section.

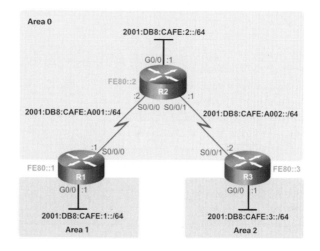

**Figure 9-17**    OSPFv3 Multiarea Topology

No special commands are required. A router simply becomes an ABR when it has two interfaces in different areas.

In Example 9-5, R1 is assigned the router ID 1.1.1.1. The configuration also enables OSPF on the LAN interface in area 1 and the serial interface in area 0. Because R1 has interfaces connected to two different areas, it becomes an ABR. Also shown are the configurations for R2 and R3.

**Example 9-5** Configuring Multiarea OSPFv3

```
R1(config)# ipv6 router ospf 10
R1(config-rtr)# router-id 1.1.1.1
R1(config-rtr)# exit
R1(config)# interface GigabitEthernet 0/0
R1(config-if)# ipv6 ospf 10 area 1
R1(config-if)# interface Serial0/0/0
R1(config-if)# ipv6 ospf 10 area 0
R1(config-if)# end
R1#
```

```
R2(config)# ipv6 router ospf 10
*Apr 24 14:18:10.463: %OSPFv3-4-NORTRID: Process OSPFv3-10-IPv6 could not pick a
  router-id, please configure manually
R2(config-rtr)# router-id 2.2.2.2
R2(config-rtr)# exit
R2(config)# interface g0/0
R2(config-if)# ipv6 ospf 10 area 0
R2(config-if)# interface s0/0/0
R2(config-if)# ipv6 ospf 10 area 0
R2(config-if)# interface s0/0/1
R2(config-if)# ipv6 ospf 10 area 0
*Apr 24 14:18:35.135: %OSPFv3-5-ADJCHG: Process 10, Nbr 1.1.1.1 on Serial0/0/0 from
  LOADING to FULL, Loading Done
R2(config-if)# end
R2#
```

```
R3(config)# ipv6 router ospf 10
*Apr 24 14:20:42.463: %OSPFv3-4-NORTRID: Process OSPFv3-10-IPv6 could not pick a
  router-id, please configure manually
R3(config-rtr)# router-id 3.3.3.3
R3(config-rtr)# exit
R3(config)# interface g0/0
R3(config-if)# ipv6 ospf 10 area 2
R3(config-if)# interface s0/0/1
R3(config-if)# ipv6 ospf 10 area 0
*Apr 24 14:21:01.439: %OSPFv3-5-ADJCHG: Process 10, Nbr 2.2.2.2 on Serial0/0/1 from
  LOADING to FULL, Loading Done
R3(config-if)# end
R3#
```

Upon completion of the R2 configuration, notice the message indicating that there is an adjacency with R1 (1.1.1.1).

Upon completion of the R3 configuration, notice the message indicating that there is an adjacency with R2 (2.2.2.2).

# Verifying Multiarea OSPF (9.2.2)

In this topic, you will verify multiarea OSPFv2 operation.

## Verifying Multiarea OSPFv2 (9.2.2.1)

The same verification commands used to verify single-area OSPFv2 also can be used to verify the multiarea OSPF topology:

- **show ip ospf neighbor**
- **show ip ospf**
- **show ip ospf interface**

Commands that verify specific multiarea OSPFv2 information include the following:

- **show ip protocols**
- **show ip ospf interface brief**
- **show ip route ospf**
- **show ip ospf database**

**Note**

For the equivalent OSPFv3 commands, simply substitute **ipv6** for **ip**.

## Verify General Multiarea OSPFv2 Settings (9.2.2.2)

Use the **show ip protocols** command to verify the OSPFv2 status. The output of the command reveals which routing protocols are configured on a router. It also includes routing protocol specifics, such as the router ID, number of areas in the router, and networks included within the routing protocol configuration.

Example 9-6 shows the OSPFv2 settings of R1.

**Example 9-6**   Verifying Multiarea OSPFv2 Status on R1

```
R1# show ip protocols
*** IP Routing is NSF aware ***

Routing Protocol is "ospf 10"
  Outgoing update filter list for all interfaces is not set
  Incoming update filter list for all interfaces is not set
  Router ID 1.1.1.1
  It is an area border router
  Number of areas in this router is 2. 2 normal 0 stub 0 nssa
  Maximum path: 4
```

```
 Routing for Networks:
    10.1.1.1 0.0.0.0 area 1
    10.1.2.1 0.0.0.0 area 1
    192.168.10.1 0.0.0.0 area 0
 Routing Information Sources:
    Gateway          Distance      Last Update
    3.3.3.3               110      02:20:36
    2.2.2.2               110      02:20:39
 Distance: (default is 110)

R1#
```

Notice that the command shows there are two areas. The Routing for Networks section identifies the networks and their respective areas.

Use the **show ip ospf interface brief** command to display concise OSPFv2-related information of OSPFv2-enabled interfaces. This command reveals useful information such as the OSPFv2 process ID that the interface is assigned to, the area that the interfaces are in, and the cost of the interface.

Example 9-7 verifies the OSPFv2-enabled interfaces and the areas to which they belong.

**Example 9-7**   Verifying OSPFv2-Enabled Interfaces on R1

```
R1# show ip ospf interface brief
Interface    PID    Area        IP Address/Mask      Cost   State Nbrs F/C
Se0/0/0      10     0           192.168.10.1/30      64     P2P   1/1
Gi0/1        10     1           10.1.2.1/24          1      DR    0/0
Gi0/0        10     1           10.1.1.1/24          1      DR    0/0
R1#
```

## Verify the OSPFv2 Routes (9.2.2.3)

The command most commonly used to verify a multiarea OSPFv2 configuration is the **show ip route** command. Add the **ospf** parameter to display only OSPFv2-related information. Example 9-8 shows the routing table of R1.

**Example 9-8**   Verifying Multiarea OSPFv2 Routes on R1

```
R1# show ip route ospf | begin Gateway
Gateway of last resort is not set

      10.0.0.0/8 is variably subnetted, 5 subnets, 2 masks
O        10.2.1.0/24 [110/648] via 192.168.10.2, 00:26:03, Serial0/0/0
```

```
O IA    192.168.1.0/24 [110/1295] via 192.168.10.2, 00:26:03, Serial0/0/0
O IA    192.168.2.0/24 [110/1295] via 192.168.10.2, 00:26:03, Serial0/0/0
        192.168.10.0/24 is variably subnetted, 3 subnets, 2 masks
O           192.168.10.4/30 [110/1294] via 192.168.10.2, 00:26:03, Serial0/0/0
R1#
```

Notice that the O IA entries in the routing table identify networks learned from other areas. Specifically, O represents OSPFv2 routes, and IA represents interarea, which means the route originated from another area.

Recall that R1 is in area 0, and the 192.168.1.0 and 192.168.2.0 subnets are connected to R3 in area 2. The [110/1295] entry in the routing table represents the administrative distance that is assigned to OSPF (110) and the total cost of the routes (1295).

## Verify the Multiarea OSPFv2 LSDB (9.2.2.4)

Use the **show ip ospf database** command to verify the contents of the OSPFv2 LSDB. There are many command options available with the **show ip ospf database** command. Example 9-9 shows the content of the LSDB of R1.

**Example 9-9**    Verifying the OSPFv2 LSDB on R1

```
R1# show ip ospf database

            OSPF Router with ID (1.1.1.1) (Process ID 10)


            Router Link States (Area 0)

Link ID         ADV Router      Age         Seq#        Checksum Link count
1.1.1.1         1.1.1.1         725         0x80000005 0x00F9B0 2
2.2.2.2         2.2.2.2         695         0x80000007 0x003DB1 5
3.3.3.3         3.3.3.3         681         0x80000005 0x00FF91 2


            Summary Net Link States (Area 0)

Link ID         ADV Router      Age         Seq#        Checksum
10.1.1.0        1.1.1.1         725         0x80000006 0x00D155
10.1.2.0        1.1.1.1         725         0x80000005 0x00C85E
192.168.1.0     3.3.3.3         681         0x80000006 0x00724E
192.168.2.0     3.3.3.3         681         0x80000005 0x006957


            Router Link States (Area 1)

Link ID         ADV Router      Age         Seq#        Checksum Link count
1.1.1.1         1.1.1.1         725         0x80000006 0x007D7C 2
```

```
        Summary Net Link States (Area 1)

Link ID          ADV Router       Age        Seq#        Checksum
10.2.1.0         1.1.1.1          725        0x80000005 0x004A9C
192.168.1.0      1.1.1.1          725        0x80000005 0x00B593
192.168.2.0      1.1.1.1          725        0x80000005 0x00AA9D
192.168.10.0     1.1.1.1          725        0x80000005 0x00B3D0
192.168.10.4     1.1.1.1          725        0x80000005 0x000E32
R1#
```

Notice that R1 has entries for area 0 and area 1 because ABRs must maintain a separate LSDB for each area to which they belong. In the output, the Router Link States (Area 0) section identifies three routers. The Summary Net Link States sections identify networks learned from other areas and which neighbor advertised the network.

## Verify Multiarea OSPFv3 (9.2.2.5)

Like OSPFv2, OSPFv3 provides similar verification commands. Refer to the reference OSPFv3 topology in Figure 9-17.

Example 9-10 shows the OSPFv3 settings of R1. Notice that the command confirms that there are now two areas. It also identifies each interface enabled for the respective area.

**Example 9-10**   Verifying Multiarea OSPFv3 Status on R1

```
R1# show ipv6 protocols
IPv6 Routing Protocol is "connected"
IPv6 Routing Protocol is "ND"
IPv6 Routing Protocol is "ospf 10"
  Router ID 1.1.1.1
  Area border router
  Number of areas: 2 normal, 0 stub, 0 nssa
  Interfaces (Area 0):
    Serial0/0/0
  Interfaces (Area 1):
    GigabitEthernet0/0
  Redistribution:
    None
R1#
```

Example 9-11 verifies the OSPFv3-enabled interfaces and the area to which they belong.

**Example 9-11**   Verifying OSPFv3-Enabled Interfaces on R1

```
R1# show ipv6 ospf interface brief
Interface     PID   Area            Intf ID    Cost   State Nbrs F/C
Se0/0/0       10    0               6          647    P2P   1/1
Gi0/0         10    1               3          1      DR    0/0
R1#
```

Example 9-12 shows the routing table of R1.

**Example 9-12**   Verifying Multiarea OSPFv3 Routes on R1

```
R1# show ipv6 route ospf
IPv6 Routing Table - default - 8 entries
Codes: C - Connected, L - Local, S - Static, U - Per-user Static route
       B - BGP, R - RIP, H - NHRP, I1 - ISIS L1
       I2 - ISIS L2, IA - ISIS interarea, IS - ISIS summary, D - EIGRP
       EX - EIGRP external, ND - ND Default, NDp - ND Prefix, DCE - Destination
       NDr - Redirect, O - OSPF Intra, OI - OSPF Inter, OE1 - OSPF ext 1
       OE2 - OSPF ext 2, ON1 - OSPF NSSA ext 1, ON2 - OSPF NSSA ext 2
O    2001:DB8:CAFE:2::/64 [110/648]
     via FE80::2, Serial0/0/0
OI   2001:DB8:CAFE:3::/64 [110/1295]
     via FE80::2, Serial0/0/0
O    2001:DB8:CAFE:A002::/64 [110/1294]
     via FE80::2, Serial0/0/0
R1#
```

Notice that the IPv6 routing table displays OI entries in the routing table to identify networks learned from other areas. Specifically, O represents OSPF routes, and I represents interarea, which means the route originated from another area.

Recall that R1 is in area 0, and the 2001:DB8:CAFE:3::/64 subnet is connected to R3 in area 2. The [110/1295] entry in the routing table represents the administrative distance that is assigned to OSPF (110) and the total cost of the routes (1295).

Example 9-13 shows the content of the LSDB of R1. The command offers similar information to its OSPFv2 counterpart. However, the OSPFv3 LSDB contains additional LSA types not available in OSPFv2.

**Example 9-13**  Verifying the OSPFv3 LSDB on R1

```
R1# show ipv6 ospf database

              OSPFv3 Router with ID (1.1.1.1) (Process ID 10)

          Router Link States (Area 0)

ADV Router       Age         Seq#        Fragment ID  Link count  Bits
 1.1.1.1         1617        0x80000002  0             1          B
 2.2.2.2         1484        0x80000002  0             2          None
 3.3.3.3         1485        0x80000001  0             1          B


          Inter Area Prefix Link States (Area 0)

ADV Router       Age         Seq#        Prefix
 1.1.1.1         1833        0x80000001  2001:DB8:CAFE:1::/64
 3.3.3.3         1476        0x80000001  2001:DB8:CAFE:3::/64


          Link (Type-8) Link States (Area 0)

ADV Router       Age         Seq#        Link ID    Interface
 1.1.1.1         1843        0x80000001  6          Se0/0/0
 2.2.2.2         1619        0x80000001  6          Se0/0/0


          Intra Area Prefix Link States (Area 0)

ADV Router       Age         Seq#        Link ID    Ref-lstype   Ref-LSID
 1.1.1.1         1843        0x80000001  0          0x2001       0
 2.2.2.2         1614        0x80000002  0          0x2001       0
 3.3.3.3         1486        0x80000001  0          0x2001       0


          Router Link States (Area 1)

ADV Router       Age         Seq#        Fragment ID  Link count  Bits
 1.1.1.1         1843        0x80000001  0             0          B


          Inter Area Prefix Link States (Area 1)
ADV Router       Age         Seq#        Prefix
 1.1.1.1         1833        0x80000001  2001:DB8:CAFE:A001::/64
 1.1.1.1         1613        0x80000001  2001:DB8:CAFE:A002::/64
 1.1.1.1         1613        0x80000001  2001:DB8:CAFE:2::/64
 1.1.1.1         1474        0x80000001  2001:DB8:CAFE:3::/64
          Link (Type-8) Link States (Area 1)
```

```
ADV Router         Age           Seq#          Link ID     Interface
  1.1.1.1          1844          0x80000001    3           Gi0/0


              Intra Area Prefix Link States (Area 1)


ADV Router         Age           Seq#          Link ID     Ref-lstype   Ref-LSID
  1.1.1.1          1844          0x80000001    0           0x2001       0
R1#
```

### Packet Tracer 9.2.2.6: Configuring Multiarea OSPFv2

In this activity, you will configure multiarea OSPFv2. The network is already connected, and interfaces are configured with IPv4 addressing. Your job is to enable multiarea OSPFv2, verify connectivity, and examine the operation of multiarea OSPFv2.

### Packet Tracer 9.2.2.7: Configuring Multiarea OSPFv3

#### Background/Scenario

In this activity, you will configure multiarea OSPFv3. The network is already connected, and interfaces are configured with IPv6 addressing. Your job is to enable multiarea OSPFv3, verify connectivity, and examine the operation of multiarea OSPFv3.

### Lab 9.2.2.8: Configuring Multi-area OSPFv2

Refer to *Scaling Networks v6 Labs & Study Guide* and the online course to complete this activity.

In this lab, you will complete the following objectives:

- Part 1: Build the Network and Configure Basic Device Settings
- Part 2: Configure a Multiarea OSPFv2 Network
- Part 3: Configure Interarea Summary Routes

### Lab 9.2.2.9: Configuring Multi-area OSPFv3

Refer to *Scaling Networks v6 Labs & Study Guide* and the online course to complete this activity.

In this lab, you will complete the following objectives:

- Part 1: Build the Network and Configure Basic Device Settings
- Part 2: Configure Multiarea OSPFv3 Routing

# Summary (9.3)

**Class Activity 9.3.1.1: Digital Trolleys**

Refer to *Scaling Networks v6 Labs & Study Guide* and the online course to complete this activity.

Your city has an aging digital trolley system based on a one-area design. All communications within this one area are taking longer to process as trolleys are being added to routes serving the population of your growing city. Trolley departures and arrivals are also taking a little longer because each trolley must check large routing tables to determine where to pick up and deliver residents from their source and destination streets.

A concerned citizen has come up with the idea of dividing the city into different areas to more efficiently determine trolley routing information. It is thought that if the trolley maps are smaller, the system might be improved because of faster and smaller updates to the routing tables.

Your city board approves and implements the new area-based digital trolley system. But to ensure that the new area routes are more efficient, the city board needs data to show the results at the next open board meeting.

Complete the directions found in the PDF for this activity. Share your answers with your class.

---

Single-area OSPF is useful in smaller networks, but in larger networks multiarea OSPF is a better choice. Multiarea OSPF solves the issues of large routing tables, large link-state databases, and frequent SPF algorithm calculations.

The main area is called the backbone area (area 0), and all other areas must connect to the backbone area. Routing occurs between the areas, but many of the routing operations, such as recalculating the database, are kept within an area.

There are four different types of OSPF routers: internal router, backbone router, area border router (ABR), and Autonomous System Boundary Router (ASBR). A router can be classified as more than one router type.

Link-state advertisements (LSA) are the building blocks of OSPF. This chapter concentrates on LSA type 1 to LSA type 5. Type 1 LSAs are referred to as router link entries. Type 2 LSAs, referred to as network link entries, are flooded by a DR. Type 3 LSAs, referred to as summary link entries, are created and propagated by ABRs. A type 4 summary LSA is generated by an ABR only when an ASBR exists within an area. Type 5 external LSAs describe routes to networks outside the OSPF autonomous system. Type 5 LSAs are originated by the ASBR and are flooded to the entire autonomous system.

OSPFv2 routes in an IPv4 routing table are identified using the descriptors O, O IA, O E1, and O E2. Each router uses the SPF algorithm against the LSDB to build the SPF tree. The SPF tree is used to determine the best paths.

No special commands are required to implement a multiarea OSPF network. A router simply becomes an ABR when it has two **network** statements in different areas.

The following is an example of multiarea OSPF configuration:

```
R1(config)# router ospf 10
R1(config-router)# router-id 1.1.1.1
R1(config-router)# network 10.1.1.1 0.0.0.0 area 1
R1(config-router)# network 10.1.2.1 0.0.0.0 area 1
R1(config-router)# network 192.168.10.1 0.0.0.0 area 0
```

The following commands are used to verify OSPFv2 configuration:

- **show ip ospf neighbor**
- **show ip ospf**
- **show ip ospf interface**
- **show ip protocols**
- **show ip ospf interface brief**
- **show ip route ospf**
- **show ip ospf database**

To use the equivalent OSPFv3 commands, simply substitute **ipv6** for **ip**.

# Practice

The following activities provide practice with the topics introduced in this chapter. The Labs and Class Activities are available in the companion *Scaling Networks v6 Labs & Study Guide* (ISBN 978-1-58713-433-3). The Packet Tracer activity instructions are also in the Labs & Study Guide. The PKA files are found in the online course.

**Class Activities**

Class Activity 9.0.1.2: Leaving on a Jet Plane

Class Activity 9.3.1.1: Digital Trolleys

**Labs**

Lab 9.2.2.8: Configuring Multi-area OSPFv2

Lab 9.2.2.9: Configuring Multi-area OSPFv3

**Packet Tracer Activities**

Packet Tracer 9.2.2.6: Configuring Multiarea OSPFv2

Packet Tracer 9.2.2.7: Configuring Multiarea OSPFv3

# Check Your Understanding Questions

Complete all the review questions listed here to test your understanding of the topics and concepts in this chapter. The appendix "Answers to 'Check Your Understanding' Questions" lists the answers.

1. Which statement describes a multiarea OSPF network?

   A. It consists of multiple network areas that are daisy-chained together.

   B. It has a core backbone area, with other areas connected to the backbone area.

   C. It has multiple routers that run multiple routing protocols simultaneously, and each protocol consists of an area.

   D. It requires a three-layer hierarchical network design approach.

2. What is one advantage of using multiarea OSPF?

   A. It allows OSPFv2 and OSPFv3 to be running together.

   B. It enables multiple routing protocols to be running in a large network.

   C. It improves routing efficiency by reducing the routing table and link-state update overhead.

   D. It increases routing performance by dividing the neighbor table into separate smaller tables.

3. Which characteristic describes both ABRs and ASBRs that are implemented in a multiarea OSPF network?

   A. They are required to perform any summarization or redistribution tasks.

   B. They are required to reload frequently and quickly in order to update the LSDB.

   C. They both run multiple routing protocols simultaneously.

   D. They usually have many local networks attached.

4. Which of the following is used to facilitate hierarchical scaling in OSPF?

   A. Autosummarization

   B. Frequent SPF calculations

   C. The election of designated routers

   D. The use of multiple areas

5. Which two statements correctly describe OSPF type 3 LSAs? (Choose two.)

   A. Type 3 LSAs are generated without requiring a full SPF calculation.

   B. Type 3 LSAs are known as autonomous system external LSA entries.

   C. Type 3 LSAs are known as router link entries.

   D. Type 3 LSAs are used for routes to networks outside the OSPF autonomous system.

   E. Type 3 LSAs are used to update routes between OSPF areas.

6. What OSPF LSA type is used to inform routers of the router ID of the DR in each multiaccess network in an OSPF area?

   A. Type 1

   B. Type 2

   C. Type 3

   D. Type 4

7. What type of OSPF LSA is originated by ASBRs to advertise external routes?

   A. Type 1

   B. Type 2

   C. Type 3

   D. Type 5

8. What routing table descriptor is used to identify OSPF summary networks that originate from an ABR?

   A. O

   B. O IA

   C. O E1

   D. O E2

9. Which command can be used to verify the contents of the LSDB in an OSPF area?

A. show ip ospf database

B. show ip ospf interface

C. show ip ospf neighbor

D. show ip route ospf

# CHAPTER 10

# OSPF Tuning and Troubleshooting

## Objectives

Upon completion of this chapter, you will be able to answer the following questions:

- How can you configure OSPF to improve network performance?

- How do you troubleshoot common OSPF configuration issues in a small to medium-sized business network?

## Key Terms

This chapter uses the following key terms. You can find the definitions in the Glossary.

# Introduction (10.0.1.1)

OSPF is a popular link-state routing protocol that can be fine-tuned in many ways. Some of the most common methods of fine-tuning include manipulating the designated router/backup designated router (DR/BDR) election process, propagating default routes, fine-tuning the OSPFv2 and OSPFv3 interfaces, and enabling authentication.

This chapter describes these tuning features of OSPF, the configuration mode commands to implement these features for both IPv4 and IPv6, and the components and commands used to troubleshoot OSPFv2 and OSPFv3.

**Class Activity 10.0.1.2: DR and BDR Election**

Refer to *Scaling Networks v6 Labs & Study Guide* and the online course to complete this activity.

You are trying to decide how to influence the selection of the designated router and backup designated router for your OSPF network. This activity simulates that process.

Three separate DR election scenarios will be presented. The focus is on electing a DR and a BDR for your group. Refer to the PDF for this activity for the remaining instructions.

If additional time is available, two groups can be combined to simulate DR and BDR elections.

# Advanced Single-Area OSPF Configurations (10.1)

In this section, you will learn how to configure OSPF to improve network performance.

## OSPF in Multiaccess Networks (10.1.1)

In this topic, you will configure the OSPF interface priority to influence the DR/BDR election.

### OSPF Network Types (10.1.1.1)

To configure OSPF adjustments, start with a basic implementation of the OSPF routing protocol.

OSPF defines five network types:

- **Point-to-point**—Two routers interconnected over a common link, with no other routers on the link. This is often the configuration in WAN links (see Figure 10-1).

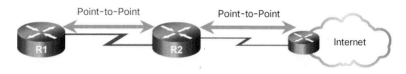

**Figure 10-1**   OSPF Point-to-Point Network

- *Broadcast multiaccess*—Multiple routers interconnected over an Ethernet network (see Figure 10-2).

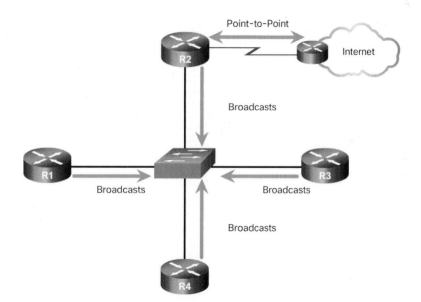

**Figure 10-2**   OSPF Multiaccess Network

- **Nonbroadcast multiaccess (NBMA)**—Multiple routers interconnected in a network that does not allow broadcasts, such as a Frame Relay network (see Figure 10-3). In this scenario, R1, R2, and R3 are interconnected over a Frame Relay network. Frame Relay does not allow broadcasts. OSPF must be configured to create neighbor adjacencies.

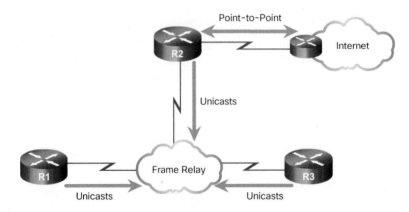

**Figure 10-3** OSPF Nonbroadcast Multiaccess Network

- *Point-to-multipoint*—Multiple routers interconnected in a hub-and-spoke topology over an NBMA network. Often used to connect branch sites (spokes) to a central site (hub) (see Figure 10-4). In this scenario, R1, R2, and R3 are interconnected over a Frame Relay network. Frame Relay does not allow broadcasts. OSPF must be configured to create neighbor adjacencies.

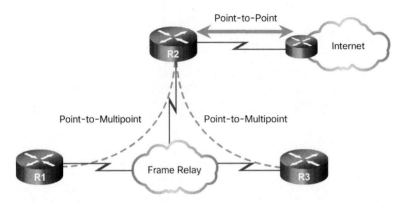

**Figure 10-4** OSPF Point-to-Multipoint Network

- *Virtual links*—Special OSPF network used to interconnect distant OSPF areas to the backbone area (see Figure 10-5). In this scenario, area 51 cannot connect directly to area 0. A special OSPF area must be configured to connect area 51 to area 0. The R1 and R2 area 1 must be configured as a virtual link.

A multiaccess network is a network with multiple devices on the same shared media, which are sharing communications. Ethernet LANs are the most common example of broadcast multiaccess networks. In broadcast networks, all devices on the network see all broadcast and multicast frames. They are multiaccess networks because numerous hosts, printers, routers, and other devices may all be members of the same network.

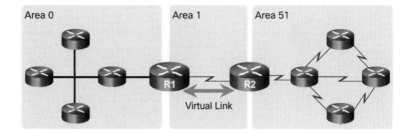

**Figure 10-5**   OSPF Virtual Link Network

## Challenges in Multiaccess Networks (10.1.1.2)

Multiaccess networks can create two challenges for OSPF regarding the flooding of LSAs:

- **Creation of multiple adjacencies**—Ethernet networks could potentially interconnect many OSPF routers over a common link. Creating adjacencies with every router is unnecessary and undesirable. It would lead to an excessive number of LSAs exchanged between routers on the same network.

- **Extensive flooding of LSAs**—Link-state routers flood their link-state packets when OSPF is initialized, or when there is a change in the topology. This flooding can become excessive.

To understand the problem with multiple adjacencies, we must use this formula:

$$n (n - 1) / 2$$

Specifically, for any number of routers (designated as $n$) on a multiaccess network, there are $n (n - 1) / 2$ adjacencies.

Figure 10-6 shows a simple topology of four routers, all of which are attached to the same multiaccess Ethernet network.

Without some type of mechanism to reduce the number of adjacencies, collectively these routers would form six adjacencies: $4 (4 - 1) / 2 = 6$ (see Figure 10-7).

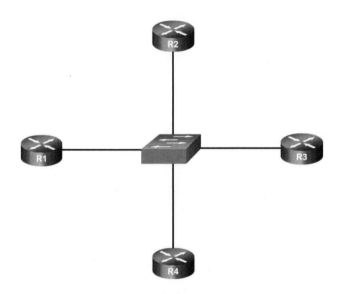

**Figure 10-6**    OSPF Multiaccess Network

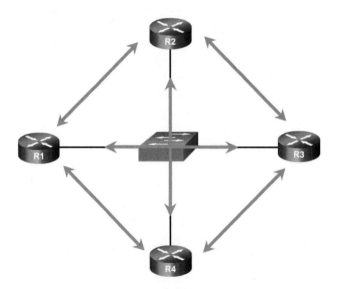

**Figure 10-7**    Establishing Six Neighbor Adjacencies

Table 10-1 shows that as routers are added to the network, the number of adjacencies increases dramatically.

**Table 10-1**   More Routers = More Adjacencies

| Routers: $n$ | Adjacencies: $n (n - 1) / 2$ |
|---|---|
| 4 | 6 |
| 5 | 10 |
| 10 | 45 |
| 20 | 190 |
| 50 | 1225 |

## OSPF Designated Router (10.1.1.3)

The solution to managing the number of adjacencies and the flooding of LSAs on a multiaccess network is the DR. On multiaccess networks, OSPF elects a DR to be the collection and distribution point for LSAs sent and received.

A BDR is also elected, to take over if the DR fails. The BDR listens passively to this exchange and maintains a relationship with all the routers. If the DR stops producing Hello packets, the BDR promotes itself and assumes the role of DR.

All other non-DR or BDR routers become DROTHERs (routers that are neither the DR nor the BDR).

In Figure 10-8, R1 has been elected as the DR for the Ethernet LAN interconnecting R2, R3, and R4. Notice that the number of adjacencies has been reduced to three.

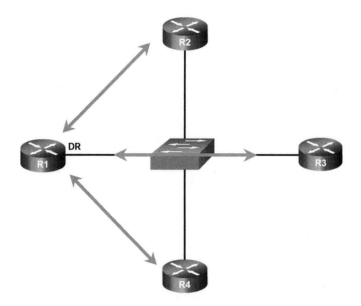

**Figure 10-8**   Establishing Adjacency with the DR

Routers on a multiaccess network elect a DR and a BDR. DROTHERs only form full adjacencies with the DR and BDR in the network. Instead of flooding LSAs to all routers in the network, DROTHERs only send their LSAs to the DR and BDR, using the multicast address 224.0.0.6 (all DR routers).

**Note**

The DR is used only for the distribution of LSAs. Packets are routed according to each of the routers' individual routing tables.

In Figure 10-9, R1 sends LSAs to the DR. The BDR also listens.

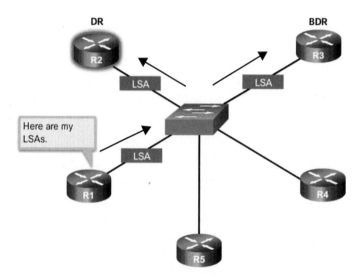

**Figure 10-9**   Role of the DR: Forming Adjacencies with the DR and BDR Only

As shown in Figure 10-10, the DR is responsible for forwarding the LSAs from R1 to all other routers.

The DR uses the multicast address 224.0.0.5 (all OSPF routers). The end result is that there is only one router doing all the flooding of all LSAs in the multiaccess network.

**Note**

DR/BDR elections occur only in multiaccess networks and do not occur in point-to-point networks.

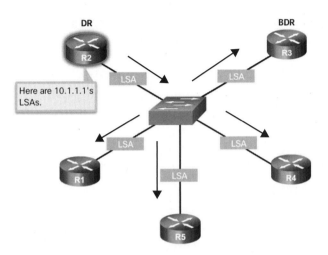

**Figure 10-10**   Role of the DR: Sending LSAs to Other Routers

## Verifying DR/BDR Roles (10.1.1.4)

In the multiaccess topology shown in Figure 10-11, three routers are interconnected over a common Ethernet multiaccess network, 192.168.1.0/28.

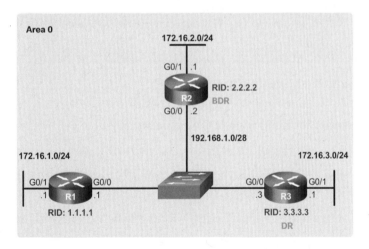

**Figure 10-11**   OSPFv2 Multiaccess Broadcast Reference Topology

Each router is configured with the indicated IPv4 address on the GigabitEthernet 0/0 interface. Because the routers are connected over a common multiaccess broadcast network, OSPF has automatically elected a DR and a BDR. In this example, R3 has been elected as the DR because its router ID is 3.3.3.3, which is the highest in this network. R2 is the BDR because it has the second-highest router ID in the network, 2.2.2.2.

To verify the roles of the OSPFv2 router, use the **show ip ospf interface** command. Figure 10-12 shows the output generated by R1.

**Note**

For the equivalent OSPFv3 command, simply substitute **ipv6** for **ip**.

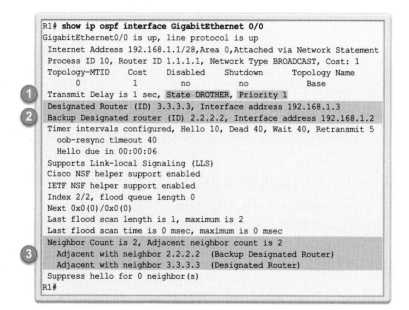

```
R1# show ip ospf interface GigabitEthernet 0/0
GigabitEthernet0/0 is up, line protocol is up
 Internet Address 192.168.1.1/28,Area 0,Attached via Network Statement
 Process ID 10, Router ID 1.1.1.1, Network Type BROADCAST, Cost: 1
 Topology-MTID    Cost    Disabled    Shutdown       Topology Name
       0           1         no          no             Base
 Transmit Delay is 1 sec, State DROTHER, Priority 1
 Designated Router (ID) 3.3.3.3, Interface address 192.168.1.3
 Backup Designated router (ID) 2.2.2.2, Interface address 192.168.1.2
 Timer intervals configured, Hello 10, Dead 40, Wait 40, Retransmit 5
   oob-resync timeout 40
   Hello due in 00:00:06
 Supports Link-local Signaling (LLS)
 Cisco NSF helper support enabled
 IETF NSF helper support enabled
 Index 2/2, flood queue length 0
 Next 0x0(0)/0x0(0)
 Last flood scan length is 1, maximum is 2
 Last flood scan time is 0 msec, maximum is 0 msec
 Neighbor Count is 2, Adjacent neighbor count is 2
    Adjacent with neighbor 2.2.2.2  (Backup Designated Router)
    Adjacent with neighbor 3.3.3.3  (Designated Router)
 Suppress hello for 0 neighbor(s)
R1#
```

**Figure 10-12**    Verifying the Role of R1

Details of the numbering in the figure are as follows:

1. R1 is not the DR or BDR but is a DROTHER with a default priority of 1.

2. The DR is R3, with router ID 3.3.3.3 at IPv4 address 192.168.1.3, and the BDR is R2, with router ID 2.2.2.2 at IPv4 address 192.168.1.2.

3. R1 has two adjacencies: one with the BDR and one with the DR.

Refer to Figure 10-13 for R2 output.

Details of the numbering in the figure are as follows:

1. R2 is the BDR, with a default priority of 1.

2. The DR is R3, with router ID 3.3.3.3 at IPv4 address 192.168.1.3, and the BDR is R2, with router ID 2.2.2.2 at IPv4 address 192.168.1.2.

3. R2 has two adjacencies: one with a neighbor with router ID 1.1.1.1 (R1) and the other with the DR.

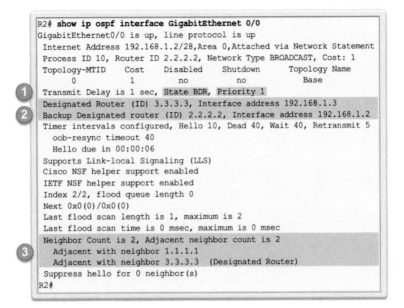

**Figure 10-13**    Verifying the Role of R2

Refer to Figure 10-14 for R3 output.

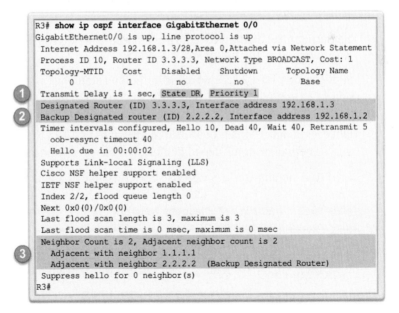

**Figure 10-14**    Verifying the Role of R3

Details of the numbering in the figure are as follows:

1. R3 is the DR with a default priority of 1.

2. The DR is R3 with router ID 3.3.3.3 at IPv4 address 192.168.1.3, while the BDR is R2 with router ID 2.2.2.2 at IPv4 address 192.168.1.2.

3. R3 has two adjacencies: one with a neighbor with router ID 1.1.1.1 (R1) and the other with the BDR.

## Verifying DR/BDR Adjacencies (10.1.1.5)

To verify the OSPFv2 adjacencies, use the **show ip ospf neighbor** command, as shown in Figure 10-15.

```
R1# show ip ospf neighbor

Neighbor ID Pri State        Dead Time  Address      Interface

2.2.2.2     1   FULL/BDR     00:00:36 192.168.1.2 GigabitEthernet0/0

3.3.3.3     1   FULL/DR      0:00:35  192.168.1.3 GigabitEthernet0/0

R1#
```

**Figure 10-15**   Verifying the Neighbor Adjacencies of R1

The output generated by R1 confirms that it has adjacencies with routers. Details of the numbering in the figure are as follows:

1. R2 (router ID 2.2.2.2), which is in the Full state, has assumed the role of BDR.

2. R3 (router ID 3.3.3.3), which is in the Full state, has assumed the role of DR.

Unlike serial links. which only display the state FULL/-, the state of neighbors in multiaccess networks varies depending on the role of the router.

Table 10-2 summarizes the various states possible in a multiaccess network.

**Table 10-2**   States in a Multiaccess Network

| State | Description |
| --- | --- |
| FULL/DR | The router is fully adjacent with the indicated DR neighbor. |
| | These two neighbors can exchange Hello, Update, Query, Reply, and Acknowledgment packets. |

| State | Description |
|---|---|
| FULL/BDR | The router is fully adjacent with the indicated BDR neighbor. |
| | These two neighbors can exchange Hello, Update, Query, Reply, and Acknowledgment packets. |
| FULL/DROTHER | This is a DR or BDR router that is fully adjacent with a non-DR or BDR router. |
| | These two neighbors can exchange Hello, Update, Query, Reply, and Acknowledgment packets. |
| 2-WAY/DROTHER | The non-DR or BDR router has a neighbor relationship with another non-DR or BDR router. |
| | These two neighbors exchange Hello packets. |

The normal state for an OSPF router is usually FULL. If a router is stuck in another state, this is an indication that there are problems in forming adjacencies. The only exception to this is the 2-WAY state, which is normal in a multiaccess broadcast network.

In multiaccess networks, DROTHERs form FULL adjacencies only with the DR and BDR. However, DROTHERs still form 2-WAY neighbor adjacencies with any DROTHERs that join the network. This means that all DROTHER routers in a multiaccess network still receive Hello packets from all other DROTHER routers. In this way, they are aware of all routers in the network. When two DROTHER routers form a neighbor adjacency, the neighbor state displays as 2-WAY/DROTHER.

The output generated by R2 (see Figure 10-16) confirms that R2 has adjacencies with other routers.

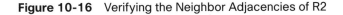

```
R2# show ip ospf neighbor

Neighbor ID Pri State        Dead Time  Address      Interface
 1.1.1.1      1  FULL/DROTHER 00:00:31  192.168.1.1  GigabitEthernet0/0
 3.3.3.3      1  FULL/DR      00:00:39  192.168.1.3  GigabitEthernet0/0

R2#
```

**Figure 10-16**   Verifying the Neighbor Adjacencies of R2

Details of the numbering in the figure are as follows:

1. R1 (router ID 1.1.1.1) is in the Full state and is neither the DR nor the BDR.

2. R3 (router ID 3.3.3.3) is in the Full state and has assumed the role of DR.

The output generated by R3, shown in Figure 10-17, confirms that R3 has adjacencies with other routers.

```
R3# show ip ospf neighbor

Neighbor ID Pri State        Dead Time  Address      Interface

① 1.1.1.1     1   FULL/DROTHER 00:00:34 192.168.1.1 GigabitEthernet0/0

② 2.2.2.2     1   FULL/BDR     00:00:39 192.168.1.2 GigabitEthernet0/0

R3#
```

**Figure 10-17**    Verifying the Neighbor Adjacencies of R3

Details of the numbering in the figure are as follows:

1. R1 (router ID 1.1.1.1) is in the Full state and is neither the DR nor the BDR.

2. R2 (router ID 2.2.2.2) is in the Full state and has assumed the role of BDR.

## Default DR/BDR Election Process (10.1.1.6)

How do the DR and BDR get elected? The OSPF DR and BDR election decision is based on the following criteria, in sequential order:

1. The routers in the network elect the router with the highest interface priority as the DR. The router with the second-highest interface priority is elected as the BDR. The priority can be configured to be any number between 0 and 255. The higher the priority, the more likely it is that the router will be selected as the DR. If the priority is set to 0, the router is not capable of becoming the DR. The default priority of multiaccess broadcast interfaces is 1. Therefore, unless otherwise configured, all routers have an equal priority value and must rely on another tie-breaking method during the DR/BDR election.

2. If the interface priorities are equal, the router with the highest router ID is elected as the DR. The router with the second-highest router ID is elected as the BDR.

Recall that the router ID is determined in one of three ways:

- The router ID can be manually configured.

- If no router IDs are configured, the router ID is determined by the highest loopback IPv4 address.

- If no loopback interfaces are configured, the router ID is determined by the highest active IPv4 address.

**Note**

In an IPv6 network, if there are no IPv4 addresses configured on the router, the router ID must be manually configured with the **router-id** *rid* command; otherwise, OSPFv3 does not start.

In Figure 10-11, all Ethernet router interfaces have a default priority of 1. As a result, based on the selection criteria listed above, the OSPF router ID is used to elect the DR and BDR. R3, with the highest router ID, becomes the DR; and R2, with the second-highest router ID, becomes the BDR.

**Note**

Serial interfaces have default priorities set to 0; therefore, they do not elect a DR and a BDR.

The DR and BDR election process takes place as soon as the first router with an OSPF-enabled interface is active on the multiaccess network. This can happen when the preconfigured OSPF routers are powered on or when OSPF is activated on the interface. The election process takes only a few seconds.

It should be noted that the automated manner in which OSPF selects a DR can results in problems if a router with inadequate resources is selected as DR.

## DR/BDR Election Process (10.1.1.7)

OSPF DR and BDR elections are not preemptive. If a new router with a higher priority or a higher router ID is added to the network after the DR and BDR election, the newly added router does not take over the DR role or the BDR role because those roles have already been assigned. The addition of a new router does not initiate a new election process.

After the DR is elected, it remains the DR until one of the following events occurs:

- The DR fails.

- The OSPF process on the DR fails or is stopped.

- The multiaccess interface on the DR fails or is shut down.

If the DR fails, the BDR is automatically promoted to DR. This is the case even if another DROTHER with a higher priority or router ID is added to the network after the initial DR/BDR election. However, after a BDR is promoted to DR, a new BDR election occurs, and the DROTHER with the higher priority or router ID is elected as the new BDR.

Figures 10-18 through 10-21 illustrate various scenarios related to the DR and BDR election process.

In Figure 10-18, the current DR (R3) fails; therefore, the pre-elected BDR (R2) assumes the role of DR. Subsequently, an election is held to choose a new BDR. Because R1 is the only DROTHER, it is elected as the BDR.

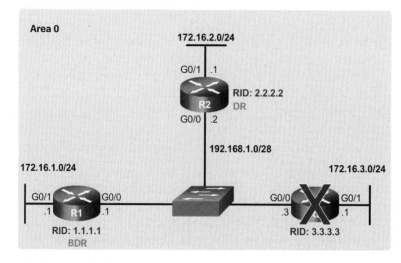

**Figure 10-18**   R3 Fails

In Figure 10-19, R3 has rejoined the network after several minutes of being unavailable. Because the DR and BDR already exist, R3 does not take over either role; instead, it becomes a DROTHER.

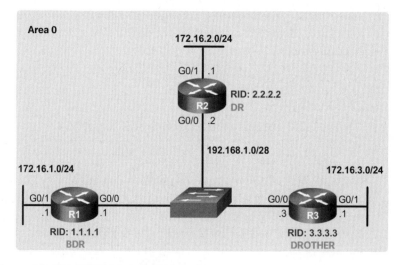

**Figure 10-19**   R3 Rejoins the Network

In Figure 10-20, a new router (R4) with a higher router ID is added to the network. DR (R2) and BDR (R1) retain the DR and BDR roles. R4 automatically becomes a DROTHER.

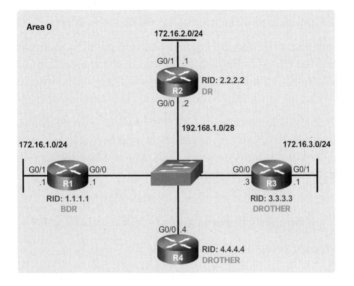

**Figure 10-20**   R4 Joins the Network

In Figure 10-21, R2 has failed. The BDR (R1) automatically becomes the DR, and an election process selects R4 as the BDR because it has the highest router ID.

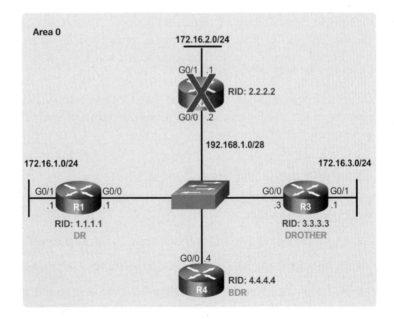

**Figure 10-21**   R2 Fails

## The OSPF Priority (10.1.1.8)

The DR becomes the focal point for the collection and distribution of LSAs. Therefore, this router must have sufficient CPU and memory capacity to handle the workload. It is possible to influence the DR/BDR election process through configurations.

If the interface priorities are equal on all routers, the router with the highest router ID is elected the DR. It is possible to configure the router ID to manipulate the DR/BDR election. However, this process works only if there is a stringent plan for setting the router ID on all routers. In large networks, this can be cumbersome.

Instead of relying on the router ID, it is better to control the election by setting interface priorities. A priority is an interface-specific value, which means it provides better control on a multiaccess network. This also allows a router to be the DR in one network and a DROTHER in another.

To set the priority of an interface, use the following commands:

- **ip ospf priority** *value* for OSPFv2
- **ipv6 ospf priority** *value* for OSPFv3

The *value* can be any of the following:

- **0**—Does not become a DR or BDR.
- **1–255**—The higher the priority value, the more likely the router is to become the DR or BDR on the interface.

In Figure 10-11, all routers have equal OSPF priority because the priority value defaults to 1 for all router interfaces. Therefore, the router ID is used to determine the DR (R3) and BDR (R2). Changing the priority value on an interface from 1 to a higher value would enable the router to become a DR or BDR during the next election.

If the interface priority is configured after OSPF is enabled, the administrator must shut down the OSPF process on all routers and then re-enable the OSPF process to force a new DR/BDR election.

## Changing the OSPF Priority (10.1.1.9)

In the topology in Figure 10-11, R3 is the DR, and R2 is the BDR. The corporate network policy states that

- R1 should be the DR and will be configured with a priority of 255.
- R2 should be the BDR and will be left with the default priority of 1.
- R3 should never be a DR or BDR and will be configured with a priority of 0.

Example 10-1 shows how to change the R1 GigabitEthernet 0/0 interface priority from 1 to 255.

**Example 10-1**   Changing the R1 GigabitEthernet 0/0 Interface Priority

```
R1(config)# interface GigabitEthernet 0/0
R1(config-if)# ip ospf priority 255
R1(config-if)# end
R1#
```

Example 10-2 shows how to change the R3 GigabitEthernet 0/0 interface priority from 1 to 0.

**Example 10-2**   Changing the R3 GigabitEthernet 0/0 Interface Priority

```
R3(config)# interface GigabitEthernet 0/0
R3(config-if)# ip ospf priority 0
R3(config-if)# end
R3#
```

The changes do not automatically take effect because the DR and BDR are already elected. Therefore, the OSPF election must be negotiated using one of the following methods:

- Shut down the router interfaces and then re-enable them, starting with the DR, and then the BDR, and then all other routers.

- Reset the OSPF process by using the **clear ip ospf process** privileged EXEC mode command on all routers.

Example 10-3 shows how to clear the OSPF process on R1.

**Example 10-3**   Clearing the OSPF Process on R1

```
R1# clear ip ospf process
Reset ALL OSPF processes? [no]: yes
R1#
*Apr  6 16:00:44.282: %OSPF-5-ADJCHG: Process 10, Nbr 2.2.2.2 on GigabitEthernet0/0
  from FULL to DOWN, Neighbor Down: Interface down or detached
*Apr  6 16:00:44.282: %OSPF-5-ADJCHG: Process 10, Nbr 3.3.3.3 on GigabitEthernet0/0
  from FULL to DOWN, Neighbor Down: Interface down or detached
R1#
```

Assume that the **clear ip ospf process** privileged EXEC mode command has been also been configured on R2 and R3. Notice the OSPF state information generated.

The output in Example 10-4 confirms that R1 is now the DR, with a priority of 255, and identifies the new neighbor adjacencies of R1.

**Example 10-4**   Verifying the Role and Adjacencies of R1

```
R1# show ip ospf interface GigabitEthernet 0/0
GigabitEthernet0/0 is up, line protocol is up
  Internet Address 192.168.1.1/28, Area 0, Attached via Network
  Statement
  Process ID 10, Router ID 1.1.1.1, Network Type BROADCAST, Cost: 1
  Topology-MTID    Cost     Disabled     Shutdown      Topology Name
        0            1         no           no             Base
  Transmit Delay is 1 sec, State DR, Priority 255
  Designated Router (ID) 1.1.1.1, Interface address 192.168.1.1
  Backup Designated router (ID) 2.2.2.2, Interface address 192.168.1.2
  Timer intervals configured, Hello 10, Dead 40, Wait 40, Retransmit 5
    oob-resync timeout 40
    Hello due in 00:00:05
  Supports Link-local Signaling (LLS)
  Cisco NSF helper support enabled
  IETF NSF helper support enabled
  Index 2/2, flood queue length 0
  Next 0x0(0)/0x0(0)
  Last flood scan length is 1, maximum is 2
  Last flood scan time is 0 msec, maximum is 0 msec
  Neighbor Count is 2, Adjacent neighbor count is 2
    Adjacent with neighbor 2.2.2.2  (Backup Designated Router)
    Adjacent with neighbor 3.3.3.3
  Suppress hello for 0 neighbor(s)
R1#
R1# show ip ospf neighbor

Neighbor ID     Pri   State          Dead Time
  Address             Interface
2.2.2.2          1    FULL/BDR       00:00:30    192.168.1.2
  GigabitEthernet0/0
3.3.3.3          0    FULL/DROTHER   00:00:38    192.168.1.3
  GigabitEthernet0/0
R1#
```

### Activity 10.1.1.10: Identify OSPF Network Type Terminology

Refer to the online course to complete this activity.

Interactive
Graphic

**Activity 10.1.1.11: Select the Designated Router**

Refer to the online course to complete this activity.

Packet Tracer
☐ Activity

**Packet Tracer 10.1.1.12: Determining the DR and BDR**

In this activity, you will examine DR and BDR roles and watch the roles change when there is a change in the network. You will then modify the priority to control the roles and force a new election. Finally, you will verify that routers are filling the desired roles.

**Lab 10.1.1.13: Configuring OSPFv2 on a Multiaccess Network**

Refer to *Scaling Networks v6 Labs & Study Guide* and the online course to complete this activity.

In this lab, you will complete the following objectives:

- Part 1: Build the Network and Configure Basic Device Settings
- Part 2: Configure and Verify OSPFv2 on the DR, BDR, and DROTHER
- Part 3: Configure OSPFv2 Interface Priority to Determine the DR and BDR

# Default Route Propagation (10.1.2)

In this topic, you will configure OSPF to propagate a default route.

## Propagating a Default Static Route in OSPFv2 (10.1.2.1)

With OSPF, the router connected to the Internet is used to propagate a default route to other routers in the OSPF routing domain. This router is sometimes called the *edge*, the *entrance*, or the *gateway* router. However, in OSPF terminology, the router located between an OSPF routing domain and a non-OSPF network is also called the *Autonomous System Boundary Router (ASBR)*.

In Figure 10-22, R2 is single-homed to a service provider. Therefore, all that is required for R2 to reach the Internet is a default static route to the service provider.

**Note**

In this example, a loopback interface with IPv4 address 209.165.200.225 is used to simulate the connection to the service provider.

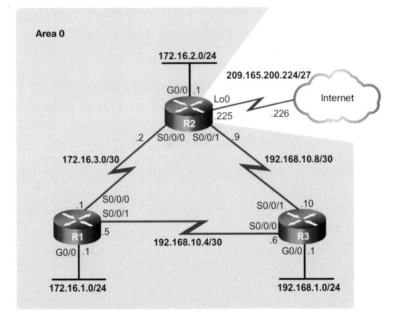

**Figure 10-22**   OSPFv2 Default Route Topology

To propagate a default route, the edge router (R2) must be configured with the following:

- A default static route, using the **ip route 0.0.0.0 0.0.0.0** {*ip-address* | *exit-intf*} command

- The **default-information originate** router configuration mode command, which instructs R2 to be the source of the default route information and propagate the default static route in OSPF updates

Example 10-5 shows how to configure an IPv4 default static route to the service provider and have it propagate in OSPFv2.

**Example 10-5**   Configuring a Default Route on R2

```
R2(config)# ip route 0.0.0.0 0.0.0.0 loopback 0 209.165.200.226
R2(config)# router ospf 10
R2(config-router)# default-information originate
R2(config-router)# end
R2#
```

## Verifying the Propagated IPv4 Default Route (10.1.2.2)

Example 10-6 shows how to verify the default route settings on R2 by using the **show ip route** command.

**Example 10-6**   Verifying a Default Route on R2

```
R2# show ip route | begin Gateway

Gateway of last resort is 209.165.200.226 to network 0.0.0.0

S*      0.0.0.0/0 [1/0] via 209.165.200.226, Loopback0
        172.16.0.0/16 is variably subnetted, 5 subnets, 3 masks
O          172.16.1.0/24 [110/65] via 172.16.3.1, 00:01:44, Serial0/0/0
C          172.16.2.0/24 is directly connected, GigabitEthernet0/0
L          172.16.2.1/32 is directly connected, GigabitEthernet0/0
C          172.16.3.0/30 is directly connected, Serial0/0/0
L          172.16.3.2/32 is directly connected, Serial0/0/0
O       192.168.1.0/24 [110/65] via 192.168.10.10, 00:01:12, Serial0/0/1
        192.168.10.0/24 is variably subnetted, 3 subnets, 2 masks
O          192.168.10.4/30 [110/128] via 192.168.10.10, 00:01:12, Serial0/0/1
                           [110/128] via 172.16.3.1, 00:01:12, Serial0/0/0
C          192.168.10.8/30 is directly connected, Serial0/0/1
L          192.168.10.9/32 is directly connected, Serial0/0/1
        209.165.200.0/24 is variably subnetted, 2 subnets, 2 masks
C          209.165.200.224/30 is directly connected, Loopback0
L          209.165.200.225/32 is directly connected, Loopback0
R2#
```

Example 10-7 shows how to verify that the default route has been propagated to R1 and R3.

**Example 10-7**   Verifying that the Default Route Is Propagated to R1 and R3

```
R1# show ip route | begin Gateway

Gateway of last resort is 172.16.3.2 to network 0.0.0.0

O*E2  0.0.0.0/0 [110/1] via 172.16.3.2, 00:19:37, Serial0/0/0
        172.16.0.0/16 is variably subnetted, 5 subnets, 3 masks
C          172.16.1.0/24 is directly connected, GigabitEthernet0/0
L          172.16.1.1/32 is directly connected, GigabitEthernet0/0
O          172.16.2.0/24 [110/65] via 172.16.3.2, 00:21:19, Serial0/0/0
```

```
C           172.16.3.0/30 is directly connected, Serial0/0/0
L           172.16.3.1/32 is directly connected, Serial0/0/0
O        192.168.1.0/24 [110/65] via 192.168.10.6, 00:20:49, Serial0/0/1
         192.168.10.0/24 is variably subnetted, 3 subnets, 2 masks
C           192.168.10.4/30 is directly connected, Serial0/0/1
L           192.168.10.5/32 is directly connected, Serial0/0/1
O           192.168.10.8/30 [110/128] via 192.168.10.6, 00:20:49, Serial0/0/1
                           [110/128] via 172.16.3.2, 00:20:49, Serial0/0/0
R1#
```

```
R3# show ip route | begin Gateway


Gateway of last resort is 192.168.10.9 to network 0.0.0.0


O*E2  0.0.0.0/0 [110/1] via 192.168.10.9, 00:18:22, Serial0/0/1
         172.16.0.0/16 is variably subnetted, 3 subnets, 2 masks
O           172.16.1.0/24 [110/65] via 192.168.10.5, 00:19:36, Serial0/0/0
O           172.16.2.0/24 [110/65] via 192.168.10.9, 00:19:36, Serial0/0/1
O           172.16.3.0/30 [110/128] via 192.168.10.9, 00:19:36, Serial0/0/1
                          [110/128] via 192.168.10.5, 00:19:36, Serial0/0/0
         192.168.1.0/24 is variably subnetted, 2 subnets, 2 masks
C           192.168.1.0/24 is directly connected, GigabitEthernet0/0
L           192.168.1.1/32 is directly connected, GigabitEthernet0/0
         192.168.10.0/24 is variably subnetted, 4 subnets, 2 masks
C           192.168.10.4/30 is directly connected, Serial0/0/0
L           192.168.10.6/32 is directly connected, Serial0/0/0
C           192.168.10.8/30 is directly connected, Serial0/0/1
L           192.168.10.10/32 is directly connected, Serial0/0/1
R3#
```

Notice that the route source is O*E2, signifying that it was learned using OSPFv2. The asterisk identifies this as a good candidate for the default route. The E2 designation indicates that it is an external route.

External routes are either external type 1 or external type 2. The difference between the two is in the way the cost (metric) of the route is calculated.

The cost of a type 2 route is always the external cost, regardless of the interior cost to reach that route. A type 1 cost is the addition of the external cost and the internal cost used to reach that route. A type 1 route is always preferred over a type 2 route for the same destination.

## Propagating a Default Static Route in OSPFv3 (10.1.2.3)

The process of propagating a default static route in OSPFv3 is almost identical to the process in OSPFv2.

In Figure 10-23, R2 is single-homed to a service provider. Therefore, all that is required for R2 to reach the Internet is a default static route to the service provider.

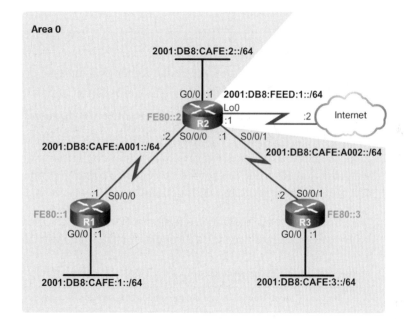

**Figure 10-23** OSPFv3 Default Route Topology

**Note**

In this example, a loopback interface with the IPv6 address 2001:DB8:FEED:1::1/64 is used to simulate the connection to the service provider.

Example 10-8 shows the current IPv6 routing table of R1. Notice that it has no knowledge of the route to the Internet.

**Example 10-8** Verifying the IPv6 Routing Table on R1

```
R1# show ipv6 route ospf
IPv6 Routing Table - default - 8 entries
Codes: C - Connected, L - Local, S - Static, U - Per-user Static route
       B - BGP, R - RIP, H - NHRP, I1 - ISIS L1
       I2 - ISIS L2, IA - ISIS interarea, IS - ISIS summary, D - EIGRP
       EX - EIGRP external, ND - ND Default, NDp - ND Prefix, DCE - Destination
```

```
          NDr - Redirect, O - OSPF Intra, OI - OSPF Inter, OE1 - OSPF ext 1
          OE2 - OSPF ext 2, ON1 - OSPF NSSA ext 1, ON2 - OSPF NSSA ext 2
O    2001:DB8:CAFE:2::/64 [110/648]
     via FE80::2, Serial0/0/0
O    2001:DB8:CAFE:3::/64 [110/648]
     via FE80::2, Serial0/0/0
O    2001:DB8:CAFE:A002::/64 [110/1294]
     via FE80::2, Serial0/0/0
R1#
```

To propagate a default route, the edge router (R2) must be configured with the following:

- A default static route, using the **ipv6 route ::/0** {*ipv6-address* | *exit-intf*} command

- The **default-information originate** router configuration mode command, which instructs R2 to be the source of the default route information and propagate the default static route in OSPF updates

Example 10-9 shows how to configure an IPv6 default static route to the service provider and propagate that route throughout an OSPFv3 domain.

**Example 10-9**    Propagating an OSPFv3 Default Route on R2

```
R2(config)# ipv6 route 0::/0 loopback0 2001:DB8:FEED:1::2
R2(config)# ipv6 router ospf 10
R2(config-rtr)# default-information originate
R2(config-rtr)# end
R2#
*Apr 10 11:36:21.995: %SYS-5-CONFIG_I: Configured from console by console
R2#
```

## Verifying the Propagated IPv6 Default Route (10.1.2.4)

Example 10-10 shows how to verify the default static route setting on R2 by using the **show ipv6 route static** command.

**Example 10-10**    Verifying a Default Route on R2

```
R2# show ipv6 route static
IPv6 Routing Table - default - 12 entries
Codes: C - Connected, L - Local, S - Static, U - Per-user Static route
       B - BGP, R - RIP, H - NHRP, I1 - ISIS L1
```

```
         I2 - ISIS L2, IA - ISIS interarea, IS - ISIS summary, D - EIGRP
         EX - EIGRP external, ND - ND Default, NDp - ND Prefix, DCE - Destination
         NDr - Redirect, O - OSPF Intra, OI - OSPF Inter, OE1 - OSPF ext 1
         OE2 - OSPF ext 2, ON1 - OSPF NSSA ext 1, ON2 - OSPF NSSA ext 2
S    ::/0 [1/0]
     via 2001:DB8:FEED:1::2, Loopback0
R2#
```

Example 10-11 shows how to verify that the default route has been propagated to R1 and R3.

**Example 10-11**   Verifying That the Default Route Is Propagated to R1 and R3

```
R1# show ipv6 route ospf
<output omitted>
OE2 ::/0 [110/1], tag 10
     via FE80::2, Serial0/0/0
O    2001:DB8:CAFE:2::/64 [110/648]
     via FE80::2, Serial0/0/0
O    2001:DB8:CAFE:3::/64 [110/648]
     via FE80::2, Serial0/0/0
O    2001:DB8:CAFE:A002::/64 [110/1294]
     via FE80::2, Serial0/0/0
R1#


R3# show ipv6 route ospf
<output omitted>
OE2 ::/0 [110/1], tag 10
     via FE80::2, GigabitEthernet0/0
O    2001:DB8:CAFE:1::/64 [110/649]
     via FE80::2, GigabitEthernet0/0
O    2001:DB8:CAFE:2::/64 [110/1]
     via GigabitEthernet0/0, directly connected
O    2001:DB8:CAFE:A001::/64 [110/648]
     via FE80::2, GigabitEthernet0/0
R3#
```

Notice that the route source is OE2, signifying that it was learned using OSPFv3. The E2 designation indicates that it is external route. Unlike with the IPv4 routing table, IPv6 does not use the asterisk to signify that the route is a good candidate for the default route.

**Packet Tracer 10.1.2.5: Propagating a Default Route in OSPFv2**

Background/Scenario

In this activity, you will configure an IPv4 default route to the Internet and propagate that default route to other OSPF routers. You will then verify that the default route is in downstream routing tables and that hosts can access a web server on the Internet.

# Fine-tuning OSPF Interfaces (10.1.3)

In this topic, you will configure OSPF interface settings to improve network performance.

## OSPF Hello and Dead Intervals (10.1.3.1)

The *OSPF hello and dead intervals* are configurable on a per-interface basis. The OSPF intervals must match, or a neighbor adjacency does not occur.

To verify the currently configured OSPFv2 interface intervals, use the **show ip ospf interface** command, as shown in Example 10-12.

**Example 10-12**    Verifying the OSPFv2 Intervals on R1

```
R1# show ip ospf interface serial 0/0/0
Serial0/0/0 is up, line protocol is up
  Internet Address 172.16.3.1/30, Area 0, Attached via Network Statement
  Process ID 10, Router ID 1.1.1.1, Network Type POINT_TO_POINT, Cost: 64
  Topology-MTID    Cost    Disabled    Shutdown    Topology Name
        0           64        no          no             Base
  Transmit Delay is 1 sec, State POINT_TO_POINT
  Timer intervals configured, Hello 10, Dead 40, Wait 40, Retransmit 5
    oob-resync timeout 40
    Hello due in 00:00:03
  Supports Link-local Signaling (LLS)
  Cisco NSF helper support enabled
  IETF NSF helper support enabled
  Index 2/2, flood queue length 0
  Next 0x0(0)/0x0(0)
  Last flood scan length is 1, maximum is 1
  Last flood scan time is 0 msec, maximum is 0 msec
  Neighbor Count is 1, Adjacent neighbor count is 1
    Adjacent with neighbor 2.2.2.2
  Suppress hello for 0 neighbor(s)
R1#
```

The Serial 0/0/0 hello and dead intervals are set to the default 10 seconds and 40 seconds, respectively.

Example 10-13 provides an example of using a filtering technique to display the OSPFv2 intervals for the OSPF-enabled interface Serial 0/0/0 on R1.

**Example 10-13**   Verifying the OSPFv2 Intervals on R1 by Using a Filter

```
R1# show ip ospf interface | include Timer
  Timer intervals configured, Hello 10, Dead 40, Wait 40, Retransmit 5
  Timer intervals configured, Hello 10, Dead 40, Wait 40, Retransmit 5
  Timer intervals configured, Hello 10, Dead 40, Wait 40, Retransmit 5
R1#
```

In Example 10-14, the **show ip ospf neighbor** command is used on R1 to verify that R1 is adjacent to R2 and R3.

**Example 10-14**   Verifying OSPFv2 Adjacencies on R1

```
R1# show ip ospf neighbor

Neighbor ID     Pri   State      Dead Time    Address         Interface
3.3.3.3           0   FULL/  -    00:00:35     192.168.10.6    Serial0/0/1
2.2.2.2           0   FULL/  -    00:00:33     172.16.3.2      Serial0/0/0
R1#
```

Notice in the output that the dead timer is counting down from 40 seconds. By default, this value is refreshed every 10 seconds, when R1 receives a Hello packet from the neighbor.

## Modifying OSPFv2 Intervals (10.1.3.2)

It may be desirable to change the OSPF timers so that routers detect network failures in less time. Doing this increases traffic, but sometimes the need for quick convergence is more important than the extra traffic it creates.

**Note**

The default hello and dead intervals are based on best practices and should be altered only in rare situations.

OSPFv2 hello and dead intervals can be modified manually using the following interface configuration mode commands:

- **ip ospf hello-interval** *seconds*
- **ip ospf dead-interval** *seconds*

Use the **no ip ospf hello-interval** and **no ip ospf dead-interval** commands to reset the intervals to their default.

Example 10-15 shows how to modify the hello interval to 5 seconds.

**Example 10-15**    Modifying the R1 Serial 0/0/0 Interface OSPFv2 Intervals

```
R1(config)# interface Serial 0/0/0
R1(config-if)# ip ospf hello-interval 5
R1(config-if)# ip ospf dead-interval 20
R1(config-if)# end
*Apr  7 17:28:21.529: %OSPF-5-ADJCHG: Process 10, Nbr 2.2.2.2 on Serial0/0/0 from
  FULL to DOWN, Neighbor Down: Dead timer expired
R1#
```

Immediately after you change the hello interval, the Cisco IOS automatically modifies the dead interval to four times the hello interval. However, it is always good practice to explicitly modify the timer instead of relying on an automatic IOS feature so that modifications are documented in the configuration. Therefore, Example 10-15 shows the dead interval also being manually set to 20 seconds on the R1 Serial 0/0/0 interface.

As indicated in the highlighted OSPFv2 adjacency message in Example 10-15, when the dead timer on R1 expires, R1 and R2 lose adjacency. The reason is because the values have been altered on only one side of the serial link between R1 and R2. Recall that the OSPF hello and dead intervals must match between neighbors.

Use the **show ip ospf neighbor** command on R1 to verify the neighbor adjacencies, as shown in Example 10-16.

**Example 10-16**    Verifying the OSPFv2 Neighbor Adjacencies on R1

```
R1# show ip ospf neighbor

Neighbor ID     Pri   State           Dead Time   Address         Interface
3.3.3.3           0   FULL/  -        00:00:37    192.168.10.6    Serial0/0/1
R1#
```

Notice that the only neighbor listed is the 3.3.3.3 (R3) router and that R1 is no longer adjacent with the 2.2.2.2 (R2) neighbor. The timers set on Serial 0/0/0 do not affect the neighbor adjacency with R3.

To restore adjacency between R1 and R2, the R2 Serial 0/0/0 interface hello interval is set to 5 seconds, as shown in Example 10-17.

**Example 10-17** Modifying the R2 Serial 0/0/0 Interface OSPF Intervals

```
R2(config)# interface serial 0/0/0
R2(config-if)# ip ospf hello-interval 5
*Apr  7 17:41:49.001: %OSPF-5-ADJCHG: Process 10, Nbr 1.1.1.1 on Serial0/0/0 from
  LOADING to FULL, Loading Done
R2(config-if)# end
R2#
```

Almost immediately, the IOS displays a message that adjacency has been established, and the state is Full.

Verify the interface intervals by using the **show ip ospf interface** command and the neighbor adjacencies, as shown in Example 10-18.

**Example 10-18** Verifying the OSPF Neighbor Adjacencies on R2

```
R2# show ip ospf interface s0/0/0 | include Timer
  Timer intervals configured, Hello 5, Dead 20, Wait 20, Retransmit 5
R2#
R2# show ip ospf neighbor

Neighbor ID     Pri   State           Dead Time   Address         Interface
3.3.3.3           0   FULL/   -       00:00:35    192.168.10.10   Serial0/0/1
1.1.1.1           0   FULL/   -       00:00:17    172.16.3.1      Serial0/0/0
R2#
```

Notice that the hello time is 5 seconds, and the dead time was automatically set to 20 seconds instead of the default 40 seconds. Remember that OSPF automatically sets the dead interval to four times the hello interval.

## Modifying OSPFv3 Intervals (10.1.3.3)

Like OSPFv2 intervals, OSPFv3 intervals can be adjusted. You can modify OSPFv3 hello and dead intervals manually by using the following interface configuration mode commands:

- **ipv6 ospf hello-interval** *seconds*

- **ipv6 ospf dead-interval** *seconds*

**Note**

Use the **no ipv6 ospf hello-interval** and **no ipv6 ospf dead-interval** commands to reset the intervals to their defaults.

Refer to the IPv6 topology in Figure 10-23. Assume that the network has converged using OSPFv3.

Example 10-19 shows how to modify the OSPFv3 hello interval to 5 seconds.

**Example 10-19**    Modifying the R1 Serial 0/0/0 Interface OSPFv3 Intervals

```
R1(config)# interface Serial 0/0/0
R1(config-if)# ipv6 ospf hello-interval 5
R1(config-if)# ipv6 ospf dead-interval 20
R1(config-if)# end
*Apr 10 15:03:51.175: %OSPFv3-5-ADJCHG: Process 10, Nbr 2.2.2.2 on Serial0/0/0 from
  FULL to DOWN, Neighbor Down: Dead timer expired
R1#
```

Immediately after you change the hello interval, the Cisco IOS automatically modifies the dead interval to four times the Hello interval. However, as with OSPFv2, it is always good practice to explicitly modify the timer instead of relying on an automatic IOS feature so that modifications are documented in the configuration. Therefore, Example 10-19 shows the dead interval also being manually set to 20 seconds on the R1 Serial 0/0/0 interface.

When the dead timer on R1 expires, R1 and R2 lose adjacency, as indicated in the highlighted OSPFv3 adjacency message in Example 10-19, because the values have been altered on only one side of the serial link, between R1 and R2. Recall that the OSPFv3 hello and dead intervals must be equivalent between neighbors.

Use the **show ipv6 ospf neighbor** command on R1 to verify the neighbor adjacencies, as shown in Example 10-20.

**Example 10-20**    Verifying the OSPFv3 Neighbor Adjacencies on R1

```
R1# show ipv6 ospf neighbor
R1#
```

Notice that R1 is no longer adjacent with the 2.2.2.2 (R2) neighbor.

To restore adjacency between R1 and R2, set the R2 Serial 0/0/0 interface hello interval to 5 seconds, as shown in Example 10-21.

**Example 10-21**    Modifying the R2 Serial 0/0/0 Interface OSPFv3 Intervals

```
R2(config)# interface serial 0/0/0
R2(config-if)# ipv6 ospf hello-interval 5
*Apr 10 15:07:28.815: %OSPFv3-5-ADJCHG: Process 10, Nbr 1.1.1.1 on Serial0/0/0 from
  LOADING to FULL, Loading Done
R2(config-if)# end
R2#
```

Almost immediately, the IOS displays a message that adjacency has been established, and the state is Full.

Example 10-22 shows how to verify the interface intervals by using the **show ipv6 ospf interface** command and verify the neighbor adjacencies.

**Example 10-22**  Verifying the OSPFv3 Neighbor Adjacencies on R2

```
R2# show ipv6 ospf interface s0/0/0 | include Timer
  Timer intervals configured, Hello 5, Dead 20, Wait 20, Retransmit 5
R2#
R2# show ipv6 ospf neighbor

            OSPFv3 Router with ID (2.2.2.2) (Process ID 10)


Neighbor ID     Pri   State          Dead Time   Interface ID   Interface
3.3.3.3           0   FULL/  -       00:00:38    7              Serial0/0/1
1.1.1.1           0   FULL/  -       00:00:19    6              Serial0/0/0
R2#
```

Notice that the hello time is 5 seconds and the dead time was automatically set to 20 seconds instead of the default 40 seconds. Remember that OSPF automatically sets the dead interval to four times the hello interval.

**Packet Tracer 10.1.3.4: Configuring OSPFv2 Advanced Features**

In this lab, you will complete the following objectives:

- Part 1: Modify OSPF Default Settings

- Part 2: Verify Connectivity

---

**Lab 10.1.3.5: Configuring OSPFv2 Advanced Features**

Refer to *Scaling Networks v6 Labs & Study Guide* and the online course to complete this activity.

In this lab, you will complete the following objectives:

- Part 1: Build the Network and Configure Basic Device Settings

- Part 2: Configure and Verify OSPF Routing

- Part 3: Change OSPF Metrics

- Part 4: Configure and Propagate a Static Default Route

# Troubleshooting Single-Area OSPF Implementations (10.2)

In this section, you will learn about troubleshooting single-area OSPF implementations.

## Components of Troubleshooting Single-Area OSPF (10.2.1)

In this topic, you will learn about the process and tools used to troubleshoot a single-area OSPF network.

### Overview (10.2.1.1)

OSPF is a popularly implemented routing protocol used in large enterprise networks. Troubleshooting problems related to the exchange of routing information is one of the most essential skills for a network professional involved in the implementation and maintenance of large, routed enterprise networks that use OSPF as the IGP.

OSPF adjacencies do not form if one or more of the following conditions exist:

- The interfaces are not on the same network.
- The OSPF network types do not match.
- The OSPF hello timer or the OSPF dead timer does not match.
- The interface to the neighbor is incorrectly configured as passive.
- There is a missing or incorrect OSPF **network** command.
- Authentication is misconfigured.
- An interface is not properly addressed or is not in the "up and up" condition.

### OSPF States (10.2.1.2)

To troubleshoot OSPF, it is important to understand how OSPF routers traverse different OSPF states when adjacencies are being established, as shown in Figure 10-24.

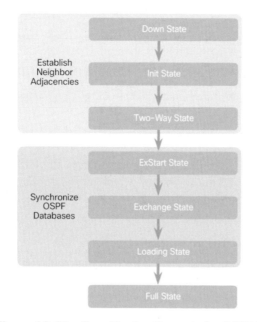

**Figure 10-24**    Transitioning Through the OSPF States

Table 10-3 lists the details of each state.

**Table 10-3**    OSPF State Descriptions

| OSPF State | Description |
| --- | --- |
| Down state | ■ No Hello packets received = Down. |
| | ■ Router sends Hello packets. |
| | ■ Transition to Init state. |
| Init state | ■ Hello packets are received from the neighbor. |
| | ■ They contain the sending router's router ID. |
| | ■ Transition to Two-Way state. |
| Two-Way state | ■ On Ethernet links, elect a DR and a BDR. |
| | ■ Transition to ExStart state. |
| ExStart state | ■ Negotiate the master/slave relationship and DBD packet sequence number. |
| | ■ The master initiates the DBD packet exchange. |
| Exchange state | ■ Routers exchange DBD packets. |
| | ■ If additional router information is required, transition to Loading; otherwise, transition to the Full state. |

| OSPF State | Description |
|---|---|
| Loading state | ■ LSRs and LSUs are used to gain additional route information.<br>■ Routes are processed using the SPF algorithm.<br>■ Transition to the Full state. |
| Full state | ■ Routers have converged. |

When troubleshooting OSPF neighbors, be aware that the Full and Two-Way states are normal. All other states are transitory, which means a router should not remain in those states for extended periods of time.

## OSPF Troubleshooting Commands (10.2.1.3)

Many different OSPF commands can be used in the troubleshooting process, including the following:

- **show ip protocols**
- **show ip ospf neighbor**
- **show ip ospf interface**
- **show ip ospf**
- **show ip route ospf**
- **clear ip ospf** [*process-id*] **process**

The following pages provide brief descriptions and examples of these commands.

Example 10-23 shows output generated by the **show ip protocols** command, which is very useful for verifying vital OSPFv2 settings.

**Example 10-23**   Verifying the OSPF Settings on R1

```
R1# show ip protocols
*** IP Routing is NSF aware ***

Routing Protocol is "ospf 10"
  Outgoing update filter list for all interfaces is not set
  Incoming update filter list for all interfaces is not set
  Router ID 1.1.1.1
  Number of areas in this router is 1. 1 normal 0 stub 0 nssa
  Maximum path: 4
```

```
    Routing for Networks:
      172.16.1.1 0.0.0.0 area 0
      172.16.3.1 0.0.0.0 area 0
      192.168.10.5 0.0.0.0 area 0
    Passive Interface(s):
      GigabitEthernet0/0
    Routing Information Sources:
      Gateway         Distance      Last Update
      3.3.3.3             110       00:08:35
      2.2.2.2             110       00:08:35
    Distance: (default is 110)

R1#
```

The command in Example 10-23 identifies the OSPFv2 process ID, the router ID, networks the router is advertising, the neighbors the router is receiving updates from, and the default administrative distance, which is 110 for OSPF.

Example 10-24 shows output generated by the **show ip ospf neighbor** command, which is useful for verifying OSPFv2 adjacencies with neighboring routers.

**Example 10-24**    Verifying the OSPF Neighbor Adjacencies on R1

```
R1# show ip ospf neighbor

Neighbor ID     Pri  State         Dead Time   Address         Interface
2.2.2.2           1  FULL/BDR      00:00:30    192.168.1.2     GigabitEthernet0/0
        0  FULL/DROTHER    00:00:38  192.168.1.3     GigabitEthernet0/0
R1#
```

The command in Example 10-24 lists the neighboring OSPF peers and identifies for each the neighbor router ID, neighbor priority, OSPFv2 state, dead timer, neighbor interface IPv4 address, and the interface through which the neighbor is accessible.

If the router ID of the neighboring router is not displayed or if it does not show the state as FULL or 2WAY, the two routers have not formed an OSPFv2 adjacency. If two routers do not establish adjacency, link-state information is not exchanged. Incomplete link-state databases can cause inaccurate SPF trees and routing tables. Routes to destination networks may not exist or may not be the most optimum paths.

Example 10-25 shows output generated by the **show ip ospf interface** command, which is used to verify the OSPFv2 parameters configured on an interface.

**Example 10-25**  Verifying the OSPF Interface Settings of Serial 0/0/0 on R1

```
R1# show ip ospf interface Serial 0/0/0
Serial0/0/0 is up, line protocol is up
  Internet Address 172.16.3.1/30, Area 0, Attached via Network Statement
  Process ID 10, Router ID 1.1.1.1, Network Type POINT_TO_POINT, Cost: 64
  Topology-MTID    Cost    Disabled    Shutdown      Topology Name
         0          64        no          no             Base
  Transmit Delay is 1 sec, State POINT_TO_POINT
  Timer intervals configured, Hello 5, Dead 20, Wait 20, Retransmit 5
    oob-resync timeout 40
    Hello due in 00:00:02
  Supports Link-local Signaling (LLS)
  Cisco NSF helper support enabled
  IETF NSF helper support enabled
  Index 2/2, flood queue length 0
  Next 0x0(0)/0x0(0)
  Last flood scan length is 1, maximum is 1
  Last flood scan time is 0 msec, maximum is 0 msec
  Neighbor Count is 1, Adjacent neighbor count is 1
    Adjacent with neighbor 2.2.2.2
  Suppress hello for 0 neighbor(s)
  Message digest authentication enabled
    Youngest key id is 1
R1#
```

The command in Example 10-25 identifies the OSPFv2 process ID that the interface is assigned to, the area that the interfaces are in, the cost of the interface, and the hello and dead intervals. Adding the interface name and number to the command displays output for a specific interface.

Example 10-26 shows output generated by the **show ip ospf** command, which is used to examine the OSPFv2 operational information.

**Example 10-26**  Verifying the OSPF Operational Information

```
R1# show ip ospf
Routing Process "ospf 10" with ID 1.1.1.1
 Start time: 00:02:19.116, Time elapsed: 00:01:00.796
 Supports only single TOS(TOS0) routes
 Supports opaque LSA
 Supports Link-local Signaling (LLS)
 Supports area transit capability
 Supports NSSA (compatible with RFC 3101)
 Event-log enabled, Maximum number of events: 1000, Mode: cyclic
 Router is not originating router-LSAs with maximum metric
```

```
Initial SPF schedule delay 5000 msecs
Minimum hold time between two consecutive SPFs 10000 msecs
Maximum wait time between two consecutive SPFs 10000 msecs
Incremental-SPF disabled
Minimum LSA interval 5 secs
Minimum LSA arrival 1000 msecs
LSA group pacing timer 240 secs
Interface flood pacing timer 33 msecs
Retransmission pacing timer 66 msecs
Number of external LSA 1. Checksum Sum 0x00A1FF
Number of opaque AS LSA 0. Checksum Sum 0x000000
Number of DCbitless external and opaque AS LSA 0
Number of DoNotAge external and opaque AS LSA 0
Number of areas in this router is 1. 1 normal 0 stub 0 nssa
Number of areas transit capable is 0
External flood list length 0
IETF NSF helper support enabled
Cisco NSF helper support enabled
Reference bandwidth unit is 100 mbps
    Area BACKBONE(0)
        Number of interfaces in this area is 3
      Area has no authentication
      SPF algorithm last executed 00:00:36.936 ago
      SPF algorithm executed 3 times
      Area ranges are
      Number of LSA 3. Checksum Sum 0x016D60
      Number of opaque link LSA 0. Checksum Sum 0x000000
      Number of DCbitless LSA 0
      Number of indication LSA 0
      Number of DoNotAge LSA 0
      Flood list length 0

R1#
```

The command in Example 10-26 identifies the process ID and router ID, as well as other assorted information, such as the last time the SPF algorithm was calculated, the number and type of areas the router is connected to, and whether authentication has been configured.

Example 10-27 shows output generated by the **show ip route ospf** command, which is used to examine only the OSPFv2 learned routes in the IPv4 routing table. In this example, R1 has learned about four remote networks through OSPFv2.

**Example 10-27**   Verifying the OSPF Routes in the Routing Table on R1

```
R1# show ip route ospf | begin Gateway

Gateway of last resort is 172.16.3.2 to network 0.0.0.0

O*E2  0.0.0.0/0 [110/1] via 172.16.3.2, 00:33:17, Serial0/0/0
        172.16.0.0/16 is variably subnetted, 5 subnets, 3 masks
O          172.16.2.0/24 [110/65] via 172.16.3.2, 00:33:17, Serial0/0/0
O       192.168.1.0/24 [110/65] via 192.168.10.6, 00:30:43, Serial0/0/1
        192.168.10.0/24 is variably subnetted, 3 subnets, 2 masks
O          192.168.10.8/30 [110/128] via 192.168.10.6, 00:30:43, Serial0/0/1
                             [110/128] via 172.16.3.2, 00:33:17, Serial0/0/0
R1#
```

When an OSPF change has occurred, such as a changed router ID, it is sometimes necessary to reset the OSPFv2 neighbor adjacencies by using the **clear ip ospf** [*process-id*] **process** command.

**Note**

For the equivalent OSPFv3 command, simply substitute **ipv6** for **ip**.

## Components of Troubleshooting OSPF (10.2.1.4)

OSPF problems usually relate to the following:

- Neighbor adjacencies
- Missing routes
- Path selection

When troubleshooting neighbor issues, use the troubleshooting flowchart shown in Figure 10-25.

First, verify whether the router has established adjacencies with neighboring routers by using the OSPFv2 **show ip ospf neighbor** command. If there is no adjacency, then the routers cannot exchange routes.

Verify whether interfaces are operational and enabled for OSPFv2 by using the **show ip interface brief** and **show ip ospf interface** commands. If the interfaces are operational and enabled for OSPFv2, ensure that interfaces on both routers are configured for the same OSPFv2 area and that the interfaces are not configured as passive interfaces.

If adjacency between two routers is established, verify that there are OSPFv2 routes in the IPv4 routing table, as shown in Figure 10-26.

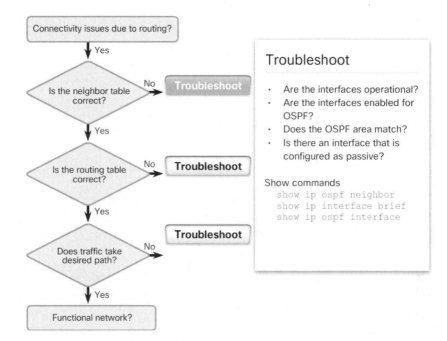

**Figure 10-25**    Troubleshooting OSPF Neighbor Issues

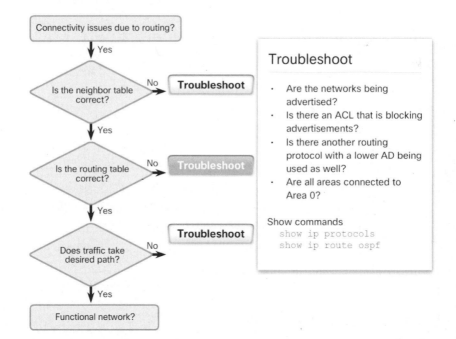

**Figure 10-26**    Troubleshooting OSPF Routing Table Issues

Use the **show ip route ospf** and **show ip protocols** commands to verify routing information.

If there are no OSPFv2 routes, verify that there are no other routing protocols with lower administrative distances running in the network. Verify that all the required networks are advertised in OSPFv2. Also verify whether an access list is configured on a router that would filter either incoming or outgoing routing updates.

If all the required routes are in the routing table but the path that traffic takes is not correct, verify the OSPFv2 cost on interfaces on the path, as shown in Figure 10-27.

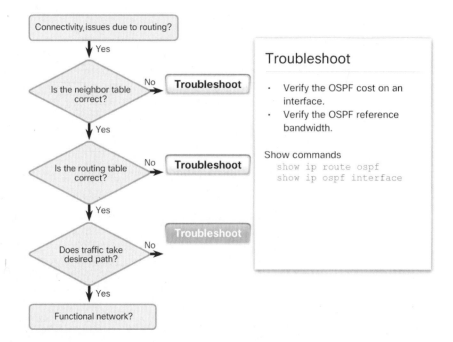

**Figure 10-27**    Troubleshooting OSPF Path Selection Issues

Useful commands for troubleshooting path selection issues include the **show ip route ospf** and **show ip ospf interface** commands to verify routing information.

Be careful in cases where the interfaces are faster than 100 Mbps, because all interfaces above this bandwidth by default have the same OSPFv2 cost.

**Note**

The commands and processes are similar for OSPFv3. For the equivalent OSPFv3 commands, simply substitute **ipv6** for **ip**.

**Activity 10.2.1.5: Identify the Troubleshooting Command**

Refer to the online course to complete this activity.

## Troubleshoot Single-Area OSPFv2 Routing Issues (10.2.2)

In this topic, you will troubleshoot missing route entries in the single-area OSPFv2 routing table.

### Troubleshooting Neighbor Issues (10.2.2.1)

The topology in Figure 10-28 is used in this section to highlight how to troubleshoot neighbor problems. In this topology, all the routers have been configured to support OSPFv2 routing. However, R1 is not receiving R2 routes.

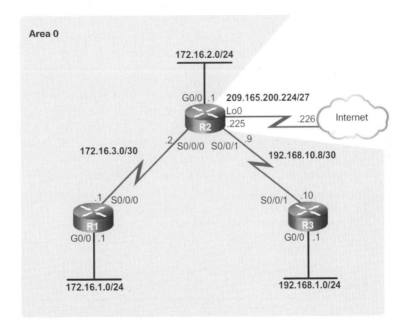

**Figure 10-28**   OSPFv2 Topology

Example 10-28 shows the routing table of R1.

**Example 10-28**    Verifying OSPF Routes in the Routing Table of R1

```
R1# show ip route | begin Gateway

Gateway of last resort is not set

      172.16.0.0/16 is variably subnetted, 4 subnets, 3 masks
C        172.16.1.0/24 is directly connected, GigabitEthernet0/0
L        172.16.1.1/32 is directly connected, GigabitEthernet0/0
C        172.16.3.0/30 is directly connected, Serial0/0/0
L        172.16.3.1/32 is directly connected, Serial0/0/0
R1#
```

The output confirms that R1 is not adding any OSPFv2 routes. This could be happening for a number of reasons. However, a prerequisite for the neighbor relationship to form between two routers is OSI Layer 3 connectivity. Therefore, you should verify Layer 3 connectivity.

Example 10-29 shows how to verify the interface status and test connectivity to R2.

**Example 10-29**    Verifying Layer 3 Connectivity to R2

```
R1# show ip interface brief
Interface                    IP-Address      OK? Method Status                Protocol
Embedded-Service-Engine0/0   unassigned      YES unset  administratively down down
GigabitEthernet0/0           172.16.1.1      YES manual up                    up
GigabitEthernet0/1           unassigned      YES unset  administratively down down
Serial0/0/0                  172.16.3.1      YES manual up                    up
Serial0/0/1                  unassigned      YES TFTP   up                    up
R1#
R1# ping 172.16.3.2
Type escape sequence to abort.
Sending 5, 100-byte ICMP Echos to 172.16.3.2, timeout is 2 seconds:
!!!!!
Success rate is 100 percent (5/5), round-trip min/avg/max = 12/14/16 ms
R1#
```

Notice in Example 10-29 that the Serial 0/0/0 interface is up and active. The successful **ping** also confirms that the R2 serial interface is active, and Layer 3 connectivity is successful.

If the **ping** is not successful, check the cabling and verify that interfaces on connected devices are configured correctly and are operational.

A successful **ping** does not mean an adjacency will form because it is possible to have overlapping subnets or misconfigured OSPF parameters. You still have to verify that interfaces on the connected devices share the same subnet.

For an interface to be enabled for OSPFv2, a matching **network** command must be configured in the OSPFv2 routing process. Active OSPFv2 interfaces can be verified by using the **show ip ospf interface** command.

Example 10-30 shows how to verify that the Serial 0/0/0 interface is enabled for OSPFv2.

**Example 10-30**    Verifying Whether OSPF Is Enabled on the R1 Serial 0/0/0

```
R1# show ip ospf interface serial 0/0/0
Serial0/0/0 is up, line protocol is up
  Internet Address 172.16.3.1/30, Area 0, Attached via Network Statement
  Process ID 10, Router ID 1.1.1.1, Network Type POINT_TO_POINT, Cost: 64
  Topology-MTID    Cost    Disabled    Shutdown    Topology Name
        0           64        no          no           Base
  Transmit Delay is 1 sec, State POINT_TO_POINT
  Timer intervals configured, Hello 5, Dead 20, Wait 20, Retransmit 5
    oob-resync timeout 40
    No Hellos (Passive interface)
  Supports Link-local Signaling (LLS)
  Cisco NSF helper support enabled
  IETF NSF helper support enabled
  Index 2/2, flood queue length 0
  Next 0x0(0)/0x0(0)
  Last flood scan length is 1, maximum is 1
  Last flood scan time is 0 msec, maximum is 0 msec
  Neighbor Count is 0, Adjacent neighbor count is 0
  Suppress hello for 0 neighbor(s)
  Message digest authentication enabled
    Youngest key id is 1
R1#
```

If connected interfaces on two routers are not enabled for OSPF, the neighbors do not form an adjacency.

Example 10-31 shows how to use the **show ip protocols** command to verify that OSPFv2 is enabled on R1.

**Example 10-31**    Verifying the OSPFv2 Settings on R1

```
R1# show ip protocols
*** IP Routing is NSF aware ***

Routing Protocol is "ospf 10"
  Outgoing update filter list for all interfaces is not set
  Incoming update filter list for all interfaces is not set
  Router ID 1.1.1.1
  Number of areas in this router is 1. 1 normal 0 stub 0 nssa
  Maximum path: 4
  Routing for Networks:
    172.16.1.1 0.0.0.0 area 0
    172.16.3.1 0.0.0.0 area 0
Passive Interface(s):
    GigabitEthernet0/0
    Serial0/0/0
 Routing Information Sources:
    Gateway         Distance      Last Update
    3.3.3.3              110      00:50:03
    2.2.2.2              110      04:27:25
  Distance: (default is 110)

R1#
```

The output in Example 10-31 also lists the networks being advertised as enabled by the **network** command. If an IPv4 address on an interface falls within a network that has been enabled for OSPFv2, the interface is also enabled for OSPFv2.

However, notice that the Serial 0/0/0 interface is listed as passive. The **passive-interface** command stops both outgoing and incoming routing updates because the effect of the command causes the router to stop sending and receiving Hello packets over an interface. For this reason, the routers do not become neighbors.

To disable the interface as passive, use the **no passive-interface** router configuration mode command, as shown in Example 10-32.

**Example 10-32**    Disabling Passive Interface on the R1 S0/0/0 Interface

```
R1(config)# router ospf 10
R1(config-router)# no passive-interface s0/0/0
*Apr  9 13:14:15.454: %OSPF-5-ADJCHG: Process 10, Nbr 2.2.2.2 on Serial0/0/0 from
  LOADING to FULL, Loading Done
R1(config-router)# end
R1#
```

After you disable the passive interface, the routers become adjacent, as indicated by the automatically generated information message.

A quick verification of the routing table, as shown in Example 10-33, confirms that OSPFv2 is now exchanging routing information.

**Example 10-33**   Verifying OSPF Routes in the Routing Table of R1

```
R1# show ip route ospf | begin Gateway

Gateway of last resort is 172.16.3.2 to network 0.0.0.0

O*E2  0.0.0.0/0 [110/1] via 172.16.3.2, 00:00:18, Serial0/0/0
      172.16.0.0/16 is variably subnetted, 5 subnets, 3 masks
O        172.16.2.0/24 [110/65] via 172.16.3.2, 00:00:18, Serial0/0/0
O     192.168.1.0/24 [110/129] via 172.16.3.2, 00:00:18, Serial0/0/0
      192.168.10.0/30 is subnetted, 1 subnets
O        192.168.10.8 [110/128] via 172.16.3.2, 00:00:18, Serial0/0/0
R1#
```

Other types of problems could also stop OSPF from establishing neighbor relationships. For instance, a problem may arise is which two neighboring routers have mismatched MTU sizes on their connecting interfaces. The MTU size is the largest network layer packet that the router will forward out each interface. Routers default to an MTU size of 1500 bytes. However, you can change this value for IPv4 packets by using the **ip mtu** *size* interface configuration command or the **ipv6 mtu** *size* interface command for IPv6 packets. If two connecting routers had mismatched MTU values, they would still attempt to form an adjacency, but they would not exchange their LSDBs, and the neighbor relationship would fail.

## Troubleshooting OSPFv2 Routing Table Issues (10.2.2.2)

A quick look at the R1 routing table (see Example 10-34) reveals that it receives default route information, the R2 LAN (172.16.2.0/24), and the link between R2 and R3 (192.168.10.8/30). However, it does not receive the R3 LAN OSPFv2 route.

**Example 10-34**   Verifying OSPF Routes in the Routing Table of R1

```
R1# show ip route | begin Gateway

Gateway of last resort is 172.16.3.2 to network 0.0.0.0

O*E2  0.0.0.0/0 [110/1] via 172.16.3.2, 00:05:26, Serial0/0/0
      172.16.0.0/16 is variably subnetted, 5 subnets, 3 masks
C        172.16.1.0/24 is directly connected, GigabitEthernet0/0
L        172.16.1.1/32 is directly connected, GigabitEthernet0/0
```

```
O          172.16.2.0/24 [110/65] via 172.16.3.2, 00:05:26, Serial0/0/0
C          172.16.3.0/30 is directly connected, Serial0/0/0
L          172.16.3.1/32 is directly connected, Serial0/0/0
       192.168.10.0/30 is subnetted, 1 subnets
O          192.168.10.8 [110/128] via 172.16.3.2, 00:05:26, Serial0/0/0
R1#
```

The output in Example 10-35 verifies the OSPFv2 settings on R3.

**Example 10-35**    Verifying OSPF Settings on R3

```
R3# show ip protocols
*** IP Routing is NSF aware ***

Routing Protocol is "ospf 10"
  Outgoing update filter list for all interfaces is not set
  Incoming update filter list for all interfaces is not set
  Router ID 3.3.3.3
  Number of areas in this router is 1. 1 normal 0 stub 0 nssa
  Maximum path: 4
  Routing for Networks:
  192.168.10.8 0.0.0.3 area 0
  Passive Interface(s):
    Embedded-Service-Engine0/0
    GigabitEthernet0/0
    GigabitEthernet0/1
    GigabitEthernet0/3
    RG-AR-IF-INPUT1
  Routing Information Sources:
    Gateway         Distance      Last Update
    1.1.1.1              110       00:02:48
    2.2.2.2              110       00:02:48
  Distance: (default is 110)

R3#
```

Notice that R3 only advertises the link between R3 and R2. It does not advertise the R3 LAN (192.168.1.0/24).

For an interface to be enabled for OSPFv2, a matching **network** command must be configured in the OSPFv2 routing process. The output in Example 10-36 confirms that the R3 LAN is not advertised in OSPFv2.

**Example 10-36**   Verifying the OSPF Router Configuration on R3

```
R3# show running-config | section router ospf
router ospf 10
 router-id 3.3.3.3
 passive-interface default
 no passive-interface Serial0/0/1
 network 192.168.10.8 0.0.0.3 area 0
R3#
```

Example 10-37 adds a **network** command for the R3 LAN. R3 should now advertise the R3 LAN to its OSPFv2 neighbors.

**Example 10-37**   Advertising the R3 LAN in OSPF

```
R3(config)# router ospf 10
R3(config-router)# network 192.168.1.0 0.0.0.255 area 0
R3(config-router)# end
*Apr 10 11:03:11.115: %SYS-5-CONFIG_I: Configured from console by console
R3#
```

The output in Example 10-38 verifies that the R3 LAN is now in the routing table of R1.

**Example 10-38**   Verifying OSPF Routes in the Routing Table of R1

```
R1# show ip route ospf | begin Gateway

Gateway of last resort is 172.16.3.2 to network 0.0.0.0

O*E2  0.0.0.0/0 [110/1] via 172.16.3.2, 00:08:38, Serial0/0/0
        172.16.0.0/16 is variably subnetted, 5 subnets, 3 masks
O         172.16.2.0/24 [110/65] via 172.16.3.2, 00:08:38, Serial0/0/0
O      192.168.1.0/24 [110/129] via 172.16.3.2, 00:00:37, Serial0/0/0
        192.168.10.0/30 is subnetted, 1 subnets
O         192.168.10.8 [110/128] via 172.16.3.2, 00:08:38, Serial0/0/0
R1#
```

**Packet Tracer
☐ Activity**

**Packet Tracer 10.2.2.3: Troubleshooting Single-Area OSPFv2**

In this activity, you will troubleshoot OSPF routing issues by using **ping** and **show** commands to identify errors in the network configuration. Then you will document the errors you discover and implement an appropriate solution. Finally, you will verify that end-to-end connectivity is restored.

## Troubleshoot Single-Area OSPFv3 Routing Issues (10.2.3)

In this topic, you will troubleshoot missing route entries in a single-area OSPFv3 routing table.

### OSPFv3 Troubleshooting Commands (10.2.3.1)

Figure 10-29 shows the OSPFv3 reference topology used in this section.

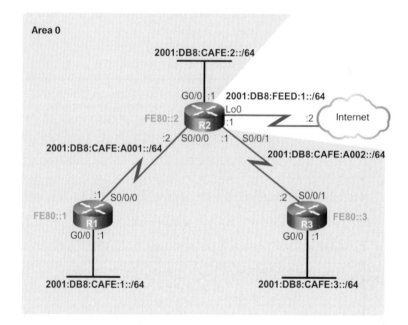

**Figure 10-29**   OSPFv3 Topology

Troubleshooting OSPFv3 is almost identical to troubleshooting OSPFv2. Many OSPFv2 commands and troubleshooting criteria also apply to OSPFv3.

OSPF commands that can be used to help in the OSPFv3 troubleshooting process include the following:

- show ipv6 protocols
- show ipv6 ospf neighbor
- show ipv6 ospf interface
- show ipv6 ospf
- show ipv6 route ospf
- clear ipv6 ospf [*process-id*] process

The following pages provide brief descriptions and examples of these commands.

Example 10-39 shows output generated by the **show ipv6 protocols** command, which is useful for verifying vital OSPFv3 settings.

**Example 10-39**    Verifying the OSPFv3 Settings on R1

```
R1# show ipv6 protocols
IPv6 Routing Protocol is "connected"
IPv6 Routing Protocol is "ND"
IPv6 Routing Protocol is "ospf 10"
  Router ID 1.1.1.1
  Number of areas: 1 normal, 0 stub, 0 nssa
  Interfaces (Area 0):
    Serial0/0/0
    GigabitEthernet0/0
  Redistribution:
    None
R1#
```

The command in Example 10-39 identifies the OSPFv3 process ID, the router ID, and the interfaces the router is receiving updates from.

Example 10-40 shows output generated by the **show ipv6 ospf neighbor** command, which is useful for verifying OSPFv3 adjacencies with neighboring routers.

**Example 10-40**    Verifying the OSPFv3 Neighbor Adjacencies on R1

```
R1# show ipv6 neighbors
IPv6 Address                              Age Link-layer Addr State Interface
FE80::2                                    28 d48c.b5ce.a120   STALE Gi0/0
FE80::3                                    28 30f7.0da3.1640   STALE Gi0/0


R1#
```

The output in Example 10-40 displays the neighbor router ID, the neighbor priority, OSPFv3 state, dead timer, neighbor interface ID, and interface through which the neighbor is accessible.

If the router ID of the neighboring router is not displayed or if it does not show the state as FULL or 2WAY, the two routers have not formed an OSPFv3 adjacency. If two routers do not establish adjacency, link-state information is not exchanged. Incomplete link-state databases can cause inaccurate SPF trees and routing tables. Routes to destination networks may not exist, or they may not be the most optimum paths.

Example 10-41 shows output generated by the **show ipv6 ospf interface** command, which is used to verify the OSPFv3 parameters configured on an interface.

**Example 10-41**    Verifying the OSPFv3 Interface Settings of Serial 0/0/0 on R1

```
R1# show ipv6 ospf interface s0/0/0
Serial0/0/0 is up, line protocol is up
  Link Local Address FE80::1, Interface ID 6
  Area 0, Process ID 10, Instance ID 0, Router ID 1.1.1.1
  Network Type POINT_TO_POINT, Cost: 647
  Transmit Delay is 1 sec, State POINT_TO_POINT
  Timer intervals configured, Hello 10, Dead 40, Wait 40, Retransmit 5
    Hello due in 00:00:08
  Graceful restart helper support enabled
  Index 1/2/2, flood queue length 0
  Next 0x0(0)/0x0(0)/0x0(0)
  Last flood scan length is 2, maximum is 6
  Last flood scan time is 0 msec, maximum is 0 msec
  Neighbor Count is 1, Adjacent neighbor count is 1
    Adjacent with neighbor 2.2.2.2
  Suppress hello for 0 neighbor(s)
R1#
```

The command in Example 10-41 identifies the OSPFv3 process ID that the interface is assigned to, the area that the interfaces are in, the cost of the interface, and the hello and dead intervals. Adding the interface name and number to the command displays output for a specific interface.

Example 10-42 shows output generated by the **show ipv6 ospf** command, which is used to examine the OSPFv3 operational information.

**Example 10-42**    Verifying the OSPFv3 Interface Settings of Serial 0/0/0 on R1

```
R1# show ipv6 ospf
 Routing Process "ospfv3 10" with ID 1.1.1.1
 Event-log enabled, Maximum number of events: 1000, Mode: cyclic
 Router is not originating router-LSAs with maximum metric
 Initial SPF schedule delay 5000 msecs
 Minimum hold time between two consecutive SPFs 10000 msecs
 Maximum wait time between two consecutive SPFs 10000 msecs
 Minimum LSA interval 5 secs
 Minimum LSA arrival 1000 msecs
 LSA group pacing timer 240 secs
 Interface flood pacing timer 33 msecs
 Retransmission pacing timer 66 msecs
 Number of external LSA 1. Checksum Sum 0x0017E9
```

```
Number of areas in this router is 1. 1 normal 0 stub 0 nssa
Graceful restart helper support enabled
Reference bandwidth unit is 1000 mbps
RFC1583 compatibility enabled
   Area BACKBONE(0)
      Number of interfaces in this area is 2
      SPF algorithm executed 8 times
      Number of LSA 13. Checksum Sum 0x063D5D
      Number of DCbitless LSA 0
      Number of indication LSA 0
      Number of DoNotAge LSA 0
      Flood list length 0

R1#
```

The command in Example 10-42 identifies the process ID and router ID, as well as other assorted information, such as the last time the SPF algorithm was calculated and the number and type of areas the router is connected to.

Example 10-43 shows output generated by the **show ipv6 route ospf** command, which is used to display only the OSPFv3 learned routes in the IPv6 routing table. In this example, R1 has learned about four remote IPv6 networks through OSPFv3.

**Example 10-43**   Verifying the OSPFv3 Routes in the Routing Table on R1

```
R1# show ipv6 route ospf
IPv6 Routing Table - default - 9 entries
Codes: C - Connected, L - Local, S - Static, U - Per-user Static route
       B - BGP, R - RIP, H - NHRP, I1 - ISIS L1
       I2 - ISIS L2, IA - ISIS interarea, IS - ISIS summary, D - EIGRP
       EX - EIGRP external, ND - ND Default, NDp - ND Prefix, DCE - Destination
       NDr - Redirect, O - OSPF Intra, OI - OSPF Inter, OE1 - OSPF ext 1
       OE2 - OSPF ext 2, ON1 - OSPF NSSA ext 1, ON2 - OSPF NSSA ext 2
OE2 ::/0 [110/1], tag 10
     via FE80::2, Serial0/0/0
O    2001:DB8:CAFE:2::/64 [110/648]
     via FE80::2, Serial0/0/0
O    2001:DB8:CAFE:3::/64 [110/648]
     via FE80::2, Serial0/0/0
O    2001:DB8:CAFE:A002::/64 [110/1294]
     via FE80::2, Serial0/0/0
R1#
```

When an OSPF change has occurred, such as a changed router ID, it is sometimes necessary to reset the OSPFv3 neighbor adjacencies by using the **clear ipv6 ospf** [*process-id*] **process** command.

## Troubleshooting OSPFv3 (10.2.3.2)

In this example, R1 is not receiving routes from R3. Example 10-44 shows the IPv6 routing table of R1.

**Example 10-44**   Verifying OSPFv3 Routes in the Routing Table of R1

```
R1# show ipv6 route ospf
IPv6 Routing Table - default - 8 entries
Codes: C - Connected, L - Local, S - Static, U - Per-user Static route
       B - BGP, R - RIP, H - NHRP, I1 - ISIS L1
       I2 - ISIS L2, IA - ISIS interarea, IS - ISIS summary, D - EIGRP
       EX - EIGRP external, ND - ND Default, NDp - ND Prefix, DCE - Destination
       NDr - Redirect, O - OSPF Intra, OI - OSPF Inter, OE1 - OSPF ext 1
       OE2 - OSPF ext 2, ON1 - OSPF NSSA ext 1, ON2 - OSPF NSSA ext 2
OE2 ::/0 [110/1], tag 10
     via FE80::2, Serial0/0/0
O    2001:DB8:CAFE:2::/64 [110/648]
     via FE80::2, Serial0/0/0
O    2001:DB8:CAFE:A002::/64 [110/1294]
     via FE80::2, Serial0/0/0
R1#
```

The output in Example 10-44 reveals that R1 receives a default route, the R2 LAN (2001:DB8:CAFE:2::/64) and the link between R2 and R3 (2001:DB8:CAFE:A002::/64). However, it does not receive the R3 LAN OSPFv3 route (2001:DB8:CAFE:3::/64).

The output in Example 10-45 verifies the OSPFv3 settings on R3.

**Example 10-45**   Verifying OSPFv3 Settings on R3

```
R3# show ipv6 protocols
IPv6 Routing Protocol is "connected"
IPv6 Routing Protocol is "ND"
IPv6 Routing Protocol is "ospf 10"
  Router ID 3.3.3.3
  Number of areas: 1 normal, 0 stub, 0 nssa
  Interfaces (Area 0):
    Serial0/0/1
  Redistribution:
    None
R3#
```

Notice that OSPF is enabled only on the Serial 0/0/1 interface. It appears that it is not enabled on the GigabitEthernet 0/0 R3 interface.

Unlike OSPFv2, OSPFV3 does not use the **network** command. Instead, OSPFv3 is enabled directly on the interface. The output in Example 10-46 confirms that the R3 interface is not enabled for OSPFv3.

**Example 10-46**   Verifying the OSPFv3 Router Configuration on R3

```
R3# show running-config interface g0/0
Building configuration...


Current configuration : 196 bytes
!
interface GigabitEthernet0/0
 description R3 LAN
 no ip address
 duplex auto
 speed auto
 ipv6 address FE80::3 link-local
 ipv6 address 2001:DB8:CAFE:3::1/64
end

R3#
```

Example 10-47 shows how to enable OSPFv3 on the R3 GigabitEthernet 0/0 interface. R3 should now advertise the R3 LAN to its OSPFv3 neighbors.

**Example 10-47**   Enabling OSPFv3 on the R3 LAN

```
R3(config)# interface g0/0
R3(config-if)# ipv6 ospf 10 area 0
R3(config-if)# end
R3#
```

The output in Example 10-48 verifies that the R3 LAN is now in the routing table of R1.

**Example 10-48**   Verifying OSPFv3 Routes in the Routing Table of R1

```
R1# show ipv6 route ospf
IPv6 Routing Table - default - 9 entries
Codes: C - Connected, L - Local, S - Static, U - Per-user Static route
       B - BGP, R - RIP, H - NHRP, I1 - ISIS L1
       I2 - ISIS L2, IA - ISIS interarea, IS - ISIS summary, D - EIGRP
```

```
        EX - EIGRP external, ND - ND Default, NDp - ND Prefix, DCE - Destination
        NDr - Redirect, O - OSPF Intra, OI - OSPF Inter, OE1 - OSPF ext 1
        OE2 - OSPF ext 2, ON1 - OSPF NSSA ext 1, ON2 - OSPF NSSA ext 2
OE2 ::/0 [110/1], tag 10
     via FE80::2, Serial0/0/0
O    2001:DB8:CAFE:2::/64 [110/648]
     via FE80::2, Serial0/0/0
O    2001:DB8:CAFE:3::/64 [110/1295]
     via FE80::2, Serial0/0/0
O    2001:DB8:CAFE:A002::/64 [110/1294]
     via FE80::2, Serial0/0/0
R1#
```

**Lab 10.2.3.3: Troubleshooting Basic Single-Area OSPFv2 and OSPFv3**

Refer to *Scaling Networks v6 Labs & Study Guide* and the online course to complete this activity.

In this lab, you will complete the following objectives:

- Part 1: Build the Network and Load Device Configurations
- Part 2: Troubleshoot Layer 3 Connectivity
- Part 3: Troubleshoot OSPFv2
- Part 4: Troubleshoot OSPFv3

# Troubleshooting Multiarea OSPFv2 and OSPFv3 (10.2.4)

In this topic, you will troubleshoot missing route entries in multiarea OSPFv2 and OSPFv3 routing tables.

## Multiarea OSPF Troubleshooting Skills (10.2.4.1)

Before you can begin to diagnose and resolve problems related to a multiarea OSPF implementation, you must be able to do the following:

- Understand the processes OSPF uses to distribute, store, and select routing information.
- Understand how OSPF information flows within and between areas.
- Use Cisco IOS commands to gather and interpret the information necessary to troubleshoot OSPF operation.

## Multiarea OSPF Troubleshooting Data Structures (10.2.4.2)

OSPF stores routing information in four main data structures, as shown in Figure 10-30.

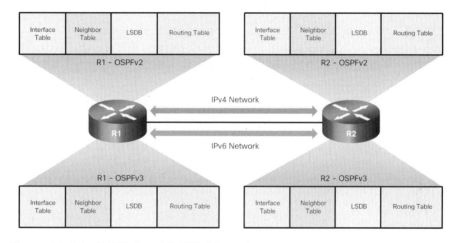

**Figure 10-30**   OSPFv2 and OSPFv3 Data Structures

Table 10-4 summarizes the OSPFv2 and OSPFv3 data structures.

**Table 10-4**   OSPFv2 and OSPFv3 Data Structures

| Data Structure | Description |
|---|---|
| Interface table | ■ This table includes a list of all active interfaces that have been enabled for OSPF.<br><br>■ Type 1 LSAs include the subnets associated with each active interface. |
| Neighbor table | ■ This table is used to manage neighbor adjacencies through hello timers and dead timers.<br><br>■ Neighbor entries are added and refreshed when a Hello packet is received.<br><br>■ Neighbors are removed when the dead timer expires. |
| Link-state database (LSDB) | ■ This is the primary data structure that OSPF uses to store network topology information.<br><br>■ It includes full topological information about each area that the OSPF router is connected to, as well as any paths that are available to reach other networks or autonomous systems. |
| Routing table | ■ After the SPF algorithm is calculated, the best routes to each network are offered to the routing table. |

Packet Tracer
☐ Activity

**Packet Tracer 10.2.4.3: Troubleshooting Multiarea OSPFv2**

In this Packet Tracer, you must troubleshoot a network with problems and fix a multiarea OSPFv2 implementation to restore communications throughout the network.

Packet Tracer
☐ Activity

**Packet Tracer 10.2.4.4: Troubleshooting Multiarea OSPFv3**

In this Packet Tracer, you must troubleshoot a network problem and fix the multiarea OSPFv3 implementation to restore communication throughout the network.

**Lab 10.2.4.5: Troubleshooting Multiarea OSPFv2 and OSPFv3**

Refer to *Scaling Networks v6 Labs & Study Guide* and the online course to complete this activity.

In this lab, you will complete the following objectives:

- Part 1: Build the Network and Load Device Configurations
- Part 2: Troubleshoot Layer 3 Connectivity
- Part 3: Troubleshoot OSPFv2
- Part 4: Troubleshoot OSPFv3

# Summary (10.3)

### Class Activity 10.3.1.1: OSPF Troubleshooting Mastery

Refer to *Scaling Networks v6 Labs & Study Guide* and the online course to complete this activity.

You have decided to change your routing protocol from RIPv2 to OSPFv2. The original physical settings of your small to medium-sized business network topology will not change. Use the diagram in the PDF for this activity as your company's small to medium-sized business network design.

When your addressing design is complete, you configure your routers with IPv4 and VLSM. OSPF has been applied as the routing protocol. However, some routers are sharing routing information with each other, and some are not. Open the PDF file that accompanies this modeling activity and follow the directions to complete the activity.

When the steps in the directions are complete, regroup as a class and compare recorded activity correction times. The group taking the shortest time to find and fix the configuration error will be declared the winner—but only after successfully explaining how they found the error, fixed it, and proved that the topology is now working.

### Packet Tracer 10.3.1.2: Skills Integration Challenge

In this skills integration challenge, your focus is OSPFv2 advanced configurations. IP addressing has been configured for all devices. You will configure OSPFv2 routing with passive interfaces and default route propagation. You will modify the OSPFv2 configuration by adjusting timers and establishing MD5 authentication. Finally, you will verify your configurations and test connectivity between end devices.

OSPF defines five network types: point-to-point, broadcast multiaccess, nonbroadcast multiaccess, point-to-multipoint, and virtual links.

Multiaccess networks can create two challenges for OSPF regarding the flooding of LSAs: creation of multiple adjacencies and extensive flooding of LSAs. The solution to managing the number of adjacencies and the flooding of LSAs on a multiaccess network is the DR and BDR. If the DR stops producing Hello packets, the BDR promotes itself and assumes the role of DR.

The routers in the network elect the router with the highest interface priority as DR. The router with the second-highest interface priority is elected as the BDR. The higher the priority, the more likely it is that a router will be selected as the DR. If the priority is set to 0, the router is not capable of becoming the DR. The default priority of multiaccess broadcast interfaces is 1. Therefore, unless otherwise configured, all routers have an equal priority value and must rely on a tie-breaking method during DR/BDR election. If the interface priorities are equal, the router with the highest router ID is elected the DR. The router with the second-highest router ID is the BDR. The addition of a new router does not initiate a new election process.

To propagate a default route in OSPF, the router must be configured with a default static route, and the **default-information originate** command must be added to the configuration. You can verify routes by using the **show ip route** or **show ipv6 route** command.

To assist OSPF in making the correct path determination, the reference bandwidth must be changed to a higher value to accommodate networks with links faster than 100 Mbps. To adjust the reference bandwidth, use the **auto-cost reference-bandwidth** *Mbps* router configuration mode command. To adjust the interface bandwidth, use the **bandwidth** *kilobits* interface configuration mode command. The cost can be manually configured on an interface by using the **ip ospf cost** *value* interface configuration mode command.

The OSPF hello and dead intervals must match, or a neighbor adjacency does not occur. To modify these intervals, use the following interface commands:

- **ip ospf hello-interval** *seconds*
- **ip ospf dead-interval** *seconds*
- **ipv6 ospf hello-interval** *seconds*
- **ipv6 ospf dead-interval** *seconds*

When troubleshooting OSPF neighbors, be aware that the Full or and Two-Way states are normal. The following commands are used for OSPFv2 troubleshooting:

- **show ip protocols**
- **show ip ospf neighbor**
- **show ip ospf interface**
- **show ip ospf**
- **show ip route ospf**
- **clear ip ospf** [*process-id*] **process**

Troubleshooting OSPFv3 is similar to troubleshooting OSPFv2. The following OSPFv3 commands are the equivalents of the OSPFv2 commands used for troubleshooting: **show ipv6 protocols, show ipv6 ospf neighbor, show ipv6 ospf interface, show ipv6 ospf, show ipv6 route ospf,** and **clear ipv6 ospf** [*process-id*] **process.**

# Practice

The following activities provide practice with the topics introduced in this chapter. The Labs and Class Activities are available in the companion *Scaling Networks v6 Labs & Study Guide* (ISBN 978-1-58713-433-3). The Packet Tracer activity instructions are also in the Labs & Study Guide. The PKA files are found in the online course.

### Class Activities

Class Activity 10.0.1.2: DR and BDR Election

Class Activity 10.3.1.1: OSPF Troubleshooting Mastery

### Labs

Lab 10.1.1.13: Configuring OSPFv2 on a Multiaccess Network

Lab 10.1.3.5: Configuring OSPFv2 Advance Features

Lab 10.2.3.3: Troubleshooting Basic Single-Area OSPFv2 and OSPFv3

Lab 10.2.3.4: Troubleshooting Advanced Single-Area OSPFv2

Lab 10.2.4.5: Troubleshooting Multiarea OSPFv2 and OSPFv3

Packet Tracer
☐ Activity

### Packet Tracer Activities

Packet Tracer 10.1.1.12: Determining the DR and BDR

Packet Tracer 10.1.2.5: Propagating a Default Route in OSPFv2

Packet Tracer 10.1.3.4: Configuring OSPFv2 Advance Features

Packet Tracer 10.2.2.3: Troubleshooting Single-Area OSPFv2

Packet Tracer 10.2.4.3: Troubleshooting Multiarea OSPFv2

Packet Tracer 10.2.4.4: Troubleshooting Multiarea OSPFv3

Packet Tracer 10.3.1.2: Skills Integration Challenge

# Check Your Understanding Questions

Complete all the review questions listed here to test your understanding of the topics and concepts in this chapter. The appendix "Answers to 'Check Your Understanding' Questions" lists the answers.

1. What information can be gathered from the routing table entry O*E2 0.0.0.0/0 [110/1] via 192.168.16.3, 00:20:22, Serial0/0/0?

   A. The edge of the OSPF area 0 is the interface that is addressed 192.168.16.3.

   B. The metric for this route is 110.

   C. The route is located two hops away.

   D. This route is a propagated default route.

2. Which command can a network engineer issue to verify the configured hello and dead timer intervals on a point-to-point WAN link between two routers that are running OSPFv2?

   A. **show ip ospf neighbor**

   B. **show ip ospf interface fastethernet 0/1**

   C. **show ip ospf interface serial 0/0/0**

   D. **show ipv6 ospf interface serial 0/0/0**

3. A network engineer suspects that OSPFv3 routers are not forming neighbor adjacencies because there are interface timer mismatches. Which two commands can be issued on the interface of each OSFPv3 router to resolve all timer mismatches? (Choose two.)

   A. **ip ospf dead-interval 40**

   B. **ip ospf hello-interval 10**

   C. **no ipv6 ospf cost 10**

   D. **no ipv6 ospf dead-interval**

   E. **no ipv6 ospf hello-interval**

   F. **no ipv6 router ospf 10**

4. A network engineer is troubleshooting convergence and adjacency issues in an OSPFv2 network and has noted that some expected network route entries are not displayed in the routing table. Which two commands provide additional information about the state of router adjacencies, timer intervals, and the area ID? (Choose two.)

   A. **show ip ospf interface**

   B. **show ip ospf neighbor**

   C. **show ip protocols**

   D. **show ip route ospf**

   E. **show running-configuration**

5. When OSPFv2 neighbors are establishing adjacencies, in which state do they elect a DR and BDR router?

   A. Exchange state

   B. Init state

   C. Loading state

   D. Two-Way state

6. A network engineer is troubleshooting OSPFv2 routing issues on two connected routers. Which two requirements to form an adjacency need to be verified? (Choose two.)

   A. Verify that both routers are using the same OSPFv2 process ID.

   B. Verify that one of the interfaces that connects the two routers is active and the other passive.

   C. Verify that one of the routers is the DR or BDR, and the other router is a DROTHER.

   D. Verify that the interfaces connecting the two routers are in the same area.

   E. Verify that the interfaces connecting the two routers are in the same subnet.

7. Which command is used to verify that OSPF is enabled and also provides a list of the networks that are being advertised by the network?

   A. **show ip interface brief**

   B. **show ip ospf interface**

   C. **show ip protocols**

   D. **show ip route ospf**

8. During verification or troubleshooting of the OPSFv3 configuration on a router, which three parameters are displayed by the **show ipv6 ospf interface** command? (Choose three.)

   A. The global unicast IPv6 address of the interface

   B. The hello and dead intervals

   C. The metric of the route that is attached to the interface

   D. The number of interfaces in the area

   E. The OSPFv3 area that the interface is in

   F. The process ID that is assigned to the interface

9. A network engineer is troubleshooting an OSPFv2 network and discovers that two routers connected by a point-to-point WAN serial link are not establishing an adjacency. The OSPF routing process, network commands, and area ID are all confirmed as correct, and the interfaces are not passive. Testing shows that the cabling is correct, the link is up, and pings between the interfaces are successful. What is most likely the problem??

A. A clock rate has not been set on the DCE interface of the serial link.

B. A DR election has not taken place.

C. The OSPFv2 process IDs on the routers do not match.

D. The subnet masks on the two connected serial interfaces do not match.

# Answers to the Review Questions

## Chapter 1

1. B and C. The Cisco Enterprise Architecture is a hierarchical design. The network is divided into three functional layers: core, distribution, and access. In smaller networks, this three-layer division of functional layers is collapsed into two layers, with the core and distribution layers combined to form a collapsed core.

2. D. Routers or multilayer switches are usually deployed in pairs, with access layer switches evenly divided between them. This configuration is referred to as a building switch block or a departmental switch block. Each switch block acts independently of the others. As a result, the failure of a single device does not cause the network to go down. Even the failure of an entire switch block does not affect a significant number of end users.

3. C and E. Providing wireless connectivity offers many advantages, such as increased flexibility, reduced costs, and the ability to grow and adapt to changing network and business requirements.

4. A. Link aggregation allows an administrator to increase the amount of bandwidth between devices by grouping several physical links together to create one logical link. EtherChannel is a form of link aggregation used in switched networks.

5. B. Cisco Meraki cloud-managed access switches enable virtual stacking of switches. They monitor and configure thousands of switch ports over the web, without the intervention of onsite IT staff.

6. D. The thickness of a switch determines how much space on the rack it will take up and is measured in rack units.

7. A and C. Routers play a critical role in networking by determining the best path for sending packets. They connect multiple IP networks by connecting homes and businesses to the Internet. They are also used to interconnect multiple sites within an enterprise network, providing redundant paths to destinations. Routers can also act as translators between different media types and protocols.

8. D and E. In-band management is used to monitor and make configuration changes to a network device over a network connection. Configuration using in-band management requires at least one network interface on the device to be connected and operational and requires Telnet, SSH, HTTP, or HTTPS to access a Cisco device.

9. B and C. Out-of-band management is used for initial configuration or when a network connection is unavailable. Configuration using out-of-band management requires a direct connection to a console or an AUX port and a terminal emulation client such as PuTTY or TeraTerm.

# Chapter 2

1. C. VTP propagates and synchronizes VLAN information to other switches in the VTP domain. There are currently three versions of VTP: VTPv1, VTPv2, and VTPv3.

2. B and E. VTP clients can only communicate with other switches in the same VTP domain. VTP clients cannot create, change, or delete VLANs. A VTP client only stores the VLAN information for the entire domain while the switch is on. A switch reset deletes the VLAN information. You must configure VTP client mode on a switch.

3. C. If its own configuration revision number is higher or equal to the received configuration revision number, the packet is ignored. If its own configuration revision number is lower, an advertisement request is sent, asking for the subset advertisement message.

4. A. By default, Cisco switches issue summary advertisements every five minutes. Summary advertisements inform adjacent VTP switches of the current VTP domain name and the configuration revision number.

5. A, B, and F. To share VLAN information, all switches must use the same version of VTP, be in the same VTP domain, and use the same VTP password (if a password is configured).

6. A and E. Transparent switches do not participate in VTP except to forward VTP advertisements to VTP clients and VTP servers. VLANs that are created, renamed, or deleted on transparent switches are local to those switches only. To create an extended VLAN, a switch must be configured as a VTP transparent switch when using VTP Versions 1 or 2.

7. A and C. VTP requires the use of trunk links. The VTP domain name, which is case sensitive, identifies the administrative domain for the switch. The VTP domain name is NULL by default.

8. B. To reset a configuration revision on a switch, change the VTP domain name. This resets the revision number to 0. Then change the name back to the original name, and it will acquire the current revision number from a VTP server.

9. A and D. The VTP revision number is used to determine whether the received information is more recent than the current version. The revision number increases by 1 each time you add a VLAN, delete a VLAN, or change a VLAN name. If the VTP domain name is changed or the switch is set to transparent mode, the revision number is reset to 0.

10. B. Each switch in the VTP domain sends periodic VTP advertisements from each trunk port to a reserved Layer 2 multicast address.

11. B. Legacy inter-VLAN routing would require four FastEthernet interfaces. Therefore, the best router-based solution is to configure a router-on-a-stick.

12. C. Router-on-a-stick requires one interface configured as a subinterface for each VLAN.

13. A and B. Legacy (traditional) inter-VLAN routing requires more ports, and the configuration can be more complex than with a router-on-a-stick solution.

14. A. The host must have a default gateway configured. Hosts on VLANs must have their default gateway configured on a router subinterface to provide inter-VLAN routing services.

15. D. The switch port must be configured as a trunk, and the VLANs on the switch must have users connected to them.

# Chapter 3

1. A. When multiple alternative physical paths exist, duplicate unicast frames from a sending host are sent to the destination. Many application protocols expect to receive only one copy of each packet, especially TCP-based protocols that use sequence number and acknowledge number to track the sequence of packets. Multiple copies of the same frame could cause application protocols to make errors in processing the packets. Broadcast storms are caused by switches flooding broadcast frames endlessly. With microsegmentation, collisions are controlled within each switch port.

2. D. The BPDU has three fields: bridge priority, extended system ID, the MAC address. The extended system ID contains 12 bits that identify the VLAN ID.

3. A, C, and E. The three components that are combined to form a bridge ID are bridge priority, extended system ID, and MAC address.

4. D. The root port is the port with the lowest cost to reach the root bridge.

5. C. Cisco switches running IOS 15.0 or later run PVST+ by default. Cisco Catalyst switches support PVST+, Rapid PVST+, and MSTP. However, only one version can be active at any time.

6. B. PVST+ results in optimum load balancing. However, this is accomplished by manually configuring switches to be elected as root bridges for different VLANs on the network. The root bridges are not automatically selected. Furthermore, having spanning-tree instances for each VLAN actually consumes more bandwidth and increases the CPU cycles for all the switches in the network.

7. C and D. Switches learn MAC addresses at the learning and forwarding port states. They receive and process BPDUs at the blocking, listening, learning, and forwarding port states.

8. A. Although the **spanning-tree vlan 10 root primary** command ensures that a switch will have a bridge priority value lower than other bridges introduced to the network, the **spanning-tree vlan 10 priority 0** command ensures that the bridge priority takes precedence over all other priorities.

9. C and D. The **show spanning-tree** command displays the status of STP for all VLANs that are defined on a switch and other information, including the root bridge BID. It does not show the number of broadcast packets received on the ports. The IP address of the management VLAN interface is not related to STP and is displayed by the **show running-configuration** command.

10. C and D. Spanning Tree Protocol (STP) is required to ensure correct network operation when designing a network with multiple interconnected Layer 2 switches or using redundant links to eliminate single points of failure between Layer 2 switches. Routing is a Layer 3 function and does not relate to STP. VLANs do reduce the number of broadcast domains but relate to Layer 3 subnets, not STP.

11. C. When all switches are configured with the same default bridge priority, the MAC address becomes the deciding factor for the election of the root bridge. All links on the same VLAN will also have the same extended system ID, so this will not contribute to determining which switch is the root for that VLAN.

12. B and D. The RSTP edge port concept corresponds to the PVST+ PortFast feature. An edge port connects to an end station and assumes that the switch port does not connect to another switch. RSTP edge ports should immediately transition to the forwarding state, thereby skipping the time-consuming 802.1D listening and learning port states.

13. A. If switch access ports are configured as edge ports using PortFast, BPDUs should never be received on those ports. Cisco switches support a feature called BPDU guard. When it is enabled, BPDU guard puts an edge port in an error-disabled state if a BPDU is received by the port. This prevents a Layer 2 loop from occurring.

# Chapter 4

1. B. Increasing the link speed does not scale very well. Adding more VLANs does not reduce the amount of traffic that is flowing across the link. Inserting a router between the switches does not improve congestion.

2. E and F. Source MAC to destination MAC load balancing and source IP to destination IP load balancing are two implementation methods used in EtherChannel technology.

3. B. PAgP is used to automatically aggregate multiple ports into an EtherChannel bundle, but it works only between Cisco devices. LACP can be used for the same purpose between Cisco and non-Cisco devices. PAgP must have the same duplex mode at both ends and can use two ports or more. The number of ports depends on the switch platform or module. An EtherChannel aggregated link is seen as one port by the spanning-tree algorithm.

4. A and C. The two protocols that can be used to form an EtherChannel are PAgP (Cisco proprietary) and LACP, also known as IEEE 802.3ad. STP (Spanning Tree Protocol) or RSTP (Rapid Spanning Tree Protocol) is used to avoid loops in a Layer 2 network. EtherChannel describes the bundling of two or more links that are treated as a single link for spanning-tree configuration.

5. C. Switch 1 and switch 2 establish an EtherChannel if both sides are set to desirable as both sides will negotiate the link. A channel can also be established if both sides are set to on, or if one side is set to auto and the other to desirable. Setting one switch to on prevents that switch from negotiating the formation of an EtherChannel bundle.

6. A. The command **channel-group mode active** enables LACP unconditionally, and the command **channel-group mode passive** enables LACP only if the port receives an LACP packet from another device. The command **channel-group mode desirable** enables PAgP unconditionally, and the command **channel-group mode auto** enables PAgP only if the port receives a PAgP packet from another device.

7. B. The command **channel-group mode active** enables LACP unconditionally, and the command **channel-group mode passive** enables LACP only if the port receives an LACP packet from another device. The command **channel-group mode desirable** enables PAgP unconditionally, and the command **channel-group mode auto** enables PAgP only if the port receives a PAgP packet from another device.

8. D. An EtherChannel is formed by combining multiple (same type) Ethernet physical links so they are seen and configured as one logical link. It provides an aggregated link between two switches. Currently each EtherChannel can consist of up to eight compatibly configured Ethernet ports.

9. A and B. LACP is part of an IEEE specification (802.3ad) that enables several physical ports to automatically be bundled to form a single EtherChannel logical channel. LACP allows a switch to negotiate an automatic bundle by sending LACP packets to the peer. It performs a function similar to PAgP with Cisco EtherChannel, but it can be used to facilitate EtherChannels in multivendor environments. Cisco devices support both PAgP and LACP configurations.

10. A, C, and F. Speed and duplex settings must match for all interfaces in an EtherChannel. All interfaces in the EtherChannel must be in the same VLAN if the ports are not configured as trunks. Any ports may be used to establish an EtherChannel. SNMP community strings and port security settings are not relevant to EtherChannel.

11. B. Hosts send traffic to their default gateways, which is the virtual IP address and the virtual MAC address. The virtual IP address is assigned by the administrator, and the virtual MAC address is created automatically by HSRP. The virtual IPv4 and MAC addresses provide consistent default gateway addressing for the end devices. Only the HSRP active router responds to the virtual IP and virtual MAC address.

12. A. VRRP selects a master router and one or more backup routers. VRRP backup routers monitor the VRRP master router.

13. A. HSRP and GLBP are Cisco proprietary protocols, and VRRP is an IEEE open standard protocol.

14. D. HSRP is an FHRP that provides Layer 3 default gateway redundancy.

# Chapter 5

1. A. BGP is a protocol developed to interconnect different levels of ISPs as well as ISPs and some of their larger private clients.

2. C. RIP was created with a metric that does not support larger networks. Other routing protocols, including OSPF, EIGRP, and IS-IS, scale well and accommodate growth and larger networks.

3. C and E. Routing protocols dynamically discover neighbors to exchange and update routing information.

4. C and D. Classless routing protocols include subnet mask information in their routing updates and therefore support VLSM and CIDR.

5. C. Time to convergence defines how quickly the routers in the network topology share routing information and reach a state of consistent knowledge.

6. A and C. A link-state packet (LSP) is sent only during initial startup of the routing protocol process on a router and whenever there is a change in the topology, including a link going down or coming up or a neighbor adjacency being established or broken. Data traffic congestion does not directly influence routing protocol behavior. LSPs are not flooded periodically, and update timers are not relevant to LSPs.

7. C and D. A link-state enabled router must determine the cost of its active links and establish adjacencies before it can send an LSP. Once LSPs are received, the router can construct its SPF tree and build its LSDB.

8. B and D. The metric of OSPF is cost, which is based on the cumulative bandwidth of the links to the destination network.

9. C. Like OSPF, EIGRP uses hello packets to establish and maintain neighbor adjacencies.

10. B. Each OSPF router views the network differently, as the root of a unique SPF tree. Each router builds adjacencies based on its own position in the topology. Each routing table in the area is developed individually through the application of the SPF algorithm. The link-state database for an area, however, must reflect the same information for all routers.

11. A. The OSPF hello packet serves three primary functions: discover OSPF neighbors and establish adjacencies, advertise parameters that OSPF neighbors must agree on, and elect the DR and BDR.

12. A and C. EIGRP uses bandwidth and delay by default, and it can also be configured to use load and reliability as metrics for selecting the best path to reach a network.

13. B. Dynamically learned routes are constantly updated and maintained by routing protocols.

14. C and D. There are several factors to consider when selecting a routing protocol to implement. Two of them are scalability and speed of convergence. The other options listed here are irrelevant.

# Chapter 6

1. A. EIGRP is designed to route several network layer protocols by using PDMs. For example, EIGRP can be used to route IPv4 and IPv6, as well as other network layer protocols. There are separate instances of PDM for different network layer protocols.

2. C. EIGRP uses the hold time as the maximum time it should wait for receiving a hello packet (or other EIGRP packets) from its neighbor before declaring that the neighbor is unreachable. By default the hold time is three times greater than the hello interval. On LAN interfaces, the default hello time is 5 seconds, and the default hold time is 15 seconds.

3. A and B. The Update, Query, and Reply EIGRP packet types require reliable delivery.

4. C. When an EIGRP multicast packet is encapsulated into an Ethernet frame, the destination MAC address is 01-00-5E-00-00-0A.

5. C. The EIGRP packet header opcode is used to identify the EIGRP packet type: Update (1), Query (3), Reply (4), and Hello (5).

6. A. The wildcard mask in the EIGRP **network** command is used to define precisely which network or subnets participate in the EIGRP process. Only interfaces that have addresses in a subnet included in a **network** command will participate in EIGRP.

7. A. The **router eigrp 100** command uses the number as a process ID to keep track of the running instance of the EIGRP process, as several EIGRP processes can be run at the same time. This number is called the *autonomous system number*.

8. E. Only successor routes are offered to the routing table.

9. D. An EIGRP router maintains a topology table that includes entries for every destination that the router learns from directly connected EIGRP neighbors.

10. B. The privileged EXEC mode command **show interfaces** is used to verify the default or configured bandwidth value on an interface. Correct bandwidth values are important for efficient routing with EIGRP.

11. A and B. Bandwidth and delay are static values that are not actually tracked by a device. Load and reliability are tracked dynamically by a device over a default period of time. MTU is not used for EIGRP metrics.

12. C. EIGRP routers use Hello packets to establish and maintain adjacencies.

13. C. Passive state means that the router topology table is stable and is converged.

14. B. The multicast address for EIGRP for IPv6 is FF02::A, which is the shortened form of FF02:0000:0 000:0000:0000:0000:0000:A

15. C. By default, the EIGRP for IPv6 process is in a shutdown state. The EIGRP for IPv6 process must be activated by using the **no shutdown** command in router configuration mode.


# Chapter 7

1. B. EIGRP for IPv4 automatically installs a Null0 summary route into the routing table when EIGRP automatic summarization is enabled and there is at least one EIGRP learned subnet. Null0 is a virtual interface that is a route to nowhere and is used to prevent routing loops for destinations that are included in a summary network but do not have a specific entry in the routing table.

2. D. Routes learned from other routing protocols that are redistributed into EIGRP are known as external routes and are assigned an administrative distance of 170.

3. A. The amount of bandwidth that EIGRP uses by default for control traffic is 50 percent of the bandwidth of the exit interface. To change this default setting, you use the **ip bandwidth-percent eigrp** command. The **ip bandwidth-percent eigrp 100 8** command sets the bandwidth for autonomous system 100 at 8 percent of the bandwidth of the interface.

4. B. For load balancing, EIGRP by default installs up to four equal-cost paths to the same destination network in the routing table.

5. B. EIGRP routers must belong to the same autonomous system for an adjacency to be successful. The autonomous system number is specified at the end of the **router** command.

6. A. If there are discontiguous IPv4 networks, automatic summarization causes inconsistent routing because routes are summarized at classful boundaries. When there is no common subnet between EIGRP neighbors, an adjacency cannot form. Mismatching EIGRP AS numbers and the lack of an adjacency will not cause inconsistent routing but a lack of routing overall.

7. D. To verify whether automatic summarization is being performed on a router, enter the **show ip protocols** command. The **show ip eigrp interfaces** command shows which interfaces are enabled for EIGRP. The **show ip interface brief** command is used to verify that the status and protocol are both up for an interface connected to a router. The **show ip eigrp neighbors** command on a router verifies the establishment of EIGRP neighbor adjacencies with other routers.

8. C. EIGRP for IPv6 uses the link-local address of the router exit interface as the source address for EIGRP messages, including hello messages.

9. A. If the connection to the successor of a network is lost and there is no feasible successor in the topology database, DUAL puts the network into the active state and actively queries the neighbors for a new successor. In a normal circumstance when the network is reachable and traffic is normal, the network is put into passive mode.

10. A and B. EIGRP uses a composite metric. By default, EIGRP uses the slowest bandwidth of all interfaces between the source and the destination and the sum of all interface delays along the path to calculate the best path. The worst reliability and the worst load on a link between source and destination can also be used to select the best path, but these are not default metric values. MTU is included in routing updates but is not used as a routing metric.

11. A. The **show interfaces** command is used to show the delay, in microseconds, of a specified interface. This command also provides the default delay value or an administratively configured value. The **show running-config** command displays only an administratively configured value. The commands **show ip route** and **show ip protocols** do not provide the delay value of each interface.

12. A. The **router eigrp 100** command uses the number as a process ID to keep track of the running instance of the EIGRP process, as several EIGRP processes can be run at the same time. This number is called the autonomous system number.

# Chapter 8

1. B. On Cisco routers, the default dead interval is four times the hello interval, and this timer has expired in this case. SPF does not determine the state of neighbor routers; it determines which routes become routing table entries. A DR/DBR election will not always automatically run; whether it runs depends on the type of network and on whether the router that is no longer up was a DR or BDR.

2. A, C, and F. Only OSPFv2 messages are sourced from the IP address of the exit interface; OSPFv3 uses the link-local address of the exit interface. Only OSPFv3 uses IPsec; OSPFv2 uses plaintext or MD5 authentication. Unicast routing is enabled by default only with OSPFv2.

3. B. Each OSPF router views the network differently, as the root of a unique SPF tree. Each router builds adjacencies based on its own position in the topology. Each routing table in the area is developed individually through the application of the SPF algorithm. The link-state database for an area, however, must reflect the same information for all routers.

4. B, D, and F. The topology table on an OSPF router is a link-state database (LSDB) that lists information about all other routers in the network and represents the network topology. All routers within an area have identical link-state databases, and the table can be viewed using the **show ip ospf database** command. The EIGRP topology table contains feasible successor routes. This concept is not used by OSPF. The SPF algorithm uses the LSDB to produce the unique routing table for each router, which contains the lowest cost route entries for known networks.

5. A. The adjacency database is used to create the OSPF neighbor table. The link-state database is used to create the topology table, and the forwarding database is used to create the routing table.

6. A. The OSPF Hello packet serves three primary functions: discover OSPF neighbors and establish adjacencies, advertise parameters that OSPF neighbors must agree on, and, when necessary, elect the DR and BDR.

7. E. Link-State Update (LSU) packets contain different types of link-state advertisements (LSA). The LSUs are used to reply to Link-State Request (LSR) packets and to announce new information.

8. B and E. OSPF router ID does not contribute to SPF algorithm calculations, nor does it facilitate the transition of the OSPF neighbor state to Full. Although the router ID is contained within OSPF messages when router adjacencies are being established, it has no bearing on the convergence process.

9. A. When electing a DR, the router with the highest OSPF priority becomes the DR. If all routers have the same priority, then the router with the highest router ID is elected.

10. A. The wildcard mask can be found by subtracting the subnet mask from 255.255.255.255.

11. C and D. There may be several reasons why routers running OSPF will fail to form an OSPF adjacency, including subnet masks not matching, OSPF hello or dead timers not matching, OSPF network types not matching, or a missing or incorrect OSPF **network** command. Mismatched IOS

versions, the use of private IP addresses, and different types of interface ports do not cause an OSPF adjacency to fail to form between two routers.

12. C. While the **show ip interface brief** and **ping** commands can be used to determine whether Layer 1, 2, and 3 connectivity exists, neither command can be used to determine whether a particular OSPF or EIGRP-initiated relationship has been made. The **show ip protocols** command is useful in determining routing parameters such as timers, router ID, and metric information associated with a specific routing protocol. The **show ip ospf neighbor** command shows whether two adjacent routers have exchanged OSPF messages in order to form a neighbor relationship.

13. A. Both versions of OSPF use the same five basic packet types, cost metric, and DR/BDR election process. Hello packets are used in both versions to build adjacencies. OSPFv3, however, uses advanced encryption and authentication features that are provided by IPsec, while OSPFv2 uses either plaintext or MD5 authentication.

14. A, B, and C. OSPFv6 messages can be sent to either the OSPF router multicast FF02::5, the OSPF DR/BDR multicast FF02::6, or the link-local address.

15. A. Because serial interfaces do not have MAC addresses, OSPFv3 automatically assigns a link-local address to them, based on the first available MAC address from the pool of Ethernet interface addresses on the router. A FE80::/10 prefix is added. The router then applies the EUI-64 process to the MAC address by inserting FFFE into the middle of the existing 48-bit address and flipping the seventh bit.

16. D. The basic command to implement OSPFv3 on a router uses the same *process-id* parameter as OSPFv2 to assign a locally significant number to the OSPF process. OSPF does not use autonomous system numbers. Following the assignment of the process ID, a prompt directs the user to manually assign a router ID. After the router ID is assigned, the reference bandwidth can be set.

17. C. The command to enable an OSPFv3 process on a router interface is **ipv6 ospf process-id area** *area-id*. In the case, the process ID is 20, and the area ID is 0.

18. B. The **show ipv6 ospf neighbor** command verifies neighbor adjacencies for OSPFv3 routers. The other options do not provide neighbor information.

19. D. The **show ipv6 route ospf** command gives specific information that is related to OSPFv3 routes in the routing table. The **show ipv6 route** command shows the entire routing table. The **show ip route** and **show ip route ospf** commands are used with OSPFv2.

## Chapter 9

1. B. A multiarea OSPF network requires hierarchical network design (two levels). The main area is called the backbone area, and all other areas must connect to the main area.

2. C. A multiarea OSPF network improves routing performance and efficiency in a large network. As the network is divided into smaller areas, each router maintains a smaller routing table because

routes between areas can be summarized. Also, fewer updated routes means fewer LSAs are exchanged, thus reducing the need for CPU resources. Running multiple routing protocols simultaneously and implementing both IPv4 and IPv6 are not primary considerations for a multiarea OSPF network.

3. A. ABRs and ASBRs need to perform any summarization or redistribution among multiple areas and thus demand more router resources than a regular router in an OSPF area.

4. D. OSPF supports the concept of using areas to prevent larger routing tables, excessive SPF calculations, and large LSDBs. Only routers within an area share link-state information. This allows OSPF to scale in a hierarchical fashion with all areas that connect to a backbone area.

5. A and E. Type 4 LSAs are known as autonomous system external LSA entries and are generated by an ABR to inform other areas of next-hop information for the ASBR. Type 1 LSAs are known as router link entries. Type 3 LSAs can be generated without requiring a full SPF calculation. Type 3 LSAs are used to carry routes between OSPF areas.

6. B. OSPF has many different LSA types, including type 1, which contains a list of directly connected interfaces; type 2, which exists only for multiaccess networks and includes DR router ID; type 3, which is used by ABRs to advertise networks from other areas; type 4, which is generated by ABRs to identify an ASBR and provide a route to it; and type 5, which is originated by ASBRs to advertise external routes.

7. D. OSPF has many different LSA types, including type 1, which contains a list of directly connected interfaces; type 2, which exists only for multiaccess networks and includes DR router ID; type 3, which is used by ABRs to advertise networks from other areas; type 4, which is generated by ABRs to identify an ASBR and provide a route to it; and type 5, which is originated by ASBRs to advertise external routes.

8. B. OSPF routes have several descriptors in IPv4 routing tables, including O, which indicates intra-area routes learned from a DR; O IA, which indicates summary interarea routes that are learned from a ABR; and O E1 or O E2, which indicate external routes that are learned from an ASBR.

9. A. The **show ip ospf database** command is used to verify the contents of the LSDB. The **show ip ospf interface** command is used to verify the configuration information of OSPF-enabled interfaces. The **show ip ospf neighbor** command is used to gather information regarding OSPF neighbor routers. The **show ip route ospf** command displays OSPF-related information in the routing table.

# Chapter 10

1. D. The metric toward this external route is 1, and 192.168.16.3 is the address of the next interface toward the destination.

2. C. The **show ip ospf interface serial 0/0/0** command displays the configured hello and dead timer intervals on a point-to-point serial WAN link between two OSPFv2 routers. The **show ipv6 ospf**

**interface serial 0/0/0** command displays the configured hello and dead timer intervals on a point-to-point serial link between two OSPFv3 routers. The **show ip ospf interface fastethernet 0/1** command displays the configured hello and dead timer intervals on a multiaccess link between two (or more) OSPFv2 routers. The **show ip ospf neighbor** command displays the dead interval elapsed time since the last hello message was received but does not show the configured value of the timer.

3. D and E. The **no ipv6 ospf hello-interval** and **no ipv6 ospf dead-interval** commands issued on each OSPFv3 interface reset the intervals to the respective default periods. This ensures that the timers on all routers match and, provided that other appropriate configurations are correct, the routers form adjacencies. The **ip ospf hello-interval 10** and **ip ospf dead-interval 40** commands are OPSFv2 commands that are used for IPv4 routing. If the **ipv6 ospf hello-interval** and **ipv6 ospf dead-interval** commands are used, the interval has to be specified in seconds. The parameter default is not valid in these commands.

4. A and B. The **show ip ospf interface** command displays routing table information that is already known. The **show ip ospf neighbors** command displays adjacency information on neighboring OSPF routers. The show **running-configuration** and **show ip protocols** commands display aspects of the OSPF configuration on the router but do not display adjacency state details or timer interval details.

5. D. The states are as follows: Down state, no Hello packets are received; Init state, Hello packets are received; Two-way state, DR and BDR election; ExStart state, negotiate master/slave and DBD packet sequence number; Exchange state, exchange of DBD packets; Loading state, additional information is sent; and Full state, routers converged.

6. D and E. The OSPFv2 process ID is local to each router and does not have to be common. Neither interface on the link connecting the two routers can be passive. Both must be participating in the OSPF area. The DR, BDR, and DROTHER status of the router has no bearing on the adjacency relationship.

7. C. The command **show ip ospf interface** verifies the active OSPF interfaces. The command **show ip interface brief** is used to check that the interfaces are operational. The command **show ip route ospf** displays the entries that are learned via OSPF in the routing table. The command **show ip protocols** checks that OSPF is enabled and lists the networks that are advertised.

8. B, E, and F. The number of interfaces in the area is displayed by the **show ipv6 ospf** command. The metric of the route that is attached to the interface is displayed by the **show ipv6 route** command. The interface global unicast IPv6 address is displayed in the **show running-configuration** command output.

9. D. The establishment of an OSPF adjacency between connected routers requires all the interfaces of the link to be in the same subnet. Each interface must be configured with correct IP addresses and the same subnet mask. Pings across serial links can be successful with correct IP addresses and different subnet masks. Successful pings verify that a clock rate has been set on the DCE interface of the serial link. The OSPFv2 process IDs on the routers are local and do not need to match. A DR election does not take place across point-to-point serial links between OSPF routers.

# Glossary

**802.1D** The original STP standard, which provided a loop-free topology in a network with redundant links. Also called Common Spanning Tree (CST), it assumed one spanning tree instance for the entire bridged network, regardless of the number of VLANs. The updated version of the standard is IEEE 802.1D-2004.

**802.1s** The IEEE STP standard defined for Multiple Spanning Tree Protocol (MSTP). It maps multiple VLANs into the same spanning tree instance.

**802.1w** The IEEE STP standard for Rapid Spanning Tree Protocol (RSTP), which is an evolution of STP that provides faster convergence than STP.

**802.3ad** *See* Link Aggregation Control Protocol (LACP).

## A

**access layer** The layer in the three-layer hierarchical network model that describes the portion of the network where devices connect to the network and includes controls for allowing devices to communicate on the network.

**Acknowledgment packets** Packets that are used to acknowledge the receipt of an EIGRP message sent using reliable delivery.

**active router** The name given to the HSRP forwarding router.

**active state** A term used with EIGRP to describe a route in the topology that is currently not stable. DUAL is actively communicating with peer EIGRP routers to find out if there is a better path to the route.

**adjacency** A relationship formed between selected neighboring routers and end nodes for the purpose of exchanging routing information. Adjacency is based on the use of a common media segment.

**administrative distance (AD)** The feature that routers use to select the best path when there are two or more different routes to the same destination from two different routing protocols. The AD represents the "trustworthiness," or reliability, of the route.

**advertised distance (AD)** *See* reported distance (RD).

**advertisement request** A VTP message sent when a summary advertisement contains a higher configuration revision number than the current value. *See also* summary advertisement *and* subset advertisement.

**all OSPF routers** A multicast group used in the OSPF routing protocol. The all OSPF routers address is 224.0.0.5.

**alternate port** Also called a backup port, a switch port in an RSTP topology that offers an alternate path toward the root bridge. An alternate port assumes a discarding state in a stable, active topology. An alternate port is present on nondesignated bridges and makes a transition to a designated port if the current path fails.

**application-specific integrated circuit (ASIC)**   An integrated circuit design that is specific to the intended application, as opposed to being a design for general-purpose use. For example, ASIC is used in Cisco Express Forwarding to route packets at a higher speed than an individual CPU could support.

**area border router (ABR)**   In OSPF, a router that connects one or more non-backbone areas to the backbone. These are the routers interconnecting the areas in a multiarea OSPF network.

**automatic summarization**   A routing protocol feature in which a router that connects to more than one classful network advertises summarized routes for each entire classful network when sending updates out interfaces connected to other classful networks.

**autonomous system (AS)**   Also known as a routing domain, a network of routers under common administration, such as a company or an organization. Typical examples of an AS are a company's internal network and an ISP's network.

**Autonomous System Boundary Router (ASBR)**   In OSPF, a router that exchanges routes between OSPF and another routing domain through route redistribution. Routes are injected into OSPF from an ASBR. An ASBR communicates the OSPF routes into another routing domain. The ASBR runs OSPF and another routing protocol.

**autonomous system number**   A number used in EIGRP that is locally assigned to identify an EIGRP process and that has no global significance. Or a number used in BGP that has have global significance and is used to identify an enterprise or service provider on the Internet.

# B

**backbone area**   In OSPFv2 and OSPFv3, the special area in a multiarea design where all non-backbone areas connect. Also known as area 0. In any OSPF network design, there must be at least one area. Traditionally, this area is numbered 0. In single-area OSPF, the lone area is area 0. In multiarea OSPF, area 0 forms the core of the network as all other areas attach to the backbone area to facilitate interarea communication.

**backbone router**   In OSPF, a router that is configured to participate in area 0, or the backbone area. A backbone router can also be an ABR or ASBR.

**backup designated router (BDR)**   In OSPF, a backup to the designated router (DR) in case the DR fails. The BDR is the OSPF router with the second-highest priority at the time of the last DR election.

**backup port**   Also called an alternate port, a switch port in an RSTP topology that offers an alternate path toward the root bridge. The port assumes a discarding state in a stable, active topology. A backup port is present on a nondesignated bridge and makes a transition to a designated port if the current path fails.

**backup router**   A VRRP router that monitors the VRRP master router. VRRP can have multiple backup routers. The role of the backup router is similar to that of an HSRP standby router.

**Bellman-Ford algorithm**   The routing algorithm of the RIP routing protocol.

**best path**   The path with the lowest metric to a destination network.

blocking state    A port state for a nondesignated port that does not participate in frame forwarding. The port continues to process received BPDU frames to determine the location and root ID of the root bridge and what port role the switch port should assume in the final active STP topology.

Border Gateway Protocol (BGP)    An exterior gateway routing protocol that ISPs use to propagate routing information.

bounded triggered update    An update sent when a network change occurs, in which the router immediately sends an update about the network change and not its entire routing table. In EIGRP, this type of update is sent only to routers that need the updated information instead of to all routers.

bounded updates    Updates that are propagated to the routers that need the updated information instead of being sent updates to all routers.

BPDU filter    A Cisco switch feature that is used to filter sending or receiving BPDUs on a switch port.

BPDU guard    A Cisco switch feature that listens for incoming STP BPDU messages and disables the interface if any are received. The goal is to prevent loops when a switch connects to a port that is expected to have only a host connected to it.

branch router    A router platform that optimizes branch services while delivering an optimal application experience across branch and WAN infrastructures. *Compare with* network edge router *and* service provider router.

bridge ID (BID)    An 8-byte identifier of switches used by STP and RSTP. It consists of a 2-byte bridge priority field and a 6-byte system ID field. The priority field is a configurable bridge priority number, and the system ID is the MAC address of the sending switch.

bridge priority    A customizable value between 0 and 65,535 (the default is 32,768) that can be configured to influence which switch becomes the root bridge.

bridge protocol data unit (BPDU)    A frame used by STP to communicate key information about the avoidance of Layer 2 loops in the network topology.

broadcast multiaccess    A type of network configuration in which multiple routers are interconnected over an Ethernet network.

broadcast storm    A condition in which broadcasts are flooded endlessly, often due to a looping at Layer 2 (bridge loop). A broadcast storm occurs when there are so many broadcast frames caught in a Layer 2 loop that all available bandwidth is consumed.

building switch block    A design that deploys routers, or multilayer switches, in pairs, with access layer switches evenly divided between them. Each switch block operates independently of the others, so a failure of a single device does not cause the network to go down. As a result, the failure of a single device or switch block does not significantly affect end users. *See also* departmental switch block.

# C

**campus LAN switch**   A distribution, access, or compact switches that may be anywhere from a fanless switch with eight fixed ports to a 13-blade switch supporting hundreds of ports. Campus LAN switch platforms include the Cisco 2960, 3560, 3650, 3850, 4500, 6500, and 6800 Series. *Compare with* cloud-managed switch, data center switch, service provider switch, *and* virtual networking switch.

**child route**   A route that is a subnet of a classful network address. Also known as a level 2 route. A child route is an ultimate route.

**classless interdomain routing (CIDR)**   An IP addressing technique based on route aggregation. CIDR allows for routers to group routes together to minimize the quantity of routing information carried by routers.

**Cisco Express Forwarding**   A Cisco proprietary protocol that allows high-speed packet switching in ASICs rather than using CPUs. Cisco Express Forwarding offers "wire speed" routing of packets and load balancing.

**Cisco IOS Software**   Cisco operating system software that provides the majority of a router's or switch's features, with the hardware providing the remaining features.

**classful routing protocol**   A routing protocol that does not carry subnet mask information in its routing updates.

**classless**   A concept in IPv4 addressing that involves defining a subnetted IP address as having two parts: a prefix (or subnet) and a host.

**classless routing protocol**   A routing protocol that carries subnet mask information in its routing updates. Classless routing protocols can take advantage of VLSM and supernet routes. RIPv2, OSPF, and EIGRP are IPv4 classless routing protocols.

**cloud-managed switch**   A switch (for example, a Cisco Meraki switch) that can monitor and configure thousands of switch ports over the web, without the intervention of onsite IT staff. This type of switch enables virtual stacking of switches. *Compare with* campus LAN switch, data center switch, service provider switch, *and* virtual networking switch.

**collapsed core design**   A two-tier hierarchical design model that collapses the core and distribution layers into one layer, reducing the cost and complexity of the network design.

**Common Spanning Tree (CST)**   The original IEEE 802.1D STP standard, which assumes one spanning-tree instance for an entire bridged network, regardless of the number of VLANs.

**composite metric**   EIGRP's metric, which combines, by default, bandwidth and delay.

**converge**   To agree on internetworking topology after a topology change.

**converged network**   (1) A network that combines voice and video with the traditional data network. (2) A network that provides a loop-free Layer 2 topology for a switched LAN through the use of spanning tree. (3) A network that provides a stable Layer 3 network in which the routers have finished providing each other with updates, and the routing tables are complete.

**convergence**   The process in which a group of internetworking devices running a specific routing protocol all agree on internetworking topology after a topology change.

convergence time   The amount of time it takes a protocol to converge.

core layer   The backbone of a switched LAN. All traffic to and from peripheral networks must pass through the core layer. It includes high-speed switching devices that can handle relatively large amounts of traffic.

cost   An arbitrary value, typically based on hop count, media bandwidth, or other measures, that is assigned by a network administrator and used to compare various paths through an internetwork environment. Routing protocols use cost values to calculate the most favorable path to a particular destination; the lower the cost, the better the path.

# D

database description (DBD) packet   A packet used in OSPF that contains LSA headers only and describes the contents of the entire link-state database. Routers exchange DBDs during the exchange phase of adjacency creation. A DBD is an OSPF type 2 packet.

data center switch   A high-performance, low-latency switch that promotes infrastructure scalability, operational continuity, and transport flexibility. Data center switch platforms include the Cisco Nexus Series switches and the Cisco Catalyst 6500 Series switches. *Compare with* campus LAN, cloud-managed, service provider, *and* virtual networking switches.

dead interval   The time, in seconds, that a router waits to hear from a neighbor before declaring the neighboring router out of service.

default port cost   A measure assigned on a per-link basis in a switched LAN. It is determined by the link bandwidth, with a higher bandwidth having a lower port cost.

departmental switch block   A design that deploys routers, or multilayer switches, in pairs, with access layer switches evenly divided between them. Each switch block operates independently of the others, so a failure of a single device does not cause the network to go down. As a result, the failure of a single device or switch block does not significantly affect end users *See also* building switch block.

designated port   In spanning tree, a non-root switch port that is permitted to forward traffic on the network. For a trunk link connecting two switches, one end connects to the designated bridge through the designated port. Only one end of every trunk link in a switched LAN (with spanning tree enabled) connects to a designated port. The selection of designated ports is the last step in the spanning-tree algorithm.

designated router (DR)   An OSPF router that generates LSAs for a multiaccess network and has other special responsibilities in running OSPF. Each multiaccess OSPF network that has at least two attached routers has a designated router that is elected by the OSPF Hello packet. The designated router enables a reduction in the number of adjacencies required on a multiaccess network, which in turn reduces the amount of routing protocol traffic and the size of the topology database.

Diffusing Update Algorithm (DUAL)   A convergence algorithm used in EIGRP that provides loop-free operation at every instant throughout a route computation. DUAL allows routers involved in a topology change to synchronize at the same time, while not involving routers that are unaffected by the change.

**Dijkstra's algorithm**   An algorithm used by the OSPF routing protocol that is also called the shortest path first (SPF) algorithm.

**directly connected network**   A network that is connected to a router's physical Ethernet or serial interfaces.

**disabled state**   A spanning tree state for a switch port that is administratively shut down. A disabled port does not function in the spanning-tree process.

**distance**   A measure that identifies how far it is to a destination network, based on hop count, cost, bandwidth, delay, or another metric.

**distance vector routing protocol**   A type of routing protocol in which a router's routing table is based on hop-by-hop metrics and is only aware of the topology from the viewpoint of its directly connected neighbors. EIGRP and RIP are examples of distance vector routing protocols.

**distribution layer**   In the three-layer hierarchical network design model, the layer that invokes policy and routing control. Typically, VLANs are defined at this layer.

**DROTHER**   A router in an OSPF multiaccess network that is neither the DR nor the BDR. DROTHERS are the other routers in the OSPF network.

**Dynamic Trunking Protocol (DTP)**   A Cisco proprietary protocol that negotiates both the status and encapsulation of trunk ports.

# E

**edge port**   A switch port that is never intended to be connected to another switch device. It immediately transitions to the forwarding state when enabled. Edge ports are conceptually similar to PortFast enabled ports in the Cisco implementation of IEEE 802.1D.

**Enhanced Interior Gateway Routing Protocol (EIGRP)**   An advanced version of IGRP, developed by Cisco. EIGRP provides superior convergence and operating efficiency, and it combines the advantages of link-state protocols with those of distance vector protocols.

**enterprise network**   A large and diverse network connecting most major points in a company or another organization. An enterprise network differs from a WAN in that it is privately owned and maintained.

**equal-cost load balancing**   A process in which a router utilizes multiple paths with the same administrative distance and cost to a destination.

**EtherChannel**   A feature in which up to eight parallel Ethernet segments between the same two devices, each using the same speed, can be combined to act as a single link for forwarding and STP logic.

**Exchange state**   A state in which OSPF routers exchange database descriptor (DBD) packets. Database descriptors contain LSA headers only and describe the contents of the entire link-state database.

**ExStart state**   A state in which the routers and their DR and BDR establish a master/slave relationship and choose the initial sequence number for adjacency formation. The router with the higher router ID becomes the master and starts the exchange.

**extended-range VLANs**   Special VLANs numbered 1006 to 4094. Only transparent VTP mode switches can create extended VLANs. *Compare with* normal-range VLAN.

**extended system ID**   A VLAN ID or a Multiple Spanning Tree Protocol (MSTP) instance ID. Constitutes 12 bits of the 8-byte BID and contains the ID of the VLAN with which an STP BPDU is associated. The presence of the extended system ID results in bridge priority values incrementing in multiples of 4096.

**exterior gateway protocol (EGP)**   A protocol used for routing between ASes. It is also referred to as inter-AS routing. Service providers and large companies may interconnect using an EGP. BGP is the only currently viable EGP, and it is the official routing protocol used on the Internet.

# F

**failure domain**   An area of a network that is impacted when a critical device or network service experiences problems.

**feasible condition (FC)**   In EIGRP routing, a condition that exists when the receiving router has a feasible distance to a particular network and it receives an update from a neighbor with a lower advertised distance (reported distance) to that network.

**feasible distance (FD)**   In EIGRP routing, the metric of a network advertised by the connected neighbor plus the cost of reaching that neighbor. The path with the lowest metric is added to the routing table and is called FD.

**feasible successor (FS)**   In EIGRP routing, a next-hop router that leads to a certain destination network. The FS can be thought of as a backup next hop if the primary next hop (successor) goes down.

**finite state machine (FSM)**   A workflow model for an algorithm that has a finite number of stages. For example, the DUAL FSM is the EIGRP route calculating algorithm, which contains all the logic used to calculate and compare routes in an EIGRP network.

**first-hop redundancy protocols (FHRP)**   A class of protocols that includes HSRP, VRRP, and GLBP, which allows multiple redundant routers on the same subnet to act as a single default router (that is, first-hop router).

**fixed configuration**   A device with a set number of interfaces.

**form factor**   The aspect of design that defines the physical size, shape, and other physical specifications of a networking device.

**forwarding rate**   A rate that defines the processing capabilities of a switch by stating how much data the switch can process per second.

**forwarding state**   A state in which an STP port is considered part of the active topology and forwards data frames and sends and receives BPDU frames.

**Full state**   A state in which OSPF routers are fully adjacent with each other. All the router and network LSAs are exchanged, and the routers' databases are fully synchronized.

# G

**Gateway Load Balancing Protocol (GLBP)**   A Cisco proprietary protocol that provides both redundancy and load balancing of data, through the use of multiple routers. Routers present a shared GLBP address that end stations use as a default gateway.

# H

**hello interval**   The frequency, in seconds, at which a router sends Hello packets.

**Hello packet**   A packet used by OSPF and EIGRP routers to discover, establish, and maintain neighbor relationships. In OSPF, Hello packets are type 1 OSPF packets and are used to establish and maintain adjacency with other OSPF routers.

**hierarchical network**   A design methodology for building networks in three layers: access, distribution, and core.

**Hot Standby Router Protocol (HSRP)**   A Cisco proprietary protocol that allows two (or more) routers to share the duties of being the default router on a subnet, with an active/ standby model, with one router acting as the default router and the other sitting by, waiting to take over that role if the first router fails.

**hello keepalive mechanism**   With OSPF and EIGRP, a small packet that is exchanged by peers to verify that a link is still operational.

# I

**ICMP Router Discovery Protocol (IRDP)**   A legacy FHRP solution that allows IPv4 hosts to locate routers that provide IPv4 connectivity to other (nonlocal) IP networks.

**in-band management**   The process of monitoring and making configuration changes to a network device over a network connection using Telnet, SSH, or HTTP access.

**Init state**   An OSPF state which specifies that the router has received a Hello packet from its neighbor, but the receiving router's ID was not included in the Hello packet.

**inter-VLAN routing**   A method of routing between VLAN segment networks. It can be accomplished by using a legacy inter-VLAN routing method with a router, a router-on-a-stick method, or by using a Layer 3 multilayer switch.

**interarea routing**   In multiarea OSPF, routing that occurs between areas.

**Interior Gateway Protocol (IGP)**   A protocol used for routing within an AS. It is also referred to as intra-AS routing. Companies, organizations, and even service providers use an IGP on their internal networks. IGPs include RIP, EIGRP, OSPF, and IS-IS.

**Interior Gateway Routing Protocol (IGRP)**   A legacy Cisco proprietary distance vector routing protocol. It has been replaced with EIGRP and has not been available since IOS 12.2.

**internal router**   An OSPF router that has all its interfaces in the same area. All internal routers in an area have identical LSDBs.

**Internet Assigned Numbers Authority (IANA)**   An organization operated under the auspices of the ISOC as part of the IAB. IANA delegates authority for IP address space allocation and domain name assignment to the NIC and other organizations. IANA also maintains a database of assigned protocol identifiers used in the TCP/IP stack, including AS numbers.

**International Organization for Standardization (ISO)**   An international standard-setting body with members from global national standards organizations. The ISO is responsible for multiple standards, including the OSI reference model.

**inverse mask**   *See* wildcard mask.

**Internet Protocol Security (IPsec)**   A framework of open standards that spells out the rules for secure communications. IPsec works at the network layer, protecting and authenticating IP packets between participating IPsec peers.

**IOS image**   The operating system image stored in flash. The file contains the IOS instruction to provide routing, switching, security, and other internetworking features.

# K

**keepalive**   A mechanism used by OSPF and EIGRP to verify that the link between two peers is still operating.

# L

**Layer 2 loop**   A loop created by redundant links such as when multiple connections exist between two switches or two ports on the same switch connected to each other. The loop creates broadcast storms as broadcasts and multicasts are continuously forwarded by switches out every port. The switch or switches eventually flood the network. Layer 2 headers do not support a TTL value, so a frame could loop indefinitely.

**Layer 3 inter-VLAN routing**   A modern inter-VLAN solution that requires Layer 3 to be enabled for routing and configured with SVIs for each VLAN. *Compare with* legacy inter-VLAN routing and router-on-a-stick inter-VLAN routing.

**learning state**   A state in which a port accepts data frames to populate the MAC address table in an effort to limit flooding of unknown unicast frames. The IEEE 802.1D learning state is seen in

both a stable active topology and during topology synchronization changes.

**legacy inter-VLAN routing**   An inter-VLAN routing solution performed by connecting different physical router interfaces to different physical switch ports. The switch ports connected to the router are placed in access mode, and each physical interface is assigned to a different VLAN. Each router interface can then accept traffic from the VLAN associated with the switch interface it is connected to, and traffic can be routed to the other VLANs connected to the other interfaces. *Compare with* router-on-a-stick inter-VLAN routing *and* Layer 3 inter-VLAN routing.

**link aggregation**   A method of aggregating (that is, combining) multiple links between equipment to increase bandwidth.

**Link Aggregation Control Protocol (LACP)**   An industry-standard protocol that aids in the automatic creation of EtherChannel links.

**link state**   Refers to the status of a link, including the interface IP address/subnet mask, the type of network, the cost of the link, and any neighbor routers on that link.

**Link-State Acknowledgment (LSAck) packet**   A packet that acknowledges receipt of LSA packets. LSAck packets are type 5 OSPF packets.

**link-state advertisement (LSA)**   Often referred to as a link-state packet (LSP), a broadcast packet used by link-state protocols that contains information about neighbors and path costs. LSAs are used by receiving routers to maintain their routing tables.

**link-state database (LSDB)**   A table used in OSPF that is a representation of the topology of the autonomous system. It is the method by which routers "see" the state of the links in the autonomous system.

**link-state information** With OSPF, refers to information about a link, such as neighbor ID, link type, and bandwidth.

**link-state packet (LSP)** *See* link-state advertisement (LSA).

**Link-State Request (LSR) packet** A type 3 OSPF packet that is used to request the pieces of the neighbor's database that are most up to date.

**link-state router** A router that uses a link-state routing protocol such as OSPF.

**link-state routing protocol** A routing protocol classification in which each router has a topology database based on an SPF tree through the network, with knowledge of all nodes. OSPF and IS-IS are examples of link-state routing protocols.

**Link-State Update (LSU) packet** A type 4 OSPF packet that carries a collection of link-state advertisements one hop farther from its origin.

**listening state** A state in which a port cannot send or receive data frames, but the port is allowed to receive and send BPDUs. The IEEE 802.1D listening state is seen in both a stable active topology and during topology synchronization changes.

**load balancing** The proves in which a networking device distributes traffic over some of its network ports on the path to the destination. Load balancing increases the utilization of network segments, thus increasing effective network bandwidth.

**loading state** A state in which the actual exchange of link-state information occurs. Based on the information provided by the DBDs, routers send link-state request packets. The neighbor then provides the requested link-state information in link-state update packets. During the adjacency, if a router receives an outdated or missing LSA, it requests that LSA by sending a link-state request packet. All link-state update packets are acknowledged.

**loop guard** An STP feature that provides additional protection against Layer 2 forwarding loops (STP loops) caused when a physically redundant port no longer receives STP BPDUs. If BPDUs are not received on a non-designated port and loop guard is enabled, that port is moved into the STP loop-inconsistent blocking state instead of the listening/learning/forwarding state.

**loopback interface** A software-only interface that emulates a physical interface. A loopback interface is always up and never goes down.

**LSA type 1** A packet sent by all routers to advertise their directly connected OSPF-enabled links and forward their network information to OSPF neighbors.

**LSA type 2** A packet sent only by the DR in multiaccess and NBMA networks to give other routers information about multiaccess networks within the same area. It contains the router ID and IP address of the DR, along with the router ID of all other routers on the multiaccess segment.

**LSA type 3** A packet used by an ABR to advertise networks from other areas.

**LSA type 4** A packet sent generated by an ABR only when an ASBR exists within an area. It identifies the ASBR and provides a route to it.

**LSA type 5** A packet originated by an ASBR that describes routes to networks outside the OSPF autonomous system.

# M

**master router**   A VRRP forwarding router with a role similar to that of the HSRP active router.

**MD5 authentication**   An algorithm used for message authentication that verifies the integrity of the communication, authenticates the origin, and checks for timeliness.

**metric**   A quantitative value used to measure the distance to a given network.

**mission-critical services**   Network services that are crucial to the operation of the enterprise.

**modular configuration**   A modular design that allows for upgrading a device with different or possibly newer interface configurations.

**multiarea OSPF**   A method for scaling an OSPF implementation. As an OSPF network is expanded, other, non-backbone, areas can be created.

**multicast address**   An address that is used to identify a group of hosts that are part of a multicast group. Sending traffic to a multicast address is more efficient than broadcasting traffic to all devices on a segment.

**mulithomed**   A situation in which an enterprise connects to two different service providers. *Compare with* single-homed.

**multilayer switch**   A switch characterized by its ability to build a routing table, support a few routing protocols, and forward IP packets at a rate close to that of Layer 2 forwarding.

**Multiple Spanning Tree (MST)**   The Cisco implementation of MSTP.

**Multiple Spanning Tree Protocol (MSTP)**   An evolution of IEEE 802.1D STP and IEEE 802.1w (RSTP) that enables multiple VLANs to be mapped to the same spanning-tree instance, reducing the number of instances needed to support a large number of VLANs. MSTP was introduced as IEEE 802.1s.

# N

**named EIGRP**   The newest version of EIGRP, available in IOS 15.0(1)M and up, which enables the configuration of EIGRP for both IPv4 and IPv6 under a single configuration mode, using Address Families. This helps eliminate configuration complexity that occurs when configuring EIGRP for both IPv4 and IPv6.

**neighbor table**   A table in which an EIGRP router records addresses and interfaces of neighbors that it discovers. One neighbor table exists for each protocol-dependent module, such as IPv4.

**neighbors**   Two routers that have interfaces to a common network. Sometimes referred to as peers. In RIP, neighbors exchange routing information. In EIGRP and OSPF, neighbors exchange routing information and keep in touch by using Hello packets.

**network edge router**   A router that delivers high-performance, highly secure, and reliable services that unite campus, data center, and branch networks. *Compare with* branch router, network edge router, *and* service provider router.

**network operations center (NOC)**   The central location from which a network is supervised, monitored, and maintained.

nonbroadcast multiaccess (NBMA)   A characterization of a type of Layer 2 network in which more than two devices connect to the network, but the network does not allow broadcast frames to be sent to all devices on the network.

normal-range VLAN   A VLAN that is numbered between 1 and 1005 and created on Cisco Catalyst switches. *Compare with* extended-range VLAN.

Null0   A virtual IOS interface that is a route to nowhere, commonly known as "the bit bucket." Packets that match a route with a Null0 exit interface are discarded.

# O

Open Shortest Path First (OSPF)   A scalable link-state routing protocol used by many company networks.

OSPF area   A logical set of network segments and their attached devices. Areas are usually connected to other areas through routers to form a single autonomous system.

OSPFv2   Version 2 of the OSPF routing protocol. It is used to support IPv4 unicast address families.

OSPFv3   Version 3 of the OSPF routing protocol. It is used to support both IPv4 and IPv6 unicast address families.

OSPF hello and dead intervals   Timers in OSPF that are used to maintain neighbor adjacency. By default, if an OSPF router does not hear from its neighbor after four hello intervals, the neighbor is considered down (dead). Configured hello and dead intervals must match between neighbors.

out-of-band management   A type of management used for the initial configuration of a device or when network access is unavailable that requires direct connection to the console or AUX port and terminal emulation software.

# P

parent route   A level 1 route that has been subnetted. A parent route can never be an ultimate route. Parent routes never include an exit interface or a next-hop IP address.

partial update   An update that only includes information about route changes, such as a new link or a link becoming unavailable.

passive state   Term used in EIGRP to describe a stable route in the topology table.

path-vector routing protocol   A routing protocol that makes routing decisions based on manually configured network policies. BGP is the only path-vector routing protocol and uses configurable attributes to make routing decisions.

Per-VLAN Spanning Tree (PVST+)   A Cisco enhancement of STP that provides a separate 802.1D spanning-tree instance for each VLAN configured in the network.

periodic update   A distance vector term describing the time period to wait until updates are transmitted to neighboring routers. The periodic update for RIP is 30 seconds.

point-to-multipoint   Multiple devices interconnected in a hub-and-spoke topology over an NBMA network.

**point-to-point** Two devices interconnected over a common link. No other devices are on the link.

**Port Aggregation Protocol (PAgP)** A Cisco proprietary protocol that aids in the automatic creation of EtherChannel links.

**Port Channel interface** The virtual interface created when configuring an EtherChannel link on Cisco Catalyst switch. Configuration tasks are done on the Port Channel interface instead of on each individual port, ensuring configuration consistency throughout the links.

**port density** The number of interfaces supported on a switch.

**PortFast** A switch STP feature in which a port is placed in an STP forwarding state as soon as the interface comes up, bypassing the listening and learning states. This feature is meant for ports connected to end-user devices.

**Power over Ethernet (PoE)** A feature that allows a switch to deliver power to a device over the existing Ethernet cabling. This feature can be used by IP phones, security cameras, wireless access points, and other switches.

**protocol-dependent module (PDM)** A component that depends on a certain routed protocol. For example, protocol-dependent modules in EIGRP allow it to work with various routed protocols. PDMs allow EIGRP to keep a topology table for each routed protocol, such as IP.

**PuTTY** A popular terminal emulation program that provides serial console and in-band Telnet/ SSH access. TeraTerm also provides similar access.

**PVST+** *See* Per-VLAN Spanning Tree (PVST+).

# Q

**quad zero** A common phrase used to describe the dotted-decimal address 0.0.0.0 used in default routing.

**Query packet** In EIGRP, a packet that is used to request specific information from a neighbor router.

# R

**rack unit (RU)** Defined in EIA-310, a unit (U) with a standard height of 4.45 centimeters (1 3/4 inches) and width of 48.26 centimeters (19 inches). Therefore, a device occupying double that height would be referred to as a 2U device.

**Rapid Per-VLAN Spanning Tree (Rapid PVST+)** A Cisco proprietary implementation of RSTP.

**Rapid PVST+** *See* Rapid Per-VLAN PVST+.

**Rapid Spanning Tree Protocol (RSTP)** The IEEE 802.1w standard that defines an improved version of STP that converges much more quickly and consistently than STP (802.1d).

**redundancy** The duplication of devices, services, or connections so that, in the event of a failure, the redundant devices, services, or connections can perform the work of those that failed.

**reference bandwidth** The number, measured in Mbps, that is used by OSPF routers to calculate cost. The default reference bandwidth is 100 Mbps. Changing the reference bandwidth does not actually affect the bandwidth capacity on the link; rather, it simply affects the calculation used to determine the metric.

**regional Internet registry (RIR)**   The generic term for one of five current organizations responsible for assigning the public, globally unique IPv4 and IPv6 address space.

**Reliable Transport Protocol (RTP)**   A protocol that is unique to EIGRP and provides delivery of EIGRP packets to neighbors. EIGRP does not use TCP.

**Reply packets**   In EIGRP, packets that are used to respond to Query packets.

**reported distance (RD)**   The total metric along a path to a destination network, as advertised by an upstream neighbor in EIGRP.

**RIPng**   An IPv6 distance vector routing protocol based on the IPv4 RIPv2 routing protocol. It still has a 15-hop limitation, and the administrative distance is 120.

**root bridge**   The root of a spanning-tree topology. A root bridge exchanges topology information with other bridges in a spanning tree topology to notify all other bridges in the network when topology changes are required. This prevents loops and provides a measure of defense against link failure.

**root guard**   A feature that provides a way to enforce the root bridge placement in the network. The root guard ensures that the port on which root guard is enabled is the designated port

**root path cost**   A cost of the path from the sending switch to the root bridge that is used to determine STP port roles. It is calculated by summing the individual port costs along the path from the switch to the root bridge.

**root port**   The unique port on a non-root bridge that has the lowest path cost to the root bridge. Every non-root bridge in an STP topology must elect a root port. The root port on a switch is used for communication between the switch and the root bridge.

**route redistribution**   The process of injecting a route from one route source into the routing process of another route source.

**route summarization**   The process of aggregating multiple routes into one routing advertisement to reduce the size of routing tables.

**routed port**   A Layer 3 switch port configured to be a Layer 3 interface by using the **no switchport** interface configuration command.

**router-on-a-stick inter-VLAN routing**   An inter-VLAN routing solution that requires a router interface to become a trunk link with a switch. The router interface is configured using subinterfaces, and each subinterface is assigned to a specific VLAN. *Compare with* legacy inter-VLAN routing *and* Layer 3 inter-VLAN routing.

**router ID**   A field in an OSPF Hello packet that is a 32-bit value expressed in dotted-decimal notation (an IPv4 address) used to uniquely identify the originating router.

**router priority**   A value that is used in a DR/BDR election. The default priority for all OSPF routers is 1 but can be manually altered from 0 to 255. The higher the value, the more likely the router is to become the DR on the link.

**Routing Information Protocol Version 1 (RIPv1)**   A legacy classful distance vector distance vector routing protocol. It has been replaced by RIPv2.

Routing Information Protocol Version 2 (RIPv2)   A classless distance vector distance vector routing protocol.

RSTP   *See* Rapid Spanning Tree Protocol (RSTP).

# S

service provider router   A router that is responsible for differentiating the service portfolio and increasing revenues by delivering end-to-end scalable solutions and subscriber-aware services. *Compare with* branch router *and* network edge router.

service provider switch   A switch that aggregates traffic at the edge of a network, while service provider Ethernet access switches provide application intelligence, unified services, virtualization, integrated security, and simplified management. *Compare with* campus LAN switch, cloud-managed switch, data center switch, *and* virtual networking switch.

SHA authentication   A type of message authentication based on Secure Hash Algorithm (SHA). SHA verifies the integrity of the communication, authenticates the origin, and checks for timeliness and is more secure than MD5.

shortest path first (SPF) algorithm   Often referred to as the Dijkstra's algorithm, an algorithm used by protocols such as STP and OSPF to determine a shortest path to a destination. The algorithm accumulates costs along each path, from source to destination, to determine the total cost of a route.

single-area OSPF   An OSPF configuration that only uses one area, the backbone area (area 0).

single-homed   An Internet access design in which the organization only has one connection to a service provider. *Compare with* multihomed.

small form-factor pluggable (SFP)   A small, compact, hot-pluggable transceiver used on switches to provide flexibility when choosing network media. SFPs are available for Ethernet, Sonet/SDH, and Fibre Channel networks.

source IP to destination IP load balancing   A type of load balancing used by EtherChannel bundled links. *See also* source MAC to destination MAC load balancing.

source MAC to destination MAC load balancing   A type of load balancing used by EtherChannel bundled links. *See also* source IP to destination IP load balancing.

Spanning Tree Algorithm (STA)   An algorithm used by STP to calculate the best path to the root switch. It also is used to determine which redundant ports to block.

spanning-tree instance   Each STP instance identifies a root bridge that serves as a reference point for all spanning tree calculations to determine which redundant paths to block. PVST+ runs one STP instance for each VLAN.

Spanning Tree Protocol (STP)   A protocol defined by IEEE standard 802.1D that allows switches and bridges to create a redundant LAN, with the protocol dynamically causing some ports to block traffic so that the bridge/switch forwarding logic will not cause frames to loop indefinitely around the LAN.

**SPF tree**   A logical construct used by OSPF to calculate the cost for a router to reach any router or network in the area. Each OSPF router builds a data structure with itself as the root and branches connecting to other OSPF peers, which in turn also have branches.

**split horizon**   A distance vector routing protocol technique used to prevent reverse routes between two routers. Specifically, it prevents a router from advertising a route back onto the interface from which the route was learned.

**stackable configuration**   A configuration in which devices are capable of being connected to other, such as devices to provide higher port density.

**standby router**   The HSRP router that monitors the HSRP active router. In the event that the active router fails, the standby router sends a coup message and takes over the active role.

**STP**   *See* Spanning Tree Protocol (STP).

**STP diameter**   The maximum number of switches that data must cross to connect any two switches. The IEEE recommends a maximum diameter of seven switches for the default STP timers.

**STP instance**   *See* spanning-tree instance.

**stub network**   A network with only one exit point. In a hub-and-spoke network, the hub networks is the stub networks connected to a central hub router.

**subset advertisement**   A VTP message that is sent in response to advertisement request messages that contain current VTP domain VLAN information, including any recent changes.

*See also* advertisement request *and* summary advertisement.

**successor**   The path to a destination. In EIGRP, the successor is chosen using DUAL from all the known paths or feasible successors to the end destination.

**summary advertisement**   A VTP message that is sent every five minutes to advertise the VTP domain name and configuration revision number to adjacent VTP domain switches. *See also* advertisement request *and* subset advertisement.

**supervisor engine**   A supervisor (or "sup") that provides centralized processing and information forwarding for a modular chassis switch. Up to two sup engines can be installed to provide a redundant active/standby failover environment.

**switch virtual interface (SVI)**   A virtual VLAN interface used to configure management interface and for inter-VLAN routing. It provides basic Layer 3 functions for a switch that does not have a dedicated physical interface for IP addressing.

# T

**TeraTerm**   A popular terminal emulation program that provides serial console and in-band Telnet/SSH access. PuTTY also provides similar access.

**time to live (TTL)**   The field in an IP header that indicates how long a packet is considered valid. Each routing device that an IP packet passes through decrements the TTL by 1.

**topology change acknowledgment (TCA) bit**   A 1-bit flag in the STP BPDU that is set to acknowledge receipt of a configuration message with the TC bit set.

**topology change (TC) bit**   A 1-bit flag in the STP BPDU that signals a topology change when a path to the root bridge has been disrupted.

**topology table**   A table that contains all destinations that are advertised by neighboring routers. There is a separate topology table for each PDM.

**trunk**   A switch port mode configured so that the switch can transmit traffic from multiple VLANs over a single link.

**type, length, value (TLV)**   The data portion of the EIGRP packet. All TLVs begin with a 16-bit type field and a 16-bit length field. Different TLV values exist, depending on the routed protocol. There is, however, a general TLV that describes generic EIGRP parameters such as sequence (used by Cisco Reliable Multicast) and EIGRP software version.

# U

**ultimate route**   A routing table entry that contains either a next-hop IPv4 address or an exit interface. Directly connected, dynamically learned, and local routes are all considered to be ultimate routes.

**unequal-cost load balancing**   Load balancing that uses multiple paths to the same destination that have different costs or metrics. EIGRP uses unequal-cost load balancing with the **variance** command.

**Update packet**   An EIGRP packet used to convey routing information to neighbors about known destinations.

# V

**virtual link**   A special OSPF network used to interconnect distant OSPF areas to the backbone area.

**virtual local area network (VLAN)**   A group of hosts with a common set of requirements that communicate as if they were attached to the same wire, regardless of their physical location. A VLAN has the same attributes as a physical LAN, but it allows for end stations to be grouped together even if they are not located on the same LAN segment.

**virtual networking switch**   A switch such as a Cisco Nexus virtual networking switch that provides secure multitenant services by adding virtualization intelligence technology to the data center network. *Compare with* campus LAN switch, cloud-managed switch, data center switch, *and* service provider switch.

**Virtual Router Redundancy Protocol (VRRP)**   A TCP/IP RFC protocol that allows two (or more) routers to share the duties of being the default router on a subnet, with an active/ standby model, with one router acting as the default router and the other sitting by, waiting to take over that role if the first router fails.

**vlan.dat**   A VLAN database file that stores Cisco switch VLAN configuration information. The vlan.dat file is located in flash memory of the switch.

**VLAN Trunking Protocol (VTP)**   A Cisco proprietary Layer 2 protocol that enables a network manager to configure one or more switches so that they propagate VLAN configuration information to other switches in the network, as well as synchronizes the VLAN information with the other switches in the VTP domain.

variable length subnet mask (VLSM)   An IPv4 feature that enables the use of different subnet masks for individual subnets. It allows a network space to be divided into unequal parts. With VLSM, the network is first subnetted, and then the subnets are subnetted again. This process can be repeated multiple times to create subnets of various sizes. VLSM creates more efficient use of address space.

VTP advertisement   A message that each switch in a VTP domain sends periodically from each trunk port to a reserved multicast address. Neighboring switches receive these advertisements and update their VTP and VLAN configurations as necessary.

VTP client   A client that functions the same way as a VTP server, but that does not allow you to create, change, or delete VLANs. A VTP client only stores the VLAN information for the entire domain while the switch is on. A switch reset deletes the VLAN information. You must configure VTP client mode on a switch.

VTP domain   One or more interconnected switches sharing the same VLAN configuration details, using VTP advertisements. A switch can be only in one VTP domain at any time and switches in different VTP domains do not exchange VTP messages.

VTP mode   VTP server, client, or transparent configuration of a switch.

VTP server   A server that advertises the VTP domain VLAN information to other VTP-enabled switches in the same VTP domain. VTP servers store the VLAN information for the entire domain in NVRAM. The VTP server is where VLANs can be created, deleted, or renamed for the domain.

VTP transparent   A type of switch that does not participate in VTP except to forward VTP advertisements to VTP clients and VTP servers. VLANs that are created, renamed, or deleted on transparent switches are local to that switch only. To create an extended VLAN, a switch must be configured as a VTP transparent switch when using VTP Version 1 or Version 2.

# W

wildcard mask   A string of 32 binary digits that a router uses to determine which bits of the IPv4 address to examine for a match. Also known as an inverse mask.

wire speed   The data rate that an Ethernet port on a switch is capable of attaining.

wireless access point (AP)   A device that connects wireless communication devices to form a wireless network, analogous to a hub connecting wired devices to form a LAN. The AP usually connects to a wired network and can relay data between wireless devices and wired devices. Several APs can link together to form a larger network that allows roaming.

# Index

# J-K-L

# O

# P

# W-X-Y-Z